A Parochial History of St. Mary Bourne, with an account of the Manor of Hurstbourne Priors, Hants.

Joseph Stevens

A Parochial History of St. Mary Bourne, with an account of the Manor of Hurstbourne Priors, Hants.
Stevens, Joseph
British Library, Historical Print Editions
British Library
1888
vi. 374 p. ; 8°.
10352.l.21.

The BiblioLife Network

This project was made possible in part by the BiblioLife Network (BLN), a project aimed at addressing some of the huge challenges facing book preservationists around the world. The BLN includes libraries, library networks, archives, subject matter experts, online communities and library service providers. We believe every book ever published should be available as a high-quality print reproduction; printed on- demand anywhere in the world. This insures the ongoing accessibility of the content and helps generate sustainable revenue for the libraries and organizations that work to preserve these important materials.

The following book is in the "public domain" and represents an authentic reproduction of the text as printed by the original publisher. While we have attempted to accurately maintain the integrity of the original work, there are sometimes problems with the original book or micro-film from which the books were digitized. This can result in minor errors in reproduction. Possible imperfections include missing and blurred pages, poor pictures, markings and other reproduction issues beyond our control. Because this work is culturally important, we have made it available as part of our commitment to protecting, preserving, and promoting the world's literature.

GUIDE TO FOLD-OUTS, MAPS and OVERSIZED IMAGES

In an online database, page images do not need to conform to the size restrictions found in a printed book. When converting these images back into a printed bound book, the page sizes are standardized in ways that maintain the detail of the original. For large images, such as fold-out maps, the original page image is split into two or more pages.

Guidelines used to determine the split of oversize pages:

- Some images are split vertically; large images require vertical and horizontal splits.
- For horizontal splits, the content is split left to right.
- For vertical splits, the content is split from top to bottom.
- For both vertical and horizontal splits, the image is processed from top left to bottom right.

A

PAROCHIAL HISTORY

OF

ST. MARY BOURNE,

HANTS.

A

Parochial History

OF

ST. MARY BOURNE

WITH AN ACCOUNT OF THE

MANOR OF HURSTBOURNE PRIORS

HANTS

BY

JOSEPH STEVENS

MEMBER OF THE ROYAL COLLEGE OF PHYSICIANS, LONDON; LOCAL MEMBER OF COUNCIL FOR BERKS,
AND LATE FOR HANTS, BRITISH ARCHÆOLOGICAL ASSOCIATION;
HON. CURATOR, READING MUSEUM.

LONDON
WHITING AND CO., 30 AND 32, SARDINIA STREET, W.C.
1888.

PRINTED BY
WHITING AND CO., 30 AND 32, SARDINIA STREET W.C.

PREFACE.

In the following pages, which have been compiled from various sources, it has been my endeavour to place before the reader some account of the different peoples who have lived in and around St. Mary Bourne. Whatever may be its shortcomings, the work is more immediately intended for the old friends and fellow-villagers among whom were passed the best years of my life, and in whom I am sure of finding an indulgent audience. It is in respect of these that familiarity of expression has been used at intervals throughout the book.

From the time when the skin-clad savage manufactured his stone implements down to the present enlightened period, several races of men have passed over the face of North Hampshire. The earlier of these, from the impediments which Nature had planted in their path, are not to be regarded as ordinary valley settlers. But we have testimony in scattered and degraded earthworks, and in rude implements, in the shape of tools and weapons, that they occupied the elevations bordering on the valleys, and they doubtless penetrated into the swampy valleys in search of fish and wild-fowl. The records which they have left in the soil are, however, in some cases so scanty and difficult to decipher, that it need not excite surprise if error should have crept into what has been written concerning them. Nevertheless, the relics which have been gathered from the surface soil, or obtained by the agency of the spade, will be of future service, if only as adjuncts to similar discoveries yet to come, in helping to bring about a more comprehensive history of the past.

Although a connected history of the parish and the manor has to a considerable extent been maintained, a portion of the narrative consists rather of some materials for a history—that section which refers to the churches, for example, which can scarcely be considered a full account of the Ecclesiastical Establishment. The same remarks apply to the Forest of Chute and Finkley, which is only incidentally connected with the Manor of Hurstbourne Priors. As regards both the manor and the churches, I am quite aware that among the public records and in private hands much valuable documentary matter yet remains to be consulted.

Where objects which are little known to the general reader are concerned, the usefulness of a book is much enhanced by the introduction of illustrations. A single glance at a stone implement, for instance, will often convey a better idea of its character than a page of letter-press. Hence the appearance in this work of figures of rude relics with which most people have but little opportunity of becoming acquainted; and these figures are more particularly necessary because the space at the disposal of the writer would not admit of a minute description of the objects. The more familiar articles figured, such as the Font and the Stocks, are added on account of their archæological interest in association with the district of which this volume treats.

For many of the abstracts from State papers in the book I am indebted to Mr. E. G. Kirk. I avail myself also of this opportunity to express my gratitude to friends for valuable notices, which I have duly acknowledged elsewhere; and at the same time desire to register my heartfelt thanks to life-long friends—a few happily still surviving—for homely references and memory-matter, forming the basis of some of the social and domestic history of the old place, and without which—documentary evidence not being obtainable—a considerable portion of what has been written could not have appeared. The plates and diagrams, with the exception of the church and its interior, the font, and the plan of Swampton allotments, were drawn by myself.

J. S.

READING, *March* 1888.

CONTENTS.

		PAGE
1.—St. Mary Bourne	. . . . .	1
2.—Old Stone Implements	. . . .	14
3.—Pit-Dwellings	. . . . .	25
4.—Eggbury Camp	. . . . .	37
5.—Polished Stone Implements	. . .	48
6.—The Romans	. . . . .	54
7.—The Saxons	. . . . .	74
8.—The Manor	. . . . .	87
9.—The Summerhaugh	. . . .	188
10.—The Churches (including the Register)	. .	200
11.—Extracts from the Old Parish Books	. .	237
12.—The Tithings (including the Village School)	.	268
13.—Pleas of the Crown	. . . .	296
14.—The Subsidy Rolls	. . . .	303
15.—The Forest of Chute and Finkley	. .	320
16.—Parochial Customs (including Provincial Words)	.	336
17.—The Chalk (including the Rarer Wild Plants)	.	345

LIST OF ILLUSTRATIONS.

FRONTISPIECE.—ST. MARY BOURNE CHURCH, HANTS.

PLATE	FACING PAGE
1.—Old Stone Implements	18
2.—Diagram of Pit-Dwellings	23
3.—Articles from Pit-Dwellings	30
4.—Plan of Haydon Fort, Wilts	45
5.—Flint Implements (Neolithic)	52
6.—Plan of Romano-British Building, Finkley	62
7.—Romano-British Articles found at Finkley	64
8.—Relics from British and Romano-British Graves	70
9.—Scolds' Bridle and Village Stocks	194
10.—The Interior of St. Mary Bourne Church	203
11.—The Cross-legged Effigy	205
12.—The Font	206
13.—Manorial Weight, and other Relics, from St. Mary Bourne	242
14.—The Chained-Bible Table	246
15.—The Map of Swampton Allotments	291

St. Mary Bourne.

🌰 🌰 🌰

AMONG the retired villages of North Hampshire, St. Mary Bourne may be considered as possessing picturesque and pleasing features, for which it is mainly indebted to the rude and scattered character of its habitations. The homes like the people have undergone but little change, or rather the change has been so slow as to be scarcely appreciable. The same may be said to characterise the hamlets of North Hampshire generally, thereby contrasting somewhat remarkably with the up-growth which has been so apparent in many of the manufacturing districts. The consequence is that these old agricultural centres have obtained the reputation of maintaining the simplicity of former times.

About forty-five years ago, when I first settled in the village, a friend inquired, "What kind of folk live at Bourne?" whereupon I replied, "The people generally live in thatched houses, and keep old Christmas." Mr. Dawson, who just previous to that time had been vicar of the parish, is stated to have affirmed from the pulpit that the village was half-a-century behind; meaning, I suppose, that in a progressive sense it was fifty years in arrear of other places. This must have been somewhat of a libel on the old place. At all events, the introduction of modern villas along the hill-sides, and particularly the adoption of a Board School, which was one of the earliest of the kind in North Hampshire, must have some time since removed any stigma that might have appertained to it on that head.

The village, nevertheless, had some pretensions to be considered old-fashioned, inasmuch as I remember being informed by an old inhabitant, a Miss Stair, who had reached the advanced age of ninety-three, that she could bear in memory having walked from Hurstbourne Tarrant to the neighbouring village of Stoke to see a sash-window, the first introduction of its kind in that district; and she further remarked, that so little had the people of St. Mary Bourne mingled with the great outside world in her early days that the passing of a post-chaise along the street was sufficient to secure half-a-holiday for the school-children. Mr. William Cobbett, in one of his " Rural Rides", relates a conversation he had with an inhabitant of Tangley, which bears out the view which has just been stated regarding the retired and primitive habits of the North Hampshire people. He says, "I rode up to the garden-wicket of a cottage, and asked the woman, who had two children, and who seemed to be about thirty years old, which was the way to Ludgarshall, which I knew could not be about *four miles* off. She did *not know!* A very neat, smart, and pretty woman; but she did not know the way to this rotten borough, which was, I was sure, only about four miles off! 'Well, my dear, good woman,' said I, 'but you *have been* at Ludgarshall?'—'No.' 'Nor at Andover?' (six miles another way).—'No.' 'Nor at Marlborough?' (nine miles another way).—'No.' 'Pray were you born in this house?'—'Yes.' 'And how far have you ever been from this house?'—'Oh! I have been *up in the parish and over to Chute.*' That is to say, the utmost extent of her voyages had been about two-and-a-half miles!"

At equal distances above and below St. Mary Bourne as the water runs are two villages, the one known as Hurstbourne Tarrant, and the other as Hurstbourne Priors. In popular phrase they are spoken of as "Up Hurstbourne",[1] and "Down Hurstbourne"; and quite locally as "Uphusband", and "Downhusband". It has been thought that *Hurst* refers to the Saxon, meaning forest, from the localisation of these places with the ancient forests of Doiley and Harewood; but the mode of writing the name Hurstbourne is a corruption of quite recent date. In the will of King Alfred the name stands as *Hysseburinan* in the Saxon will, *Husseburn* or *Husseburum* in the Latin text of the same will. Might the *hys*, meaning *his*[2] or *of him*, refer to the place as the property of the king, for it formerly belonged to him? Husseburn is a Saxon form, and might come from the Anglo-Saxon *hus*,[3] *æs*, n., a house or dwelling. In *Domesday Book*, Hus-

---

[1] It was called Huphusseburn as early as the time of Henry III. *Testa de Nevill* (p. 234) states that " Punz. Blanchard holds Huphusseburn of the feoffment of the Lord Richard King of England, for half a knight's fee, of the Lord the King in chief."

[2] Bosworth, *Anglo-Saxon Dictionary*.   [3] *Ibid*.

borne Tarrant is given as *Esseborne*, and Husborne Priors as *Eisseburne*. As early as 1167 the names of the two villages are written *Esseburna Regis* and *Hesseburna Prioris*. In a charter of Henry II Hurstbourne Priors appears as *Ecclesia de Hesseburna;* and in the Pipe Rolls, 1 Richard I, the title is written *Husseburn*. Bishop Godfrey de Lucy's charter of 1191, and a charter of Henry I, also give the name as *Husseburn* (*Ecclesia de Husseburn*). In the list of vicars the name is written Husborne and Husbourne till 1575, when the *r* is first introduced, the name then appearing as Hursborne Priors; but the *t* is a yet later introduction. I observe that Speede's early map of Hampshire gives *Husborntarr* in the hundred of Pastrae, for Hurstbourne Tarrant; and *Husborne* for Hurstbourne Priors, in the hundred of Evingar. The term is written Hursbourne in Warner's *History of Hampshire;* but Brayley and Britton, in their *Beauties of England and Wales* (1805), write the word *Hurstbourne*, showing that the *t* was an innovation of about the end of the eighteenth or the beginning of the nineteenth century.

The adjunct Tarent or Tarrent is derived from the connection of this place with the nunnery of Tarent in Dorsetshire, which possessed the manor and tithes of the parish, as also those of Vernham Dean adjoining it, for several centuries anterior to the Reformation. Hurstbourne Tarrant was a demesne of the Crown at the time of the Conquest, and it is mentioned as a royal manor with a church, and it was obligated, in common with Basingstoke and Clere, to provide an establishment for the king for one day.[1] In the other case, Priors was, at the time of *Domesday*, Church property, and had always been abbey land, and being held by the bishop it derived its name from that connection. In Saxon times Edmund the Elder held Hurstbourne Tarrant; but the manor and its tithes were granted by Edward VI, with other property in Hampshire, to the first Marquis of Winchester, for the maintenance of Netley Fort (named Letteley in Warner's *Hampshire*), and for the retaining and supporting there of one captain, one gunner, one porter, and six soldiers. That Vernham Dean formed part of the original manor of Hurstbourne Tarrant is rendered certain from a return in the *Calendarium Rotulorum*, 7th of King John, that Henry de Bernevalle held *Fernham* manor, a member of Hursborne manor.[2]

Bourne as a place-name appears to be derived from the *burn* or brook which flows along the valley. It comes probably from the Celtic *bron*, Anglo-Saxon *burne*.[3] Bourne is a common adjunct in

[1] Moody, *Sketches of Hampshire*, p. 164.
[2] Moody, *Hampshire Domesday*, p. 42.
[3] Bosworth, *Anglo-Saxon Dictionary*.

village names, and in some instances, as in Winterbourne, the title refers to the periodic character of the stream. In *Domesday*, the *burne* of the Saxon becomes changed into *bourne* or *borne*, as in Esseborne, Haliborne and Sireborne or Sirebourne. The stream is also known as the Test, Upper Test, as distinct from a branch of greater volume called the Lower Test, which runs from Ashe and Overton through Whitchurch, and joins the upper stream near Longparish. It has been stated that the Test is mentioned in a boundary of the West Saxons as *Terstan*[1]; and in 909 the Terstan was a boundary of Whitchurch. Mr. B. B. Woodward[2] states that "the old British name, preserved under the Latin *Trisanton* and the English *Terstan*, belongs to the river throughout its course." It is difficult to conjecture the meaning of these words, save that they bear some reference to the irregular and winding nature of the stream. The term Test conveys the impression that its etymology bears a Celtic significance in *es*, the *T* apostrophised rendering the reading as *T'est*, the water; and *es* is more strongly marked in the place-name *Esse* of *Domesday*, which refers to the present village of Ashe, at which place the lower stream takes its rise.

The Upper Test is an intermittent stream, but not intermittent at St. Mary Bourne in the sense of some "bournes", which run only once in two or three years. And the term "intermittent" applies only to St. Mary Bourne, and that portion of the valley between it and the watershed, as at about a mile and a half lower down there is some water always present. Mostly the water ceases flowing in the autumn, and returns in the late winter months or early spring. I have observed that in several places up the valley the water flows a little after it has discontinued running in others; in these cases there is no doubt the dry places represent spots above the then saturation-level in the chalk, the water reaching the lower outlets underground. In wet times, such as that of 1869, and those following 1879, the water flows all the winter; and occasionally, on the return of spring, with fresh accessions of water, there is an overflow of the banks, the water making its way along the main street.[3] I find that in 1869 the water-level in January was five feet above its level in 1854 (which was a dry season) in February. The season in 1869 was wet, and so exceedingly mild that the fields were clothed with green; and on the 9th of January the hepatica, snowdrop, crocus, anemone, and double violet flowered in the gardens; daffodils came

---

[1] *Diplomatarium Anglicum Ævi Saxonici*, pp. 145-47.
[2] Woodward and Wilks, *History of Hampshire*, vol. i, p. 374.
[3] The water was unusually high in 1883. The main street became a watercourse, and a temporary bridge was erected for the use of foot-passengers.

into flower, as did primroses and scented violets in favourable places, and catkins appeared on the hazel.[1] During the dry season of 1854-5 there was scarcely any water at all during the summer; in fact, the water-level in February 1854 was four feet below the surface-level in the watercourse at St. Mary Bourne; and as the springs continued low until 1859 it appeared as if the brook would become permanently dry.

The water usually begins to make its appearance in the river-course in January; it did so this year (1887); but sometimes it is delayed till February and even March. Commonly, however, the brook attains to a considerable bulk in February, reaching its culmination in May, and remaining somewhat stationary till the end of June. I mean stationary in so far as the river-bulk is concerned, as at about this time the onward flow becomes impeded by aquatic vegetation, which chokes up the course, causing some stagnation, and rendering the stream more swollen than it would be from the actual supply it receives from the springs. Another source of obstruction is the frequent penning back of the water where the brook flows through water-meadows, in order to force the herbage.

The river-supply here, as elsewhere, is regulated by the rainfall. The hills act as condensers of atmospheric vapour, which falls as rain over the extended chalk surface of the watershed, which here attains to a maximum elevation of 974.5 feet.[2] The valley runs at a greater or less right angle to it, and therefore intersects the general plane of saturation. The water percolating downwards becomes absorbed by the chalk to the extent of from one-twelfth to one-ninth of its weight, or at the rate of two gallons to the cubic foot.[3] The chalk is very tenacious of water; and it circulates freely only in the faults and numerous cracks and fissures which penetrate the chalk in all directions, and more or less throughout its total thickness.[4] Large supplies of water are obtained, as at Brighton and other large towns, by sinking below the line of saturation, and driving headings in various directions in order to tap some of the fissures. It is not many years since two men nearly lost their lives at Brighton in carrying out an operation of this kind, from the water coming in so rapidly. The fissures when drawn upon generally increase in size by use and yield a large quantity of water. The water from the

---

[1] Note extracted from Village Records. (J. S.)
[2] Ordnance Map.
[3] Dr. John Evans, F.R.S., *Physiography*, p. 13.
[4] There is a difference in the porosity of chalk according to its density, which varies in the several members of the upper cretaceous group.

surface takes up what carbonic acid it meets with and carries it into the chalk, solution of the chalky material taking place quite near the surface, as may be seen in the pipes and pots filled with surface-materials washed in or sunk in ; but water containing carbonic acid might be carried to great depths in chalk and other limestone rocks by means of faults and fissures before losing its dissolving power. Such underground currents bearing carbonic acid are the means of forming caverns, with stalactites, etc., in carboniferous limestone rocks.

In places on the chalk hills beds of brick-earth and clay-with-flints occur, and along the line of the watershed at the head of the Upper Test valley patches of clay and other materials belonging to the Tertiaries of the Reading and Woolwich series are present.[1] In such, the clay being quite impervious to water, the water flows over it, and through any porous materials below, such as sand, etc., and finding its way into fissures in the chalk it enlarges these apertures both by its chemical and mechanical action, and sudden sinkings of the ground sometimes occur. Into these swallow-holes large quantities of water obtain access to the chalk, and form underground currents. The nodules of flint also, in the upper chalk, render this material more porous to water in places where they occur ; so that in boring for water a supply is often obtained immediately on traversing a stratification of flints. These waterways so readily communicate with water stored at a higher level, that the water in a deep boring in the bottom of a valley will rise higher than the level of the stream running through it, and overflow into its course.

The chalk constitutes magnificent underground reservoirs, in which vast volumes of water are not only rendered and kept pure, but stored and preserved at a uniform temperature of about 10° C. (50° F.), so as to be cool and refreshing in summer, and far removed from the freezing-point in winter.... There is reason to believe that the more this stratum is drawn upon for its abundant and excellent water, the better will its qualities as a storage medium become. Every million gallons of water abstracted from the chalk carries with it in solution on an average a ton and a quarter of chalk through which it has percolated, and thus makes room for an additional volume of about 110 gallons of water. The porosity or sponginess of the chalk must therefore go on augmenting, and the

---

[1] A narrow outlier of this series lies on the summit of the Chalk Down, south-east of Walbury. (*Memoirs of the Geological Survey*, No. 12, p. 28.)

yield from wells[1] judiciously sunk ought, within certain limits, to increase with their age.[2]

Intermittent springs are caused by the fluctuations that take place, according to the amount of rainfall, in the line of saturation, which is generally more or less inclined. This inclination is towards those places where the water finds its way to the surface in the form of springs. It is found to vary at different times; sometimes the inclination is at an angle of 20 feet to the mile, and sometimes 25 feet; and at others the slope is not greater than 12 feet to the mile.[3] Although the line of saturation varies according to the amount of rain, there must be a perennial source of supply to the streams which constantly flow, or the waters would cease flowing. These receive their water from underground reservoirs, and are independent of any immediate rainfall. But in intermittent springs, the supply being capricious, the brooks supplied by them are capricious also, and they cease to flow when the rain which temporarily raises the line of saturation is drained away.

The rain which makes its way through the chalk during the winter months raises the level of the subterranean reservoir on account of the water filling in from above faster than it can find its way out by the springs; and although there may be no rain during the summer of sufficient bulk to penetrate to the reservoir, yet the water already there continues running and the level gradually falls, and the variations in the level may be observed in the fall of

---

[1] The following are the depths of some of the principal chalk wells, as well as of some of the superficial wells, commonly called diproles, which lie along the line of the Upper Test valley:—

Littledown Well	245 feet
Bottom of Vernham Street Well	210 ,,
Vernham Well at the George Inn	135 ,,
Upton Well	99 ,,
Hurstbourne Tarrant { Green's Well	37 ,,
Hurstbourne Tarrant { White's Well	30 ,,
Hurstbourne Tarrant { Batchelor's Well	31 ,,
Stoke Wells	from 12 to 18 ,,
St. Mary Bourne { Colebrook's Well	8 ,,
St. Mary Bourne { Gale's Well	8 ,,
St. Mary Bourne { The Police Well	10 ,,
St. Mary Bourne { Page's Well	12 ,,

These wells lie in the gravel, except the Police Well, which is sunk 2 feet in the chalk. In August 1887, after the extreme dry summer, Colebrook's Well contained 3 feet 6 inches of water; Gale's, 4 feet 6 inches; and the Police Well, 6 feet 6 inches of water.

[2] Rivers Pollution Commission (1868), p. 101.

[3] This index refers to a chalk valley; but the permanent saturation slopes vary somewhat in different chalk districts. (Evans, *The Hertfordshire Bourne*, in Trans. of Watford Nat. Hist. Soc., vol. 1877, p. 138.)

the water in the wells. The wells are a most excellent gauge of the saturation levels of the district. During long-continued rain all the water above that which the chalk holds by capillary attraction gravitates downwards till it arrives at the point where the chalk is already charged with water. In the bottoms of valleys with streams flowing along them this saturated rock will be found near the surface; but the rain falling on hills such as those of Combe and Hippenscombe will have to descend hundreds of feet before its descent is arrested by the spaces in the chalk already occupied by water; and then its bulk, added to that already there, will of course bring about a more elevated line of saturation. Friction is found to be a chief factor in keeping the bottoms of the valleys charged with water, and in preventing the water under the hills from finding some means of escape. Could friction be removed the surface of the saturated rock would present a nearly dead level, and the rain would escape at the lowest vent almost as quickly as it penetrated the ground.[1]

It has been usual to state that the Upper Test stream takes its rise in a spring near Upton; but this is only one of its sources, the water making its way out at a variety of places along the bed of the stream, the volume of water increasing as it flows onwards. According to seasons there is a difference in the point of rising of from five to seven miles in the Upper Test valley. After unusually protracted rain the saturation-line of the chalk becomes sufficiently elevated to cause an overflow of the wells as high up as Vernham, when there is considerable flooding of the roads, and the water enters the lower floors of houses. At these times the hills are almost completely saturated, and the plane of saturation corresponds with the figure of the land-surface. The well at the George Inn, Vernham, is 135 feet in depth, which shows not merely the extreme elevation of the water when the well overflows, but the contingencies that it is calculated are likely to arise in obtaining water in very dry seasons. The average depth at which water is obtained at Vernham from the various wells is ninety feet.

The following are a few notices furnished by old inhabitants in reference to the rising of the water in the upper reaches of the valley.

[1] *Physiography*, a lecture delivered at the Institute of Civil Engineers, 1884-5, by Dr. John Evans, F.R.S. The following are some other references to literature concerning intermittent springs:—The *Hertfordshire Bourne*, in Transactions of the Watford Nat. Hist. Soc., March 1877, by Dr. J. Evans, F.R.S.; *Memoirs of Geolog. Survey of Great Britain*, Whitaker, vol. iv, 1872, pp. 391-2; also, same author, *Appendix* in *Memoir of Geolog. Survey*, 1881; also, *Proceed. Geologists' Assoc.*, vol. viii, part III, p. 138; also, *Presidential Address*, Norwich Geolog. Society, 1884, p. 288. These refer to the saturation-level, not to the "Bournes" themselves. Geological Magazine, vol. ii, No. 4, 1885, pp. 148-150, *Intermittent Streams in Berkshire*, by Prof. Rupert Jones, F.R.S.

Mr. Criswick Child, of Vernham Manor, sends me an extract from the Old Vernham Dean parish church-book:—

"... Be it remembered that in the year of our Lord, 1774, March 15th, the springs was so high in Vernham's Dean, that the Dean Well run over for a week, and the houses was so full of spring water for upwards of forty poles above the George Inn, that the inhabitants was forced to open trenches to draw it off, which caused a river all down the bottom, and many quit their houses, and also springs at the same time rose in the ditch in Conholt bottom near three furlongs."

"The springs were very high in the beginning of the year 1828, many wells in the Dean run over, which caused a large breadth of the down, called Berry-dean, to be covered with water, and made quite a river in the road below Assam's fields, which continued many weeks. The springs were up in Conholt bottom at the same time. The winter of this year was remarkably mild; and the summers of 1825-1826 excessively dry and hot."

An old inhabitant states that when he was thirteen years old, in 1814, the well by the George Inn at Vernham Dean overflowed.

Mr. Child himself states that he has seen the cottage well above the parish schools in Berry-dean run over, and that the water ran down the Dean by Hen Barn through Upton to Hurstbourne. At the same time, he adds, a swift stream came from the Netherton valley (a neighbouring vale extending down from the watershed of Combe), the two becoming confluent in Hurstbourne village. This union has been called from early times "the meeting of the Cock and Hen".

Mr. J. H. Gilmour, of Hurstbourne Tarrant, furnishes twenty-eight years' experiences. He states that the watercourse crosses the road five times between Hurstbourne and Upton, a distance of a mile and a half; and the course is complete to the Hen-pit, a quarter of a mile beyond Upton, where it becomes lost. It is most rare that water rises higher up the valley than this. He has known the water rise in all the hollows twice since 1857, and fill the low-lying grounds as far up as Vernham School, the pits in Bury Dean common being full. The highroad is then a watercourse for a mile and a half, till Hen-barn is reached. He has never heard of it coming down Hippenscombe and Fosbury valleys; but aged people say the well in the centre of Vernham village ran over about the time of the Crimean war, and at that time Conholt bottom was full, although there is no way of egress for it from there into the Hurstbourne valley. When the water rises in Hen-pit it is always found to do so in Cock-pit; but when the water overflows these it invariably rises in other springs higher up both valleys. During the floods just alluded to the springs rose quite a mile up beyond the Cock-pit, which is as far up as Netherton barn, and nearly as high up as the "Saxon landmark, Wodens or Wansdyke", which here crosses the Netherton vale. The watercourse is distinctly traceable to the divisions between Faccombe and Hurstbourne parishes, where it is lost. When the water was so high at Vernham, Mr. Gilmour was told that it ran out of the farmyard at Netherton. He has seen the "Cock and Hen" meet twice, in 1876-7 and in 1883. They have very nearly done so several times, but they receded just as the gravel-pits at the Dean at Hurstbourne got full. There are several springs in these pits; but in 1885 there was no water even in the main river-course, and the people were in great straits.

Among the papers of the late Mr. John Page, of St. Mary Bourne, were found some notices relating to floods and small-pox in the village in 1797; and it is in justice to a useful and consistent man to make a few remarks at this point on his life. He died in 1884, at an advanced age, and was a very old inhabitant. He was one of the earliest of the Primitive Methodists who preached in the surrounding villages over half-a-century ago—a time when, the mission being young, some moral courage was requisite; Mr. Page having himself informed me that it was not unusual for him, when preaching, to be assailed with stones. The first place of meeting of the Society was Mr. Farr's kitchen at Binley. Mr. Page's house was at all times open for the reception of preachers, and he entertained among others Mr. Hugh Bourne, the founder of the connexion. He also entertained Mr. Joseph Arch on his visits to the village in the cause of the labourers. He was a pioneer of temperance, he having signed the pledge in 1838. At the introduction of a School Board Mr. Page became a member of it, and continued to sit at the Board till the time of his death.

The following notice of the floods appears under the head of "John Bull His account of the floods and Small Pox, Written by his Fathers orders December ye 23rd, 1797."

"... A Memorandom of a flood Sunday, February ye 8th, People at Church obliged to be Carryed Home in Carts and with Horses, the Waters Rising so fast while Morning Service continued between 11 and 12 o'clock, Being the third Flood in a fortnight by Snow and Sharp frost and Quick thaws. Jany. ye 28th, February ye 1st; but ye 8th of February was Heavy and Shocking, the Banks of the water Courses brake out and the Street full of Water and no Passing."

A comprehensive view of the physical features of the Upper Test valley is obtained from the top of Spring Hill, so called from the little spring which issues at its base. The hills extend away northward in graceful sweeps, each one appearing almost a repetition of the preceding one. There is considerable sameness in the scenery of North Hampshire; the elevations have softened outlines, and are never precipitous, which arises from the chalk out of which the entire district is moulded being a material of tolerably uniform texture and solubility. Sometimes a huge roll of chalk stretches for a long distance unbroken, then the line is split, and a bluff-head appears in the distance like a big mole-hill. White roads wind along the hollows between the hills, and the villages extend along the lines of the watercourses. A different distribution of passage-way appears to have obtained in times past, the very ancient roads being mostly traceable along the higher grounds. An illustration of this is furnished by a trackway which formerly traversed the entire length of the parish of St. Mary Bourne, and which bore, as part of it still bears, the unimportant title of Hungerford Lane. Much of it has of late years been appropriated as waste land; but where it still remains drove the grass has monopolised the unused surface. Where traversing woodland the unchecked bramble and hazel have reduced its dimensions to a mere copse-lane. The banks and ditches which still remain in places, however, mark the outlines of what was formerly a sturdy road.

Thirty years ago, on the top of the hill known as Fivelanes-end (being the spot where Hungerford Lane crosses the St. Mary Bourne road to Andover), a direction-post stood,[1] bearing on its arms "Hungerford" and "Winchester", showing that the lane must have been at one time a main road. It is an old packhorse way, and was probably used for centuries as such, when no other method of traversing the country was possible from the swampy state of the valley in winter, and when the rugged hills were not convenient for vehicles. As late as forty years ago, when there were no county bridges, fords were of frequent occurrence, not less than three such occurring between St. Mary Bourne and Hurstbourne Tarrant. And when in winter the brook became swollen and the road flooded travellers were compelled to traverse the outlying water in journeying from village to village.

Swamp-ton, the name of one of the St. Mary Bourne tithings, lying along the valley, has been thought to point to the condition just described; but the word is written *Suantune* in *Domesday*, and doubtless has its origin in the Anglo-Saxon *suan*,[2] a swain, herdsman, or servant, in reference to the serfs of the manor at the time of the survey.

The packhorse-road is still observable at Lower Week, and traversing the hills west of St. Mary Bourne it continued onwards to Hurstbourne Tarrant, where it appears to have taken the line of the

---

[1] The notices regarding Hungerford Lane refer to thirty years ago, as since that period a considerable part of the lane which extended from Bedlam's Copse to Lower Week has been grubbed and demolished.

[2] Bosworth, *Anglo-Saxon Dictionary*.

hill-country through Tangley to Hungerford, a portion of the direct Roman road through the former place being called Hungerford Lane on the six-inch Ordnance Map. The road is doubtless older than the period of the Conquest, the name *gang*,[1] which is applied to a passage over the brook near Stoke village implying that there must have been a ford at this point in Saxon times. It was the custom of the Saxon people to designate their roads according to their width; *anes wænes gang* representing their four-feet road, or single waggon-way; and *twegna wænes gangweg* their eight-feet or double waggon-track,—a disposition which assorts with the dimensions of some of our winding country lanes. In places where the packhorse-road is still used the sunken state of the way below the banks on either side suggests long usage without adequate repairs.

The traffic extended from Southampton to places inland by way of Hungerford; and the packhorse-man—for the biped packman hawked his wares about the country at the same time—was the carrier of the period over hilly districts to remote places which could not be reached by the road-waggon, and his packages consequently contained a medley of commodities—bales of woollens from Andover or Newbury; for there were branch roads traversed by the packmen in various directions, knitting the villages with the country towns. The visits of the packman were anxiously looked for, as he was the bearer of news-letters and the herald of news on war, peace, parliamentary changes, and concerning marriage and death. Among the traditions of village life his name is associated with tea, tobacco, and hollands, which bore the reputation of being smuggled. The late Mr. John Moore, who died at the advanced age of ninety, placed in my possession two black, rudely made, squat, globose bottles which had contained spirits obtained of a packman by his grandfather. They are of about the date of the end of the seventeenth century, and probably contained hollands. The packhorses travelled in lines laden with bundles or panniers, the baskets being about three feet in length, two feet in depth, their width being about one or two feet. The horses' backs were padded, and the panniers were suspended by hooks attached to a curved billet of wood which crossed from side to side; and it has been suggested that the inn-sign known as the "Crooked Billet" derived its name from this apparatus.

In my possession are several small globular bells of pleasant tinkling sound, which were picked up in the village from time to time. They are of the seventeenth century, and there is little

---

[1] *Gan, gangan*, to go; *gang-weg*, a gang-way. (Bosworth, *Anglo-Saxon Dictionary*.)

doubt were worn by packhorses. One specimen has a transverse bar of iron attached to it for fixing apparently to a cross-bar. They are smaller than the bells which were formerly worn on the market-teams of the farmers, although the early examples of market-bells were globular. Such bells were once universal among the farmers; and the object of their employment, in addition to any small pride in their use on the part of the employers or carters, was the necessity of warning any counter-traffic in narrow roads during the night or early morning. Another motive that I have heard stated was the scaring away the demons of the night from obstructing the wains by putting what the carters call "spells" on the wheels.

At the period of the packhorses and later the country was infested with footpads and highwaymen, and there was but little security to life and property. One of the fraternity named Bolter frequented the roads between Newbury and Winchester. At the latter place he met a felon's well-merited fate; and the wife of a tailor named Brown, then living at St. Mary Bourne, attended the execution in order to be brought in contact with the dead felon's hand, under the impression that she should receive cure of some local malady. This incident may help to elucidate the superstitious beliefs which were then current among the peasantry.

Old Stone Implements.

(PALÆOLITHIC.)

NOTHING that has been written since conveys a more comprehensive impression of the topography of the district, and the character of the soils of the more elevated parts of North Hampshire than that which was penned by Mr. W. Cobbett fifty years ago. He writes of it as a nice country of continual hill and dell, with now and then a chain of hills higher than the rest, and these are woods or downs. The undulations are endless, and the variety in the height, breadth, length, and form of the little hills has a very delightful effect. The soil, which to look on it appears to be more than half flint-stones, is very good in quality, and in general better on the tops of the lesser hills than in the valleys. It has great tenacity, and does not wash away like sand or light loam. It is a stiff, tenacious loam, mixed with flint-stones; bears saintfoin well, and all sorts of grass, which make the fields on the hills as green as meadows, even at this season (November), and the grass does not burn up in summer.

In a country so full of hills one would expect endless runs of water and springs; but there are none. No water-furrow is ever made in the land; no ditches round the fields; and even in the deep valleys, such as that in which this village (Hurstbourne Tarrant) is situated, though it winds round for ten or fifteen miles, there is no run of water even now. The grass is fine and excellent in quality in the long and narrow valleys such as this. The soil is much shallower in the vales than on the hills. In the vales it is a sort of hazel-mould on a bed of something approaching to gravel; but on the hills it is stiff loam, with apparently half flints, on a bed of something like clay first (reddish, not yellow), and then comes the chalk. Sometimes in spring-thaws and thunder-showers the rain runs down the hills in torrents, but is gone directly. The woods, which consist chiefly of oak, thinly intermixed with ash, and well set with underwood of ash and hazel, but mostly the latter, are very beautiful. They sometimes stretch along the top and sides of hills for miles together; and as their edges or outsides joining the fields and the downs go winding and twisting about, and as the fields and downs are naked of trees, the sight altogether is very pretty. The trees in the deep and long valleys, especially the elm and the ash, are very fine and lofty; and from distance to distance the rooks have made them their habitation. This sort of country, which in shape is irregular and of great extent, has many advantages. It is dry under foot, and has good roads, winter as well as summer, and with very little expense. Saintfoin flourishes; fences cost little; wood, hurdles, and hedging-stuff are cheap. There is no shade in wet harvests, and the water in the wells is excellent.[1]

The reddish clay here spoken of exists as a gravelly or clay-gravelly subsoil over hundreds of acres between the top-soil and the chalk, which is always found at a moderate depth beneath. These clayey under-soils mark the lines of the ancient forest-tracts, at all events the denser portions of them, before the times of disafforestation, as the oak will not flourish on a subsoil of chalk. Large copses still extend over some of these areas. Beds of reddish-brown clay of irregular outline lie on the chalk, or are let down into pot-holes which have come from solution of the chalk, and the flints of the chalk have mixed with the clay and formed clay-with-flints.[2] The flints are unworn, and lie mostly near the bottom of the beds, and the beds are on the upper chalk. An old brickfield of this material occupies the highest point of the hill above Stoke hollow on the north of it.[3] There are also areas of high level gravels above the valleys, more or less pebbly, and of the thickness of a few inches to a few feet between the surface-soil and the chalk. These have been deposited at some time since the period of the plastic clay.

The map of the Geological Survey lays the whole district down in chalk; but places on it fringes of gravel along the river-courses, and also marks out certain areas of not more perhaps than a hundred acres in extent as belonging to the Woolwich and Reading series.[4] The mottled clays are all found on the present elevated ground.

[1] Cobbett, *Rural Rides*, pp. 10-11.
[2] *Memoirs of the Geological Survey*, No. 7, pp. 63-64.
[3] Stevens, *Geolog. Notices of North Hants*, Trans. Newbury Dist. Field Club, p. 75.
[4] There are three outliers of this series in Harewood Forest, from which bricks are made from the red-mottled clay; but the Eocene beds are so thin that there are some doubts whether it might not be brick-earth. At the north-east corner of Doles Wood, by Stoke Hill Farm, there is a ferruginous loam dug for making bricks. And there is a small outlier of the Woolwich and Reading beds between Doily farm and Stoke. (Bristow and Whitaker, *Memoir of Geolog. Survey*, No. 12.)

In the Report accompanying the map it is stated that brick-earths cover considerable tracts; and that they are believed to be formed by the re-arrangement of previously existing materials,[1] meaning older beds. But these brick-earths generally bear a very close resemblance to the true plastic clay, not merely in the colour and character of their clay, but in the constituents of their beds. The beds on Berehill, east of Andover, look like patches of Eocene dropped into gullies or pot-holes. They show the variously coloured clay lying on greenish sand with green or black-coated flints above the chalk, and carry the characteristic shells of *Ostrea Bellovacina*, mostly fragmentary; and I have picked out sharks' teeth from the same deposits.[2]

It has been suggested in accounting for the sparseness of the Eocenes in North Hampshire that they might have occupied a shallower sea, on account of the anticlinal axis through Shalbourn and Burghclere having already existed at the time of the deposition of the Eocenes, the districts now Berkshire and South Hampshire occupying comparatively deep bottoms in the sea of that period.[3] However that may be, the clays of the old Eocene sea-bottom and the materials of its beach have furnished the constituents of the brick-earths, clay-with-flints, and the pebble and other gravels which now overspread North Hampshire, with the aid of flint-gravel derived from the chalk; and this was carried out at an immense expense of time, and while the land was slowly rising and becoming drier.

If you survey the Upper Test Basin from an elevation on the west side of the valley, say from Wallop hill between St. Mary Bourne and Hurstbourne Tarrant, the height being five hundred feet above the level of the sea, its outlines will be seen to be somewhat pear-shaped, the tail-end representing the valley as it contracts in running southwards. The line of the hills formed by the chalk elevations sweeping round from above Hippenscombe and Combe to the high lands above Woodcot forms the rim of the basin; and from it the minor hills and hollows slope downwards from the north and north-west towards the valley. The hollows have no water-courses, although strewn along them are relics of the denudation of the chalk, which they must have obtained as feeders to the main valley. That the denudation of the chalk is not due to marine action we have the authority of Mr. Whitaker.[4] The rounded contour of the hills,

---

[1] *Memoirs of Geolog. Survey*, No. 12, p. 45.

[2] Stevens, *Geolog. Notices of North Hants*. Trans. Newbury Dist. Field Club, p. 77.

[3] C. B. Clarke, *Introduction to the Flora of Andover*, p. 4.

[4] W. Whitaker, F.G.S., *On Subaërial Denudation, and on the Cliffs and Escarpments of the Chalk, and the Lower Tertiary Beds*, Geolog. Magazine, 1867.

and their graduated slopes, indeed, the uniformity of outline which characterises the entire district, are indicative that the operations which have brought their superficies to what we see them were sub-aërial, that the work has been done by "rain and rivers". The graduated slope of the Upper Test Valley on the east, and its more abrupt embankment on the west, under which the present stream tends to cling, point clearly to river action.

Flexuous valleys such as that of the Test could scarcely have been cut out by any other than river erosion. The valley in its upper sources is tolerably deep, it being in depth at Hurstbourne Tarrant about 250 feet from the upper part of the west escarpment, and the depth is much the same from Wallop hill and Stoke hill. The drainage, further, has always since tertiary times followed the same lines as at present, or from north to south. There are no sufficient gaps in that portion of the ridge forming the watershed of the Upper Test valley district by which any extraneous water could have obtained access from the north of the ridge to assist in the denudation. The lowest connecting depression is behind Fosbury, where the height above sea-level cannot be less than 700 feet, the cutting-out therefore south of the ridge below that level must have been due to the existing rivers, with whatever assistance they might have derived from climatic disturbances.

The Upper Test river, and the Anton, which is separated from it by the small watershed, Hurstbourne ridge, belong to the same drainage system; but they at no time drained a larger area than the present one. The depth and general distribution of the valley-gravel over the general area of both valleys show that at some time the streams must have had a much greater volume, and have been less confined in their operations. At Stoke I found the depth through the valley-gravel to the chalk to be $8\frac{1}{2}$ feet; and at two points at St. Mary Bourne 10 feet; the measurements being taken where the houses extend along the floor of the valley. The depth, however, varies considerably, as the floor of the valley, although approximately level is not really so when estimated by the depth of the superficial wells or "dip-holes", which varies at St. Mary Bourne from about 8 feet to 12 feet.

The gravels lying along the floor of the valley and extending somewhat up the lower slopes are all fluviatile. They belong to the low-level series, geologically named *post-pliocene, pleistocene*, or *quaternary;* and they are made up of materials derived from many sources. Among their contents are sand, fragments of chalk-flints; some water-worn, others larger and very little worn; and very largely materials from the high-level gravels. And it is not unusual to observe rounded flints stained blackish, evidently from the base of the Woolwich and Reading beds. In further evidence of chalk denudation casts are met with of *Inoceramus, Pecten, Spondylus, Pleurotomaria, Terebratula, Rhynchonella, Echini* of various species, and sponge remains,[1] etc., in flints which have come from that formation. It is not unusual to find in such beds rude records of man in the shape of chipped flint implements, and the bones of extinct mammalia. The evidences are not abundant, but they are sufficiently conclusive that the maker of the "old stone" tools, the earliest man of whom we have any knowledge from his handiwork, must have been an inhabitant of the Upper Test Valley, and that he had the Mammoth for his contemporary.

The gravels have received but little investigation, or, rather, few opportunities have been furnished for making investigations, there being no sections from gravel-diggings for road-repairing, or for the foundations of houses. But in 1862, in removing material for the erection of new buildings at Bourne farm, on the north slope of the embouchure of Warwick hollow, a molar of Mammoth (*Elephas primigenius*) was dug out. It lay under about four feet of gravelly clay without flints, on some white river-sand. The elevation here is 7 or 8 feet above the general valley-level. The bed slopes upwards on the north-west inclination of the hollow; and there is a broken dip from it down to the present watercourse. The drift has the appearance of being deposited by the action of the back-water of the river as it swept into the hollow when the water occupied the level of the stratified deposit. In the material dug out from another part of the same drift I found the flake, fig. 3. It is reddish-yellow in colour, similar to that of the clay, and I have no doubt that it is *Palæolithic.*

The tooth is a lower left molar (pl. 1, fig. 5), and therefore slightly concave on its grinding surface. Its length is 9 inches, and its depth through the 10th plate 5 inches. The broadest span of its grinding surface is $2\frac{3}{4}$ inches; and its weight $4\frac{1}{2}$ lbs. The lamellar divisions of the crown are seventeen or eighteen, the last four or five of which have only just come into use. It was consequently not a shelled tooth; but must have died with the animal. From the number of plates it must be a fifth or sixth molar; and as its angles are very little worn, it could not have travelled far from where the animal died, or rather where the bones separated from decomposition, as there is room for the supposition that the carcass might have drifted down with the flood-water of the valley.

[1] A variety of identified fossils from the flints of the Upper Test Valley are in the Reading Museum.

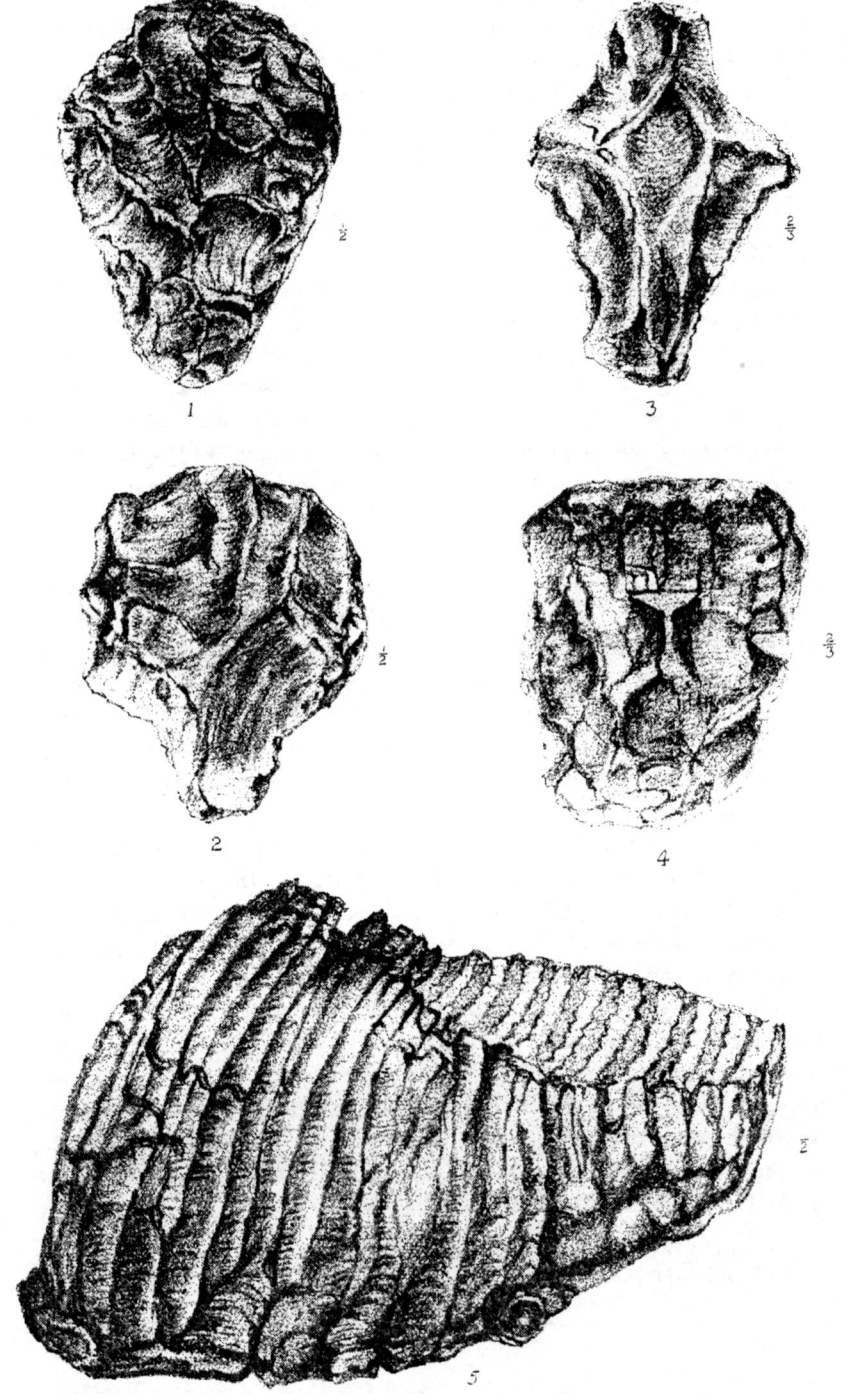

Pl. 1.

On April 30th, 1868, a small oval drift implement was found in the Vicar's garden, in some dark reddish undisturbed gravel from the depth of 5 feet. It was in length 3½ inches, its diameter being about 2½ inches. My attention was called to it by the Vicar's son, Mr. Charles Lockhart, who furnished me with these particulars. The garden stands in about the centre of the valley. The core, fig. 4, a flake or two, and three rudely-wrought implements, I found in the river-course, in valley-gravel which had fallen in from the undermining of the gravel in digging to obtain river-sand. The obtusely pointed form (pl. 1, fig. 1), and the trimmed flake (fig. 2), came from the same gravel when a cutting was carried through it in order to diverge the river-course, and build a bridge below Spring-hill, at a point where the gravel slopes downwards from the east.[1] There is no doubt that with favourable opportunities these discoveries may be added to; but they are sufficient to show that the *Neolithic* or later stone implement maker, whose flint relics occur so abundantly along the hills above the river-course, was preceded by the very much earlier nomad whose rude tools and weapons of flint are confined to the drift formations of the valley.

Whatever manner of men they were who contrived to eke out a precarious subsistence by means of implements so rude and seemingly unmanageable, they must have occupied the district at an immensely distant period, and when its features were very different from those of the present day. They must have traversed the hills and vales for flesh and fish in small scattered families, and with wild food within their reach were doubtless miserably poor, their small constructive capacity and the conditions of climate rendering it difficult of obtainment. In the midst of powerful and fierce animals,

---

[1] The Mammoth's tooth and the drift implements from the Upper Test Valley now form part of the Reading Museum collection; and are arranged with a large and varied series of *Palæolithic* implements and mammalian remains obtained by me from the drifts of the Thames Valley at Reading since 1879, when they were first discovered at Grovelands. This deposit occupies an elevation above the present Thames level of 82 feet. In 1880-1, some very fine implements, chiefly of the lengthened pointed forms, were found on the Caversham side of the Thames, in high-level drift, at 119 feet above Thames level. They occupied an old palæolithic floor under denuded gravel. In addition to these I have obtained implements from the following formations: the middle drift of Redlands, Reading; the high-level gravels at Purley (the implements being in the possession of Mr. F. Wilder); in the low-level gravels with Mammoth, etc., at Taplow, Bucks; at Maidenhead; on the Henley road, Caversham, in middle drift, with Mammoth's tusks, teeth, etc.; in low-level drift at Newbury; also from the Earley cutting on the Great Western Railway, Reading. See Lieut.-Col. Cooper King, F.G.S., *History of Berkshire;* and Stevens, *Transactions of Berks and Reading Archæolog. and Architectural Soc.*

whose contentions for food were as great as their own, the struggle for life must have been protracted and severe. The qualities of these men must have been of the enduring, passive rather than active.

As a mere outline of the operations which are believed to have effected the scooping out of the valley of the Upper Test, and the neighbouring high-level chalk-valleys, it is considered that the coarseness of the sands, the general distribution of the materials along the valleys, and the absence of mud sediments, indicate that the rivers were more voluminous and violent. To have favoured these conditions the land was more elevated and the climate colder.[1] The land-surface was at the outset comparatively level; but the drainage had been determined by the southern dip, and perhaps the drainage-lines had been outlined by the sea. The winters were subject to greater vicissitudes then, and they were of greater severity. The accumulations of ice and snow, particularly on the more elevated lands, furnished the materials of floods. These, becoming loosened in the spring by change of temperature, with a heavy rainfall, sent down large bodies of water with floating ice, which attacking the lines of least resistance carved out the hollows, and carried the harder and more indestructible materials from the older tertiaries and the chalk, with whatever animal and vegetable remains came within the force of the current, and spread them over the lower ground. Similar wearing operations, together with solution of the chalk-surface, and the disintegrating effects of frost, continued year by year over an indefinite period, the operations gradually becoming gentler, brought the face of the country to its present state of hill and valley. The drift deposits are not everywhere uniform. Along the valley-bottoms are distributed coarse sand, and very coarse gravel, made up largely of broken flints derived from the destruction of the chalk, which is sometimes called white "water-gravel". But where there was any protection from current-action the drifts differ, as in the eddies at the junction of the streams, where are found finer gravel and sand; and where the water was more languid, layers of fine river-sand, such as that on which lay the mammoth's molar. In this way are left in favourable places, deposits of sand, sand and gravel, and occasionally a finer muddy sediment known as brick-earth. The drifts have been

---

[1] Bearing on these difficult subjects, among many others the following papers may be referred to:—*Proc. Royal Soc.*, March 27th, 1862; also Prestwich, Memoir on Sheet 7, *Geolog. Survey*; also, by the same author, a paper read at the opening of the Blackmore Museum, Salisbury, 1867, printed in *Trans. Wilts. Archæol. and Nat. Hist. Soc.;* also Mr. Godwin-Austen, *Journ. Geolog. Soc.*, vol. vi.

wasted by subsequent denudation, and the valley-gravels have been disturbed by the rivers which have cut through them and re-arranged their materials, and man's hand has operated in changing the course of the streams; but it is in the remains of these old river-beds that we are to look for the surviving evidences of the men who occupied North Hampshire at that time, and of the animals that lived with him.[1]

Of the earlier races who have passed over the face of North Hampshire we may reckon on the following, according to our present

---

[1] Prof. J. Prestwich, in a paper read before the Geological Society on May 25th, 1887, largely curtails the time stated by Dr. Croll as necessary to have effected valley-denudation. Dr. Croll had referred the date of the glacial epoch to an earlier phase of orbital eccentricity commencing 980,000 years ago, subsequently regarding it as coinciding with a minor period of eccentricity that began 240,000, and ended 80,000 years since; this last estimate being supported by the amount of denudation that had subsequently taken place. It was thought by Prof. Prestwich that the efficacy of the increased eccentricity of the earth in producing the glacial epoch was very doubtful, for as similar changes in the eccentricity had occurred 165 times in the last 100 millions of years, there must have been many glacial epochs, some of which must have been very severe; but of such glacial epochs there was no valid evidence. He questioned also the succession of cold and warm periods as being due according to Mr. Croll to the earth's eccentricity; but was more likely dependent on changes in the distribution of land and water, and not due to cosmical causes. The time requisite for such interglacial periods as were supported by geological evidence was more likely hundreds than thousands of years. Recent observations in Greenland had shown that the movement of ice in large quantities was much more rapid, and consequently the denudation produced was much greater than formerly supposed. The average rate of progress in several large iceberg-producing glaciers in Greenland had been found to be 36 feet daily. Prof. Prestwich limited the duration of the glacial epoch from 15,000 to 20,000 years, including the time during which the cold was increasing, or pre-glacial time, and that during which the cold was diminishing, or post-glacial time. The evidence which had been adduced by Dr. Hicks, Mr. Skertchly, and others, as to the occurrence of human relics in pre-glacial times had induced Prof. Prestwich to change his views as to the age of the high-level gravels in the Somme, Seine, Thames, and Avon rivers, and he was disposed to assign these beds to the early part of the glacial epoch, when the ice-sheet was advancing. The advance drove the men then inhabiting Western Europe to localities not covered with ice. Man, he thought, had occupied the country a short time before the land was overwhelmed with ice, he was therefore pre-glacial. He thought that at the close of the glacial epoch the final melting of the ice might have occupied 8,000 to 10,000 years. The former estimate of one foot being removed in 6,000 years, on which Dr. Croll founded his hypothesis of 80,000 years having elapsed since the glacial epoch, was insufficient, as a heavier rainfall, and the disintegrating effects of frost would produce more rapid denudation. Prof. Prestwich thought that *Neolithic* man made his appearance in Europe 3000 to 4000 years B.C., but he may have existed for a long time previously in the East, as in Egypt and Asia Minor large states flourished at an earlier date than 4000 B.C. (*Nature*, June 16th, 1887.)

evidence. 1st. The *Palæolithic* men of the Mammoth period, who have so far as can be shown no descendants, unless the Esquimaux have some pretensions.[1] England then formed part of the European continent. 2nd. Dark, short, narrow-skulled tribes, who may be called *Silures;* whose burial-places are the long barrows, sometimes chambered, containing stone implements of the *Neolithic* type; and whose descendants are present, as their appearance testifies, particularly in South Wales and Ireland, though they now speak a Celtic tongue. 3rd. A taller, broad-skulled people, fair in hair and complexion (*Celtæ*), and possibly allied to the modern Finns. These, judging from the contents of the round tumuli, used polished stone and bronze implements and weapons, and eventually conquered and mixed with their predecessors. Last came the invading tribes from Gaul (*Belgæ*), who, although using bronze, had introduced iron before the Roman conquest.

[1] The Esquimaux are thought to have some alliance with the Cave-men (see Boyd Dawkins, *Cave Hunting*); and as the Mammoth belonged to a temperate fauna, the low-level gravels of the south of England might be comparatively late. Mr. B. Dawkins (*Early Man in Britain*) affirms that the Cave-men are not lower than the Australians; and in art, as shown by their remarkable carvings on bone, teeth, etc., he was higher than his successor in Europe in the Neolithic Age. There were two types of men in the Pleistocene period, quite distinct, the Drift-man, and the so-called Cave-man. I say so-called, because *reliquiæ* of the older man have been found in caves; but at a lower level than those of the other, and his relics are ruder. There are no traces of pottery or spinning associated with the life of the Cave-dweller, and he in our part of the world shows no connection with domesticated animals, or with cultivated seeds. But he used fire, probably obtained by rubbing dried sticks together. He was a feral wanderer, in the hunter stage of human progress. Mr. Dawkins shows how close is the relation of the true Cave-dweller to the Esquimaux, in the character of his implements, methods of obtaining food and of cooking it, modes of preparing skins for clothing; and particularly in his remarkable skill of depicting figures on bone. From the researches of Mons. Julien Fraipont, Prof. of Animal Palæontology in the University of Liége, into the human remains found in a cave on the banks of the Orneau, in the commune of Spy, province of Namur, there is but little doubt that the older race, who occupied Europe during the early Mammoth Age, are practically extinct. This race have now been shown in their osteological relations to possess lower affinities than any race now existing; and the discoveries at Spy bear out the views which have been entertained regarding the inferiority of type of the previously discovered Neanderthal and similar human crania. (*Nature*, April 14th, 1887, p. 564.)

GROUP OF PIT-DWELLINGS DISCOVERED AT HURSTBOURNE SIDING,

Sept. 23rd, 1871.

(*See the accompanying diagram.*)

---

1. Pit pear-shaped; entrance south; length 22 ft. from mouth of entrance-passage to end of dwelling, the passage measuring in length 7 ft.; greatest diameter of pit, 12 ft.; depth at centre, 4 ft.; was rudely pitched with flint stones, and large flints were found round its circumference, and along the sides of the alley, some of which were built up in courses without mortar. When the flints were removed, and carted away, they were reckoned at twelve cart-loads. This pit was 21 ft. from the end of Pit 3. For the contents of Pit 1 see Plate III.

2 and 3. Pits partly opened, but they could not be completely examined on account of their extending underneath the Station pales and yard: the portions examined were 5 ft. in diameter.

4 and 5. Entrances of pits, pointing south, which could not be examined on account of their extending beneath the Station road. The portions opened were 6 ft. in length, and 16 ft. from each other: entrance 4 was 52 ft. from Pit 2.

6. Appeared to be the passage of a pit partly completed. Its length was 7 ft.; and it was 46 ft. from Pit 7.

7. Pit completely investigated. It opened east, and was 38 ft. from Pit 5; length from mouth of alley to end of pit, 42 ft.; greatest diameter, 13 ft. 6 in.; depth at centre, 4 ft.; entrance-passage, 3 ft. in width at centre. For the contents of this habitation see Plate III.

8. Almost circular hole, 5 ft. 4 in. by 4 ft. 6 in.; at 9 ft. from Pit 7. Its depth was 3 ft.; and as its contents were animal bones, some of which had been exposed to fire; also snail shells, together with charred flints and charcoal ashes; and as fire had been used in the hole, as shown by the chalk walls of the hole, coupled with its contiguity to Pit 7, it was thought to be a cooking-hole.

A site in the Station garden from which animal bones, etc., were removed, in digging a well, was thought to be another habitation.

* About 10 ft. of Romano-British wall was laid bare at the south-east corner of the enclosure; in clearing it out we found scraps of Romano-British pottery, a small piece of Samian, besides roof-nails, and a bronze buckle.

The pits were dug in the chalk, and the floors of those not pitched with flints were formed by the solid chalk. The removed material consisted of gravelly soil washed into the pits from the adjoining slopes.

Pl. II.

Pit-Dwellings.

THE site of the hut-circles described on the previous page was brought to my notice by a labourer engaged in forming a yard adjacent to Hurstbourne Siding, a new station on the Basingstoke and Salisbury Railway, situated at about half a mile distant from, and south of, St. Mary Bourne. The man had been employed in excavating some Roman buildings at Finkley during the previous summer, and having become somewhat expert in the recognition of rude objects of antiquity, and finding that the subsoil of the yard contained calcined stones, broken pottery, and other evidences of past occupation, he called my attention to the matter, which led to the discovery of nine early habitations, of which, from their situation, two only could be completely investigated, and five others partially. The pits extended along the brow of the hill, and they evidently formed part of a *vicus*, which from the character of its contents had been occupied during a lengthened period. The situation had been favourably selected for the obtainment of water from the Upper Test river, which runs immediately below it on the west, the pit-huts being about fifty feet above the valley level; and that the buildings were not confined to the yard was obvious from the fact that similar remains, together with various animal bones, had been dug up in forming the garden appertaining to the station. At the time that the habitations were being explored, the survey for the six-inch Ordnance Map was in process, which led to a notice of the site appearing on the Government map.

The chief points of interest in the consideration of these remains are the sloping entrances, the large flints forming the pitching and outside walls of Pit 1, and the cooking-hole outside of Pit 7. Circularity of outline and central fireplaces are also observable in these early habitations (see plate ii). A few flint stones irregularly placed, among which some wood ashes were mixed, indicated that these were the hearths around which the domestic operations had been carried on, and it was here chiefly that the relics left by the occupants of the pits were discovered.

It appears that sloping entrance-passages had not hitherto been observed in England. In a note on the subject from Mr. Albert Way, in July 1872, he remarks that "he remembers no instance of the troglodytic dwellings with an approach by slanting passages, although they have occurred in France." There seems, however, nothing very remarkable that such a simple arrangement should have suggested itself in lieu of the rude ladder which has been considered the method sometimes adopted, and which it is conjectured was the mode of obtaining access to the underground dwellings investigated at Highfield, near Salisbury.[1] Mr. Way further remarks on the discovery of the lip of a cowry in Pit 1 (plate iii, fig. 10) as curious and uncommon. That it had been purposely cut from the shell and used for some purpose is evident from the worn condition of the crenulations of the lip. The use of flints for pitching, and in building the foundation walls of Pit 1, finds a parallel in some habitations explored by Mr. Edmund Kell at Gallibury and Rowborough in the Isle of Wight, an account of which appeared in vol. xi of the *Transactions of the British Archæological Association*. British remains of a similar kind have been observed on the Island, as at the base of Newbarns Down; but the pits at Gallibury and Rowborough were completely explored. The depressions numbered sixty in the two villages, and were in shape round or oval. Their diameter varied from 15 ft. by 15 ft., to 55 ft. by 46 ft., their depth varying from 1 ft. to 7 ft. The articles found in them were unimportant; but some of the circles were found to contain flints. In the neighbourhood were inclosures apparently for penning cattle; a drainage pond had supplied water from the hills; and the pits were in near relation to an earthwork for the protection of the inhabitants in times of danger. The greater diameter of Mr. Kell's pits in proportion to their depth must have been due to the gradual washing in of their sides.

The pottery found in and around the pits at Hurstbourne Siding was of the commoner kinds of Romano-British, with fragments of hand-made British ware of coarse clay with flint-grit. Pottery similar in character is found on the same line of elevation, on the farm of Mr. Andrew Twitchin, and scraps of similar texture were frequent in the soil turned up in grubbing Hogdiggen copse, on the same farm, some years ago. Indeed, along the line of the Roman Portway several

---

[1] Mr. E. T. Stevens, *Flint Chips*, p. 57; also Pits at Highfield, near Fisherton, *Wilts County Mirror*, June 15, 1866. These pits were reached by a circular descending shaft, and Mr. A. Way, in a note of July 8th, 1872, suggested that a rude ladder was probably used.

sites occur where pottery is ploughed up, showing how general must have been the occupation of the district during the Romano-British period.

Portions of mealing-stones were found among the *reliquiæ*, notably a large section of one in Pit 1, a fragment in Pit 3, and an entire saddle-quern near the fireplace of Pit 7, in all five, whole or in fragments, were dug out during the excavations. Their material is a hard-grit sandstone, but the entire specimen is of sarsen sandstone, and most likely came from the tertiary formation which once overspread North Hampshire. Two of the rubbing-stones were worn on their surfaces probably from pulverising grain. Several hand-stones or mullers were found lying contiguous to them, showing by their battered surfaces that they had been employed for crushing or bruising. The specimen represented on the plate is of flint, and is abraded on one facet, the other retaining the natural crust for grasping in the hand. Instruments for hand-mealing must have been in common use among the pit-dwellers throughout England. Mr. E. T. Stevens furnishes an account (see list of references) of two concave querns of the simplest type which were taken from the pit-habitations at Highfield; and curiously enough Dr. Blackmore discovered the cast of a grain of wheat in breaking open a lump of the clay which had covered one of the pits. Professor A. H. Church (see *Guide to the Corinium Museum*) states that a number of querns have been found at Cirencester, some of which show scoring on their surfaces. In size they are similar to those from Hurstbourne, having diameters varying from 10 inches to 20 inches. The Honourable W. O. Stanley has given details of several rubbing-stones and mortars with their pestles taken from some circular huts, which were explored by him on the farm of Ty Mawr, Anglesey, in 1862.[1] One of these relics was a slab of coarse-grained sandstone, hollowed in the course of grinding; and an oval rubber lay near it, measuring 1 foot by 5 inches, which was flat on one face and convex on the other. The grain was probably prepared by parching it before crushing. The hollow condition of the understone prevented the grain from escaping, as in the ordinary mortar, while the muller was so shaped as to render it easily grasped while it was pushed backwards and forwards by the hands. Similar simple forms of handmills are in use among most tribes in the infancy of agriculture. They are mentioned by Dr. Livingstone, and Sir Samuel Baker, as employed among the native Africans. The latter furnishes the following interesting notice relative to an apparatus of this kind. He writes:—

---

[1] Hon. W. O. Stanley, *Ancient Circular Dwellings in Holyhead Island*, Archæologia, vol. xxvi; Journ. Brit. Archæolog. Assoc., vol. vii.

"I must have swallowed a good-sized millstone since I have been in Africa, in the shape of grit rubbed from the moortraka or grinding-stone. The moortraka, when new, is a large flat stone weighing about forty pounds. Upon this the corn is ground by being rubbed with a cylindrical stone with both hands. After a few months' use half of the grinding-stone disappears, the grit being mixed with the flour; thus the grinding-stone is actually eaten. No wonder that hearts become stony in this country."[1]

The materials used in constructing querns in England differ somewhat in different districts, according to the localisation of any particular stone adapted for shaping them; and it is not unusual to find that the material was imported from one district to another. The hard sandstone, plentiful in some localities under the title of "Greywethers", or "Druid-stones", appears a likely material to have been used in the South of England; yet grain-rubbers of this stone are not prevalent. The gritstone from the Upper Greensand, so well known for making rubbers for sharpening scythes and other cutting tools, is more frequently selected. But the stone most in use is derived from the various coloured sandstones and gritstones of the coal-measures and new red sandstones.

Old red sandstones and pudding-stones of the old red conglomerate also were often selected for constructing querns, the latter being the material of which the Wroxeter (*Uriconium*) specimens were made. The Pen Pits, near Penselwood, Somerset, were thought by Dr. Buckland to have been quarries where the Britons dug their millstone material; but other antiquaries have regarded the pits as the remains of a British village, this latter view having met the acceptance of Mr. Thomas Kerslake, in 1882,[2] and, at an earlier period, of Mr. William Cunnington, an able exponent of Wiltshire antiquities. The pits were considered as numbering 20,000, covering an area estimated at 700 acres, on the Greensand formation. Sir Richard Colt Hoare[3] states what is known in reference to their being human abodes; but the later researches of the Rev. H. H. Winwood, subsequently confirmed by those of Lieut.-General Pitt-Rivers,[4] go far to prove that they mark the sites of old quarries worked by the Britons in order to obtain suitable loose material, without quarrying the hard rock, for making querns or millstones. Broken quernstones, some partly dressed, were found in the pits; and specimens are not uncommon in the surrounding villages, which are said to have come from the pits. They vary in diameter from 9 inches to 2 feet.

[1] *The Albert Nyanza*, vol. i, p. 65.
[2] Thos. Kerslake, *Caer Pensauelcoit*, 1882.
[3] Sir R. C. Hoare, *Ancient Wilts*, p. 35.
[4] Lieut.-Gen. Pitt-Rivers, *Report on Excavations in the Pen Pits, near Penselwood, Somerset*, 1884.

Sufficient evidences were not found in the shape of pottery, bones, or other relics to justify the opinion that the depressions are the remains of habitations.

In Berkshire, near Faringdon, similar depressions occur, traditionally called Cole's Pits,[1] which were considered by the Hon. Danes Barrington[2] as British habitations; but which Mr. Godwin-Austen stated resulted from working underneath the sand for ironstone. The "Grimes'-graves," in Norfolk, were quarried for the purpose of obtaining flint for shaping implements during the Neolithic age[3]; and those remarkable shafts and caverns on Cissbury Hill, in Sussex, which so largely filled the attention of scientific observers a few years ago, were excavated for the same purpose.[4] In the chalk districts of England some of the depressions observable on the surface might have come from chalk or marl digging for agricultural purposes, as the ancient Briton, like the modern farmer (Pliny, *Natural History*), knew the advantage of a porous material such as chalk in rendering newly grubbed soils more workable and productive.

Bones were present in various places, not merely in the dwellings and cooking-hole at Hurstbourne, but were mingled with the soil surrounding the pits. They consisted of fragments of the skulls and long bones of the Celtic ox (*Bos longifrons*); portions of antler, and a bored tine of red deer (*Cervus elaphus*); facial bones and tusks of pig (*Sus Sp.*); skull and horn-cores of goat (*Capra hircus*); bones apparently of dog; teeth of a small kind of horse; and bones of the hare or rabbit. Some of the long bones were split in their long axes; others were blackened as if they had been toasted; and one specimen, now in the Reading collection, bears scorings as if made with teeth. Some small articles

---

[1] Stevens, *Nature*, Oct. 1885, p. 560.

[2] Hon. Danes Barrington, *Account of some Remarkable Pits in Berks*, Archæologia, vol. vii.

[3] Rev. W. Greenwell, *Grimes' Graves, Norfolk*, Journal Ethnograph. Soc., 1871, p. 419.

[4] Col. A. L. Fox, *Hill Forts, Sussex*, Archæologia, Feb. 6, 1868; also Col. A. Lane Fox, *Excavations in Cissbury Camp, Sussex*, Journ. Anthropolog. Institute, 1876; also Mr. E. Willet, *On Recent Excavations at Cissbury*, Brighton and Sussex Nat. Hist. Soc., 1875. Also Stevens, *Flint Works at Cissbury*, Sussex Archæological Collections, vol. xxiv. The following are some other notices concerning Pit-Dwellings :—Rev. A. C. Smith, *Guide to Brit. and Roman Antiquities of North Wiltshire Downs*, 1884; Stevens, *Pit-Dwellings*, Brighton and Sussex Nat. Hist. Soc., 1872; also, *Nature*, vol. v, 1872; Mr. W. H. Cunnington, *Brit. Dwelling-Pit at Beckhampton*, Wilts. Archæolog. and Nat. Hist. Soc., 1886, vol. xxiii; Mr. C. Warne, *Ancient Dorset*, p. 12; Mr. Spence Bate, *Prehistoric Antiq. of Dartmoor*, Jour. Anthropol. Institute, July 1871; Bateman, *Vestiges of Derbyshire;* Rev. A. Hume, *Remarks on Querns*, Arch. Camb., Second Series, vol. iv, p. 89.

ARTICLES FOUND IN PIT-DWELLINGS AT HURSTBOURNE SIDING,

During September and October 1871.

(*See the accompanying Plate.*)

---

1. Knife, apparently of deer-antler, from Pit 1.
2. Bone needle, with eyelet partly removed, from Pit 1.
3. Marrow-scoop or awl, from British dwellings, Finkley.
4. Bone awl, from   ditto   ditto.
5. Bone awl, from Pit 7.
6. Holed Romano-British pottery, from Pit 7.
7. Holed stone, from Pit 1.
8. Quartzite grain-crusher (*Quern*), and flint muller, from Pit 7 (dimensions of quern, 10 in. long diameter, by 8 in.; height, 7 in.).
9. Chalk spindle-whorl, from Pit 7.
10. Lip of cowry (*Cypræa sp.*), from Pit 1. It had apparently been used as a rasp or polisher, the crenulations of the lip being considerably worn.
11. Nodule of burnt clay, from Pit 1.
12. Lump of clay-iron-stone scored on its face, from Pit 7.
13. Piece of stone grain-rubber, worn and blackened on its interior, which might have been used for the purpose of parching grain, from Pit 1.
14. Quartzite whetstone, from Pit 7.
15. Half of a quartzite hammer, from near Pit 1. A British gold coin also was found close to Pit 1; it is slightly concavo-convex, and of the same type as fig. 6, plate B, page 61-2, in Dr. Evans's *Ancient British Coins*. It is there described as ranging somewhat extensively, particularly its coarser varieties, in the south-west districts of England. The type appears in Ruding, pl. 1, fig. 10; in Poste's *British Coins*, p. 139, No. 5. Mr. Durden, of Blandford, has a specimen; and Mr. Whitbourn one, found near Basingstoke. Similar coins are also found in silver and copper.

In addition to the above, various cut bones were found in the dwellings, including a bored *ulna* (see plate), and a tine of deer-antler (*Cervus elaphus*), hollowed apparently for a socket. The whole of the series is now in the Reading Free Museum.

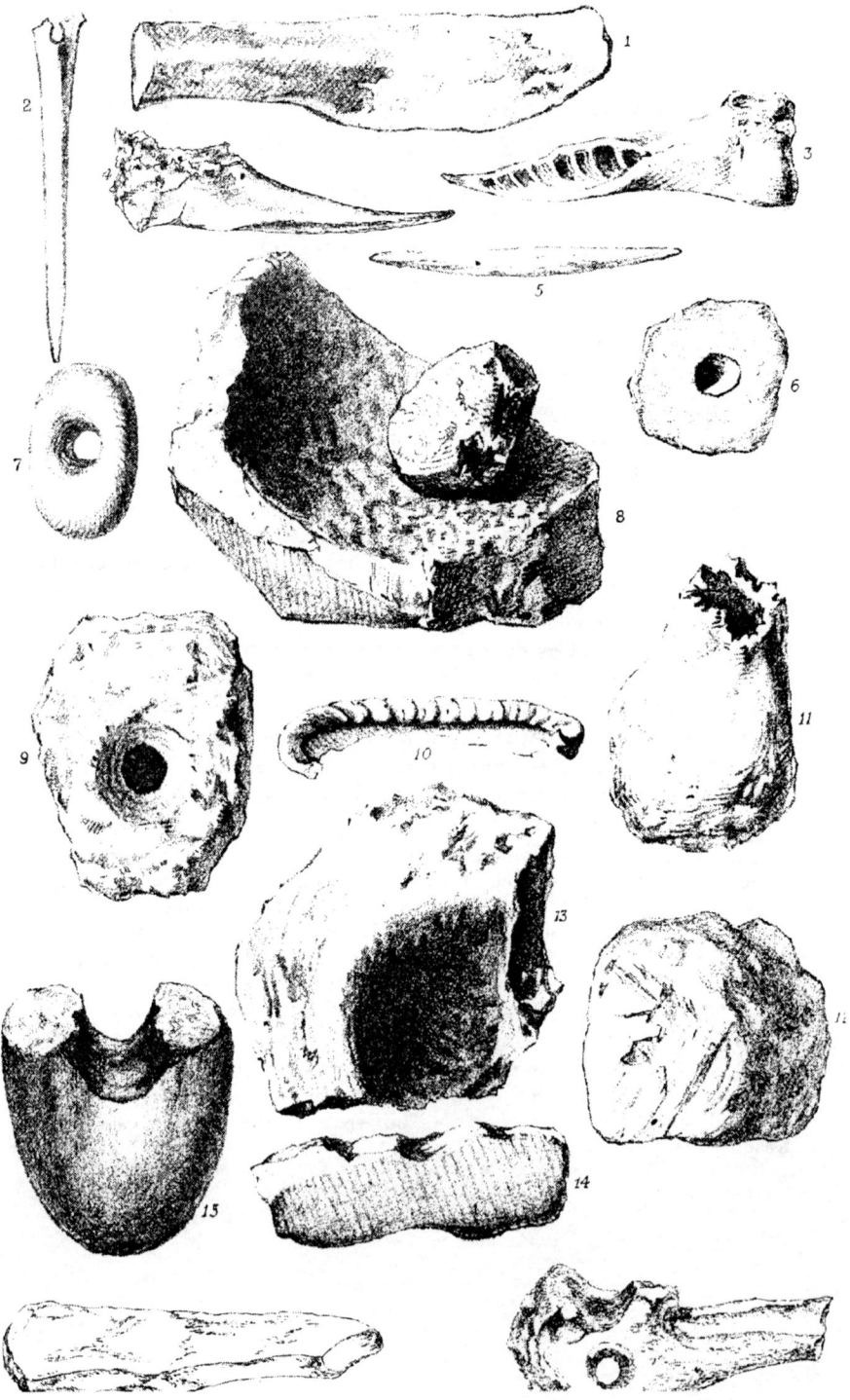

Pl. III.

gipsies sling their kettles in front of their cabins. The contracted nature of the pits, with no other means of exit for the smoke than the narrow entrance, and perhaps a hole in the roof, must, at all events during summer, have rendered out-of-door cooking almost a life-necessity. Mr. E. T. Stevens found evidences of exterior cooking at the pit-huts examined by him at Highfield, near Salisbury (*Flint Chips*, p. 59). Mr. Schoolcraft also states that the method is adopted by the Navajoe Indians, who live in circular huts, and occasionally under rock shelters (*Schoolcraft*, part iii, p. 70).

With regard to stone-boiling, it is evident that stones which have been so extensively calcined must have served some purpose in association with fire. I have found similar stones mostly irregularly circular, and all bearing the appearance of having been repeatedly fired, at most of the sites where flint implements occur. In a few instances I have found them in shallow holes in the earth, denoting apparently that these were temporary camping grounds. Such places occupied chalky platforms above the water valley, suitably chosen perhaps on account of being elevated, and the spots less densely wooded. Under the name of "milk-stones", calcined flints have been noticed by Sir J. Clarke Jervoise, Bart., he having met with them in the Eastern division of Hampshire, and considered that they were used for cooking purposes (*Archæolog. Journal*, vol. xx, p. 371). The charred stones found in the Hurstbourne pits were of two kinds, the one already referred to, and a form of irregular shape, with flattish facets, and much blackened, conveying the impression that they had been used in constructing earth-ovens for baking or smother-roasting. The clean, circular, porcelainous-looking stones were used probably after the manner adopted by various savage races of heating stones in the fire, and then distributing them among the flesh intended to be cooked, in some receptacle in the ground made to take the place of a cooking-pot. Mr. Tylor, in his *Early History of Mankind*, p. 262, states that the Assineboins, or stone-boilers, dig a hole in the ground, take a piece of raw hide and press it down to the sides of the hole, and fill it with water; this is called a "paunch-kettle"; they then make a number of stones red-hot in a fire close by, the meat is put into the water, and the hot stones dropped in until it is cooked. The Mimacs and the Souriquois boil in the same way[1]; and the Indians of the north-west coast of America widen their canoes by stone-boiling.[2] The South Sea Islanders adopt similar primitive methods in cooking their pigs and other food.[3] There are traditions among the High-

[1] *Schoolcraft*, vol. i, p. 54.
[2] *Naturalist in British Columbia*, vol. ii, p. 256.
[3] Sir J. Lubbock, *Prehistoric Times*, p. 380; and Tylor, *Early History of Mankind*, p. 266, etc.

landers of a similar method of preparing their feasts after hunting. They made a pit and lined it with smooth stones, and near it placed a heap of flat flint stones. The stones as well as the pit were properly heated with heather. They then placed the venison at the bottom, and a stratum of stones above it, and continued placing the stones alternately till the pit was full; the whole was then closed in with heath to confine the steam.[1] A similar use, I am inclined to believe, was made of the blackened stones found at Hurstbourne Siding.

A clumsy method of earth-baking has more than once been described to me by members of that "vagabond and useless race", as styled by Cowper, whose tawny skins, wandering instincts, unity, and patriarchal mode of life proclaim an Eastern origin—the gipsies. These wanderers were accustomed to frequent the waste places around St. Mary Bourne, Hogdiggen-corner between that parish and Whitchurch being one of their favourite haunts. Here fifty years ago might have been seen, especially during the time of the revel, a motley group of lean-looking men, tawdrily dressed women, with bare-headed and shoeless children, baskets of tin-ware and trinkets, dogs of mongrel aspect, donkeys, tent-cloths, and tent-rods. The gaudily-painted van of later days was hardly in existence then. Their tents were of two kinds, one circular with a semi-elliptical entrance-hole, the other sufficiently lengthy to enable the inmates to extend themselves full length. In front of the tents were suspended their cooking utensils. In my early days I had frequent opportunities of observing the habits of a gipsy family of the well-known Blacks of Berkshire. Whether they were of the pure blood of those low-caste wanderers who spread over Europe a few centuries ago from India, speaking a broken-down Hindu dialect, I am not in a position to state. According to their tribal habits they slung their kettle in the pleasant nooks in out-of-the-way places of the county, their cattle running free, and often pasturing on the common lands used by the English cotters. The leader at that time was known as "Old Tom Black". He was a stout-made, sturdy fellow, who with his brothers frequented the fairs and revels then in vogue; and it was remarkable how accurate was his knowledge concerning the dates and other particulars of every feast, fair, and revel throughout Berkshire and the adjoining counties. The older members excelled at "single-stick", or "backsword-playing", and it was their habit to practise their skill against the sapling oaks that grew in proximity to their tents, in the absence of a living opponent. The association of the gipsies with pleasant English

[1] Hon. W. O. Stanley, *Ancient Circular Habitations in Holyhead Island*, p. 9.

scenery, the picturesque character of their lives, and their animal beauty have at all times rendered them favourite subjects of the painter and poet; but the latter takes a liberty with even their degraded habits when he states the summary of their food as

> "Flesh obscene of dog
> Or vermin, or at best of cock purloin'd
> From his accustomed perch."

To the last, however, no exception can be brought, while the first is never eaten, as few fare better than the gipsies. But the hedgehog and the cock were not unfrequent dishes, and were sometimes cooked in their integuments, the plan being adopted probably in times of scarcity, or when secrecy was necessary, and it might be a survival of a method once general. The process consisted of placing the animal on embers in a hole in the earth, and covering it well with more embers, and over these placing a sod of turf, and banking the sides well up with embers and ashes. The skin retained the moisture without any extraneous covering; and the method had the advantage in the case of poultry that the feathers told no tales. In some cases the hedgehog was skinned and enveloped in a coat of wet clay before being consigned to the glowing embers; it was then said to be peculiarly savoury when cooked. The gipsy-nooks of England are now being fast absorbed, and these wandering people made more conformable to settled habits. The feasts and revels which fostered their vagabond mode of life are slowly yielding to the better tone and purpose of the English people, and it is hoped that they will shortly be numbered with their concomitants—the ducking-chair, pillory, and stocks—among the things of the past.

The circular method of building the pits corresponds with that of constructing habitations among all prehistoric races;[1] and the plan is mostly adopted among existing savages. In the numerous villages recorded by Mr. C. Warne, F.S.A.,[2] along the elevated grounds of Dorset, all the huts were circular or oval; and the same throughout Wiltshire,[3] Gloucestershire, Devonshire,[4] and the English counties generally where such remains have been explored; in Wales also;[5] and on the moors of Scotland. Among existing examples Dr. Living-

---

[1] Col. A. Lane Fox, *Primitive Warfare*, 1868.
[2] Charles Warne, F.S.A., *Dorsetshire; Its Vestiges—Celtic, Roman, Saxon, and Danish.*
[3] Rev. A. C. Smith, *British and Roman Antiquities of North Wiltshire Downs*, 1884.
[4] Mr. Spence Bate, *Prehistoric Antiquities of Dartmoor*, July 1871.
[5] Hon. W. O. Stanley, *Circular Dwellings in Anglesey*, Archæologia, vol. xxvi, p. 483.

stone states that he could not instruct the natives of Central Africa to build otherwise than circular. The North American Indians have both winter and summer houses, which are somewhat modified in form in different tribes, but on the whole are somewhat alike, those of the Dacotahs being formed of sapling rods stuck in a circle in the ground, and the tops meeting form a conical frame, over which buffalo-skins are extended for protection from the weather. Their summer wigwams are made of bark.[1] The native of Tahiti—with his

> "Cocoas and bananas, palms and yams,
> And homestall thatch'd with leaves,"—

builds a more open sanitary dormitory, not circular, the floor of which he strews with soft hay.[2] The hut of the Fuegian is a pit-dwelling, or tent, constructed of trees, with a hole at the top for the escape of the smoke.[3] It is needless to multiply examples; but it may be further cited that the Australian, a degraded human type, builds his hut barely high enough to enable him to sit upright in it[4]; and the equally squalid Tasmanian, according to Cook, was houseless, had no covering of any kind, and could not even construct a canoe for the purpose of fishing.

We have now to inquire, who were the occupants of these pits, and at what periods were they inhabited? It has been stated that a piece of well-built wall was discovered at the south-east corner of the enclosure, and with it some Romano-British pottery and a scrap of Samian. It is clear, therefore, that the elevation was occupied by the Romano-Britons. But some of the relics speak of occupation long anterior to this. The flint implements found in the earth of the pits and along the hill quite establish that the site, if not the dwellings, was occupied by the people of the Neolithic Stone Era; and Mr. Boyd Dawkins considers that pit-dwellings may be dated as far back as that period.[5] The querns, spindle-whorl, bone articles, and the pottery may be attributed to the Britons anterior to the arrival of the Romans; and which appears to be satisfactorily determined by the British coin which was found while removing the earth from the circumference of Pit 1. It is of the ordinary gold of these coins, and its weight is 96 grains; in this particular corresponding to the coins of the same type described in *Ancient British Coins*, by Dr. J. Evans. Thus, a similar coin on Plate B, No. 6, p. 61, weighs $96\frac{1}{4}$ grains; others

---

[1] Sir John Lubbock, *Prehistoric Times*, p. 421.
[2] *Ibid.*, p. 372. [3] *Ibid.*, p. 432.
[4] *Ibid.*, p. 346.
[5] Boyd Dawkins, *Early Man in Britain*, p. 266.

from Wareham 94 grains; and another found near Poole, Dorset, 95 grains. The Hurstbourne specimen is an uninscribed, debased form.

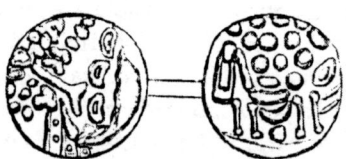

British Coin found at Hurstbourne Siding.

Obverse—Laureate head, face to the right; extreme left a sort of frill, which represents the back hair; bar across the centre, the bandlet across the wreath, the crescent at the end signifies the ear; three crescents under each other, the top one the most open, represent the front hair; dotted band intended for neck drapery; the bulbous object in front of the crescents is in place of face and chin.

Reverse—Disjointed horse facing to the left; eyelike object on the right is intended probably for a wheel or head of another horse; legs are the four straight lines ending in bulbs; pellets on the upper part in curved lines, 5, 4, 3, 1; upper crescent under pellets with curved body and pellets joined by bars, the head, neck and back of the animal; crescent in the centre between the legs, probably the belly; single pellet below the crescents, intended for a chariot-wheel.

Among numismatists this coin is known as a degraded copy of the Greek *stater* of Philip II of Macedon. The stater bears on its *obverse* the laureate head of Apollo (by some thought to be young Hercules) representing Philip; the *reverse* containing a biga, with a charioteer, the name of Philip being beneath.

The weight of the Macedonian stater, according to Dr. John Evans, was 133 grains; and the stater came to be first imitated in Gaul about 300 years before Christ. The weight of the Philippus it appears became reduced to 120 grains before its modified copies were introduced into Britain from Gaul. After these modified forms reached this country a gradual diminution in their weight took place, till the coins came to weigh no more than 84 grains. The original copy of the stater was a tolerably good imitation of the obverse and reverse on the stater; but during a course of years the copies became more and more transformed the further they receded from the original prototype. And not merely did the coins become degraded in their resemblance to the originals, and as we have already noticed in their diminution in weight, but the character of the gold became gradually debased. Taking into consideration the time requisite to bring about all this, with other concomitant circumstances, Dr. Evans thinks there are sufficient grounds for believing that there was a native currency in some parts of Britain, as early as, if not earlier than, 150 years before Christ.

As Dr. Evans writes:—"Assuming the diminution in weight to have been constant, and that the Philippus of 133 grains was first imitated B.C. 300, and that the weight had become reduced to 84 grains in B.C. 20, the date at which the weight of 120 grains (that of our British prototype) would have been reached, is B.C. 226, but it is possible that the ratio of diminution was rather less rapid at first than subsequently. Looking at all the coincident circumstances, we may, I think, fix on B.C. 150, as the approximate date for the commencement of the British coinage."[1]

Concerning the British coin in its bearing on the occupation of the Hurstbourne pits, it must have taken a considerable time for the extension of the British coinage over the different parts of the country; and bearing in mind that the Hurstbourne coin is not one of the lowest standard in weight, it may be considered that its presence testifies to the occupation of the site by the Britons at a date not later perhaps than 100 years anterior to the Christian era.

Glancing at the construction of the habitations, the presence of large flint stones around Pit 1, and forming its floor; and the scattered flints which were observed in one of the dwellings which could not be sufficiently examined, lead to the inference that some of the huts had their substructures of flint, on which perhaps were placed conical roofs composed of rafters lashed together at the centre, and protected by an outside coat of peat, sods of turf, or rushes. Some of these dwellings might have been constructed of wattles plastered with mud or clay. We have evidence that their inhabitants spun thread; and the mealing-stones testify that they were agricultural. They were associated with the ordinary domesticated animals; and the woodlands which then extended over the clay districts of North Hampshire, and penetrated as forests far into Wiltshire, of which portions remain in the present woods of Chute, Finkley, and Harewood, were doubtless frequented by them during their hunting excursions.

---

[1] Much learned matter regarding the origin and progress of the British coinage will be found in *Ancient British Coins*, pp. 17-32, Dr. J. Evans, F.R.S.

Eggbury Camp.

THE pit-dwellings which have just been described are not the only relics of the British period which have been found on the elevations above the Upper Test river. On the opposite or west side of the valley broken Romano-British pottery and a bone pin were dug out in levelling some ground on Gravel-hill; and at Eggbury, alongside of the British earthwork known as the Castle, in a small paddock several pit-like depressions were observed in 1872 during the improving of the entrance to Mr. Vincent's yard. The hollows contained a quantity of animal bones together with calcined stones. The district appears to be prolific in relics of a people who occupied the platform on which the camp is seated, and who most likely frequented it as a stronghold. Although it might have been used by the Belgic people in later times, it was in all probability outlined by the earlier Celtæ as a centre for their small scattered communities. Evidences of the Romano-Britons were discovered here by Mr. Vincent, who while digging in the entrenchment for the purpose of forming a pond on the east side of the camp, in 1847, found pottery with two coins (second brass of Gallienus and Claudius Gothicus). I have picked up flakes, cores, and similar relics of the Later Stone Era within the fortress; and two fine celts were found in 1863, in an adjoining field, by a ploughman in the service of Mr. Vincent. The camp is near the Roman Portway, which runs south of it at the distance of 800 yards, but appears to have no connection with it by road. In shape it is irregularly square, as it appears on the six-inch Ordnance map, and encloses about an area of 12 acres, and is 430 feet above sea-level. A considerable part of the rampart has been destroyed, and the ditch is filled in, that portion which commands the valley on the west being in the best state of preservation; and here the embankment reaches to about the height of 10 feet. On the north-west angle might have been erected a signal-post in connection with similar beacons on Beacon and Danebury hills, which appear in the distance. Two entrances are traceable, that on the west being the more visible; while there are signs of one on the east, with traces of a road, supposed to have connected the camp with the old way from Newbury to Winchester.[1] In addition to the discoveries made in the encampment an iron flight arrow (Pl. XIII, fig. 4) was ploughed up here in 1870.

Richard of Cirencester's *Itinerary* is not regarded as satisfactory; but a commentator remarking on his site of Vindomis, says—

"Of the next station we can merely offer a conjecture. As the country of the Atrebates and their capital *Calleva*, or Silchester, is by our author described as lying near the Thames, in distinction from that of the Segontiaci, whose capital, *Vindomis*, was further distant from that river, and near the Kennet, one point only appears to suit the distances, which bears the proper relation to the neighbouring stations, and at the same time falls at the intersection of two known Roman roads. This is in the neighbourhood of St. Mary Bourne, and affords reason for considering Egbury Camp, or some spot near it, as the capital of the Segontiaci."[2]

There are grounds for the belief that Vindomis should be found *in the neighbourhood* of St. Mary Bourne; but sufficient relics have not been discovered there or at Eggbury, which is only about a mile distant from it, to lead to the opinion that that village was the actual site of a Roman station. Vindomis was a British settlement, and granting that it was situated anywhere in North Hampshire, was a Belgic village, probably merely a cluster of mud huts at the time of the conquest of Hampshire by Vespasian with the second legion. Afterwards the Romans converted it into one of their stations, and about 320 it came to form a link in Antonine's 15th Iter. The Segontiaci were an older tribe in Britain than the Belgæ, the latter having penetrated into this country about 500 years before the invasion of Cæsar, and occupied the south and west of Hampshire, but eventually extended into the northern parts of the county, Venta (Winchester) being their chief city. The whole of these Celtic tribes came from the east or southeast; and the Segontiaci appear to have occupied the same position relative to the Belgæ, as did the Ancalites and the Bibroci in their relation to the Atrebates.[3] The Segontians were largely scattered

---

[1] H. Maclauchlan, *Silchester*, Archæolog. Journal, 1851.

[2] Mr. Leman's observations to Mr. Hatcher's edition of *Richard of Cirencester*, 1809, p. 156.

[3] The Belgæ, according to Cæsar, differed from the Celtæ, and there are reasons for believing that they were of German extraction or Teutonic. (Wright, *Celt, Roman, and Saxon*, p. 3.) Professor Rolleston states that the skulls of the earlier and later Celtic races differed; the former or true bronze users were *brachy-cephalic*

over North Hampshire, and it is likely that they occupied Silchester (*Calleva*) as their chief town; and it may be inferred that they inhabited the districts round St. Mary Bourne prior to the Belgic people.

Silchester is called *Caer Segeint* by Nennius, who wrote about the 8th century. By Henry of Huntingdon it is named *Caer Segon*, derived, doubtless, from the term *sægon* appearing on a block of stone which was taken from the ruins, and which has been interpreted as signifying that the place was inhabited by the Segontiaci as their principal city. The tribe is mentioned by Cæsar as one that was conquered by him, and is placed by Cæsar after the Cenimagni, and before the Ancalites.[1] The inscription on the stone runs thus:—

DEO HER

SAEGON

T. TAMMON

SAEN. TAMMON

VITALIS

OB HONO

The full text of which has been rendered as follows by Mr. Ward:—
DEO HERCULI SÆGONTIACORUM TITUS TAMMONIUS SÆNII TAMMONII VITALIS FILIUS OB HONOREM.[2] This legend is read as a dedication by Titus Tammonius, son to Sænius Tammonius Vitalis. May not the reverse relationship rather be indicated, viz., to the Hercules of the Segontiaci?[3]

Dr. Horsley, who placed Vindomis at Farnham, considers Silchester *Calleva Atrebatum*. Having fully examined the distances between the stations as stated in the *Itinerary*, with the actual distances between the known stations, he thus accounts for the place being the residence of the Segontiaci as well as the Atrebates:—

(round crania); but, he writes, "the few skulls which I have been able to examine, or read of, from interments of what is called the late Celtic period, the period intervening between the close of the Bronze age and the establishment of the Roman power in this country, have been *dolicho-cephalic*" (long-headed). There was a vast difference, however, between these people and the dolicho-cephalic inhabitants of these Islands in the Stone age; they were more powerful, and were light instead of dark-haired. (Greenwell and Rolleston, *Remarks on Prehistoric Crania, British Barrows*, p. 636.)

[1] Cæsar, *De Bello Gall.*, v, 21; also Mr. D. Maclauchlan, *Silchester* (Archæological Journal, Sept. 1851).

[2] *The History and Antiquities of Silchester*, printed by Sam. Chandler, Basingstoke, 1821, p. 2; also see Gough's *Camden*.

[3] A Julius Vitalis, natione Belga, is commemorated in an inscription at Bath; but it does not appear whether he belonged to the British Belgæ (Woodward, *Hist. of Hants.*, p. 195).

"The Segontiaci are not mentioned at all by Ptolemy; and possibly in his time, and also when the *Itinerary* was written, might be joined to the Atrebates, and looked upon only as a part of that people; so that what was before a city of the Segontiaci, might then justly be termed a city of the Atrebates." (*Brit.-Romana*, p. 442.)

The origin of the term *Galleva*, or Calleva, might be traced probably to *gual*, a wall or rampart, and the form obtained of *Gual Vawr*, the Great Wall (see Appendix to *Archæologia*, vol. xxvii, p. 416).

History gives but little precise information relative to the boundaries of the British tribes. From an old map taken from *Richard of Cirencester* by Stukeley, and introduced by Mr. W. Hewett in his *Hundred of Compton*, it appears that the Thames river separated the Dobuni from the Atrebates, and that the Atrebates lived on the north side of the Kennet, the Segontians occupying the south of that river up to the borders of North Hampshire, and between the Atrebates and the Belgæ, the latter tribe living throughout Hampshire[1] and extending into the West. This arrangement, if historically correct, must refer to the Segontiaci after their expulsion from Hampshire by the Belgic people. In order to reach Berkshire the Segontians must have taken the route over the elevated chalk range forming the boundary of Hampshire on the north, and most likely entrenched themselves in the large earthwork known as Walbury camp.

There is an extended earthwork, the Devil's Dyke, part of which lies midway between St. Mary Bourne and Andover, and to some extent forms the boundary of the two parishes, which carries, in its construction and the line of country traversed by it, the impression that it was thrown up as a military line between the Segontiaci and the Belgæ. The ditch being on the west or towards the Roman settlement at Finkley forbids the idea that the work could have been intended as a cover to the station which undoubtedly stood there. Throughout its course, the position of the vallum relative to the ditch implies that it was erected by dwellers living along the south of the line. Many years ago I traced the line as far as the condition of the work rendered it practicable. In his paper on the "Belgic Ditches, etc.,"[2] Mr. Edwin Guest conjectures that the Dyke east of Andover is continuous with an ancient earthwork which stretches south of Beacon Hill near Amesbury, a fragment of which still remains to the south of Walbury. He further thinks that the line near Walbury and Andover might have been the boundary of a Belgic settlement,

---

[1] The same location of the British tribes is represented on the map, *Britannia Romana*, in Camden.

[2] Dr. E. Guest, *On the Belgic Ditches, etc.*, Archæolog. Journal, July 1851, No. 30.

whose capital was Winchester. Following the dotted line which I have traced on a map of North Hampshire, the Dyke is distinct in Wherwell Wood, where it comes in contact with the Roman road from Winchester.[1] On Tinker's hill, tracing the Dyke northward, the earthwork is much degraded, the ditch is filled in, but the rampart stands well up; and the curve on the hill implies command of the flats lying towards Andover. In the fir plantation at Finkley the work is more complete than at any part of its course, the bank being 10 or 12 feet above the level of the ditch in places, and the entire work embraces about the width of 32 feet. But the ditch was in early times much deeper, as could be seen at the time the railway was constructed, which cuts through the Dyke at the foot of Tinker's hill. A triangular mass of earth lying on the chalk at the base of the present ditch showed that the original fosse was several feet below its present level. Leaving the plantation the Dyke becomes lost in Trinley bottom, where it crosses the Roman road, but its line is well shown on the south-west of Week farm. It then runs on to Hackwood copse and through it to Frenches, and onwards through Dowles to Hurstbourne Tarrant common lands, and over those to Ragwood where it becomes difficult to trace, but it appears to join an earthwork from the west, which has erroneously been styled Wansdyke. This Dyke coming from Chute heath runs through Tangley to Pill-heath, then on to Ball's wood, and through Wilster copse to Netherton hanging, where it consists simply of a wide ditch between two banks. It then passes on through the wooded district below Faccombe. Now this remarkably flexible earthwork has been stated as cutting off the open country from the woodlands, but it does nothing of the kind. It is a work which traverses hill and dale, open and forest, and I should regard this as signifying that it was an acknowledged division line of territory. It is too extended for temporary military purposes; but built on military lines, and held on the south and south-east by the stronger, it was, I believe, although probably only for a time, a recognised tribal boundary. This boundary places the chalk range, overlooking the vale of Kennet, and Walbury camp on the north of it; the earthwork must therefore have been within the territory of the Segontiaci. Along the line of the Dyke in places pits have been observed, which have been considered British villages. Such habitations are present at Finkley; and a series of depressions in the chalk is noticeable in Frenches[2] close to

[1] The Devil's Dyke is very likely a continuation of the boundary line locally called Van-dyke, near Bransbury.
[2] Rev. E. Kell, *Account of a Discovery of a Roman Building in Castle Field*, Journ. Brit. Archæolog. Assoc., vol. for 1867, p. 268.

the Dyke. Some of these were investigated by me some years ago; but nothing was found save some small horse-shoes, the kind apparently that were worn by forest ponies. The pits occupied rising ground, slanting inwards in cave-like fashion; and the excavated material appears to have been placed over the mouths of the excavations for additional shelter or to shelve the water from the entrances.[1]

Walbury Camp.

Walbury Camp occupies the highest position that the chalk reaches in the south of England. On the south it directly overlooks the Test Basin, the fertile Kennet valley lying below it on the north. It is evidently a British *Oppidum*—the stronghold of the tribes formerly located in the surrounding districts. It is irregularly bell-shaped, as represented on the six-inch Ordnance Map; and its dimensions are about 550 yards from north to south, and 783 yards between the gates. It has two gateways which trend nearly east and west, and which open towards the ridges of the neighbouring downs, evidently with the object of commanding the entire view of the surrounding country and every approach to the hills; and there are some breaks in the northern rampart, which were most likely minor gates for the use of the guard and for the obtainment of forage from the rich Kennet vale beneath. At the east entrance the defences on the north are double, which appears to arise from a traverse which ascends the hill on the north-east, and which runs up to the east gate, the sharp bank of which forms an outer cover to the fosse. Immediately below the camp on the east, and also on the west, some pits are seen, which are stated on the Ordnance Map as chalk pits. The ramparts at the west gate are thrown backwards so as to form a re-entering angle, and thus to obtain a cross-fire upon the causeway over the ditch. As in the case of most British camps, but little regard seems to have been paid to the amount of space inclosed, the line of ramparts being drawn round the brow in the position best suited for defence. Where the ascent is easy the defences are more powerful, but where the approaches are difficult the ditch is slight or entirely absent. A good illustration of this appears on the south of Walbury. Such places might have had the addition of a stockade. Whoever were the aborigines who built this camp, their object seems to have been, from the necessities of their position, to occupy the strongest features of the country. And it has been

---

[1] Stevens, *Flint Implements found at St. Mary Bourne*, p. 20, Tennant, Strand, 1867.

thought that, to secure this, the considerations for the supply of fuel and water were sacrificed. But I would suggest that a people who could have so accurately adapted their defences to the natural advantages, and, indeed, the disadvantages of the situation, could not have been without the knowledge of furnishing their fortification with the necessary requirements of its occupants. Imposing as are still these ancient earthworks, it should be borne in mind that we do not behold them in their pristine boldness and sharpness, but weathered and degraded by the storms of ages.

The above details, generally, are not the characteristics of a Roman camp. The Romans, who at no time had large forces in Britain, had to contend against undisciplined numbers, for Cæsar writes of the Britons—"*hominum est infinita multitudo.*" Having therefore to use economy and skill, they, according to Vegetius, never extended their garrisons beyond what they could man with effect, while water and other necessaries were never neglected in their military arrangements.[1]

A well-worn trackway, which extends along the crest of the range, runs straight through Walbury, and has been for centuries used by drovers with their flocks travelling from the west of England. I have thought that the term Walbury is Celtic-Saxon, and relates to this usage. The Teutons called bordering tribes *Walsche*, that is Welsh or foreigners. The Teutonic root appears in the form of the prefix *wal*, which has its equivalent in the Celtic *gal*, meaning strange or foreign; hence the German *waller*, a stranger, and *wallen*, to wander.[2] The camp might, therefore, have been assigned by the Saxons the "Strangers' Camp", on account of the Celtic shepherds having frequented it in their wanderings over these hills. The stamp of the Cymric or Welsh is apparent in some place-names in this immediate district. In the Celtic-Saxon *combe*, a hollow; in the Welsh *pen*, in Hippenscombe, the *head* or *top* of the combe or hollow; in Faccombe, and yet more pointed in the Welsh Kimmer, or Cymmer, a confluence of waters; also in Tidcombe, the long combe. Lower down the Norse appears in Ibthorp. The prefix *wal*, might, however, have come from the Celtic *gwal*,[3] *s.f.*, a rampart.

In July, 1871, I found flint implements scattered over the face of the soil for some distance round the flagstaff in this entrenchment. They consist of well-wrought scrapers, some cores, flakes, arrow-tips, and a neatly-trimmed spear-head, which having only recently

---

[1] *Vegetius*, lib. I, c. xviii.
[2] Taylor, *Words and Places*, pp. 42, 43.
[3] Owen's *Celtic Dictionary*.

been brought to the surface during farming operations have but little calciferous patination, probably from their coming from a clayey undersoil. It is the first discovery of the kind along these hills, and in so far as it establishes occupation by the Neolithic or late stone workers, it correlates Walbury with Cissbury Hill in Sussex. The latter camp, however, appears to have been used as a manufactory of flint implements, excavations conducted there some time since by Colonel A. Lane Fox,[1] now General Pitt-Rivers, and some others, proving that pits of considerable depth had been sunk, and horizontal shafts conducted from their bases some distance into the chalk in search of material. The instruments employed in the excavations were picks of red-deer antler, and shovels of the blade bones of *Bos longifrons* and pig,[2] which led to the conclusion that metal implements could not then have been known. It might be that the tools of the Polished Stone Age found on Walbury are the work of an early Celtic wave, although no implements of bronze have turned up in support of this. The entire range of hills from east to west is scored with trackways and earthworks; and it is not improbable that the simpler camps are the work of the Neolithic people as a protection to their tribal villages.[3] These they stockaded, and lived within them in common with their herds of horned cattle and horses. But the stronger of these earthworks—possibly, in some instances, the earlier ones strengthened—are most likely the handiwork of the Gael or true Celts, who were probably the first of the Celtic races who trod through Western Europe to the shores of the Atlantic, and who might have entered Britain 1500 years before the Christian era.[4] They were followed by the bronze and iron-using Belgæ, who still pushing westward might have further strengthened those rude fortifications according to the exigencies of the moment. The earlier Celtic races conducted their operations with implements of polished stone; but they had learned besides to mould bronze chisels, reaping-hooks, daggers, lance-heads, rings, buttons, bracelets, and other articles,

---

[1] Col. A. L. Fox, *Excavations in Cissbury Camp, Sussex,* Journ. Anthrop. Inst., 1876.

[2] Mr. E. Willett, *Excavations at Cissbury,* Brighton and Sussex Nat. Hist. Soc., 1875.

[3] It seems almost incredible that extended and deep earthworks could have been excavated with instruments of stone, but Gen. Pitt-Rivers points out that the Neolithic people constructed camps of great power, which they defended with their slingstones and arrows, being well acquainted with the art of war. (*Hill Forts of Sussex*, Archæologia, vol. xlii.)

[4] Lieut.-Col. Cooper King considers the early earthworks Celtic. (*History of Berkshire.*)

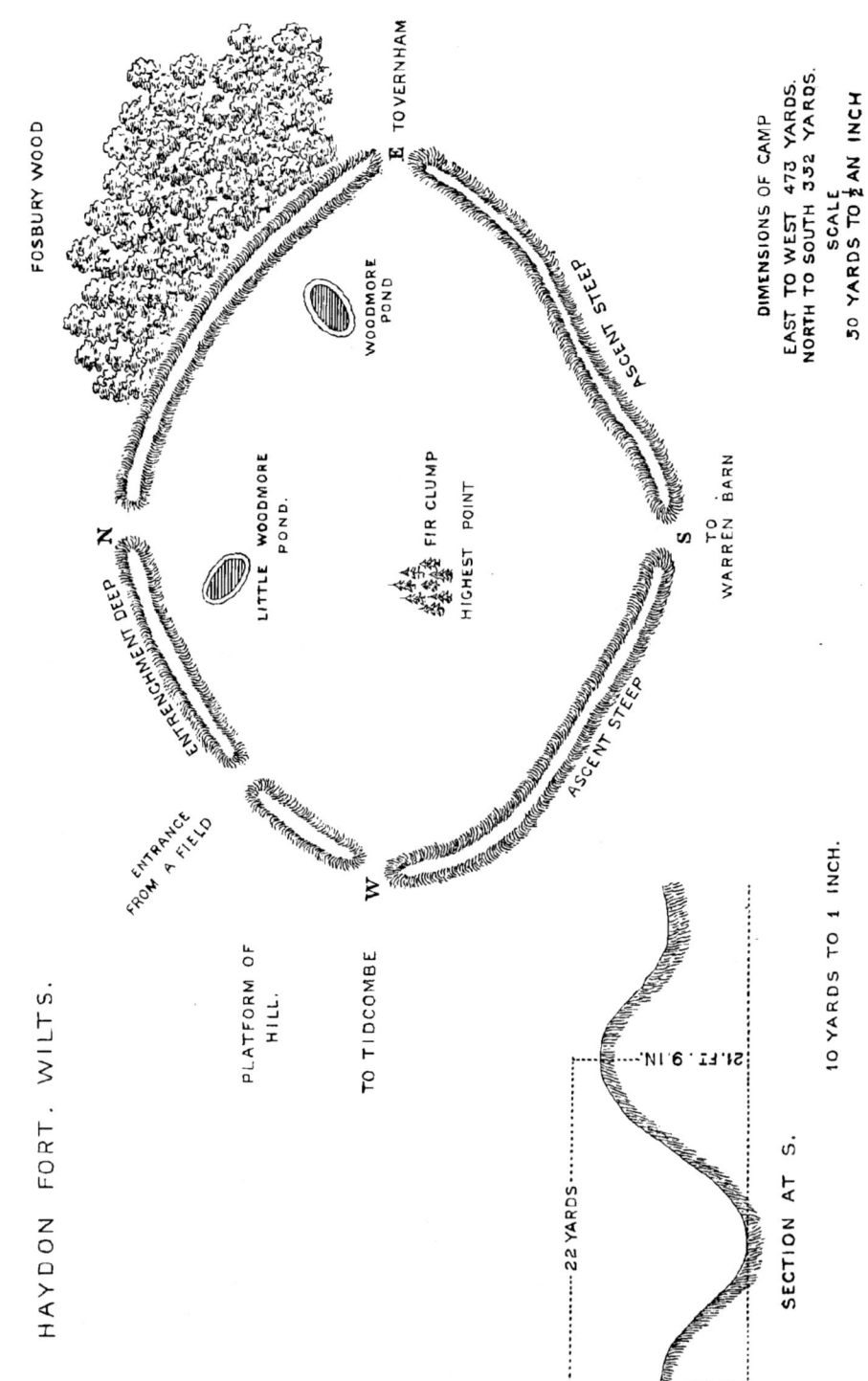

having discovered that a tough alloy of copper and tin was of greater avail in war, and in the arts, than such brittle and unmanageable material as flint.

Haydon Fort.

From the summit of Walbury, directing the eye south-westwards, an entrenched hill appears over the intervening country. This camp is called Haydon Fort, and by the older writers "Knoll Ditches". It is about three miles distant, on the extreme border of Wiltshire, and occupies the position one could imagine the Romans would have chosen in watching the movements of the Britons in Walbury. Between the two fortresses earthworks are observable in places on the hill sides; and what appears to be a British village extends over the southern slope of Combe Wood. That Haydon is a Roman military work there can be no question; and, although in the first instance it was probably one of their *castra exploratoria*, might have ultimately become a place of more permanent occupation. Its dimensions are 352 yards from north to south, and 473 yards from east to west (see *diagram*). It is, as in most Roman camps, quadrangular, with the angles rounded off. The ramparts are lofty, and in places the entrenchments are deep and formidable. The *fossa*, or ditch, evidently furnishes the name of Fosbury, the village close by it. The openings are at the four cardinal points; and there are ample provisions for water in two ponds which are never known to be without water. A portion of Fosbury Wood occupies the site, and the interior contains depressions, which might be hut circles. In cutting through the embankment at the west entrance, I am informed some iron spear-heads were found, and I have a formidable iron arrow-head from the same source, which appears to be Roman (Plate XIII, fig. 3). The raspberry, most likely another Roman introduction, grows within the fortress. In further testimony to the place being Roman, the Roman road from *Venta*, or Winchester, runs up to this hill, and after making a remarkable curve at the end of Chute park, on account of the steep valley (which deviation conducts it in front of a small hostelry at Scots' Poor), it continues in a direct line to the station *Cunetio*, on the Kennet, at Mildenhall.

But when may it be inferred that the Romans overran the Hampshire valleys? It would appear that, in the conquest of Britain, the Emperor Claudius undertook the invasion of our island in earnest, in an expedition which took place in the year 43, under the command of Aulus Plautius. And later, Vespasian under Plautius made war against the Britons, and according to Suetonius defeated several powerful tribes, took a number of towns (*oppida* or fortified posts), reduced the Isle of Wight, and fought thirty battles. And as the towns were in the western districts, and the peoples stated to have been the Belgæ, the Durotriges, and the Damnonii, it is likely as the Belgæ were located in Hants, Wilts, and Somerset, that North Hants was included in his conquests.

The Romans could have had no difficulty in obtaining water, as in addition to the ponds, as conquerors they had means of communication with the neighbouring valleys. But how could the Britons, during even a short sojourn on these hills, have been supplied? Failing water, the camp theory breaks down. I say camp theory, because there is room for regarding these earthworks as places used temporarily, under emergencies, when the Britons took shelter in them with their families and flocks. It seems almost impossible that a small invading force, such as the Roman, could have effectually barred such extensive areas. For temporary use it is likely the ponds would have been sufficient; and as the Romans would hardly have been driven to form ponds, the tanks still present on Haydon convey the idea that this fortress was British before it was Roman. It is not to be inferred that the present ponds were in existence in British times; most likely they were constructed for the use of the sheep in summer pasturing within the area of the fortress. But such a simple method of obtaining water could not have escaped the sagacity of the Britons; and the present reservoirs may be looked on in the light of a survival. Mr. Lansley of Vernham informed me that in 1844 he had assisted in cleaning out the larger tank, when a stone commemorating the date was fixed in the centre of the pond, and since then the water had never been sufficiently low to enable the surface of the stone to be seen. There are some depressions in Walbury marked on the large Ordnance Map as "gravel pits", which I believe were sunk in order to obtain clay for brick-making. One of these hollows, in July 1873, was full of water and aquatic vegetation, and it had been well supplied all the summer. It had the appearance of a properly-constructed pond, and I have no doubt that the clay remaining at the base and sides was sufficient to render the pit a natural water-tank. During their operations on these hills, such natural basins would have suggested to the Britons an easy method of storing surface water. Where camps are situated at sufficiently low levels, water might have been obtained perhaps during wet seasons by springs flowing at higher elevations; but sites such as the watershed on which Walbury is situated could be supplied only by night clouds emptying their contents into reservoirs known as "Dew ponds"; and that these furnish an almost perennial supply on elevated downland districts there is ample evidence. On the same line of hills there is a large pond on Ladle-hill above Burghclere, respecting which, in reply to an inquiry, Mr. S. Wentworth, of Burghclere Farm, furnishes the following experience. He writes, October 25th, 1880:—

"From my own observation I cannot but think that your opinion as to how the early Britons obtained their water on the hills the correct one. I know of a number of ponds on the hills in Hampshire and Wiltshire, which constantly supply several hundreds of sheep all through the summer months, and scarcely ever fail, even when those under the hills have been dry some time. These ponds must be filled by fogs and mists since there is no surface from which the rain-water can run into them. This has been the opinion of numbers of farmers in Wiltshire as long as I can remember."

The Rev. A. C. Smith, of Yatesbury Rectory, Hon. Secretary to the Wilts Archæological and Nat. Hist. Society, writes to me his views on the same subject. He says:—" I live in a district where such 'Cloud' or 'Dew-ponds' are in constant use. The farmers have now found out their value, and I can point to many new ones puddled at great expense on the tops of our hills (Wilts). I have seen such in process of making, and it is really wonderful how the clouds at night keep them full, discharging water enough to admit of the daily supply of large flocks of sheep, as well as evaporation. They are filled in the first place by means of snow, which is carted into them in great quantities on favourable opportunities."[1]

---

[1] See also *Dew-Ponds*, pp. 21, 110, 113, Rev. A. C. Smith, M.A., *Guide to British and Roman Antiquities of North Wilts Downs, One Hundred Square Miles round Abury*, 1884.

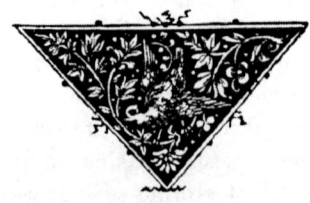

Polished Stone Implements.

(NEOLITHIC.)

E have hitherto considered the Celtic races (*Indo-European*); but there are evidences of an earlier and a ruder people, "Allophylian",[1] of whose presence on these hills there are ample traces in their tools and weapons of stone. It has been stated that flint implements occur in the low-level gravels of the Upper Test valley in association with remains of Mammoth, but those are all rudely chipped into form; whereas the implements of the later stone-workers were, at least a good many of them, sharpened at their edges by grinding on a grindstone. Many of the polished axes are beautifully outlined throughout, and when hafted must have been model weapons of their kind, and have placed their owners in a more self-dependent position as artisans and warriors. They made rude pottery, which they fashioned with the hand; but the vessels are of coarse texture, the clay being amalgamated with flint-grit. And they spun thread with the spindle, and weaved their flax into fabrics. They were in the extreme infancy of agriculture, relying for subsistence chiefly on hunting, and on their herds, which they pastured on the herbage of the hills, and gradually extended their range along the elevations above the valleys as the character of the country permitted. Theirs were small tribal communities, each

---

[1] To these early races, which we loosely describe as primitive, or as aboriginal or primeval, Dr. Pritchard has suggested the application of the conveniently indefinite term "Allophylian". Dr. Pritchard remarks they "appear to have been spread, in the earliest times, through all the most remote regions of the old continent to the northward, eastward, and westward of the Indo-European tribes, whom they seem everywhere to have preceded; so that they appear, in comparison with these Indo-European colonies, in the light of aboriginal or native inhabitants."—*Natural History of Man*, p. 186; also Dr. D. Wilson, *Archæology and Prehistoric Annals of Scotland*, pp. 161, 162.

tribe probably, as common among savages, jealous of its neighbour, and therefore often in a state of warfare. What little tilled land they had was under the protection of their fortified camps; and the great forest tracts were their hunting-grounds in common.

At the time of the Polished Stone Age many of the remarkable animals that had inhabited Britain during the Old Stone Period had died out or retreated; but in Europe were now to be found the grizzly and brown bears, the elk, reindeer, and wild boar, the great wild ox (*urus*), the wolf, and fox, besides the common rodents. But the Neolithic farmer had brought with him those useful domestic animals, the dog and horse, the domestic ox, the pig, the sheep, and the goat; to him we are indebted for these harbingers of the wealth and civilisation of the country.

The early Celts had to encounter difficulties similar to those of their predecessors, for finding they had to contend against a country overrun with forest, and where the valleys were difficult to penetrate from marsh and jungle, confined their operations chiefly to the hills and uplands. We thus find that the downlands on the chalk, indeed the elevations generally throughout England, are rich in aboriginal remains. The Celts nevertheless made considerable advance in tillage where there were no great natural impediments to overcome. With their bronze axes they were enabled to effect some clearings in the woodlands, and thus increase their arable and pasture. They had passed the nomad stage of civilisation, and lived in settled communities in villages. The term *Aryan*[1] applied to them goes some way in proof that they were cultivators of the soil. But the early Britons, as we have previously noticed, were also stone-workers. To them, there is no doubt, is due a large proportion of the higher forms of polished and chipped weapons, which in places are so plentifully distributed over the surface of the ground—the finished hatchets, scrapers, and the barbed and leaf-shaped arrow-heads, such as abound, for example, in the neighbourhood of Wallingford. Such prolific localities convey the impression that they were centres or manufactories from which other districts were supplied.

The gradual progression from the hills into the valleys of the earlier inhabitants had its influence in the formation of parochial boundaries, Mr. W. Topley, in a paper read at the meeting of the British Association at Brighton, in 1872, and which he has since repeated, having observed that generally throughout the chalk

[1] In Sanskrit *Arya* is applied to tillers of the soil; and it appears connected with the Latin, *Arara*, and the old English, *Ear* "to plow" (Fiske, *Excursions of an Evolutionist*, Article, "Our Aryan Forefathers", p. 86).

districts the long axes of the parishes extend along the lines of the valleys at right angles to the watersheds from which the valleys run.

Passing along the hills, I find that Faccombe has furnished flint implements, a notice occurring in a record of "finds" that in 1868 a polished flint hatchet, and some ruder forms, were found in a field in the occupation of Mr. Willis, of Kimmer farm. In the adjoining parish of Ashmansworth also, a carter, who had made some acquaintance with the character of stone implements, sent me a miscellaneous assortment of stone tools, etc., which he had found on Ashmansworth Farm. Among these was a broken polished celt, which had been re-chipped at both ends in order to restore its usefulness. Proceeding southwards on the hilly lands bounding the Upper Test Valley some pits looking like the remains of British dwellings are present in Gaston Copse, overlooking the village of Stoke; and there is an entrenchment just within the wood, consisting of a single bank and ditch. Two or three of these pits are close alongside of the cutting through the wood; but I could find no pottery or other signs of occupation in the mould scratched out by the rabbits from the sides of the pits; and in one or two in which exploratory holes were dug no relics of any kind were found to indicate that they had been inhabited. We should not be hasty in assigning every work of this kind to the British era, as it is not improbable that some of the depressions observed here, and in other woods appertaining to the ancient forest, may be attributed to the charcoal burners, who carried on a considerable industry in the woodlands of this district in past times. It was common, however, for the Britons to entrench themselves in woods. Sir R. C. Hoare (*Ancient Wilts*, vol. ii) speaks of large settlements of the British people in the woods of Grovely and Stockton, in Wiltshire. Cæsar and Strabo also write of the homes of the Gauls as being located in the outskirts of forests and fenced round with timber. The name of the copse, *Gaston*, appears to carry a ghostly significance. It is also written *Garstun*, which is defined as *Gærs-tun*,[1] a grass meadow or enclosure. Whatever bearing they may have on the occupation of the pits, there are ample traces of early human industry in their vicinity. The soil of the brow of the hill on the north-east of the copse abounds with flint chips, and cores of flint left as refuse in working implements from material obtained most likely from the chalk which here comes up quite near to the surface. The elevation above the level of the valley is about 200 feet. I find that in August 1866, the chipped flint-celt (Pl. v, fig. 2), was found here, and is the first recorded discovery of the kind in

---

[1] Bosworth, *Anglo-Saxon Dictionary*.

this district. The soil furnished fewer specimens after repeated ploughings; but at the outset some neatly chipped celts, picks, and scrapers lay on the surface, with hammer-stones and cores, of which some of the latter were so symmetrically cut as to lead to the idea that they were wrought for some particular purpose, perhaps for sling-stones.[1] (Pl. V, fig. 9.)

Farther south on the west side of the valley, Home-field overlooking the village of St. Mary Bourne is a site which was occupied by flint-workers, similar evidences lying strewed on the soil as at other localities. The field extends westward of Derrydown copse, which also bears the title of *Punygar* or *Punygre* Wood; the former perhaps from the Anglo-Saxon *deor*,[2] a deer, *deerdown*, and the latter is commonly understood as meaning *Coney-gear*, a rabbit-warren.[3] Yet farther south, the fields above Chapmansford yield flint implements in places; and the lands extending north and south of the ancient ox-drove, a holed quartzite hammer having been picked up at Lower Week in 1861.

It would require considerable space to detail every place in and around St. Mary Bourne where instruments of flint have been discovered, and to furnish particulars of the specimens, but there is one site on which I lighted in 1866, which requires a word of comment. It is seated on the brow of the hill east of the village in Breach field. Breach is understood as meaning land preparing for another crop.[4] Here, after fresh tillage, implements of various forms could be found on the surface. The polished hatchet (fig. 1), the partly polished pick (fig. 3), the winged and oval scrapers (figs. 10, 13, 15), and the leaf-shaped and barbed arrow-heads (figs. 16, 17, 18), came from this site. One of the leaf-shaped (fig. 17), bears a notch apparently for fastening more securely to the arrow-shaft. Several halves of polished axes were picked up here, which appear to have broken in use immediately outside of the sockets in the club-handles (fig. 1). The stemmed-dart (fig. 12) was found in the same field; and at various times I took away bags of refuse and other materials, among which were exquisitely wrought flakes,[5] some of which had

---

[1] Stevens, *Notes on some Worked Flints found at St. Mary Bourne*, Wilts. Archæolog. and Nat. Hist. Soc., 1867, vol. xi, pp. 106-112.

[2] Bosworth, *The Anglo-Saxon Dictionary*.

[3] Halliwell's *Dictionary of Archaic and Provincial Words*.

[4] Rev. A. C. Smith, *Guide to Brit. and Roman Antiq. of North Wilts. Downs*, p. 40.

[5] Dr. John Evans, *Stone Implements of Great Britain*, pp. 62, 250-253; Stevens, *Descriptive List of Flint Implements found at St. Mary Bourne*, 1867; Stevens, *Relics of Early Races in the Upper Test Valley*, Berks Archæolog. and Architect. Soc., 1879-80. These implements now form part of the collection in

done work as scrapers or otherwise; cores which had been battered and left, rudely-rounded handstones for pounding or throwing, or for use as hammers; and wedges which had been shaped from cores. Holes were observable about the field containing "pot-boilers", which conveyed the impression that the spots had been camping-grounds. As in the case of the gipsies who usually return to their long-used haunts, this was a site probably frequented by some wandering family or clan of the Polished Stone Age.

Following the line of this elevation northward other places of occupation by the people of the Later Stone Age occur on the east of Wake's wood, commonly called *Wexwood* copse; and on the brow northward of this copse, at a place known as the *Nores*, most likely from the Anglo-Saxon *Norð*,[1] north, stone implements were frequently found, and forwarded to me by Mr. Alfred Medhurst, the proprietor of the land, and by Richard Gilbert, his carter. Of these, the partly-polished adze (Pl. v, fig. 8) is a rare form. It is broken on the working edge from use. The celt (fig. 3) is also rubbed at its broader cutting end; and the narrow pick with truncate butt (fig. 4) is polished. The leaf-shaped form (fig. 6), and the fabricator (fig. 7) came from the same locality, together with a quartzite rubbing-stone, considerably polished and worn on its larger facets. In 1885, I received a small box of implements from Richard Gilbert, which he had picked up while working on a farm in the occupation of Mr. Eyles, of Eggbury; among these were two neatly-chipped flint knives, some flakes, and a large chisel with its wider end somewhat square, also some well-cut scrapers (fig. 14). There are features which these localities possess in common: they occupy low hills overlooking water, the elevations varying from about 100 to 150 feet above the level of the Upper Test river; and the land not being particularly plastic was at no time probably densely covered with forest. Flint from the upper chalk for the manufacture of implements was not difficult to obtain. Wild animals which the Neolithic folk hunted for food must have been abundant and close at hand; while at a few miles distant lay the downs over which they had the opportunity of driving their cattle for food. It will not be necessary to furnish further detail; but the following enumeration of

---

the Reading Museum. They were exhibited with articles from the Pit-Dwellings, St. Mary Bourne, at the Brighton Meeting of the British Association in 1872; and a case of the same implements was present at the opening of the Blackmore Museum, Salisbury, in September 1867; and the implements were referred to in the opening address by Dr. J. Evans, on *Man, and his Earliest Known Works*, printed in Trans. of Wilts. Archæolog. and Nat. Hist. Soc., 1868, p. 6.

[1] Bosworth, *Anglo-Saxon Dictionary*.

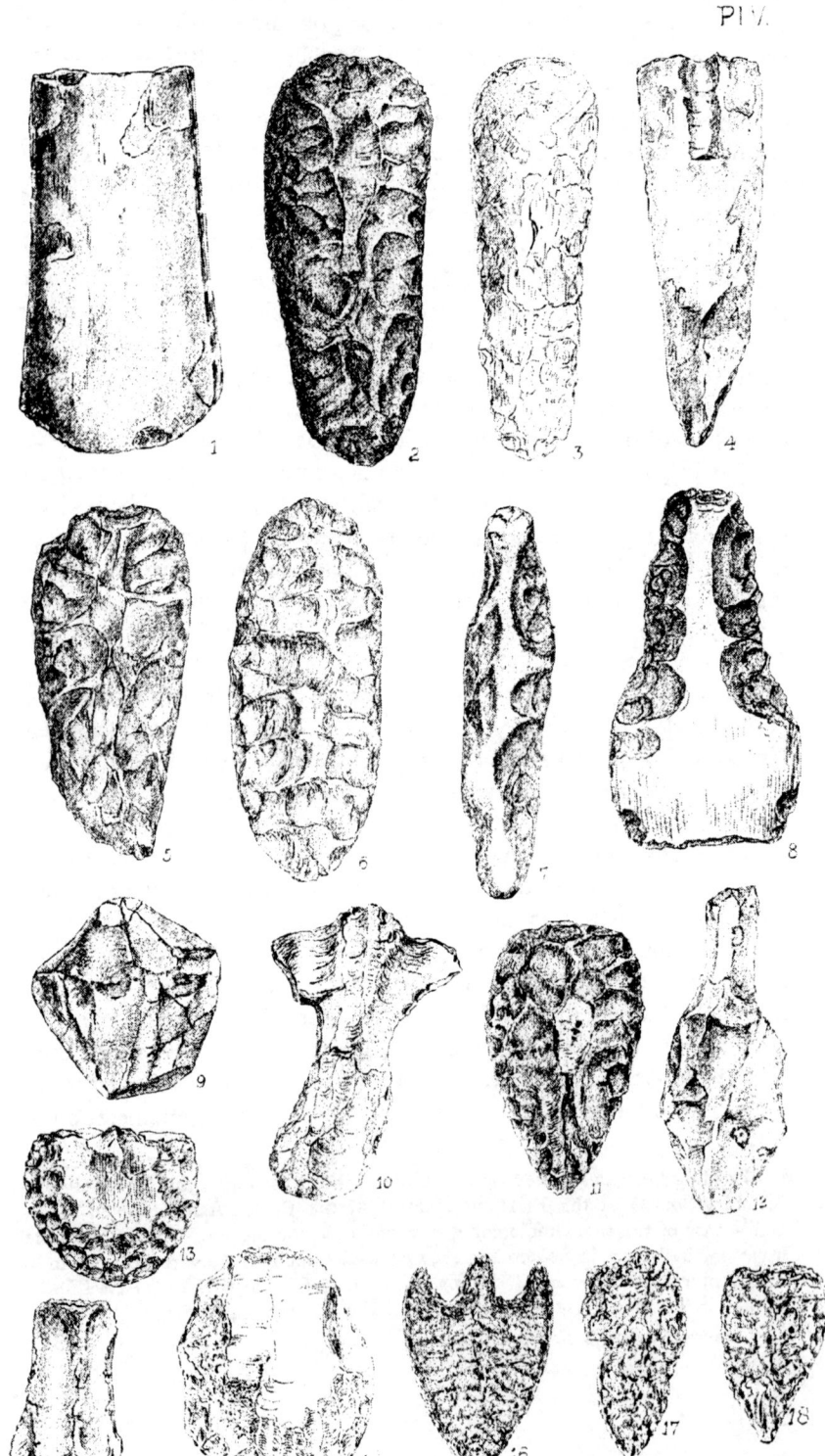

localities where I have found instruments of various forms will serve to show how generally the hills above the Test river were traversed by stone-using people,—Warwick, Stoke, and Upper Week, in the parish of St. Mary Bourne, Hurstbourne Tarrant, Enham,[1] Finkley Farm, Andover, Abbots' Anne, Leckford, Wherwell, Longparish, Tufton Warren, Tufton farm near Whitchurch, Whitchurch, and Hurstbourne Priors.

The people who wrought these tools and weapons—if some of them are not attributable to the early Celtic immigrants—are considered to have been a small dark-visaged race, who were Iberian or Basque in type, and identical with, or cognate to, the present population of the Western Pyrenees. In cranial character they were somewhat peculiar, having, as a rule, skulls long from behind forwards in proportion to their width, which have been styled "boat-shaped." The addition to the length of the skull, however, was chiefly posterior. Some of their descendants are still traceable in Ireland, and Wales, examples being conspicuous in the small swarthy Welshmen of Denbighshire.[2] It has been suggested that they bear some affinities to the Australian natives.[3] But the British stone-workers being potters, herdsmen, and to a small extent agriculturists, were probably above the culture-level of the Australians, and although in the infancy of civilisation could not have been completely savage. They extended themselves over Spain, France, Belgium, and the whole of Briton and Ireland. They were everywhere conquered by the Celts, who instead of exterminating them mingled with them, and the mixture of the two races is still perceptible in some of the people of these islands.

[1] The Ashmolean Museum contains flint implements and fictile ware collected at Enham, I believe, by a Mr. Pycroft.

[2] Prof. Huxley, *Critiques and Addresses*, p. 167.

[3] International Congress of Prehistoric Archæology, Norwich, vol. 1868; Prof. Huxley, F.R.S., *Distribution of the Races of Mankind*, p. 94. For more intimate information regarding the various races in their homes, burial-places, and their cranial affinities, I refer the reader to W. Boyd Dawkins, *Cave Hunting;* Huxley and Laing, *Prehistoric Remains of Caithness;* Dr. D. Wilson, *Prehistoric Annals of Scotland;* Dr. Thurnam, *Anthropol. Mem.*, vols. i and ii (*Crania Britan.*); Greenwell and Rolleston, *British Barrows;* W. Boyd Dawkins, *Early Man in Britain.*

The Romans.

WHEN later the legions of Rome established a footing in our island, some of the hill fortresses again became the seats of obstinate warfare, the native Briton having to assume the defensive. Occasional earthworks, more or less rectangular, are met with on elevations in association with Celtic remains, which are believed to be Roman, and which were occupied by that people in the reduction of the British *Oppida*.[1] From the absence, however, of any traces of the Romans in so many of the British earthworks, it would appear that the invaders confined their work of conquest chiefly to the lowlands, and turned to account the minor hills that lay in their line of march. The lofty eminences were not so necessary to a people with a military organisation so perfect as that of the Romans. Their operations were directed against the more accessible towns and villages scattered along the flats. These they appropriated, and connected by means of military highways with stations situated on them that could be reached by easy marches. These thoroughfares are now often traceable; and with the almost imperishable character of the masonry of their walled towns, bear testimony at the present day to the completeness of the Roman occupation.

As the Britons had communications by road between their villages, the Romans in the appropriation of their villages must have to a great extent followed the same lines. But where the British ways from the incapacity of their makers to overcome difficulties followed the natural features of the country, the Roman thoroughfares ran straight. The Portway extending from Silchester (*Calleva*)

---

[1] Charles Warne, F.S.A., *Dorsetshire, its Celtic, Roman, Saxon, and Danish Vestiges*, 1865, p. 239.

to Old Sarum (*Sorbiodunum*) is an example of this, as it sweeps along a tract of open country between lines of broken hills in the distance, bearing British earthworks on Ladle, Beacon, and Quarley hills on the north, and on Tidbury, Buryhill, Rooksbury or Balksbury, and Danebury southward. The entire series appear to menace attack on the part of an enemy coming from the district of the Avon. They show how hotly the line must have been contested in prehistoric and in early historic times.

In addition to their highways the Romans had bye-roads connecting their farms and outlying villages, and their military roads were united by branches called *Vicinal* ways (*Viæ vicinales*), one of which must have joined the Portway with Eggbury Camp.

A road of the British period runs somewhat in the same direction as the Portway, but in the neighbourhood of St. Mary Bourne it lies south of it. It is altogether distinct from what has been supposed to be the Ikeneld Street, which lies north of the Roman road, if Stukeley's view is correct that it extended from Streatley on the Thames by Ashmansworth, Tangley, and Tedworth. That some early line ran in that direction is shown by a piece of straight drove extending westward between Kimmer and Faccombe, which is called the "Street." But it will not be necessary to discuss this matter, seeing how various are the opinions concerning it on the part of Leland, Henry of Huntingdon, Robert of Gloucester, Roger de Hoveden, Stukeley, Willis, Dr. Ingram, and others. And its name as various, *Ryknield, Ikenild, Hikenild, Ikeneld, Hanildestrete, Iknield, Icening, Hicknel, Hykeneldstret, Ryknildstrete, Kikeneldstrete,* etc. Mr. Woodward[1] states that in ancient deeds a road named *Hicknelway*, followed the line northward and crossed the Portway east of Andover. This is the direction taken by the Roman road from Winchester to Cirencester; but there is no doubt that the true street is often confounded with its branches.

A British road left Silchester at the time it was a Celtic camp; but its gateway does not correspond with the west gate of the Roman city, but appears to have come away from the earthwork between the west and south entrances.[2] On its line relics of ancient date are present in the shape of large tumuli, called "Baughurst barrows"; and there is a small block of Greywether sandstone locally spoken of as the "*Imp Stone*" (*Nymph Stone?*[3]), which marks

---

[1] Woodward and Wilks, *History of Hampshire*, vol. iii, p. 191.

[2] Silchester, *Archæolog. Journ.*, Sept. 1851, p. 231. Maclauchlan.

[3] Had Nymph Stone any association with the visit of Queen Elizabeth to Silchester Heath on the 5th Sept. 1601; when at the shire boundary she met the Sheriff of Hants, and a grand cavalcade consisting of the chief families of the

possibly a parochial boundary. Tradition assigns to it a mysterious origin, and it might be a Roman milestone. It stands at about a mile from the west gate; but the tumuli are of the period of the British road.

Sketching shortly the line of the Portway, it leaves the old Roman city (Silchester) at the west gate, and must have traversed Pamber Forest, although there are no stones marking its course; but on leaving the forest its supposed line through the fields from surface indications is pointed out by local residents. Thence it is conjectured to have proceeded north of the bridge dividing the parishes of Tadley and Pamber. Crossing between Wolverton (*Wolves'-town*) and Ewhurst (*Yew-forest*) it runs close to Foscot, so-called probably from the road being entrenched on the elevation; and thence about a mile north-west of Hannington, where it is distinctly traceable. Proceeding onwards by Freemantle Park it takes the course by Walkridge, Ridgeway Heath, and Ridgeway Copse, names indicative of the Roman line. Crossing the Whitchurch and Newbury turnpike it plunges into Bradley Copse, and thence between Lark's Barrow and Eggbury Camp to the village of St. Mary Bourne, crossing the valley south of the village at a point where in past times there was a ford into Quarley meadow. Passing through Derrydown Copse, west of the village, it takes the line of the pathway to Flesch Stile, and from this point follows the course of the Andover road by Finkley, till it leaves it to ascend the hill to Eastanton, whence its course is north of Andover by Foxcot, Monxton, Amport (name derived from this connection), and on the north of Grately, from which point it lies almost parallel to the Salisbury and Andover railway to its destination Salisbury, or rather to the station *Sorbiodunum*.

It is stated by Camden[1] that "a military road called *Longbank* and *Grymesdyke*, pitched with flints, runs from the south gate of the town (Silchester) to the north gate of Winchester"; and the notice is referred to because I am in a position to show that the Portway was constructed of flint stones—the solid base of it, although it probably had a facing of some other material, perhaps fine gravel. In 1879,[2] on account of a portion of the road extending from Derrydown Copse to Flesch Stile being obstructive to ploughing, Mr. Berry, the tenant, determined on grubbing the material, when it was found that the floor of this ancient highway consisted of a solid mass

county? Thence she visited Basing, where she remained thirteen days, and on leaving, Sept. 18th, the Queen created ten of the Hampshire gentry knights.

[1] *Britannia*, Gibson's edition, p. 107.
[2] Note in *Journ. of Brit. Archæolog. Assoc.*, March 1879, p. 192.

of pitched flints. The pitching laid at from four to eight inches under the soil, and a good deal of pecking was requisite to remove the stones. When removed and placed in heaps for carting away it was found that a piece of the road comprehending a square, of which twenty-four feet formed one of its sides, contained twelve cart-loads of flints. The width of the pitching was twenty-four feet. This portion of the way, as in the case of that traversing the opposite side of the valley, could always be traced during summer from the difference in the vegetation growing on it. Through the adjoining copse the road is quite traceable, its outlines being marked by small embankments, and some stones lie about which might have assisted in its construction.

As in other cases where Roman thoroughfares extend traces of occupation by that people are never absent, so in the district now under notice the Romans have left ample evidences of their presence; indeed the face of the country for some miles round Andover must have been dotted with residences of high or low degree from the relics of the people still to be found on the surface of the fields. The main road had its milestones at stated intervals, the Roman mile (*mille passus*); and inns and post-houses (*Diversoria* and *Caupones*) for the use of travellers had their stated sites. Even in British times, according to Dr. Guest,[1] tolls were exacted at the boundary lines of the tribes, and he imagines that such were taken at the point where the Devil's Dyke crosses the road between Andover and St. Mary Bourne. Bearing on occupation, the name Cold Harbour is met with on the Portway, a small farmhouse of that title occurring at a very short distance from Eggbury Camp, which might strengthen its pretensions to be considered a station. And a place of the same name stands at the point where the Roman road from Winchester to Cirencester crosses the Test. The name is stated by Sir R. C. Hoare, Mr. Charles Warne, and others, as derivable from *Col*, an eminence, and *Arbhar*, an army; and such places are noticed as of frequent occurrence in connection with Romano-British remains in Wilts and Dorset.[2]

With reference to the more important of the remains on the north and north-west of Andover, they consist of the often-quoted Bacchus pavement at Thruxton, which occupied the space of about sixteen feet square, representing Bacchus seated on a panther or leopard; the inscription reading "QUINTUS NATALIUS NATALINUS ET BODENI", the letters V. and O. being all that could be traced in a

---

[1] *Athenæum*, No. 2002, July 28th, 1866.
[2] Sir R. C. Hoare, *Roman Era*, pp. 96-97; Charles Warne, *Ancient Dorset;* Rev. A. C. Smith, *Guide to Brit. and Roman Antiquities*, pp. 81, 203, 217, 222.

lower line. The pavement formed part perhaps of the floor of a banquet room. It lay only at a short distance from the Portway; and from the coins found there and the character of the design the pavement is referred to about the beginning of the fourth century. An engraving of the pavement is present in the Salisbury volume of the *Proc. of the Archæolog. Institute.*

At Redenham,[1] north of Thruxton, important remains have been found, comprehending the basement rooms of a Roman building, of which there were four running south-east and north-west, and measuring about 40 ft. in diameter by 17 ft.; the middle rooms were 13 ft. in diameter, and the end apartments 6 ft. A chamber containing a flue was found; and pavement in which were ornamental red bricks. Since these discoveries the Rev. C. Collier has made some interesting researches at Redenham, at the site of a Roman camp; and also investigated some dwellings of the British period.

A short distance north of the Thruxton pavement were found five skeletons in graves; and coins of the Constantines were picked up on the same site. And further southward a considerable extent of the bases of Roman buildings have been investigated in the parish of Abbot's Anne, resulting in the removal to the National Collection of some designs in tessellation. Figures of these are shown in Woodward and Wilks,[2] viz., 1, 2, 4, 6, and 7, of which the first is an octagon centre in colours, with a plain circular border; the second a cruciform centre with *guilloche hem*, with outside plain circles. The others are fragments. The late Hon. and Rev. S. Best, who worked among these remains, removed some domestic articles, coins, etc., to the Andover Museum. The coins, as stated to me by the late Mr. Samuel Shaw, range from A.D. 37, to about A.D. 353; and the list received of him includes those of *Antonia* (wife of *Drusus, sen.*), *Trajan, Antoninus Pius, Julia Domna* (wife of *Severus*), *Tetricus, Claudius Gothicus, Carausius, Allectus, Crispus, Magnentius,* and a coin of one of the *Constantines.* The field from which the remains were disinterred is known as Minster Field, formerly possessed by Hyde Abbey from the will of Edward the Elder.

In 1865, a short notice appeared in the *Andover Advertiser* from Mr. S. Shaw, stating that he had obtained some Roman coins from the slope and base of Bere Hill, in front of the old clay-pits. They are listed as consisting of a "large *denarius*, reading IMP. C. P. LIC. VALERIANVS AUG.—head radiated. *Rev.,* APOLLINI PROPUC

---

[1] Woodward and Wilks, *Hist. of Hampshire*, p. 160; and Rev. C. Collier, *Andover and its Neighbourhood*, in Wilts. Archæolog. and Nat. Hist. Magazine, vol. xxi, p. 295.

[2] *History of Hampshire*, p. 196.

(*sic*)—Apollo with a bow and arrow (*date* 254-260). A clipped small *denarius*, DN. VALENTINIANVS IVN. P. F. AUG.—head diademed. *Rev.*, URBS ROMA—Rome helmeted, sitting on spoils, spear in one hand, and a globe with a victory in the other. In the *Exergue*, AQPS—struck at Aquileia (?) (*date* 364-375). A third brass, CONSTANTINO POLIS—helmeted head. *Rev.*, no legend, Victory, with spear and shield. In the *Exergue*, TRS., struck at Treves." These coins are generally ascribed to the era of the *Constantines*. Mr. Shaw had previously received from the same locality a "fine *denarius* of *Hadrianus*, and a third brass of *Maximianus*; also a second brass of *Trajanus*, and a third brass of *Gallienus*," and others which were illegible. The series show additional evidence of Roman occupation, on this occasion on the south-east of Andover, and not far from the Roman thoroughfare from Winchester to Gloucestershire, which coming from the direction of Barton Down, and Newton Stacey, crossed the Test river, and Harewood Forest, and taking the line of the present road near the "Queen Charlotte" inn, joined the Portway below Eastanton. From St. Mary Bourne, Mr. Shaw's cabinet contained a *denarius* of *Gordianus Pius* (large size) found at Eggbury, and a fine *Solidus* of *Valentinianus*.

In April 1866, some labourers engaged in preparing a fresh watercourse at Lower Link, in the parish of St. Mary Bourne, called my attention to some pottery at the depth of about six feet. It was coarse Romano-British culinary ware; and at the same depth occurred an iron knife, and a *denarius* of *Gordianus* in *billon*. In the upper part of the same meadow, near some cottages called the Orchard, in grubbing some underwood a quantity of pottery of the same character was found distributed beneath the soil; there were also remains of foundations of coarse flints; and portions of two if not three skeletons were removed. They had been interred in oak coffins fastened with stout nails or screws; from the position of some portions of the facial bones and teeth, the bodies had been placed with their heads westward.

A notice occurs in a *Journal of the Brit. Archæolog. Association*[1] of the finding of some Roman relics on the Portway south of Flesch Stile, on Lower Week Farm. At the site hollow sounds were heard in driving or walking over it; and in Oct. 1878, a sink of the ground occurred revealing a circular shaft of some depth, which might have been a well. In filling the shaft in with earth obtained close by, the removal of the soil revealed rims and other portions of several kinds of Romano-British ware, and a fragment of a stone vessel, apparently

---

[1] Stevens, March 1879, vol. xxxv, p. 93.

a *mortarium*. And mingled with these remains were facial, jaw, and long bones of *Bos longifrons* and pig.

The buildings now to be noticed lie due east of Andover, and claim attention on account of the strong evidence furnished by them of the localisation of the site with the station Vindomis, Vindonum, or Vindunum of Antonine's 15th Iter. The first building explored lies somewhat south-east of and at about a mile distant from the crossing of the Roman roads, on an elevated platform called Castlefield on Tinker's Hill, east of the Devil's Dyke, and separated by the Dyke from the site selected for *Vindomis* by Sir Richard Colt Hoare. It is also divided from the Finkley fields by the Ox-drove, an early British trackway to the Metropolis. The remains were investigated in May, 1867, by the Rev. E. Kell,[1] and the late Mr. C. Lockhart. The building, which faced north-north-west, consisted of one large apartment of 66 ft. 6 in. in length, and 41 ft. in width, with an entrance or portico of the dimensions of 22 ft. by 14 ft. In this *Atrium* were two fire-places, apparently on the right and left of the entrance. The walls were 3 ft. in width, of flints embedded in strong mortar; and the floor was pitched with flint stones, which were laid on a prepared basis of coarse gravel and chalk. The room was heated by means of four open fire-places, which contained wood ashes, the fires being laid on clay hearth-stones, of which a restored specimen is now in the Andover Museum. The roof had been supported on two tiers of pillars, seven in each tier, with square stone bases; and the roof had been covered in with stout roof-tiles, some of which contained the ordinary roof-nails. Three circular holes paved with stones were found at the entrance end of the building, which being discoloured with fire were thought to be furnace holes. The usual forms of Romano-British pottery were unearthed in rims, sides, and bases, and there were fragments of Samian, two of which bore portions of the potters' names. The pottery was recognised as similar to that found at Crockle in the New Forest. A fragment of a handsome jug, a bronze signet ring, bronze handle of a knife of peculiar form (Pl. VII, fig. 21), a lead weight 4 ins. long, 10½ ins. in circumference, two fragments of mealing stones, and some pieces of glass vessels were among the more noticeable objects. But there was no window-glass or tesselations. There were further some rusted articles, such as iron knives, rings and nails, an iron arrow-head (Pl. VII, fig. 8), an iron bit of strong form; and a bronze design resembling a portico (Pl. VII, fig. 20), which bears a mediæval character. Bones were present of the usual domestic animals common at Roman

---

[1] Rev. E. Kell, *Discovery of a Roman Building in Castle Field*, Journ. Brit. Archæolog. Assoc., 1867, pp. 268-281.

sites; and the following coins were recognised, chiefly third brass —*Maximianus, Victorinus, Claudius, Carausius, Allectus, Diocletian, Constantinus, Constantius*, and *Licinius*, and seven others illegible, including three *minimi*. Mr. Samuel Shaw has, from Andover Down, *Constantius*, a second brass; *Crispus*, a third brass; and from Finkley farm, a minim of *Arcadius;* a third brass of *Allectus;* a third brass of *Decentius*, and a lead *denarius* of *Antoninus Pius*. The Andover Museum contains a small vase from Finkley; and the late Rev. S. I. Lockhart possessed a fine bronze fibula found on Tinker's Hill (Pl. VII, fig. 19). Here, then, was opened up a powerful but coarse form of building, supporting a heavy stone roof, which was thought to have had open fire shafts at the various hearths. It was considered to have been an inn (*Diversorium*), at all events a public building along the line of the Roman Portway. It might, however, from its furnaces and large fire-places have been a common room for the use of soldiers (*patrol*), particularly as the building occupied an elevated position above the plain below, where ample traces have been found of Roman occupation.

The field where the Roman remains were found on the flats at Finkey had long been an object of curiosity from the scraps of pottery and roof tiles which came to the surface after ploughing; and more than once the bailiff, Mr. Golding, who for many years had superintended the farming for Mr. Hooper, remarked to me on fresh arrivals after working, "here are some more of the old chimney-pots," in allusion probably to the place bearing the name of the "Old Town." But it was not till May 1871 that steps were taken to determine what buildings lay beneath the soil. From some injury to a plough from coming in contact with a sunk wall, the late Mr. Thomas Longman requested me to superintend the clearing away of the earth from the foundations; and the work was commenced on the 19th May,[1] and continued more or less till September, the last entry in my note book bearing date September 18th. The diagram shows the ground plan of the building as it stood at the time the Survey for the six-inch Ordnance Map was in process, when Mr. Calderwood, an officer of the Survey, obligingly gave me the accompanying copy, and a diagram of the same appears on the six-inch map.

Sir Richard Colt Hoare, when he investigated the *vestigia* of this district, fixed the site of Vindomis at 600 yards south of the Portway, and 200 yards west of the Devil's Dyke; whereas the foundations

[1] The notices in this paper are taken from a register of each day's proceedings, in which diagrams are entered showing the additions opened up day by day.

were found at 400 yards south of the Portway, and 300 yards west of the Dyke. Nearly opposite, at about 200 yards north of the Portway, stand two solitary round barrows; but these most likely belong to the British period. The foundations when laid bare were not removed for more than two years, and Mr. Longman at one time talked of surrounding the place with fir trees in order to their preservation; but ultimately the flints were removed, and used in building the wall and stabling at the farm. The site of the buildings is known as Nuttle Field, which once stood within the precincts of the forest of Chute and Finkley, and there is evidence in a Survey of Finkley Park, of 1652, that great and little Nuttle copses occupied this and neighbouring fields, of which fifty acres were "bare and void places". And as the forest occupied the district before the year 1300 the land might not at an earlier period have been cultivated. This might have some bearing on the facies of the spot at the time when a Roman station occupied the cross roads, for there certainly must have been a station here whatever might have been its name. It is not likely that a warlike people as were the Romans, bent on conquest and the organising of those whom they succeeded in mastering would have omitted to strengthen such a post as Finkley.

The plan of the building[1] may be briefly stated as extending 60 ft. along the north face; and 54 ft. along the south wall; its length from north to south being 84 ft. all but a few inches. There were six if not seven apartments, the north room (1) being an exceedingly long one, if there was no division in it at the central entrance (2) (*see plan*). Behind this were three apartments (3, 4, 5), the central one measuring 19 ft. by 18 ft., with perhaps a dormitory on each side, each one of about the dimensions of 17 ft. by 9 ft. Behind all extended what appeared to be a court-yard (9) pitched with large flint stones for about half its length; and as heavy roof-tiles in fragments were found alongside the walls it had been wholly or partially covered in. The walls were constructed of flint with strong mortar containing powdered brick; and were from 24 to 26 inches in width. Plaster had been used in the interior bearing traces of colour in bright crimson; and a few coarse red tesseræ were picked up, but there was no constructed tesselation. The floor of the central room had been paved with 4 in. tiles; and the hearth which was found in the corner (6) was laid with square red paving bricks. There were two entrances, the one at the south end (10), so far as could be ascertained from the broken state of the wall measuring 7 ft. in the opening; that in the east wall (8), measuring 6 ft. in width. Here there must have

---

[1] Stevens, *Roman Remains at Finkley*, Trans. Brit. Archæolog. Assoc., vol. 1872, pp. 327, 336; also Trans. Newbury Dist. Field Club, vol. 1.

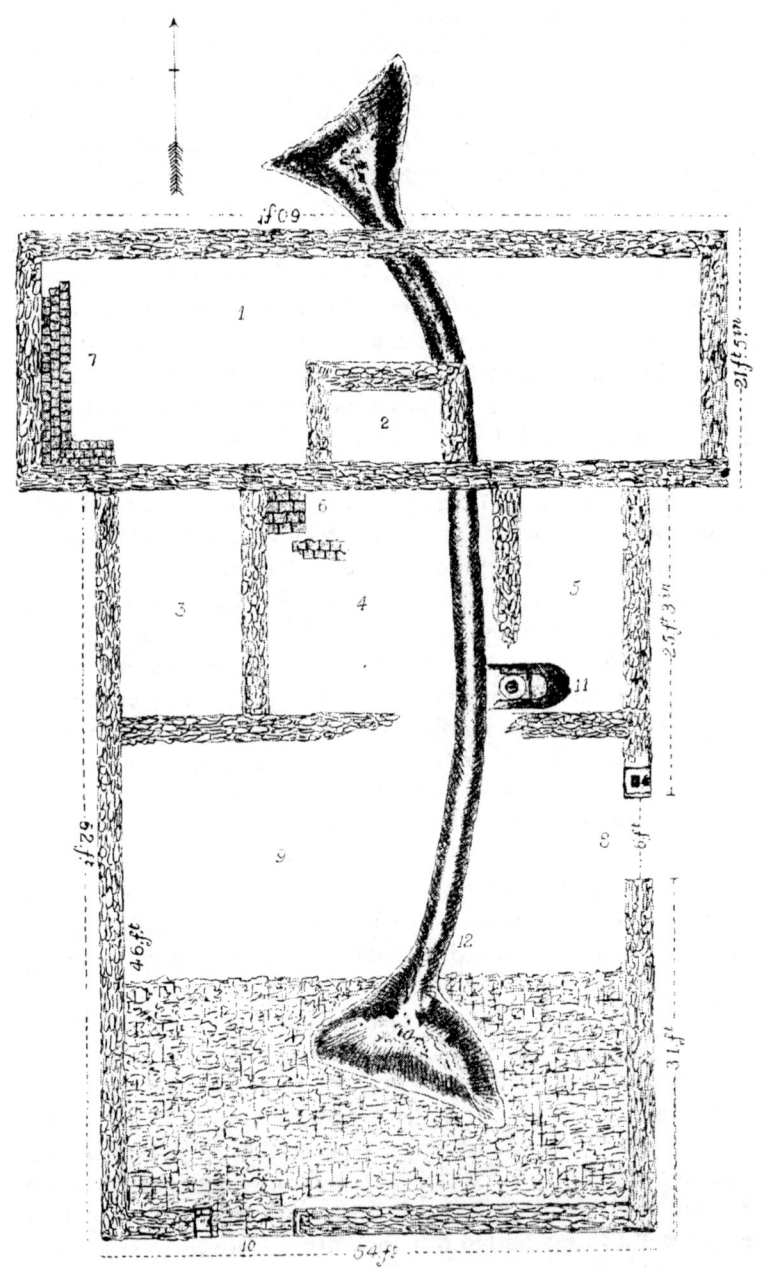

ROMANO-BRITISH BUILDING DISCOVERED
AT FINKLEY, HANTS, 1871.

been a gate, a massive square sandstone block bearing a mortice-hole having occupied the north side (with no corresponding one south), which stone is now in the Surgeon's garden at St. Mary Bourne. From the character of the fire-places, and the quantity of ashes, the fires must have been on the hearth as in the building in Castlefield; and the walls might have been wholly or partially of flint, roofed with heavy stone tiles, of which specimens were recovered bearing nail holes. Some broken red flanged tiles also were present; and the usual accompaniment of oyster shells and bones of the Celtic short-horn, *Bos longifrons.*

The testimony to Roman occupation found within the building, and alongside of its walls, consisted of rims, handles, feet, etc., of the fictile ware usually found at Romano-British sites, in red, buff, and black, representing a variety of forms; also some pieces of "mock-Samian" (*a terra-cotta surface coloured*), twelve fragments of Samian, some scraps of glass, and a polished speculum of about the diameter of a shilling. A small thumb-pot, which was found fractured (Pl. VII, fig. 1) is represented.

Coins in second and third brass, fifteen in number, from Trajan to Valens, representing occupation from A.D. 98 to A.D. 378, of which the following were partly decipherable:—

Third Brass.—POSTVMVS.

Second Brass.—The letters TRAIANO can be traced with difficulty. *Rev.,* ...... AVGVSTI ...... S.C. in the field (senatus consulto).

A denarius in base silver. IMP. LIC. GALLIENVS. P. F. AVG.; radiated head of the emperor. *Rev.,* LAETITIA. AVGG.; female figure standing.

Third Brass.—Illegible, apparently a TETRICVS. *Rev.,* illegible, except ...... AVGG.; figure standing.

Third Brass.—DN. VALENS ......; jewelled wreath round the head. *Rev.,* doubtful, apparently RESTITVTOR; emperor standing; *exergue,* P.LON.

Small Third Brass.—P. I. MAX. THEODORAE. AVG.; head of empress with jewelled wreath. *Rev.,* illegible; female standing with an infant in her arms (she was wife of Constantius Chlorus); *exergue,* PTRS.

Third Brass.—GALLIENVS ...... *Rev.,* uncertain; a chamois.

Second Brass.—AVGVSTA; head of the empress; the name is illegible, but is probably Julia Domna, the wife of Septimius Severus. *Rev.,* VESTA; S.C. in the field.

Third Brass.—GALLIENVS. AVG.; head of the emperor with radiated crown. *Rev.,* APOLLIN. CONS. AVG.; a Centaur.

Third Brass.—IMP. CONSTANTINVS. AVG.; head of the emperor laureated. *Rev.,* illegible, probably Soli invicto comiti; *exergue,* PLN.

Two illegible *minimi.*

Coins found in Nuttlefield, but not in the excavations:—

Third Brass.—IVL. CRISPVS......CÆS.; head laureated, javelin and shield. *Rev.,* BEATA. TRANQVILLITAS; altar, with a globe on it, inscribed VOTIS XX.; *exergue,* ST.

Third Brass.—D.N. CONSTANTINVS. N.C.; head, VICTORIAE. *Rev.,* ...... Two Victories supporting a shield inscribed VOT. P. R.

An English penny (an Edward), silver, much clipped.

Coins found on the site, in the possession of the late Mr. Saml. Shaw, of Andover :—

Lead denarius.—ANTONINVS . PIVS. *Rev.*, an altar; CONSECRATIO.
Third Brass.—ALLECTVS . P . F . AVG. ; crowned head. *Rev.*, a galley......;
VIRTVS . AVG.

Some peculiar relics in iron, sifted from an accumulation of ashes and *débris* in a corner (7) of the large apartment (1 in the plan), and certainly a fireplace on the hearth, if not the site of a workshop, appeared to stamp the building as used by military people. The sifting was done in dry weather, and resulted in finding among sundry articles fifty-two recognisable arrow-heads. I say recognisable, because as with all the iron things, long association with porous earth had rusted away the angles, and degraded the surfaces as to render it difficult to know what manner of articles they were. We nevertheless succeeded in finding thirty in fair condition, of which twenty-eight specimens occupy a card in the Reading Museum. They are all flight arrows barbed, without tangs (Pl. VII, figs. 14), and when new must have been much larger. Some stout bolts were found with them, which might have been for use with the crossbow (fig. 13).

Among the *débris* were bent nails looking like partly-wrought arrow-heads, with scraps of charcoal, and a quantity of slag or clinker resulting from iron forging. There were also small wedge-like tools for chipping off rough edges, and punches for drilling, the series implying that the arrow-heads were wrought here. Nails of various kinds and sizes, such as roof-nails, hob-nails, spikes, horse-shoe nails, and large circular *caliga* or sandal-nails (fig. 17) were present ; and plates of peculiar form with shanks for fixing, conveying the impression that they were intended for attachment to belts or doublets (figs. 5, 6, 12). A peculiar horse-shoe was unearthed, but whether Roman or recent is doubtful. Three iron fibulæ, one of which was of a peculiar design with pin (fig. 4); a thumb-punch or awl (fig. 16), apparently for stabbing leather ; a large ring or armlet (fig. 15); knives of different patterns (figs. 18), and keys (figs. 10, 11) ; and a third brass coin of Valens, came from the same sifting. In other parts of the building were obtained a bronze fibula, a bronze buckle, and some bronze rings (figs. 2, 3, 7, 9).[1] During the working a Romano-British grave was explored, which will be noticed later.

We have so far the Roman mark on the remains, but other relics

---

[1] The whole of these articles, with some broken pottery and other objects from Finkley, now form part of the Reading Collection.

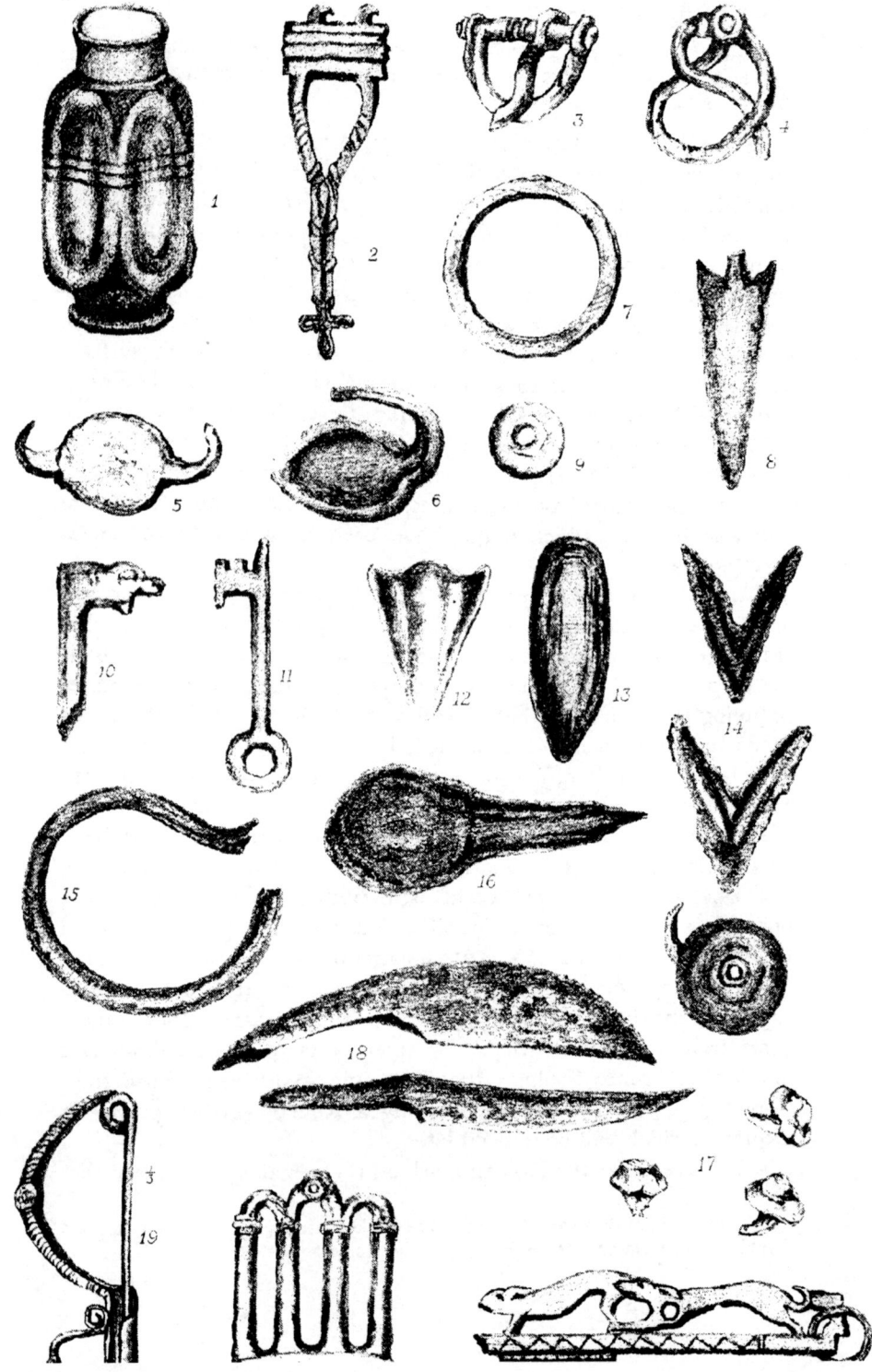

came to light which show that the Britons had been on the spot. From some moved soil lying in a depression in the chalk it was suspected that remains of interest lay deeper; and trenching revealed a kind of passage leading to dilatations at each end, which proved to be circular pits (No. 12 in the plan); but as the work was severe, the trench or passage being in length 95 ft., only a portion of the pits was cleared out. Enough was disclosed to show that they had been occupied, we having found a chalk-whorl similar to that obtained at Hurstbourne Siding; a section of a grain-rubber, some cut bones pointed as if for piercing (Pl. III, figs. 3, 4), pot-boilers, rubbing-stones or crushers, and bones of the Celtic ox, goat or sheep, and pig. Here it is evident that an early tribe must have lived, their pit-homes furnishing some protection as well as security from cold; and that the Romanised Britons subsequently built their residence on the same site. From indications observed about the field it is likely that these are not the only relics of that early period; and careful search along the same platform would, it is my belief, result in finding additional traces of the British people.

There is nothing particularly remarkable in these foundations; they were solid and useful but not pretentious, and their chief interest centres in their association with the Roman thoroughfares, and the indications which accrue therefrom in the line of marking the district as the site of the disputed station *Vindomis*. Sir R. C. Hoare states, after a careful survey of the Finkley fields:—

"The resident farmer at Finkley showed us a tile with indented marks on it, which we immediately proclaimed to be of Roman manufacture. We picked up several fragments of pottery, and observed marks of old enclosures in the cornfields."[1]

Sir R. C. Hoare further writes, after reviewing what others had written on the subject:—

"The recent survey of the rival stations, and the discovery of a new station at Finkley farm, induce me to agree with them in placing Calleva at Silchester."[2]

Mr. C. Roach Smith expresses similar views, and furnishes additional evidence for placing Vindomis at Finkley, he says:—

"Simultaneously with the excavations made at Silchester (by Rev. J. G. Joyce) may be noticed the investigations being made by Dr. Stevens at Finkley, between St. Mary Bourne and Andover, where Sir R. C. Hoare was, I think, the first to place the site of Vindomis. The Rev. E. Kell and Mr. C. Lockhart, a few years since, discovered the foundations of buildings (*not at Finkley, but near, in Castlefield*); and Dr. Stevens is now adding to the revelation of remains which justify us in being quite satisfied upon this site stood the *mansio* or *mutatio*, which, at this very distance, under the name of Vindomis comes next to Calleva."[3]

---

[1] *Ancient Wilts*, vol. ii, p. 49. [2] *Ibid.*, p. 54.
[3] C. Roach (Wyeth) Smith, *Silchester*, from The Builder, October 15th, 1871.

It is Iter XV of the *Itineraries* which places *Vindomis* in association with *Calleva;* but Vindomis occurs also in Iter XII, where it appears to occupy a more important and crucial position than in Iter XV. *Calleva* is named on three occasions in the *Itineraries*, which shows its importance as a local military centre.[1] The *Itinerary* stands in the name of *Antoninus Augustus*, its date being about 320.

SILCHESTER TO EXETER.

Iter XV.—A Calleva Isca Dumnuniorum, M.P. CXXXVI (*sic*).[2]

	M.P.[3]	Corrected.	M.P.	
Vindomi	xv	Vindomi-	xv	Finkley Farm.
Venta Belgarum	xxi	Venta Belgarum	xxi	Winchester.
Brige	xi	Brige	xi	Broughton.
Sorbioduni	viii	Sorbiodunum	viii	Old Sarum.
Vindogladia	xii	Vindogladia	xvi	On Gussage Down.
Durnovaria	viii	Ibernio	xiv	On Bere Down.
Muriduno	xxxvi	Durnovaria	xii	Dorchester (Dorset).
Isca Dumnuniorum	xv	Moridunum	xxxvi	Seaton.
		Isca Dumnuniorum	xv	Exeter.

Nothing can be added regarding the situation of *Calleva* beyond what has already been written; but the weight of authority is overwhelming on the side of Silchester.[4] A word might be uttered in

[1] Lieut.-Col. C. King, *Hist. of Berkshire*, p. 43.

[2] This must be an error, the sum total of the numerals being CXXVI; according to the corrected numbers P.M. CXLVI is the more likely. The distance between Old Sarum and Dorchester is about thirty-nine English or forty-two Roman miles, which gives a total M.P. CXLVIII in the corrected Iter. This discrepancy of twenty-two miles is a strong proof of the omission of a Station; now supplied by the introduction of Ibernio. (Warne, *Ancient Dorset*, p. 166.)

[3] M.P., *Mille Passus*, the Roman mile, equivalent to about 1,611 Roman yards. The English mile measures 1,760 yards, or 149 yards more than the Roman.

[4] Among others the following writers place Calleva at Silchester:—Sir R. C. Hoare, *Ancient Wilts*, vol. ii; Mr. T. Wright, *The Celt, Roman, and Saxon;* Mr. C. Warne, *Ancient Dorset;* Rev. J. G. Joyce, the investigator of Silchester, *Newbury Dist. Field Club Trans.*, vol. i; Rev. T. C. Wilks, *Hist. of Hants;* Mr. Gordon M. Hills, in a paper in *Journ. Brit. Archaeolog. Assoc.*, 1878, founded on the measurements of Ptolemy; Lieut.-Col. C. King, *Hist. of Berks*, 1887; and, as we have already noticed, Mr. C. Roach Smith. Other sites found for it are Wallingford, Coley or Reading, Henley, and Farnham. Of these Mr. Hewett (*Hund. of Compton*) states Streatley as Calleva, and Silchester as Vindomis; Mr. Hedges, *Hist. of Wallingford*, places Calleva at Wallingford and Vindomis at Silchester; Nennius, Camden, Stukely, and Dr. Beeke place Vindomis at Silchester. Richard of Cirencester, not thought reliable, assigns Eggbury Camp as Vindomis; Mr. Reynolds and Dr. Beeke place Calleva at Reading; Mr. Horsley leans to Farnham as Vindomis, but chooses Silchester for Calleva; Mr. Reynolds selects the Vine as Vindomis; Dr. Milner, the Winchester historian, adopted Wallingford as the site of Calleva. The Rev. Beale Poste, at the New-

reference to the physiography of the district. Here is a walled station receiving a road from London (*Londinium*) on the east which, passing out on the west, traverses in its course a natural and easy line of country. The way by Reading or Wallingford might suit Bath; but these towns are too far north to have been selected to reach Exeter by Salisbury and Dorchester in Dorset. The Romans could surmount any obstacles, but they did not waste their energies in crossing water valleys and lines of hills when the natural lie of the country rendered such pioneering unnecessary.

Respecting the disputed question of, Where is *Calleva?* Mr. C. Roach Smith observes:—

"It is rather remarkable that Silchester should have been deprived of its right to represent the ancient *Calleva*. Yet old writers, from Camden downwards, transposed it with *Vindomis*, a *mansio*, or *mutatio*, between Calleva and *Sorbiodunum* (Old Sarum). This would never have been the case had they considered that the places which commence and terminate the *Itinera* were invariably of importance; they were, in fact, towns and walled. The intermediate stations were usually establishments, more or less extensive, to supply horses and carriages for the public service, to rest the soldiers on their march, and for the general purposes of traffic. Remains, therefore, will always be found of the former; and it is essential they should be apparent, as at Silchester, which thus stands obviously prominent. The placing Calleva at such places as Henley and Wallingford denotes as much want of care and judgment in studying the system on which the *Itinera* of Antoninus is founded as making Calleva and Vindomis change places."[1]

It will be noticed that, in Iter XV, Winchester or *Venta* is included, and *Brige*, a small station between it and Sorbiodunum. The route is thus a double one, *Venta Belgarum*, the chief town of the Belgæ, being added to indicate its position in relation to Calleva, so that the traveller in journeying thither might know how he could from it reach Sorbiodunum. Vindomis is mentioned twice in the *Itineraries* in connection with Sorbiodunum, and once only in association with Calleva; the latter is therefore not more necessary in determining the position of Vindomis than is the former. Indeed, not so essential, inasmuch as whatever difficulty there might be concerning Silchester as Calleva, there can be none regarding the identification of Sorbiodunum with Old Sarum. Vindomis, therefore, was a station, regardless of distance, one stage eastward of Sorbiodunum. The distance, XV Roman miles from Calleva, suits Eggbury or St. Mary Bourne, but it does not quite meet the requirements of Finkley. There are, however, insurmountable difficulties in almost every Iter in the

bury meeting of the British Archæolog. Assoc., 1859, placed Vindomis at Silchester; and Mr. T. Wright, *Celt, Roman, and Saxon*, selects Whitchurch or St. Mary Bourne as Vindomis.

[1] C. Roach (Wyeth) Smith, *Silchester*, from The Builder, October 15th, 1871.

adjustment of distances. Mr. Horsley says that the Romans measured only the horizontal distance, without regarding the inequality of surface; or that the space between station and station was ascertained from maps. This idea receives support from the fact that the *Itinerary* miles bear a regular proportion to the English miles on *plains*, but fall short of them on *hilly ground*. Another opinion is that the *Itinerary* miles were not measured by an invariable standard, but in the distant provinces were derived from the common measures of the country. A third difficulty made by the compilers of *Itineraries* is that they did not reckon the fraction of a mile; but stated the amount in round numbers. If to these are added the frequent corruptions of numbers there is difficulty in ascertaining the exact space even between any two posts which are sufficiently near to afford a foundation for a correct measurement.

In Iter XII of modern Itinerants,[1] there is a combination of the *Itinera* XII and XV of Camden; the intention of the combination evidently being to show the line of communication between *Britannia Secunda*[2] of the Silures, and the south-west stations of *Britannia Prima*, through Gloucestershire. It is a medley of journeys, but is not difficult of interpretation. As the object here is to show the general bearing of the Iter, in so far as it tends to throw light on Vindomis, it will not be necessary to take more than the prominent points, the Iter being so complicated with Vicinal ways as to render it anything but plain sailing if the stations are taken as they follow. One journey is intended to take the traveller from *Uriconium*, through Wales to *Isca Dumnuniorum* (Exeter). Beginning with the initiatory station *Uriconium* or *Viriconium* on the Severn, the central point in South Wales would be perhaps *Isca Silurum*, once a grand city, and the place of the Second Legion, on the Usk, some of its massive masonry still remaining at Caerleon. Turning south-eastward *Burrium* may be named, which is identified with Usk. In the same direction, on the Wye comes *Blestium*, now Monmouth, on a bend of the river. Following the same line *Ariconium*, now called Weston, may be reached; and from Weston the journey could be continued to *Glevum*,[3] Gloucester, on the Severn. If from Gloucester it was intended to journey southward along the line from *Corinium*, Cirencester, to *Venta*, Winchester, the station on the junction of the roads near Finkley must have been passed. And thus it is that *Vindomis* occupies so prominent a position in that portion of Iter XII which refers to the stations in the south and south-west of England. It was

---

[1] Wright, *Celt, Roman, and Saxon*, Appendix; *Itinerary of Antoninus*.
[2] Camden's *Britannia; Roman Map; Romans in Britain*.
[3] The last four stations are in Iter XIII.

the key to *Venta* southward, and to *Sorbiodunum* on the west, and thence to Dorchester and Exeter, *Isca Dumnuniorum*, as in Iter XV. The station might not have been confined to Finkley on the east, but it must have been at, or near, the intersection of the roads. Looking at the question in all its bearings there is no doubt that an important station stood there; and no other place more completely meets the requirements of the *Itinerary* in reference to the site of *Vindomis* than Finkley.

Interments.

Accident has occasionally favoured the investigation of interments in the district around St. Mary Bourne; but no systematic explorations have been attempted of the tumuli. It is probable that the Upper Test Valley was a burial-place of the British era, as three circular barrows are still present between St. Mary Bourne and Stoke. One, with a denuded crest, occupies Longhouse meadow, and two smaller mounds stand at the foot of the embankment within the hedgerow on the west side of Quarley meadow at Stoke.[1] In 1854, a similar tumulus was carted away by Mr. Robert Holdway, the owner of the land, from a meadow on the east side of the highway between Stoke and Hurstbourne Tarrant, its removal being necessitated in order to cut a watercourse through the meadow. Sufficient observations were not made of the entire arrangement of the tumulus; but from the relics which were removed from it there is no doubt that it was of the British period. The objects, which are now in my possession, were retained by the late Vicar, the Rev. S. I. Lockhart, and each specimen was accurately labelled and dated. Much of the earth taken from the base of the barrow is stated as blackened, and

---

[1] These tumuli lie in close relation to the river-course; and the association calls up the suggestions made by Mr. Phené, and some others, that the placing tumuli near water may be looked on as symbolical. It is remarkable that barrows have been observed clustered near water-springs, as at the seven barrows, Lambourne, and at Abury; and to come nearer home, at Litchfield. At this last place a "bourne" rises quite among the mounds of the dead; and in persistently wet seasons, as during the rainy winter of 1872-3, a spring bursts forth, and turns the turnpike into a river-course as far as Litchfield. It more frequently rises lower down; but in 1872 it issued near the border of the down. The heathen custom of placing a coin (*obolus*) in the mouth of the dead is well known as a Roman custom associated with water; and it is possible the placing Celtic barrows in proximity to water may be a symbol of Nature worship, connected with the heathen practice of conveying the dead across water in the direction of the declining sun, as symbolical of the passage of the spirit. (J. S. Phené, F.S.A., *Uniformity of Design in the Works of the Earliest Settlers in Britain*, Journ. Brit. Archæolog. Assoc., March 1873, pp. 27-36.)

apparently contained ashes. The remains (Plate VIII) are quite of the round-tumulus type. They consist of (1) a small circular hand-made vessel of coarse clay, rudely fired, and blackened on its interior. The dimensions of this vessel are 1¾ in. in height, and 2½ in. across its mouth; (2) a holed stone, polished, of the size of the figure, which might be a pendant or charm; (3) the half of a hard-grit sandstone rubber, much worn on all its facets, and is the kind of implement which would be employed in facing fig. 2. The other article, fig. 4, appears to be the half of a globule of native ironstone. It contains a large percentage of iron, and is evidently not manufactured. Sparks can be obtained from it with a flint flake; and I believe it to be a *briquet* or *strike-light*. These are all the particulars I have been able to obtain; but they are quite sufficient to testify that the interment was British.

At the time of clearing out the Romano-British building at Finkley, in 1871, in removing some earth 6 ft. from the east entrance (11 on plan), within the precincts of the building a small trench was found, which proved to be a grave containing a cremated interment. It was 6 ft. in length and 5 ft. in depth, and extended down into the solid chalk. The remains were found in a small oval cist or pan 3 ft. by 2 ft. About 7 in. above the level of the floor of the cist a small platform of chalk extended 2 ft. by 2 ft., which had the appearance of being made for the use of the person depositing the remains. The cist contained four vessels, all crushed, of Romano-British ware. The fragments of the larger vessel were embedded in ashes which had evidently filled its interior; and among the ashes lay the head of a tibia of a child of the age of about six years. The vessel was of the ordinary dark-coloured pottery, and of the shape usually employed for cinerary purposes. The other fragments belonged to a small reddish globular-shaped vessel, with a sunk line round its swell, and a small *patera* of similar colour; and with these the restored *ampulla* (fig. 6) of blue-black material, plain with frilled neck. Its dimensions are, height 5 in., greatest width 4½ in. The pottery was of the same character as that usually found at Romano-British sites in North Hampshire. The pan was covered in with two hollow sandstone slabs, corresponding with a slab found near one of the fireplaces; and these slabs were cemented together with a thick layer of mortar. Above the slabs were broken tiles and bricks, pieces of pottery, fragments of fractured bones of animals, not discoloured by fire, and other *débris*, which had the appearance of being thrown in to fill the grave; and from this it was inferred that the interment was of later date than the building. It was distinctly a Romano-British interment.

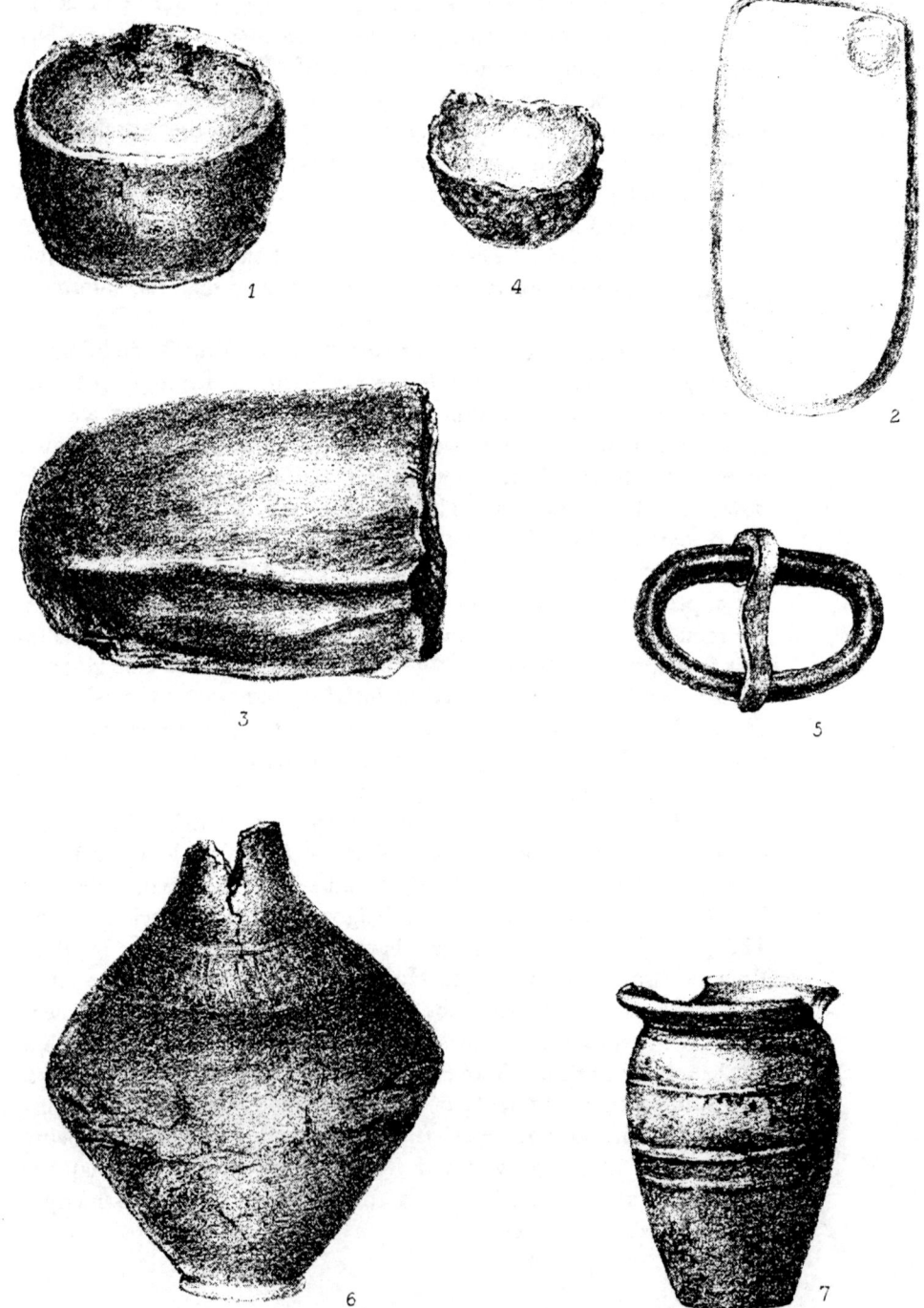

Pl. VIII.

In March 1875, a labourer named John Allen, who had often called my attention to remains which he deemed worth notice during his labours, met with a skull and some other human bones while excavating a road through the south end of Derrydown copse on the west elevation of the valley at St. Mary Bourne. It lay on the brow of the hill, on the chalk, at the depth of three feet. And close to the skull, but immediately underneath it lay an iron buckle (fig. 5). The skull is globose, of fair capacity, and of the following superficial dimensions :—

Length	6' 5"
Vertical height	6"
Extreme width	5' 5"
Circumference	20' 2"

The superciliary ridges are softened. The whole of the facial bones are absent. As access could be obtained to its interior I found its measurements to be—

Greatest length	6' 2"
Do. width	5' 3"

The late Professor Rolleston, who examined the skull, thought that from the circumstance of the buckle the interment might be Saxon.

THE FIRGROVE INTERMENT.[1]

A ploughman engaged in his ordinary work on Firgrove Hill, near Longparish, in June 1879, came on a human skeleton lying in the chalk-rubble, immediately underneath the top soil; and from observations made on the spot, with diligent inquiry into the various particulars, I was enabled to find that the bones occupied a shallow grave of about 5 ft. in length, 3 ft. in width, and 1½ ft. in depth, on the brow of the hill, at the distance of 60 yards from the fir plantation. There were no signs that a tumulus had covered the grave, and there are no tumuli near. The body lay on its left side, with its head towards the north, and the feet southward, the face pointing due east. The knees were bent upwards towards the chest; the right leg crossed the left one, the right arm crossed the chest, and the left arm was flexed so as to bring the hand up towards the face or under it, as people often repose during sleep. The teeth were well preserved, and the remains appeared to be those of a female. The bones were friable and became fragmentary on removal, probably from the bones becoming saturated as the grave shallowed. A small vessel (perhaps to contain food) occupied the grave, and was only at a short distance from the face. It was found to be 3¾ in. in height, 3 in. dia-

---

[1] For this and the succeeding interment, see Stevens, *Journ. Brit. Archæol. Assoc.*, vol. xxxvi, pp. 123-4.

meter of mouth, 1½ in. at its base, and capable of containing six ounces of fluid (fig. 7). As Firgrove is the property of the Earl of Portsmouth, the vessel was presented to, and now is in the possession of, Lord Lymington. It is good kiln-baked, wheel-turned Romano-British ware, in colour brownish-black, and very similar to the pottery found at Romano-British sites in North Hampshire.

From the character of the attendant vessel the Firgrove interment appears to be of much the same period as a burial which was found at Cruxeaston Rectory in December 1856. The rectory is distant from Firgrove about seven miles. Here was found the skeleton of a female accompanied with a Romano-British vessel; but the vessel in this case bore the peculiar depressions on its sides made by the pressure of the thumb when the clay was wet, and known as a thumb-pot. Such vessels are of well-known type, and have been found in other parts of Hampshire, particularly at the old pottery works in the New Forest. In the Cruxeaston interment the body was found with its head lying westward, and the feet eastward; but it appears that no very accurate observations were made as to the side position of the body. If, however, the body was laid west and east, supposing it was not supine, the face would have pointed north or south, as the body lay on its left or right side. These remarks refer to the possibility that the mode of arranging both of these bodies in the grave point to solar worship among the Romano-Britons. The Rev. Canon Greenwell has, in his great experience of Celtic interments, extending to observations made in 234 tabulated[1] cases, stated that—

"When the head has pointed to the west or the adjoining parts to north and south of it, by far the larger number of bodies were laid on the right side; whereas when the head pointed to the east and its adjacent parts, the larger number of bodies were laid on the left side. From this fact I infer that the habit was generally to place the body in the grave facing the sun. When the head was north or south, the face would look east or west according to the side on which the body was laid, the position being regulated by the time of day at which the burial took place; but when the head pointed to east or west, it must, to face the sun, have been placed, in the one case on the left, in the other on the right side; and so we find as a rule that the bodies have this relative position of side and head. It is true that such does not appear to have held good in every case; but the proportion is too large, and the facts fit in too accurately with the supposed custom, to admit of the coincidence being merely an accidental one."

The Cruxeaston skull is a graceful, well-shaped oval, but small; but the greater portion of the frontal is absent, the temporals also and the lower margins of the parietals, and all the facial bones except half of the upper maxilla. The other bones present are the upper halves of the right radius and ulna, two cervical vertebræ and the axis,

[1] Rev. William Greenwell, M.A., *British Barrows*, Introduction, pp. 25, 26.

and two-thirds of the upper end of the right femur. This last bone shows that extensive necrosis existed at its lower third. The tibial end of the bone is absent; but the broken extremity of the upper portion shows that caries extended completely through the shaft of the bone, and that fracture must have been present at the time of death.[1]

In reference to the Firgrove interment it may be stated that those who settled in Britain in Roman times seem to have adopted the Roman forms of burial. In early times, according to ancient writers, it was the practice of the Romans to bury their dead entire, the custom of incineration being later. But in Britain both usages appear to have been adopted simultaneously. The people were made up of various races, each one probably following the usage most in accordance with its prejudices. The body found at Firgrove, therefore, was an inhumation, where the flexed condition appears to denote that an ancestral Celtic form was followed, at the same time that Romano-British pottery of the period was placed beside the dead.

[1] The bones, together with the British and Roman pottery found with the Stoke and Finkley interments, are now among the Reading Collection; but the Cruxeaston vessel was removed by the Rev. Mr. Owen, the curate of the church there.

The Saxons.

THE earliest notice that I have been able to find concerning Hurstbourne Priors, occurs in the following Charter of Bishop Denewulf (DCCC. II.),[1] in which the church receives mention. I give the Anglo-Saxon and its translation.

[Denewulf] bisceop lyfde Beornulfe his mege þæt he moste þa inberðan menn hamettan to Eblesburnan. nú hebbe ic hi hamet . Lufe ⁊ hire ðreo bearn . ⁊ Luhan ⁊ his seax bearn .

Þonne geærendodon me ða hiwan on Wintanceastre ðet þa men mostan on þan londe wunien . hæfde swa ic swa minra freonda swelce hit hæfde . þonne weron þær ðreo witeþeowe men burbærde . ⁊ ðreo ðeowberde ða me salde bisceop ⁊ þa hiwan to ryhtre æhta . ⁊ hire team .

Ðis wes gedon ða man þa cyricean halgode æt Hysseburnan . on ðara manna gewitnesse þe hira naman her neoðan standat .

Bishop Denewulf has allowed Beornulf his kinsman to house the inborn people at Ebbesborne. I have now housed Lufe and her three children, and Luha and his six children.

Then the convent at Winchester sent me word that the men must dwell on the land, whether I or any of my friends had it. There were then three penal serfs, three boor-born, and three serf-born : these the bishop and the convent gave me in lawful possession, with their families.

This was done when the church was hallowed at Husseburne, in witness of the men whose names stand here beneath.

This evidently refers to the consecration of the church in 802.

In the will of King Alfred, styled his " second will ", under the head of "*Incipit Secundum Testamentum Alfredi regis incliti, in lingua Saxonica*", occurs the following relating to the disposal of his land at Hurstbourne Priors, known also from time immemorial as Lower

---

[1] *Diplomatarium Anglicum Ævi Saxonici. Miscellaneous Charters, etc., concerning the West Saxons*, translated by B. Thorpe, pp. 151-2, 1865.

Hurstbourne, Hants (A.D. 885 ?).[1] The *Hysseburinan* of the Charters Mr. Kemble identifies with Hurstbourne Priors, near Whitchurch, and there is no doubt that he is correct, as in the Charter it is called *Nether* Hurstbourne [*Neoðerian Hysseburinan*].

Ic Alfred, Ƿest-seaxena cinge, (cinʒe), mið Godes gife, and mid þisse geƿittenesse, gecƿeðe hu ic ymbe min yyfe, [wille] æftest minum dæge: æriest (æpeɼt) ic an Eadƿearide minan yldrian (ylðþan) suna þese (þæɼ.) landes æt Striætneat on Truconscipe, and Heoritigtunes, and þa boc-land ealle þe Leof-heah hylt, and þa land æt Earumtune, and æt Cylfantune, and æt Burinhamme, and æt Ƿedmori; and ic eom fyrimbig to þam hipum æt Ceoðrie þæt hy hine ceosan on þa geriað þe ƿe æri (æp.) gecƿeðen hæfðon, mið þam land (lande) æt Ciptune, and þam þe þær to-hyriað; and ic him an þæs landes æt Cantuctune, and æt Bedemdan, and æt Fefesige, and Hysseburinan, and æt Suttune, and æt Leoðruðan, and æt Apeltune. And ealle þa boc-land þe ic on Cent habbe, and æt þam Nyðerian Hysseburinan, and æt Cyselðene, agyfe man in to Ƿintanceastrie, on þa geriað þe hit min fæderi æri gecyeðe, and þæt min sundori feoh þæt ic Egulfe oðfæste on þam Neoðerian Hysseburinan.

I, Alfred, King of the West-Saxons, by God's grace, and by means of this testimony, declare how I will (dispose) concerning my estates, after my day.

First, I give to Edward, my eldest son, the land at Stratford, in Cornwall, and Hardington [? in Somersetshire], and all the deed-conveyed lands that Leofheah holds, and the lands at Carhampton [in Somersetshire], and at Chilhampton [in Wiltshire], and at Burnham, and at Wedmore [both in Somersetshire]. And I make my request to the families at Chedder [in Somersetshire] that they would choose him [to be their lord] conformably with the stipulations that we formerly agreed to[2]; with the land of Chewton [also in Somersetshire], and that which thereto pertaineth. And I also give to him the land at Quantock [in Somersetshire], and at Bedwin [in Wiltshire], and at Pewsey [in Wiltshire], and at Hurstbourne [Hurstbourne, in Hampshire], and at Sutton [in Hampshire or in Wiltshire], and at Leatherhead [in Surrey?], and at Alton [Alton Berners in Wiltshire?].

And all the deed-conveyed land that I have in Kent, and at Down Hurstbourne [Hurstbourne Priors, Hants], and at Chisledon [in Wiltshire], let it be given to Winchester, on the stipulations that my father formerly made; and my separate property at Lower Hurstbourne which I gave in trust to Ecgulf.

[1] *Liber Monasterii de Hyda*, Lansdowne MS., British Museum, translated by E. Edwards, p. 62.

[2] "These families at Chedder", Manning writes, "were the Ceorls who occupied the tenemental lands there. They were so far analogous to those who

After bequests to his younger son, and to his daughters, and bequests to other kinsfolk, and to his officers, and to the bishops, with some charitable bequests, the will makes the following provisions:—

"And I will that those to whom I have given my freehold land shall not let it go, after their own lifetime, away from my kindred. But if it so be that they have no children, it shall go to my nearest of kin. And I especially desire that it remain in the male line so long as I have any [male descendant] that shall be found worthy of it. My grandfather bequeathed his land to the spear-side, and not to the spindle-side."

The "Boc-land" (*deed-conveyed*), referred to in the will of King Alfred, was land held by Charter, or deed, in contradistinction to *Folk-land*. Book-land was free. At an earlier period lands were conferred by the delivery of a staff, spear, arrow, or drinking-horn, or by a turf. Boc-land was held in perpetuity, and could be conferred by will. Folc-land, on the contrary, was the land of the people, either held in common, or parcelled out in the *folc-gemot*, or district Court. It could not be held in perpetuity, but reverted to the community.

Leland (*Collect.*, vol. ii, pp. 428-30), in his list of *Fundatores principales*, professedly condensed from Rudborne, gives the following benefactions:—"*Alfstanus dux, filius Ethelredi, dedid ecclesiæ Winton, Merden* [in Hursley] *et Eggebyri* [in St. Mary Bourne Parish]."

In the account of the endowments of the Cathedral contained in Rudborne, and the *Annales Wintonienses* [as compared with the lists in the *Taxatio Ecclesiastica*], among the possessions in Hampshire not recorded in *Domesday*, appears the following:—901, ten [hides] "*manentes*" in Stoke [*Stoce be Hysseburna*]; Codex Diplomaticus, No. 1077, given by Edward the Elder (the Latin text of this follows with a translation).

Charter of King Eadward the Elder relating to a gift of land, etc., at Stoke, in the Parish of St. Mary Bourne, and at Hurstbourne Priors. (DCCCC.)[1]:—

in the succeeding feudal times were called 'privileged villeins', as that they could not be compelled to hold their lands against [without ?] their own consent." (*Will of King Alfred*, note 1.)

"Charters of Eadwig, Eadgar, and Eadmund", writes Mr. Thorpe, " are dated from the Royal Palace at Chedder; the 'hiwan', here mentioned, are probably either the vassals attached to the Palace, or the inmates of an Abbey there, both having legal power to choose their lord." (*Diplomatarium Anglicum Ævi Saxonici*, pp. 487.)

[1] B. Thorpe, *Diplomatarium Anglicum Ævi Saxonici*, pp. 143, 144.

Regnante imperpetuum Domino nostro Ihesu Christo, et omnia de summo cæli apice visibilia et invisibilia ordinabiliter gubernante, presentisque vitæ semper curriculo cotidie decrescente. Quapropter ego Eadward, gratia Dei Angul Saxonum rex, litterarum memoriæ commendare procuraverim, quod in diebus avi mei Æðelwlfi regis et Ælfredi regis patris mei factum fuerat; hoc est quod ille Aðulf rex moriens commendavit Ælfredo regi, filio suo, illam terram æt Ceolseldene et æt Sweores holte, ea conditione, quod ille Ælfred rex, post obitum suum, dimitteret eandem terram illi familie venerabili in Wintonia civitate, specialiter ad refectorium suum, habendam et possidendam perfruendamque perpetualiter, cum silvis, campis, pratis, et pascuis, atque omnibus ad se pertinentibus, in sempiternam hereditatem. Attamen ego Eadward rex utramque præfatam terram ab illa venerabili præfata familia in Wintonia civitate comparavi, dedique pro utraque præfata terra x. *manentes in illo loco qui dicitur æt Stoce be Hysseburnan*, cum omnibus hominibus qui in illa terra erant quando Ælfred rex obiit, et etiam cum illis omnibus hominibus qui tunc fuerunt æt Hisseburna quando Ælfred rex viam universe carnis adiit. Sunt autem utræque terræ ab omni censu mundiali et regali libere et expedite, excepta expeditione, et arcis et pontis constructione.

Since our Lord Jesus Christ reigns for ever, and in due order governs all things visible and invisible from the loftiest height of heaven, and the span of the present life is daily decreasing: Therefore, I, Eadward, by the grace of God, King of the Anglo-Saxons, have procured it to be committed to the record of writing, that in the days of my grandfather Æðelwlf the King, and Ælfred the King my father, it happened thus, that he Aðulf the King when dying committed to Ælfred the King, his son, that land at Ceolseldene and at Sweores holte, under the condition, that the same Ælfred the King, after his death, should demise the same land to that venerable household in Winchester city, specially for their refectory; to have and possess and enjoy for ever, with woods, fields, meadows, and pastures, and all things thereto appertaining, as a perpetual inheritance. Nevertheless, I, Eadward the King, have bought both the aforesaid land(s) from the venerable household aforesaid in Winchester city, and have given for both the aforesaid land(s) 10 hides or holdings in that place which is called "at Stoke by Hysseburn", with all men who were in that land when Ælfred the King died, and also with those men who were then "at Hysseburn" when Ælfred the King departed the way of all flesh. And both lands are free and discharged from all secular and royal tribute, except "expedition" (*i.e., service in the King's wars*), and the building of castle and bridge.

The ten hides here mentioned as belonging to Stoke by Hurstbourne, together with the men living thereon, and those at Hurstbourne, were in the year 900 given by Edward the elder to the *Old Minster*, at Winchester, under an arrangement made with the Monks that certain lands at Ceolsdene [*Chiseldon, Wilts*] should be transferred to the New Minster. It appears that the necessity for this change came about from the fact that King Ethelwolf on his death left to his son Alfred lands at Chiseldon, and other places, with the conditions stipulated that King Alfred should leave these same lands to the Old Minster, which King Alfred faithfully did. Now, King Alfred and his Queen were buried in the Old Minster; but their remains were subsequently removed to the New Minster. The land at Chiseldon, the special object of which, as a bequest, was the benefit of King Alfred's soul, was left properly enough, as we have seen, to the Old Minster. But, on the removal of the bodies of the King and his Queen from the old building to the new one, the King and the property left for his particular benefit became parted, and this rendered it necessary that the Chiseldon property should be transferred to the New Minster, which was accordingly done, the Stoke and Hurstbourne property being given in its place to the Old Minster.

It had been a cherished idea in the mind of King Alfred in the decline of his life to build a new monastery, in order to the higher education of the children of his nobility; and to effect his purpose he selected a Monk named Grimbald from the Monastery of St. Bertin, in Picardy, in which he himself had passed some portion of his early life. His desire was, however, not to be completed in his lifetime, but it was left for his son Edward to finish the building, and endow it. At its completion Grimbald became the first Abbot; but died within a year after his appointment, and was canonised. In the Old Minster of the Bishop lay the bones of Alfred; but it is stated that the Canons of the old foundation held some superstitious notions about the ghost of the Royal King not resting in peace, but wandering at night about the cloisters, and thus at length they resolved on removing his remains, and those of Queen Ealhswith to the New Minster.[1] This was their ostensible reason; but the true one was the disagreements between the occupants of the two Minsters. The bells of the one were rung while the service was going on in the other, and the choral services interfered with those in the adjacent church; and it has been thought that the occupants of the two churches did not live in a state of Christian brotherhood.

At the time of King Edward the Elder (*Miscellaneous Charters*, p. 145) it is stated what were the services of the Churls at Hurstbourne, meaning the duties that the labourers had to carry out on the land.[2] The following is the Anglo-Saxon and its translation.

---

[1] *Liber de Hyda*, see Introduction by E. Edwards.
[2] *Diplomatarium Anglicum Ævi Saxonici;* also, *Transcripts of Anglo-Saxon Charters*, published by the Historical Soc., vol. iv (*Charter* 977), by J. M. Kemble. Also, *Brief Historical Notices of Hurstbourne Priors and St. Mary Bourne* (J. Russell Smith, London), pp. 8-9, 1861.

The Services of the Tenants at Husseburn.

Her synd gewríten þa gerihta þæ ða ceorlas sculan don to Hysseburnam . Ærest æt hilcan hiwisce feowerti penega tó herfestes emnihte . ⁊ vi . ciricmittan eálað . ⁊ iii . sesðlar hlafhwetes . ⁊ iii . æceras geérian on heora agenre hwile ⁊ mid heora agenan sæda gesawan . ⁊ on hyra agenre hwile on bærene gebringan . ⁊ þreo pund gauolbæres . ⁊ healfne æcer gauolmæde on hiora agienre hwile . ⁊ þæt on hreace gebringan . ⁊ iiii . foðera aclofenas gauolwyda to scidhræce . on hiora agenre hwile . ⁊ xvi . gyrda gauoltininga eác on hiora agenre hwile . ⁊ to Eastran two ewe mid twam lamban . ⁊ we [talað] two geong sceap tó eald sceapan . ⁊ hi sculan waxan scéap ⁊ sciran on hiora agenre hwile . ⁊ ælce wucan wircen ðæt hi man háte . butan ðrim . an to middanwintra . oðeru to Eastran . pridde tó gangdagan .

Here are written the services which the churls have to render at Hurstbourne. First, for every family forty pence at the autumnal equinox, and 6 church-measures of ale, and iii . sesters of loaf-wheat; and to plough three acres, in their own time, and sow them with their own seed; and in their own time to bring [the produce] into the barns; and three pounds of gafol-barley, and half an acre of gafol meadow, in their own time; and to bring it in a rick; and iiii . fothers of cloven gafol-wood for a shingle-rick, in their own time ; and xvi rods of gafol-palings, also in their own time. And at Easter two ewes with two lambs. And we reckon two young sheep as an old sheep. And they shall wax [grease] and shear the sheep, in their own time; and they shall do every week what they are ordered, excepting three: one at Midwinter, a second at Easter, and a third in the Rogation days.

"In their own time", means the time granted to the Churls for carrying out their own occupations. The *pound* alluded to was a much larger quantity than the present pound; and "gafol" refers to tribute, rent or tax. The word comes from *gifan*, to give, as expressing tribute, and does not particularly mean money, but payment by personal service, such as labour rendered to the lord on the land or road, or providing draught or carriage by beasts, or produce in the shape of corn, ale, honey, etc. This kind of tenure was only partial in Saxon times, but it became universal afterwards under the feudalism of the Normans. The "xvi rods of palings" most likely mean enclosure, that the Churls had to enclose some portions of the lord's demesne to that extent. A similar duty of enclosing the parks of lords of manors was incumbent on the tenants in the thirteenth century,[1] who paled-in certain portions according to their holdings.

Much has been written regarding the amount of freedom enjoyed by the Churls. Cowel writes that the *Ceorle* or Churl was in Saxon

---

[1] *Coram Rege Roll*, 12th Edward I.

times a tenant at will, of *free condition*, who held some land from the Thane on conditions of Rent and Service. They were of two kinds, one that hired the Lord's outland or tenementary land; the other that tilled and manured the *inland* or *demesne*, yielding work and not rent, and were thereupon called his Sockmen or Ploughmen. [*Vid. Spelman on Feuds.*]

Probably they had hardly so much freedom as here expressed. There is no doubt that the Churls cultivated the land on the open field system, somewhat after the manner of the Villeins at the time of *Domesday*. In the land boundaries [*see those of Hurstbourne Tarrant*] the Churl's acre receives mention, and the tilled *lince* or lynchet, which was an acre strip in open fields formed into a terrace by always turning the sod downwards in ploughing a hill-side. In the specified duties of the Churls on the Hurstbourne Priors manor, it is stated that every week they were to do what they were bid, except three weeks, and this appears clearly to denote that, however distant their condition was from serfdom, they could not have been free.

There is a dialogue of Ælfric,[1] of the tenth century, which is written in Saxon and Latin, of which the following is a translation, which, placed in the shape of question and reply, permits the Saxon ploughman to express his own condition.

"What sayest thou, ploughman? How dost thou do thy work?"

"Oh, my lord, hard do I work. I go out at daybreak driving the oxen to field, and I yoke them to the plough. Nor is it ever so hard winter that I dare loiter at home, for fear of my lord, but the oxen yoked, and the ploughshare and coulter fastened to the plough, every day must I plough a full acre, or more."

"Hast thou any comrade?"

"I have a boy driving the oxen with an iron goad, who also is hoarse with cold and shouting."

"What more dost thou in the day?"

"Verily then I do more. I must fill the bin of the oxen with hay, and water them, and carry out the dung. Ha! Ha! hard work it is, hard work it is! because *I am not free*."

The ploughman was not free, but his services were not particularly severe. His labour in ploughing, feeding, and watering his cattle, and in cleansing their stable was not harder, as mere work, than the duties of an ordinary carter in the nineteenth century. The labour was evidently not so much the difficulty as the want of freedom, as he says, "Hard work it is, *because* I am not free."

The Saxon *Theows* or slaves must be regarded as in a different position. They were more completely slaves than the *Servi* of *Domesday*. The Charter of Denewulf, already noticed, expresses three

---

[1] Seebohm, *The English Village Community*, p. 166. (*Cotton MS.*, Tib. A. iii, f. 58b, British Museum.)

several grades of serfdom, "three penal serfs, three boor-born, and three serf-born", and that they were given in lawful possession with their families. The slaves did the work of the manor-house of the most servile kind; and they could be bought and sold in the market, and exported commercially to distant lands. Slavery was their heritage; and Mr. Kemble states that freemen sometimes sold themselves into slavery under the pressure of extreme want.[1]

The open method of field cultivation among the Saxons is of considerable antiquity, and can be traced back to the time of Ine, who was King of the West Saxons in 688. The laws of this chief were republished by King Alfred, under the title of the "*Dooms of Ine*". Taking them as a genuine record of that period, they represent the settled agricultural usages among the West Saxons in the second half of the seventh century. Among other references to the social life of the people is one which shows definitely the holding of lands in common, having their divisions into acres, and the use of pasture lands in meadows, which were divided into strips or doles similar to the method observed at a much later period in the case of the Lammas lands. The extract below, taken from the Code, shows the arrangement then existing regarding the use of the common meadows by the Churls or labourers.[2]

Be Ceorles Gærs-tune.

[XLII] Gif ceoplaʃ ʒæpʃ-ʈun hæbben ʒemænne. Oþþe oðeɲ ʒebál-lanð ʈo ʈýnanne. ⁊ hæbben ʃume ʒeʈýneð hioɲa bæl. ʃume næbban. ⁊ ... eʈʈen hioɲa ʒemænan æcepaʃ oþþe ʒæpʃ, ʒán þa þonne þe ꝥ ʒeaʈ aʒan. ⁊ ʒebeʈe[n] þam oðɲum þe hioɲa bæl ʒeʈýneðne ....

Of a Ceorle's grass-tun [meadow].

[42] If ceorls have common meadow or other land *divided into strips* to fence, and some have fenced their strip, some have not, and ... [stray cattle?] eat their common acres or grass, let those go who own the gap, and compensate the others who have fenced their strip ....

In the Charter of King Edward (DCCCC) concerning the services of the Churls, a land-boundary is given, in which Hysseburnan (*Hurstbourne Priors*) and other places in the same district receive mention.[3]

Ðis synd þa landgemero.

Ærest of Twyfyrde andlang weges to Fearnhlince. þanan andlang weges to Æsesbeorge. þanan on gerihte to þære pirigan. þonne ⁊ lang weges on Ceardices beorg. þonne on Wiðig-

These are the land-boundaries.

First from Twyford along the way to Farnlinch; thence along the way to Æsesbeorg; thence right on to the pear-tree; then along the way to Cerdic's hill; then to Withygrove;

---

[1] *Saxons in England*, vol. i, p. 196.
[2] Thorpe, *Laws of King Ine, Ancient Laws, etc., of England*, p. 55; F. Seebohm, *The English Village Community*, pp. 109-10.
[3] *Diplomatarium Anglicum Ævi Saxonici*, pp. 145-47.

grafe . þonne on ðone weg þe scyt ofer ða díc . þonne andlang weges on þa coppedan ác . þanan andlang weges of [oð] he to wuda lið . þonne on gerihte on Stodleage suþewearde . þonne andlang Mearcweges útt wið Feldbeorga . þonne andlang Mearcweges to þan hagan be suþan Feárnleáge . andlang hagan útt to Ubbanleáge stigele . þonne ⁊ lang hagan to Wocces geate . þanan andlang hagan ón Tyrwenes sledes heafad . þonne andlang hagan útt to Bitan cnolle on ðone lithagan . andlang þære þorngræfan þwyres ofer Hysseburnan on Gosdæne . þonne andlang þæs weges þe lið andlang Gosdæne þwyres ofer in Waldes weg . þonne andlang weges on þonne beorg æt Wæcces treówe . þanan onbutan Higdune þornes to Bruneshamme . þonne andlang hagan to þam grundeliesan pytte . þanan on gerihte andlang hagan to Hremmes dene . þ̄ andlang hagan on ðære ealdan mapolder be suþan Tutan mære . þonne andlang hagan on Sotceorles æcer . þanan ofer ða dæne úpp be wyrtwalan . þonne onbutan ðone garan on þone piwinðlan . þonne onbutan þone garan on þone biwinðlan . þonne andlang Mearcweges to Wifan stocce . þanan andlang þæs ealdan weges to Bradan lea . þonne an westeweard Geapan garan . þanan to þære haran apoldre . þonne ⁊ lang díc útt on Terstan on þone syþeran steð . þonne ⁊ lang steþes . þ̄ beneoðan Beamwær on þone norþere steþ . andlang staðes æft on Twyfyrde .

then to the way that leads over the ditch; then along the way to the copped oak; thence along the way which leads to the wood; then right on southward to Studley; then along the boundary way out towards Felborough; then along the boundary way to the 'haga' south of Farleigh; along the 'haga' out to Ubley stile; then along the 'haga' to Wockes gate; thence along the 'haga' to the head of Tyrwen's 'slade'; then along the 'haga' out to Bita's knoll to the 'lithaga', along the thorn-grove across over Hussebourn to Gosden; then along the way that leads by Gosden across over to Walde's way; then along the way to the hill at Wecke's tree; thence round Higdon (Highdown) thorns to Brun's ham; then along the 'haga' to the bottomless pit; thence right on along the 'haga' to Raven's dean; then along the 'haga' to the old maple south of Tuta's mere; then along the 'haga' to Sotchurl's field; thence over the dean up by the 'wyrtwal'; then round the 'gore' to the windle-tree; then round the 'gore' to the windle-tree; then along the boundary to 'Wifan stock'; thence along the old way to Bradley; thence to Geapa gore; thence to the hoar apple-tree; then along the dike out to the Terstan to the south bank; then along the bank; then below Beamweir to the north bank; along the bank again to Twyford.

These ancient landmarks comprehend a boundary of some importance, and embrace a considerable West Saxon district. Some of the names mentioned are recognisable. The country included in the boundary extended from Twyford on the Test (Terstan) southward, to Highdown hill (*Haydon?*), on the extreme north border of Wiltshire; and back from Highdown to Twyford. The boundary ran east to Farley; then across the country to Hurstbourne, which would be the right line to Highdown from Farley. Wecke's-tree is mentioned; and there are three places named Week in the neighbourhood of Hurstbourne Priors. A portion of Hurstbourne Tarrant is called the Dean; and there is a Bradley between St. Mary Bourne and Lichfield. The "Old Way" appears to refer to the Harrow-way, a name evidently derived from the Anglo-Saxon *har*, hoar or ancient (*Hoarway?*); and this ancient way is at the present time crossed by the Dike (Devil's Dyke), which lies between Andover and St. Mary Bourne. From the Dike back to Twyford it would appear that the boundary followed the Test River (*Terstan, its old name*), traversing its south bank and crossing over to the north bank in its course to Twyford.

The word "haga", which so frequently appears in the Twyford boundaries, means *hedge*. It shows that fields bounded by hedges—Anglo-Saxon, *haga*, or *hæge*, G. *hage*, meaning the Common Hawthorn (*Cratægus oxyacantha*)—had become largely parcelled out at a very early period in the history of the Germanic races.

The disposal of the Hurstbourne property by the will of King Alfred was followed by a bequest of the same property by his son Edward the Elder, of which the following is a copy in Latin and English text. There is a reference here to a place named *Adstock* (Stoke), one of the tithings of the parish of St. Mary Bourne, of which an account appears in a Charter, already given, of the same King Edward (A.D. DCCCC).

Charter of Edward the Elder.[1]

Regnante imperpetuum Sancta Trinitate! Præsentisque vitæ curriculis subterlabentibus, atque omnibus, propemodum regum gestis oblivioni traditis, aut ignorantia id agente vel incuria regum ac magistrorum ignaviter torpescente ac lacescente; quapropter ego Edwardus divina indulgente clementia Anglorum Saxonum rex, literarum memoriæ commendare procuravi, quod proavus meus Egberhtus rex possidebat quinquaginta manentes praetio comparatos in illo loco qui dicitur Hursborne, et alios decem in loco qui dicitur Adstoke, qui ad præfatum pertinent locum, scilicet

The Holy Trinity ever reigning. And of this present life fleeting away, and all worthy acts of Kings in a manner handed over to oblivion, or else ignorance or the negligence of Kings and governors lazily torpid and sluggish effecting the same. For which reason I, Edward, King of the Anglo-Saxons, have caused to be committed to remembrance, by writing, that my great-grandfather, King Egbert, possessed fifty tenants, obtained by valuable consideration, in that place which is called Hursborne, and ten others in the place which is called Adstock (Stoke), which belong to the aforesaid place, to wit, Hurs-

---

[1] J. M. Kemble, *Ancient Charters*, vol. ii, published by the English Hist. Society.

Hursborne. Cumque proavus meus moriens commendavit eandem terram filio suo Adulpho regi avo meo, at ille viam universitatis ingrediens reliquit eandem terram filio suo Alfredo regi patri meo in diebus suis, ea condicione ut ipse moriens demitteret eandem terram venerabili familiæ beatorum apostolorum Petri et Pauli in Wentana civitate, in perpetuam hæreditatem habendam et possidendam; intus ad refectorium fratrum, cum silvis, campis, pratis, et pascuis, atque ad se rite pertinentibus. Hec autem donatio, Deo, autore, ita confirmata est cum superno chirographo in cruce domini nostri Jesu Christi, pro redempcione piaculorum Adulphi regis et Alfredi regis, necnon et antecessorum suorum, simul et pro æterna libertate animæ meæ et omnis successuræ posteritatis meæ eadem condicione comprobata est, ut nullus episcopus nec etiam præsens familia, nec insuper subsequens possit illam terram amovere ab illa familia perpetualiter, neque pro pecunia, neque pro alia terra, quamdiu fuerit homo super terram, vel petra in terra, sed hæreditas ipsa beatis apostolis Petro et Paulo commendata perpetualiter ab omni servitute mundiali et regali libera remaneat, excepta expedicione et arcis et pontis constructione; hac quoque causa imperavi istum hæreditarium librum noviter scribi, quia iste antiquus hæreditarius liber, olim scriptus, non habebatur; si quis vero post hac illum hæreditarium librum vel alium quemlibet contra hanc nostram defensionem in propatulo adduxerit, ab omni Christianitate irritus fiat et ad nihilum valeat; si quis hoc nostrum decretum custodire et augere voluerit, adaugeat omnipotens omnia præsentis sibi et futuræ vite bona. Si quis vero, (quod non optamus,) contra nostrum hoc decre-

borne. And whereas my great-grandfather dying committed the same land to King Adulph, my grandfather, and he going the way of all flesh, left the same land to his son King Alfred, my father, in his days, on this condition, that he dying should pass the same land to the venerable brotherhood of the blessed apostles Peter and Paul in the City of Winchester, to be had and possessed in perpetual inheritance, for the domestic sustentation of the brethren,—with the woods, fields, meadows, and feedings to them lawfully belonging. And this gift, by the dictation of God, is so confirmed with the heavenly chirograph in the cross of our Lord Jesus Christ, for the atonement of the sins of King Adulph and King Alfred, and also of their ancestors at the same time, and for the eternal deliverance of my own soul and of all my posterity hereafter to come: it is upon the same condition confirmed that no bishop, nor yet the present brotherhood nor the subsequent, may be able to amove that land from that brotherhood permanently, nor for money, nor for other land, so long as there shall be a man upon the earth, or a stone in the earth, but that same inheritance, permanently committed to the blessed apostles Peter and Paul shall remain free from all worldly and regal service, except military expedition and building of castle and bridge.

For this cause also I have commanded this book of Inheritance to be written anew, because that ancient book of inheritance heretofore written will not have credence. But if indeed hereafter any one shall scandalously question this deed of inheritance, or any other whatsoever, against this our confirmation, let him be cut off from all Christian society, and be brought to nought. If any one will

tum machinari, aut infringere aliquid voluerit, sciat se graviter racionem redditurum in die judicii ante tribunal Domini, nisi prius hic digna emendaverit pœnitentia ante mortem.

desire to preserve and increase this our decree, may the Omnipotent increase to him all the advantages of the life present and to come! If again (which we by no means wish) any one should desire to cunningly devise or disannul anything against this our decree, let him know that he will have to render a grievous reckoning on the day of judgment before the judgment-seat of our Lord, unless he shall first here have undergone a suitable penance before his death.

The following translation from the Saxon of a portion of one of the Charters of Eadgar[1] (961) relates to Hurstbourne Tarrant or *Regis*. It comprehends the boundaries of Hurstbourne Tarrant; and it is introduced as some of the place-names here written are the same as those mentioned in the Twyford boundaries.

"These are the Landboundaries to Hursbourn [Ðis sind ða landgemæra tó Hisseburnan].

"First Begmære; from Begmære to Coganmere; from Coganmere to Guttescumbes head; thence to Hengist-pathe's gate; from that gate along the enclosure to Standene; from Standene to Hennadene; from Hennadene to Thyrranmere; from Thyrranmere to Dhorcmere; from Dhorcmere to Lillan ridge; from Lillan ridge to Ruwan [rough] Hill; from Ruwan Hill to Woon-lince [tilled lynchet?]; from Woon-lince to Geoc meadow to Cissan antsigo; thence to White-fences; thence to Gosdene; from Gosdene along the valley to Bittan Hill-top to the wood; from Bittan Hill-top to Wocces [Weeks?] gate; from Wocces Gate to Lidgate; from Lidgate to Wesan [west] house southward; thence to Tanmere; from Tanmere to Begmere. Then there are those same XV hides at Eastune. First to Eferfearn, to the Yellow-bank, thence to Hyldan Mound; then along the road as far as Ceapmanna-dale [Chapman's-dell]; from Ceapmanna-dale thence to Portmanna under Hill; thence to Bigwindlan; thence ever by the stream on to Ceorl's-acre, from Cheorl's-acre unto Wonstoc; from thence to Stocce-Thweores [Stoke-poores?] over Brodan [broad] lea to Horsleaga-dene; from that valley to the Bottomless-pit; from that pit to Hacan pound-fold, back again to Eferfearn.

"In the year of our Lord's incarnation DCCCCLXI., this Charter is written, these Witnesses consenting, whose names are set down here below."

The boundaries of Hurstbourne Tarrant, as I have already noticed, include place-names mentioned in the Twyford boundaries, showing that the Twyford line extended in the direction indicated in the notices regarding those boundaries. In addition to Hurstbourne, "Wocces-gate", "Gosden", and the remarkable name, "Bottomless-

[1] J. M. Kemble, *Codex Diplomaticus Ævi Saxonici*, vol. vi, p. 40.

pit", occur in both. It is impossible at this time to recognise, save in a few instances, the places named, but *Hennadene* undoubtedly refers to Hendean, between Upton and Vernham. Saxon boundaries are not to be considered as necessarily following the present parochial boundaries, inasmuch as they embrace in many cases districts wider than the present parishes. They are usually described as proceeding from some well-marked point, and passing on to other well-marked points they go back to the place from which they start. Thus, the Hurstbourne boundary starting at Begmere ends at Begmere. It is interesting to note that certain of the names point to the open-field system as the method of cultivation at that time on the lands of the Saxon manor of Hurstbourne.[1] *Gore* and *Geapa's gore* in the Twyford boundaries refer to the *gore* or *goredacre*, which means strips in open fields pointed or tapering at one end, because the shape of the field would not admit of the land being cut up into regular strips. *Sotchurl's field* and *Geoc meadow*, in the boundaries of Twyford, and *Churl's-acre*, in the boundaries of Hurstbourne, show that among the tillers of the land the *Ceorl*, who was in the lowest grade of husbandmen, had his plot of ground. It is evident, therefore, that the Saxon villages were open fields, which had their division into furlongs and strips, having their headlands and linches; and that the holdings contained their small meadows. *Lince* or *lynch* has already been explained under the head of the Services of the Churls of Hurstbourne Priors. Pound-fold, or pound for the impounding of stray cattle, was an appendage of the Saxon manor, and had its keeper or *Punder*—an institution which has survived down to the present day.

[1] See a similar example, under the head of Boundaries of Hardwell, in Hampshire, appended to a Charter (*Hist. Monasterii de Abingdon*, vol. i, p. 57), by which King Edward, son of King Alfred, gave the estate to the Abbey of Abingdon. (F. Seebohm, *The English Village Community*, pp. 107-108.)

The Manor.

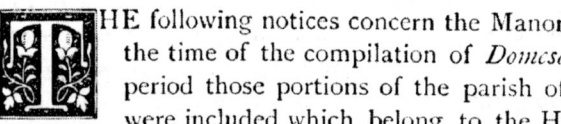

Hurstbourne Priors.

[DOMESDAY, 1086.]

THE following notices concern the Manor of Hurstbourne at the time of the compilation of *Domesday Book*. At that period those portions of the parish of St. Mary Bourne were included which belong to the Hundred of Evingar. Swampton, one of the tithings of St. Mary Bourne, is in the Hundred of Clere, and receives separate mention in *Domesday*.

The county at the time of the Survey was divided nominally into fifty hundreds; but whether there were fifty or forty-seven, as one or two of them are not accurately defined, is of no great consequence. Some of them retain their ancient names, and are apparently of the same extent now as they were at the time of the Conqueror.

The hundreds are subdivided into about three hundred manors, of which seventy-five were held by the king, and one hundred and three by ecclesiastical persons and establishments.[1] The rental of the county appears to have been about £2,640, of which two-fifths belonged to the Bishop of Winchester, and other ecclesiastics and ecclesiastical institutions.

In writing of the hundred, the tithing should receive mention, and the parish. A tithing is a district originally composed of ten freemen, heads of families, who were sureties for each other to the king and his people; the term tithing (a tenth) denoting the number of householders of which it was composed. The presiding officer of the tithing was called a tithing-man. Ten of those tithings originally constituted the hundred, whose chief was denominated *Hundredes-ealdor*, or Ealdorman (Elder of the people), the presiding officer of the hundred-court.

---

[1] H. Moody, *Introduction to Translation of Domesday Book*, p. 1.

A parish is that circuit of ground which is committed to the charge of one parson, vicar, or other minister, having care of souls therein. In the early ages of Christianity in this island parishes were unknown, or at least signified the same that a diocese does now. When the *dioichia* (diocese), or the district over which the bishop exercised his spiritual functions, was divided into lesser portions for the superintendence of his clergy, a word of similar import was adopted, *paroichia* (parish), and in ancient times the words were used indiscriminately.[1]

The word parish is, however, derived from the Anglo-Saxon priest-shire, the share, division, or jurisdiction of a priest. It has been supposed that parishes were first erected by the Council of Lateran (A.D. 1179), but there is no doubt that their origin is of earlier date, they being mentioned in the laws of King Edgar, about the year 970, implying that England then had some division into parishes. It seems pretty clear that the boundaries of parishes were originally ascertained by those of a manor or manors, since it seldom happens that a manor extends itself over more parishes than one, though there are often many manors in one parish; but, at present, the boundaries of the one afford no evidence of the boundaries of the other.[2]

DOMESDAY, A.D. 1086.

(*Esseburne, Hantescire.*)

Extended Latin Text.

Ipse episcopus tenet *Esseburne*. Semper fuit in monasterio. Tempore Regis Edwardi, et modo, se defendit pro 38 hidis. Terra est 51 carucatæ. In dominio sunt 4 carucatæ; et 55 villani, et 38 bordarii, cum 45 carucis. Ibi 14 servi, et 5 molini de 25 solidis; et 30 acræ prati. Silva de 20 porcis. T. R. E. valebat 36 libras; et postea, 26 libras; modo, 40 libras.

De hoc manerio tenet Goisfridus, de episcopo, 5 hidas, in eadem villa. Tres taini tenuerunt, de episcopo, et non potuerunt ire quolibet. Tres aulas habuerunt. Et ibi sunt 3 carucatæ in dominio; et 19 bordarii, et 2 servi, et molinus de 12 solidis et 6

Translation.

The Bishop himself holds Esseburne (Hurstbourne Priors). It was always abbey land. In the time of King Edward, it was, and is now, assessed at 38 hides. The land is 51 carucates (sufficient for 51 plough-teams). In demesne there are 4 carucates; and 55 villeins, and 38 borderers, with 45 ploughs. There are 14 serfs; and 5 mills of 25 shillings (value in money); and 30 acres of meadow. Wood of 20 pigs (the pannage of). In the time of King Edward (the Confessor) it was worth 36 pounds; and afterwards 26 pounds; now (it is worth) 40 pounds.

Of this manor, Goisfrid holds of the bishop 5 hides, in the same vil-

---

[1] Charles Sandys, F.S.A., *Consuetudines Kanciae*, p. 65.
[2] Blackstone's *Commentaries*, p. 111.

denariis, et 20 acræ prati. Valuit 8 libras. Modo, 6 libras.

De eodem manerio, tenet Richerius, de episcopo, 2 hidas. Alnod tenuit, nec quolibet ire potuit. Ibi est, in dominio, una carucata, et 9 bordarii, et 3 servi, et 5 acræ prati. Silva de 3 porcis pasnagio. Valet 40 solidos.

De ipso manerio, tenet Willelmus, de episcopo, 2 hidas, dimidia virgata minus. Sawinus tenuit, de episcopo, et non potuit ire quolibet. Ibi est una carucata, cum uno villano; et 12 bordarii, cum una carucata; et 4 acræ prati. Valuit 6 libras; modo 40 solidos. Lewinus tenet, de episcopo, unam hidam, cum ecclesia; et ibi habet 7 boves in carucata, et 2 acras prati. Valet, et valuit, 50 solidos.[1]

lage. Three thanes held them of the bishop, and they were not able (at liberty) to go anywhere (meaning, that they were tied to the manor). They have three halls (*i.e.*, each had a house of that description). And there are 3 carucates in demesne; and 19 borderers, and 2 serfs, and a mill of 12s. and 6d. (value); and 20 acres of meadow. It was worth 8 pounds: now (it is worth) 6 pounds.

Of the same manor, Richerius holds of the bishop 2 hides. Alnod held them; nor was he able (at liberty) to move anywhere. There is, in demesne, one carucate, and 9 borderers, and 3 serfs, and 5 acres of meadow. Wood for the pannage of 3 pigs. It is worth 40 shillings.

Of the same manor, William holds of the bishop 2 hides, *minus* half-a-virgate. Sawin held them of the bishop, and was not at liberty to remove. There is one carucate, with one villein; and 12 borderers, with one carucate; and 4 acres of meadow. It was worth 6 pounds, now 40 shillings. Lewin holds of the bishop one hide, with the church; and he has 7 oxen (in a plough-team?) and 2 acres of meadow. It was, and is, worth 50 shillings.

There were, therefore, three holders under the Bishop in the Hurstbourne manor; and Lewin the priest, who held some land of the Bishop, in addition to the church. The entry *ibi habet* vii *bov' in caruc'*, Mr. F. J. Baigent suggests, refers to seven ploughed bovates of land, or the right to pasture seven oxen; if the former, the bovate being equivalent to the half-virgate of 15 acres, renders the holding, in addition to the one hide, 105 acres. It is likely that the five hides held by Goisfrid represent the land which afterwards came to Emma de Roches; if so, it later came to Fawconer and Brocas (see *Fawconer*).

[1] An extended Latin text of *Domesday*, with translation, appears in the *History of Hampshire*, by Richard Warner, Junr., 1789; there is also a translation, with Latin text, by Henry Moody, together with a facsimile copy of the original *Domesday of Hants*, in photo-zincography.

Of Richerius more will appear later. These tenants appear to have held largely in other parts of Hampshire (see *Domesday*), particularly Willelmus, if he is the same as the Willelmus described as the son of Azor.

During the Saxon period, in the time of King Edward, Hurstbourne manor was rated at 38 hides, and it was assessed at the same in the *Domesday* Survey; and as the hide was then the unit of measure it will be necessary to determine its value. Carucate is used for hide in some districts, the word meaning both plough and plough-team, and as in the case of the hide, the carucate varied in area. The Hundred Rolls of Bedfordshire and Buckinghamshire state that there were circumstances under which it differed as largely from 80 to 200 acres.[1] The hide also differed greatly, although its normal rendering was 120 acres, or equal to 4 virgates of 30 acres each, this being the normal value of the virgate, which in its turn largely varied. To furnish a few examples: In the Hundred Rolls of Huntingdonshire, the hide of 120 acres obtains in twelve cases out of nineteen, although in the table there is a variation in the hide of from 120 to 240 acres; while the virgate varies as widely, or from 15 up to 48 acres. Taking the normal estimate of 120 acres for the hide, the manor of Hurstbourne comprehended 4,560 acres.

This manor now comprises the parishes of Hurstbourne Priors and St. Mary Bourne, with an area of 10,800 acres.[2]

There is evidence that the hide contained but 96 acres,—" Virgata terræ continet viginti quatuor acras; et quatuor virgatæ constituunt unam hidam" (MS. formerly belonging to Malmesbury Abbey, quoted by Spelman). Intermediate between the estimates of 120 and 96 acres comes that of the *Dialogus de Scaccario* (in the Black Book of the Exchequer), which gives 100 acres to the hide; and with that computation the well-known passage in the paraphrase of Beda, ascribed to King Alfred, will be found to agree very well:—" Est autem mensuræ ejusdem insulæ, juxta æstimationem Anglorum, mille ducentarum familiarum,"—the hide in its primal sense, being (it is supposed) a quantity deemed sufficient to maintain one family, and capable on average land of being kept in tillage by a single plough. " Hida autem Anglice vocatur terra unius aratri cultura sufficiens per annum" (Henry of Huntingdon, *Historia*, lib. vi (A.D. 1008).[3] The late Mr. J. M. Kemble is in favour of a smaller estimate than any of these (see *Saxons in England*); but on the whole the larger estimate has been generally accepted by antiquaries.

[1] *The English Village Community*, p. 40; also F. Seebohm, *Hundred Rolls*, p. 37. [2] Henry Moody, *Domesday*, and translation, p. 42.
[3] *Liber Monasterii de Hyda*, Glossary, pp. 370-71.

At the time of the *Domesday* Survey England was covered with manors, the manors in their simplest form being the estates of manorial lords, each having its small village community living in villenage upon it. The home farm or demesne belonged to the manor house, and was cultivated by the tenants in villenage. The land extended around the village in open fields; and in the village were the small homesteads of the tenants, their holdings consisting of bundles of strips scattered about the open fields; and all the tenants had rights of pasture for their cattle after the harvesting of their crops, as well as the green commons of the manor.

There were two classes of tenants, the Villeins [*Villani*], and the Borderers [*Bordarii*]. Both classes held by base service. The first, or Villeins proper, held in hides, half-hides, virgates, or in bovates, according to the oxen allotted to them, or contributed by them to the manorial plough-team consisting of eight oxen, each villein commonly contributing a pair. The normal holding was the virgate or yard-land, which consisted of about 30 acres in scattered acre or half-acre strips, each a furlong in length, and a perch or two in breadth, separated by turf balks. The country lanes often kept to the lines of the balks and headlands which separated the arable fields, or they skirted the division between the ancient arable and the moorland or open pasture. We can thus account for most of the old by-ways called droves in the parish of St. Mary Bourne, which are but relics of the open-field system, or adopted at the time of the division of the land into allotments.

These holdings passed with the strips of land by re-grant from the manorial lord from one generation of serfs to another in unbroken regularity, always to a single successor whether the oldest or the youngest, varying somewhat according to the custom of the manor, and were possessed in some cases for generations by members of the same family, and were often recognised by the family name of the holders. The object was, however, not the preservation of the tenant, but of his services as representing the yardland to the lord of the manor. At the date of *Domesday* the Villeins were the most important tenants in villenage, and were more numerous than the *Bordarii*, or cottage tenants, the former numbering about 38 per cent., and the latter embracing about 32 per cent. of the entire population.[1] There appear to have been no absolutely free tenants at the time of the Survey. It was at a later period that the demesne lands were let out to permanent tenants in freehold.

Next to the Villeins were the smaller occupiers, the Borderers, or Cottiers, probably from the Saxon *bord*, a cottage. They possessed

---

[1] Seebohm, *The English Village Community*, p. 90; also pp. 96-97.

commonly no oxen, and therefore had no ploughing. In some manors, however, they appeared to rank as a lower grade of Villeins, and held small allotments in the common fields, in strips varying up to five acres in extent, and sometimes more. The Cottiers were bound to do domestic work, and supply the lord's table. Their services were of a more trivial kind than those of the Villeins, but their duties were above those of the next class, the Serfs; and were of the kind which would most easily merge into the condition of the modern labourer. In the case of all the tenants in the earlier stage of villenage the payments were made in produce, for which in later times a money payment was substituted. From this we obtain an insight into the origin of the term farmer. Those who held the outlands of the lord as tenants had to render to him certain necessaries as rent, this they called *feorme*. But after the time of Henry II the food became changed for money; nevertheless, in letting land, the word remained under the head of *farmer*. (*Spelman on Feuds*, chap. vii; *vide* Cowel.)

The lower class, or Serfs (*Servi*), embraced about 9 per cent. of the population. They were more numerous in the south-west of England, and were at that time fast merging into the class of Cottiers. They mingled with the labourers and household servants on the lord's demesne, and were acquiring habits of freedom, and passing away from the condition of the *Theow*, which may be considered as representing their condition in Saxon times.

Tithes[1] (*decimæ*) are first expressly mentioned in the constitution of Egbert, Archbishop of York, A.D. 750. They then belonged to the common treasure of the diocese; and seem to have been paid into the hands of the Bishop, and distributed by him among his clergy, in such proportion as their services deserved. But when churches were founded and endowed with glebe, or certain portions of land appropriated to the resident minister, the Bishops were easily prevailed on to appropriate the tithes also (reserving some share to themselves) to the ministers officiating within the districts from whence they arose; the necessity of maintaining a number of itinerant priests being now at an end, their cathedrals, by the munificence of princes, and gifts of private individuals, being amply endowed for the maintenance of themselves and their college of priests who attended on the service of the cathedral church. Before tithes were paid, or churches endowed, the clergy lived upon the oblations and contributions of the people, which were doubtless very considerable.

Hurstbourne [*Hysseburne*], as we have seen, was a manor of the royal demesne until by Charter-grant it became monastic property,

---

[1] Introduction to Hutchins's *Dorset*, p. 90; and Brady's *History*, p. 102, note *m*.

and the church was manorial. Relating to tithes it appears that, in A.D. 837,[1] Ethelwulf granted one-tenth of the whole land of England to the Church. Under the head of "Accession of Ethelwulf and his administration of the Government" occurs the following passage:—
"*In regem sic sublimatus, Alstanum, Schirborniæ episcopum, habuit in rebus forensicis maxime cooperatorem. In rebus vero ecclesiasticis, sanctissimum patrem Swythunum, cui dedit præsulatum Wyntoniensis ecclesiæ, cujus providentia et consilio decimam partem omnium terrarum in manibus suis existentium, ecclesiæ dedit Anglicanæ, perpetuis temporibus possidendam.*" Respecting this gift Mr. F. Seebohm writes:—

"There is nothing intrinsically impossible even in the alleged but doubtful donation of King Ethelwulf of one-tenth of the whole land of England by one stroke of the pen to the Church. It has been said that he could not do it, except on the royal domains, without robbing the landowners and their tenants of their holdings. It would be so if the holdings were blocks. But there is nothing impossible in the supposition that a Saxon king should enact a law that every tenth strip ploughed by the common ploughs throughout the villages of England should be devoted to the Church." . . . . "Whatever may be said as to the donation of Ethelwulf, whether it be spurious or not, there are other proofs that something of the kind was afterwards effected."

"In No. xxv (Thorpe, p. 328) of the *Excerptiones* of Archbishop Egbert (A.D. 735-66) it is ordained that 'to every church shall be allotted one complete holding (*mansa*), and that this shall be free from all but ecclesiastical services.' . . . . The *Domesday* Survey proves that, in a great number of instances at least, room had been made in the village community for the priest and his virgate."[2]

The humble position of the secular clergy is shown at the time of *Domesday* in the mention of priests among the villeins of the manor. Bearing on this there is an entry in the Church Register of the neighbouring hamlet of Woodcot. The Register commences in the year 1587, and contains various entries relating to the Kingsmill family, one of which refers to a "Master of Artes", who is stated as being a servant to one of the Kingsmills.

Under the Saxon laws tithes appear not to have been taken in the shape of tenths, as the tenth sheaf, but in land, every tenth strip being left for the Church by the ploughmen, if, indeed, the ploughing was not performed by the common ploughs, in return for the services rendered by the priests. In the laws of Æthelred, 978-1016 (Thorpe, p. 146), it was ordered that every man should give his *churchshot*, and just tithe, *as the plough traverses the tenth acre*. Although *Domesday* furnishes but small reference to churches and their tithes, Mr. F. Seebohm cites one example of the tithes being taken in absolute strips and acres. It refers to the church of Wallop, the place from

[1] *Liber de Hyda*, pp. 22-23; *Chronicle of Ethelwulf*, A.D. 837-57.
[2] *The English Village Community*, pp. 114-15.

which sprung the family of the present Lord of the Manor of Hurstbourne, the Earl of Portsmouth. It states that "to the church there pertains one hide, also half of the tithes of the manor, also the whole Kirkshot. And of the tithes of the *Villani*, XLVI. *pence, and half of the acres.* There is in addition a little church to which pertains VIII *acres of the tithes.*"[1]

According to *Domesday* there were five mills belonging to the manor, of the value of twenty-five shillings; and a mill is stated as attached to the *demesne*, which is valued at twelve shillings and sixpence. This one might have been a water-mill, and the others hand-mills. The number refers to five pairs of stones, which were not of large size, and when worked by manual labour were each turned by a single wheel. Water-mills were largely used at the time of *Domesday*. Religious houses had their malt-houses, mill-houses, stables, etc., as part of their out-buildings. From the *Charta de Foresta* of Henry III (Manwood, ff. 6-11), we find that persons had houses and farms, and even woods, in the King's forest; and the Charter provides that they may there, on their own lands, build mills on the forest streams, sink wells, and dig marl-pits, for the same purpose, probably, as at the present day chalk is dug and strewed over the ground with the object of rendering heavy land more porous and productive. Under the head of *Molendinum*, we find *Molendinum fullonicum*, a fulling-mill; *Molendinum ad ventum*, a windmill; *Molendinum aquaticum*, a water-mill; *Molendinum equitium*, a horse-mill, and *Molendinum molare*, a grinding or grist-mill.[2] Mills were in some cases not only rented by a money value, but by the additional payment of eels.

The pannage (*pasnagium*) of hogs refers to the custom of permitting those who had a right to common of pannage to turn out pigs to roam in the woodlands, upon the payment of a nominal sum, for the purpose of feeding on the beech-mast and acorns. The time was called the pannage-month, which in some cases, in the New Forest for instance, lasted from September 25th to November 22nd. In *Domesday*, under *Clatinges*, p. xviii.*a*, we find, "*Silva inutilis*", that is, a wood which has no beech, oak, ash, nor holly, but only yews or thorns, equivalent to the entry, "*Silva sine pasnagio*", under *Anne*, p. xix.*a* (see, also, Ellis, *Introduction to Domesday*, vol. i, p. 99); whilst under *Borgate*, p. iv.*b*, we find, "*Pastura quæ reddebat* XL *porcos est in forestâ Regis.*"[3]

Of the Hurstbourne manor, it will be observed that Goisfrid held five hides under the Bishop. And it appears from the *Domesday* record that this same Goisfrid (*Goisfridus*) held three hides of the

---

[1] F. Seebohm, *The English Village Community*, p. 117.
[2] Interpreter, Dr. Cowel, *Molendinum*.
[3] Wise, *The New Forest*, p. 35, footnote.

lands of the manor of Easton (*Estune*), in *Falelie* hundred. He also held at Weston under Durand of Gloucester; and at *Bradelie*, in a manor belonging to Overton, he held five hides. In the manor of Fareham (*Fernham*) Goisfrid possessed four hides, which had been held by Hercus; and of the land at Shalfleet (*Seldeflet*) he is recorded as holding two-and-a-half yardlands, and one ploughland, together with two villeins, and one borderer.[1]

It is further noticeable in connection with the Hurstbourne Priors manor that three *Thanes* had held possession of the land then enjoyed by Goisfrid under the Bishop, and it is stated that they were fixed to the spot (*could not remove*), and that each had a hall. In some other notices in *Domesday* Thanes are spoken of as at liberty to go where they would, which points that there must have been considerable difference in the rank and privileges of those Saxon gentlemen. According to Kelham and Selden there were three degrees of Thanes, viz., those of Royal rank, a middle order, and the inferior Thanes (*Thani regis*, *Thani mediocres*, and *Thani minores*). The intermediate were about equivalent to lords of manors. The *Thani regis* were those who actually served the King in Court and Commonwealth; while those who held the title by inheritance were "Middle Thanes". In addition to these two degrees, Ceorls, or inferior landowners, or mercantile persons, could become Thanes by the acquisition of sufficient landed property; but only entitling them to the rank of *Thani minores*. The Thanes who could move might perhaps be reckoned among the *Thani mediocres;* although the remark that "they could go whither they would", seems to imply that they had not inherited but had acquired freedom of locomotion. The Hurstbourne Thanes were most likely the next in degree to the Ceorls, who before becoming Thanes were often "*adscripti glebæ*", tenants for life.

The hall of the Thane had no pretensions to be considered architectural. It was commonly built of wood, rarely stone was introduced; but in later Saxon times stone was in use for both houses and churches. There was no difficulty with regard to timber, as trees of fine stature were obtainable in clearing the forests. It was oblong in shape, with doors at the opposite ends, and constructed of huge trees morticed at the four corners, with logs between, filled in or caulked with tow or other materials, or the sides were wattled. The roof was supported with cumbrous pillars called "roof-trees"; and the roof was thatched. The hearthstone occupied the centre, on which were burnt large logs, the smoke escaping through an opening in the roof. All the rooms were on the ground-floor, the ladies' sleeping-apartments being separated from the dwelling-place by the arras; and the walls

---

[1] Henry Moody, *Hampshire Domesday Book*, extended and translated.

in the higher-class houses were ornamented with tapestry, elaborately weaved and embroidered by the ladies of the household. On the walls hung the arms and armour of the occupants, and the seats consisted of benches called " mead-settles", arranged along the sides, as the "settles" are still placed at the present day in some village public-houses. On these sat the Saxon chiefs drinking their favourite beverage, mead, or "sweet-beer", out of the horns presented to them by the waiting damsels. The door was commonly open, and all comers were free to enter, particularly at midwinter; but there was a most rigid gradation exacted in the grouping of visitors according to their various social stations.[1]

It is stated by Mr. F. Seebohm[2] that the estates mentioned by Alfred, with their villages, which the Normans would have called manors, were *hams* (names frequently occurring in the south of England)'; and that the *tuns*, in common with the *hams*, were private estates with their attendant hamlets. The manorial lord over these was a *Thane*, who had his demesne lands, and his *gafol*-land, or *geneat*-land, which was land in villenage, and cultivated by *geneats*, or persons holding by service, as in the time of the Conqueror. As in later times, this gafol-land was made up of hides and yard-lands; and the villein tenants were in two classes: [1] the *geburs* (villeins proper), who held the yard-lands; and [2] the *cottiers*, with their smaller holdings. Beneath these two classes there were the slaves (*theows*), occupying a similar position to that of the *servi* of the time of *Domesday*.

When the Saxons first introduced the spade they were permitted to settle on the spot, each one having a portion of land allotted to him in the clearings of the manor on the Royal demesne. Hurstbourne was a manor of the king's demesne, until it became by charter the property of the Monastery. The land was measured out to the settlers by rods into acres; and these were ploughed by the common ploughs. On these clearings the tenants built their log houses, and thus set up a new *ham*, or *tun*, or *worth*, the word *tun* bearing reference to the fencing of the settlement (*tynan, to hedge in*).[3] This new hamlet the king might grant to a *thane* who superintended the work as *bocland*, and thereby it became his inheritance or manor. Although words change so vastly in course of time, I have thought that such names as Wootton, in Hampshire, might refer to such a cluster of Saxon huts in the forest, formed of timber, and mean *Wood-town.* The term lot, again, as applied to certain holdings in

---

[1] J. F. Hodgetts, *On the Scandinavian Elements in the English Race*, The Antiquary, No. 82, p. 137.   [2] *The English Village Community*, p. 128.
[3] Bosworth, *Anglo-Saxon Dictionary.*

the parish of St. Mary Bourne and elsewhere may be of quite recent date; but there is no doubt that the word can sometimes be traced to the early parcelling out of land in Saxon times. Thus, in the *Chronicles* of Simeon of Durham, where mention is made of the removal of St. Cuthbert's bones to Durham, at that time under forest, the document states that the eradication of the wood should be the first care, "*eradicata itaque silva, et unicuique sorte distributa*", and then that the clearings should be distributed *by lot*. It is not improbable that the peculiar windings of some of the old lanes in Hampshire originated in the necessity of avoiding the early lands parcelled out among the Saxon residents; or some parts might have been grubbed and others forest, the winding roads being necessary in order to reach the grubbed portions.

Richerius.

We have seen that Richerius at the time of *Domesday* held two hides of land under the Bishop, in the manor of Hurstbourne Priors. He was a Clerk, or Priest, and held in other manors in Hampshire, notably at Chilton Candover[1] (*Candevre*, in *Maneberge* hundred), where he held one manor of the Bishop. At Barton Stacey (in *Bertune* hundred) he held Bransbury, and claimed under the Bishop. At South Stoneham[2] (*Manebridge* hundred), it is stated, "Richerius the Clerk holds the church belonging to the manor, together with two other churches, near *Hantone*, which are dependant on this as the mother church." He also held lands of the King, *in capite*, and of the Bishop; and the tithes of the town of Hantone (Southampton), and of the *King's lands* belonging to the living. It is difficult at this time to ascertain which were the two churches near Southampton dependent on that of South Stoneham. Perhaps the spot on which subsequently stood the priory of St. Dionysius may have been occupied by a small church or chapel; and if the chapel at the hermitage of the Holy Trinity, and Virgin Mary, on the west bank of the river opposite to the valley of Itchen, and which gave its name to the present "Chapel Mill", was standing at the time of the Conquest, these might have been the two minor churches held by Richerius. The *Domesday* Survey does not state the situation of the land of the King held by Richerius, or of the land from which part of the tithes possessed by him arose. Portswood is a manor and tithing comprehending part of the parish of South Stoneham, within the county of the town of Southampton, which belonged to the King. It is

[1] Richard Warner, *Domesday*, p. 55.   [2] *Ibid.*

not improbable, therefore, that Portswood may have been the land held by Richerius of the King *in capite*. The name "*Kingsland*", at the present day, distinguishes a district in the parish of St. Mary, which now forms part of the town of Southampton; but which at the time of the Conquest was situated outside of the bounds of Hantone. If the land of the King may be supposed to have been held by Richerius in respect of the chapel at the hermitage, there are some grounds for believing that "Kingsland" may have been "the land of the King" in question.[1]

In the list of persons who were privileged by the Conqueror to possess their houses in Hantone tax free (*vide Mortimer*), occurs the name of Richerius de Andely, as holding four houses. Now, this Richerius de Andely became the founder of a family who held considerable property in Hampshire, and elsewhere, and filled many important offices under the Crown. At the time of the Conquest he was attached to the court of William of Normandy. In a pamphlet concerning the parishes of Hurstbourne Priors and St. Mary Bourne,[2] it is stated in regard to this d'Andeli that he was—"*un clerc ou un fils de la gaie science, attaché à la cour du Conquérant. Il est même probable qu'il fût le chef de la famille des poètes ou trouvères, Roger et Henri d'Andeli, qui ont brillé dans le province de Normandie pendant le 13e siècle.*"

Whatever office Richerius de Andely might have filled at the court of the Conqueror, it is probable that he was the chief of the family of whom Roger and Henry d'Andely were eminent in the province of Normandy in the thirteenth century. Whether their name came from a town in Normandy, their probable birthplace, or whether it was ancestrally derived, it is evident that they were members of a distinguished family, who possessed the lordship of d'Hermanville-sur-Vienne, in the Department of Caux. It appears in the records of Philippe-Auguste that Roger d'Andely was one of the knights who held a fief of the Duke of Normandy by military service; and it is found that, in 1201, one of the name was appointed as the Governor of the Château de Lavardin by King John.[3]

It has been inferentially suggested that Richerius of the *Domesday* manor of Hurstbourne Priors is the same person as Richerius de Andely,[4] who received a grant of houses in Hantone (Southampton) of

---

[1] Duthy, *Sketches of Hampshire*, p. 400.

[2] John Russell Smith, *Brief Historical Notices of the Parishes of Hurstbourne Priors, and St. Mary Bourne, Hants*, 1861, p. 14.

[3] *Cart. Roll. A.*, 3rd John; also, L'Abbé De la Rue, *History of the Troubadours*, vol. iii, pp. 196-8.

[4] *Brief Historical Notices of Hurstbourne Priors, etc.*, p. 17.

the Conqueror. It is shown that Richerius the Clerk held at various places in Hampshire, including churches at or near Hantone, with one hide, and the tithe of the manor; and as it is stated that Richerius d'Andely was "un clerc" in the train of Norman William, and the names being similar, it is not improbable that Richerius the Clerk and Richerius d'Andely are one. Irrespective of this there is room for the belief, although no documentary statement of the fact has been found, that the Dandelys possessed Week or Wyke manor; and there is also sufficient to justify the inference, in the *Brief Historical Notices*, that the cross-legged effigy in St. Mary Bourne Church represents one of that family. Hurstbourne was divided into two principal manors, *interius* and *exterius*; and if the Dandelys held in either it must have been in *exterius*, which contains Wyke manor. As the interior manor, which may be called Hurstbourne proper, was always priory land there is nothing particular (*i.e.*, eventful) in its history till after the Dissolution. But the exterior manor underwent changes of ownership; and it will be found that it was associated with the names of, probably, Dandely, but certainly with those of De Roches, Fawconer, Brocas, and others.

There are frequent notices of the Dandelys or Daundelys in the Public Records. According to *Foss's Judges*, Maurice Dandely or Aundely was a Westminster justice before whom fines were levied in 1219; and he served as a justice in various counties till about 1230.[1]

In 1235, the custody of the Manor of Gillingham, with the park and its appurtenances, and the manor and appurtenances of Mar, were committed to Robert of Aundely by King Henry III.[2]

In 1274, the Bishop of Winchester held half a knight's fee in chief, in Nether Werston, in the Hundred of Blagrave, Wilts; and Robert Daundely held the same half fee of the Bishop. And in the Hundred of Dunton the Bishop of Winchester held one knight's fee in chief in Fallerstone; and William of Brewes [Brewer?] held the said fee of the said Bishop. The Bishop also held the fourth part of one knight's fee of the King in chief, and Robert Daundely held the said tenement of the Bishop.

In the *Parliamentary Writs*, it appears that in 1297 Hugh Daundely was returned for Northampton, as holding lands or rents to the amount of £20 and upwards, yearly value, either *in capite* or otherwise, and as holder he was summoned under the general writ to perform military service in person, with horses and arms, in parts beyond the seas. In 1300, John Daundely was returned for Somerset

---

[1] *Rot. Claus.*, i, 516; ii, 77.
[2] *Abbrev. Rot. Orig.*, 20th Henry III.

and Dorset as holding lands *in capite* or otherwise to the amount of £40 and upwards, yearly value; and in 1301, Hugh Daundely, of Northampton, was summoned to perform military service in person against the Scots. In 1316, Roger Daundely certified as Lord of the Hundred of Mainsborough, and of the township of Chilton, in the county of Southampton. In 1322, John Daundely, Knight of the Shire, was returned for Northampton; and John Daundely obtained his expenses for attendance at the same Parliament. In 1322, Nicholas Daundely, manucaptor of John of Northampton, was returned for Northampton. In 1324, John Daundely was Sheriff of Northampton.

There is a notice of Walter de Andely, which was confirmed by his son Walter, of grants of land, with eighteen acres of Ruggenore wood, held of Chiltecandere (Chilton Candover) manor, to the Hospitallers of Baddesley, Hampshire. Baddesley was acquired by the Hospitallers in the thirteenth century; and on the 17th July 1304, Baddesley Church was appropriated to the English Priory of St. John of Jerusalem by deed of the Bishop.[1]

Walter de Andely gave a tenement at Portsmouth to the Canons of Christchurch Priory.

Godfrey de Andeli or Daundeli witnessed with others the gift by Edward de Foxcote of his Chapel of Foxcote, to the Church of St. Mary, at Andover. And with it he gave in frankalmoign, to be held by service of praying for himself, his family, and kinsfolk, the tithe of his demesne, and eight pence tithe of land held in villenage at Foscote. In Harl. MS. 532, the limitation of eightpence is omitted, and the grant runs as *totam decimam suam de dominico suo de Foscota et de villanis*.[2]

In 1338, the King committed to Robert Daundely the county of Southampton[3]; and in the same year to him was entrusted the custody and keeping of the King's Castle of Winchester, with the appurtenances, to hold,[4] etc.

Rolls of the Exchequer, or Pipe.

The Great Rolls of the Exchequer (*Mag. Rot. Pipæ*, known as the Pipe, because it was the channel or pipe for conveying the revenues into the Treasury) were formerly the records of the accounts of the Court of Exchequer, and contained the accounts of the whole revenues of the Crown, digested under the heads of the several

---

[1] Woodward and Wilks, *History of Hampshire*, vol. iii, pp. 58-59.
[2] *Ibid.*, vol. iii, p. 168.
[3] *Pat. Roll*, 12th Edward III, Ro. 16.
[4] *Abbr. Rot. Orig.*, 12th Edward III, Ro. 27.

counties, and were annually written out in order to the charging and discharging of the Sheriffs and other Accountants.

The earliest Pipe Roll preserved is that of the 31st Henry I[1] (1130), which is the most ancient record of the Exchequer, excepting *Domesday*.

The Crown-lands as they are set forth in the Pipe Rolls consist of the following elements:—(1) The Farms,[2] or ancient allodial estates originally assigned to the national King in the earliest Saxon period, or acquired by the territorial sovereign in the later Saxon period, and which were known since *Domesday* as Ancient Demesne of the Crown. (2) The feudal estates, knights' fees, baronies, or honours which the Crown had occupied by way of resumption,[3] escheat, or forfeiture, whether as lord of the fee or lord paramount in the last resource. (3) The Forests, expressed in the accounts rendered for the assessed fines of Assart.[4]

There was a fixed charge against each Sheriff, he compounding for the same in a fixed sum to the Crown, and receiving proportionate allowance in case of any diminution of the Crown-lands through alienations, etc. The Sheriff might be considered the Farmer-General of the Crown, who collected the rents of the King's tenants or "Debtors", who formed a class of small cultivators; and any grants in the shape of alms, or for repairs, etc., made from time to time by the King, were accounted for by the Sheriff or by his Bailiff, and were allowed in the discharge, upon sufficient warrant being shown. Thus, it will be seen that in the account rendered by Sheriff Briwer, in Chancellor's Roll, No. 14, 39*s*. 2*d*. is remitted in discharge for repairs.

The freeholders of the county had the election of the Sheriffs and therefore their offices were not determined by the death of the King.

In the Pipe Roll, 3rd and 4th Henry II, I find no mention of Hurstbourne Priors; but there are several notices of sums rendered in the manor of Hurstbourne Tarrant. But in the Roll, 1st Richard I, 1189-90, under *Sydhantescr'*—

"Henry de Bernevall renders account of £20, in coin, in Hurstbourne [*et Henr' de Bernevall . xxli. nuo. in Husseburn*]."

In another Roll of Richard I (Rot. 5, memb. 2) occurs an entry of payment of *pannage*—

---

[1] F. S. Thomas, *Handbook to the Public Records*, p. 243.
[2] *Fundi Regii.*
[3] *Dialogus de Scaccario*, ii, 10.
[4] *Notes on the History of the Crown Lands*, Antiquary, vol. xiii, p. 3.

"Id Vic redd Comp de . xxiiii*s*. ꝫ . ix*d*. de pasnag ꝫ p'q'isitio'ib; de Husseburn. h. anno. "In thro libauit. Et Quiet' est."

"The same Sheriff renders [his] account of 24*s*. 9*d*. the perquisites of pannage of Hurstbourn this year.
"[He has] paid it into the Treasury. And he is quit."

In the 1st of Richard there is an entry of £24 2*s*., in coin, of which account is rendered later; and this I believe refers to a subsequent entry, in which it is stated—the same Sheriff renders account of £18 2*s*., in coin, of the outgoings (*de exitu*) of Hurstbourne, and which appears to have been paid in gifts by the King's Brief. (Rot. 12, memb. 1.)

Under the head of *Hesseburna, Hantescr'*, 3rd year of Henry II, appears the entry:—

"Hamo Boterell renders [his] account [to the Sheriff] of £42, in bullion, in Hesseburna [*et Ham. Botterell . xlii li. bl. in Hesseburna*]."

In the fourth year of Henry II, 1157, occurs a precisely similar entry.

These entries might refer to Hurstbourne Tarrant, inasmuch as Hamo Botterell is found rendering account of 20*s*., the dues of the Brills of Doiley Forest. [*Comp. [de] . xxs. de censu Brollii de Diggerlai.*] (3rd Hy. I, Rot. 7, memb. 2.)

Again, 2nd Henry II—"*Hamo Boterell. deb.—xx . de censu foreste de Digerlea.*" This is not quite clear.

In the same list—"Mathias Croc renders [his] account of 60*s*., of the farm of the forest of 'Witingelega' (Whitingly) of the Brills of Andover. [*Math's Croc redd Comp de . lxs. de firma foreste de Witingelega . ꝫ de Brolliis de Andieura.*]
"*In th . lxs. Et Quiet' est.*
"Paid into the Treasury 60*s*. And he is quit."

The chief use of *Testa de Nevill* is to ascertain the principal landholders *temp*. Henry III, and Edward I, and the tenures by which they held their estates. But there are no references apparently to Hurstbourne Priors. A place called *Benetleg* is named (p. 232), which might be Binley. And William de Feritate holds *Stokes* as part of his barony of Normandy (p. 235). And, again (p. 236), the same holds Weston and the *vill* of *Stokes* in barony since the conquest of England; but there are several places of this name in Hampshire.

In the Chancellor's Roll, or duplicate of annual Accounts of the Exchequer, 3rd of King John (1201). Amercements of Henry de Nevill.

The above renders his account of 20*s*. received of Mathew Oisel. The same renders account of half a mark for the village (*vill'*) of Husseburn. In the same year the Prior of Husseburn renders account of one mark for old waste.

Will. Briwer renders account of £6 16s. 6d. of the farming of Husseburn for the half-year. Paid into the Treasury £4 16s. 4d.; and in the repairs which he has had in the above farming, 39s. 2d.

The £4 16s. 4d., with 39s. 2d., make the total of £6 15s. 6d., so that there is an error of 1s.

7th King John, 1205, m. 9 (*Rot. Lit. Claus.*). The King, etc., to the Barons of the Exchequer, etc.

"Know ye that Brien de Insula, and Alex. de Refham, and Alex. de Dorset have paid into our Treasury, by the hands of Philip de Lucy, at Gillingham, upon the morrow of St. Martin's day, xv marks (*the value of the mark in silver was* 13s. 4d.), subsequently x marks, the fine of William de Scat (*alias de Scalaris or Scales*) for the village (*vill'*) of Husseborn. I command you that they may remain quit. *Witness, Peter de Stoke,* xiii Nov."

[Fines were paid to the King; and the King alone could grant pardons, unless the Crown had made a special grant at any time to the manorial lord.]

17th King John, 1215 (*Rot. Lit. Pat.,* m. 21). The King to John, son of Hugo, etc.

"We order you that without delay you shall restore to liberty Robert Foliot and Nicholas, men of our venerable father in God, I—Bishop of Bath, who were seized in his wood of Essebirn by the men of the Bishop of Salisbury, and that their horses and all their possessions, which were taken away from them shall, without delay, be restored to them. Witness, etc. At Wilton, 28th June, in the 17th year of our reign."

The Patent Rolls (*Cal. Rot. Pat.*) contain grants of offices and lands, restitutions of temporalities to Bishops, Abbots, and other ecclesiastical persons; confirmations of grants made to bodies corporate; grants made in fee farm; patents of creation; and licences of all kinds which pass the Great Seal, Commissions, etc.[1]

Patent Roll, 16 Hen. III, 1231, m. 16; states the liberties granted to the Bishop, Prior, and Monks of St. Swithin.

"Henry the King, etc., greeting. Know ye that we out of regard to God and for the health of our soul, and of the souls of our ancestors and heirs, have given to God and the church of St. Swithun of Winchester, and to the venerable father P. Bishop of the same church and his successors Bishops of the same Church, and to the Prior and Monks there serving God, all the amercements of their men (*i.e.,* tenants in Hurstbourne and other places), and lands and fees, which amercements would appertain to us or our heirs or to our Sheriffs or constables or foresters or other our bailiffs if we had not granted them to the aforesaid Bishop and his successors and to the aforesaid Prior." The King also grants them all chattels forfeited by their men; and that no sheriff, constable, or bailiff of the King shall have "power or entry" into their lands or fees, "except attachments of pleas of the Crown". "They shall for ever be quit of all escapes of thieves and other prisoners. They shall also be quit from toll through all the King's land, from suits of shires and hundreds (*i.e.,* courts of Counties and Hundreds), and from the repairs of castles

---

[1] Thomas, *Handbook of the Public Records,* Appendix, p. 452.

and all other works." (Names of witnesses given). Dated at Lambeth, 20th January. They also had letters to the Sheriff of Southampton to cause the said Charter to be read in his full County (Court), etc.

Assize Roll, Southampton.

M.5.20 } 2.   8 Edw. I, 1279.

Roll 1. Pleas of Juries and Assizes before Solomon of Rochester and his associates, Justices in Eyre, at Winchester, in the octaves of St. Martin, 8 Edw. I.

Roll 28. A day is given to the Prior of St. Swithin's, Winchester, Defendant against the Lord the King, of a plea that he should render to him the Manor of Husseburne, from the day of Easter in 15 days at Wylton, at the prayer of William de Gyselham.[1]

[There appears to be nothing further concerning this in the Assizes held at Wilton in the Easter term 9th Edward I.]

There is a duplicate of the last extract in the "*Quo Warranto*" Rolls, 8th and 9th Edward I ; which Rolls are pleadings to try by what right parties held or claimed manors, liberties, privileges, etc.

Coram Rege Roll, Trinity term, 12th Edward I, 1283, No. 86, m. 7.

"These are the services which the Lord Bishop of Winchester has been accustomed to receive and have from the Prior, '*obedienciarii*', and Monks of St. Swithin of Winchester, and from their men, that is to say :—

"The free men of the said Prior, and obedienciarii of the manors of Havonte, Drokenesford, *Husseburn*, Wytchurch, Berthon without Winchester, and of their own manors, ought to keep the fair of St. Giles while it continues, at the will of the Lord Bishop. They (the Prior and obedienciarii) agree to this for their villains (*i.e., tenants at will or copyholders*), but the free men (*i.e., the freeholders*) must answer for themselves.

"Also the Lord Bishop ought to have the wardship and marriage of certain free men of the said Prior and obedienciarii. It is agreed, saving to the Prior rents, heriots, reliefs, escheats, and amercements for whatsoever cause."

These are the services which the Prior and his tenants owe to the Manor of Clere :—

"The whole township of Husseburn (*inter alia*) ought to enclose 20 perches there, as often as it shall be necessary." [This refers to the enclosure of the Bishop's Park there with palings, as will be seen by a notice which follows, which was supplied from the archives of Winchester.]

---

[1] William de Giselham was the King's Attorney. He disputed claims that tended to infringe the liberties of the Crown, such as rights of free warren, claims to hold liberties of gallows, tumbrel, and assize of bread and beer, as in the case of the Abbot of Bec (*de Becco*), who was summoned by the Attorney, in the reign of Edward I, to show cause why he claimed to hold in his manors of Anne Beck and Coumbe (*Combe*) the liberties of view of frankpledge, gallows, tumbrel, and assize of broken bread and beer. As Attorney Royal he also lodged complaints when the villeins failed to attend and do suit at the King's Hundred Courts, etc.

"Also the Prior's tenants of Stoke, Wyke, and Bylygh ought to enclose 19 perches there, as often as it shall be necessary."

"They agree that they will enclose as they have been accustomed."

"Also the Prior shall find one tenant who shall keep the Bishop's meadows at Husseburne in hay-time. They agree that it shall be done to him as it has been accustomed to be done."

"These are the services which the Prior's tenants owe to the Manor of Overton":—"The whole township of Husseburn owes yearly for release of ploughing at Overton, 25s." (This was a commutation of the "works" or "dayworks" formerly performed by the tenants of Husseburn in Overton, for a fixed yearly sum or rent, in lieu of personal service.)

Various other obligations of the Prior towards the Bishop in the city of Winchester are described. The fair of St. Giles is again mentioned.[1]

The enclosure or palings of the Bishop's park at Highclere had to be maintained by the tenants and inhabitants of the episcopal or church manors of the neighbourhood. The following were the allotments relating to Husseburne Priors in the time of Edward I[2]:—

Freeholders of the Manor of Husseburne Priors:

Peter de Chalgrave, to enclose three perches, and to guard the fair of Saint Giles (near Winchester).

Robert Durvent, to enclose two perches and to guard the fair.

John de Middleton, to enclose one perch and to guard the fair.

Richard de Knolle, to enclose two perches and to perform the same service of guarding the fair of St. Giles.

The entire village (or township) of Husseburne, to enclose twenty perches of the same Park.

The tenants of the Prior of Saint Swithun's (Winchester), of Stoke, Wyke and Bylygh (now called Binley), to enclose nineteen perches.

The entire village of Husseburne pays yearly (to the Bishop) 25s. for release from the customary service of ploughing.

The Charter Rolls (*Rotuli Chartarum*) are royal grants of lands, honours, dignities, hereditary offices, liberties, and other estates of inheritance to the nobility and commonalty; and of lands, liberties, privileges, immunities, and other estates in mortmain to ecclesiastical, eleemosynary, and lay corporations, etc.[3]

Charter Roll, 13th Edward I, 1284, m. 27. For the Prior and Convent of St. Swithin's, Winchester.

I. Royal Charter, inspecting and confirming a Charter of John Bishop of Winchester, settling the ancient dissensions touching the election of Prior and the appointment of Ministers.

II. "The King to Archbishops, etc., greeting. We have inspected the Charter

---

[1] It seems that disputes between the Bishop and Prior had lasted for many years. The Patent Roll of 40 Henry III contains a Royal Charter relative to peace and concord" then made between them, the King being personally present in the Chapter.

[2] This extract is supplied to me by Mr. F. J. Baigent.

[3] *Handbook to the Public Records*, Appendix, p. 457.

which the venerable father John Bishop of Winchester has made for himself and his successors to our beloved in Christ the Prior and Convent or Chapter of St. Swithin, Winchester, touching the grant, remission, quitclaim, and all kind of action which the same Bishop had or could have in the Manors of the Priory of St. Swithin, Winchester, in these words : To all faithful people of Christ to whom the present writing shall come, John, by divine permission, Bishop of Winchester, greeting in the Lord everlastingly. Know all of you that we for us and our successors do grant, remit, and quitclaim to our beloved in Christ the Prior and Convent or Chapter of St. Swithin, Winchester, and their successors, all right and claim, and all kind of action, which we have or had or could have in the manors of the Priory of St. Swithin, Winchester, that is to say . . . [many names here follow] . . . of Husseburn . . . with all hamlets, appendages, and other appurt's, to the aforesaid manors howsoever belonging . . . in customs, administrations, possessions of temporalities, and in all temporal things belonging to the aforesaid, by whatsoever name they may be called ; so that neither we nor our successors, nor any one in our name or for us, shall be able to claim, demand, or challenge any right or claim in the aforesaid in future . . . saving always to us and our successors, warrens and chaces in our lands and fees and in those of our men, and in the lands and fees of the aforesaid Prior and Convent and of their men, where and in like manner as we and our predecessors have been accustomed to have them ; and saving likewise to the same Prior and Convent and their successors, warrens and chaces in their lands and fees, and in those of their men, and also in the lands and fees of us and our successors, and of our men, where and in like manner as the same Prior and his predecessors have been accustomed to have them ; and saving always to us and our successors the services and customs which the Prior of Winchester and his predecessors, and his men, have been accustomed to do from any of their Manors or tenures. And the Prior and the 'obedienciarii' shall do to us and our successors the services and customs which they and their predecessors used to do to us and our predecessors . . . Given at Winchester on Tuesday next after the feast of the Translation of the blessed Thomas the Martyr, A.D. 1284 . . . And we (the King), holding ratified and acceptable the grant and remission aforesaid, grant and confirm them for us and our heirs, as much as in us is, to the aforesaid Prior and Convent and their successors, as the Charters and letters patent aforesaid reasonably do testify . . . [names of witnesses] given by our hand at Westminster on the 15th day of May."

III. Royal Charter inspecting and confirming a "Composition" between the Bishop of Winchester and the Prior and "obedienciarii", touching the election of the Prior and appointment of "obedienciarii", and servants, and touching certain manors, about which there had been many disputes. The Prior and Convent gave up certain manors to the Bishop.

Charter Roll, 18th Edward I, 1289, m. 23.

"The King to Archbishops, etc. Know ye that whereas for the health of our soul and those of our ancestors and heirs we granted by our Charter to John Bishop of Winchester, and his successors, *chaces* in all his demesne lands and woods, both of his own fees and of those of his men (*tenants*), and also in all the demesne lands and woods of the Prior and Convent of St. Swithin, Winchester . . . both of their own fees and those of their men (including *Hurstbourne*), as well within the metes and bounds of our forest as without . . . so nevertheless then the same Bishop . . . shall not place nets to take such venison ; so also that the Prior and Convent abovesaid . . . and others shall have their chaces in the same lands, tenements, fees, and woods where and in like manner as they had in the times of Adelmar, John, and Nicholas, formerly Bishops of Winchester ; we—

although we have learnt by a certain Inquisition . . . that the said Prior ought to course (*currere*) . . . in all the lands and woods (including *Hurstbourne*) of the same Prior and his men in the County of Southampton, except the lands and woods which are in the chace of Crundale . . . and except other chaces and warrens where the said Prior has lands,—nevertheless, at the request of the said Bishop, and with his assent and goodwill, we have granted for us and our heirs to the said Prior and his successors that they may have a chace in all their own demesne lands and woods both of their own fees and of the fees of their men of Crundale . . ." [The Inquisition above referred to is recited.] Hunting privileges are also granted to the Prior in all his demesne lands and woods where he has chaces, with power to destroy woods, and bring the lands into cultivation; and with a proviso that he shall not use nets [names of witnesses given]. Dated at Westminster 14th July.

Charter Roll, 29th Edward I, 1300, No. 54, contains a grant of Free Warren in Hurstbourne, and Wyke.

"The King to Archbishops, etc., greeting. Know ye that we have granted, and by this our charter confirmed, to our beloved in Christ the Prior and Convent of St. Swythin of Winchester, that they and their successors for ever may have free warren in all their demesne lands of Berton next Winchester . . . Husseburne, Whitcherche, Wyke . . . in the county of Southampton . . .; so nevertheless that those lands be not within the metes of our Forest; so that no one may enter those lands to hunt in them, or to take anything which may appertain to warren, without the licence and goodwill of the same Prior and Convent or of their successors, upon forfeiture to us of ten pounds. Wherefore we will, etc. These being witnesses [names given]. Given by our hand at Northampton on the 26th day of December. (' For a fine made before the Treasurer.')"

1316.—Among the *Parliamentary Writs*, there is a notice that Richard, Prior of St. Swithin, was certified as Lord of Hurstbourne Priors, St. Mary Bourne, Stoke, Wyke, Binley, Whitchurch and Freefolk, in the Hund. of Evingar. Richard or Richardus de Enford was Prior in 1309, confirmed August 25th.

Patent Roll, 15th Edward II, 1321, p. 1, m. 22.

"The King to all, etc. We have granted and given licence for us and our heirs, as much as in us is, to John Waspray, that he may give and assign three acres of land with appurts. in *Husseburne Priors*, and to John Shirfield that he may give one messuage, one mill, and two acres of meadow with appurts. in Overton Priors—which [premises] are held of the Prior and Convent of St. Swithyn, Winchester, and which are worth 6s. by the year . . . to the aforesaid Prior and Convent. Witness the King at Westminster on the 1st day of August." [The Prior and Convent had some years previously (10 Ed. II) obtained a Royal licence to acquire lands to a certain value; which the King granted at the request of John de Sendale, the Bishop.]

Patent Roll, 3rd Edward III, 1328, p. 2, m. 12. Exemplification of liberties for the Bishop and the Prior of Winchester, "for their chases", as in Charter 18th Edward I.

Patent Roll, 6th Edward III, 1332, p. 1, m. 13, gives permission to the Prior of St. Swithin to impark his woods at Hurstbourne, etc.

"The King to all to whom, etc., greeting. Know ye that of our special grace we have granted and given licence for us and our heirs, as much as in us is, to our beloved in Christ . . . Prior and the Convent of St. Swithin of Winchester, that they shall be able to enclose their woods of Muchelmersh, *Husseburn*, Whitchurch, Wotton, etc., and to make parks thereof, (*imparcare boscos suos*), and to hold those woods so enclosed and made parks of, to them and their successors for ever, without trouble or hindrance of us or our heirs, or of our justices, escheators, sheriffs, or other bailiffs or ministers whomsoever; provided nevertheless that those woods be not within the metes of our Forest. (*By Writ of Privy seal, 23rd day of March.*)"

Boscus (*bosc.*) can hardly apply to wood in the ordinary sense, but to brake or bush; and would seem to refer to waste lands with open spaces for cattle amidst bramble, etc., similar to the commons of the present day.

Patent Roll, 9th Edward III, 1334, p. 2, m. 30. The King confirms to the Prior of St. Swithin, Winchester, 30 marks yearly from the profits of the fair of St. Giles's at Winchester, granted to him by former Bishops of Winchester, whose Charters are recited. (See *Coram Rege Roll*, 12th Edw. I.)

Inquis. p. m., 9th Edward III, 1335. (This is really an Inquisition *ad quod damnum*.) It concerns Nicholas de Hanyton, who was a tenant of the Priory, at Hurstbourne, and apparently a freeholder.

"Inquisition taken at Winchester before Robert Selyman, Escheator of the Lord the King in Co. Southampton, 14th Feb., 9th Edw. III. The Jurors say that it is not to the damage of the King or of others if the King grant to Nicholas de Hanyton that he may give and assign one messuage, one carucate of land, 40 acres of wood, and 20 acres of pasture, with appurt[s]. in Medestede and Hattyngle to the Prior and Convent of St. Swithin of Winchester, in part satisfaction of £40 worth of lands and tenements which King Edward II licensed them to acquire. There remain to the said Nicholas £6 (worth) of land and rent in Husseburne, Sparkeforde, and Croundale, which are held of the said Prior by the service of 2s. by the year. The lands and rent remaining to the said Nicholas are sufficient to do the customs and services due from the lands given and from those retained, and to sustain all other charges which he used to bear, as in suits, views of Frankpledge, aids, tallages, watches, fines, redemptions, amercements, contributions, etc.; and the same Nicholas can be placed in Assizes, Juries, and other 'recognitions', as before the said gift, so that the country will not be burdened more than usual."

DUTIES OF THE HURSTBOURNE TENANTS OF ST. CROSS.

Hurstbourne Priors Church formerly belonged to the Hospital of St. Cross, Winchester; and the Harleian MS. No. 1616, contains a register of the estates belonging to the Hospital before the year 1386, together with the names of the tenants, and the duties they had to perform in their holdings. The following is a translation of the original document.

[Consuetudinar' Homū Dom' S'cti Crucis in villa de Husseburn'.]

Thomas le Frie holds a house and piece of land thereto, one virgate of land containing 27 acres of land in the whole, freely for all services by 6s. 8d. at the feast of St. Michael.

Ralph the Ysemonger holds a house and piece of land thereto, by 3s. at the four terms of the year for all services.

Thomas Hughet, of Wyk, holds certain land which is called the Breche by 6s. in the feast of St. Michael for all services.

Richard Maydenlove holds a house and piece of land thereto, which was of William the Vacher (Cowherd), by 18d. freely for all services at the four terms of the year. The same holds part of certain land which is called the Hyde, freely by 13s. 4d. at the four terms of the year for all services.

Roger Ailewarde holds a house and piece of land thereto, and 9 acres of land by 4s. at the four terms of the year, that is to say, at three singular terms 10½d., at the fourth term 16d.

John the Carter holds a house and piece of land thereto, and three acres of land in one open field, and three acres of land in another open field, by 18d. on the terms aforesaid, and shall give for chirchseed three hens and one cock at the feast of St. Martin, if he shall have a wife. And if he shall not have a wife, he shall give two hens, and oweth to wash and shear the lord's sheep with one man for one day, and shall have nothing, and oweth to hoe the lord's corn with one man for one day, and shall have his dinner once in the day, that is to say, bread and ale, and two messes, flesh, fish, or cheese. And he shall turn the lord's hay with one man, and shall come at two bind days in the autumn, that is to say, at the bind day with one man, and shall have his dinner, that is to say, bread, and one mess and cheese, and at the other bind day with two men, and shall have his dinner, that is to say, bread, and two messes and ale. And he oweth one day's work to mow the Prior's corn, and he shall have one sheaf of barley or drag at the grange of the Holy Cross by custom. And if he shall gather the lambs, wool, and cheese of the tithe of the said parish, with the sergeant of Whitchurche, then he shall have one lamb, one fleece, and one cheese; nor can he marry his son nor his daughter, nor sell the horse foaled to him, nor the ox calved to him, without the licence of the lord. Also to drive the beasts of the said house of the Holy Cross when need shall require, to have his dinner there.

Ralph, the son of Martin, holds the third part of certain land which is called the Hyde by 13s. 4d. at the four terms of the year for all services, which tenement Adam the Cowherd heretofore held.

Robert the Skinner holds a house and piece of land thereto, and two acres of land which Adam the Cowherd heretofore held, by 12d. at the aforesaid terms, and he does service in like manner as John the Carter.

Also the same holds a house and piece of land thereto, and six acres of land which Nicholas the Cof held, by 18d. at the aforesaid terms, and he does service in all things in like manner as John the Carter.

Robert Gunnore holds and does service in like manner as John the Carter.

John Gonaire holds and does service in all things in like manner as John the Carter.

John the Nuhyre holds and does service in all things in like manner as John the Carter.

John Alain holds a house and piece of land thereto which was his father's, and four acres of land, by 13½d. at the terms aforesaid, and he shall give and do service in all things as the aforesaid John the Carter. Also the same holds one piece of land freely for all services by 2s. at the aforesaid terms. Also the same holds the third part of certain land which is called the Hyde by 13s. 4d. freely for all services at the aforesaid terms.

Margery, the relict of Richard Cole, holds a house and piece of land thereto, and seven acres, by 3s. at the four terms of the year, and does service in all things in like manner as John the Carter.

Julian Cokegild holds a house and piece of land thereto by 18d. at the said terms, and does service in all things as John the Carter, besides two hens at Chirchseed.[1]

John Baniot holds a house and piece of land thereto, which Robert Dodeman held, by 12d. at the same terms, and he shall give at Chirchseed two hens, in like manner as the aforesaid Juliana.

Richard Conk holds a house and piece of land thereto by 2s. at the aforesaid terms, yet he shall only come to one day's work, once in the autumn, and he shall have his dinner in like manner as the others. Also the same holds one piece of land by 2d. at two terms freely for all services.

John Fari holds a house with a piece of land thereto, ten acres of land which Silvester the Carter held, by 4s. 6d., and shall give at chirchseed three hens and one cock, and shall do service in all things in like manner as John of Whytechurche.

All the afore-written villans hold in common a certain marsh by 3s. 6d. on the feast of St. Michael. All the aforesaid shall be quit of the pannage of hogs, if they had any.

---

[1] Churchseed was a sum paid for first-fruits, to be paid at Martlemas, or the feast of St. Martin in November. (Brady's *Hist.*, p. 129.)

All the aforesaid villans shall have in common when they carry in their chirchseeds eight pence.

Be it remembered that the house at Holy Cross shall pay 12*d.* yearly for the place of the court of Bourne to John, the heir of Bourne.

The sum of the whole rent of assize by the entire year £4 6s. 7½*d.*, that is to say, at every three terms 17*s.* and at the feast of St. Michael 35*s.*

The sum of the hens, thirty-eight hens.[1]

At the time of the "Customary", the Manor of Hurstbourne which appertained to St. Cross Hospital was held by tenants in villenage, in open fields, and the agricultural operations were conducted on the common field plan. The lands were occupied in strips, varying up to the virgate or yardland, which in the case of the holding of Thomas le Frie is stated as containing 27 acres. These strips were not all joined together in one field, as may be seen in the holdings of John the Carter, who "held 3 acres of land in one open field, and 3 acres in another open field." The yardland of thirty acres was the normal holding of the villein with two oxen. The strips were not hedged off or parted otherwise than by "balks", or slips of unploughed turf land, mostly separating strips of two acres each. This method was adopted in order to carry out the cultivation of the common fields on the three-field rotation of crops (or the two-field system as the case may be), viz., those of tillage, grain, and fallow. The three-field plan was adopted on the common lands at Hurstbourne (see *Kingsmill v. Oxenbridge*, 1598). This system of tillage was necessary in order that a certain portion of the open fields should be brought in with grain at one time, to meet without inconvenience the right the tenants possessed in common of turning out their cattle after the corn was carried. At Hurstbourne, the customary tenants as well as the copyholders pastured in common after a notice being given of three days.

The tenants in 1386, time of Richard II, were fast becoming free. The week's work as servile villeins was not exacted, and the rents were mostly paid in specie. Some held quite free, as Thomas le Frie; others paid partly in money, and at the same time rendered service,[2] as in the instance of John the Carter. And the terms of holding of John Alain show that his was a life tenancy, he having

---

[1] *Brief Historical Notices of the Parishes of Hurstbourne Priors and St. Mary Bourne*, pp. 30, 1, 2, 3.

[2] Among the tenants of the Wallop Manor, four gave no personal service, but rendered payments in money in full of all dues (*quatuor tenentes nativi pertinentes ad prædictum manerium*), and others, twelve in number, paid their service in part by personal labour (*sunt ibidem, duodecim tenentes nativi*).

succeeded his father. Life tenancy was the rule under the manorial system at Hurstbourne Priors. In the fourteenth century, however, although the earlier restrictions were becoming obsolete, the tenants were not free men. 1. It was necessary that the lord's licence should be obtained for the marriage of the daughter. 2. The lord's licence was necessary for the sale of oxen, etc. 3. Tenants were obligated to use the lord's mill, and to do service at his court. 4. Certain *bind days* were to be observed.

As early as the reign of Henry III, the lords of manors appear to have felt it necessary to protect their rights against the encroachments of their tenants. Thus, the Act known as the *Statute of Merton* (20th Henry III, 1235) recites:—

"Because many landowners, who have enfeoffed Knights and their freeholders of small tenements in the great manors, have complained that they cannot make their profit of the residue of their manors, as of wastes, woods, and pastures, the same feoffees having sufficient pasture, as much as belongeth to their tenements. It is provided that when such feoffees bring an assize of novel disseisin [which means an unlawful dispossessing a man of his land] for their common of pasture, and it is known before the justices that they have sufficient pasture for their tenements, and that they have free egress to and from their tenements to their pasture, let them be content therewith."

The Hurstbourne tenants under St. Cross held a marsh in common; and the place at which the Manor Courts were held was rented by the Prior at 12*d.* a year. The place at which John the Carter and others did service was the home farm, attached to the Grange, at which lived the Prior's Bailiff. It was his duty to superintend the daily work of the tenants, inspect the ploughs and ploughing, and see that a proper day's work was completed. Over the Bailiff was the Steward, who held the Manor Court, and there made inquiry whether there were any withdrawals of customs, rents, or services, or of suits to the courts, markets and mills of the lord of the manor, and as to alienations of lands. At the Court-leet meetings one of the principal duties of all tenants, free and serf, was to be a jury for the trial or acquittal of offenders. It was the Steward's province, further, to acquaint himself with the condition of the implements required in agriculture; and to supervise the arrangement of the land whether in the three-field or the two-field system. Other officials in the completion of the *villata*,[1] were the Blacksmith (*Faber*), and the Carpenter, who repaired the iron-work and wood-work of the implements, and in return had their small holdings among the tenants free of ordinary services. In addition, there was the *Punder*, the officer who had charge of the fences, and impounded stray cattle, for which, in virtue of his office, he held some land as long as he continued in office. The

---

[1] *Villata, i.e.*, the village community.

Pound (*Pound-fold*) is among the last remnants of the system yet remaining in our villages, and is sometimes used. The pound of Hurstbourne Priors is not now in existence; but it formerly stood on the margin of the highway opposite the Home farm, the place probably it had occupied for centuries. Among the commoners' rights, according to Wingrove Cook, in addition to their tillage and pasture, they were allowed turves of *fire-bote*, a reasonable quantity for the fuel of the chimneys attached to their houses, and a reasonable quantity of *estovers* for the repair of their fences and farm implements. The complete self-dependence of these small communities is expressed in the names of the people still living around the manor. Thus, Baker, Butcher, Tailor, and Carter all denote callings. Then we have Reves or Reve, the Bailiff who collected the petty rents; Waterman, Fisher, and Weir were associated with the manorial fisheries; Bevis attended to the oxen; Talley had charge of the tallies, and Toller of the tolls. Summerbee appears to refer to a thoroughly Saxon industry, the care of the apiaries, the cultivation of the bee being universal in the days when mead was a chief article of consumption. And there is one name which bears reference probably to the early village festivals, Bower. Churcher, Clark or Clerk, and Sexton probably held Church offices. Leaving out of account the large number of surnames which are manifestly derived from occupation or residence, it is interesting to note a few cases where family names have multiplied from loose pronunciation. Thus, in names of more than one syllable, the corrupt use of one or more syllables has brought about such names as Lee from Allee, Merry from Merryfield, Gibbs from Gibbons, Vince from Vincent, Lance from Lansley, loosely pronounced Lancely. These are a few instances, but such changes have become almost innumerable in the course of time.

Calendars to the Inquisitions (*Cal. Inquis. post mortem*). These are taken by virtue of writs directed to the escheators of each county or district, to summon a jury on oath, who were to inquire what lands any person died seized of, and by what rents or services the same were held, who was the next heir, and of what age the heir was, that the King might be informed of his right of escheat or wardship. The Inquisitions also state whether the tenant was attainted of treason, or was an alien, in either of which cases the lands were seized into the King's hands. They likewise show the quantity, quality, and value of the lands of which each tenant died seized; and they are the best evidence of the descent of families and of property.[1]

In the *Post Mortem* Inquisitions there are some notices relating to the possession of the manor of Wyke by the Beyntons. It was then

---

[1] F. S. Thomas, *Handbook to the Public Records*, Appendix, p. 453.

styled Daundelese Wyke. The notices further relate to certain property in the parish of St. Mary Bourne.

It appears that, in 1422, Nicholas Beynton held Daundelese Wyke manor, and the manor of Chilton "Candever", in Hampshire; and the manor (*maner'*) of "Fallerdeston", as well as the manor of Nether Wroughton, in Wiltshire.[1] In 1466, time of Edward IV, John Beynton (*miles*) held the manor of Chilton "Candever", and Daunderley manor (*maner'*), in Hampshire, and other property in Wiltshire, Somersetshire, and Dorsetshire,[2] etc.

In 1476, Robert Baynton, of Farleston, Soldier, attainted in the 12th year of Edward IV, held the manor of Chilton Candever (*Candover*), etc., also "Daundele Wyk" manor, and the manor of Swampton; and in "Maryborne" he held a messuage and rent (*mess' et redd.'*); and other property in Gloster, Somerset, Dorset, Oxon, and Wilts.[3]

In 1479, John Mone, also Mawne, held the manor of Whitchurch; and in Burne (*Bourne*) one messuage and forty acres of land (1 *mess' 40 acr' terr'*.).[4]

We have seen that no record has been recovered of any member of the Dandely family having held Wyke; but the holding by the Beyntons of "Daundele Wyk" jointly with Candover and Farleston, which places were held by Robert Daundely, points in the direction of Wyke having also been held by him. The proximity of Wyke to Foxcot, the gift of the chapel of which to the church of Andover was witnessed by Godfrey Daundele, implies that this member of the family lived in the district. In the Inquisitions concerning the possession of the manor by the Beyntons the title is written Daundelese, Daunderley, and Daundele; and, again, Daundelese Wyke, when in the possession of Sir George Nevill. This was in the fifteenth century; and it was called Dauleswyke[5] in the time of Henry VIII. The name was now evidently wearing out. It might, therefore, be inferred that the name was derived from the association of the manor with the Daundelys, and particularly when we find the name of the family, in connection with property in the county, and as Sheriffs, written Andely, Dandely, Daundely, and Daunderley.

Charter Roll, 21-24th Henry VI, 1445, No. 12. By this Charter the King restores the powers and privileges of the Prior and Convent, in

---

[1] *Inquis. post mortem*, 9th Henry V, No. 43.
[2] *Ibid.*, 5th Edward IV, No. 3.
[3] *Ibid.*, 15th Edward IV.
[4] *Ibid.*, 19th Edward IV, No. 51.
[5] Dauleswyke reminds one that Dowles' Wood joins that manor; the names are very similar, and it is likely that the whole of the property was under the same manorial holding. At all events the suggestion is worth noting.

respect to the tenants of the various manors, including Hursborne Priors, belonging to the Prior and Convent, the powers and privileges having from various causes become loosely obeyed. (See *Charter Roll*, 13th Edward I.)

"For the Bishop of Winchester and the Prior and Convent of St. Swithin of Winchester.

"The King to Archbishops, Bishops, etc., greeting. Know ye that whereas our very beloved great uncle Henry, Cardinal of England, Bishop of Winchester, and his predecessors, late Bishops of Winchester, and also our beloved in Christ the Prior and Convent of the Cathedral Church of St. Swithin of Winchester, and their predecessors, have well, freely, peacefully and quietly used and enjoyed certain liberties . . . And now . . . we have learnt that lately on account of the obscurity of certain general words in Charters and letters . . . they have been and are hindered from using and enjoying them . . . We to the praise, glory, and honour of the most high and undivided Trinity, and of the most blessed, most glorious, and undefiled Virgin Mary, mother of our Lord Jesus Christ, and from the special devotion which we bear and have to the glorious Confessor Saint Swithin, the singular patron of the said Cathedral Church, in which certain bodies of divers of our noble progenitors are honorably buried . . . have granted . . . to the aforesaid now Prior and Convent that they and their successors for ever shall have all and all manner of fines for amercements, for trespasses, and for licences to agree, and all amercements and issues forfeited, and all things which to us and our heirs can appertain of year, day, and estep, of all their men and tenants, as well wholly tenants as not wholly tenants, residents, and other residents whomsoever, of and upon the lands (including *Hursburne*), tenements, fees, and possessions of the same Prior and Convent and their successors, in whatsoever courts," (*i.e.*, those at Westminster and Assize Courts, etc. Thus the fine of any man of Hurstbourne amerced in the Common Pleas would belong to the Prior), " of us and our heirs . . . Also all manner of goods and chattels of felons, fugitives, outlaws, persons attainted, convicted, and condemned, and put in exigent for felony, and of felons *de se*, being such men, tenants, residents, and non-residents, and other residents whomsoever . . ." (Similar grants are made to the Bishop in his lands and fees.) Names of Witnesses given. "Given by our hand at Westminster on the 15th day of March, 24 Henry VI." By the King, and of the date aforesaid, by authority of Parliament.

According to the *Patent Rolls*, a grant of the manor of Week, then called *Daundelese Wyke*, with the appurtenances, was made to George Nevill, Knight, and his descendants, on July 1st, 1485; together with the manor of Chilton Candover, and the advowson of the Church of Chilton.[1] The grant consisted of 600 acres of land, 25 acres of meadow, 300 acres of pasture, 300 acres of wood (*bosc'*), and 100 acres of heath, in Chilton "Candever", Daundeles Wyke, and Swampton.

And at St. Mary Bourne he held by military service one messuage of ten shillings per annum rent.

De Banco Roll (Common Pleas). Trinity, 1 Hen. VII, 1485, Roll 394.

[1] *Patent Roll*, 3rd Richard III.

"*South'ton.*—Thomas Hunton, Prior of the Cathedral Church of St. Swithin of Winchester, appears against Henry Hopkyn of Overton, husbandman, of a plea wherefore by force and arms he entered the free warren of the same Prior at Hursburne Priors, and hunted therein without the Prior's licence and consent, and took and carried away hares, rabbits, pheasants, and partridges, to his great damage, etc. Deft. does not appear; and the Sheriff having been ordered to attach him, returns that he has nothing, etc. Therefore let him be taken, so that he be here in the octaves of St. Michael."

Fauconer or Fawconer.

Grant of lands in Husborne by Emma de Roches to Ralph le Fauconer, A.D. 1263.[1]

This is the final agreement made in the King's court at Winchester in the third week from Easter day in the 47th year of the reign of King Henry III (April 15-21, 1263), between Ralph le Fauconer *plaintiff* (by William le Fauconer in his stead), and Emma de Roches *deforciant* (by Roger le Moneter in her stead), concerning a messuage and a carucate of land with appurtenances in Husseburne, on the plea of the warranty of a charter between them. To wit, that the said Emma acknowledges the messuage and land aforesaid to be the right of Ralph, as that which the same Ralph has by the gift of the aforesaid Emma,—to be held by the said Ralph and his heirs of the said Emma and her heirs for ever, together with the hide of land and all other lands and tenements with appurtenances, which the same Ralph held of the fee of this Emma, in the same village on the day this agreement was made. Paying annually to her and her heirs eight marks of silver (£5 6s. 8d.), namely two marks on each quarter day, and to do the foreign service, as much as belonged to the three hides of land of the same fee in the same village, for all services, suits of court, and exactions. Emma and her heirs to warrant it for ever. The same Ralph remits and quits claim, for himself and his heirs to the said Emma and her heirs for ever, his whole right and claim in all the lands and tenements with appurtenances, which Martin de Roches, son and heir of this Emma, held by the grant of the same Emma in North Far[e]ham, on the day this final agreement was made, and afterwards the same Ralph gave the said Emma a falcon-gentil.

Patent Roll, 6th Edward III, 1332, p. 1, m. 31. Refers to exchange of land in Wyke manor.

"For the Prior of St. Swithin, Winchester.

"The King to all to whom, etc., greeting. Holding ratified and acceptable the grant and confirmation which John le Fauconer, of Hussebourn Priors, since the publication of the statute enacted concerning the not putting lands and tenements

---

[1] Copy of Grant was furnished by Mr. F. J. Baigent.

to mortmain, made by his Charter to our beloved in Christ, Alexander, Prior of the church of St. Swithin of Winchester, and to the Convent of the same place, of forty-five acres, one rood, and nine perches and a half of land in the *Vill* of *Hussebourn*, in the field called Wykenesham" (probably a "common field" or "open field"), "next to the wood Thurnyngelege, in exchange for so many acres of land in the same vill in the field called Wynerde. To have and to hold to the same Prior and Convent and their successors in exchange as aforesaid of the chief lords of that fee, by the services due and accustomed for ever. We grant and confirm them" (*i.e.*, the grant and confirmation above mentioned) "for us and our heirs, as much as in us is, as the charter aforesaid reasonably testifies. At Westmister, 25th day of January."

The land thus given in exchange belonged to Wyke manor, which was part of Fawconer's manor, inasmuch as *Wykenesham* refers to a field near the farm-dwelling at Wyke; and the wood *Thurnyngelege*, meaning Thorny-hedge, is evidently the Thorngrove or Thorny-grove of the present day at Wyke.

Lay Subsidies, Southampton, $\frac{173}{19}$. Aid for making the King's eldest son a Knight.

Inquisition, 21st Edward III, 1346.

"In the Hundred of Eyngar.

"John le Fauconer holds in Hussebourn, half a fee, which was of William le Fauconer."

Lay Subsidies, Southampton, $\frac{173}{66}$. Certificate of holders of land. 13th Henry IV, 1411.

"Nicholas Faukener has lands and rents in Husborne Priors, and Middleton, which are worth by the year beyond reprises—20*l*."

There is no doubt that the lands and rents in Hurstbourne relate to Fawconer's manor, which name is derived from its association with that family. It formed a separate manor under the head of Hurstbourne Fawconers or *exterius*. Part of it was formerly down, and is still called Fawconer's down.

Lay Subsidies, Southampton, $\frac{173}{78}$.

Inquisition at Basingstoke, 24th June, 6th Henry VI.

"Hundred of Evinggar.

"John le Fauconer holds in Husseborn Priors half a Knight's fee, which was late of John le Fawconer."

NOTE.—A Knight's Fee (*Feodum Militare*), is as much inheritance as is sufficient yearly to maintain a Knight with convenient revenue, which Camden (*Britan.*, p. iii) writes was £15 in the time of Henry III; but which Sir Thomas Smith rates at £40 (see *Repub. Angl.*, lib. 1, cap. 18). In *Coke on Littleton* (fol. 69), a Knight's fee is stated as containing twelve ploughlands, or 680 acres. "*Virgata terræ continet* 24 *acras,* 4 *Vergatæ terræ* make one hide, and five hides make a Knight's fee, whose relief is five pounds" (Cowel, *Interpreter*). The Knight's fee, however, varied at different times, and in different places, both in value and extent of land; and the possessor of an entire Knight's fee was bound to attend his lord to the wars for forty days in every year, if called upon.

Among special royalties and privileges claimed within the hundred of Basingstoke, were the return of writs, liberty of gallows, and assize of bread and beer, etc., granted to the men of Basingstoke by Henry III; the assize of bread and beer at Maplederwell, taken without warrant by Ela Basset; gallows at Basing, and assize of bread and beer in all his lands within the hundred, claimed by John de St. John; Reginald Fitz Peter, Walter de Merton, William de Braybeof, Peter de Codray, and *William le Fauconer*, had chase of hares and foxes within the hundred.[1]

William Fawconer was Sheriff of Hants in 1437. He bore arms: *Sable*, three falcons *argent*, beaked, legged, and belled *or*. *Crest:* A garb *or*, banded *argent*. The family were, up to and later than 1575, still settled in the county.

In Fuller's *Worthies*, among the names of the "Gentry in Hampshire" returned into the Tower by the Commissioners, in the 12th year of Henry VI, appear those of William Fawconer and Johannes Fawconer.

In 1552, a Richard Fawconer was seated at Hurstbourne, of which mention occurs in the *Visitation of Hampshire* of that year. This Richard Fawconer married Elinor, daughter of George Ranbrigge, by Berry stated as Pembridge, co. Southampton, by whom he had issue Richard Fawconer, of Hursbourn, who died *s. p.*, and three daughters, Elizabeth, Margaret, who married William Sottewell, of Chute, co. Wilts, and Alice, sister and co-heir, who married Richard Kingsmill, Attorney of the Court of Wards to Queen Elizabeth. She was his first wife, and the issue of the marriage was a daughter, Constance, who was Sir Richard's sole heir, and who married Sir Thomas Lucy, Knt., co. Warwick.

A branch of the same family was, during eight generations, settled at Kingsclere. The first of the name, according to the *Visitation* of 1634, was Richard Fauconer, the last mentioned being Constance, who died young.

The following is an abstract of the Funeral Certificate of Richard Kingsmill, Esq. (*Coll. Arm.*, i, 16*f*, 103).

The Right Worshipful Mr. Richard Kingsmill, of High-clere, in the County of Southampton, Esquire, surveior of the Court of Wardes and Leverees (*liveries*), married to his first Wyffe Alice, the dooughter of Richard Faulconer of Hurstbourne, and Co-heire to her brother Richard Faulconer, by which Alice he had issue Constance, his only doughter and heire, married to Sir Thomas Lucy of Charlecot, in the County of Warwick, Knight, who by her had issue Thomas Lucy,

---

[1] Woodward and Wilks, *Hist. of Hampshire*, vol. iii, p. 215.

Richard, George, William, Robert, Francis, Elizabeth, Anne and Brigid. He ended this transitory lyffe at High-clere the 17th of September, anº. 1600, and was in the parish Church there worshipfully according to his estate committed to the earth, and his ffuneral solemnized the 7th of October following.

Principal Mourner Sir Thomas Lucy. The Assistants, Mr. George Kingsmill, Justice of the Common pleas, and Mr. William Kingsmill. The penon borne by Mr. William Wroughton, William Camden, Clarenceux, and William Smith, Rouge Dragon, attending and serving at the said funerall.

[Signatures of the Heralds, etc., and then follows the description of the Arms.]

In this abstract there is a remarkable conjunction of names. The Sir Thomas Lucy, of Charlcot, was probably a member of the family of Sir William Lucy of Shakespeare; and William Camden, Clarenceux, was doubtless the great antiquary and historian, who died in 1623.

In the Will of William of Wykeham, dated January 1403, occur the following bequests.

To the Abbot of the Monastery of Hyde a Cup of Silver Gilt, with a Cover, of the price of £10. To each Monk of the same in priest's orders XLs., to each Monk in inferior orders XXs.

To the Hospital of the Holy Cross, near Winton, a pair of vestments, with a chalice, and a pair of silver dishes, with a *Fer de Moulin* engraved in the bottom of the same in the form of a cross.

In the Codicil, William Faulkner, Richard Wallop [*and others*], to each of them 100s., or a silver Cup of the same value.

De Roches.

It will be seen under the head of Fauconer, by a grant which was made to Ralph le Fauconer, in the year 1263, that Emma de Roches possessed land at Hurstburne prior to that period.

By an *Inq. p. m.*, 5th Edward I (No. 12), Aug. 13th, 1276, it appears the Martin de Roches, deceased, held land in the manor of Stiventon; and also the manor of Bradele. He held eight marks of rent of the Bishop of Winchester in Husseburn by the service of one Knight's fee; also other lands in Candevere and Stoke Charte [Charity?].

Hugh de Roches is stated as his brother and next heir, aged 40 years.

Later, a Martin de Roches, by an *Inquis. p. m.*, 49th Edward III, 1374, died seized of Stiventon and Bradeley manors, with lands at Husseburn, Candevere, and Stoke Charte.

With reference to Martin de Roches it appears that Geffery de Roches, by his wife Emma, had two sons, Hugh of that name, and Martin, who died 5th Edward I, *s. p.*; and that Hugh Roches was the father of John de Roches, who married Beatrix ......, 1305. John de Roches died 5th Edward II, leaving Sir John de Roches, Knt., who married Joan, daughter and heir, 2nd Edward III, and from their union came Mary, his daughter and heir, who married Sir Bernard Brocas, 1st Richard II.[1]

The property at Hurstbourne of the 5th Edward I, held by Martin de Roches, was evidently held later by Sir Bernard Brocas (see *Inq. p. m.*, 1st Hen. IV, *Brocas*). The land of the value of *8 marks of rent* (£5 6s. 8d.) was part of Fawconer's manor, otherwise Hurstbourne *exterius*, of which Week was the manorial residence. (See *De Banco Roll*, 16th Hen. VII.)

Brokas, or Brocas.

Feet of Fines, Divers Counties, Mich., 7th Ric. II, 1383, No. 95. (Old No. 16.)

"Fine between Master Arnald Brocas, clerk, John de Chitterne, clerk, Peter Golde, clerk, William Hermyte, chaplain, and Henry Holte (Plaintiffs), and (Sir) Bernard Brocas Kt. (Deforciant), concerning certain Manors and lands in several counties, including the Manors of Beaurepeyr, Northfarham, Hoo, Bradele, Hanyngton, and Brokkesheved, and 4 messuages, 1 mill, 5 carucates of land, 12ª meadow, 30ª wood, and 8 *marks of rent* in Froille, Basyng, Eldestoke, Suthewyk, Basyngstok, *Husseburne*, and Stratfeld Mortymer in co. South'ton. The said Bernard acknowledges the premises to be the right of the Plfs.; to hold to them and the heirs of the said Peter."

[The Plfs. were probably trustees for Sir Bernard Brocas.]

Inquis. p. m., 1st Henry IV, 1399, p. 1, No. 17. (Sir) Bernard Brocas, Knt., deceased. Writ dated 22nd Feb. Inquisition taken at Basingstoke.

"The jurors say that Bernard Brocas held in fee the Manors of North Fareham and Brockesheved, etc. William is the son and heir, aged 20 years and upwards. Bernard died 28th Jan. last. Bernard Brocas, Knt., father of the said Bernard, by Fine of 7th Ric. II, granted to Master Arnald Brocas, clerk, John de Chitterne, clerk, Peter Golde, clerk, and others, the Manor of Beaurepere, Bradele, and 4 messuages, one mill, 5 carucates of land, 12 acres of meadow, 30 acres of wood, and 8 *marks of rent*, with appurt's, in Froille, Basing, Eldestoke, Suthewyk, Basyngstoke, *Husseburn*, and Stratfeld Mortemer, which are *not* held of the King in chief. John Chytterne, the surviving feoffee, granted the same manor, lands,

---

[1] Berry's *Hampshire Genealogies*, Part I, p. 90 (from the *Visitation* of 1634). But it appears from Capt. Montagu Burrows (see *Brocas of Beaurepaire and Roche Court Pedigree*) that Mary de Roches had previously married Sir John Borhunte, who died before 1360.

and rent to Ralph de Lenham and John Shirlond, who in 19th Ric. II granted to William Bishop of Winchester, John Bishop of Salisbury, and others (trustees), some of whom in the 20th Ric. II granted and demised to the said Bernard Brocas (just deceased) the manors of Bradele and Styvynton, and the said lands in Basyng .... for 8 years, at the yearly rent of £50. The lands thus leased belonged during the said term to Joan widow of Bernard the son, according to the King's letters patent of the 15th Feb. .... granting to her all the goods and chattels forfeited by the same Bernard, the son, to the King."

From the *Visitation* of 1634, and from the Harleian MS., it appears that there was a Sir Bernard Brocas, Knt., who was buried at Guildford; and who left issue Sir Bernard Brocas, Knt., who in his turn was the father of a Sir Bernard Brocas, Knt., from whom descended Sir John Brocas, Knt., of the time of Edward III.[1] Now this Sir Bernard Brocas had three sons—Sir John Brocas, Knt., who died *s. p.*; Sir Oliver Brocas, Knt., who married Margaret, daughter of Thomas Hever; and Sir Bernard Brocas, Knt., who married Mary, sole daughter and heiress of Sir John de Roches, and became through her master of the King's buckhounds, and obtained also the lands of Roches Court, and other property. He held the office of Chamberlain to Anne of Bohemia, wife of Richard II, and died in 1396, having been born in 1347. Sir Bernard Brocas was a legatee under the will of Sir Nicholas de Lovaine, dated September 20th, 1375. And in 1388 he obtained licence to enlarge the area of Beaurepaire Park with one hundred acres of land and wood at Bromley St. John, belonging to Sherborne Priors. He was interred in Westminster Abbey; and at his funeral £40 was spent on the hearse, with banners, pennons, twenty-four torches, black cloth drapery, wax tapers, etc. The modern epitaph on the Brocas tomb in the Abbey is considered not quite reliable.

By an Inquisition of 1378, John Brocas, who died *s. p.*, son of Sir Oliver Brocas, held lands in Hampshire, and in Berkshire (*Anno 2, Rich. II, Johannes Brocas filius Oliveri, Mil',—Bray, 2 acr' prat'.*).

Sir Bernard Brocas, by his wife Mary, had three children—Johanna, who married Robert Dyneley; Ralph Brocas, and Sir Bernard Brocas, Knt., who was attainted 1st Henry IV (Sir *Bernard Brocas, beheaded* 1399-1400—*C. Inq. p. mort.*). The wife of Sir Bernard was Johanna, thought to be a Vernon of Little Beligh, Essex; by whom he had four sons—William, his first son and heir; Gilbert,

---

[1] Capt. Montagu Burrows (*Brocas of Beaurepaire and Roche Court Pedigree*) states that there was a Master Bernard de Brocas, who was lord of Beaurepaire in 1353; but that Sir John de Brocas, who died in 1365, was the father, by his wife Margaret, of Sir Oliver Brocas, and of Sir Bernard Brocas, who by Mary, the widow of Sir John Borhunte, became the father of Sir Bernard Brocas, who was attainted 1st or 2nd of Henry IV.

Thomas, and Bernard Brocas, of Alton, the ancestor of the old line of the Beaurepaire family.

Sir Bernard Brocas was carver to the Queen; but the transactions of his life fill an unfortunate page in the history of the period, for having joined in the conspiracy to reinstate Richard II on the throne, he was attainted of treason, and executed in 1399. "*Bernardus Brokays et I Schevele milites alii quoque plures acceperunt similem mortis sortem,*"—that is, they were drawn, hanged, and beheaded.[1]

We have already seen that *Hurstbourne* is included in the lands specified as held by Bernard Brocas in the return of 1399. And in the notices of Bray in the *Cal. Inquis. post mortem*, it appears that his wife Johanna held land there—*Anno 7, Hen. VI. Johanna, que fuit uxor Bernardi Brocas, Chivaler attinct' tempore Hen. IV*,

Cokham[2] } *Maner membr'*.
Braye

Henry IV granted, *per servit' debit'*, to William Brocas, eldest son of Sir Bernard Brocas, the manors and other property forfeited to the King, of which Sir Bernard had been seized.

William Brocas was twice Sheriff of Hants, in 1428 and in 1435. He died 35th of Henry VI, leaving by his wife Sibilla one son, William Brocas of Beaurepaire. By his will, dated March 4th, 1454, he desired that his body should be buried in the church of St. Andrew, at Sherborne. Johanna his widow (2nd wife, who was Johanna Sandes), in 1470, died seized of various manors, messuages, lands, mills, etc., in Hampshire, all of which are specified; but as Hurstbourne is not named among them, it is probable that the Hurstbourne estate had passed out of the possession of the family.

The next in succession was William Brocas, Esq., the younger, who married Agnes, daughter of Thomas Bekingham, leaving a son, John Brocas. He died April 22nd, 1483, and was interred at St. Bartholomew's, in Smithfield. The property, at his death, included Beaurepaire manor, Stephyngton manor, Roches Court, and other lands. His widow afterwards married Robert Attemore, and as her first husband bore the name of Brocas de Bradleigh, the return made in 1484, after her death, included the manor of Bradleigh, with the advowson of its rectory.

John Brocas, Esq., married for his first wife Anne, daughter of Edward Langford, Esq., his second wife being Ann, daughter of John Rogers of Freefolk, from whom descended William Brocas.[3] John Brocas was Sheriff of Hants in 1482; and he died May 10th, 1492.

---

[1] Woodward and Wilks, *History of Hampshire*, vol. iii, p. 260, note.
[2] Rev. C. Kerry, *History of the Hundred of Bray*.
[3] Berry, *Hampshire Genealogies*, Part I, p. 90.

William Brocas, Esq., succeeded to the Beaurepaire estates, and was united to Mary, daughter of John Griffin, by whom, according to Berry, he had a daughter, Edith, his sole heir, who, by her alliance with Ralph Pexsall, Esq., conveyed the Beaurepaire estates into the Pexsall family. On this head, however, there are differences of opinion, it being stated that Ralph Pexsall married the eldest sister of William Brocas, who was made co-heir to her father John Brocas.[1] Be that as it may, Ralph Pexsall married Edith Brocas, heiress to William Brocas, and they both lie buried in the Brocas chapel of the church of Sherborne St. John.

The issue of this marriage was Sir Richard Pexsall, Knt., who was Master of the Buckhounds, and died in 1571. He was married twice—first to Lady Elinor, daughter of the Marquis of Winchester, afterwards to Elinor, daughter of John Cotgrave, co. Chester. The offspring of his first union were four daughters—Eliza, Margaret, Anne, and Barbara, of whom Anne, the eldest daughter, became united in marriage to Bernard Brocas of Alton, her fourth cousin twice removed, thus carrying the Beaurepaire estates back into the Brocas family.

Their son was Sir Pexali Brocas of Beaurepaire, Knt., who married Margaret, daughter of Sir Thomas Shirley of Wiston-Neston, co. Sussex, Knt., of whom was born Thomas Brocas, who was the last hereditary Master of the Buckhounds. He married Elizabeth, daughter of Sir Robert Wingfield of Upton, co. Northampton, and died in 1663, leaving a family of five sons and two daughters.

Thomas, son of Thomas Brocas, married Mary, daughter of Philip Catelyn, Esq. She died in February 1693; and their son, Thomas, died in 1715, at the age of 66, he having married, for his 2nd wife, the daughter and heiress of Edmund Webb. She died in 1708.

With regard to the younger branch of the family from whom descended Bernard Brocas, who came back to Beaurepaire, taking the direct line, it appears that Bernard Brocas, a younger son of the Sir Bernard who suffered for treason, settled at Alton, 1st of Henry IV. He married for his first wife Sibilla Croke, from whom descended Bernard Brocas, who married Emmeline Erwyn; and from their union came Bernard Brocas, whose wife was Anne Morell of Dunstable. The offspring of this union was John Brocas, who married Elizabeth, daughter of ...... Marshall, and who had issue Robert Brocas of Horton Hall, co. Bucks. He, in turn, wedded Dorothy, daughter of Richard Ruthall, co. Bucks, from whom descended William Brocas of Thedingworth, co. Leicester, and Bernard Brocas, the younger son,

---

[1] Woodward and Wilkes, *History of Hampshire*, vol. iii, p. 261.

who was united to his cousin Anne, daughter of Sir Richard Pexsall of Beaurepaire.

The Vine, or Vyne, as it is also spelt, was for a time the property of the Brocas family, perhaps through the marriage of Emlyn Sandes with Bernard Brocas of Alton, grandson to the Bernard who married Mary Roches.[1]

Several monuments erected to the ancient holders of Beaurepaire occupy the aisle bearing the family name in the church of Sherborne St. John.

Brocas bore, *Sable*, a lion rampant guardant *or;* while their crest was a Moor's head *rayonne*. The Moor's head relates to a family legend. The Roach coat was, *Sable*, two lions passant guardant, in pale *argent*, otherwise two leopards *argent*, armed *gules*.[2] Pexsall bore, A cross engrailed flory *sable*, between four Cornish choughs, proper, sometimes given as martlets.

De Banco Roll (Common Pleas), Easter, 16th Hen. VII, 1500, Roll 321.

"*South'ton.*—John Brocas gent., John Swayne, William Talbot, and Richard Bromfeld were summoned to make answer to William Wygmore wherefore they took his cattle and detained them on 20th March, 16 Hen. VII, at Husburn, in a place called Court place alias Court Heys—viz. 20 cows and 9 horses, to his damage of £20. Defs. say they acted as bailiffs of William Brocas of Beaurepere, and that one John Faukener was formerly seized in fee of certain tenements called 'Faukoners Maner' in Husburn, whereof the *locus in quo* was parcel, and held 'that tenement' of one Wm. Brocas, Esq., as of his Manor of North Fareham, by homage, fealty, and the yearly rent of 8 marks. The said Manor of N. F. and the said services descended to the said Wm. Brocas of Beaurepere as kinsman and heir, viz. son of John, son of William, son of the said Wm. Brocas, Esq. 'Faukeners Maner' has descended to one John Faukener of Husburn, whose homage and fealty not having been done, and £42 13s. 4d. of the said rent being in arrear, for 8 years last past, Defs. distrained Plfs. cattle in the said place, as parcel of Faukener's Maner. Plf. says that the said John Faukener of Husburn on 12 Oct., 15 Hen. VII, demised Faukeners Maner to him for 20 years; so he prays the aid of the said J. F., who is therefore summoned to be here in Trinity term, when he caused himself to be essoined 'de malo veniendi'. He also failed to appear in Mich'as term, when the case was ordered to proceed without him. After further pleadings, issue was joined as to whether the *locus* was within the fee of Wm. Brocas or not."

[No verdict or judgment recorded.]

Ellis Wynne.

After the Dissolution of religious houses in 1535, it appears by the *Augmentation Decrees* that Ellis Wynne was granted the custody of the Hurstbourne manor, he having obtained the same from the Prior and Convent of St. Swithin. (*Augmentation Decrees*, vol. ii, fo. 1346.)

---

[1] Woodward and Wilks, *Hist. of Hampshire*, vol. iii, p. 262.   [2] *Ibid.*, 262.

Memorandum.—That, in the term of St. Hilary, namely the 24th January, in the 33rd year of King Henry VIII, Ellis Wynne came into court. The writing acknowledges, under the Convent Seal of the Monastery of St. Swithin, Winchester. To all and faithful, etc., William Basyng, Prior of St. Swithin, Winchester. Know ye that we have given and granted to Ellis Wynne the Stewardship of our inner Manor of Hursborne, and the Custody of our Park there, and he to receive £5 for the same, payable at Easter and Michaelmas.

Patent Roll, 33rd Hen. VIII, 1541, p. 9, m. 38(6).

" Grant by the King to the Dean and Chapter of Winchester of various Manors and lands in the county of Southampton, and all commons, fisheries, courts, etc., in various parishes, towns, or hamlets, including Wyke (Hurstbourne *exterius*), lately belonging to the Monastery of St. Swithin."

Ministers' Accounts, 32-33, Hen. VIII, 1540-1 (No. 109, m. 45), give particulars of the lands of the Priory of Swithin, at Hurstbourne Priors, after the Dissolution.

Site of the Monastery and certain Manors, etc.—Account of William Kyngesmyll, clerk, Dean of the Church of Holy Trinity of Winchester. He renders no account of the issues of the said Site and Manors (specified) with appurt's in various places (including Wyke), for that the King has granted them to the Dean and Chapter, etc. But he accounts for the rents reserved to the Crown by the letters patent to the Dean and Chapter.

Manor of Hursborne with the Members.—Account of Ellis Wynne, Bailiff of the Lord the King there.

Arrears from the preceding year . . . . 14*l*. 0*s*. 3*d*.
Rents of Assize as well of free as of customary tenants there, as appears by a certain Rental . . . . . 20*l*. 0*s*. 6*d*.
Farm of the Manor with the demesne lands, etc., and the works of customary tenants, demised by the late Prior and Convent to John Milles by Indenture for a term of years . . . . . 13*l*. 10*s*.
Farm of the Interior Manor of Hursebourne, with 8 couples of conies every week between Pentecost and the Purification of B. V. Mary [formerly] to be delivered to the late Prior and Convent at the said Monastery, and the herbage of 7 geldings, two cartloads of hay, and the herbage of 20 sheep pasturing within the Park in summer ; which things were reserved to the late Prior and Convent in the Indenture made by them to the said Ellis of the Custody of the said Manor and Park, and have been appraised by the King's officers, 4*l*. 16*s*. 8*d*.
Farm of one Mill in Hursebourne, demised to Richard Cowpar by Indenture between the late Prior and Convent and him for a term of years ; he doing the repairs " as well under the water and in the water as upon the water" at his own charges . . . . . . 20*s*.[1]

---

[1] Among the arrears (at the end) it is stated that £11 was due from *Christopher* Cowpar for the Mill in Hursebourne.

Farm of another Mill called Robhodismyll, demised to Robert Kegill by the late Prior and Convent . . . . . 25s. 4d.
Farm of the warren of conies within the said Manor of Hursebourne, called Bradley, demised to John Milles by the late Prior and Convent . 46s. 8d.
    Sum of the Farms . . . . 22l. 18s. 8d.
Perquisites of Courts, 21s. 2d. from two turns and courts held there this year, including 4s. for the cert-money of the Leets, 10s. for fines of lands, and 5s. for heriots, as appears by the Roll of the same.
Rents of Assize, as well of free as of customary tenants in *Borne* as by the Rental, 28l. 10s. 7d.
Perquisites of Courts there—110s. 8d. from 2 turns and Courts held this year, including 6s. for cert-money of the Leets, 65s. for fines of lands, and 37s. 8d. from heriots.
Rents of Assize (as above) in *Stoke* . . . 19l. 8s. 4d.
Perquisites of Courts there—23s. 8d., including 4s. for cert-money, 10s. for fines, 6s. 8d. for heriots, and 6d. for the fines of Cecily Bulpitt (4d.) and Isabel Bright (2d.) for licence to substitute under tenants in certain lands.
Rents of Assize in *Bynley* (as above) . . . 15l. 18s. 11d.
Perquisites of Courts there—11s., including 2s. for cert-money and 8d. for heriots.
Rents of Assize in *Wike* (as above) . . . 15l. 19s. 11d.
Perquisites of Courts there—4s. 7d., including 3s. for cert-money.
Rents of Assize in *Egbury* (as above) . . . 14l. 5s. 3¾d.
Perquisites of Courts there—2s. 8d., including 2s. for cert-money.
   Sum Total of the Receipts with the Arrears 159l. 16s. 0¾d.
                      Whereof—
Fee of Sir William Poulett, Kt., Lord Seynt John, Steward of the said Manor, 26s. 8d. Livery of John Milles, Farmer of the Manor of Hursebourne, 6s. 8d. Wages of a Reap-reeve (Messor[1]) for custody of the King's Woods in Stoke, parcel of the Lordship, 3s. Wages of another Reap-reeve for custody of the King's Woods in Wike, 3s. Stipend of the Auditor's clerk writing this account, 4s.—Total, 43s. 4d.
Repairs on the houses of the Manor this year, in the works of carpenters and tylers, tiles, etc. . . . . . 26s. 10d.
Moneys delivered to the King's Receiver . . 139l. 3s. 7¾d.
Arrears due from divers offices and tenants.
John Longe owes 6s. 8d. for a heriot, due from his lands in *Borne*.
 [Then follow other manors belonging to St. Swithin's.]

There should be a similar account for each following year down to the time when the manor was granted out of the Crown.

*Chapter House Books, A*⁶⁄₁. Contains a Valor of the lands of St. Swithin's, 26th Henry VIII. Hurstbourne manor is given with its members.

Out of the same manor of Hurstbourne Priors Thomas Crumwell, and Gregory Crumwell, and also Thomas Wriothesly and Thomas Rithe had grants, as shown by the following orders in abstract.

Augmentation Decrees, vol. iii, fol. 1076. *Memorandum*—That on the 20th of November, in the 33rd year of King Henry VIII, Gregory,

---

[1] This term was usually applied to the overseer of the harvest-field.

Lord Crumwell, came into the Court of Augmentations and acknowledged a writing in these words—Know ye, etc.

We the Prior and Convent of St. Swithin, Winchester, have given and confirmed to Thomas Crumwell[1] and Gregory Crumwell, and assigns, £20 out of our manor of Hurseborne, with the appurtenances, in our County of Southampton.

Same *Decrees* (vol. ix, fol. 56). In Easter term, namely May 10th, in the 33rd year of King Henry VIII, Thomas Wriothesly and Thomas Rithe came into the Court, etc. The writing was acknowledged as in the previous abstract.

Grant of four marks out of the manor of Hursborne, with the appurtenances, in our County of Southampton.

Edward, Duke of Somerset.

In the first year of Edward VI, a grant of the manor of Hurstbourne was obtained by Edward, Duke of Somerset, formerly Earl of Hertford, in support of his dignity, by writ of Privy Seal, dated Westminster, July 23rd, 1547.

The writ comprehends "The Lordships and Manors of Hursbourn *interius*, and Hursbourn *exterius* (*Southampton*), and the park, and liberty of the park of Hursbourn, and all lands, etc., called Hursbourn, belonging to the late dissolved priory of St. Swithin, in the city of Winchester, and all messuages, houses, etc., in the tenure of John Mills, to the said priory lately belonging.

"The Water Mill called Hursbourn Mill, and the Fuller's Mill, called Robwood Mill, in Hursbourn, and all the lands, etc., in the tenure of Richard Cowper and Robert Kegill in Hursbourn, to the said priory lately belonging.

"The Warren of Badley (*Bradley*), with the appurtenances in Badley and Hursbourn, to the said priory lately belonging. The water-mill and one messuage, and two yardlands, in the tenure of Thomas Power in Bourne (*St. Mary Bourne*), Southampton, to the said priory lately belonging. The Dovecot, with the appurtenances, in the tenure of Ellis Wynne, in Hursbourn, and the several fishery of the water called Colleslake, in Bourn, in the tenure of John Mills, to the said priory lately belonging, in chief for one-fortieth of a Knight's fee at a rent of 26s."

[1] In Chalmers's *Biographical Dictionary*, it is stated that, "On the 17th of April 1539, Thomas Crumwell was advanced to the dignity of Earl of Essex, and soon after constituted Lord High Chamberlain of England. The same day he was created Earl of Essex he procured Gregory his son to be made Baron Cromwell or Crumwell of Oakham." This must refer to the Gregory, Lord Crumwell, and the Thomas Crumwell, his father, the favourites of Henry VIII.

Patent Roll, 1st Edward VI, 1547, p. 4.

"Grant to Edward, Duke of Somerset, of the Manors of Hursborne, Hursborne Interius, and Hursborne Exterius, and the Park of Hursborne, late of the Priory of St. Swithin; a watermill and fulling-mill in Hursborne called Robwood's mill: the warren of Badley in Badley and Hursb.; a fishery in Borne called Colleslake; a dovecote in Hursborne, etc. To hold by Knight's service. 23rd June (1547)."

SOMERSET.

Camden, in his *Britannia*, refers to the distinguished family of St. Maur, "corruptly called Seymour", and states that about the year 1240 Gilbert Marshal, Earl of Pembroke, was obliged to assist William St. Maur in an expedition against the Welsh. From this St. Maur was descended Roger of St. Maur, Knight, who married one of the heiresses of the well-known John Beauchamp, Baron of Hache. At a later period came Sir John Seymour, one of the commanders who suppressed the insurrection of Lord Audley and the Cornish rebels in 1497, and who subsequently participated in the French wars of Henry VIII. Sir John was in the train of King Henry on his famous interview with the French monarch Francis I, in 1520, and with his Royal Master he received the Emperor Charles V, on the latter's visit to England in 1522.

Of Sir John Seymour's offspring, Thomas, created Lord Seymour of Sudeley, married Queen Catherine [Parr], widow of Henry VIII, and was constituted Lord Admiral of England. Being convicted of high treason, he was beheaded on the 10th of March 1548-9. Jane Seymour, the eldest daughter of Sir John, was married to Henry VIII, by whom she was the mother of Edward VI.

The eldest son of Sir John, Sir Edward Seymour, became successively Viscount Beauchamp and Earl of Hertford. After the death of Henry VIII, to whom he was executor, the Earl was constituted Lord Treasurer of England, being already one of the Council to the young King, his nephew. Not being a Baron of the United Kingdom, he was created Baron Seymour of Hache on the 15th of February 1546-7, and the following day was advanced to the dukedom of Somerset. He received a grant of the office of Earl Marshal for life, and was appointed by patent Protector and Governor of the King and his realms, with an income of 8,000 marks so long as he should exercise that high office. The Protector Somerset thus attained a position of power and dignity almost unexampled in a subject; but his brilliant and ambitious career had a gloomy ending, for having come into collision with the Earl of Northumberland, who had obtained considerable power, he, in union with other opponents of Somerset, brought a charge of conspiracy against him to molest the Privy

Council. He was tried for felony, and found guilty, and was executed on Tower Hill, on the 22nd of January 1552.

The honours of the dukedom were for a time forfeited, but they were revived in the year 1660, in the person of Sir William Seymour, second Duke of Somerset, who had taken a distinguished and gallant part in favour of the Stuarts during the civil wars.

William Seymour, the third Duke of Somerset, died of small-pox in 1671, at the age of nineteen, unmarried; and the landed property at Tottenham, Savernake, and other places, went to his sister and heiress, Lady Elizabeth Seymour, who married the Earl of Ailesbury. John Seymour, the fourth Duke, succeeded to the title. He was the uncle of the late Duke, and married Sarah Alston, the Duchess of Somerset, who founded the Hospital at Froxfield, in Wiltshire. This Duke died at Amesbury, in April 1675, without issue, and the title passed to a younger branch, the Lords Seymour of Trowbridge, who were residents at Marlborough Castle, their representative at that time being Francis Seymour, who was born in January 1657. Francis became the fifth Duke in 1675, when he was in his eighteenth year; but he held his title for a very short period, for on reaching the age of twenty-one, when on his travels in Italy, he was shot at the entrance of his inn, in mistake for some one else, by one Horatio Botti. An account of his death may be seen in the British Museum (Lansd. MS. 722, fol. 133).

Extract from the SEYMOUR PEDIGREE, *showing the succession of the family after the death of* PROTECTOR SOMERSET.

EDWARD, EARL of HERTFORD, younger son of PROTECTOR SOMERSET.
|
EDWARD, LORD BEAUCHAMP, died 1612.

```
┌─────────────────────────┬──────────────────────────────────────────────────┐
WILLIAM, MARQ. of         FRANCIS, LORD SEYMOUR = FRANCES, d. of Sir Gil-
HERTFORD, second          of Trowbridge. Built "the   bert Prynne of Alling-
DUKE of SOMERSET          Castle", at Marlborough,    ton, near Chippen-
[restored], died 1660.    1640. Died 1664.            ham.
        │                         │                          │
        │                  ┌─ 1st ┤                          ├─ 2nd.
HENRY, LORD               JOHN, fourth = SARAH, foundress of Frox-  = LORD
BEAUCHAMP,                 DUKE of       field Hospital and Broad     COLE-
died 1654, in              SOMERSET,     Town Charity. Died           RAINE.
father's life-             died s. p., 1675.   1692.
time.
        │
┌───────┴─────────────────────────────────────┐
WILLIAM, third DUKE of SOMER-         ELIZABETH. = Mar. EARL of
SET, died unmar., 12th Dec. 1671,                   AILESBURY.
    æt. 19.
```

a |

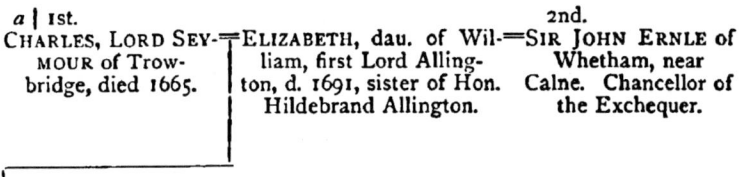

FRANCIS, *fifth* DUKE of SOMERSET. Born 17th Jan. 1657; shot at Lerici, 20th April; buried at Great Bedwyn, 15th Oct. 1678, *s. p.* The title passed to his brother CHARLES, *the sixth* [the "PROUD"] DUKE.

The will of Henry VIII contains bequests to the Earl of Hertford, John Gates, etc. (December 30th, 1546).

Executors.—Lord Wriothesley, Chancellor of England; Earl of Hertford, Grand Chamberlain, and others.

Bequests.—Lord Wriothesley, £500; Earl Hertford, £500. "Also for the special love we bear our trusty Councillors, we give and bequeath unto them such sums as are tolled upon their heads." £200, Sir Thomas Cheney; £200, Sir Thomas Seymour, brother of the Earl of Hertford, executed, 14th March 1549; £200, John Gates, who is one of the witnesses.

Sir Mychael Lyster.

In the Subsidy Roll of 37th Henry VIII, 1545, Sir Mychael Lyster is stated as holding lands in Hurstbourne; but the name does not appear later, in the Subsidy of Elizabeth, 1592. The land held by Sir Mychael was Wyke manor.

Sir Mychael Lyster married Elizabeth, daughter and sole heir of Senaire de la Bere, in co. Hereford, of whom was born Richard Lister, who wedded Mary, daughter of Thomas Wriothesley, Earl of Southampton; and his son and heir, who was twenty-one years of age in 1577, married Elizabeth, eldest daughter of Richard Southwell of Woodrising, co. Norfolk.

The monument of Sir Richard Lyster, in St. Michael's Church, Southampton, he having been buried March 17th, 1554, was commonly taken for the tomb of the first Earl of Southampton, until Sir Frederic Madden, in 1845, exposed the error in a paper read at the Winchester meeting of the Archæological Institute, wherein he traced the descent of the Chief Justice from his grandfather, Thos. Leyster of Wakefield. Sir R. Lyster held considerable property in land in Hampshire. His daughter, Elizabeth, married Sir Richard, father to Sir Michael Blount.

Among the Sheriffs of Hampshire, Michael Lister, Mil., 37th Henry VIII, appears; and also Michael Lister, 3rd Edward VI.

Feet of Fines.—Southampton, Michaelmas, 38th Hen. VIII, 1546.

"Fine between (Sir) Michael Lyster, Kt. (Plaintiff), and Andrew Baynton, Esq. (Deforciant), concerning the Manor of Wyke, otherwise Dauleswyke, and 10 messuages, 10 cottages, 300^a land, 40^a meadow, 200^a pasture, 100^a wood, 200^a furze and heath, and 100s. of rent, with appurt^s in Wyke, otherwise Dauleswyke, Hursbourne, and Born (*St. Mary Bourne*), which Elizabeth Baynton, widow of Edward Baynton, Kt., holds for term of her life of the inheritance of the said Andrew, who grants the reversion to the said (Sir) Michael."

Sir John Gate.

Sir John Gate, sometimes written Gates, held a grant of the manor of Hurstbourne after the attainder of the Duke of Somerset. He possessed the property in 1553, one year after the Duke's death. Sir John Gate took part in the attempt to place the Lady Jane Grey on the throne, and was arrested at the same time with the Earl of Northumberland, who was the leader in the rebellion, the Earl of Warwick, several of the Dudleys, the Marquis of Northampton, the Earl of Huntingdon, and Sir Thomas Palmer. He was convicted of high treason, and was beheaded, together with the Duke of Northumberland, and Sir Thomas Palmer, on the 22nd of August 1553.

Calendar and Inventory.—Particulars for Grants, Edward VI. Gate, Sir John, Knt., Vice-Chamberlayn of the King's Household, Chancellor of the Duchy of Lancaster, and one of the four principal Knights of the Privy Chamber.

May 10th, 7th year Edward VI, Sec. 4.—Request to purchase (1) Farm of the manor of Ringwood (South^n), late of Edward Duke of Somerset. *Memorandum.*—Summary and particulars of sale. [Rated for Sir John Gate, Kt., 10th April, 7th Edward VI.]

(2) Constableship of Castle of Christchurch, late of Edward Duke of Somerset. [Items crossed out.]

(3) Farm of the manor of Hursborne, otherwise Pryors Hursborne (Suth^n), and of the tithes of the manors of Saint Mary Borne, Wyke, Stoke, Bindley (Suth^n), and Eggbury, late of Edward Duke of Somerset, and formerly of the Priory of St. Swithin, Winchester.

Patent Roll.—7th Edw. VI, 1553, p. 7. Grant to Sir John Gate, Knt., of the manors of Hurseborne alias Priors, and Hursborne Interius, mills, etc., the tithes (tithings) of St. Mary Bourne, Wyke, Stoke, Byndley, Egbury, Swampton, etc., 15th May.

Particulars for Grants.—7th year Edward VI, Section 4. Sir John Gate, Knt., Grantee.

Com. South'n.—Portion of the possessions of Edward, late Duke of Somerset, and previously portion of the possessions of the late Priory of St. Swithin, Winchester.

Manor of Hurseborne, alias Priors Hurseborne in the said county, is worth in—

Rent of the Customary Tenants there per annum . . xix*li.* vij*s.* j*d.*
Farm of a corn mill there called Hursborne Mille, with appurtenances, demised to Robert Cowper by copy of Court [Roll], per annum . . xx*s.*
Farm of a fulling mill there [*molend' ffullonic'*] called Rodwoode Mille, with appurtenances, also one Messuage, and xiij acres marsh land [*Marisc'*], demised to Robert Kegill by copy of Court [Roll], p. ann. . . . xl*s.*
Farm of a Rabbit Warren there, called Badley [Bradley], demised to John Milles by Copy of Court [Roll], p. ann. . . . . xlvj*s.* viiij*d.*
Farm of the outer site of the Manor of Hursborne aforesaid, with all houses and buildings thereupon standing, also all lands, meadows, fields, and pastures, also works of customary tenants there in money not rented with certain stock (*Stauro*), as well living as dead, as demised to John Milles, Elizabeth his wife, and to Robert and William, their sons, by Indenture, dated the 6th day of April, Anno Reg. 26 of the late King Henry VIII, for a term of 50 years. Rendering thence p. ann. . . . . xiij*li.* x*s.*
Farm of the Interior Manor of Hursborne, also aforesaid, viij pair of Rabbits every week between the feasts of Pentecost and the Purification of the Blessed Mary; every year to be delivered, together with price of herbage of seven *Eunuchs* [Geldings?] (in the MS., *Herbag'* vij[tem] *Eunchor'*), and eight muttons [wether sheep] (viij[to] *Mutton*, in MS.), within the Park there every year to be pastured in summer time. Per ann. . . . . iiij*li.* xvj*s.* viij*d.*
Farm of a certain Dovecote [*Columbar'*] beneath the Manor of Hursborne aforesaid. Demised to Elis Wynne, at will. P. ann. . vj*s.* viij*d.*
Certain rents there p. ann. . . . . . iiij*s.*
Perquisites of Court there . . . . qua casualia

Reprises, viz., in—

Fees of the Bailiff there, for his official expenses; if outgoing. P. ann. . xl*s.*
And is clearly worth per ann'm . . . . xlj*li.* xj*s.* j*d.*

This paragraph is in English in the MS. :—

Memorandum.—That the ffarme of the Interior Mannor above charged at iiij*li.* xvj*s.* viij*d.* was used and occupied to thuse [the use?] of the said late Duke, Notwith-stonding Elys Wynne hathe a lease thereof for certen yeres.

Item, whether the same Interior Mannor be gruᵃnted (*sic*) to any p'son by ye King's Matie or not it is unknowen to me.

Manor or Tithing of Saynt Maryborne is worth in—

Rent of Free Tenants there p. ann. . . . . xij*s.*
Rent of all the Customary Tenants there p. annum . . xxij*li.* xiiij*s.* vj*d.*

Manor or Tithings of St. Maryborne—

Farm of a Watermill in Saynt Marieborne afores'd, with one Messuage, two virgates of land pertaining, demised to Thome Powre by Copy of Court [Roll], per annum . . . . . . vj*li.* x*d.*

Certain Rents there per annum	vjs.
Perquisites of Court, ordinary years . . .	Causa q' supra.
	xxix*li*. ijs. iiij*d*.

Manor or Tithing of Wyke is worth in—

Rent of Free tenants there per annum	vijs.
Rent of Customary tenants there per ann'm. . .	xv*li*. xjs.
Certain rents there p. ann.	iijs.
Perquisites of Court, ordinary years, ut supra .	xvj*li*. xijs.

Manor or Tithing of Stoke is worth in—

Rent of Free tenants there p. annum . . .	viijs.
Rent of Customary tenants there p. ann. . .	xviij*li*. xixs. vij*d*.
Certain rents there p. ann.	iiijs.
Perquisites of Court there, ordinary years . .	vjs. viij*d*. (*sic*).
	xix*li*. xjs. viij*d*.

Manor or Tithing of Byndley is worth in—

Rent of all the Customary Tenants p. ann. . .	xv*li*. xviijs. vij*d*.
Certain Rents there p. ann.	ijs.
Perquisites of Court there, ordinary years . .	viijs. (*sic*).
	xvj*li*. xjs.

Manor or Tithing of Eggebury is worth in—

Rent of the Free tenants there per ann. . . .	xvjs.
Rent of Customary Tenants there per ann. . .	xiij*li*. ixs. iiij*d*.
Certain rents there p. ann.	ijs.
Perquisites of Court there, ordinary years . .	ijs. viij*d*. (*sic*).
	xiij*li*. vijs. vij*d*.
Total.—Sum total clear (*Sm'a Totis clar.*). Annual value. Premises aforesaid beside. Reprises abovementioned . .	cxxxvj*li*. xiiijs. iiij*d*.

Reprises, viz., in—Fees or wages of John Fitz Williams de Kingesley, Keeper and Governor of the Chief House and Park of Priors Hursborne aforesaid, and Master of the Drift of Wild Animals in the said Park, also Seneschal (Steward) of the Manor aforesaid, and Keeper of all Rabbits being in the said park, at £11 16s. per annum. To have and to receive to the said John for the term of his life, namely, for the office of Keeper of the House, 60s. 8d. for the year. For the exercise of the office of Master of the Drift of Wild Animals in the Park aforesaid, at 60s. 8d. for the year. Also for the office of Seneschal (Steward) of the Manor aforesaid, at 100s. for the year, in all as above as to the same John granted by Letters Patent of the Lord the King Edward VI, bearing date the last day of April in the sixth of Edward VI aforesaid, for as in the same more plainly appears, per annum £16 16s. (this sum includes the "ffee of cs.")

[English in MS.]

Add herto ye sume of v*li*. under wrytten all owed to Ellys Wynne by cause ye warra't is to have all charges, etc.

"And so it is worth clear per annum, cxx*li*. xiiijs. q͞s."

[English in MS.]

Memorandum.—That there is a ffee of c*s*. by yere grunted to Elys Wynne for terme of his lyffe by L'res patentes of the late Priory of Saynt Swythyns in Wynchester for Keping of the House and Parke aforesaid ou'r and beside the ffee above reprised, which Elys is yet lyving.

Executed the xxvij day March A°. 1553

By WILLIAM KYNYATT, Auditor.

For Sir John Gates.

It will be seen by the *Ministers' Accounts*, 32nd and 33rd of Henry the VIII, and by the *Particulars for Grants*, just stated, that the lands of all the manorial tithings were cultivated as common lands; and that the tenants were in two classes, " free and customary". The several tithings were then styled manors as well as tithings. The free tenants were in very small proportion to the customary tenants. The demesne lands were often tilled by the free tenants or copyholders, who not unfrequently cultivated portions of the common fields at the same time. There was then a small watermill at St. Mary Bourne. Indeed, these little agricultural communities were almost entirely self-dependent, and received but little help out of their own districts for food, clothing, for agricultural implements, or for the repair of dwellings. The officials engaged under the manorial lord in the management of the free and customary tenants were, as had been already observed, the Seneschal or Steward, and the Bailiff. But there were some minor officials, as the " reep-reeve", who was the overseer of the harvest-fields, and had the custody of the woods of the manor. The rents are stated as " Rents of Assize", meaning that the tenants paid in a fixed sum, as distinguished from a variable rent (see Cowel, *Interpreter*). The lord of the manor had besides certain yearly profits growing out of fines, amercements, etc., which were entitled " Perquisites of Court". One of these was the " Fine of a Heriot", which consisted in the custom of taking a fine in the shape of a beast, or probably its value in money, at the time of a tenant's death. The custom appertained to the Hurstbourne Priors manor, and was paid in money, as stated in the accounts of Ellis Wynne, who was the bailiff of the King; although in another place he is denominated as the Steward of the *inner* manor. On the obtainment of licence from the Manor Court, the tenants could, on certain lands, substitute under-tenants, the payment for which was a sum in some cases as small as 2*d*. " Cert-money" was another fine of the Court of the manorial system of Hurstbourne. It was a charge of the lord of the manor on the heads of his tenants for providing them with a Court-leet. The fine was sometimes styled head-money, or head-pence, as well as cert-money; in some manors the charge was a penny per *poll*. The tax must have been of advantage to the tenants, in enabling them to do their suit at the Court-leet, nearer home, instead of having to attend the Sheriff's court or other court. "Amercements" were also fines; but in these cases they were exacted by the lord in his Court for petty offences. The offender was amerced in a small sum by throwing himself on the mercy of the Court. When the amercements were too grievous, a release was given, the fine being deducted in the accounts of the bailiff or the collector of rents. It has now been seen what were the services of the tenants at the time of Domesday; also in the middle of the fourteenth century, when the tenants paid in money, or in both services and money; and again in the middle of the sixteenth century, when the land was held by money payments only.

A few years later, in the 7th year of the reign of Elizabeth, 1564 (see *Memoranda Roll*, 35), the tithing of St. Mary Bourne contained 35 messuages, 4 tofts, a mill, a dovecote, 10 cottages, 4 gardens, 41 virgates of land, equal to 1230 acres; 10 acres of meadow, 22 acres of pasture, and 2 acres of wood. At the same time the Wyke tithing contained 11 messuages, 6 tofts, 13 virgates of land, or 390 acres; 37 acres of pasture, and 5 acres of wood. The tithing of Stoke contained 18 messuages, 4 tofts, 3 cottages, 2 gardens, 20 virgates of land, or 600 acres; and 4 acres of wood. Binley tithing contained 16 messuages, 3 tofts, 27 virgates of land, equal to 810 acres; and 10 acres of wood. The tithing of Eggbury contained 17 messuages, 30 virgates, or 900 acres of land; and 10 acres of pasture. A messuage is a house with a little land assigned to it; a cottage had no land attached to it, or very little; a *toft* is a place where a messuage once stood. There being such a small number of cottages shows that the occupants of the messuages were all workers on the land; and the land being stated in one lump, as that of St. Mary Bourne, which consisted of 41 virgates, refers to the whole as common fields, cultivated by the entire community of the tithing. The gardens, of which there were only four in St. Mary Bourne, were most likely the gardens of the freeholders. The quantity of land here given for the virgate is the normal estimate of 30 acres; but it is likely that the virgate in this case represented a smaller quantity, as we have already seen that the virgate varied from 15 up to 48 acres.

Oxenburgh, or Oxenbridge.

Cal. Inquis. p. m. for Grants. Philip and Mary. Oxenbrye Sir Robert, 25th July 1558; 5th and 6th Philip and Mary. No request to purchase.

Grant. Farm of the manor of Husborne, otherwise Priors Husborne, and the *Decennas* (tithings) of St. Mary Borne, Wyke, Stoke, Byndeley, and Eggbury, Suth'n, late of Sir John Gate. Rated for Sir Robert Oxenbrye.

Farm of the Park of Pryours Husborne, al's Husborne Priory (Suth'n). Mem. and Pars. rated for Oxenbrye (Memb. 7).

The sum paid for the manor by Sir Robert Oxenbridge was two thousand seven hundred and ninety pounds thirteen shillings and ninepence; and the purchase included all the bucks and does in the park, and all the woods in the said park of Hursbourn, called Roundhill, Callow Coppice, Bramblebury, Pond Coppice, and Lodge Coppice, also the Fulling Mill, called Robwood's Mill, and a messuage, and thirteen acres of land in Hursbourn, in the occupation of Robert Kegill, and a Water Mill, and a messuage, and two rods of land in Borne, in the occupation of Thomas Power,—the whole amounting to the clear annual value of one hundred and thirty-nine pounds ten shillings and eightpence, granted *in capite*, and one-fortieth of a Knight's fee.

Patent Roll. Philip and Mary, p. 5. Robert Oxenbridge. Manor of Hursborne, alias Priours Hursborne, alias H. Pryour; Badley Warren; 2 mills; St. Maryborne, Wyke, Stoke, Byndley, and Eggbury [tithings?]; 1 Watermill, etc., in St. Maryborne; late of Sir John Gates, attainted. To hold *in capite*, etc.

Exchequer, L. T. R. Memoranda Roll, Easter, 7 Eliz. (Roll 35). By which Sir R. Oxenbridge obtains title to the manors of St. Mary Bourne, Wick, Stoke, Binley, and Eggbury, as part of the manor of Hurstbourne Priors.

"*South'ton.*—The Sheriff was commanded to distrain Robert Oxenbridge, Kt., tenant of the Manors of Seynt Marye Borne, Wicke, Stoke, Byndeley, and Egburye, to do homage and fealty for the said Manors, which John Gate, Kt., had of the gift of King Edward VI, and to show by what title he holds them."

[The grant to Gate is recited.]

"Oxenbridge appears and complains that he has been distrained unjustly, because he says that the said supposed Manor of Seynt Marye Bourne contains

35 messuages, 4 tofts, one mill, one dovecote, ten cottages, 4 gardens, 41 virgates of land, 10ᵃ meadow, 22ᵃ pasture, and 2ᵃ wood, in Seynt Mary Borne, and from time immemorial it has been commonly known by the name of the tithing of Seinte Marie Borne : That the supposed Manor of Wyke contains 11 messuages, 6 tofts, 13 virgates of land, 37ᵃ pasture and 5ᵃ wood, in Wike, and is known as the tithing of Wyke : That the supposed Manor of Stocke contains 18 messuages, 4 tofts, 3 cottages, 2 gardens, 20 virgates of land, and 4 acres of wood in Stocke, and is known as the tithing of Stocke : That the supposed Manor of Bynley contains 16 messuages, 3 tofts, 27 virgates of land, and 10ᵃ wood, in Bynley, and is known as the tithing of Bynley : That the supposed Manor of Eggburye contains 17 messuages, 30 virgates of land, and 10ᵃ pasture in Eggbury, and is known as the tithing of Eggburye : That the said tithings or townships [*decennæ sine villatæ*] are and from time immemorial have been hamlets of the Manor of Husborne, otherwise called Priours Husborne, otherwise called Husbourne Prioure : That on 30 July, 5 and 6 Philip and Mary granted to him, the said Robert Oxenbridge, the said Manor of Husborne with its members, whereof the said messuages, tofts, lands, etc., were and are parcels [the grant is shortly recited] : That in Easter term, 6 Eliz., he made a fine with the Queen for respite of his homage and fealty for one year.

"After several adjournments the Attorney General (Gilbert Gerrard, Esq.) appeared, and replied that the Manor of Seynte Mary Bourne is an entire manor of itself, whereof the said 35 messuages, etc., are parcel ; and the same as to the other Manors : That the said Manors ought to be in the Queen's hands by reason of the attainder of the said John Gate, Kt. : That the said messuages, tofts, lands, etc., were never parcel of the Manor of Hursborne, etc.

"The matter was referred to Justices of Assize, to be tried at Winchester Castle on 15th July, when a Jury found that the said messuages, tofts, lands, etc., were parcel of the Manor of Hursborne. Judgment was accordingly given that Oxenbridge should depart *sine die* with regard to his alleged unlawful entry into the said supposed Manors."

The family of Oxenburgh or Oxenbridge held the manor of Hurstbourne Priors for exactly three-quarters of a century. They were originally located in Sussex, Forde or Brede Place being their ancient seat. The manor of Brede comprises part of the township of Hastings, and derives its name from the small river Brede, which was once of larger volume, and hence the Anglo-Saxon *bred* or *brad*, broad, was applied to it. Oxenbridge as a family name is now nearly or quite extinct in Sussex. Its derivation is thought to have come from *Acken, Oaken,* or Oxene-bridge, in the form of "Oxenebrug", as it occurs in a Saxon Charter for Dorset, given in the *Codex Diplomaticus*, No. 397. In the time of Edward III, John de Oxenebrigge was a juror in an Inquisition relating to the Echinghams, taken July 6th, 1329. There appears to have been a Jordan de Oxenbridge of Sussex, manucaptor [surety] of Nicholas Waselyn ; he was distrained to receive knighthood, 26th June 1278. The residence of this John was Attegate, in Beckley, on the river Tillingham, the family name still existing in a farm of some hundred acres at Iden. The family resided at Beckley till the time of Richard II, when one branch having, according to Leland, married the heiress of Alard (the Admiral) and assumed his arms, and having also purchased Ford Place, in Brede, of Joan atte Forde, removed thither; and the family continued to flourish in Sussex throughout the fourteenth and fifteenth centuries, and up to some time in the sixteenth century.

The first connected pedigree is found in Harl. MS. 1,562, and the pedigree is continued in the *Visitation of Hampshire* down to the year 1634. The earliest name in the pedigree is that of John de Oxenbrigge of Beckley; and from him descended three brothers, Thomas, Walter, and Geoffrey. From Thomas, the elder, sprung two important branches, those of William and Robert Oxenbridge. William, the first of these, was a Commissioner for Oaths in 1433. He had a son, Sir Thomas Oxenbridge, Knt., who owned Gosle, in Beckley, and died *circa* 1512. This Sir Thomas formed an alliance with the family of Moningham, he marrying the heiress of William, Lord Molines, and inheriting the estate of that nobleman. Dorothy, his daughter and heiress by this marriage, wedded Sir Thomas Digby of Olney, Bucks, who was knighted by Henry VII after the battle of Bosworth Field.

The junior branch, with which we are more particularly interested, as being the line from which proceeded the Hampshire family, produced a Robert and a John, the former of whom was one of the Conservators of the Peace for Sussex in 1430, and who died before 6th September 1433 (*Inq.*, 12th Hen. VI), while the latter, John, is named as one of the gentry of the county in the list of 1434. Martyn Oxenbridge, a brother of the two just mentioned, was the founder of a branch which became extinct in the second generation. They had an only sister, Mary, who married the so-called Edward, Lord Hastings, who is believed to be the person who had the celebrated litigation of twenty years' duration with Lord Grey de Ruthyn, concerning the arms, *Or*, a maunch *gules*. A "maunch" is known heraldically as a lady's sleeve. As old Drayton says, in his *Barons' War*—

"A Ladie's sleeve high-spirited Hastings wore."

The Court of Chivalry determined against Hastings, and he was condemned in heavy costs, and imprisoned for sixteen years for disobeying the decision of the Court. At the time of his death he bequeathed his curse on his descendants, if they did not make an effort to vindicate his claim. John, the second brother, had descendants down to the fourth generation.

The elder of the three, Robert Oxenbridge, had a son of the same name, who settled at Brede, now known as Brede Place, at which residence he was a freeman in 1483. He purchased Bixle in 1459; and in 1458 and 1465 he was Commissioner for Embankments, and in 1474 Commissioner for settling the ordinances of Romney Marsh. He married Anne, daughter of ...... Lyvelode, who died February 27th, 1493. His will bears date 16th April, 1483; and the testator died March 9th, 1487. Both the husband and wife lie in the Lady Chapel, in the Church of St. George at Brede, and there is a brass to their memory on the floor of the church. There is a remarkable story extant of this member of the family, he being supposed to have been the "Old Oxenbridge", the *Ogre*, who daily devoured young children for his dinner, and who was cut asunder by his neighbours with a wooden saw, which was shaped by the people at "Groaning Bridge", in Brede. Mr. Mark Anthony Lower thinks that the story must have been derived from some forgotten legend of higher antiquity.

There was a John Oxenbridge, a notable member of the family, who was Canon of Windsor in 1509, and founder of the Oxenbridge chantry in St. George's Chapel. He was a benefactor to the Chapel, and died in 1522. The Oxenbridge arms are over the door, with the quaint rebus of *an Ox, the letter N, and a Bridge*. He was Sir Robert's sixth son, in a family of ten children, consisting of six sons and four daughters.

The eldest son, Thomas Oxenbridge, was a lawyer of some repute. He appears to have obtained the confidence of Richard III, as he was in all the Sussex Commissions of the Peace issued by that King; but he afterwards gave his adhesion to Henry VII, and was elected a Sergeant-at-law in the 11th of Henry VII. His will bears date the 12th of November 1496. To his wife Anne, who survived him, he bequeathed his house at Ford, and most of his lands in Brede till her second marriage, or till his heir should reach his twenty-fourth year.

From his brother, Sir Goddard Oxenbridge, descended Sir Robert Oxenbridge, who purchased the manor of Hurstbourne Priors. Sir Goddard succeeded to the estate at Ford, and he added both to his estate, and to his family position, by his alliance with two wealthy families; the first wife being Elizabeth, daughter and co-heir of Sir Thomas Echingham, Knt., and the second, Anna, daughter of Sir Thomas Fynes, brother of Lord Dacre. He was thrice Sheriff of Surrey and Sussex, viz., in 1506, 1512, and in 1519; and on the 24th of May 1522, he was one of the Knights, etc., summoned to attend the Lord Legate (Wolsey) at Canterbury, and formed part of the retinue of the Cardinal on the landing of the Emperor Charles V at Dover. His will bears date 17th of June 1530. In it he directed his body to be buried in "our Lady's Chapel at Brede"; and that a tomb should be erected with his coat armour, and the ensigns of knighthood. These instructions were faithfully carried out, as his monument in stone stands against the south wall of the chancel of Ford Place. It shows a full-length figure in the usual attitude, the head resting on a helmet, and a lion at the feet. The base of the tomb bears shields of the Oxenbridge arms, impaling those of Echingham, Dacre, and Fynes.

From the *Inquisition p. m.* it appears that Sir Goddard left his wife, "Dame Anne", his mansion and tenement of Ford, in the parish of Brede, other lands and tenements in Brede, in Sussex (with some exceptions), she paying yearly to Robert Oxenbridge, his son, during her life 20 marks; and if she should marry, then Robert was to possess such lands to him, and his heirs, and was to pay his mother an annuity of 40 marks. The will gives, further, a lengthened statement of his bequests, of his large landed property in various parts of Sussex and Surrey, to his other children, with some legacies to certain servants. The jurors found that Sir Goddard died on the 10th of February 1531; and that Anna, his widow, died on the 24th of May 1531; and that Thomas, the eldest son, was thirty years of age and upwards.

From the style of the architecture of the house at Brede, and as Sir Goddard for the first time calls it Ford Place, it is believed that he rebuilt the mansion. Mr. Mark Anthony Lower states that "it is for the most part of later date than the settlement of Robert Oxenbridge there, and belongs to the earlier years of Henry VIII, when a great impulse was given to the building of large houses, which superseded the plain, low-pitched old manor-houses of post and panel." Mr. Jas. Parker (*Domestic Architecture*, vol. iii, p. 315) considers it "a tolerably good house of the time of Henry VIII, with alterations and additions of the time of Elizabeth." But Mr. C. Durrant Cooper says, "it was of the latter part of Henry VII's reign, for Thomas Oxenbridge died in November 1497, or in the early part of the reign of Henry VIII, Sir Goddard dying in February 1531."

Sir Goddard Oxenbridge, by his first wife, left an elder son, Thomas Oxenbridge, who outlived his father only nine years. Thomas Oxenbridge was twice married; first to Elizabeth, daughter of Sir George Puttingham, Knt., and second to Faith, daughter of Sir Richard Devenish, Knt. He was thirty years of age at the death of his father; and he died on the 28th of March 1540, his escutcheon and arms being in Brede Church. His *Inquisition p. m.* was taken at Echingham on the 15th of July 1540. Sir Thomas left a son, Andrew, and two daughters, Ursula and Elizabeth. The jurors found that Andrew, at the time of taking the inquest, viz., 28th March, was five years old and upwards, and Elizabeth, his daughter, was eleven years old and upwards.

The son Andrew was of Trinity College, Cambridge, and public orator in 1561. He subsequently became an LL.D. but, adhering to the Catholic faith, and denying the supremacy of the Queen, he was, in 1583, imprisoned in Wisbeach Castle, and afterwards at Winchester. He, however, subsequently took the oath of supremacy, as one of the following entries, which I have found among the *State Papers Domestic*, testifies. These papers also refer to his imprisonment.

Oct. 16th, 1580.—George Carleton and Humfrey Michell to the Council. Reasons why they could not thoroughly acquaint their Lordships of the state of the recusants in Wisbeach Castle. The prisoners are eight in number—Watson, Feckman, Younge, Windham, Oxenbridge, Mettam, Wood, Bluet. Desire to know if their servants are to have free access to them, and whether they should have their meals together.

1582, June (?).—List of the notablest Recusants yet remaining prisoners in Winchester, and elsewhere :—Wm Burley, Nicholas Scroope, James Braybrook, Dr. Oxenbridge, and others.

1583, May 14th.—The Oath of Allegiance taken by Sir Andrew Oxenbridge ; and as touching matter of religion he is willing to renounce any error of which he can be convinced by any learned man, being sent by authority.

Another remarkable member of Sir Goddard Oxenbridge's family was his daughter Elizabeth, who married Sir Robert Tirwhitt of Leighton, co. Huntingdon, before 1546. In May 1546, Lady Tirwhitt was Lady-in-Waiting to Queen Catherine Parr, her husband being Master of the Horse. She was in attendance on the Queen at the time of her accouchement and fatal illness at Sudeley Castle, in September 1548. In 1546, the Duke of Norfolk appeals to Lady Tirwhitt as one of the suite of both his nieces, " whom it had pleased the King's Highness to marry", to testify what malice both those nieces bore to him. (Burnet, *Hist. of the Reformation*, iii, Pt. II, p. 259.) On the 17th February 1549, the custody of the person of the Princess Elizabeth, and her good conduct and government, were committed by the Council to Lady Tirwhitt, in consequence of the misconduct of Mrs. Catherine Ashley. Sir Robert describes his wife as "not sane [*learned*] in divinity, but half a scripture Woman."

The purchaser of the Hurstbourne and Dunley estates, in Hampshire, from Sir John Gate, and who came to Hurstbourne Priors to live, he having let his property at Brede, was Sir Robert Oxenbridge, Knt., son of Sir Goddard Oxenbridge, by his second wife. He represented East Grinstead in Parliament in 1547, and 1552, and the county of Sussex in 1554, 1555, 1557 ; and he was Sheriff of Sussex in 1551, and Sheriff of Hampshire in 1568. Sir Robert was appointed Constable of the Tower of London by Queen Mary in 1556; and in his capacity as Constable he conveyed Lord Stourton, and his four servants, in March 1556-7, from the Tower to their execution at Salisbury, for the murder of the two Hartgills.

In the *State Papers Domestic* I find some notices concerning Sir Robert Oxenbridge, at the time he held the office of Constable, and as a Commissioner in Hampshire :—

May 4th, 1558.—Warrant to pay the wages and entertainments of Sir Robert Oxenbridge, Constable of the Tower, and the Guard and Warders of the same; amounting in the whole to £580 4s. 2d. *per annum.* Dec. 12th, 1558.—Charges of Sir Robert Oxenbridge for himself and 40 men serving in the Tower, from 19th Nov. to 12th Dec. 1558.

Jan. 10th, 1567.—Commission by the Queen to Lord Chidiock Powlett, Sir Robert Oxenbridge, and others, touching inquiry into concealed lands belonging to suppressed religious houses, within the counties of Southampton and Berks.

Sir Robert married Alice, a daughter of Thomas Fogge, Esq., of Ash, Kent, by whom he had a son and heir, and two daughters, Mary and Margaret, the former of whom married Francis Tuke of Kent; and the latter wedded John Power of Husburne. He died on the 17th November 1574, æt. 65, and was buried in Hurstbourne Church, 15th December 1574. By the Inquisition taken at Winchester on the 5th March 1575, it was found that he died seized as of his fee of the manor of Hursborne, and the park and lands in Hants, lately belonging to Sir John Gate, Knt., and of other lands and tenements there, which were demised for the term of forty-one years, if he should so long live, and then for the same term after his death, if his wife Alice should so long live, and remain his widow, at a rent of £139 1s. 1½d., half of which was to be for the use of his wife, and the residue for her as the guardian of his son and heir until he should come of age. It appears, further, that on the 21st June 1574 he made his will, leaving his wife the Hurstbourne property for life, in lieu of dower and thirds. On the marriage of his son Robert, his heir, Sir Robert Oxenbridge left his Sussex property to the sole use of his son and Barbara his wife, and their heirs, and in default to the use of the said Robert and his heirs male, with remainder to Andrew Oxenbridge. Other premises in Sussex he left to the use of Sir Robert for life, and then to his son Robert and Barbara his wife, with the same remainders over. The jury found that Sir Robert died 17th November 1574, and that Robert his son was thirty years of age and upwards. It appears that Sir Robert died in the same year that he made his will. Among others of his expressed wishes was that a tomb should be erected suitable to his degree of a Knight, ornamented with the warlike insignia appertaining to his profession, and bearing an epitaph. (The tomb of Sir Robert Oxenbridge and his wife stands on the north of the chancel in Hurstbourne Priors Church.)

Sir Robert left his personal property, jewels, and plate, to be equally divided between his wife and his son Robert, with the provision that should either of them act contrary to his directions, such one should be deprived of all benefit under the will. He left to his daughter a copyhold of his manor of Hursebourn, worth £36 per annum, together with small legacies to his servants. He requests that in lieu of all comers partaking of the refreshment provided at the funeral, that two bullocks and six sheep may be killed, one quarter of wheat made into bread, and one tun of beer brewed, and given to the poor of Whitchurch, Longparish, and surrounding places. His executors were his wife Elizabeth and his son Robert.

Lady Oxenbridge, his widow, appears to have lived till 1583, inasmuch as on the 15th September 1583, Robert Oxenbridge (the only son), by an indenture made between him of the one part, and Gabriel White and Stephen White of the other part, demised to them his lands in Husborne, then late in the occupation of Alice his mother, for the use, after his decease, of his wife Barbara for her life, if she should remain unmarried, and if not, then to raise her an annuity of £60 a year; subject to which, and to the following annuities to his six younger sons, the property went to his eldest son Robert. These annuities were—to Goddard, £26 13s. 4d. a year; William, £20; Henry, £20; Gabriel, £20; Richard, £20; and John, £20, when they should attain the respective ages of twenty years. On the *Inquisition p. m.* which was taken at Andover, April 16th, 1591, it was found that in addition to the Hampshire property he was in possession of the lands in Brede, Udimore, and Rye, lately belonging to his father, and that by his will, dated 21st May 1587, he left the whole of his Hants property, and lands called Bunges and Mabbands in Brede, to his wife for life, and then to his son Robert and his heirs male, with remainders successively to his other six sons and their heirs male, with the ultimate remainder to his own right heirs; and Forde and the remainder of his property to his son Robert and his heirs for ever; and also that he died at Husborne, 22nd January 1591, leaving Barbara, his widow; and that his son Robert was then twenty-two years old and upwards. Barbara, the widow of this Sir Robert, went to live at Upper Week.

The next in succession was also a Sir Robert Oxenbridge, eldest son of the preceding one, whose wife was Elizabeth, second daughter and co-heiress of Sir Henry Cock of Broxbourne, Herts, Knt.; relict of Robert West, son and heir of Lord De la Warre. She afterwards married Sir Richard Lucy, Knt., and died in 1645. During the reign of Elizabeth no member of the Oxenbridge family sat in Parliament; but on the accession of James, in 1603, Sir Robert sat for the county of Hants. By indenture, dated 2nd July 1599, he demised his estates in Hants to Sir Henry Cock, Edward Lewknor, Esq., and Edward Cason, for a term of years, to pay the rents to his wife for life, or whilst she remained unmarried, and in the event of her marriage to pay her an annuity of £74 a year. Sir Robert was Sheriff of Hants in 1596. He died at Husborne on the 28th May 1616, the Inquisition being taken at Winchester on the 5th September 1616.[1]

He left five sons and one daughter; and by his will of February 8th, 1616, he gave ten pounds towards the repair of Hurstbourne Church, and five pounds towards the repair of the chapel at Bourne. He left small sums to the poor of the neighbouring parishes. To his wife for life he left his coach, mares, and two geldings, the house and household stuff at Hursbourn, and two hundred pounds per annum from his manor of Hursbourn; the rent (£140 per annum) of his farm at Wyke (leased to Paul Alexander, Gent.), and several articles of plate, provided she remained single; and to each of his sons, Henry, William, John, and Charles, £200 apiece; and the household stuff at Broxbourn, Herts, after the decease of Lady Cock, to his only daughter Ursula, on her attaining the age of sixteen years, all his sheep at Hursbourn, and £280, the value of seven hundred wether sheep on the farm at Wyke, which are to be paid for by Paul Alexander on the termination of his lease; mentions a brother to whom he leaves £50, and leaves his three sisters money to buy plate; various

---

[1] In the book of St. George's funeral proceedings there is a record of the "proceedings of the Right Worshipfull Sir Robert Oxenbridge, Knt., on Thursday the 20th June 1616, at his house at Hursborne Pryars, in the countye of Southampton, who departed this mortall life on Tuesday the 28th of May 1616:—2 conductors; pore men in gownes, 48. *Servants to Strangers*—Mr. Wm. Oxenbridge's man and Geo. Hamon; Mr. Kempe's man and Mr. Woodwarde's man, Mr. Lambert's man and Mr. Fran. Harwell's man, Mr. Jo. Knight's man and Sir Walter Tichborne's man, Sir Rich. Tichborne's man. The *standert* borne by Mr. Fran. Kempe. *Servants* to the defunct: Geffrey Mills and William Kidgell, Danyell Wyatt and Tho. Penton, Henry Puckridge and Willm. Brooker, Jasper Mannings and Nicholas Gray, Tho. Atkinson and Tho. Faldoe, Henry Hall, sen. *Gentm. in cloakes:* Mr. Peter Noys and Mr. Lambert, jun., Mr. John Oxenbregg and Mr. Godard Oxenbregg, Mr. Edw. Woodward and Mr. Thomas Lambert, Mr. John Knight and Mr. Fran. Harewell, Sr. Walter Tichborne and Sr. Richard Tichborne; Mr. Elmes, *Vicker*, and Doctor Johnson, *preacher;* Mr. Rich. Oxenbregg, the *Penon, Healm* and *Crest*, Richmond. *Sword* and *Targe*, and *Coate of Armes*, Wyndesore.—The *Corpes*.—Mr. Robt. Oxenbrigg, chiefe mourner; Mr. Henry Oxenbregg, Mr. Willm. Oxenbregg, Mr. John Oxenbregg and Mr. Willm. (*sic*) Oxenbregg, assistants to the chiefe mourner.—Knights and Gent. Without blacks." (Harl. MS. No. 1368, p. 31.)

sums to his servants; mentions having a lease of the parsonage at Hursbourn and St. Mary Bourne; and that his son Robert is to have the estates.

The following notices relating to Sir Robert, who died in 1616, are taken from the *State Papers Domestic*:—

1608, Feb. 10th.—Letter to Sir Robert Oxenbridge to permit Sir Thomas Tyringham to follow the King's buckhounds into his grounds.

1608, April 24th.—Licence to Sir Oliver Butler to travel for three years to and from the Spa in Company with his wife and Goddard Oxenbridge. [Goddard Oxenbridge was a brother of Sir Robert.]

1608, April 17th.—Sir Henry Cock to Salisbury:—Wishes to go into Hampshire to see his daughter Oxenbridge.

1611, Nov. 5th.—Sir Robert Oxenbridge to Salisbury:—For dismissal of a second suit brought against him by Sir E. Lucy, touching the lease of the manor of Punsburn, bequeathed to him by Sir H. Cock.

The Oxenbridges lived in knightly degree at Hurstbourne Priors until 1638, when Sir Robert Oxenbridge, the last of the race at Hurstbourne, and his four brothers having died without issue, their only sister, Ursula, wife of Sir John Monson, the second Baronet, became sole heiress of their large estate. Their descendants were elevated to the peerage as Barons Monson; so that the representation of the Oxenbridges may be supposed to vest in the present and seventh Lord Monson of Gatton Park, Surrey, and Burton Hall, Lincolnshire.

The Sir Robert of 1638, was member for Whitchurch, 1620, and for Hampshire, 1623. J.P. for Hants, 1625. He survived all his brothers, and died unmarried, June 1638, and was buried in Hurstbourne Church. He made his will, 25th January 1637, and expresses therein his desire to be buried without ostentation at Hurstbourne. He leaves five pounds towards the repair of Hurstbourne Church, and three pounds towards repairing the church at Bourne; and fifty pounds for the poor of Hurstbourne and St. Mary Bourne; and requests that the fifty pounds given for a similar purpose by Mr. Kemp may be immediately paid over: leaves to his kinsman, Edmund Oxenbridge of Dunley, a rent-charge out of the manor of Hursbourn of two hundred pounds, and in default to his brother Robert, to be paid by Sir Henry Wallop, and his son and heir Robert Wallop, Esq. (see *Chancery Proc., Mounson v. Oxenbregge*, etc.); and one-third of his manor of Hursbourn Fawconer, and his quit rents of the manor of Brede, and other property in Sussex: leaves ten pounds to his sister, Lady Monson, to purchase a ring, for a remembrance of him, she not requiring a more substantial gift, as God had blessed her with a large estate. He also leaves to his servants certain legacies.

Arms of Oxenbridge.

ARMS.—*Gu.*, a lion rampant *ar.*, within a bordure *vert*, charged with eight escallops *or*.

CREST.—A demi-lion rampant *ar.*, tail forked, holding in the dexter paw an escallop *or*.

Pedigree of the OXENBRIDGE FAMILY *after the purchase of the Hurstbourne Estate.*

SIR ROBERT OXENBRIDGE, Knt., son of Sir Goddard Oxenbridge. Came to live at Husburn Priors, Hants. *Ob.* 17th Nov. 1574, æt. 65. Buried in Husburn Church. =Mar. ALICE, one of the dau. and heirs of Thomas Fogge, Esq., of Ash, Kent.

ROBERT OXENBRIDGE. *Ob.* at Husborne, Jan. 22nd, 1591. =BARBARA, dau. of Sir Thomas White, Knt., South Warnburg, co. Hants. When a widow lived at Upper Week, in the Parish of St. Mary Bourne.

MARY, called "*Katherin*" in the certificate of her father's funeral. Mar. F. Tuke, Esq., Kent.

MARGARET, wife of John Power of Husborne.

SIR ROBERT OXENBRIDGE. *Ob.* at Husborne, May 26th, 1616, æt. 47. Bur. in Husborne Church. =ELIZABETH, 2nd dau. and co-heir of Sir Henry Cock of Broxborne, Herts.

2. GODDARD OXENBRIDGE, died *s. p.* 1634.

3. WILLIAM OXENBRIDGE of Dunley, in the Parish of St. Mary Bourne, Hants.

4. HENRY.
5. GABRIEL.
6. RICHARD.
7. JOHN.

1. ELIZABETH.
2. SUSAN.
3. ANNE.

1. EDMUND OXENBRIDGE of Dunley.

2. ROBERT OXENBRIDGE of Piddle Trenthyde, co. Dorset. Epitaph in Husborne Church.

1. CATHERINE.
2. ELIZABETH.
3. MARY.

1. SIR ROBERT OXENBRIDGE, Knt. Survived all his brothers. *Ob.* unmarried, June 1638. Buried at Husborne.

2. HENRY OXENBRIDGE, æt. 19, 1616. *Ob. s. p.*

3. WILLIAM OXENBRIDGE, æt. 18, 1616. *Ob. s. p.*

4. JOHN OXENBRIDGE, æt. 16, 1616. *Ob. s. p.*

5. CHARLES OXENBRIDGE, æt. 7, 1616. *Ob. s. p.*

URSULA, heiress of her brothers. Mar. Sir John Monson, 1627.

Chancery B. and A. Miscell., 1st Series, p. 26, No. 83. *Mounson* v. *Oxenbregge* and others.

"1638, 17 Oct.—[Abstract of the] Bill of Sir John Mounson of Burton next Lincoln, Kt. of the Bath, and Dame Ursula his wife, shewing that Sir Robert Oxenbregge of Husborne Priors, in co. Southampton, Kt., deceased, was seized of divers messuages, lands, etc., in Husborne Priors, Stoake, Binley, Ashmersworth, Swampton, Cullmeston, alias Kympston, Clidesden, Bourne, Weeke, and Crocker Stoake in the said county, and of a third part of divers messuages, lands, etc., in Stoake, Binley, etc., and of all that messuage or farm in the parish of Husborne Priors, called Somersets, to the yearly value of £1,500. Sir Robert conveyed the premises or some part of them to Sir Henry Wallopp, Kt., and Robert Wallopp, Esq., his son, in trust to grant to Sir Robert a yearly rent charge of £200. Sir Robert died about 4 June, 14 Chas. I, without issue, whereupon such lands as he died seized of descended to the said Dame Ursula as sister and heir, and such lands as were conveyed to the Wallopps ought to be held in trust for her. But one Edward Oxenbregge, gent., the said Sir Henry and Robert Wallopp, Wm Smith, gent., Robert Oxenbregge, Thomas Pecke, Francis Palmes, Walter Marshall, John Harris, John Palmer, John Coldeston, Richard Fuller, John Campion, Isaac Lane, Henry Foyle, Robert Harwood, and James Goldston, have published some writing purporting to be a grant of a rent charge of £200 by the year issuing out of certain lands, and pretended to be made by the Wallopps to Sir Robert, and another writing purporting to be a grant and assignment by Sir Robert to the said Edw. Oxenbregge and his heirs of the said rent charge, and another writing not executed, and if the same were sealed by the said Sir Henry and Robert Wallopp, 'the same was so done at such time as the said Sir Robert Oxenbregge was not of capacity to accept thereof by reason of his weakness both of his body and understanding, caused by extremity of sickness,' and the said Edw. Oxenbregge, or some one else, antedated the (second?) grant, and the name of Sir Robert was not written by himself, but some person 'did guide or lead' his hand. Sometimes Edw. Oxenbregge makes title to the said lands and rent, by colour of a writing which they (Defts.) divulge to be the last Will of Sir Robert; but if Sir Robert made any such Will, he did not bequeath any of the said lands to Edw. Oxenbregge, as he thereby only mentions his 3rd part of the Manor of Husborne Falkoners, or some 'out rents', whereas Sir Robert was not seized of any such manor, but of certain lands in Husborne Priors and Husborne Falkoners, all which are held of his Majesty by Knight's service *in capite*."

Statement of John Palmer, physician, as to Sir R. Oxenbridge's condition when he signed the first Grant. (The Abstract seems to be inaccurate in some places. The original Bill may be found elsewhere.) Taken at Taunton, 29th April, 14 Chas. I.

"11. Answer of John Palmer, gent., one of the Def^{ts}. About May last he 'was sent unto by Sir Robert Oxenbridge Kt. deceased (he living above fifty miles from him), for his advice in physic, and when this Deft. came unto him he found him very sick of a high dropsie with many other infirmities.' Palmer stayed with him till about 10 June, when Sir Robert died. Pleads ignorance as to the lands and the conveyance to the Wallopps, etc. As to the grant by Sir Robert to Edward Oxenbridge, he saith that in June last, in the night time, he being in Sir Robert's chamber, there came into the room the other Def^{ts}, Mr. John Harris, Mr. Edward Oxenbridge, Mr. Francis Palmes, and Mr. Wm Smith, but what other persons were present Palmer remembereth not; 'who all came about the said Sir

Robert's bedside; and the said Mr. Harris having a writing in his hand, he did desire the said Sir Robert to set his hand and seal to it. And the said Sir Robert Oxenbridge being then in a slumbering trance, by stirring of his body by some of the parties before named, he did speak after a muffling fashion in this Def.'s hearing: "No, no", and no other words did he hear him use at that time; but this Def. saith that he sate a pretty distance from his bed upon a trunk, and the other parties last before named were near him and might hear him more distinctly. And then the said Mr. Harris did take a pen, and did put it into [his] hand, and did guide him to write his name and to set his seal to it, and desired him to deliver it as his act and deed, which he could not do without his help.' Palmer subscribed his name, after persuasion. Mr. Harris said 'they would new do it, if Sir Robert came to better memory.'"

[The original Bill, and the Answers of the other Defendants, are probably to be found elsewhere.]

The following Bill contains a confirmation of the first Grant, which was made by Sir R. Oxenbridge when he was ill.

Chancery B. and A. Miscellaneous: 1st Series, part 13, No. 105. *Oxenbridge* v. *Mounson.*

"1639, 15 June.—1. Bill of Robert Oxenbridge of Dunley, in co. South., Esq., alleging that Sir Robert Oxenbridge of Hursborne Priors . . . . deceased was seized in fee of the Manor of Hursborne Priory, and of a third part of the Manor of Hursbourne Faconers, and of the messuages and farms of Weeke and Summersetts (so called from its possession by the Duke of Somerset in 1547), and divers other lands in the parish of Hursborne Priors. By Indenture, dated 15 January, 11 Chas. I, for a great sum of money, he conveyed the premises to Sir Henry Wallopp of Forley Wallopp, Kt., and Robert Wallopp, his son and heir apparent. The said third part of the Manor of H. Faconers was inserted in the conveyance, without the knowledge of Sir Robert O.; and Sir Henry W. and Robert W. admitted the mistake, and by some Deed assured the said third part to Sir R. O. The Wallopps having a great part of the purchase moneys in their hands, Sir R. O. was desirous to have a rent-charge of £200 per annum, and by Ind're 22 Jan., 13 Chas. I, in consideration of £3,400, they granted him a rent-charge of £200, issuing out of all that capital messuage or farm of . . . . . . in the parish of Hursborne Priors, then in the tenure of Ric. Hellier, and out of all other their lands in the tythings of Weeke, St. Mary Borne, and Stoke, and payable yearly at the farm house of Weeke, on 23 Feb. and 23 August, by equal portions. By two Deeds, dated 1st May (one of them not delivered till after) last, Sir R. O. assigned the said rent-charge to Edward Oxenbridge, Plf.'s elder brother and his heirs. The Wallopps attorned to the first grant, but whether they did so to the second Plf. knoweth not. The reason why the second grant was made, was because Sir Robert 'was very dull and heavy when he sealed and delivered the first grant, and did not much express himself; therefore, for fear question after might be moved whether he was of perfect understanding and memory at the time of the sealing and delivery thereof, the said second grant was made' . . . . . 'when without all controversy and apparently he was of perfect memory and understanding', etc. Sir Robert made his Will on 25 Jan. 1637[-8], bequeathing to his kinsman, Edward Oxenbridge of Damley, Gent. (meaning the said Edw. O.), the said rent-charge 'out of the Manor of Hursborne Priors; also his third part of Hursborne Fakners, with all the quit rents thereto belonging, to the said Edward and his issue male, remainder to Robert his brother (Plf.) and his male issue, etc.; also quit rents out of the Manor of Breed and other places in Sussex. To his sister, the Lady Mounson, meaning Dame Ursilla, wife of Sir John Mounson (whom God hath otherwise blessed with a great estate)', he bequeathed £10 for a ring or piece of plate. He made Edward Oxenbridge his executor. He died about 10 June last, without issue. Edward proved the Will, and afterwards died on 12 May instant, 1639, without issue. But Sir John Mounson and Dame Ursulla, his wife, Sir Henry Wallopp and Rob. Wallopp, have combined to deprive Plf. of the said rent-charge and of the said third part of the Manor of Hursborne Faknors, and give out that Sir Robert, when he sealed the said Deeds, was not of sane memory; Dame Ursilla being sister and heir at law to Sir Robert, Sir J. M., and Dame U., also allege that Edward Oxenbridge was to have only a life interest, because the word 'heirs' was accidently omitted in the Will," etc.

"1639, 25 June.—II. Answer and Demurrer of Sir John Mounson and Dame Ursula, his wife. Plf. ought to sue at the Common law. Defs. plead ignorance as to the alleged conveyances, and object to make further assurances to Plf. as claimed," etc., etc.

Early Chancery Proceedings, Series 2, bundle 573. *Kingsmill* v. *Oxenbridge* and others.

This document, among other particulars, refers to the cultivation of the demesne lands by the customary tenants and copyholders.

"16 Oct. 1598.—Complaint of Richard Kingismill, Esq., Surveyor of H.M. Court of Wards and Liveries, and Elizabeth, his wife—[the s'd Richard and his ancestors have been] seized of a capital messuage in Hursborne, in the parish of Hursborne Priors, called 'Kingesmille's House', with lands called 'Kingesmille's demesne lands', sometime the lands of one Richard Fawcknour, deceased. [They] have used from time immemorial to depasture and feed in a close or ground in Hursborne called Southfield, which was wont to be sown with wheat every third year, after the wheat was cut and carried, and public warning given according [to the custom there], by the space of three days and three nights, with all their cattle and 'rudder beasts', *levant* and *couchant* in and upon [the premises], together with the cattle of the copyholders and customary tenants of the said Richard Kingismill of his [Manor of Faucknours] Hursborne, whereof the said house and demesnes are parcel, they having land in the said close or field, and together with . . . the customary tenants and Copyholders of the manor of Hursborne Priors, now the manor of Robert Oxenbridge, Esq., also holding tenements in the said close or field, and also holding together with the cattle of some of the customary tenants and copyholders of Mr. ...... Bennett, D.D. [Master of the] Hospital of St. Cross nigh Winchester, and the Confreers and Brethren of the s'd Hospital, and his and their predecessors, pasturing in the same close and field. Kingismill and wife hold for life, remainder to Sir Thomas Lucie, Kt., and dame, etc. . . . Plaintiffs complain that def'ts and their tenants deprive them of their common of pasture by altering 'the course and nature of the tillage of the land.'"

"II. Sir R. Oxenbridge argues the various agricultural points raised in the bill, and denies that he or his tenants had done anything to pltfs. injury."

III. Replication. [The Bill is in a very decayed state.]

Chancery Decree Rolls, 1st Division, part 96, No. 17, 44 Eliz. *Poore* v. *Oxenbridge.*

"Whereas Elizabeth Poore, widow of Geoffrey Poore, exhibited her Bill of complaint against Sir Robert Oxenbridge, Kt., and Henry Hall, declaring that Robert Oxenbridge, Esq., deceased, was seized in fee of the Manor of Hursborne Priors, in co. South'n, and in consideration of a great sum of money, did, on 4 April, 32 Eliz., grant by copy of Court Roll to the said Geoffrey and Plf., and Robert Poore, their son, one messuage and 5 yard-lands called Chapmans Ford, with one pasture called Standhurste, and two crofts of land lying in Chapmans Ford, and 4 coppices containing 10 acres, and one water-mill to grind their own corn, and one parcel of land cont'g 1½ acre, sometime parcel of Uttmershe; all being customary lands of the said Manor; with a proviso that if the grantees should grind any kind of wheat, barley, or grain of any tenant within the Manor in the said Mill, that their estate should be void and cease. Geoffrey died about four years before the date of the Bill, and Plf. was admitted. During Geoffrey's lifetime the said messuage and all the houses belonging were burnt by casualty, and the said Robert forced them to new-build the same, 'almost to the utter undoing of them'. After new-building the tenement and houses, Geoffrey began to repair the mill, although it had previously been in decay, but died before it was finished. Plf. finished it, 'and did grind thereat her own corn only, and the corn of strangers, not tenants of or within the said Manor', giving to every miller and loader that she kept there express commandment not to take in any corn of any tenant within the Manor. But Sir Robert Oxenbridge, Kt., son and heir of the said Robert Oxenbridge, Esq., being Lord of the Manor, made an entry into the said messuages, land and mill, and made a lease to the other Def., Henry Hall, his servant, to try the title against Plf., and prosecuted an '*ejectione firmæ*' in the Queen's Bench against John Poore, Plf.'s son, who occupied under her, Sir Robert giving out in speeches that by grinding some grain of some tenant or tenants within the Manor, Plf.'s estate was void. Plf. feared to stand to trial with Sir Robert at the Common law, 'for that he was a man of great power in the said County, and a Justice of the Peace,' etc.

"To the premises Sir Robert made Answer that Plf., by the instigation of Robert Poore, her son (who 'thought likewise in time to make benefit thereof himself'), ground at the said Mill by her gristers and millners, the corn and grain of divers tenants of the Manor of Husborne Priors, for which she was presented at divers Courts of the Manor. By means of this undue practice, 'the out custom unto the Mill called Pratsdowne Mill was utterly decayed, insomuch as one Jenkin, who had before time taken the said Mill at a certain yearly rent, and lived well thereon, was utterly undone thereby', and forced to give up the Mill to Sir Robert, which had ever since stood still without any tenant or custom," etc.

[Henry Hall in his Answer confessed the lease made to him. Witnesses were examined as well in this Court as by commission in the country.]

"It seemed unto this Court, that albeit in law the said condition was broken, and so the Plf.'s said estate was void, yet the matter of the said breach being but of no great value, by grinding some of the corn of some of the tenants dwelling near unto the said Mill, 'without her privity'; therefore, in consideration of her age and poverty, and that she is not likely to live long: It is decreed in this term of St. Michael, on 9 Nov., 44 Eliz., by Sir Thomas Egerton, Lord Keeper, that Plf. may hold the said copyhold lands, tenements, and mill, according to her estate granted by the copy, performing the said condition henceforth."

The following notices concerning the Oxenbridge family are extracted from the *Calendar of State Papers Domestic.*

1603.—Aug. 21st, James I, and the Queen at Hurstbourn.[1]

[1] There is a tradition worth notice, and which I have many times heard repeated by people long resident at St. Mary Bourne, that when James II was retreating in disguise from the Prince of Orange in 1688, he passed through the village of Bourne, and inquired "where Will. Kingsmill lived." Lord Macaulay, in his *History from the Accession of James II*, furnishes an account of the King's visit to Andover on the occasion of his retreat, and it is probable it was at that time that he made his way through St. Mary Bourne.

1627, Feb. 28th.—Sir John Hippisley to Buckingham.

Sends a letter of intelligence, and has sent word into the Downs to the King's ship; wishes they were strong enough to encounter this fleet. Captain Oxenbridge, who has just come in, will take the 'States' man-of-war, and see what he can do.

1627, May 7th.—Sir Robert Oxenbridge and Henry Reade to Sec. Conway.

Send for his information an examination and copy of a letter. Have written to Mr. Windebank, one of the clerks of the Signet, the nearest Justice of the Peace to Oakingham, to take examinations of persons resident there.

1627, Nov. 19th.—The King to Sir Rob. Oxenbridge and Sir Henry Wallop, etc.

Commission to execute martial law upon soldiers billeted in Hants.

1628, Feb. 27th.—Capt. John Oxenbridge to Nicholas.

Has stayed a Frenchman who pretends to be of Rochelle, but he fears him. Sir John Hippisley has her under command. Begs him to acquaint Sir Henry Mervyn.

1634, April 22nd.

Oath which John Oxenbridge of Magdalen College, Oxford, and a tutor there, procured to be taken to himself by certain of his pupils. It promises obedience to his government in hair and clothes, studies performances of religious duties, company and recreation.

1635 (?)—Petition of G. Savage to Sec. Windebank.

Petitioner in 1630 and 1631 lent two sums of £100 to Sir R. Oxenbridge, Henry Oxenbridge, and W. Bagworth. The two former being dead, and their executors absenting themselves, Bagworth pretends to be his Majesty's servant, being a postmaster at Andover. Petitioner prays for leave to take a legal course against him.

1637, Dec. 2nd.

Certificate of Dr. William Harvey and Dr. Daniel Oxenbridge as to the state of health of Sir Thomas Thynne.

1638, April 27th.

Note of the sums of £100 lent by the Countess of Castlehaven to Sir R. Oxenbridge and others.

1652, Aug. 20th.—The day's Proceedings of the Council of State.

Clement Oxenbridge to be check master to the Commissioners for sale of Dutch prizes, as well as to the collectors, and to have instructions accordingly.

1652, Sept. 24th.

The Council of State to sit to-morrow at 9 a.m. Colonels Thompson and Harvey, the treasurers at Drury House, and Mr. Oxenbridge to attend.

1652, Dec. 27th.

Order on report from the Sub-Committee on Mr. Oxenbridge's business to request Council that his salary of £250 a year, as clerk of the check to the collectors for prize-goods, be increased to £300, on his acting also for the Commissioners for Dutch Prizes.

1653, June 30th.—Council of State to Clement Oxenbridge, and all others concerned in the inland and foreign post.

John Manley having contracted for, and farmed these offices, we authorise him to enter on his duties this night, to receive and carry all packets, and to receive the profits to his own use. And you are required to permit him to do this without interruption.

1653, July 1st.

The Posts committee to adjust the accounts of Mr. Malyn, Mr. Oxenbridge, and the rest of the new undertakers, and to report.

1654, Jan. 30th.

Petition of Clement Oxenbridge and F. Thomson on behalf of the first undertakers for reducing the postage of inland letters to half the former rates, to the Protector.

1654, Aug. (?)

Prize goods officers, H. Blake, R. Blackwell, John Sparrow, R. Hill, commissioners, and Clement Oxenbridge, controller to the Admiralty Committee.

1661, Aug. 2nd.

Account of the State of the Post Office, showing that it is managed by those who were active for Cromwell and the late government.

Aug 1st, Major Wildman a subtile leveller and anti-monarchyman.

2nd, Oxenbridge a confidant of Cromwell, and betrayer of many of the King's party.

1662, Nov. 10th.—Clem. Oxenbridge to Mr. Godolphin.

Begs his influence to obtain for Mr. Gill some employment in writing Latin, Belgic, or French ; he knows all the intrigues of the office, and is trusty in matters of great consequence.

1663, March 1st.

Petition of Thomas Bushell, master workman of the Royal Mines, to the King for directions that he and Clement Oxenbridge, his surety, may be sworn servants of the Privy Chamber, the mode of royal protection being thought not proper.

1665 (?)

Information of Rob. Turner, that he is compelled to transfer his prosecution of the prize collectors to Mr. Peck for want of money, and wishes Parliament to be informed that some of the guilty cause delay by their bribes. With notes against Clem. Oxenbridge, comptroller of the prize office, who endeavours to stifle the King's right in the prize business, as he tried formerly to ruin the Duke of Buckingham.

NOTE.—Authorities consulted:—Sussex Archæolog. Collections, *Notices concerning the Oxenbridge Family*, by W. Durrant Cooper, F.S.A., vol. viii ; also *Notes on Old Sussex Families—Oxenbridge*, M. A. Lower, F.S.A., vol. xxiv ; *Strype's Annals*, vol. iii ; *Hist. of the Reformation*, vol. iii ; *Machyn's Diary, Synopsis of the Peerage*, vol. ii ; *Brief Historical Notices of Hurstbourne Priors and St. Mary Bourne; Hampshire Genealogies*, Berry, Pt. II ; *Parliamentary Writs*, Palgrave, vol. i ; *Hist. of Hampshire*, Woodward and Wilkes.

Welhop, or Wallop.

Sir Henry Wallop, of Farley Wallop, co. Southampton, succeeded the Oxenbridge Family as the possessor of the Manor of Hurstbourn, he having purchased the same of Sir Robert Oxenbridge 10th Charles I, 1634. Previous to the purchase Sir Henry had held the property under a deed of mortgage.[1] The purchase included the manor house of Hurstbourne together with its park, also the orchard, gardens, brewhouse and outhouses belonging to the same, the whole estimated to contain three hundred and fifty acres more or less.

The arable and pasture lands comprehended eight hundred acres, and the coppice and woodland three hundred and seventy-eight acres. The indenture, after particularising the various pieces of land, states,—"and all that customary corn mill, with the appurtenances, called Hurstbourn Mill, all which said manor house, park, closes, fields, meadows, etc., now are, or late were, in the tenure or occupation of the said Sir Robert Oxenbridge, or of his under tenants, in the parish of Hurstbourn, tything or hamlet of Egbury, now or late in the tenure of William Oxenbridge, John Bright, John Godden, Widow Newell, Widow Bright, William Penton, Thomas Penton, John Broadway and Henry Gower; and all those messuages, lands, etc., within the tything, hamlet, village, or limit of Stoke, in the parish of Hurstbourn [should be, in the Parish of St. Mary Bourne], now or late in the occupation of Simon Golding, Henry Grey, George Grey, Jeffery Ilderwill, and Richard Bunny; and the manor of Swampton, County of Southampton; and also all that capital messuage with the appurtenances called Weke House, and all those other messuages, farm lands known by the name of Herne's tenements, Ilderwill's tenements, farm lands called Symly Coppice, Jackbit Coppice, Rownehill Coppice, Drod Coppice, Court Garden, and Drod Mead, situate and being in Week and Stoke, late in the tenure of Paul Alexander, and sometime parcel or reputed parcel of the manor of Hurstbourn Priors (excepting the third part of his manor of Hurstbourn Fawconer)."

The Wallop family is of considerable antiquity; and some members of it have filled important offices in the country since the time of the Conquest. It has been always understood, and the name Matthew *de* Wallop, which was the title of one of its early members, favours the opinion, that the Wallops were settled at Wallop as Saxon

---

[1] *Chancery Miscell., Oxenbridge* v. *Mounson.*

manorial lords anterior to the Conquest of England, and that the family name is derived from that place. A small tributary to the Test issues forth in the parish of Wallop, which from the length of its course has been called the "nine-mile-water", out of which Camden has offered what appears to be simply a happy suggestion. He says (*Britannia*, Gibson's ed., p. 138): " The Test takes in another small river called *Wallop*, or rather *Wellop*, that is (if we interpret it from our ancient language), *a little fountain on the side of a hill*, which gives name to the ancient and knightly family of the Wallops, who live near it." At the time of the Conquest, according to Warner,[1] (*Jus Anglorum ab Antiquo*, p. 82), four brothers, Englishmen, are mentioned in *Domesday* as possessing Wallop, in Hampshire.

It appears that during the reign of King John Winchester contained four Mews for the use of the king's hawks (*Rot. Lit. Claus.*, vol. i, p. 553). These Mews were evidently re-establishments made by the king, inasmuch as a *Domus havoc*, or *Mews*, was present in Winchester long anterier to this (see *Liber Winton.*, p. 537). Concerning the Mews in the time of King John, one of the *Charter Rolls* grants certain lands to Matthew de Wallop, Warden of Winchester Castle, for the service of mewing at his own cost the King's birds, "*quas ponemus infra castellum Winton, ad mutandum*".

The lands granted for the service were at Candover, and in the manor of Woodcote. Bramdean, which contains the finest Roman pavement in Hampshire, lies within the limits of Woodcote manor, which manor was formerly held by the service of guarding the gaol of Winchester. It is found that in 1362, Alicia, wife of Valentine Beeke, held it by the above tenure. A Charter of 1346 gave land at Woodcote and the custody of Winchester Gaol to Neil Fitz-Robert. At a yet earlier date Mathew de Wallop held by gift of King John 100s. worth of land in the *Villa de Bramdena*, in the hundred of *Esselei*, by the service of keeping the gaol at Winchester. Henry de Bramdena held 20s. worth of land at Bramdean by a similar service. The original grant was conveyed in a Charter Roll, 5th of King John [*m*. 7, p. 126], date April 27, 1204; by which the King grants to Matthew de Wallop the custody of the King's houses, and of the gate of the castle, and of the gaol of Winchester, with the land of Wudecote, and one hide of land in Candeura (Candover), and all other things appertaining to the same custody: To hold to him and his heirs of the King, by the service of mewing at his and their own cost the King's birds, which the King shall place in the Castle of Winchester to be mewed; and of finding one servant to mew and keep

---

[1] Warner, *Hist. of Hampshire*, vol. ii-iii, p. 103.

them during the whole season of mewing; and also of finding the cost of three hounds in the same castle for the same season. In the 9th year of John, the King grants to Matthew de Wallop, his servant, 208 acres of land in Wallop, which was Stephen de Bendenges. (*Claus.*, 9 John, m. 4.) In the 15th of John, the King orders him to deliver Nicholas de Hevill (who was in his custody at Winchester) to Robert de Gaugy. (*Pat.*, 15 John, m. 11.) In the 6th of Henry III, the Sheriff of the County of Southampton had command to deliver to Matthew de Wallop those lands which were in the King's hands in Wallop. (*Claus.*, 6 Hen. III, m. 18.)

Matthew de Wallop had a son, John de Wallop, who was the possessor of Wallop in 1228, and who doubtless is the same person as John de Walhop, also written Walhope, who possessed lands in Ireland in the reign of Edward I. From the following notices, taken from the *Calendar of State Papers relating to Ireland*, it is evident that the Wallops held lands in Ireland at an early date.

Close Roll, 6th Edward I, m. 7, June 22nd, 1278.

The King notifies to his Justiciary of Ireland that he grants in fee to John de Walhop for his long service 30 pounds' worth [of land] in the King's waste lands in Ireland; and commands the Justiciary to deliver those lands to the said John, and when he has done so, to certify the King thereof.

Inquisitions p. m., 7th Edward I, (No. 58), Nov. 15th, 1279.

Return of the Justiciary to the foregoing Writ, stating that he could not personally attend to its execution when he received it, and as John de Walhop would not wait till he could go to the place where the land was to be assigned, he had appointed John de Kent, clerk, 'approver' of the King's lands, and the Sheriff of Connaught and others, to make the 'extent' which he sends.

On the back is the "extent" of nine vills of land made at Roscommon on the Monday after Michaelmas. Names given, etc.

Charter Roll, December 27th, 1279.—The Justiciary of Ireland to the King.

That he had by direction of the King's Council of that County, and by oath of Knights and Freemen, assigned and delivered to John 3½ carucates of land in Ballihaulis, and 1½ carucates in Balliotyre, whereof each acre is extended to 12 pence in mountain easements, to hold by the service of 1½ Knight's fee, when the King's royal service runs.

This grant of land was most likely made for services rendered in Ireland during the rebellion in the time of Henry III, and in the beginning of the reign of Edward I.[1]

January 6th, 1280; 9th Edward I.

Mandate to Robert de Ufford, justiciary of Ireland, to cause John de Walhope to have of the King's gift, in the park of Glencree, 7 oak trees fit for timber.

---

[1] Cox's *History of Ireland*, p. 71.

January 2nd, 1282.

Grant to William de Odingeseles of custody of the land and heir of John de Wallop, who held of the King *in capite* in Ireland; to hold until the age of the heirs, with the marriage of the heirs without disparagement.

Nov. 15th, 1282.

John de Wallop prays the King to give him, in order to make his house in Ballimaeihores, 1½ carucates, with 50 acres of land for Knighthood, *inbote* and *hausebote*, in the wood of Glencree, and 4 Irishmen who have been four years on the land. [*Inbote* means *free ingress;* and *hausebote* refers to a sufficiency of timber for repairs.] (See *Housebote*, Cowel.)

May 21st, 1283, 12th Edward I.

Mandate to Stephen, Bishop of Waterford, justiciary of Ireland, having taken from Margery, who was the wife of John de Walhope, an oath that she shall not marry without the King's licence, he cause to be assigned to her, out of her husband's lands and tenements in Ireland, her dower, according to law and custom of these parts.

April 1st, 1300, 29th Edward I.

The King notifies to John Wogan, justiciary of Ireland, that the King has taken homage of William de Walhope, uncle and heir of Margaret, daughter of John Walhope, of all the lands and tenements in Ireland, held of the King *in capite* at her death, and restores the lands. Mandate to the justiciary, that having taken security from William for payment of his relief, he cause seizin of the lands to be given to William.

This John de Wallop had two sons, first, Richard Wallop, who died *s. p.*; and second, Sir Robert Wallop, otherwise Walhope, who was living in 1281, time of Edward I, and who also died without issue. According to Berry's *Genealogies*, they had an only sister, Alice Wallop, who became heir of her brother, Sir Richard Wallop, and married Peter de Barton, of West Barton, co. Southampton. Warner, in his *History of Hampshire*, states differently, that Sir Robert de Wallop, who died in the second of Edward I, left an only daughter and heir, Alice, who became the wife of Peter de Barton, of whom was born William de Barton, who wedded Joan, daughter and heir of Herbert de Denmead, from whom descended Richard, who assumed the name of Wallop, and who was returned to Parliament for the county of Southampton in the second year of Edward III, the Parliament at that time being held at Salisbury.

Sir Robert de Wallop, the grandfather of the present Sir Richard, was an eminent man, and was appointed with Gilbert de Clare, Earl of Gloucester, Humfrey, Earl of Hereford, and others, to make the award, which consisted of forty-three articles, between the King and the Commons, which was proclaimed in the castle of Kenilworth in the fifty-first of Henry III. (*Stat.*, 51st Hen. III.)

Sir Richard Wallop, the grandson, married Alice, daughter of Sir

Roger Hussey, Knt., of Beechworth Castle, Surrey. In 3 Edw. III, he, in company with John de Grymstede, was returned member for the county, to the Parliament then held at Salisbury, but subsequently adjourned to Westminster, where they sat only eleven days.[1] The descendants of Sir Richard were three sons, Thomas, John, and Richard; of whom John Wallop was one of the members for Wilton in the 21st and 22nd of Edward III.[2] Sir Richard Wallop, the father, was active in the public service; he having been appointed a Justice of the *quorum* for the county of Hants in the 1st of Henry V, and a Justice of the gaol-delivery at Winchester. In the 2nd of Henry V, he was appointed one of the Commissioners to inquire into the sect of the Lollards[3]; and in the 9th of Henry V he was returned to Parliament as one of the Knights for the county of Southampton in company with Sir Richard Brocas.[4]

Thomas Wallop, the eldest son, succeeded to the estates of his father; and married, in the sixteenth year of Edward III, Margaret, daughter of ...... Wellington, Esq., of Stockbridge, Hants. He died on November 27th, 33rd Edward III, leaving a son, John Wallop, who at the death of his father was eight years of age. Sir Thomas Wallop died seized of the manors of Soberton, Wilberton, Over-Wallop, and Nether-Wallop, in the county of Southampton.

There are some discrepancies regarding the marriage of John Wallop, but Berry states that his wife was named Alice, and that she was the daughter of ...... Bushey of Stamford, co. Somerset; of whom he had issue Thomas Wallop. It appears that John Wallop was one of the members for Salisbury in the Parliament held in the 2nd of Henry IV, and that he died in the 16th of Henry VI.

Sir Thomas Wallop, his heir, was a Knight of the shire for the county of Southampton in the 2nd of Henry V.[5] His wife was Margaret, daughter and co-heir of Nicholas Valoynes, Lord of Farley and Cliddesden, in co. Southampton, of whom were born four sons. John Wallop, the eldest of these, not only became successor to his grandfather's estates, but likewise inherited through his mother the manors of Farley and Cliddesden, and took up his residence in the manor-house of Farley, which was a noble structure, and the seat of Sir William de Valoynes in the reign of Henry III. Indeed, Farley became the chief residence of the Wallops till it was destroyed by fire in the year 1667. It was not rebuilt till 1733, when it was restored by John, the first Earl of Portsmouth. According to Fuller's *Worthies*, this John Wallop was Sheriff of Hampshire in the thirty-

---

[1] Prynn's *Brevia Parl.*, vol. i, pp. 102, 103.   [2] *Ibid.*, vol. iv, p. 1166.
[3] *Pat.*, 2nd Henry V, p. 1.   [4] *Prynn*, vol. i, p. 128.
[5] *Prynn*, vol. i, p. 81.

third year of Henry VI; and also in the first year of Edward IV. In the twelfth year of Edward IV, Prynn states that he was chosen to serve in Parliament for the county of Hants with Sir Maurice Berkley. His body lies in the chancel of Farley Church, where there still remains a tomb erected to his memory, with male and female figures in the costumes of that period. It is stated by Warner that the inscriptions and brass plates were removed at the time of the civil war, when Farley was garrisoned by the Parliamentary army. The church of Farley was in a ruinous condition, and was rebuilt by the first Earl of Portsmouth. John Wallop, Esq., married Joan, daughter of Richard Holte, Esq., of Colrythe, co. Southampton, by whom he had born three sons, Richard, Robert, and Stephen; also two daughters—Margery, wife of John Kirby of Stanbridge, and Margaret, who married John Vaux of Odiham, in the county of Southampton.

Richard Wallop, Esq., the eldest son, succeeded his father. He was Sheriff of the county in the seventeenth year of Henry VII; and the same year he was to have been made a Knight of the Bath, in honour of the marriage of Prince Arthur, the King's eldest son; but it appears from the will of Elizabeth, his wife, that he died about the time the honour was to have been conferred on him. His wife, Elizabeth, was daughter and co-heir of ...... Hampton, Esq., of Old Stoke, Hants. It appears from the will of his widow, of date 10th September 1506 (*Ex Regist. Holgrave*, q. 38), that she directs her body to be buried in the parish church of Farley, near that of her late husband. She bequeathed, to the maintaining the lights and other ornaments in the churches of Farley and Old Stoke, such money as should arise from the sale of 100 sheep. She was a benefactress of several other churches; and bequeathed a legacy to Giles, son of Stephen Wallop, in order that he should be brought up as a priest.

The next representative of the family was Sir Robert Wallop, the brother and heir of the late Sir Richard, who was subsequently knighted, and filled the office of Sheriff of the county in the 1st, 7th, and 15th of Henry VII. In the 5th year of Henry VIII[1] he was nominated by Act of Parliament "as one of the most discreet persons, justices of the peace, for assessing and collecting by a poll-tax a subsidy of £163,000." His will bears date August 22nd, 1529; but he lived six years after, as is apparent by the probate, dated June 16th, 1535.

He directed his body to be buried in Farley Church within the

---

[1] *Rot. Parl. An.*, 5th and 6th Henry VIII, Dorso 31.

chancel, next to his father's tomb; and bequeathed to the mother church of St. Swithin 10s., and 20s. more, because he was a brother of the chapter-house there. He left legacies to several churches, and the issues and profits of the manor of Cliddesden to charitable uses for the space of twenty years. The residue of the profits of the said manor he bequeathed to Rose, his wife, whom he made sole executrix, to dispose of in deeds of mercy and charity. He left to Oliver Wallop, his nephew, and his heirs, all his lands and tenements in Andover; and stated that he wrote his will with his own hand, and had it subscribed by persons of note in order to prevent disputes. As he left no issue, his estate devolved on his nephew and heir, Sir John Wallop, son and heir of Stephen Wallop, youngest son of John Wallop last mentioned; which Stephen married a daughter of Hugh Ashley, Esq., of Wimbourn St. Giles, co. Dorset; from which marriage proceeded three sons—Sir John Wallop, already named, Sir Oliver Wallop, and Giles, a priest (*Ex Regist. Holgrave*, qu. 38).

Sir John Wallop greatly distinguished himself as a commander, and in several embassies during the reign of Henry VIII ; and early received the honour of knighthood. In the fourth year of Henry VIII, under the title of Sir John Wallop, he served under Sir Edward Howard; and in 1514, sixth of Henry VIII, he was Admiral and Commander-in-Chief of the Fleet;[1] and was despatched in 1515 to harass the coast of Normandy, in redress of an attack made by the French on the English coast, under Pierre Jean le Bidoulx, better known as "Prior John." The French commander had taken the opportunity when the coast was unguarded, and burnt the small fishing-place, Brighthelmstone, including the chantry of St. Bartholomew, which stood near the site of the present Town Hall. In retaliation, Sir John Wallop landed at various places on the French coast, and burnt their shipping and destroyed their towns.[2] Dr. C. Brewer, in his *Dictionary of Phrase and Fable*, assigns the origin of the word "Wallop", as meaning a *thrashing*, to the reprisals of Sir John Wallop, when he burnt twenty-one French towns and villages.

Sir John Wallop was one of the Chief Commanders who, in the fourteenth year of Henry VIII, landed in Brittany on July 1st, and took by assault the town of Morlaix[3]; and in the same year he was in the expedition into France under the Earl of Surrey. In the fifteenth year of Henry VIII he attended the Duke of Suffolk in the taking of Bray, Roy, and Montdidier, in France. He was employed by the King on special missions to the Princes of Germany, and

[1] *Hall's Chronicles*, p. 47.
[2] Lord Herbert, *History of England*, vol. ii, p. 21.
[3] *Hall*, p. 100, and *Hollinshed*, p. 873-4.

also to Queen Mary of Hungary. In the twentieth of Henry VIII he obtained the office of Ranger of Ditton Park,[1] and steward of the manor for life; and on June 23rd he was appointed Lieutenant of the Castle of Calais.[2] He was sent as Ambassador to the French King, Francis I, in the twenty-fifth of Henry VIII, and continued at that Court[3]; and in 1535 he was ordered to expostulate with the French monarch for advising the German people to own the supremacy of the Bishop of Rome.[4]

In 1535 he had made to him a grant of the advowson of the parish church of Obbyrkirk in the Marches of Calais.[5] He continued Ambassador to France till 1537, when he was recalled to attend the christening of Prince Edward[6]; and the same year he was in nomination for one of the Knights of the Garter.[7] After this, Sir J. Wallop was sent to assist the Emperor Charles V in the defence of Lower Germany against the King of France, and for that purpose landed at Calais in 1543[8]; and on his return he was made a Knight of the Garter; and as a mark of the King's favour Sir John wore his robes of the Order out of the royal wardrobe when he was installed.[9] Sir John was twice Commissioner with Lord Cobham, and others, for the delivering of hostages in Edward VI's time, concerning the treaty of Valloigne. The last Commission was on Nov. 16, 1550, when he was the first named to hear and determine all controversies relating to the titles of lands and possessions, lordships and territories, as well within the King's limits, as within the limits of the French King, on the Marches of Calais.[10]

At the death of Henry VIII, Sir John Wallop appears not to have been in England, being at that time engaged in the King's service abroad. In the reign of Edward VI, he was the sole commander of the English forces used for the defence of the English territories in France. While on service at Guisnes he died, in July, in the fifth year of Edward VI,[11] and was interred at the same place, without leaving issue.[12]

His will is dated May 22nd, 1551.[13] After the preamble some peculiar legacies occur, thus:—" I give and bequeathe to my singular good Lord, the Duke of Somerset's Grace, one of the two great guylt cuppis that King Ferdynando, King of Romayns, did give to me,

---

[1] Bill, Sign, 20th Henry VIII.
[2] *Ibid.*, 22nd Henry VIII.
[3] Strype's *Memorials*, vol. i, p. 153.
[4] *Ibid.*, p. 225.
[5] Bill, Sign, 27th Henry VIII.
[6] *Strype*, vol. ii, p. 3, 4.
[7] Anstis's *Register of the Order of the Garter*, vol. ii, p. 407.
[8] *Herbert Præd.*, p. 239.
[9] *MS. in Bibl. Cotton. Julii, F.* 11.
[10] *Strype*, vol. ii, p. 174.
[11] Anstis, p. 429.
[12] Vincent and Charles.
[13] *Ex Regist. Buck.*, qu. 24, in Cur. Prærog. Cant.

being the King's ambassador with hyme. I give and bequeath to my very good Lord Therle of Warwick, thother greate gilt cupp, the fellow of the same. To my Lorde Therle of Wiltshire, my great gilt boll with a cover, that I brought out of France with me. To my loving brother Sir Thomas Chayne, Lord Gwarden of the Five Ports, my great gilt cupp that the King of Pole dyde give me, and my mules. To my loving Frende, Sir William Herbert, Knight, Master of the Horse, one of my three new bollys with a cover gilt, bought at Bruges. To Sir Edward Wotton, Knight, my gilt cupp with a cover, whiche I and my wife did use to drynke caudels in . . . To my brother Oliver Wallop, my gown furred with sables, and all my stuf of household which I now have at my house of my manor of Farley." After stating many similar personal legacies, the testament states that he bequeaths to all his servants half a year's wages, and five pounds towards the repair of the church at Guisons. He bequeaths the manor of Bury and Barlich, co. Somerset, and the manor of Morebach, co. Devon, to his wife Elizabeth, with the stipulation that from the proceeds she shall pay his debts, and some annuities. And at her death he leaves the said manors to his brother, Oliver Wallop, and to his heirs male. He then asks, in consideration of his life's services, and having not only spent the revenues of his offices, but also the rents and profits of his own lands, his debts to the Crown may be remitted, or part thereof, " the rather that there was nyne hundred Crownys due to me for the ransom of French prysoners that were taken, whiche prysoners I delivered to his Grace's Counsayll's Commandment without any money paying for their ransom to me due."[1]

The following extracts are from the *Calendar of State Papers Domestic for Ireland*, and refer to Sir John Wallop :—

Aug. 27th, 1520.

The great O'Neill brake his appointment. The Lord Lieutenant entered the counties of O'Neill and M'Mahon on Aug. 11th, and compelled them to make peace, as Sir John Wallop can declare.

May 2nd, 1524.

Letters patent granting to Thomas Stevyns, on the surrender of Sir John Wallop, the office of Bailiff and Receiver of the Lordship of Trim.

Aug. 23rd, 15...

Thomas Crumwell to Sir John Wallop, the King's Ambassador, resident at the Court of France. Directs him in what manner to justify the King's actions in the matter of the divorce, and the execution of Sir John More (?), and the Bishop of Rochester, etc. [Sir Thomas More was executed 6th July 1535.].

---

[1] The peculiar methods of spelling many of the names of persons and places throughout these pages are due to following the spelling in early books and documents.

Sir John Wallop was twice married; first to Elizabeth, relict of Gerald, son of the Earl of Kildare; and second to Elizabeth, daughter of Sir Clement Harleston, Knt., of "Okinden", co. Essex. She survived him, but left no issue; and his estate devolved on his brother and heir:

Sir Oliver Wallop, Knt., so created for his gallant conduct in the battle of Musselborough[1] in 1547, the honour being conferred on him in the camp of Roxborough by the Duke of Somerset. He had livery of the manors of Bury and Barlich, in the 6th of Edward VI, by the decease of Elizabeth, the wife of Sir John Wallop. He was Sheriff of the county of Hants in the last year of Queen Mary; and died at Farley on the last day of February, in the eighth year of Elizabeth. He was twice married; first to Bridget, daughter of ...... Pigot of Beechampton, co. Bucks, by whom he had a daughter, Rose, who married Walter Lambert, Esq.; and three sons, of whom Sir Henry Wallop succeeded to his estate.

William, the second son, was member of Parliament for Lymington,[2] in the 18th of Elizabeth; and there is a monument to his memory in the church of Weald, co. Southampton. He was a Justice of the Peace, once High Sheriff of Hampshire, and twice Mayor of Southampton. He was thrice married, but left no issue. Richard Wallop, the third son, was seated at Bugbrooke, co. Northampton. Sir Oliver Wallop's second wife was Anne, daughter of Robert Martin, Esq., of Athelhampston, co. Dorset.

Sir Henry Wallop, who succeeded Sir Oliver, was greatly distinguished in the reign of Queen Elizabeth, he having held many important offices, and was knighted by the Queen[3] at Basing in 1569. He was chosen one of the members for Southampton to the Parliament first held at Winchester in 1572, and which continued its sittings for nearly twelve years. He became a leading member of the House; and was appointed in 1575, with all the Privy Council of the House, to consider a petition to the Queen concerning the reformation of discipline in the Church. Sir Henry almost lost his seat by a technical error in 1580, Fulke Greville being elected in his place on the supposition that Sir Henry was disqualified from sitting on account of his being in the Queen's service.

Sir Henry was one of the thirty-three Hampshire Justices who in 1585 might write themselves of the *quorum*. In addition to his other offices he was Constable of Christchurch Castle, the fee for performing the duties of the same in the time of Elizabeth being

---

[1] *Nom. Equit.*, in Bibl. Cotton., Claudius, C. 3.
[2] Wallis's *Not. Parl.*, in Com. Southamp. MS.
[3] *Cat. of Knights*, MS. *penes meips*.

£8 0s. 9d. To him belonged the duty of carrying to gaol the felons in Westover liberty.

During the rebellion in Ireland Sir Henry raised a company of men, and in 1580 went to the assistance of the Lord Justice, then besieging the castle of Askeyton, which place he garrisoned on its surrender.[1] In the same year, on August the 14th, he was constituted Vice-Treasurer, and Treasurer of War in Ireland. On Lord Grey of Wilton resigning his government of Ireland in 1582,[2] he delivered the sword to Adam Loftus, Archbishop of Dublin, Lord Chancellor, and to Sir Henry Wallop, Treasurer of War in Ireland, whom the Queen afterwards appointed Lords Justices on September 1st, 1582. Under their administration the rebellion under Gerald Fitzgerald, Earl of Desmond, was quelled, the Earl being taken prisoner by a common soldier, and afterwards executed.

In the presence of Sir Henry as one of the Lords Justices it is related in the *Chronicles of Ireland* (*Præd.*, p. 180) that a remarkable trial by battle took place in 1582, in the Court of the Castle of Dublin. The fight occurred between two kinsmen of the family of the O'Connors, who having charged each other with sundry treasons in the late rebellion, desired a trial by battle. The Lords Justices having consented to it, and all things being prepared according to the customary laws in such cases, and the Lords Justices, the Lords of the Council, Judges, etc., sitting in their places, each one according to his degree, the appellant, stripped in his shirt, was brought before the Court with only his sword and target, and when he had done his reverences to the Lords Justices and the Court, was set on a stool; the defendant was likewise brought in, in the same order, and with the like weapons, and placed over against the appellant. After the challenge was read, each combatant took an oath of what he averred, and that it was true, and would justify the same both by sword and blood. Then the signal being given to engage by sound of trumpet, the appellant did not only disarm the defendant, but also, with the sword he took from him, cut off his head, and on the point thereof presented it to the Lords Justices, who thereupon acquitted him.

During the Irish Parliaments, which met in 1585, Sir Henry Wallop took an active part in carrying out various measures; and on April 26th, 1587,[3] he was commissioned with others to dispose of the forfeited estates in Ireland. And on January 5th, 1595, he, with Sir Robert Gardiner,[4] was appointed to conclude peace with the famous Tyrone, and the Irish rebels; both being

---

[1] *Chron. of Ireland*, in Holinshed, vol. i, p. 167.
[2] *Ibid.*, p. 177.
[3] Cox's *History of Ireland*, p. 395.
[4] *Ibid.*, p. 408.

persons of gravity and conduct, according to the testimony of Camden. He was, in June 1595,[1] appointed one of the Commissioners for propagating the province of Munster, in Ireland, with English inhabitants, and for compounding with the possessors of lands in that province. He appears not to have taken part in any other commissions; but he continued of the Privy Council, and filled the office of Vice-Treasurer, and Treasurer of War, until his death.

With the object of introducing English residents, he first purchased a lease of the Abbey of Enniscorthy, and the Castle and manor, with the lands appertaining thereto in the county of Wexford. This was in March 1584-5. On May 11th of the same year, Sir Henry had a lease of the lands of the Bishop of Fernes[2]; and in the 28th of Elizabeth he purchased lands of Dermont Mac Morishe and of three of his brethren in the county of Wexford. In the twenty-ninth year of Elizabeth he made purchases of a lease of the priory of Selskar, in the county of Wexford, and of lands in several towns in the same district. In all of these transactions he appears to have acted in a judicious and impartial manner, and to have gained thereby the thanks and consideration of the leading residents in the county of Wexford.

One of the more noticeable passages in the life of Sir Henry is his entertainment of Queen Elizabeth and her Court for some days at Farley Wallop in 1591, on her route from Southampton, at which place the Queen had been entertained with much ceremony, mention occurring in the Corporation records of the "great charge the town was att in the receiving of the Queen's Majestie". On that occasion she went by Portsmouth and Titchfield to Southampton, and thence on the 13th of September to the seat of Sir Henry Wallop.

For the services he had rendered to the Crown, the Queen, by the advice of the Council, grants and confirms to Sir Henry Wallop, his heirs and assigns, the Abbey of Enniscorthy; also the Castle of Enniscorthy, in co. Wexford, to hold by the service of the twentieth part of a knight's fee, as of the Castle of Dublin. The grant was made on November 4th, 1590.

The health of Sir Henry Wallop began to decline a year before his death, which occurred in Dublin on the 14th April 1599. In 1598 he obtained licence of Queen Elizabeth to alienate and convey[3] to Lewis Basset, Esq., Oliver Wallop, Esq., his second son, Richard Harper, and John Brown, his Castle, manor, and Abbey of Enniscorthy with the appurtenances, etc., in co. Wexford, in trust to the use of his last will and testament.

[1] Rymer's *Fœd.*, vol. xvi. [2] *Ex Origin. penes præhon. Joh.' Com. Portsmouth.*
[3] *Ex Orig. Patent.*, 40th Elizabeth.

William Wallop, one of his younger sons, became a soldier, and died in service in Brittany; and subsequently, during his father's life,[1] Oliver Wallop was killed during the War in Ireland, on August the 14th, 1598.

I have met with a few notices in the *Calendar of State Papers*,[2] Irish series, concerning affairs in which Sir Henry Wallop was engaged, thus:—

July 21st, 1570 (Elizabeth).—Sir Henry Wallop, and Sir William Kyngesmyll to Cecill. Measures which they have taken for furnishing the country with arms and armour. Many refuse to pay the reasonable sums assessed upon them for increase of armour. [*Several similar notices.*] June 28th, 1590.—Notices of Warrant to the Exchequer for payments to Sir Henry Wallop (£10,000, one sum), for the payments of wages to the officers and army in Ireland. Nov. 11th, 1596.—The Queen to the Officers of the Exchequer. "Large sums being required for Ireland, we will pay to you £20,000, to Mr. Henry Wallop, Treasurer of War there, for wages and food." June 11th, 1597 (Elizabeth).—" Sir John North has died and left his lady a mean widow; also Sir Thomas Wroughton, and old Duns. Sir Henry Peyton is made Lieutenant of the Tower, and Sir Henry Cock to be Cofferer of the Household . . . . This term Capt. Lay of Somersetshire was condemned in the Star Chamber, in 500 marks, and to stand in the pillory for chopping and making sale of his soldiers . . . . Being weary of idleness, I am going to Ireland with Mr. Wallop [son of Sir Henry], but will be back before Bartholomew-tide. Private news." (Printed in the *Letters of Chamberlain*, edited by Miss Williams for the Camden Society, pp. 1-5.)

Sir Henry Wallop married Katherine, daughter of Richard Gifford, Esq., of Sombourn, Hants; by whom he had issue three sons, the two younger of whom, as we have already noticed, died unmarried. He had also three daughters—Anne, who married Richard Paulet of Heriard, co. Southampton; the second became the wife of Nicholas Halswell, Esq., co. Somerset; while the third, Winifred, wedded Sir Richard Gifford of Sombourn, co. Southampton. The will of Sir Henry bears date March 31st, 1599.

By an *Inquisition p. m.*, 41st of Elizabeth (p. 1, No. 6), it appears that Sir Henry Wallopp, Knt., deceased, was seized of the manors of Farley Mortimer, *alias* Farley Wallopp, Clydesden, Over Wallopp, etc., etc. By his will he bequeathed the manor of Allington, etc., to Lady Katherine his wife for life; and annuities to William Phillipps and John Leonard. Sir Oliver Wallop, father of Sir Henry, conveyed the manor of Worley (*Worlbury*), in Somerset, to Sir Henry, and Lady Katherine, then his wife. Sir Henry Wallop, his eldest son and heir, was at his father's decease aged twenty-six years and upwards.

[1] Camden's *Elizabeth*, in *Hist. of England*, vol. ii, p. 612.
[2] The notices from the *Calendar of State Papers* are copied as they appear in the edited volumes.

Sir Henry, his only surviving son, was left his father's sole executor. Among minor bequests, Sir Henry left Dame Catherine, his wife, 700 ounces of plate, and a third-part of all his furniture at his seat at Wallop, and at his houses of Farley and Enniscorthy, except the bed of crimson velvet, with the furniture thereto belonging, in his chamber, called the best chamber of Farley: also all her jewels, and her coach and horses, and their furniture, and three geldings for her use. He directs his body to be decently buried within two days after his decease. He was buried in St. Patrick's Church, Dublin; and there is an inscription on a plate of brass,[1] on which among other matter it is stated that he " faithfully served Queen Elizabeth as Vice-Treasurer and Treasurer at War by the space of Eighteen years, and eight months, and was Lord Justice within this realm, jointly with the Lord Chancellor of this realm, almost by the space of two years .... in which time the wars of Desmond were ended, and his head sent into England."

Richard Wallop, a member of the Wallop family which had settled at Bugbrooke in Northamptonshire, was the third son of Sir Oliver Wallop of Farley, Knt.,[2] and brother of Sir Henry Wallop, Knt., Treasurer of Ireland. Richard Wallop married Mary, daughter and co-heir of Thomas Spencer of Everton, co. Southampton, by whom he had six sons and four daughters. The eldest son was Richard Wallop who, on his retirement from the severe and lengthened duties of a barrister, obtained the appointment of Cursitor Baron of the Exchequer on March 16th, 1696. He did not long enjoy his well-merited promotion, he having died on the 22nd August 1697. During his forensic experience he became widely known and respected in the various Courts in which he pleaded, and might be classed among the most successful barristers of his time. He was called to the bar of the Middle Temple in February 1646, and was appointed a bencher in 1666. There are no reports concerning his career till 1661; but after that period the numerous trials in which his name figures sufficiently testify to the estimation in which he was held as a counsel. His political tendencies are obvious from the fact that his services were generally retained against the Crown, during the reign of Charles II and James II.[3] He was the leading counsel for Lord Stafford in 1680; and was selected to defend the Duke of York in 1681. He was on the defence in the case of Thomas Rosewell for high treason; and his name will be permanently associated with that of Richard Baxter, whom in his memorable trial in

---

[1] *Borlase*, p. 137.
[2] Berry, *Hampshire Genealogies*, p. 42.
[3] Foss's *Judges*, p. 697. *State Trials*, vols. vii-xi. Woolrych's *Jeffreys*, p. 145.

1685, reign of James II, he defended. During this trial, as in many other cases, he was treated with brutality by Judge Jeffreys, who appears to have entertained a peculiar antipathy to him, although every other judge treated Mr. Wallop and his arguments with respect. In the Baxter case, Jeffreys remarked, "I observe you are in all these dirty cases, Mr. Wallop."[1] There is no doubt that this unprincipled judge could not tolerate anyone who stood between him and his victims. These incivilities, or rather persecutions, attended all cases in which this judge occupied the judgment-seat; and were peculiarly disgusting from the fact that Mr. Wallop had attained to an advanced age.

Sir Henry Wallop, the heir of the late Irish Treasurer, and the purchaser of the Hurstbourne estates in 1634, was born on the 18th of October 1568,[2] and was knighted by the Earl of Essex in Ireland, in 1599. He was elected one of the members for Andover in the 39th year of Elizabeth; and one of the Knights for the county of Hampshire in the 43rd of Elizabeth. In the third year of the reign of James I he was Sheriff of Shropshire,[3] he having acquired by his marriage with Elizabeth, the only daughter and heir of Robert Corbet, Esq., of Morton-Corbet, Salop, the manor and seat of Red-Castle, and divers other manors and lordships in Salop. On February the 16th, 1617, he obtained a grant of free warren[4] in his manors of Hampshire, Wiltshire, and Salop. He became one of his Majesty's Council in the 15th of James I,[5] under Lord Compton, then President of the Marches of Wales; and in 1622[6] he was appointed a commissioner for advancing the woollen manufactory in that Principality.

It is stated by Stow that Sir Hamden Powlett and Sir Henry, as Knights of the Shire, were on Wednesday, November 9th, 1603, charged with the duty of taking as prisoners to Winchester, Henry, Lord Cobham, and Thomas, Earl Gray.[7] On the following Saturday, November 12th, Sir Henry Wallop, Sir Francis Pares, and Sir Richard, son and heir to the High Sheriff, Sir Benjamin Tichbourne, did the same duty by George Brooke and the other conspirators.

Sir James Deane of Deane, by will, August 19th, 1607, left in trust to Sir Henry Wallop, and several others, a rent of £21, charged on his manor and farm of Ashe, 20s. of which was to be spent yearly in repairing the causeway between the church-gate and the Angel inn, and £20 to be given to the Basingstoke schoolmaster. Sir

---

[1] Lord Macaulay, *History of England from the Accession of James II*, People's Edition, vol. i, p. 233.
[2] *Ex Regist. de Farley.*
[3] Fuller, *In Com. Salop.*
[4] *Ex Orig. Pat.*, 14 James I.
[5] *Rymer*, vol. xvii, p. 29.
[6] *Ibid.*, p. 410.
[7] *Annals of King James.*

James Deane, also by his will, August 19th, 1607, founded almshouses for six old people of Basingstoke, chosen by the past bailiffs of the town, and two from Ashe and Deane. For their maintenance he left Sir Henry Wallop, and others, in trust a rent of £55, charged on his manor or farm of Ashe, now part of the Portal estate.[1]

The following are some notices from the *Calendar of State Papers*, in which the name of Sir Henry Wallop appears:

Sept. 19th, 1601, Elizabeth. Knebworth.—John Chamberlain to Dudley Carleton, at Paris. "Came to the Churching of Lady Wallop. She is very proud of her little boy. The Queen is at Basing, a house of the Lord Marquis [Winchester]."

March 26th, 1608, 7th James I.

Warrant to make to Sir Oliver Lambert a lease in reversion for 41 years, to commence at the expiration of his present lease, from the Crown, of certain Termon lands in the County of Cavan; and a lease in reversion for a like term of years of certain parsonages, belonging to the Abbey of Selskar, in the County of Wexford, which he holds as assignee of Sir Henry Wallop, both at their present rents.

June 24th, 1609.—The King to Sir Arthur Chichester.

Directs him to make a grant in fee farm to Sir Henry Wallop, of all the rectories, chapels, tithes, and the hereditaments lately belonging to the dissolved Abbey of Selskar, in the county of Wexford, which were now or of late in the possession of Richard Sinnot, Esq., deceased, of the said Sir Henry Wallop, or Sir Oliver St. John, to hold in fee and common soccage of the King's Castle of Wexford, at a rent of £76 per annum, being the usual rent paid for forty years past.

March 6th, 1611.—Rents and revenues belonging to the Crown of Ireland, 1597.

A brief declaration of the state of all the rents and revenues certain, belonging to the Crown of Ireland, as the same stood, partly charged in the account of Sir Henry Wallop, Knt., late Vice-Treasurer and Treasurer at War there made, for one year ended at Michaelmas, 1596, and partly collected out of other records remaining in several offices there certified to the Right Honble. William, Lord Burghley, late Lord High Treasurer of England, in July 1597.

May 10th, 1614.—Sir Ralph Winwood to [Carleton]. Troubles with the recusant Irish Parliament.

Several of them were sent for to England, and refusing to submit were sent to prison. Impositions give a rub to the English Parliament. Sir Thomas Parry disgraced, and put out of Parliament for trying to bring in Sir Walter Cope, and Sir Henry Wallop for Stockbridge, they not having been chosen.

May 12th.—Chamberlain to Carleton.

Sir Thomas Parry suspended [from the Chancellorship of the Duchy of Lancaster], and he, Sir Walter, Sir Henry Wallop, and Sir John Chamberlain discharged the House, as untruly elected.

---

[1] Woodward and Wilks, *Hist. of Hants*, vol. iii, p. 237.

December 4th, 1616.—Licence to Sir Henry Wallop to hold the Court in the manor of Farley Wallop and others, co. Hants.

July 3rd, 1619, James I.—Thomas Locke to Carleton.

Has suggested Mr. Henry Wallop or Sir Walter Cope [for Carleton's projected gift of a peerage], also mentioned Paulet, but he was disliked.

August 2nd, 1628, Farley Wallop.—Sir Henry Wallop to the Mayor of Southampton, sends the last Commission of Oyer and Terminer for Hants, with a list of the Commissioners' names.

January 1630.—Petition of Thomas Taylor and Elizabeth his wife, and their sixteen children, to the same (Justices of the Peace for co. Devon).

State the circumstances of the dispute between the petitioners and Sir Kenelm Digby. The matters are triable at the next Winchester Assizes. Sir H. Wallop, the Sheriff, is the professed enemy of the petitioners in respect of suits in the Star Chamber between Thomas Taylor and Sir Henry, for abetting the first notorious riot committed by Sir John Savage, the author of all this mischief. The lands, lives, and goods of the petitioners are now at stake. Sir Kenelm Digby and Sir Henry Wallop having exhibited informations to this Board to make petitioners odious to the State and Civil Government, they pray to be allowed certain counsel.

January 23rd, 1630, Farley Wallop.—Sir Henry Wallop, Sheriff of the county of Hants, to the Council.

Relates endeavours made by himself and his Under-Sheriff to remove Thomas Taylor out of the Manor House at Bradley, and to give possession to Sir Kenelm Digby, as his Majesty's farmer thereof. The persons in possession resisted with firearms; the Sheriff's party answered with ordnance, but were ultimately obliged to retreat.

February 10th, 1630, Charles I.

A later letter to the Council from Sir Henry Wallop in reference to the holding of the house at Bradley. States that possession had been rendered to Sir Kenelm Digby.

Sir Henry being very aged[1] was not present in Parliament in 1641, when the protestation was taken by both houses. His death took place on November 16th, 1642, at the age of seventy-four; and he was buried in the ancestral vault at Farley, in which grave also lies Lady Wallop. They had an only son, Robert Wallop, and five daughters,[2] of whom Elizabeth, Katherine, and Theodocia died unmarried; while Anne, born 1602, wedded John Dodington of Breamore, co. Southampton; and Bridget married Sir Henry Worsley, Bart., of Appuldurcombe, co. Southampton.

Sir Robert Wallop, successor to his father, was born on July 20th,

---

[1] *Rushworth*, vol. iv, p. 244.
[2] Nicholas Charles, Lancaster Herald, *Ex Collect., temp.* Jas. I.

1610.[1] He wedded Lady Anne, daughter of Henry Wriothesly, Earl of Southampton, sister to Thomas Wriothesly, the Lord Treasurer.

Sir Robert Wallop must have taken part at an early period of his life in the affairs of the county of Hants, as he subsequeutly did in Parliamentary matters, inasmuch as among *The Calendar of State Papers Domestic, temp.* Charles I, 1626, November 19th, there is an entry of Robert Wallop being one in a Commission issued by the King to execute martial law upon soldiers billeted in Hants. In the same Commission appear the names of Sir Henry Wallop, Robert Oxenbridge, and many others.

It will be seen in the list of Members of Parliament for Andover, that Robert Wallop, Esq., was elected for the Borough in 1623 with John Shuter, Esq.; in 1627 he was elected to serve with Ralph Conway, Esq.; in 1639 he was returned with Sir Richard Wynn, Bart.; and in 1640 he was chosen to serve in the Long Parliament, his co-member on that occasion being Sir Henry Rainsford, Knt.; but he dying early in 1641 another election was rendered necessary, when after a severe contest between Sir Henry Vernon, a Royalist, and Sir William Waller, a Parliamentarian, the former was returned; but he being afterwards unseated by a resolution of the House of Commons, Sir W. Waller took the seat, so that Andover became represented by two supporters of the Commonwealth.

The writ for Andover on the return, dated the 19th of October 1640, reads thus, omitting details :—" 16th Charles I, between the Sheriff of the one part and ye Bailiff, approved men and Burgesses of ye Borough of Andover of the other part, whereby the aforesaid Bailiff, approved men and Burgesses of ye Borough aforesaid, in their Guildhall aforesaid, on the day and place aforesaid assembled, have elected Robert Wallop, Esq., and Sir Henry Rainsford Knight, their Burgesses, to be at Westminster," etc. Mr. Wallop took an active part in the support of Sir Harry Vane and the Independents; and it was through his influence that Sir Harry was returned for Whitchurch, Hants, in 1659, although he had the active opposition of the Court party to contend against; he, however, persisted in his endeavours, and not only succeeded in the cause of his friend, but he himself was chosen for the county. It is well known that Sir Harry Vane took an active part in the Civil War between Charles I and the Parliament; and that he was beheaded on Tower Hill on the 14th of June 1662.

In the Parliament of 1654 Edward Hooper, Esq., the elder, sat for

---

[1] *Ex Regis. Eccles. Farley.*

the county of Hants with Richard Cromwell, Richard Norton, Richard Major, John St. Barbe, Robert Wallop, Francis Rivet, and John Bulkeley. Robert Wallop sat for the county in 1656.

Among the Commissioners appointed by an order of the 16th of November 1643, for making the weekly collection in Hampshire, the name of Robert Wallop appears. It was provided that the Committee, or a *quorum* of four, afterwards reduced to three, of their number, should, beginning from February 18th, 1643, levy weekly upon "Papists and Delinquents", £930 16s. in Kent, £345 13s. 6d. in Surrey (excepting Southwark and the part of the county within the lines), £680 16s. in Sussex, and as much in Hampshire, excepting the Isle of Wight. By an order of March the 30th, 1644, the forces to be maintained by that subsidy were established at 3,000 foot, 1,200 horse, and 500 dragoons. They were commanded by Sir William Waller, Sergeant-Major-General, under the Earl of Essex.[1] The service of the troops was confined within the limits of the associated counties, beyond which they might not be moved without the consent of Sir William Waller and the Committee. No free quarter was allowed in the associated counties.

It is evident that Mr. Robert Wallop held a good position in the House of Commons, and was a diligent and painstaking member, as his name is of frequent occurrence as serving in Committee. Thus, —*Calendar of State Papers Domestic,* January 10th, 1650. *Memorandum*—Robert Wallop in the Isle of Wight, and at Winchester, concerning troops, defences, etc., as a Member of the Council of State.

1650, February 16th. *The Commonwealth.*—Act of Parliament appointing a Council of State, until February 17th, 1650-51. Among the members of this Council appear the names of Robert Wallop, Sir Henry Mildmay, Edmund Ludlow, John Bradshaw, Lord General Fairfax, Oliver Cromwell, Lord Lieutenant of Ireland, Oliver St. John, and several others. The Council were to exercise the following powers :—

To oppose and suppress all who maintain the pretended title of Charles Stuart, the elder son of the late King, or any of the King's issue, or the pretended title of any other single person whomsoever to the Crown of England, Ireland, or Wales.

To order all the forces by sea or land ; to use all means for the advancement of trade ; to advise of anything concerning the good of this Commonwealth, etc., etc. [There were many other clauses, but they were all to the same effect.]

---

[1] Woodward and Wilkes, *Hist. of Hampshire*, vol. iii, p. 146, *note.*

1650, February 19th. *Council of State.*

Mr. Wallop with others placed on the Committee to carry on the affairs of the Admiralty and Navy for a fortnight.

1650, March 2nd.

In addition to the above, power to carry on the affairs of Ireland.

1650, August 16th.

Mr. Wallop, and others named, to be a Committee to consider papers, petitions, etc., concerning Barbadoes, the business of, and to advise with the merchants.

1650, December 16th.

To write to Mr. Wallop and the rest of the Commission for Hampshire to cause one troop of their Horse Militia to be in readiness for preserving the peace of the country, which is considered to be endangered.

1651, April 16th. *Council of State.*

To Robert Wallop and Richard Cromwell, regarding the great waste of timber for ship-building.

1651, December 2nd.

Mr. Wallop was one of a Committee of 21 members of the House of Commons for carrying on the affairs of Ireland and Scotland.

1652, November 22nd.

He was appointed one of the *Council of State* for the ensuing year.

1652, February 8th. *Council of State.*

Mr. Wallop, Col. Fielder, Mr. Love, Col. Thompson, and Col. Morley, to be a Committee to consider the proposal of Peter Priaulx, and others of Southampton, concerning the finding of coal in Hampshire.

After the return of Charles II, Mildmay, Col. John Hutchinson, Col. Francis Lassels, William, Lord Monson, James Challoner, Robert Wallop, Sir James Harrington, and John Phelps, were the only survivors of the judges of Charles I who did not receive sentence of death in 1660. Col. Hutchinson, though he had signed the death-warrant, obtained his pardon, but was fined, and declared incapable of holding public office. Col. Lassels, who had not joined in the sentence, was in like manner fined. The other six, though they had no hand in the death-warrant, were, nevertheless, for the offence of sitting in the High Court of Justice, sentenced to perpetual imprisonment, their blood being attainted, and their estates confiscated.

1660, August 1st, Charles II.

Daniel Wicherley of the Inner Temple, for a letter to the Dean and Chapter of Winchester, to renew to him and his brother-in-law, only son of the late William Shrimpton, the lease of Whitchurch Farm, the interest in which he was obliged to assign to Robert Wallop, who bought the reversion of the lease, but which is now forfeited, he being exempt from the general pardon. Had the great honour and happiness of receiving his Majesty at his house, when the late King came up with his army from the west; and Mr. Shrimpton suffered much in entertaining forces.

1660, October 1st.

Dean and Chapter of the Holy Trinity, Winchester, for allowance of timber from Husborn Park, forfeit by attainder of Robert Wallop, and formerly belonging to the church, that they may rebuild their demolished cloisters, library, dwelling-houses, etc., etc.,; they have no place for meetings, church timber being so generally wasted and destroyed.

Bearing on the above a notice occurs in the Cathedral accounts of which the following is an abstract. It bears date 20th May 1654, six years earlier, and evidently refers to a date anterior to the attainder of Sir Robert Wallop:—

" Itt being generally known that Trinity Churche, neere Winton, though it be a very emenent and usefull place for preaching and learning gods word, yett itt doth dayly decay for want of Reparacion: Wee whose names are subscribed to prevent the mischeife that may happen by delay doe willingly contribute by way of advance mony for the presentt towards the reparacion of the said Churche such summes as are subscribed and hereunder mentioned to our severall names." [Among other subscribers appears " Robte. Wallopp Esqr. £05 00s. 00d."]

The sentence on Mr. Wallop, and his fellow-prisoners, which was that of imprisonment in the Tower during their lives, involved also the terrible ordeal of being taken once a year to and under the gallows; and that it was carried out we have the authority of Mr. Pepys, in his *Diary*, thus:—"Jan. 27th, 1661. Going to take water upon Tower-hill, we met with three sledges standing there to carry my Lord Monson, and Sir Henry Mildmay, and another, to the gallows and back again, with ropes about their necks; which is to be repeated every year, this being the day of their sentencing the King. Lord Monson was the second son of Sir Thomas Monson, Bart.; created by Charles I Viscount Castlemaine of the Kingdom of Ireland; notwithstanding which, he was instrumental in his Majesty's death; and in 1661, being degraded of his honours, was sentenced, with Sir Henry Mildmay and Mr. Robert Wallop, to be drawn on sledges, with ropes round their necks, to Tyburn, and back to the Tower, there to remain prisoners for life. Sir H. Mildmay had been recognised by Charles I, who made him master of the jewels; but he sat a few days as one of the King's Judges. He died at Antwerp."

1661, March 19th. London. Letter from John Ward to Col. Michell, Wingerworth, near Chesterfield.

It goes to show that Mr. Robert Wallop might have purchased his pardon had he been able to pay a sufficiently high price for it. Among other matters the letter states, "that the last levy of Poll money is much disliked in the city, but none of the members opened their mouths about it. *Mr. Wallop has not yet got his pardon; they ask high for it.*"

1661, July 25th.

Petitions were presented simultaneously on this date to the House of Lords, by Lord Monson, Sir Henry Mildmay, and Mr. Wallop, praying the Lords to commiserate their condition, etc.[1] Accompanying the Petition of Sir H. Mildmay is the following certificate of his medical attendant :—"Certificate of Dr. E. Warner that Sir Henry Mildmay is suffering from a rupture, and that if the sentence of drawing him in a sledge from the Tower to Tyburn were put in execution it would endanger his life."

1661, *House of Lords, Calendar*, July 25th. Petition of Sir Robert Wallop. (*L. J.*, xi, 320.)

"To the Right Hon'ble the Lords assembled in Parliament.

"The humble peti'con of Robert Wallop, Esq. In all humblenesse sheweth.

"That (lying under the insupportable burthen and sense of the just displeasure of the Hon'ble House of Commons manifested in their sentence lately pronounced against him ; And being app'hensive that the cause inducing that hon'ble House soe to proceede against him was for his appearing in the p'tended high Court of Justice for tryal of this late Matie) Yo^r pet^r. ever did, and doeth from His soule abhorre and detest that most horrid and execrable murther of his late Matie ; And his appearing in that p'tended Court was for noe other cause but that hee might gaine an advantage thereby of being instrumental in the uprightnes of his heart to p'serve ye life of His late Matie. That being surprized with the suddennesse of his last appearing before ye hon'ble House of Commons, hee had not opportunity by any other evidence than his owne personal assertion and protestac'on to prove ye truth of what is herein alleaged.

"That ye Bill for paines, penalties and forfeitures (wherein yor pet^r is most unhappily included) being transmitted from the House of Com'ons to your Lo^{pps}.

"Yo^r pet^r doeth therefore most humbly beseech your good Lo^{pps} to co'miserate his most sad and deplorable condic'on, and to extend yor mercie to him and his distressed wife and Children ; and for cleering the Integrity of his intentions in this matter, that hee may haue libertie before ye passing of the sayd Bill to produce his testimony and proofe before your Lo^{pps}.

"And yor pet^r (as in duty bound) shall ever pray, etc.

"Ro : WALLOP."

House of Lords, Calendar, July 2nd, 1661.

Engrossment of an Act for reparation and satisfaction to be made unto John, Lord St. John of Basing, Earl of Wilts, and Marquis of Winchester, out of the manors and lands of Robert Wallop, Esq., for the sum of ten thousand pounds heretofore granted unto him by the then pretended Parliament out of the said Marquis of Winchester's estate. Brought from the Commons this day, rejected 12th July. (*L. J.*, xi, 295, etc. Parchment collection.)

1661, August 23rd. *Whitehall.*

Warrant for a grant to Lord Treasurer the Earl of Southampton, and three others, of the forfeited estates in England and Ireland of Robert Wallop, who married Lady Anne, sister of the said Earl, permitting him to dispose of the same, or any other part thereof, for the benefit of her and her family, but not *compelling him* thereto.

---

[1] *Historical Manuscripts Commission*, Appendix to Seventh Report, pp. 150-1.

1662, Jan. 17th.

Petition of Robert Wallop [his most disconsolate subject] to the King, for remission of the dreadful punishment which remains to be inflicted on him,—his most grievous affliction is the sense of His Majesty's indignation for his great offence in taking the precious life of the late King, altho' he ever abhorred that execrable murder, and was only present in the pretended Court to preserve his Majesty's life,—is so reduced by fever that he could never recover from any heavy punishment.

Certificate by William Hearst, physician, that the petitioner is so weak from long illness that there would be no probability of his recovery if he were exposed to the air at this season of the year.

With note (by Nicholas) that this punishment being ordered by Parliament, the King does not think fit to dispense with it.

1662, Jan. 16th.   Petition.

Petition of Robert Wallop, prisoner in the Tower, to the King, to take pity on an old man, forsaken by his nearest relations, and give him liberty of free air before he dies,—on security for his appearance, as was granted to John Downes, a fellow prisoner condemned to die. Has guilt laid on himself and family for want of due information. His pretended friends have failed him in order to gain advantage by his estates, and thus has been censured by the Parliament of 1660, and lost the good opinion of King and people.

Breviate of the Case of Robert Wallop.

Sat twice on the trial of the late King, but only at the request of His Majesty's friends, in order to try to moderate the furious proceedings, and failing therein left the others to themselves. On the Restoration was in treaty for his pardon, and the warrant was signed, when his friends declined to proceed unless he would pay £4,000 more the debts of an extravagant son; and whilst he paused, the Act of Oblivion passed, and he was sentenced in Parliament.

1662, June 21st.   *The Tower.*   Sir J. Robinson to Sec. Nicholas.

Has taken a suspicious person, who brought a letter to Mr. Wallop, and will not say from whom it comes. Encloses—T. L. to Robt. Wallop. Pities his losses and crosses; exhorts him to constancy, and offers him consolation; hopes some deliverance is at hand. Begs relief for himself; is at a desperate point, not having heard a word from any one for ten months (Apl. 13th, 1662).

1666, July 9th.

Warrant from Lord Arlington to Sir John Robinson, to permit Mrs. Wallop to remain prisoner with her husband, and one maid servant to attend her. (*Minute.*)

1666, Nov. 2nd.

In a list of 32 persons confined in the Tower, on the above date, occurs the name of Robert Wallop, 1667, May 30th. Of 36 persons—" One Robert Wallop, committed by Parliament."

It appears that he never obtained his liberty, but died in the Tower on the 16th November 1667, at the age of 57. He was buried among his ancestors at Farley, and was succeeded in his estates by his son. It is remarkable that in the same year the family mansion at Farley was destroyed by fire, and many rare and valuable papers were burned.

Henry Wallop, Esq., son and heir of Sir Robert Wallop, succeeded to the estates. He was elected one of the members for Whitchurch, Hants, in the first Parliament after the Restoration, May 8th, 1661; but the Parliament being very prolonged, Sir Henry died before it was dissolved, viz., on January 25th, 1679, aged 44. He was buried at Farley. His wife was Dorothy, youngest daughter, and one of the co-heirs of John Bluet, Esq., of Bluet Hall, co. Devon. His wife was many years his survivor, and was also interred at Farley, where there is an inscription to her memory in the church on black marble. They had issue four sons. Robert, born February 20th, 1654, and died, as did Charles the youngest son, while their father was living. Henry Wallop, Esq., second son, born May 18th, 1657 (see *Farley Registers*). He was successor to his father, and became a member for Whitchurch, in the Westminster Parliament of March 6th, 1678-9[1]; as also in that which met at Oxford on March 21st, 1680-1; and in the Parliament of James II, as well as in the first two Parliaments of William and Mary. He died unmarried on the 28th Dec. 1691, at the age of 34.

John Wallop, Esq., his only remaining brother, succeeded him as his heir. He married Alicia, third daughter and co-heir of William Borlase, Esq., of Great Marlow, Bucks, son of Sir John Borlase, Bart. This John Wallop was buried with his ancestors, at Farley, on January 29th, 1694. He had issue five sons and two daughters, his wife surviving him. Of these, Bluet Wallop, born August 8th, 1684; 2nd, Henry, born November 27th, 1686, and died March 9th, 1690; 3rd, John, who became first Lord Viscount Lymington, and afterwards Earl of Portsmouth; 4th, William, born April 30th, 1692, and died on the following June; 5th, Robert, who after travelling in Germany, France, and Holland, died at the age of 19,[2] on January 27th, 1714, and was buried at Farley; 6th, Elizabeth, who was born September 19th, 1685, and was buried at Farley, May 4th, 1700, unmarried. Mary married Henry, Lord Herbert of Cherbury, and was First Lady of the Bedchamber to Anne, Princess of Orange. She died October 19th, 1770.

His eldest son, Bluet Wallop, Esq., succeeded to the estates, and died unmarried in the twenty-fourth year of his age, October 30th, 1707, wherefore the estates devolved on his next brother and heir—

John Wallop, Esq., who was born on the 15th April 1690, and who became the *first* Earl of Portsmouth.[3] His Lordship was twice

---

[1] B. Willis, *Ex Collect.*

[2] See inscription in the chancel of Farley Church.

[3] The town of Portsmouth gave no honorary title to the nobility till King Charles II created one of his female favourites, Louisa de Querovaille, Baroness Petersfield, Countess of Fareham, and Duchess of Portsmouth for life. She

married; first, to Bridget, daughter of Charles Bennet, Earl of Tankerville; second, to Elizabeth, daughter of James, Lord Griffin, and widow of Henry Grey, Esq., of Billingbeer, co. Berks. The first Lady Portsmouth died October 12th, 1738; the second in August 1762; both were buried at Farley. John Wallop constituted one of the Lords of the Treasury in 1717. He was created Baron Wallop of Farley-Wallop, co. Southampton, and Viscount Lymington, by patent, on the 11th of June 1720, 6th of George I. He was made Lord Warden and Chief Justice in Eyre, north of the Trent, in 1732; Lord Lieutenant and Custos Rotulorum, co. Southampton; Lord Warden and Keeper of the New Forest, and of the manors and parks of Lyndhurst, and of the hundred of Rudberg, in 1733; Vice-Admiral of the county of Southampton and of the Isle of Wight in 1734; Governor and Captain of the Isle of Wight and of Carisbrook Castle in 1735; and created Earl of Portsmouth, by patent, on the 11th of April 1743, 17th of George II. The Earl died on Nov. 23rd, 1762, and was buried at Farley.[1]

His Lordship sat in Parliament for the county of Hants, March 17th, 1714-15; he also became one of the members for Andover. He had no children by his second union; but by Lady Bridget he had issue—1st, Bridget, born February 20th, 1716, and died unmarried, June 26th, 1736; 2nd, John Wallop, Viscount Lymington, who was born on the 3rd of August 1718, and who married, in 1740, Catherine, daughter and heir of John Conduit, Esq., a niece of Sir Isaac Newton, to whom Sir Isaac gave an estate at Kensington, which was ultimately sold by the Earl of Portsmouth. Sir Isaac was very partial to his nephew, Mr. John Conduit, who succeeded him as master and warden in the Mint. When Sir David Brewster was preparing his *Life of Sir Isaac Newton*, he, in 1837, applied to the Honble. Newton Fellowes, one of the trustees of the Earl of Portsmouth, for permission to inspect the MSS. and Correspondence of Newton, which had come into the possession of the Portsmouth family

---

had only one son, who was created Duke of Richmond. (Warner's *Hampshire*, p. 102.)

Louisa de Querovaille, or Queroville, Duchess of Portsmouth, was sent over to England by Lewis XIV, in the train of the Duchess of Orleans, to bind Charles II to the French interest; this she did effectually, and the business of the English Court was constantly carried on in subserviency to that of France. She occasionally dissembled love, the vapours, or sickness, and rarely ever failed of working the easy monarch to her point. Her polite manners and agreeable temper rivetted the chains which her personal charms had imposed upon him; she had the first place in his affections, and he continued to love her to the day of his death. Her beauty, which was not of the most delicate kind, seemed to be very little impaired at seventy years of age. She died Nov. 1734, aged 89. (*Granger.*)

[1] Berry's *Hampshire Genealogies*, part 1, p. 43.

through Miss Conduit. These papers are carefully preserved, and although there are no reasons for believing that they contain any matter which can be considered peculiarly interesting to science, nevertheless, being the correspondence of so eminent a philosopher as Newton the papers will always be regarded as precious. One of these documents, in the handwriting of Mr. Conduit, published by Mr. Turnor in his *Collections*, p. 172, contains a remarkable conversation of Sir Isaac Newton with Mr. Conduit, in which are crudely detailed some "conjectures" which had come into the mind of the great astronomer concerning the constitution of the planetary bodies. A lengthened account of the Newton Manuscripts (relating to Sir Isaac Newton and the Mint) may be seen in the Eighth *Report* of the Historical MSS. Commission.

John Wallop, Esq., commonly called Lord Viscount Lymington, was a member for Andover in 1747 and 1748; and he died on April the 15th, 1749, leaving—1st, John, who became the *second* Earl; 2nd, Henry, who was Groom of the Bedchamber to King George III, and who died in 1794; 3rd, Barton, who was born in 1747, and who married, in 1771, Miss Camilla Powlett Smith, of Cruxeaston, Hants. Barton Wallop was Master of Magdalen College, Cambridge. He left (with a daughter Urania, wife of the Rev. Henry Wake) a posthumous son, William Barton, a captain in the army, who married Miss Ward, and died in 1824.

Some other children were descended from John, the *first* Earl, viz.: 3rd, Borlase Wallop, born June 3rd, 1720. He served in the Foot Guards, and as Aide-de-Camp to General Wentworth, at Carthagena, in 1741, and died the same year, unmarried. There was, 4th, a daughter Mary; and, 5th, Charles Wallop, born December 12th, 1722, and who, 1747, was elected a member of Parliament for Whitchurch, Hants. He died unmarried, August 11th, 1771; 6th, Anne, who died March 7th, 1759; 7th, Bluet Wallop, born April 27th, 1726: he was Page of Honour to the King, whom he attended in the campaign in Flanders; and was present at Culloden under the Duke of Cumberland. He was member for Newport, Isle of Wight, in 1747, and died, aged 23, June 6th, 1749; 8th, Elizabeth; 9th, Henry; and, 10th, Bennet Wallop, who died infants.

John, the *second* Earl, was born in 1742. He married, on August the 27th, 1763, Urania, daughter of Coulson Fellows, Esq., of Hampstead, Middlesex, and of Eggesford, Devonshire. Mr. Fellows was returned a member for Huntingdonshire from 1741 to 1754. The Earl died on the 16th of May, 1797, and left issue—John Charles, the *third* Earl; Newton, the *fourth* Earl; Coulson, who married, April 2nd, 1802, Catherine Townley, only daughter of Maurice

Keatinge, Esq., and died August 31st, 1807. Urania-Anabella, died December 17th, 1844; Henrietta-Dorothea, who married, 19th January 1816, the Rev. John Comyns Churchill, and died, 10th June 1862. Berry notices other children, viz. : William Fellows Wallop, Camilla-Mary, and Emma Maria Wallop.

John, the *second* Earl of Portsmouth was succeeded by his eldest son, John Charles Wallop, who became possessed of the Eggesford property by the maternal line.

The following entry refers to John, *second* Earl of Portsmouth. *Recoveries*, Mich., 4th Geo. III, 1763 :—

"Recovery by Henry Arthur Earl of Powis, against Joseph Banks, Esq., of the Manors of Husborne Priors, Swampton, Over Wallop, etc., and lands, tenements, rents, common of pasture, and free fishery in Husborne Priors, Swampton, Egbury, Binley, Stoake, Week, Wadweek, Dunley, *alias* Doundley, and many other places, including St. Mary Bourne. John Earl of Portsmouth was vouchee."

The *third* Earl was born on the 18th December 1767. He was twice married—first, to the Hon. Grace Norton, sister to William, Lord Grantley, on the 19th November 1799; but she dying without issue on the 15th of November 1813, a second union followed, which led to some remarkable events. The Earl's second wife was Anne, the eldest daughter of John Hanson, Esq., of Bloomsbury Place, London. The marriage took place on March 7th, 1815; but it was annulled by a decree of the Lord Chancellor in 1828. A daughter was the issue of this marriage, who was declared illegitimate. The Earl lived at Hurstbourne Park until the time of his death; but he was pronounced by the verdict of an inquisition as not of sound mind. His life was quite harmless, his time being chiefly employed in riding about and taking part with his neighbours, cottagers or otherwise, in any small social matters. He took great interest in all weddings and christenings at the parish church, and was commonly to be seen at the village festivals and sheep-shearings. He was also fond of bell-ringing, and was often present in the belfry, and superintended the ringing on festive occasions. His mode of conveyance from place to place was by means of a heavy, well-made oak cart, in shape similar to the ordinary farmer's field-cart, in which he sat surrounded with rugs, with his back resting against the high head-piece, and his feet towards the foot-board. His attendant and driver for many years was William Tayler, an intelligent labourer, who lived in a cottage at Prats Down, close alongside of the park. In driving, Tayler sat on the head of the cart, carrying a carter's whip, which was an object of interest to the Earl. And of the horse which drew the vehicle the Earl was justly proud, it being a handsome cob of the Suffolk breed, and of the colour of the genuine Suffolk "Punch." The Earl was a hale, robust-looking man, and not without dignity, as anyone was made to feel who was unduly free in accosting him. His medical attendant at Hurstbourne House was for some years a Dr. Greenhead, whose family, chiefly consisting of daughters, afterwards formed the well-known "Cremona Band", and gave concerts with stringed instruments at some of the principal towns in the south of England. John Charles, the *third* Earl, died July 14th, 1853, and was succeeded by his brother—

Newton, the *fourth* Earl, who was born on the 26th June 1772. On succeeding to the estates of his maternal uncle, Henry Arthur Fellowes, Esq., of Eggesford, he, by licence bearing date the 7th August 1794, as Newton Wallop, second son of John, Earl of Portsmouth, and his issue, was authorised to take the surname and bear the arms of Fellowes only, consequently the arms of Fellowes were exemplified by him, and were to be borne by his issue. The Earl married, first, January 30th, 1795, Frances, fourth daughter of the Rev. Castel Sherrard, and by her he had issue—1st, Henry Arthur Wallop, born 1799; and died, unmarried, 17th February 1847; 2nd, Henrietta Caroline, married, 14th December 1826, to Joseph Chichester Nagle, Esq., of Calverleigh, Devon, and died January 2nd, 1880. Her husband died eight hours afterwards.

His Lordship, the *fourth* Earl, married, secondly, 24th June 1820, Catherine, second daughter of Hugh, first Earl Fortesque, and by her (who died 17th April 1854) had—1st, Isaac Newton, the present, and *fifth* Earl, and three daughters—1st, Catherine, who married, on the 29th July 1843, Seymour Phillips Allen, Esq., Cresselly, co. Pembroke, grandson of Lord Robert Seymour, and has issue; 2nd, Hester Urania, who married, October 26th, 1847, Ralph Merrik Leeke, Esq., of Longford Hall, Salop, and has issue; 3rd, Camilla Eleanor, who married, 8th June 1852, the Honble. Dudley Fortesque, late M.P. for Andover.

The *fourth* Earl died on the 9th January 1854, and was succeeded by his surviving son, Isaac Newton, the *fifth*, and present Earl; who, on inheriting his title, adopted the *surname* and *arms* of Wallop.

Isaac Newton Wallop, Earl of Portsmouth, Viscount Lymington, and Baron Wallop of Farley Wallop, co. Southampton, was born on the 11th of January 1825, and became the *fifth* Earl at the decease of his father, on the 9th January 1854. He married, on the 15th February 1855, Lady Eveline Herbert, sister of the Earl of Carnarvon, and has issue—1st, Newton, Viscount Lymington, formerly M.P. for Barnstaple; and in 1886 elected M.P. for the South Moulton Division of Devonshire. He was born on the 19th Jan. 1856, and married

Beatrice Mary, daughter of Sir Joseph Pease, M.P.; 2nd, John Fellowes, Private Secretary to the Governor of Tasmania, born December 27th, 1859; 3rd, Oliver Henry, born 13th January 1861; 4th, Robert Gerard Valoynes, born 6th July 1864; 5th, Arthur George Edward, born 12th October 1867; 6th, Frederick Henry Arthur, born 16th February 1870. Daughters—1st, Catherine Henrietta, born 1856; married, 7th December 1876, Charles George Milnes Gaskell, Esq., of Thornes House, Wakefield, and of Wenlock Abbey, Shropshire, and has issue; 2nd, Eveline Camilla, born 1858; 3rd, Rosamund Alicia, born 1861, married, 15th February 1882, Augustus Langham Christie, Esq., eldest son of William Langham Christie, Esq., of Glyndebourne, Sussex, and Tapeley Park, co. Devon; 4th, Dorothea Hester Bluet, born 1863; 5th, Gwendolen Margaret, born 1866; 6th, Henrietta Anne, born May 29th, 1872.

CREATIONS.—Viscount, etc., 11th June 1720; Earl, 11th April 1743.[1]

ARMS.—Fellowes: *Az.*, a fesse indented *erm.*, between three lion's heads erased *or*, murally crowned *arg.*

CREST.—A lion's head, erased, *or*, murally crowned, *arg.*, and gorged with a collar indented *erm.*

ARMS OF WALLOP (which the present Earl bears).—*Arg.*, a bend wavy *sa.*

CREST.—A mermaid, holding in her sinister hand a mirror, in the other a comb, all ppr.

SUPPORTERS.—Two chamois or wild goats *sa.*

MOTTO.—*En suivant la vérité.*

SEATS.—Hurstbourne Park, co. Southampton, and Eggesford House, co. Devon.

---

[1] Notices of the pedigree of the Wallop family have been obtained from Richard Warner's *History of Hampshire*, 1789; and from Burke's *Peerage, Baronetage, and Knightage*, 1883.

Hurstbourne Park.

The finely wooded demesne surrounding the mansion of the Earl of Portsmouth consists of about one thousand acres, in the parishes of Hurstbourne Priors and Whitchurch, the area in the latter parish being about forty acres. The ground undulates, but rises boldly from the east, south, and west, becoming more richly wooded in the centre of the park, the timber here extending away in fine avenues of trees, in which the elm, beech, and chestnut are conspicuous. Lofty ashes are observable; and the general foliage is enriched by the presence of the edible chestnut; while the under-shrubs consist mostly of whitethorns, of which some are bare and gnarled with age. Below all the common bracken, and the hardy male fern, reach sufficient stature to shelter the fallow-deer with which the park is richly stocked. The arrangement of the timber of to-day must have been due to the ancestors of the present proprietor, as the park appears not to have been so densely furnished when the old mansion known as the "Grange" occupied a site at the foot of the sharp elevation now clothed with a belt of beeches, at a short distance on the north-east and somewhat above the level of the graveyard of the village church, which closely joined it. The house appears to have faced south, or somewhat south-west; and beyond a terrace in the front of the mansion stretched a sheet of water, which was introduced by the diversion of the Upper Test river, which ran west of the present stream. This adaptation was carried out in the time of William III,[1] after the Dutch fashion, in order to enhance the picturesque surroundings of the residence. A weir appears to have occupied the water at its south end, of which there is evidence in the name of a meadow, known as "Weir meadow". Almost parallel to the mansion on the rising ground west of the church stood the home farm; and at a short distance northward of the farm was seen the manorial mill. The site of the house appears on the six-inch Ordnance Map, and it there bears the title of "The Grange".

There is a painting of the old house in the "Wallop" room of the present mansion, executed somewhat after the early Dutch style, with perhaps no great accuracy of detail as regards perspective. It conveys the idea of the building having stood more elevated than one would imagine from its known site; but this is due probably to the comparative absence of timber in the picture on the adjoining eleva-

---

[1] White, *Post Office Directory of Hants, Hurstbourne Priors.*

tions. On the rising ground at the back of the Grange, and rather in the line of the present mansion, stood a curious-looking retreat, a kind of summer-house or tea-room, which still traditionally bears the name of "Chinese-house", from one of the rooms being lined with Dutch tiles. The Grange of the picture has the appearance of a house that had undergone alterations at several periods. It has a plain centre with ornamental wings after the Italian, which were probably seventeenth century additions. The wings bear a cupola on each roof; and a denticulated moulding traverses the front of each wing at the level of the spring of the window-arch. And the windows have proportionately great height, with semicircular heads, implying that the apartments within were lofty. The chimneys of the centre are plain structures extending in a straight line along the roof, as do a string of dormer-windows in the centre of the roof, and I should imagine indicate that this portion of the building could not be later than the beginning of the sixteenth century. I have no doubt that either part of the same, or an older structure, stood on the spot at a much earlier date, as I have furnished a notice that a house called the Grange was in existence in 1386, reign of Richard II. But there is a notice of the Grange in 1255, 40th of Henry III. (*Pleas of the Crown.*)

During the time that the manor appertained to the Priory of St. Swithin, there is no doubt, from the tenor of the notices of that period, that it was a country residence of the Prior when he came among his vassals. It has been reported to me that there was a retreat close by known as the "Prior's Walk"; and the old house is commonly spoken of as the "Priory". In the *Thesaurus* of Acton, of the 8th of King Stephen, the place is called the Priory. And in the time of Elizabeth, 1594, there is a Bill, Wilde *v.* Goulding, touching lands held of the manor of *Hurstbourne Priory*. Remains of the foundations of an ancient structure are still observable where the water issues from the culverts underneath the private road over the river-course at the back of the church; and a few years ago I observed fragments of stone-work lying in the shallows of the river at this point. The ecclesiastical establishments of that time were necessitated to be completely self-dependent in all their domestic arrangements. At Hurstbourne a bee-house stands now where, or near where, an apiary must have stood since probably the days of the Saxons. The apiary is so constructed that the bee-master can cultivate his hives on the roof while living in the apartments underneath. Malt-house, brewery, bakery, a vineyard and winepress, fish-ponds, home-farm, and mill were all adjuncts to the manorial estates of the Middle Ages.

We find that, in 1263, time of Henry III, Ralph le Fauconer, otherwise Fawconer, held property at Hurstbourne, and later other members of the same family, notably John le Fawconer, in the reign of Edward III, William le Fawconer in 1437, and Richard Fawconer in 1552. The manor was then divided into *interius* and *exterius*, the latter bearing also the title of Fawconer's manor. The residence of the manor was called " Court-place", *alias* " Court-Heys"; and as the Fawconers held *exterius*, or Fawconer's manor, the family must have lived at Court-place. Week-house, in the parish of St. Mary Bourne, is stated as the manor-house appertaining to Fawconer's manor, near which residence there is a site known as Court-garden, which plainly expresses that it was the garden of the manor-house at the time it was a more important residence. The name Court-place evidently refers to the holding of the manor-courts there. It will be observed in the account of the tithings that previous to 1612, Edward Lord Beauchamp occupied " Weeke", and that immediately after it came into the occupation of Paul Alexander. Richard Fawconer, in 1552, possessed a house and land in Hurstbourne, which afterwards became the property of Richard Kingsmill, and were held by him as "Kingesmilles house and demesne lands".

In 1541, Ellis Wynne held the custody of the manor (including both *interius* and *exterius*), and most likely lived at the Grange. John Fitz-Williams de Kingesley was Governor of the Chief House and Park of Hurstbourne Priors, and Steward of the Manor under the King (Edward VI), in 1551-2, and he must have occupied the Grange. The manor was held by the Duke of Somerset from the 1st of Edward VI, 1547, until 1552, when it came into the hands of Sir John Gate. This was one year after the death of Somerset; and probably was obtained by him for the part he took in assisting the Duke of Northumberland in disposing of his rival Somerset. Whether Sir John Gate lived at the Grange there is nothing beyond the fact that he possessed the property to determine. The estate was sold to the Oxenbridges in 1558; and some members of the family lived at the Grange till 1634, when the manor was bought by Sir Henry Wallop of Farley, whose family, or some of their dependants, John Heath having occupied the place in 1657, became the occupants of the Grange until the present mansion was built in 1785.

The modern residence is in the Italian style, and is the work of John, the second Earl of Portsmouth. It was built by Mr. Meadows in 1785, after designs by James Wyatt,[1] who was at that time the fashionable architect. It consists of a centre and two uniform wings, connected by colonnades. The east wing contains a handsome library and chapel, the west one is chiefly occupied by the offices and

---

[1] Brailey and Britton, *Beauties of England and Wales*, p. 234.

servants' rooms, while the centre, constituting the general family residence, has some noble apartments. The shrubberies at the posterior are tastefully designed and planted, and the stables and other out-offices are such as befit the character of the mansion. The house stands on a commanding elevation, considerably above the level of the site of the old house, and on the south and west extends wide and varied scenery, embracing most of the timber-clothed elevations standing between it and Winchester.

Members of Parliament.

ANDOVER.

Among the parliamentary representatives of the Borough of Andover appear the names of some members of the ancient family of Wallop, the ancestors of the Earl of Portsmouth. It appears from the Government "Blue Books" that Andover returned members from the time of Edward I, 1295. From the year 1307 until 1586 there is no mention of any member being returned for the Borough; and this is probably due to the fact that, in earlier times the burgesses being called on to pay the expenses of their parliamentary representatives, they did not think it advisable to send any.

1623-4, Jan. 7.	Robert Wallopp, Esq.
1625, April 29.	Sir Henry Wallop, Knight.
1627-8, Feb. 29.	Robert Wallop, Esq.
1639-40, March 12.	Do.
1640, Oct. 19.	Do.
1714-15, Jan. 29.	John Wallop, Esq., Farley Wallop.
1715, April 1.	James Brudenell, Esq., *vice* John Wallop, Esq., who elected to serve for the County of Southampton.
1741, May 5.	John Wallop, Esq.
1747, June 29.	John Wallop, Esq., commonly called Lord Viscount Lymington.
1749, Nov. 25.	John Griffin Griffin, Esq., *vice* John Wallop, deceased.
1796, May 25.	Coulson Wallop, Esq.
1802, July 5.	Newton Fellows, Esq.
1806, Oct. 31.	Do.
1807, May 5.	Do.
1812, Oct. 6.	Do.
1818, June 18.	Do.
1831, May 2.	Henry Arthur Wallop Fellowes, Esq.
1832, Dec. 10.	Do.

Members of Parliament.

WHITCHURCH, HANTS.

The borough of Whitchurch sent two members to Parliament from the 28th of Elizabeth until 1832, when it was, jointly with Ludgershall and Stockbridge, disfranchised by the Reform Act. The following list comprehends some members of the families of Oxenbridge and Wallop, who held the manor of Hurstbourne Priors.

1620-1. Sir Robert Oxenbridge, Knt.

1623-4. Sir Henry Wallop, Knt.

1625. Sir Robert Oxenbridge, Knt.

1625-6. Do.

1660. Robert Wallop, Esq., Farley Wallop.

1660, June 18. Henry Wallop, Esq., Farley Wallop, *vice* Robert Wallop, who was discharged from attendance.

1661. Henry Wallop, Esq., Farley Wallop.

1673-4. Richard Ayliffe, Esq., Whitchurch, *vice* Henry Wallop, Esq., deceased.

1678-9. Henry Wallop, Esq.

1679. Do.

1681. Do.

1685. Do.

1688-9. Do.

1689-90. Do.

1691-2. Christopher Stokes, Esq., Whitchurch, *vice* Henry Wallop, Esq., deceased.

1741. John Wallop, Esq.

1741-2. William Stopher, Esq., *vice* John Wallop, Esq., who elected to serve for Andover.

1747. Charles Wallop, Esq.

1768. Henry Wallop, Esq., Hanover Square, Middlesex.

Sheriffs of Hampshire.

APPERTAINING TO HURSTBOURNE PRIORS MANOR.[1]

Dandely, or Daundely.

Robertus Daundelin	- - -	13th Edward III.
Robertus de Daundelin	- - -	14th do.
Willielmus Audele (Andele?)	- - -	21st and 23rd Richard II.
Robertus Doniley[2] (Dandely?)	- - -	13th Henry VI.

Brokas, or Brocas.

Willielmus Brokas	- - -	14th Henry VI.
Bernard do.	- - -	35th do.
Johannes do.	- - -	22nd Edward IV.
Bernard Brocas	- - -	30th George II.

Fauconer, or Fawconer.

Willielmus Fauconer	- - -	16th Henry VI.

Lister.

Michael Lister	-	Mil.	- 37th Henry VIII.
Michael Lister	-	-	- 3rd Edward VI.

Oxenbridge.

Robertus Oxenbridge	-	Mil.	- 10th Elizabeth.
Robertus Oxenbridge	-	Arm.	- 38th do.

Wallop.

Johannes[3] Wallop	-	Arm.	- 33rd Henry VI.
Johannes Wallop	-	Arm.	- 1st Edward IV.
Richardus Wallop	-	Arm.	- 17th Henry VII.
Robertus Wallop	-	Arm.	- 1st Henry VIII.
Robertus Wallop	-	Arm.	- 7th Henry VIII.
Robertus Wallop	-	Arm.	- 15th Henry VIII.
Oliverus Wallop	-	Mil.	- 5th and 6th Philip and Mary.
Oliverus Wallop	-	Mil.	- 1st Elizabeth.
Willielmus Wallop[3]	-	Arm.	- 42nd do.
Henricus Wallop	-	Arm.	- 44th do.
Henricus Wallop	-	Mil.	- 2nd James I.
Henricus Wallop	-	Mil.	- 5th Charles I.
John Wallop	-	Mil.	- 6th William and Mary.

[1] William Berry, *Genealogies, County of Hants*, Part II, 1833.

[2] Doniley sounds like Dandely, and might refer to a member of that family, as the name is so variously spelt.

[3] The first is the 30th Henry VI, and the second 41st of Elizabeth, according to the *Topographer*, 1789.

The Summerhaugh.

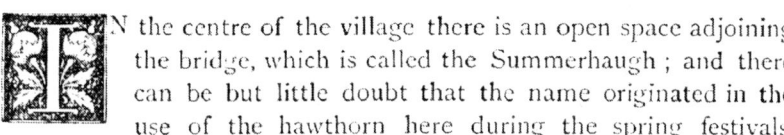

IN the centre of the village there is an open space adjoining the bridge, which is called the Summerhaugh; and there can be but little doubt that the name originated in the use of the hawthorn here during the spring festivals. *Haw*, from the Anglo-Saxon *haga*,[1] a hedge, whence "*haglia*" or *haghaw*, the provincial name of the berry of the hawthorn. Aged people remembered when the place was decorated with green boughs, and a Maypole was erected at Whitsuntide. Similar rejoicings were conducted at Hurstbourne Tarrant, also with a Maypole, which I recollect was in existence at Mr. Stephen Knight's, the "Cooper's Arms", in 1850. It was painted white, with a spiral coil of blue round it from base to apex.

The blowing of horns, an old custom on May-day, had its survival at St. Mary Bourne, fifty years ago, in boys making "May-horns" of willow-bark twisted in a spiral manner. But the May-day rejoicings at that time had dwindled down to a band of half-washed chimney-sweeps decorated with coloured papers and ribbons, who danced round a walking bower, which enclosed a female of their order, the representative probably of Maid Marian of the olden times. They extracted what music could be elicited from the contact of shovels and brushes. Later, our village festival survived as "Garland Day", when all that remained to tell of the rejoicings of the past were little children bearing miniature bowers from house to house, chanting "Please to see my garland".

The annual revel was held in the Summerhaugh on what is

---

[1] Bosworth, *Anglo-Saxon Dictionary*; also *Hawthorn, the thorn of haws, hayes or hedges*, A.-S. *hagaðorn* or *hegeðorn*, an interesting word, as being a testimony to the use of hedges, and the appropriation of plots of land, from a very early period. (R. C. A. Prior, M.D., *Popular Names of British Plants*, p. 105.)

known as "Bourne Revel Monday", and the Monday following it was the appointed day of the revel at Hurstbourne Tarrant. The Sunday preceding it was regarded as the first day of the feast, and such there is no doubt was the case in the early days of the festival. Its observance on Sunday appears to associate the feast with the dedication of the parish church, although no known records are extant in corroboration of this.

Although the origin of feasts in villages—in some instances called Wakes, in others, where sports and pastimes have been added, Revels—is wrapped in some obscurity, it is generally understood that such gatherings were instituted in honour of the patron-saints of the churches; and that the early festivals, if they were not so at the outset, ultimately became dedication rejoicings. Historically, there is no doubt that fairs were held in England in Roman times; and that they were afterwards introduced into the village-life of the Saxons. But, in so far as they assumed a familiar shape, and became a settled usage, they were due to the Normans. They appear to have been initiated by prescription, without any special authority, and were associated with religious observances under the sanction and patronage of the Church, eventually becoming controlled by the Church, to which establishment the tolls derived from stalls, etc., furnished a fertile source of revenue. Subsequently they became linked more directly under the authority of the Crown, royal charters being instituted in regulation of the times for holding fairs, in giving liberty of sale of certain wares, the appointment of tolls, fines, etc., and also for granting power to introduce new markets and fairs. Blackstone says:—" Fairs and markets, with the tolls belonging to them, can only be set up by virtue of the royal grant, or by long and immemorial usage and prescription, which presupposes such a grant."

Fair introduces another phase of these proceedings. The festival of the beginning in some cases merged into a mart or fair of wide proportions. As villages grew into towns, and new places sprung up, the increasing populations needed the introduction of food and wares from distant localities in order to the purchase of their yearly supplies; and as sufficient space was requisite, advantage was taken of the open hills and neighbouring downs. Whence we have Tan Hill fair in Wiltshire, Weyhill fair or fairs near Andover, and St. Giles's fair, near Winchester. This last, in the time of Henry III, extended to sixteen days. It was instituted by a charter of William Rufus, who gave it by way of revenue to Bishop Wakelyn, to be held for three whole days. In the time of Edward III, 1349, the Bishop of Winchester had granted to him by charter the privileges and profits of this fair.[1] The nuclei of these gatherings on hills probably had their initiation in processions and festivals in honour of pagan deities. The "Mop" or Statute fairs held at Michaelmas, in Hampshire, Wiltshire, and Berkshire, brought together servants seeking to be hired, wearing badges of their callings; the cowherd, carter, and shepherd being each distinguished by some article associated with his labour. And in earlier times bricklayers, carpenters, and other mechanics assembled in rows, everyone bearing some instrument used in his trade.

Whatever might have been the appointed times of holding these festivals, it is clear from what followed that they were "kept" much too frequently. At that period the churchyards were not properly fenced, and the stalls for the sale of wares were erected, and the revelry was conducted, in the churchyards and around them, and excesses took place within the buildings, to the detriment of secular matters, and to the disregard of the decency and reverence which was due to buildings erected for religious observances. The churches were strewed with rushes on those occasions, as there was no sort of flooring save the naked earth.[2]

Stringent enactments were consequently passed restraining the meetings, and appointing proper times for holding them. Thus, by the *Statute of Wynton* (Winchester), attributed to the reign of Edward I, but probably of earlier date, it was enacted (c. 6)—

"And the King commandeth and forbiddeth that from henceforth neither Fairs nor Markets be kept in the Churchyard for the Honour of the Church."[3]

1321. Reign of Edward II.

There is supposed to have been enacted that no officer of the Crown should hold inquest of Markets, fairs, tolls, etc., levied without licence of the King.

1328. Act, 2nd Edward III, c. 15.

"No person shall keep a fair longer than he ought to do"; and 1331, Edward III, c. 5, "The Penalty if any do sell Wares at a Fair after it is ended."

1448. Henry VI, 27th of, c. 5.

Act directed against "the scandal of holding Fairs and Markets on Sundays, and on High Feast Days", which practice had in earlier times been very general.

Also by an *Act of Convocation*, passed by Henry VIII, in the year 1536, reducing the frequency of carrying out Feasts.

The Church of St. Mary Bourne is dedicated to St. Peter the

---

[1] G. W. Kitchin, D.D., *A Charter of Edward III, confirming and enlarging the Privileges of St. Giles's Fair, Winchester*, 1349.

[2] At the Feast of the Dedication in ancient times the parishioners brought rushes wherewith to strew the church; and from this the festivity itself obtained the name of "Rush-bearing". (Brand's *Popular Antiquities*, p. 298.)

[3] C. Walford, F.S.A., *Fairs Past and Present*, p. 25.

Apostle, whose festival falls on the 29th of June[1]; and as it was the custom to hold the dedication festivals on the Sundays following the dedication days, the first Sunday in July appears to properly represent the day known as "Bourne Revel Sunday". But the traditional day of the revel has always been understood to come on the first Monday following the 12th of "Old July". The difference in date might be due to the alteration of the Calendar in 1752[2]; at all events the date of St. Peter's day and the present date of the feast-day do not meet the requirements of the case. It is probable that the date was altered in later times to suit the convenience of the supporters of the revel. In whatever way the dates might have fallen out of order, could we but glance back into the thirteenth century it is likely we should see the manorial villeins setting up the booths for the feast in honour of their patron-saint, and dragging huge boughs into the church for the purpose of decoration, as regularly as the anniversary came round. The old custom was observed at St. Mary Bourne, up to the discontinuance of the revel, of the villagers arraying themselves in their holiday attire, and visiting from house to house for the purpose of rejoicing.

St. Mary, as an adjunct to the place-name, in its association with the brook (St. Mary's burn or brook), conveys the impression that it was intended as an invocation to her as the patron-saint for the flowing of the water in the early spring; or as a thanks-offering for the supply, following its deprivation during the autumn or winter, the stream being intermittent. At the time of fixing the name very little could have been known concerning the relation of effect to cause; such a simple matter as a periodic waterflow was commonly ascribed to supernatural influence. In the thirteenth century it is written "St. Maries Borne", which suggests what has just been stated. Wells and springs in early Catholic times were commonly dedicated to saints. There was an abundance of holy wells and sacred springs, which had their patron-saints, and the waters were believed to possess healing qualities. The fountains were consecrated and blest, spirits were thought to preside over them, and feasts were held in their honour after the manner of the *Fontinalia* of ancient Rome, which were religious feasts in honour of the water-nymphs, when the springs were crowned with flowers, and nosegays were thrown into them.

[1] The custom of kindling fires on elevated places, called *Baal-fires*, in honour of *Beltan*, was observed in early times on St. Peter's Day. (Sinclair, *Statistical Account of Scotland*.)

The following appear to be the dates associated with St. Peter:—Peter and Paul, SS., Ap., June 29th; Peter—Octave, July 6th; Peter, St., *ad Vincula*, Aug. 1st; Peter, *in Cathedra*, Feb. 22nd. (W. D. Selby, *The Jubilee Date-Book*.)

[2] The new style was adopted in Great Britain and Ireland in 1752; but it was introduced by Pope Gregory XIII and adopted in other countries as early as 1582.

Probably something of the kind was carried on at St. Mary Bourne in early times.

It was the custom from time immemorial of pedlars and petty hawkers to bring their wares, and expose them for sale; but the habit has now dwindled down to the introduction of stalls for the sale of toys and sweets for children, at places where these gatherings are not wholly abandoned. A few such vendors make their appearance at St. Mary Bourne, at a club named in commemoration of the early festival the "Bourne Revel Club". This club is held on the first Monday after the 12th of July, which, as we have seen, is regarded as the proper day of the revel. The clergy in the olden time conducted services and preached both before and during the festivals, a practice which still has its survivals in the services which are held at the annual meetings of village benefit-societies.

The revel associated with the feast has been discontinued for over sixty years; but before that period it was in a waning condition. The stage on which "single-stick" and wrestling were conducted was erected over the stream opposite the "Plough" inn. There was then no bridge for horse and waggon traffic; but simply a ford, and a wooden structure for foot-people, with a turnstile at one end to prevent any but pedestrians using it. The "sports" lingered for several days; and were the means of calling together an assemblage of gipsies, vagabonds, and "gamesters", as they were called, who were regular frequenters of the revels for the purpose of contending for the prizes. The prizes consisted chiefly of hats, of the value of half-a-guinea. Sometimes a "gold-laced hat" for "old gamesters" was offered; and small prizes were given to those who succeeded in breaking one head. A head was not considered broken unless the blood flowed an inch. An umpire, vulgarly called "umsher", directed the proceedings. When the play became irregular or languid he suspended it for a time by crying "bout"; and after a short pause it was resumed on his calling "play". On an appeal, if successful, he called "blood", if not, it was met with "no head", or "play on". In all stage-matters his decision was final; although, as one may imagine, in such society it was often violently cavilled at. Records of the revel proceedings have not been retained; but the names of the following gamesters have been reported to me as having been present at the revel at St. Mary Bourne, or who were accustomed to attend similar meetings in the neighbouring county of Berkshire:—

Thomas Black, Berks.
Samuel Ayres.
Harry Seeley.
Simon Stone.
George Stacey.

Michael Preston, Berks.
David Goodyear, Hants.
Uriah Wall, Somerset.
...... Giles, Purton, Wilts.
Maurice Pope, Hants.

Among the St. Mary Bourne residents who engaged in these contests some members of the Bunce and Goodyear families are mentioned; one of the latter family, David Goodyear, whose name appears on the list, died in the lunatic asylum, Fareham, the injuries he had received to the head at the revels having in his later days caused disease to the brain. In reply to an inquiry, he said he believed his malady was due to "clouts on the head he had received on the stage". Two men named Bantam and Wheeler of Longparish contended at the revels, and a rivalry existed between them, which they arranged to determine at one of the Hurstbourne revels, when Wheeler had an eye knocked out during the encounter. The chief wrestlers at the later revels were members of the Annett family of Hurstbourne Tarrant; but "Farmer" Holdway of Stoke, better known as "Holdey", engaged in the wrestling matches, and would exhibit the scars on his legs which he had received from kicks during his early encounters. Of the others named on the list Black and Ayres were of the fraternity of gipsies. Simon Stone, who frequented most of the Berkshire and Wiltshire revels, in his best days was thought to have had no equal at "backsword-playing"; and George Stacey was equally noted with the "sticks" and as a wrestler. But Seeley was considered a remarkably cool, quiet player, and probably was the equal of any. He has been immortalised by Mr. Thomas Hughes, in his description of Seeley's method of conducting a match on White Horse Hill, Berks, at the "Scouring of the White Horse". He writes:—"But nothing puts out old Harry Seeley; no upper cut can reach his face, for his head is thrown well back, and his guard is like a rock; and though the old blue shirt is cut through and through, he makes no more of the welts of the heavy stick than if it were a cat's tail. Between the bouts his face is cheery and confident, and he tells his friends to 'hold their noise, and let him alone to tackle the chap', as he hands round his basket for the abounding coppers." The "basket" was the guard to the hand on the hilt of the stick.

The same men, or rather those who happened to be in the district, attended the revel at Hurstbourne Tarrant on the following Monday. And as a sample of the kind of amusement usual at these meetings I give the following account of a "backswording match" at Hurstbourne Revel, published in the pages of the *Wiltshire Archæological and Natural History Magazine*,[1] by the Rev. Canon Jackson, who was at that time Curate of the neighbouring hamlet of Combe, Hants. The Rev. Canon writes:—" It was during my stay at Combe

[1] Notes on the Border of Wilts and Hants; by the Rev. J. E. Jackson, F.S.A., vol. xxi, p. 334.

that I was witness to a rustic amusement, once very popular, but of which I have heard nothing for so many years that I fancy it must have nearly died out. If so, it becomes an archæological reminiscence. This was then called a backswording match; the same pastime which in one of his 'Spectator' papers Addison says he saw at Bath in 1703. He describes it as 'a ring of cudgel-players, who were breaking one another's heads in order to make some impression on their mistresses' hearts.' I saw it in 1825, at a revel at Hurstbourne, halfway between Combe and Andover. In the middle of the village, on an open space, a wooden stage was erected, about three feet high from the ground, fenced with ropes to protect the combatants from being thrown or falling off. What the prize at Hurstbourne was, whether a mistress's heart, or a cheese, a new hat, or a purse of money, I do not remember; but it ought to have been something singularly attractive, the Queen of Beauty should have been eminently beautiful, the cheese of prime quality, the hat very smart, or the purse very heavy, to induce fellows to stand up and have their heads cracked in the way I saw done for the amusement of a gaping crowd. Of that crowd of gapers I confess with shame that I was one: but at that time of life it was looked upon as fun; and the more so because the combatants themselves seemed to consider it in much the same light. These village gladiators fought in pairs, in turns, and the winner was he who succeeded in breaking most heads, or, in breaking the head of him who had broken most others. The three principal performers were: (1) a stupid raw youth, who represented Wiltshire; (2) a short, thick-set quiet little man, who stood for Somerset; and (3) the Hampshire hero (the favourite of course), a thin wiry dark-featured gypsy, with aquiline nose and the eye of a hawk, who skipped about as if he were made of gutta-percha. They fought bare-headed, with the left arm fastened to the waist, so that they might not use it to ward off blows. To hit an opponent on the face was against rules; but to hit him on the top of the head was the grand point, and the grandest of all to hit him so as to produce blood. Never shall I forget that gypsy's keen eye looking out for the effect of his blow, and how joyfully, when he saw it, he called out 'Blood', and dropped his weapon. The Wiltshire man was very soon disposed of, but when it came to the final match, the sturdy cautious little man cracked the gypsy's head, and Somerset won the day."

In the Summerhaugh, close to the bridge, in front of the paling of the late Mr. Henry Poore's dwelling, appropriately stood the village Stocks. I well remember the apparatus, which consisted (Plate IX, fig. 2) of a pair of leg-holds, with the usual iron loops and fastenings, on each side of a central whipping-post, the post being provided at

Pl. IX

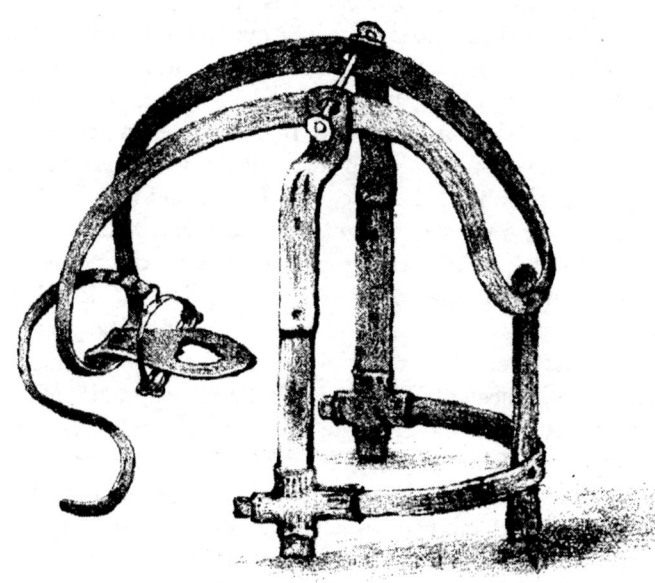

1

its upper part with wrist-bolts on either side, in which the culprit's hands were secured while undergoing the process of flagellation. In its latter days the instrument had become rickety, and had lost its leg-holds on one side; but in its perfect state it was as represented on the plate. Although for some years it had ceased to be employed as an instrument of punishment, and was regarded rather as an object of curiosity, the worn condition of the apertures to secure the legs appeared to show that it had seen much active service.

Entries in the Parish Books relating to Vagrants:

1729.—Apl. ye 9th. Agreement by the Masters of ye Parish that there shall be no use money given out of the Church or Poor Book to any Vagrant or traveller by any officer of ye Parish.

1741.—Pd. Vagabond Money £6 16s. 3d.

1742.—Gave to travellers with the pass at several times 7s.

Although the dates of these entries are later than the time when the Stocks and Whipping-post were in chief demand for the punishment of vagrants, their employment was frequent down to a period later than the dates. In ancient times vagrancy was a penal offence, necessitated by the number of people who were compelled to beg from being thrown upon the world in consequence of the suppression of religious houses. The desperate condition of the more lawless of these vagrants drove them to acts which might have been averted probably by more beneficent treatment. Henry VIII, however, had but little compunction in carrying out his resolves, he thus instituted severe enactments, such as the Acts of the 22nd and 27th of his reign for the suppression of vagrancy. The treatment need not be detailed, but it included whipping at a cart's-tail, or in the Stocks, till the backs were bleeding, cutting out the gristle of the ear, branding with the letter V (*vagabond*), imprisonment on bread and water, and even death. Burn, in his *History of Parish Registers*, cites frequent cases, as in the Registers of Wadhurst, Brentford, and Mentmore, of whipping as rogues and vagabonds of men, women, and children, the gipsies getting an unusual share of such treatment. There were clauses in the Bills permitting begging under certain conditions, as in the case of persons that were "impotent"; but the treatment just stated was commonly inflicted.

But at the time of the above entries workhouses had been established, in which the poor were employed, and outside of which they could not obtain relief. This occurred in 1723, time of George II; and there is no doubt that the *passes* mentioned as given to travellers were to enable them to reach their several parishes. As impediments were often placed in the way of paupers proving their parishes, by overseers and others, a good many of them were compelled to wander from place to place before obtaining a final settlement, thus necessitating a greater outlay in the shape of "Vagabond money" than probably was necessary.

Forty years ago it was a common practice for beggars to present themselves at the back-doors of houses, exhibiting ugly-looking sores and distorted limbs to excite charity. The limbs were awkwardly bandaged, in a crooked manner, intended to convey the idea that the limbs were diseased, when they were only purposely distorted. The sores I afterwards found were kept open by means of an application made from the Common Mezereon (*Daphne Mezereum*), a plant which was then found wild in the Hampshire woods; but which has since been in a great measure exterminated, by the shrub being used as an ornament in shrubberies and gardens. These "artful dodgers" had, as beggars generally have now, a series of marks, or hieroglyphics, to denote to their fellows coming after them what was the character of the inmates of houses so marked, in so far as they were likely to prove remunerative in case of begging. One very common mark was a small cross made with chalk on a door-post or gate, which implied that the people within were not favourable to begging. They had other symbols which denoted that the occupants might give food, or that it might not be safe to beg. These people had, besides, methods of showing, after the manner of a paper-chase, what route had been taken by their fellows; a stroke or a fork on a gate or paling at cross-roads telling which road had been selected. They also suspended scraps of rag or paper on hedges to indicate their line of march.

The Stocks were removed from the Summerhaugh about the year 1850. They disappeared suddenly, and were removed as I afterwards understood for use as firewood. In this unseemly manner perished an implement that deserved a better fate, if only as a relic of antiquity. But it was more than simply an antiquated object, as it had played a conspicuous and by no means unimportant part in the parochial history of several centuries. At first it was a legal instrument of punishment[1]; but ultimately it came to be used chiefly as an alehouse appendage to check brawling and drunkenness; and for which purposes it was greatly in requisition during and after the time of the revel. I was informed by an aged inhabitant forty years ago that in his younger days he had often witnessed its employment;

---

[1] Stocks were not the only punishment for offenders, as the tumbrel or ducking-stool was in vogue for those who trespassed against the excise, such as millers, bakers, and those who sold bad ale. The late Mr. S. Shaw told me that he once saw a baker drawn through the town of Andover on a hurdle for selling bread of short weight.

and that "during feast times human legs were commonly to be seen protruding from the holes on both sides of the post". The last person who underwent the punishment was old John May, for drunkenness. He had been for some years the parish clerk, but was dismissed for intemperance, and was at length submitted to the ordeal of "sitting in the stocks", for over-indulgence in his unfortunate propensity.

Formerly there were stocks in each of the several tithings. At Swampton the apparatus adorned the green, near where the village school formerly stood; at Stoke the site of the instrument was near the blacksmith's shop; and at Eggbury this menace to the wrong-doers of the hamlet was erected alongside of the pond, where it might be considered as filling the place of a ducking-chair.

The stocks and the common pound for the use of the tenants of the manor were provided by the manor Court, their provision coming among the presentments of the homage of the Court of the Manor.

Another instrument of punishment of a more unusual character, a Brank, or Scold's-Bridle, was discovered in the Upper Test Valley in 1864; and if we may judge from the freshness of the leather cheek-bands connecting the iron hoops at the sides, it must have been used as late as at the end of the eighteenth century. It was found at Vernham, among some old iron, by Mr. Davis, Sen., a blacksmith living in that village, who presented it to me. The implement, which may now be seen in the Reading Free Museum, side by side with a Brank which was preserved in the prison at Reading, and which had been used for a similar purpose, is of unusual character, and differs in many particulars from all others that I have had an opportunity of inspecting (Pl. IX, fig. 1). It is a helmet composed of open ironwork, formed so as to encase the head down to a level with the neck. The top of the helmet is composed of two bands of stout hoop-iron, which pass from behind forwards over the head, and down in front of the face to immediately opposite the mouth, where they terminate in a strong loop. In this loop a tongue-plate, or gag, is made to slide backwards into the mouth, and pressing on the tongue restrains it from being used. It is chiefly in the sliding tongue-plate that this instrument differs from other bridles, the gag being usually fixed to the face-piece. This Brank has, further, a kind of stirrup attached to the tongue-plate for the reception of a strap or rein, by which the wretched gagged creature was led about amidst the cries of a mocking crowd. The base of the stirrup is composed of two bars, one fixing the stirrup to the tongue-plate, while the other is made to act as a lever to the gag, and thus furnished the conductor with considerable liberty in inflicting punishment to the mouth. The following are the dimensions of the Brank:—Length, from behind forwards, 9¼ ins.; width between the ear-plates, 6 ins.; circumference of the neck-plate, 17½ ins.; height of the side-plates, 8 ins.; length of the cranial hoops from the occiput to the nose-piece, 17½ ins.; length of the connecting pin at the vertex, 2¾ ins.; height of the stirrup, 3½ ins.; width of ditto at its back, 3½ ins.; length of the tongue-plate and slide, 4½ ins.; width of ditto at the centre, 1¾ ins. In addition to the removable tongue-plate this instrument differs from other branks in its mode of application; there being no hinges or openings at the back of the helmet it must have been forced down on the head from the vertex. Although these rude appliances for correcting scolding women are sufficiently common in municipal towns, I am not aware that in any instance a specimen has been found in a village; or that there are any parochial records of the use of such an implement in villages.

The Ox-Drove or Harrow-Way.

This ancient drove has existed probably from the earliest times, one of the names by which it is familiar being evidently of Saxon origin; Harrow-way, from the Anglo-Saxon *har*,[1] hoar or ancient, *Hoarway*.[2] It has from time immemorial been used for conveniently driving sheep to and from the various fairs; and drovers with their cattle from the West of England were accustomed to traverse the road in their journeys towards the metropolis. The way had its inducements in being expansive and retired; and the banks and hedgerows furnished some scanty food for the cattle, at the same time that a long journey could be traversed without the inconvenience of turnpikes. A portion of its course forms the boundary between the parishes of Hurstbourne Priors and St. Mary Bourne; and at one point a stream formerly ran across it, which necessitated its being forded by travellers, till about thirty years ago, when a bridge was made to span the ford at the direction of the Earl of Portsmouth. The site bears the name of Chapmansford, from the use of the ford by drovers, from the Saxon *ccap*,[3] a chattel, and *man, es, m*—a Chapman or dealer. In the Subsidy Roll of 1327,[4] the name of Rob^{to} Chapmansford appears as paying in that year iii*s*. iii*d*. to the

---
[1] Bosworth, *Anglo-Saxon Dictionary.*
[2] This definition has already been given (see *The Saxons*).
[3] Bosworth, *Anglo-Saxon Dictionary.*
[4] *Subsidy Roll*, 1st Edward III, 1327.

Crown, showing that the tenant of the land close by obtained his name from the ford. The drove receives mention as the *Okwey* (Ox-way) in 1323, time of Edward II,[1] in a perambulation of the Forest of Chute, as forming part of a boundary. In early times streams were crossed by fording when they were shallow. As civilisation advanced ferries were established; but when, as in Roman times, great military ways were constructed, bridges were introduced across the principal fords. In certain districts the Saxons had bridges; and bridges were built by the Normans; but they were rickety wooden structures, often out of repair, and the tolls were heavy, and were made a source of feudal revenue. In some country districts fording continued down to the nineteenth century.

[1] *Perambulation, Chutes, Hants,* 16th Edward II, 1323.

The Churches.

Charter of Henry de Blois.

HE date of this Charter is not fixed, but 1157 is assigned as the year in which it was granted. A translation of the Charter appears in the thirty-first *Report* of the Commissioners appointed in pursuance of the Act, 6th William IV, c. 71,[1] and presented to both the Houses of Parliament by command of Her Majesty, 1837. Among the revenues of the Hospital of St. Cross, Winchester, the church of Hurstbourne Priors is included:—

"All these things I, with the assistance of Divine Grace, have appointed to be observed in the aforesaid house of God for ever, to be continually and faithfully fulfilled by you, but preserving in all things the canonical jurisdiction of the Bishop of Winchester, that the appointment and administration of the Prior of the said Hospital may be by the hands of the said bishop; and that the rents, together with all the appurtenances, bestowed upon the said Hospital by me, may remain without disturbance or misapplication for the purpose of the said Hospital; among which appurtenances we have thought it right to enumerate the following by their proper names:—The Churches of Fareham, of Nursling, of Milbrook, of Twyford, of Hinton, of Alverstoke, of Exton, of *Hurstbourne* (including St. Mary Bourne), of Whitchurch, of Chilbolton, of Woodhay, of Alton, of Wintney, of Stockton, of Ovington, with all their appurtenances and apperdages, and the tithes of demesne of Waltham, and other rents assigned to them in the city of Winton: and if any person hereafter shall take upon himself to appropriate or diminish the said rents, or to disturb or deteriorate the statutes and customs of the aforesaid House of God,

---

[1] *Notes and Queries*, 1st Series, vol. xi, pp. 42-44, contains a Translation of the Charter of Bishop De Blois. The Charter is also to be found in Pontissera's *Register*.

which have been confirmed by the authority of the Holy See and of the King, let him incur the anger of Almighty God, and of the Bishop of Winchester, and of all good men, unless he shall study to amend his fault by fitting satisfaction. But to you and your successors, benefactors of the poor, while you preserve our constitutions without breach, may there be peace and mercy from the Lord Jesus Christ" (p. 843).

St. Mary Bourne Church.

The parish church is situated in the tithing of St. Mary Bourne, immediately below the Summerhaugh, and midway between it and the Roman road, which crossed the valley at about 250 yards south of the church. It occupies a tolerably central position in relation to the several outlying tithings.

It has been seen that the Charter of Bishop De Blois bears date about 1157; and this date corresponds somewhat with the period of the earliest existing church architecture, the chancel-arch being considered as early twelfth century work.

The orientation of the church is not strictly east and west, but its line points almost east-north-east, or about 20 degrees north of east.

The present structure is long and low, and contains work of several periods. The tower is of the Perpendicular period, in three stages, cased with coarse stucco, with quoin-stones at the angles, and string-courses of stone at the various stages. It has stone-coped battlements; and its height from the battlements to the level of the road is fifty feet. The tower walls are three feet in width up to the level of the floor of the bell-loft, from that point to the battlements their width is two feet. There are four windows in the bell-loft, with square heads, vertical stone mullions, and horizontal labels. These windows are protected with weather-boards. The belfry window, looking west, is of about the date of 1420. The arch and dripstone are pointed, and the lights are in three tiers with stone dressings. The above date represents the lower part of the tower; but the upper portion, including the battlements, is evidently later, and might have undergone restoration at the latter part of the seventeenth century.

It would appear that a good deal of repair and restoration must have taken place about that time, embracing the north wall of the church, which is also coarsely stuccoed, and the introduction in the north aisle of inferior wood windows, which have just recently been replaced with stone windows. The present Perpendicular north door was patched up at the time that the church was re-pewed.

In the *Calendar of the State Papers Domestic*, vol. xvi, Part II, p. 432, June 25, 1640, I find the following entry, which appears to bear reference to the date of the repairs :—

The Wardens and parishioners of Downe Husborn, and St. Mary Bourne, co. Southampton. Referred to the Chancellor of Winchester to view the Church of Downe Husborn, and the Master of the Hospital of St. Cross to view the Church of St. Mary Bourne, and report on the ruins and necessary repairs, the first session of Michaelmas term.

The nave has a leaded roof of low pitch; and there are north and south entrances. The walls of the church and chancel are of faced flint, two feet six inches in width, and are strongly buttressed; and a stout buttress supports the south wall at the point where the wall-tomb occupies the Week aisle. The roof of the south aisle bears a plain stone parapet, which is Perpendicular, of the date of about the end of the fourteenth century. It has an ogee base moulding with a corbel-head in the south-east angle, and is capped with a weather roll. There must have been a similar parapet over the north aisle, which was removed most likely at the time of the restoration of the north side of the church; and I had thought that the capstones were utilised in building the front church wall, which from the church records bears date 1676, but the caps do not quite correspond with those of the south parapet. The north aisle was probably of the same width as the south chapel, and had corresponding windows, for on examining the roof of the tower it appears that the beams which carry the lead roof are of old material (timber used before). One of the beams has a moulding worked on its edge, similar to those on the tie-beams over the south aisle; and there is a mortice cut in it for fixing to the purlin, which appears to denote that the north wall having given way it was not rebuilt on the original foundation, perhaps from want of funds; but that the north aisle was reduced to its present width, and the removed timber was used in the tower, which was undergoing repair at the same time.

The chancel is gabled and tiled, and has side and angle-buttresses in three stages; and a heavy stone string-course extends through the walls, embraces the buttresses, and returns underneath the east window. A low recessed priests' door occupies the south wall, but it is now bricked up.

Previous to the restoration of the chancel by the Earl of Portsmouth in 1855, the roof had a much lower pitch, and the walls were connected with iron tie-rods, which spanned the chancel.

The interior of the church consists of north and south aisles, with nave and chancel; and the following are their several dimensions :—

INTERIOR OF ST MARY BOURNE CHURCH.
HANTS.

Nave	67 ft. 8 in. by 16 ft. 7 in.
North aisle . . .	67 ft. 8 in. by 6 ft.
Between north and south doors .	36 ft.
Belfry	16 ft. 3 in. by 13 ft. 5 in.
Chancel	38 ft. 5 in. by 18 ft. 4 in.

The vestry is simply the east end of the north aisle.

The nave was repaired, and the church fitted with a new pulpit and seats in 1855-6, the cost being £470, furnishing accommodation for 338 people. The chancel was restored at the same time by the lay Rector, when the Decorated east window was introduced. Previous to that time the belfry tower was reached by a spiral stair, which was removed, and an awkward ladder substituted. At the same time, the singing gallery, which stood immediately in front of the belfry arch was removed, and the organ placed where it now is. The organ is the gift of the late Mr. John Moore, and bears date Jan. 1st, 1853; maker, Brice, London.

Before the re-pewing, the pulpit stood in the centre of the church, on the north side of the nave, and faced south; but the new pulpit stands on the south side of the chancel-arch, and faces west. The old pulpit was removed to the vicarage, and occupied a site in the Vicar's dining-room.

The nave is bounded on the south by six heavy quadrangular piers, with plain chamfered capitals; and the arches and labels are obtusely pointed. The piers have two-third angle-shafts, in hollows, with corresponding capitals, some of which are simply roundels; others are foliated or bear horse-shoe designs. On the north side the arcade consists of six pillars, five arches, and a semi-arch, which abuts on the wall. The pillars, capitals, etc., are late or transition Norman of about the date of Henry II.

The chancel-arch, of earlier date than the nave, is semicircular Norman, with plain imposts. It bears a plain wedge-shaped moulding with a bead-roll; and the dimensions of the wall-shafts are, height 6 ft. 2 in.; width 1 ft. 9 in. The span of the arch is 16 ft. 7 in.; and its height at the centre is 15 ft. 3 in. The east chancel window is quite new; but the side windows are well recessed and splayed, and are in the early Decorated form of about 1320. It is evident that these windows were at one time more elevated, as parts of the earlier arches appear to lie behind the later arched walling; and traces of the old window mouldings are obscurely seen underneath the modern wall plaster. The chancel rails are of polished oak; and in the south wall there is a piscina with a drain. It has obtusely pointed cusps, and is of about the same period as the side windows.

There is nothing remarkable in the oak and plastered roof, which is heavy, of transverse collars and tie-beams, resting on stout wall-pieces, which are coarsely braced. The roof is of about the date of 1590 or 1600; and the south porch was most likely built about the same time.

The south or Week aisle is 34 ft. 9 in. by 17 ft. It was formerly probably a chapel associated with the manor of the same name. The windows are plain late Decorated; the side windows in two lights, and the east window in three. The east window contains quatre-foils, and there are signs of colour in some of the glass panes, perhaps from age or inferior glass. A cinque-foiled piscina with pointed cusps occupies the south wall, which is stated as of about the fourteenth century; but it may be earlier. And immediately near it, in the east angle, a broken bracket projects from the wall, which most likely carried an image. An altar probably stood here.

At the time that the church was re-seated some fine encaustic tiles were taken from the Week aisle. They are of the date of the end of the thirteenth or the beginning of the fourteenth century. The tiles are decorated, and thickly glazed. Some are plain, with simply an indented cross. Others evidently form part of a design, as they contain portions of a corresponding circle, which is dotted, with a foliated border. Others, perhaps central tiles, bear rude human heads decorated with foliage. I should imagine that they originally formed the paving of a manorial chapel. The patterns are inlaid, the figures being formed as moulds, which were filled with white clay, and the tiles were then coated with a yellow or yellowish-green glaze, producing a bright yellow or green pattern on a brown ground.

Two notice-boards lie in the belfry, which were removed at the time of the re-pewing. One states that "The Clock (Church-clock) was given by Mr. Richard Poare of Hurstbourne Priors, a native of this Parish, and was put up at his expence in 1826."

The other announces that "Mrs. Hannah Longman, widow of Mr. John Longman, Gent., of Apsley Farm, in 1807 gave the Chandeleer in the centre Aisle of the Church."

The Royal Escutcheon stands over the south door within the entrance; and in reference to it I find among the Church Expenses:—

Apl. 17th, 1805,	Pd. for the Coat of Arms .	£2 12s. 6d.
„	Pd. for puting up the same .	2s. 6d.

As there was no special Act at that time that I am aware of for placing the Royal Arms in churches, I have inferred that it was done in honour of His Majesty (George III), on the victories obtained by Nelson, and his death at Trafalgar, which occurred in 1805.

Pl. XI.

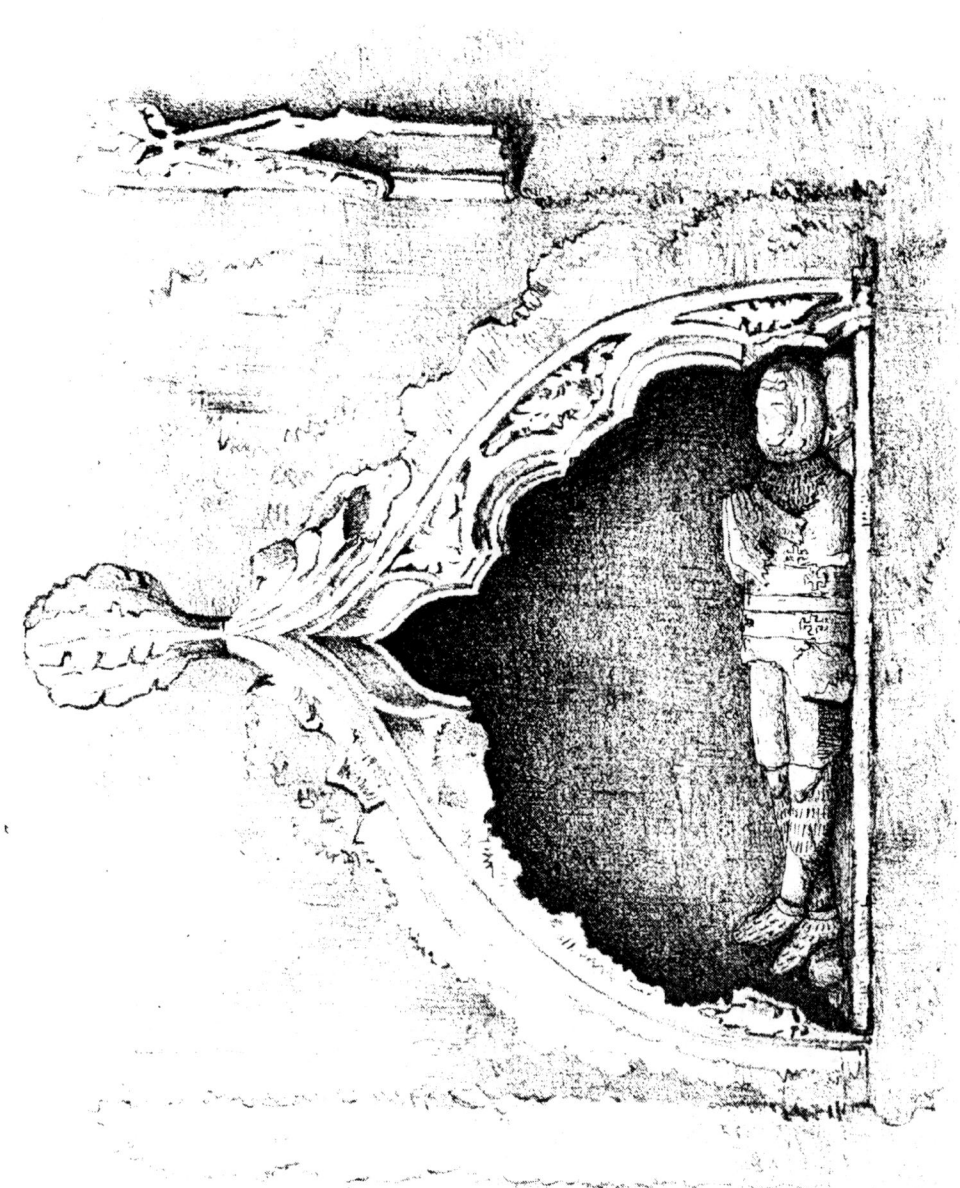

CROSS-LEGGED EFFIGY
IN ST MARY BOURNE CHURCH, HANTS.

THE CROSS-LEGGED EFFIGY.

On a low wall-tomb in the south or Wyke aisle rests the cross-legged effigy of a knight in stone. It is life-size; but the sculpture is in bad condition. The head appears to have been replaced by a rude imitation in plaster or stone, and the left or exposed side of the figure is considerably mutilated. The effigy is represented as habited in the quilted gambison, over which is the sleeved hauberk of chain-mail; and chausses of chain-mail encase the feet and legs. And there are apparently *poleyns* or knee-plates. The hands, resting on the chest, are pressed together, as if enclosing some object, perhaps a heart, as in other examples of the same period. The head is supported by an angular stone block; and at the feet reclines the figure of some animal so mutilated as to be undistinguishable. The broken crockets and finials on the canopy and wall-shafts imply that the tomb must have been a handsome one in its perfect state. Mr. Blore believes the figure to be of about the year 1280, *temp.* of Edward I; and considers that in its perfect state it was no doubt a beautiful specimen of the art of the period; at the present time its chief interest arises from the arms being represented on the surcoat, a circumstance which rarely occurs at so early a period. The Rev. Charles Kerry considers the tomb hardly so early as this, and places it at about A.D. 1327. The width of the slab on which the figure lies is 26 ins.; the length of the slab 6 ft. 6 ins.; and the height of the canopy 5 ft. 4 ins. (see plate). It is not rightly known what knight is here represented; but it is considered to be an effigy of one of the Dandelys. It can hardly be Sir Richard, as the date of the tomb is later than his period. It has been seen that the family held in various parts of Hampshire, and inferentially in Wyke manor; but what is known of the Dandelys in connection with Wyke comes through the Beyntons (see *Beynton, Inquis. post mortem*). The arms borne by the effigy are similar to those of Sir Richard Dandely (*ar.*, two bars *gu.*, each charged with three crosses croslet *or*). It might certainly represent a member of that family.

It has been stated that the cross-legged effigy represents one who had been a crusader. That a Sir Roger des Andelys served in the Barons' wars we have the testimony of a document upon the History of France, published by the Government. It is called *Histoire de la Croisade contre les Hérétiques Albigeois,* in the original Provençaux (A.D. $\frac{1209}{1217}$), and translated into French by M. C. Fauriel. At page 61 occurs this passage:—

"When the Count of Montford was invested with the Viscountship, and they had given to him Carcasson with its appendances, he was greatly troubled that so few of his friends were willing to remain with him. The greater number were desirous of returning to Paris, the country was wild and mountainous, and they were not willing to be slaughtered in the passes. However there remained with him (I know not how many) eight or ten of the boldest and most valiant of the barons, among whom were Simon, surnamed of Saissy, also the Norman, Robert of Pegu, William d'Encontre who (by the faith I owe to St. Denis) daily strove to increase in fame, Don Guy the brave and fearless Marshal, Robert de Forceville, Lambert de Crecy, Raivier de Chanderon, and Raval of Agin, Don Pons de Beaumont, and Don John his Cousin, the Viscount de Saintes, *Roger des Andelys*, Roger de Sessart, Hugh de Lascy, and others whose names I have not learnt."

Also at page 479, A.D. 1217, in the attempt to surprise Toulouse, among several of the same names appears that of *Roger d'Andely*.

THE FONT.

The St. Mary Bourne Font, from its design and character, is evidently of the same period, and probably the work of the same artificer as those of East Meon, St. Michael's, Southampton, and the Cathedral Font at Winchester. Respecting the three latter a notice occurs in the *Proceedings of the Archæological Institute*, which was read at the meeting of the Institute at Winchester in 1845, in which the belief is expressed that all these fonts are the handiwork of the same designer. The writer says, "there can be little doubt that they are all three the work of the same hand, and they are among the finest Norman fonts that have come down to us. A much higher antiquity has been assigned to them, but there is no good reason to suppose them earlier than the middle of the twelfth century." Representations of the sculptures on the East Meon font appear in *Archæologia*, vol. x, p. 185. The subjects are thought to represent the Creation of Eve; the Temptation by the Serpent; the Expulsion of Adam and Eve from Paradise, and their instruction in the arts of husbandry and spinning.

The basin of the St. Mary Bourne font is of the same massive square form as the other three; and the sculpturings, although differing as regards the designs, have the same rude and somewhat bulbous character—a peculiarity which is so commonly found to attend the work of the twelfth century. The stone out of which it is wrought has been thought to be Purbeck, or black marble, or basalt; but there is no doubt that it is hewn from a block of slate.[1] The font stands on a modern round sandstone plinth, the four original corner pillars, on which it rested after the manner of the Winchester font,

[1] This is the opinion of Prof. Rupert Jones, F.R.S.

THE FONT.

having been removed, perhaps destroyed, as the font itself shows signs of rough usage in places. It contains a drain, and its dimensions are as under:—

Length of sides	3 ft. 7 in.
Height of do.	12½ in.
Do. of Pedestal	1 ft. 9 in.
Diameter of Basin	2 ft. 6 in.

The designs on its top and sides are rude, and characteristic of an earnest although rugged period. Those on its upper surface, surrounding the basin, represent drinking doves at the north and east corners; while the west angle bears what appears to be a sheaf of corn, the opposite or south corner containing apparently a phœnix. The east and north sides of the basin are decorated with vine branches, bearing leaves and clusters of fruit (Plate XII); but the sculptures on the south and west facets are, on the former an Anglo-Norman arcade surmounted with doves and bottles; on the latter also an arcade, with the introduction over each capital of a *fleur-de-lis*.

In reply to an inquiry as to the symbolical nature of the decorations, Mr. James Parker states that he is aware the font has been ascribed to Bishop Walkelyn in the eleventh century, but he believes there are no grounds for such a statement. Very much of the work which has been attributed to Henry I is really the work of Henry II. Undoubtedly part of the carving represents grapes; but from the character of the leaves the treatment is conventional. The vine is doubtless symbolical, but it is doubtful whether the worker thought of the symbolism as a rule. It became a conventional ornament, and was used as such whenever suitable. The drinking doves form a pretty design and nothing more, and are not intended to symbolise any special doctrine; but they are admirably adapted to fill the spaces. The dove may be taken as symbolical, at the same time it might have been suitable to the designer to fill up the structure he had to decorate. The drinking dove is not specially Christian, but is a common Italian feature, and is observable in the mosaic decorations of houses, as well as in church tesselations. The whole of the three or four fonts above-named, judging from their details, are probably of the date of Henry II.

In an article entitled "Underground Southampton", in the *Antiquary*, vol. xiv, August 1886, the Hampshire fonts, of the same character and period as the St. Mary Bourne font, are believed to be of Byzantine, and not of Norman origin.

There are but few inscriptions in the Church; the chancel contains a tablet in memory of Lieut. William Easton, R.N., 1837, son of a former vicar of the parish; and there is also a tablet in memory of the father, the Rev. William Easton, who was vicar of the parish for seventeen years. He died on the 20th November, 1834, aged 68 years.

Close to the tablet of the Rev. William Easton is one in memory of his wife, Anna, who died September 21st, 1845, aged 79 years.

Within the communion rails there is a stone which bears the following inscription:—"Here lyeth the body of Smith Stone, vicar of this Church, Born July 23rd, 1682, Dyed April 1st, 1724. Also John the Son of Smith and Jane Stone, Born June 26th, 1719, Dyed August 20th, 1720."

The Churchyard.

The ground of the village churchyard has the appearance of being raised considerably above its original level, probably from the accumulated remains of the villagers which have been interred here for many centuries. The surface of the ground in consequence, particularly in places, is much higher than the highway which runs close alongside of it. A cursory inspection of the memorial stones conveys the almost painful reflection that so many of those who lie beneath, and who a few years since were the chief movers in parochial matters, have now no representatives in the parish. On the south of the church several plain altar tombs close to the road are appropriated to the Longman family, who for a lengthened period occupied the Week hamlets; and members of the same family lived at Apsley, and Wadwick, also called Warwick. But at this moment the male line is extinct in the parish. The last male representative was the benevolent owner and occupier of Wadwick, whose family tomb stands beneath the wall at the east end of the graveyard, in a plot of ground presented for burial purposes by himself and brother. The marble tomb is distinguished by a broken lily, in reference to a daughter who died early. Close by it, as if implying that those who were remarkable for lengthened residence desired to be near each other in death, is the tomb of Mr. John Moore, the last of his family; the name if ancestrally the same, which it most likely is, is found in the list of parochial residents in the time of Edward III. The earlier Moores lie on the north side of the church; one of a line of gravestones bearing an inscription to the memory of William Moore, who died in 1789. He was father of the late John Moore, and was a churchwarden with Robert Longman in 1785. The inscription reads thus:—

> A loving Uncle a Friend sincere
> Loved by most People lies buried here
> Kind to the poor of the meaner sort
> We hope that Christ will reward him for't.

"A loving Father" is not an uncommon commencement on tombstones, but "A loving Uncle" is somewhat novel.

The Holdways are also lengthened residents, but they have all passed away in so far as St. Mary Bourne is concerned, the last of the name being the late generous lady occupant of Haven Hill. The family-tomb, an enclosed pyramid, stands near the yew-tree on the south of the edifice, and bears the inscription "*Be ye also ready*", in reference to the husband of the lady, who died in consequence of an accident, and to whose memory the widow erected and endowed the village almshouses. The name of Dowling was associated with agriculture in the parish forty years ago, members of the family of that name then living at Link and St. Mary Bourne, and later at Middle Week; but they have now for some time ceased to be parochial residents. Tombs of several members of the family occupy sites on the south of the church and chancel. The Herberts are also extinct in the parish; their tombs lie on the north, east, and south-east of the edifice. An altar-tomb on the south-east covers the remains of one of the last members of the family, who was the first resident surgeon of the parish, the record stating that he exercised the duties of that office for fifteen years.

It is remarkable that there are not more records of the Vicars. We have notices of Stone and Easton in the chancel, and the latest vicar and some members of his family occupy a small plot close to the chancel, surrounded with a low wicket-paling; but the graves bear no details. The absence of early memorials of the dead may perhaps be accounted for by the quite late introduction of stones in village churchyards. Till the seventeenth century, tombstones of the ordinary kind were almost unknown, and very few until the beginning of the eighteenth century, so that many generations have been laid to rest without any external notices; and their dust has mingled with the later dead; and the few, mostly head and feet stones, which were erected in the seventeenth century have crumbled or fallen, and have been removed. The earliest recognisable inscription is that of a Longman, and it is not earlier than the beginning of the eighteenth century (see *Extracts from the Old Parish Books*).

The Browns, Parhams, Taylors, and Vincents of Eggbury, whose graves lie eastward of the chancel, have all left the district; and the tomb of the present Hooper family of Stoke stands close by;

but these families had no ancestrally lengthened association with the parish. But the Mundays lying southward of the church are of some parochial antiquity; and the Poores, whose graves are close by, have an extended village record, a John Poore and a Thomas Poore being resident in "Borne" before 1545. And the name is still vital in the parish. Among those who have for centuries placed their dead in the graveyard Gibbons is an example, known as Gibbe in 1327, and now often styled Gibbs. Churcheye, now Churcher or Kercher, appears at the same date. Mills, formerly spelt *Mylles; Becley*, afterwards Beckley; Bray; Hayes; Bright; Izorne; Purver, at one time *Purvyer*, a purveyor or victualler probably; Harris, once spelt *Harrys;* Sims, in past times *Cynes*, and Phillpott, were connected with the parish in 1545. Carter, Fisher, and Sutton are also early residents. Their dead were the "rude forefathers" of the hamlet.

There was another family of Holdways, who were possessed of land at Stoke, whose dead lie on the south-east of the church. They are also parochially extinct. The Neales, who lie not far distant from the Holdways, are yet respected residents; as also are the Medhursts, whose graves are on the north of the church, near the north gate; and although the name has been well known in the parish for several generations, it is not on the early documents. The same may be stated with regard to the Eyles's, whose ancestral memorials of worthy people are to be seen on the east of the church, near the grave of the late vicar. William Day, lying in the east part of "God's Acre", and many years a churchwarden, is of quite modern date in the village. The names Collins and Colebrook are comparatively late; but Baker, whose grave is on the east of the chancel, appears on an early church register. Wedge, Gale, Biggs, Crooks, Bull, and Broad are names of some parochial antiquity. One labourer's record should be copied, which may be considered suitable probably to many other hard-working men who lie unrecorded, that of William Bower, at whose last illness I was present thirty-six years ago. On an old-fashioned wood label, extending from end to end of the grave, and supported with head and feet posts, it is written that—

For forty years [he was] the faithful and respected farm servant of Mr. Robert Longman, of this parish. He maintained himself by his own honest earnings during life. Died May 1851, aged 77 years.

Mary Goodyear the centenarian lies at the foot of the grave of the recently buried vicar.

𝕮𝖍𝖆𝖗𝖎𝖙𝖎𝖊𝖘.

As the sums are not large it will not be necessary to enter into lengthened details; but there are certain charities, which have been bequeathed for benevolent purposes, the interests of which are annually distributed among the poor of the parish of St. Mary Bourne, by the vicar and churchwardens. They consist of the following, of which notices are specified on a board suspended in the church. The entire sum at interest is £755, made up of £50 left by William Batchelor in 1797; £100 by Robert Longman in 1814; £45 by Mrs. Hannah Longman in 1838; £30 by Thomas Sutton in 1843; £130 by William Longman in 1844; and £200 by Thomas Longman in 1858. The late Mr. John Longman of Warwick also left, in 1879, the annual interest of £200.

Immediately above the Summerhaugh, opposite the vicarage, a serviceable and benevolent addition to the village was made by Mrs. Sarah Holdway, in memory of her husband, who died in 1855, of four almshouses for the use of the aged poor of the parish. Mrs. Holdway died in December 1883, and left by her will an endowment in perpetuity of four shillings weekly to four residents in these houses. They are well and durably built, and form a quiet and comfortable retreat for the old people after the heat and burden of a life of labour. A slab erected over the doorways of the central buildings bears the following inscription :—

IN MEMORIAM
ROBERTI HOLDWAY
OB : VIII^{vo} . DIE AP : MDCCCLV .
HANC DOMUM IN USUM PAUPERUM
ÆDIFICAVIT VIDUA MDCCCLXII .

It is worthy of record that a centenarian died in one of these houses in December 1883; Mary Goodyear, who had occupied one of the houses for some years, having entered her 101st year.

The Church of St. Mary Bourne appears as part of the endowment of St. Cross Hospital, consolidated in the same benefice with Hurstbourne Priors. (The Charter of De Blois is contained in Harl. MS. 1616.)

According to the *Valor Ecclesiasticus*, in the 26th of Henry VIII, or 1534-5, the yearly revenue of the hospital was £281 13s. 5d., and the amount expended in the charity £197 9s. 3d., leaving as its value £84 4s. 2d. But a detailed account, dated eight years earlier, makes the value to be £496 18s. 4½d., and the yearly expenses £406 14s. 1½d.

This account of the 18th of Henry VIII, derived from a *Compotus* for the year ending Michaelmas, 1526, contains among the receipts "pensions" from Waltham, Upham, Exton, Alverstoke, Stockton, Woodhay, Hinton, Nursling, Chilbolton, Milbrook, Ovington, Alton Canons, Farley, and Baughurst, in all £58 5s.; and other receipts from Whitchurch, Owselbury (granted to the hospital, it is supposed, in the Cardinal's time), Twyford, Fareham, *Hurstbourne* and *St. Mary Bourne*, Ashton (granted at the same time as Owselbury), Mill of St. Cross, houses in St. Cross, houses in the Soke of Winton and Sparkford, the Hospital of St. John at Fordingbridge, Free Chapels of Cold Henley, and of Itchenswell, Crondall Rectory, Sutton, Yately, and Aldershott Chapels, the Rectory of St. Faith, and the Chapel of St. James (otherwise called St. James of Henley-on-the-Hill, near Winton, or White Monastery); together with miscellaneous receipts, such as the produce of sales of skins, wood, suet, and the property of a deceased brother, which, with the pensions before spoken of, amounted to £496 18s. 4½d.[1]

Land Revenue. Church Goods, Hants. Priors Husborne, No. $\frac{445}{14}$

"The Ornaments the' to Willm Sylvester, £v vis. viiid."

NOTE.—The £v is very indistinct in the document.

St. Mary Borne.

Not Paid.—"The Ornaments the' to John Harbard, xxiijs. iiiid."

"For a Chalis '*imbizeled*'..." (no entry to this).

"John Bedham; pledge for Brekestone, xls."

The interpretation of this appears to be that Bedham had made himself surety for Brekestone in the performance of some contract, or for his appearance. The entry might refer to a *Frankpledge* (see Pleas of the Crown). The name of Brekestone appears in the tithing of "Borne", in the Subsidy List of the 34th of Henry VIII. He was a "thonger", a maker of thongs, and represented probably the harness-maker of recent times. The name disappears from the Subsidies after the time of Edward VI.

Inventory of Church Goods at St. Mary Bourne (from the Parochial Records, April 22nd, 1600).

A Silver Communion Cup and Cover. One pewter flagon and plate for bread. One Holland table cloth, and a napkin. A scarlet cloth, pulpit cloth, and cushion. Delivered to Robert Hardway (Holdway?) to be kept in behalf of the parish.

---

[1] Woodward and Wilks, *Hist. of Hampshire*, vol. i, p. 239.

Thesaurus rerum Ecclesiasticarum (Acton). Diocese of Winchester, Deanery of Andover. Hurstbourne Priors, 1142.

Priory	7s. 5½d.
Clear annual value	£32 6s. 9d.
Yearly tenths	£1 5s. 11½d.

Taxatio Ecclesiasticæ. Pope Nicholas IV. In the year 1288 Pope Nicholas the Fourth granted the tenths to King Edward the First for six years, towards defraying the expense of an expedition to the Holy Land; and that they might be collected to their full value, a taxation was begun by the King's precept, in the year 1288, and finished, as concerns the province of Canterbury, in 1291. It is an important record, because all the taxes, as well to our Kings as to the Popes, were regulated by it, until the survey made in the year 26th of Henry VIII, under the head of *Valor Ecclesiasticus*. The following charges were made on Hursbourn Priors; Deanery of Andover (*Decanatus de Anndever*).

Vicar' de Husseborne Prior, "taxation"	£5 0s. 0d.
Tenths (*decimæ*)	10s.
Taxatio bonor' Temporaliu' Religiosor' in Archidiaconatu' Wynton' (Prior de Sĉo. Swithino.).	
Husseburn	79 18s. 9d.

Inquisitiones Nonarum (Inquisition of the Ninths.) These are taken by virtue of a commission directed to the assessors and venditors, January 26th, 15th Edward III, pursuant to Stat. 14th Edward III, which granted to the King a subsidy of the ninth lamb, the ninth fleece, and the ninth sheaf. In order to obtain correct information, the assessors and venditors were directed to take inquisitions upon the oath of the parishioners in every parish.[1]

Parish of Hurstbourne Priors (*Paroch' de Hussebourn Prioris*). 1340—14th Edward III. The names of the men of the same parish, Walter at Mere, Ralph Dymmok, Richard le Frie, John Hughet, being sworn upon their oath, say that the ninth of the sheaves, fleeces, and lambs of the aforesaid parish of Hurstbourn Priors is worth in the aforesaid xiv year £8 2s. And they say that the ninth aforesaid could not amount to the tax of the church aforesaid in the aforesaid year, for this, that the aforesaid church is endowed of a certain jurisdiction, which is worth by the year 6s. 8d. And they say that the tithe of hay and of other small tithe, with the oblations and mortuaries, is worth by the year 39s. And they say that the ninth of the temporalities of the Prior of St. Swithin, Winchester, in the same parish, was worth in the aforesaid xiv year 60s., whereof the church of St. Swithin was from old time endowed.

[1] F. S. Thomas, *Handbook to the Public Records*, Appendix, p. 453.

Grant to the Vicar of Husborne of a certain tenement in St. Marie's Borne, August 16th, 1390, 14th Richard II (*translation*)[1]:—

To all the faithful of Christ to whom this present writing shall come, Robert Ruddeborne, prior of the church of St. Swithun's, Winchester, and the Convent of the same place, send greeting everlasting in our Lord. Be it known unto you all that, with unanimous assent and consent, We have delivered and granted in fee farm, by this present indented deed, to Sir John Graunte, vicar of the church of Husborne, a messuage with the adjoining curtilage and all their appurtenances, in St. Marie's Bourne, which Henry Riotts a *neif* formerly held of us, being the same messuage with the adjoining curtilage which Isabella Waspray lately held of us for the term of her life. The entire messuage aforesaid and the adjoining curtilage with all their appurtenances to be had and held at fee farm by the aforesaid John, vicar of the church, and his successors, vicars of the same church, of us and our successors for ever, paying annually for the same to us and our successors the fee farm rent of 13*s*. 4*d*. of good and lawful money of England, in equal portions at the four principal terms of the year, for all services and demands. And if it shall happen, that the aforesaid fee farm rent of 13*s*. 4*d*. shall be in arrear and unpaid for a half year after the day of any payment in any of the abovementioned terms (which God forbid), then it shall be well and lawful for us, the prior and convent, and our successors to distrain upon the said messuage and curtilage and all its appurtenances, and the distraints thereupon seized, to take and carry away, and retain, until the aforesaid fee farm of 13*s*. 4*d*., with damages and expenses, shall be fully satisfied to us and our successors. And if there shall be found not sufficient on the aforesaid messuage and curtilage to distrain for the arrears of the aforesaid fee farm to the value of 3*s*. 4*d*., then it shall be well and lawfull for us, the aforesaid Prior and Convent and our successors, to re-enter upon the said messuage and curtilage with their appurtenances, and to hold to ourselves and our successors, our former estate therein for ever, notwithstanding this present indented writing. In testimony whereof, to that part of our present indented writing remaining with Sir John, the aforesaid vicar, and his successors, we have caused our common seal to be appended; and to the other part of this indented writing remaining with us and our successors, Sir John, the aforesaid vicar, has placed his seal, and for the greater acknowledgment of this transaction, Sir John, the aforesaid vicar, has procured its ratification by the seal of the deanery of Winchester being placed to this part. These being witnesses—Sir John Sandys, knight; Robert Chomeley, Edmund Spirecoke, Richard Pauncefote, Nicholas Fawkener, John Harries, Richard Attmere, Thomas att Clive, John Coupere, and many others. Given in our chapter house at Winchester on Tuesday the morrow of the Assumption of the Blessed Virgin Mary, namely on the sixteenth day of the month of August, in the year of our Lord one thousand three hundred and ninety, and in the 14th year of the reign of King Richard the Second, after the Conquest.

Valor Ecclesiasticus. The "Valor" was formed to give effect to Stat. 26th Henry VIII, c. 3, which gave the first-fruits and tenths to the King.

In order to the new assessment and valuation of ecclesiastical property, a survey was appointed to be made by Commissioners to be sent into every part of the kingdom. The Commission is dated 30th January, 26th of Henry VIII (1535). This assessment or survey

[1] I am indebted to Mr. F. J. Baigent for the translated copy of this Grant.

superseded that known under the name of the Taxation of Pope Nicholas (*temp.* Ed. I). The Survey contains a valuation of every form of ecclesiastical property.

Exchequer, Treasury of Receipts, Miscell. Books, A⅙. (Formerly County Bags, Southampton, No. 23.) Monastery of St. Swithin, Winchester.

The yearly value of all manors, lands, etc., belonging to the said Monastery, certified by Henry Broke, Prior of the same, to Stephen, Bishop of Winchester, and other the King's Commissioners associated to the same Bishop by the King's Commission in the Taxation of the Tenth of the possessions of all spiritual persons, granted to the King by virtue of the Act of Parliament of the 26th of Henry VIII.

Hursborne with Members.—The Manor of Hursborne with certain lands in the Prior's hands there with perquisites of Court, sale of wood, and other appurt's, one year with another . . . . 38*l*. 6*s*. 6*d*.
The Manor of Boren with appurt's by the year . . 28*l*. 16*s*. 11*d*.
The Manor of Stok with appurt's by the year . . 19*l*. 10*s*. 6*d*.
The Manor of Benley [or Denley] with appurt's by the year . 16*l*. 1*s*. 9*d*.
The Manor of Wyke with sale of wood and other appurt's there 16*l*. 1*s*. 2*d*.
The Manor of Egbury with appurt's by the year . . 14*l*. 7*s*. 3¾*d*.
Whereof in the fee of Tristram Fauntleroy the Auditor . 26*s*. 8*d*.
And in the fee of the Receiver of Rents there by the year . 6*s*. 8*d*.
Allowances 33*s*. 4*d*.
And there remains clear . . . . . 131*l*. 10*s*. 9¾*d*.

[This appears to be a *full* copy of the Return known as the "*Valor Ecclesiasticus*", of which the printed Return is only an abstract.]

The following valuation of the Vicarage of Hurstbourne Priors appears in vol. ii of the *Valor Ecclesiasticus.*

Deanery of Andover (*Decan. Andover*), 1535. The Vicarage of Hurstbourne Priors. John Arthur, now Vicar (*Joh'es Arthure, modo Vicarius*).

Rectory appropriated to the Hospital of St. Cross in the County of Southampton, Deanery of Winchester, is worth in form of lands, called Glebe lands, tithes, oblations, as appears by the said paper book . . 13*l*. 6*s*. 8*d*.
Reprises in procurations, as appears by the said paper book . 7*s*. 5*d*.
And is worth beyond . . . . . 12*l*. 19*s*. 2*d*.
The tenth thereof . . . . . 25*s*. 11¼*d*.

The tithes at the present time are given in the Winchester Diocesan Calendar as worth £309, in addition to the great tithes, which formerly belonged to St. Cross Hospital, Winchester, but are now the property of the lay rector, the Earl of Portsmouth, and which are given as £1,702. The glebe land in the parish of St. Mary Bourne consists of 57 acres of arable, rented in 1886 by Mr. John Eyles at 10*s*. per acre; and there are about six acres of meadow land.

The vicarage house standing in the village of St. Mary Bourne is a rickety structure; but it has no particular history, and is of about the date of the half-timber houses in the parish.

Both Hurstbourne Priors and St. Mary Bourne are included in the Deanery of West Andover, which in the year 1290 included, as it at present includes, a considerable area. In 1340, the following thirty-one manors and parishes belonged to the Deanery; some of the manors, as that of Hurstbourne Priors, containing more than one parish:—Andevre, Wallop *inferior*, Wallop *superior*, Anne-de-Port, Throkelestone, Fifhide, Cumeton, Shipton, Todeworth, Querle, Anne-de-Beke, Anne Abatis, Clatforde, Godeworth, Whitchurch, Husseborne Priors, Wherewell, Middleton, Ludeshulve, Wodecote, Crokeesstone, Burghclere, Alta Clera, Wydehay, Hussebourne Regis, Faccombe-cum-Tangele, Coumbe, Enham, Penyton, and La Woe.

In 1535, 27th of Henry VIII, the parishes of the Deanery were the same as those just enumerated, substituting Lynkynnolde for Anne-de-Beke or Tangley. John Carewe was Rector of Lynkynnolde, and the value was £7 6s. 8d. In 1290, the Abbot of Gloucester's holdings at Littleton and Lyngeholte were reckoned together at £15.

Within the Deanery, in 1535, were reckoned Wherwell Abbey (*Anne Colt, Abbess*), worth £403 12s. 10d. gross, and £339 8s. 7d. net yearly value; the rectory or prebend of Wherwell (*Mr. Richard Pikehurst*), worth £46 15s. 7d., but charged with procurations, alms, and a pension, 44s. 7d.; the rectory or prebend of Hursbourn Tarrant (*Richard Arche*), worth £42, subject to a charge of 11s. 1d. for procurations and synodals; rectory or prebend of Myddleton (*Dr. Fawne*), worth £21, less 50s. 8d. for procurations, pensions, and alms; the rectories of Whitchurch and Husborn Prior, appropriated to St. Cross Hospital. Amport appropriated to Chichester Cathedral. Combe appropriated to the College of Windsor. Goodworth to Wherwell Monastery; and Nether-Wallop to the vicars-choral of York Minster. Shipton to the Abbey *de Newark in Com. South'n, Winton "dioc"* — twenty unappropriated rectories and eleven Vicarages.[1]

Calendar of State Papers Domestic, vol. iv, 1596, November 10th, Richmond. The Queen to Dr. Bennett, Dean of Windsor, and Master of St. Cross.

We request a grant of a lease in reversion, for 60 years, of the parsonage of Husborn belonging to St. Cross, under the usual rents and covenants. We require you to send the lease by the bearer, though intending to pay the usual fine. We expect no difficulty, as the lease has been demised to others before.

---

[1] Woodward and Wilks, *History of Hants and Isle of Wight*, vol. iii, p. 172.

1597, vol. iv, pp. 14, 305, 485, Part I, August 4th.

Indenture of lease between Robert Bennett, Master, and the brethren of the house or hospital of St. Cross, near Winchester, of the one part, and the Queen of the other part. Recites that John Incent, late Master, and the then Brethren, by indenture of the 22nd Sept., 22nd Henry VIII, demised to Walter Chandler, Merchant, of Winchester, and to Cicely his wife, the parsonage of Husborn and St. Maryborne appropriate to the said house and hospital, for 30 years, at the yearly rent in the said indenture expressed; that afterwards, W Meadow, Master, and the Brethren, on the 20th Feb., 1st Edw. VI, demised the reversion of the same to Thomas Chandler and Jane his wife for 41 years, they to pay yearly 40 quarters of pure and clean wheat of good measure, 60 quarters of good barley malt, and £33 6s. 8d.; also to the Vicar of Husborn (being resident upon his vicarage, and keeping hospitality there) four quarters of good wheat, and four of barley malt; if the said Vicar be not resident there, the said wheat and barley to be delivered at the house of St. Cross; also to pay yearly to the said Master and Brethren 20s. for certain tithes named, and 6s. 8d. as the rents of two tenements and lands in St. Maryborne, belonging to the house of St. Cross. Also that the said Robert Bennett, and the brethren of the said house, for the said yearly rents, have demised and let to her Majesty, and to her heirs and successors, the said parsonage of Hursborne and St. Maryborne, together with all the houses, barns, tithes, profits, and spiritual commodities to the same belonging, with certain exceptions, for 50 years, commencing from the determination of the last recited lease to Thomas and Jane Chandler.

Exchequer, Decree Book, Trinity, 12th Wm. III, fo. 167, 26th June.

South'ton. — Whereas Isaac Thornegate and Thomas Izerne, Plfs., did, in Trinity term, 11 W^m III, exhibit their Bill against Dorothy Wallopp, widow, Def., setting forth that they had for two years been farmers of the Parsonage of Hursburne and St. Mary Burne, appropriated to the Hospital of St. Crosse, in the County of Southampton, and of all tithes, both great and small, profits, and commodities whatsoever, arising within the said parish, "and that the same ought to be paid in kind, or some composition for the same": That Def. occupied 100 acres of meadow within the said parish, and mowed and made the same into hay, worth yearly £100, the tithe being worth about £10; and also occupied about 200 acres of coppice or woody ground, and did yearly fell 13 acres or more, worth £60, the tithe being worth £6: That Def. refused to set out the tithes, or make any satisfaction for the same, etc.: To which Bill Def. answered, setting forth the number of acres (in her occupation), etc., and alleging that no tithes had ever been paid in kind for the said meadow: that in satisfaction of all tithes of hay belonging to her, the grass growing on four acres of meadow lying in Honey Mead and Stoke Meade, parcel of her meadows, hath time out of mind been always received and taken by the Bishop of Winchester, his farmers or agents, as a customary payment in lieu of all tithes: That she carried the underwood by her felled and cut without setting out the tithes, no tithes in kind having ever been paid for the same: That the underwood in her possession was formerly parcel of the lands belonging to the Priory of Hursburne, "and being so vested in the Church, [she] is advised the same is exempt from the payment of tithes": To which Answer the Plfs. rejoined, and the cause being at issue, divers witnesses were examined on both sides, and their Depositions published: And the said cause came to be heard this day in Serjeants' Inn Hall in Fleet Street before Sir Edward Ward, Lord Chief Baron, and two other Barons [named], when the proceedings were read, as also the Ministers' Accounts 33-34 Henry VIII, and a grant of the Manor of Hursburne by King Edward VI, in his 6th year, to Sir John Gate, and another grant by Philip and Mary to Sir John Oxenbridge, whereby it appeared that the Manor of Hursburne Pryors was parcel of the Abbey of St. Swithin in Winchester; and it appearing that no tithe of hay and wood had been ever paid in the memory of man, and the Plfs. declining to try it at law, the Court were of opinion that the Plfs. ought to have no relief in this cause. It is thereupon ordered and adjudged that the Bill be dismissed, with moderate costs, to be taxed.

List of the Vicars.

The following account of the Vicars is derived principally from the episcopal archives, Winchester. It relates to the vicarial appointments from 1283 down to the latest induction in 1843.[1]

The Church of Saint Andrew the Apostle at Hurstbourne Priors is a vicarage in the gift of the Bishop of Winchester.

The vicarage was, until recently, a peculiar; that is, a benefice exempted from the archidiaconal visitations, and the incumbent had the power of proving and granting probate to the wills of the parishioners.

The Church of Heseburn, with the chapel of Burne, is named in a bull of Pope Clement III, dated at the Lateran Palace on the 19th March 1187-8.

On the 1st of December 1283, at Wolvesey, Bishop John de Pontinara collated Adam de Steinburg, chaplain, to the vacant vicarage of Husseburne.

On the 5th March 1314, Brother Henry Wodelok, Bishop of Winchester, collated John de Merewelle, priest, to the vacant vicarage of Husseborne, with the obligation of perpetual residence.

On the 8th April 1333, at York, the venerable father the Lord John de Stratford, by the grace of God Bishop of Winchester, in the tenth year of his consecration, collated William de Lutulbury, deacon, to the vacant vicarage of the parish church of Hussebourne Priors, of his patronage and diocese, and to his collation fully belonging; and also canonically instituted him perpetual vicar of the same with the burden of residence, according to the form of the constitution of the Lord Othobon (cardinal and legate of the apostolic see in England) made and enacted thereon. And he has letters of institution for himself, and also of induction addressed to the official of Winchester under the usual form.

On the 9th February 1348-9, at Esshere, Bishop William de Edyn-

---

[1] The list of vicars has been furnished to me by Mr. F. J. Baigent of Winchester, from the *Archives*.

don, collated Walter Passelewe, priest, to the perpetual vicarage of Bourne and Husseburne, vacant by the death of its late vicar.

On the 4th June 1359, at Southwark, Bishop William de Edyndon collated John de Mershton (*alias*) Botiller, priest, to the vacant vicarage of the church of Bourne and Husseburne, and canonically instituted him perpetual vicar of the same, with the burden of residence, etc.

On the 8th January 1375-6, at Highclere, William de Wykeham, Bishop of Winchester, collated Richard Etyngdon, priest, to the vicarage of Bourne and Husseborne, vacant by the death of Sir John de Merston, its late vicar.

On the 31st January 1380-1, at Southwark, Bishop William de Wykeham collated Sir John Graunt, priest, to the perpetual vicarage of Husseborne Priors, vacant by the death of Richard Tailler, its late vicar.

[The deceased vicar is the one collated as Richard (de) Etyngdon, the former name being that of his birthplace and the second name (Tailler) his patronymic.]

On the 23rd October 1400, Richard Metford, Bishop of Sarum, at his manor of Poterne, instituted Sir John Payn, priest (late perpetual vicar of the parish church of Enford in the diocese of Sarum), to the vicarage of Husseborne Priors, *vice* Sir John Graunt, its late vicar, who exchanged for the vicarage of Enford.

On the 6th January 1401-2, Richard Metford, Bishop of Sarum, at Remmesbury, instituted Sir John Mere, otherwise called Hakebourne (late rector of West Woodhay, Berks), to the vicarage of Husseborne Priors, *vice* Sir John Payn, its late vicar, who exchanged for the rectory of West Woodhay.

On 13th February 1406-7, at London, Dr. Henry Bowet, Bishop of Bath and Wells, instituted Sir Stephen Austrewelle (late vicar of the parish church of Tymbesburgh, Somerset), on the collation of Henry Beaufort, Bishop of Winchester, to the vicarage of the parish church of Husborne Priors, *vice* Sir John Mere, its late vicar, who exchanged for Tymbesburgh.

On 31st March 1407, at Farnham, Bishop Henry Beaufort collated Sir John Snappe (late canon and prebendary of the prebend of Bursale in the collegiate church of the Holy Cross, Crediton, in the diocese of Exeter) to the vicarage of the parish church of Husborne, *vice* Sir Stephen Austyswylle, its late vicar, who exchanged for the canonry aforesaid.

On 10th January 1409-10, at Southwark, Bishop Henry Beaufort collated Sir Robert Carpenter (late rector of Greatham in the archdeaconry of Winchester) to the vicarage of Hussebourne, *vice*

Sir John Snappe, its late vicar, who exchanged for the rectory of Greatham.

On the 20th February 1410-11, at Sarum, George Louthorp, Treasurer of the Cathedral Church of Sarum, instituted, on the collation of Henry Beaufort, Bishop of Winchester, Sir John Maydekyn (late vicar of the parish church of Alwardebury in the diocese of Sarum) to the vicarage of the parish church of Husebourne Priors, *vice* Sir Robert Carpenter, its late vicar, who exchanged for the vicarage of Alwardebury aforesaid.

Sir John Palmere. (The institutions are defective from 1417 to 1446.)

On 28th October 1447, at Southwark, William Wayneflete, Bishop of Winchester, collated Sir John Grene (late vicar of Andover) to the vicarage of the parish church of Saint Marie's Bourne, vacant by the resignation of Sir John Palmere, its late vicar, by reason of his exchanging for the vicarage of Andover with the aforesaid Sir John Grene.

On 3rd December 1449, at Southwark, William Wayneflete, Bishop of Winchester, collated Sir John Perburne, chaplain, to the vacant vicarage of the parish church of St. Marie's Bourne (*de Borne Sanctæ Mariæ*).

On 13th October 1450, at Wolvesey, William Wayneflete, Bishop of Winchester, collated Sir John Baldewyn, chaplain (late vicar of Wherewell), to the vicarage of Bourne St. Marie's, *vice* Sir John Parborne, who exchanged for the vicarage of Wherewell.

On 11th June 1456, at Farnham, William Wayneflete, Bishop of Winchester, collated Sir William Dawsone, chaplain, to the vacant perpetual vicarage of the parish church of Husseburne, and of right in his collation and gift.

On 7th July 1472, at Southwark, Bishop William Wayneflete collated Sir John White, chaplain, to the vicarage of Burne St. Marie's, vacant by the death of Sir William Dawsone, its late vicar.

Sir Thomas Gray occurs as vicar of Husborne Priors in September 1517, and as non-resident.

Mr. Thomas Prutt was vicar of Husborne Priors in September 1520.

On 27th August 1527, Dr. Richard Fox, Bishop of Winchester, collated Sir Roger Blakelow, chaplain, to the perpetual vicarage of the parish church of Husborne Priors, vacant by the free resignation of Thomas Prutt, its late vicar, made on the 10th August 1527.

Sir John Arthure was vicar of Husborne Priors in June 1532.

On 8th July 1561, Dr. Robert Horne, Bishop of Winchester,

collated Richard Mill, clerk, to the perpetual vicarage of the parish church of Husborne Priors, vacant by the death of John Arthure, its late vicar.

On 9th May 1575, Nicholas Bacon, Lord Keeper of the Great Seal, presented, on the petition and recommendation of Lord de la Ware, Richard Mylles, clerk, to the vicarage of Husbourne Priors, vacant by lapse of time, in his (the Lord Keeper's) gift. Instituted by Bishop Horne on 1st October 1575,[1] as Richard Mills, clerk, to the perpetual vicarage of the parish church of Hursborne Priors, lawfully vacant, on the presentation of Queen Elizabeth, its true patron this time by reason of lapse of time.

On 12th December 1581, John Watson, Bishop of Winchester, collated Samuel Cole, M.A., to the perpetual vicarage of the parish church of Hursborne Priors, vacant by the death of Richard Mills, its late incumbent.

On 25th April 1583, Bishop Watson collated Henry Tanner, clerk, M.A., to the vicarage of the parish church of Hursborn Priors, vacant by the free resignation of Samuel Cole, its late incumbent.

On 9th May 1588, Bishop Thomas Cooper collated Thomas Goffe, clerk, to the vicarage of the parish church of Hursborn Priors, vacant by the death of Henry Tanner.

On 30th January 1603-4, Bishop Thomas Bilson collated William Elmes, clerk, B.A., to the vicarage of Husborn Priors, vacant by the resignation of Thomas Gough, clerk, by reason of his exchanging for the vicarage of Barton Stacy. This William Elmes appears to have been a careless and negligent man, as in October 1618, proceedings were taken in the Consistory Court against Mr. Elmes, Vicar of Hursborn Priors—1. For losing the Common Prayer Book; 2. For that the clerk burieth the dead; and 3. For neglecting to say service on Sundays, and evening prayers.

On 16th March 1630-1, at Winchester House, Southwark, Bishop Richard Neile collated Walter Marshall, clerk, M.A., to the perpetual vicarage of the parish church of Husborne Priors, in the county of Southampton, vacant by the death of William Elmes, its late vicar and incumbent. He was still vicar here on 13th September 1641.

Mr. Alexander Gregson, clerk, occurs as vicar of Hursborne Priors in September 1642. The date of his collation to it has not been discovered. He resigned this vicarage apparently, as he did not die until 1678.

[1] This double institution was owing to the right of presentation, on the vacancy of 1561, belonging to the Crown, by the previous vicar's suspension therefore not being in the Bishop's gift that turn.

On 24th October 1660, Bishop Brian Duppa collated William Toomer, clerk, to the vicarage of Husborne Priors.

On 24th January 1661-2, Bishop Brian Duppa collated John Claybrooke, clerk, to the vicarage of Husborne Priors.

On 20th December 1678, Bishop George Morley collated John Winter, clerk, M.A., to the vicarage of Husborne Priors, vacant by the death of John Claybrooke, clerk, its late incumbent.

On 4th October 1691, Bishop Peter Mews collated William Morse, clerk, to the vicarage of Husborne Priors, vacant by the resignation of John Winter, its late incumbent.

On 3rd December 1711, Bishop Sir Jonathan Trelawney collated Edward Middleton (B.A. of Wadham College, Oxford, on 13th October 1711) to the vicarage of Husband Priors with St. Mary Borne. He resigned this vicarage by reason of his institution to the rectory of Minstede on the 1st July 1714.

On 31st July 1714, Bishop Jonathan Trelawney collated Charles Turner, clerk, to the vicarage of Husborne.

On the 2nd July 1724, Bishop Richard Willis collated Charles Warner, clerk, to the vicarage of Husborne Priors, etc. He was ordained to the priesthood by Charles Trimnel, Bishop of Winchester, on 30th September 1722. On the 2nd September 1725, he was instituted to the rectory of Shirborne Saint John, and collated to the vicarage of Whitchurch on 20th October 1740. He held all these preferments at the time of his death, which occurred at the latter part of 1745.

On 12th January 1745-6, Bishop Benjamin Hoadley collated John Blair, clerk, M.A., of Queen's College, Oxford, B.A. on March 18th 1733-4, to the vicarage of Husborne Priors, etc. The same Bishop, on the 24th January in the same year, collated him to the vicarage of Whitchurch. He held the two vicarages with the chapelry of St. Mary Borne for 37 years, and died on 7th January 1783, aged 70 years; buried at Whitchurch.

On the 25th March 1783, Bishop Brownlow North collated George Owen Cambridge, clerk, M.A. (Queen's College, Oxford, B.A. 17th June 1778; Merton College, M.A. 30th June 1781).

On 10th January 1787, Bishop Brownlow North collated John Washington, clerk, of Trinity College, Cambridge, B.A. 1775, to the vicarage of Husborne Priors, etc. The same Bishop had collated him to the vicarage of Whitchurch on the 3rd April 1783, in succession to the Rev. John Blair, and resigned it for this vicarage, which he held until 1803, and then resigned it by reason of his collation on the 6th April to the rectory of Chilcombe, which he held up to the time of his death. He died on 22nd February 1812, aged 61 years, and was buried in Winchester Cathedral on the 29th February.

On the 10th June 1803, Bishop Brownlow North collated Daniel Williams, clerk, to the vicarage of Husborne Priors, etc.

On the 28th January 1808, Bishop Brownlow North collated Matthew Hodge, clerk (of Balliol College, Oxford, B.A. 5th February 1799, and M.A. 6th December 1804), to the vicarage of Husborne Priors, etc.

On the 24th December 1817, Bishop Brownlow North collated William Easton, clerk (of Wadham College, Oxford, B.A. on 12th June 1789), to the vicarage of Husborne Priors, etc.

On the 10th December 1831, Bishop Charles Richard Sumner collated George Francis Dawson, clerk, to the vicarage of Husborne Priors, etc.

On November 11th, 1843, Charles Richard Sumner, Bishop of Winchester, collated Samuel John Ingram Lockhart, clerk, M.A. (of Lincoln College, Oxford, B.A. on 19th October 1826, and M.A. on 9th July 1831), to the vicarage of Husborne Priors and St. Mary Bourne. He was formerly domestic chaplain to the Bishop of Quebec. He died on the 26th January 1887, aged 85 years. He was interred in the village churchyard, in an ordinary grave, on Saturday, January 29th. The coffin which contained the remains was made from a tree which was planted by the deceased about forty years previously, and which had been cut down under his instructions, and sawn into planks about six years before his death. These were made into a coffin by Mr. Batsford, a carpenter living in the village, from a design drawn by the vicar himself. Nails or screws were not permitted to be used; but the coffin was joined together with pegs formed of the same wood as the coffin. The coffin bore no plate or fittings; and at the grave it was covered with the deceased's cloak, over which rested his surplice in lieu of a pall.

The Rev. Richard Burton was ordained to the curacy of Hurstbourne Priors with St. Mary Bourne on July 7th, 1850; and he held the curacy six years. Mr. Burton was then appointed incumbent of Woodcot by the Earl of Carnarvon, the appointment taking place in July 1856; but he resigned the duties in October 1876, on account of failing health.

The Rev. Watkin Temple succeeded to the curacy of both parishes in July 1856; and filled the appointment for ten or eleven years, he having left in 1866 or 1867. During the time of his curacy the National Schools at St. Mary Bourne were erected, chiefly through his exertions.

LIST OF VICARS, FROM 1670 TO 1759.

(Extracted from the Parochial Records of St. Mary Bourne.)

I have published this list as I found it, as it supplies one name, that of Jas. Plowden, 1753, which is not included in the previous list.

1670-4. John Claybrook.	1723. Charles Warner, Curate.
1689. John Winter.	1743. C. W. Warner, Vicar.
1706. William Morse.	1751. J. Winbolt, Curate.
1714. Charles Turner, Curate.	1753. Jas. Plowden, Vicar.
...... Middleton, Vicar.	1759. John Blair, do.
1717-21. Smith Stone, Apl. 22nd.	George Hunter, Curate.

The Churchwardens of the Parish of St. Mary Bourne.

From A.D. 1664 to A.D. 1887.

The office of churchwarden is of very ancient origin. In the fourth century St. Augustine refers to certain officers in the church called *seniores Ecclesiastici*. These officers were not ordained persons, but yet had some concern in the care of the church. They were entrusted with the treasure and management of the outward affairs of the church. These persons may be looked upon as the ecclesiastical ancestors of our present race of churchwardens. (Smith's *Christian Antiquities*, i, 39; *Bingham*, ii, 19.) In the *Provincial Constitutions* of Reynolds, Archbishop of Canterbury, published in 1322, in Edward the Second's reign, we find churchwardens thus referred to:—

"We enjoin Archdeacons and their officials in their visitations of churches to cause the vessels, vestments, books, and other things belonging to the said offices to be written down, and have a special regard to the fabric of the church, and especially of the chancel, and that they fix a certain time for the supplying such defects as they find therein under some penalty, and let them make inquiry by themselves and such as belong to them whether there be anything to be corrected either as to things or persons in the parish where they perform their office of visitation, and let such excesses be corrected either at that time or at the next Chapter."

1664. Wm. Peirse and Thos. Brockley.	1674. Jas. Issorn.
1665. Thomas Brown.	1675. John Nicholas.
1666. John Batchelor, senr.	1676. Robert Longman, senr.
1667. Robert Thorngate.	1677. John Batchelor, junr.
1668. John Philpot.	1678. John Moore.
1669. Robert Welsh.	1679. Wm. Poore.
1670. Thomas Knight.	1680. Robt. Poore (since ye election of 2 every year).
1671. Wm. Adnams.	
1672. Richard Holdway.	1682. Wm. Waterman and Robert Longman.
1673. Wm. Phillis.	

The Churches.

1683. Robt. Thorngate and Richd. Holdway.
1684. John Monday and Edwd. Ratty.
1685. Matthew Rumbold and John Nicholas.
1686. Hy. Bray and Wm. Batchelor.
1687. Wm. Bond and Richard Berkley.
1688. Hugh Hellyer and Hy. Lambden.
1689. Robert Hall and Robert Carter.
1690. George Purvey and Thomas Lambden.
1691. John Kidgell and Thos. Berkley.
1692. John Batchelor and John Moore.
1693. Robert Longman and Isaac Thorngate. (Thorngate was objected to by the Vestry.)
1694. Robert Longman and Wm. Batchelor.
1695. Wm. Batchelor and Henry Bray.
1696. Hy. Bray and Thomas Frome.
1697. Robert Longman.
1698. Michell Hedges and Robert Longman.
1708. Richard Hall and John Goodall.
1709. John Carter and Thomas Berkley.
1710. John Searle.
William Poore.
1711. Thomas Beckley, junr.
John Beckley, sen.
1712. John Longman.
Henry Poore.
1713. John Longman.
Henry Poore.
1714. John Moore.
Robert Holdway, jun.
1715. *Leaf lost in book.*
1716. Mr. Hodges.
John Longman.
1717. John Carter.
William Green.
1718. William Green.
John Longman.
1719. John Munday.
Michael Hedges.
1720. George Selfe.
John Bolter.
1721. John Poore.
John Harbour.
1722. William Moore.
Gilbert Cole.
1723. Francis Flower.
Henry Carter.
1724. Francis Flower.
Henry Carter.
1725. John Longman.
James Batchelor.
1726. Mr. Rolfe.
Mr. Hedges.
1727. Farmer Green.
Mr. Edward Gale.
1728. John Longman.
Richard Beckley.
1729. John Longman.
Richard Beckley.
1730. Robert Holdway.
John Searle.
1731. Edward Gale.
Henry Poore.
1732. Edward Gale.
John Munday.
1733. Edward Gale.
John Munday.
1734. Robert Rolfe.
Francis Flower.
1735. John Longman.
John Poore.
1736. John Longman.
John Poore.
1737. John Herbert.
Robert Rolfe.
1738. William Longman.
John Herbert.
1739. John Bailey.
John Holdway.
1740. John Bailey.
John Holdway.
1741. John Longman.
John Batchlor.
1742. John Longman.
John Batchlor.
1743. Edmund Ratty.
Thomas Beckley, senr.
1744. Edmund Ratty.
Thomas Beckley, senr.
1745. John Holdway.
Joshua Vincent.
1746. John Longman.
Thomas Dowling.
1747. Edmund Rolfe.
John Herbert.
1748. Edmund Rolfe.
John Herbert.
1749. James Longman.
Isaac Holdway.
1750. Farmer James Longman.

Q

1750. Isaac Holdway.
1751. John Longman.
William Poore.
1752. John Harbutt.
Thomas Dowling.
1753. John Harbutt.
Thomas Dowling.
1754. William Arundell.
James Longman.
1755. William Arundell.
James Longman.
1756. Thomas Cordery.
Thomas Poore.
1757. Thomas Cordery.
Edmund Ratty.
1758. John Harbutt.
William Piper.
1759. John Herbert.
William Philpott.
1760. Edmund Rolfe.
John Moore.
1761. William Poore.
Thomas Beckley.
1762. William Poore.
Joseph Brown.
1763. Thomas Beckley.
John Moore.
1764. William Poore.
James Longman.
1765. James Piper.
Isaac Holdway.
1766. James Piper.
Isaac Holdway.
1767. John Moore.
Paul Holdway.
1768. John Fry.
James Longman.
1769. John Holdway.
John Longman.
1770. William Poor.
Edmund Ratty.
1771. Thomas Beckley.
James Longman.
1772. Thomas Beckley.
James Longman.
1773. Thomas Beckley.
James Longman.
1774. Thomas Beckley.
W. Poor.
1775. Thomas Beckley.
W. Poor.
1776. William Philpott.
Joseph Brown.
1777. Thomas Beckley.
Joseph Brown.
1778. Henry Poor.
Thomas Dowling.
1779. James Longman.
Earl Vincent.
1780. Joseph Brown.
William Poor.
1781. Richard Bull.
Thomas Philpott.
1782. William Longman.
Isaac Holdway.
1783. John Holdway.
William Hooper.
1784. John Herbert.
Charles Holdway.
1785. Robert Longman.
William Moore.
1786. Thomas Dowling.
John Ray.
1787. James Wedge.
Richard Bull.
1788. William Poore.
Richard Tanner.
1789. William Poore.
Richard Tanner.
1790. Robert Longman.
Paul Holdway.
1791. William Longman.
Robert Longman.
1792. Thomas Purver.
John Holdway.
1793. Richard Bull.
Isaac Holdway.
1794. William Poore.
William Hooper.
1795. Robert Longman.
William Poore.
1796. John Herbert.
William Wedge.
1797. William Longman.
Charles Holdway.
1798. Richard Bull.
Richard Tanner.
1799. Robert Longman.
William Moore.
1800. William Poore.
John Holdway.
1801. William Longman.
William Poore.
1802. Isaac Holdway.
John Farr.
1803. William Hooper.

1803. Richard Bull.
1804. Robert Longman.
    Thomas Farr.
1805. Robert Longman.
    Thomas Purver.
1806. Charles Holdway.
    George Dowling.
1807. John Herbert.
    William Holdway.
1808. Richard Bull.
    Robert Longman.
1809. Robert Longman.
    George Dowling.
1810. James Longman.
    John Poore.
1811. Isaac Holdway.
    Charles Holdway.
1812. William Wedge.
    William Poore.
1813. Richard Longman.
    William Hooper.
1814. James Longman.
    John Farr.
1815. Thomas Longman.
    Robert Vincent.
1816. Charles Holdway.
    Henry Poore.
1817. Robert Longman.
    William Holdway.
1818. William Dowling.
    Thomas Purver.
1819 James Longman.
    John Herbert.
1820. Thomas Longman.
    John Longman.
1821. Robert Munday.
    Isaac Holdway.
1822. William Hopkins.
    Robert Longman.
1823. James Longman.
    Thomas Hooper.
1824. James Longman.
    Thomas Hooper.
1825. Thomas Longman.
    John Herbert.
1826. William Dowling.
    Robert Longman.
1827. John Longman.
    Robert Longman.
1828. John Longman.
    Robert Holdway.
1829. Thomas Longman.
    John Herbert.

1830. John Herbert.
    Thomas Longman.
1831. John Longman.
    William Dowling.
1832. Thomas Purver.
    Thomas Hooper.
1833. John Moore.
    H. B. Vincent.
1834. Thomas Longman.
    Isaac Holdway.
1835. Mr. Herbert.
    John Longman.
1836. Robert Longman.
    James Dance.
1837. William Longman.
    Lloyd Herbert.
1838. William Dowling.
    John Brown.
1839. Edward Wedge.
    William Dowling.
1840. Thomas Longman.
    John Moore.
1841. W. Longman.
    H. B. Vincent.
1842. John Longman.
    John Herbert.
1843. Robert Holdway.
    G. A. Vincent.
1844. Walter Dowling.
    Thomas Hooper.
1845. John Moore.
    Lloyd Herbert.
1846. Thomas Longman.
    Thomas Piper.
1847. Thomas Longman.
    H. Poore.
1848. Thomas Longman.
    H. Poore.
1849. John Moore,
    Thomas Longman.
        And the same to 1853.
1854. John Moore.
    Robert Holdway.
1855. Thomas Longman.
    Walter Dowling.
1856. Thomas Longman.
    W. Day.
        And the same to 1858.
1859. John Lywood.
    W. Day.
        And the same to 1862.
1863. Edwin Lywood.
    W. Day.

1864. Edwin Lywood.
W. Day.
1865. John Eyles.
W. Day.
And the same to 1873.
1874. John Berry.
W. Day.

The same to 1883, when Mr. Day died.
1884. John Berry.
Dr. Phillips.
The same to 1886.
1887. J. C. Hooper.
John Berry.

The Church Register.

The Church Register commences in 1661, 13th of Charles II. Registers appear not to have been general till towards the end of the sixteenth century, although, according to Burn, the institution of Parish Registers commenced in 1501, 16th Henry VII. The St. Mary Bourne Register consists of several books, which with some of the later churchwardens' account-books are kept in an iron safe in the vestry. The earlier Register is not in very good condition, but is fairly readable; and the earlier caligraphy is better done than the later. Up to 1676 the writing is neatly engrossed, its uniformity implying that the entries were made by the same person. Later, the writing changes frequently, as if entrusted to the parish clerk of the period, or to some village official. Probably more people then knew how to write, and there was not the necessity to employ a competent penman. On the first page of the Register the name "Goodman Baker, May ye 20th," appears, it is therefore likely that he was the copyist; or it might have been the Vicar, at that time the Rev. John Claybrook.

Many of the names registered at that time are the same, but there are some that are not the same, as those of the present inhabitants. There are occasional peculiarities in the spelling, burials and marriages being sometimes spelt "buryalls", and "marriges". The affidavits were obtained at Whitchurch. From 1683 to September 1685, the Vicar then being the Rev. John Winter, the affidavits of burial were usually not supplied till after the interments, at all events they are dated later; and such occurs occasionally afterwards.

There is very little out of the ordinary routine in the entries. On the first fly-leaf there is a record that "Susanah, the wife of Stephen Burgis, was delivered of 3 children, 2 sons and 1 Daughter, May 31st, 1756, and buried June 3rd, 1756, all in one coffin." This is evidently a later entry written on an earlier register.

1699.—Mary, the daughter of Richard and Martha Hall, was born Nov. 28th, but not 1699, Baptiz'd.

At the beginning of the eighteenth century the register is not so well written; but it is kept better from 1726 to 1751, and in uniform writing. The churchwardens' book also of about 1775 is not very "scholarly" arranged. The money is stated as "gothered", and as "uncoleckted". It appears, further, that in 1706, October the 10th, "Sachariah Jolly and Mary Horne was maried". On the whole, however, the church accounts were kept in a simple and effective manner from 1686 to about 1850. After that time the general arrangement is involved.

1708.—Arrangement of ye Tithe at Easter that for time to come if there be any Reporations done to ye Church that the workmen Shall be A Lowed noe Strong bear att a parish charge. And ye Churchwardens but 12s. and 6d. att ye Visitation—witness our hands (the churchwardens).

1715, March ye 19th.—Jane Beckley, daughter of Richard and Jane Beckley, born but not baptiz'd, being an Anabaptist.

1729.—Paid ye dial £1 15s. (sun-dial).

1733.—Received of Mr. John Munday for a seat in ye church, £3 3s.

1738, Nov. 5th.—Rachel Hegar, a Traveller, was buried.

1740, Feb. ye 8th.—Mary Stanley, a traveller, daughter of Richard and Millie Stanley, travellers, baptiz'd. (Evidently gipsies: the name is still well known in the district.)

1742.—The name Neave appears on the Register. He is the first recorded Schoolmaster.

1746, March 29th.—A young child, Stranger, was buried.

Occasionally there are familiar entries, Christian names being omitted, as,—1747, March ye 24th, Widow Bunny was buried. 1749, Oct. 9th, Joseph Portsmouth's wife was buried. (Rebecca is spelled "Bekkah".)

1759, Sept. 16th.—Mary Rudder was burried in a Meadow plot at Egbury—3 graves in a meadow plot. (These burials are referred to in The Tithings.)

Feb. 27th in the year 1781.—A high wind that blowed all the sheets of Lead except two from the Tower of the chancel in the middle Ile.

1782, Apl. 3rd.—Pd. for an Act against swearing 6d.

1783, Oct. 1st.—An Act of Parliament now takes place at 3 pence each for Registering.

1784.—Entries of several being "burried by the Parish". "Thomas, son of Thomas and Sarah, was baptised some day in Dec. 1784."

1787.—David Cox pd. for repairing the Great Bridge 19s. 9d.

1790, May 2nd.—Sarah, the Daughter of Sam'l and Elizb'th Paddick was baptised.

Feb. 14, 1794.—Amy, Daughter of Mary Phillips, was born. Baptised Mar. 25th, 1796. Base born.

Ann, Daughter of John and Sarah Purver, alias Phillpott, was baptised.

1784, April.—Thomas Hopgood's bill for repairing the great Bridge; and planks and piles under the Church Wall, £6 18s. 1d.

In 1813 and 1814, only three marriages are recorded in each year, probably on account of the younger men having gone as soldiers.

1803, Apl. 12th.—Pd. making the Sir plice 10s. 6d.

1804, Apl. 4th.—Puling in the Pigg Dying in the church yard 1s.

This appears to imply that the fences were not kept in repair at that time.

1805, Apl. 17.—Pd. for drawing Jonas Broad round ye tower 4s.

This refers to one of a long-standing family of bricklayers in the parish. He was most likely repairing the tower, and was suspended in some movable apparatus.

We have seen notice of a sun-dial in the churchyard, of which the following is a further notice.

1807.—Pd. £1 11s. 6d. Ed. Dodd's Bill for drawing the Sun Dial (re-drawing?).
1814.—Wm. Hayter's Bill for the iron chest and Register Book, £5 5s.
1818.—The Repairs to the Church amounted to about £85 18s. 6d.
1831.—Tasker's bill for iron gates to porch £5 2s. 6d.
1835.—New Prayer Book £2 5s.
1840.—George Gibbons made clerk. (He was Clerk for forty years.)

There is a notice dated Wednesday, Oct. 25th, 1848, that a new piece of land to enlarge the churchyard was consecrated. The Bishop was to plant a yew-tree, which was to be called "The Bishop's Yew". (This was done on the day of consecration.) The land here alluded to enlarged the graveyard on the east; and was presented to the parish by the late Mr. Thomas Longman of Diplands, and the late Mr. John Longman of Warwick. Among the church records are the following notices of bills concerning the same :—" For consecrating the piece of additional Burial ground, £19 7s. 4d."; and " Messrs. Earl and Smith's bill for conveying the piece of ground, £22 11s. 9d."

Among the papers is one executed on May 20th, 1884, by which Ann Elizabeth Longman of Wadwick, in the parish of St. Mary Bourne, "under an Act for the Consecration of Churchyards, of 1867", Grants and Conveys to the person or persons in whom the churchyard of the parish church of St. Mary Bourne is now vested, and his successors, a piece of land of 27 perches, on the north side of the churchyard, as an addition to the churchyard for burial purposes.

1861.—Cloth on Communion Table, given by Lady Portsmouth. Two chairs and two stools, by Lord Portsmouth; Two Communion Books, by Rev. Watkin Temple; Carpet, by Henry Hansard, Esq., in the Chancel. (This was Mr. Hansard of the House of Commons, who then lived at Dipland House.)
1861.—For tolling bell at the Prince Consort's death, 4s.
1880.—Repairing the Bassoon, 14s.
1886.—The amount of Christmas charities distributed, £41 3s. 3d.

The Church Clerk entered all the burials from 1801 to 1812, and the baptisms from 1802 to 1812. Thomas May was then Clerk, and he made the following notes of events, in the book of baptisms, in very good writing :—

1808.—A snowstorm, lasting the 19th, 20th, and 21st April, afterwards very cold.

1808, Apl. 23rd.—The Shandelear was put up; gave by Mrs. Hannah Longman.

1808, March 13th.—The Rev. W. Hodge, Vicar, preached the first time at Husband and Bourne, very March day and cold.

1801, Nov. 4th.—A great rain on the day Mr. Holdway was buried.

1801, Nov. 6th.—Great snow on the day Mrs. Longman was buried.

1809, Oct. 18th.—Robert Moore of East Woodhay fell from his horse in Hurstbourne Tarrant, and not spoke afterwards.

At the time the church was re-seated, it is evident from a plan which was found in the vestry chest that it was contemplated making an entrance at the west end through the base of the tower as at Hurstbourne Priors. In the plan as it was carried out the seats were divided into free and appropriated. The appropriated pews were provided with doors; and as it was found impossible to levy a rate £1 each was charged on the pews. This was found to answer very well in reference to the expenses. The pew assessments were adopted in 1871, when there was a balance against the parish of £21 15s. 2½d.; seven years later, in 1877, this sum became gradually liquidated, and the parishioners had a balance of £7 14s. 3¼d.

Aged persons, from the Burials Book:—

John Collins	died 1826	aged	99
Richard Bull	„ 1835	„	91
Hesther Wedge	„ 1835	„	90
William Longman	„ 1844	„	92
Lucy Moore	„ 1846	„	92
Mary Colebrook	„ 1868	„	92
William Bunce	„ 1869	„	97
William Holloway	„ 1872	„	92
William Hatton	„ 1872	„	91
Edward Wedge	„ 1873	„	90
Hannah Benham	„ 1874	„	90
Sarah Wedge	„ 1874	„	93
John Moore	„ 1878	„	90
Samuel Cowley	„ 1878	„	91
James Purver	„ 1878	„	91
Mary Goodyear	„ 1883	„	100, and 8 months.

Remarks on the preceding.—The ages were imperfectly recorded in the burials previous to 1826; but there is no instance of a centenarian in the century ending 1887 except Mary Goodyear.

Baptised in 1786, 27. Died in 1786, 10.
Do. in 1886, 9.   Do. in 1886, 19.

These figures give the differences in a century; but they show an increased death-rate in 1886, with a decrease in the birth-rate, as represented by the baptisms. The greater number of deaths in 1886 is most likely due to the increased population, which at the beginning of the present century was only half what it is now; but one year may be exceptional, and hardly a fair test either way. The decrease in the baptisms in 1886 may be accounted for by the fact that at the earlier period all were baptised at church; while at the later period the baptisms were shared by the various chapels of the parish.

The following table, taken from the Church Register, is intended to show the growth of education, in so far as writing can be taken as an estimate of education ; and it may be looked on as a considerable criterion in a rural population where the three *R*'s (mostly minus the arithmetic) embraced the curriculum during the greater portion of the period from 1813 to 1887. Taking periods of 25 years the figures read thus :—

From 1813 to 1837	. .	74.5	could not write.
,, 1837 to 1862	. .	59.2	,,
,, 1862 to 1887	. .	31.9	,,

Again, taking the 16 years before the passing of the Education Act of 1870 (which created the Board School), and the 16 years which have passed since—to 1886, when the figures terminate—it will be seen that the average for the former period is 46.2 (who could not write), while the average for the latter period of 16 years is 32.3.

A.D.	Number of Persons Married.	Number who could not write.	A.D.	Number of Persons Married.	Number who could not write.	A.D.	Number of Persons Married.	Number who could not write.
1813	6	4	1837	6	2	1865	12	5
1814	6	6	1838	12	10	1866	14	2
1815	8	8	1839	26	18	1867	12	2
1816	16	14	1840	20	10	1868	10	4
1817	14	10	1841	16	12	1869	14	8
1818	10	6	1846	14	7	1870	12	3
1819	10	8	1847	22	15	1871	12	4
1820	24	18	1848	16	11	1872	16	6
1821	8	4	1849	10	6	1873	22	8
1822	20	16	1850	14	9	1874	16	5
1823	8	8	1851	10	4	1875	18	6
1824	12	12	1852	16	10	1876	16	7
1825	24	16	1853	32	22	1877	22	6
1826	8	2	1854	16	1	1878	22	5
1827	16	12	1855	16	13	1879	10	4
1828	8	8	1856	20	10	1880	22	7
1829	10	4	1857	8	5	1881	18	5
1830	20	16	1858	22	15	1882	6	3
1831	18	14	1859	14	7	1883	14	4
1832	8	8	1860	12	3	1884	14	5
1833	34	28	1861	16	4	1885	6	1
1834	2	2	1862	14	13	1886	4	1
1835	18	12	1863	6	3	1887	2	—
1836	4	2	1864	10	1	Ending in April.		

Hurstbourne Priors Church.

The village church of Hurstbourne Priors (dedicated to St. Andrew) contains some relics of archæological interest. There is not probably a parochial church throughout the country which can claim a higher antiquity, the notice referring to it in the Charter of Bishop Denewulf quite confirming that a Saxon edifice stood, most likely on the same site as the present church, at the beginning of the ninth century (802). The structure, as we now see it, is modern, it having been completely restored, and the present tower built in 1870, by the present Earl of Portsmouth, the outlay being £1,200 (see notice in the church). Previous to this, the tower carried an unsightly belfry of wood; and some years earlier a wood porch stood in front of the tower, but it was removed in order to exhibit the Norman arch at the entrance. At the restoration of the church, the space occupied by the old tower was taken into the nave in order to furnish additional space; and the present tower, which is 54 feet in height, was erected in front of where the old one had stood. Hurstbourne Priors Church has always occupied the position of parent church, that of St. Mary Bourne being an attached chapelry; and one church only receives mention in *Domesday*, that of Hurstbourne. Hurstbourne Church occupies the parent position in the will of Sir Robert Oxenbridge of 1616, in which, in a bequest in aid of repairs, it is stated that he gave "ten pounds towards the repair of Hurstbourne Church, and five pounds towards the repair of the chapel at Bourne". Most of the existing church architecture is quite recent; but the mortuary chapel, now used as a vestry, on the north side of the chancel, is most likely of about the middle of the sixteenth century. Part of the south chancel wall is also of earlier date; and there are remnants of Transition Norman in the *chevron* mouldings of the half-circle arch, and capitals of the doorway at the west entrance. Late Norman work is also recognisable in the arch and imposts between the chancel and the chapel on its north side; and the capitals of the columns, which are now placed as *sedilia* in the chancel, are of the same period. These range from about the middle of the twelfth to the middle of the thirteenth century. They appear, indeed, to correspond in date with the earlier work in the neighbouring church of St. Mary Bourne. The entire church has a light airy appearance, the modern windows being Perpendicular. By the re-arrangement of the interior, the pew-room was adapted to furnish sittings for 250 people.

In reference to a former Lord of the Manor, the tomb of Sir Robert Oxenbridge is an imposing object. It stands on the north side of the chancel, between it and the robing chapel, and inscriptively bears reference to another member of that family. In its *tout ensemble* it quite fulfils the stipulations laid down in the will of Sir Robert of 1574, who was Constable of the Tower, that a "tomb should be erected suitable to his degree of a Knight, ornamented with the warlike insignia appertaining to his profession, and bearing an epitaph." The monument, of about the date named in the will, evidently carries out all this; but the object seems to have been one of display rather than of heraldic accuracy, the figure of the Knight being encased in the military trappings of an earlier period. The canopy of the tomb is Ionic with circular-fluted corner columns, which are supported on similar pillars at the four angles of an altar-tomb, which rests underneath the canopy. But these lower columns are architecturally so unsuited for the work they have to do in carrying the pedestals of the upper columns, as to lead to the inference that the lower tomb was either an adaptation, or that during its construction an alteration was made in the design to render it more suitable to the degree of a knight, and that the work was done by different sculptors. On the slab underneath the canopy rest the full-length figures of Sir Robert and his wife. Figures of their descendants, seven on each panel, with their faces eastward, are in the attitude of prayer for the souls of the departed.

Although the artisans of that period in England made but inferior monumental specimens, such were locally produced, at all events they were furnished in the metropolis. Nevertheless, the higher sculptured tombs were the work of foreign artists; they came, as in the case of many other art works of that period, from Italy or Holland. And it is most likely that the Oxenbridge monument, following the ordinary patterns of the gilded and painted specimens which are styled Renaissance, came into this country from a foreign workshop.

The inscription on the north side of the monument is in places illegible. It, however, states that the tomb contains the body of Sir Robert Oxenbridge, Knt., son of Godard Oxenbridge, and sometime Constable of the Tower, in the reigns of Mary and Elizabeth; and also the body of his wife, a daughter of Thomas Fogge, Knight at Arms, of whom he had born sons and daughters. The inscription bears date, December 15th, 1574.

A moulding on the south side of the tomb contains the following inscription, in two lines, respecting Sir Robert Oxenbridge, of Piddle Trenthide, co. Dorset :—

The Churches.

> Robertus Oxenbregg de Pidle Trenthyde
> in Com: Dorset Armiger Prætati Filii a Patri
> Nepos Monumentum Hoc Labefactatum
> et Squalore Obrutum Antæ Pietatis
> Memor Anno Domini 1705 Redintegrabit
> et Juxta Politus Jacet Qui Obiit
> Julii Die 27 Anno Ætatis Suæ 88
> Annoque. Domini 1707.

At the time the repairs were in process at Hurstbourne Church, in making some alterations in the floor, one side of the Oxenbridge vault was laid open, when its interior was observed to contain eleven coffins.

The Bells.

The tower contains six bells, which from their dates were the introductions of different periods.

The treble bell, of 1667, bears the word Signe, with the letters A.S., and a symbol made up of two bells and a battle-axe, inclosed in a fillet, with C.K. in the field, and H.K. on opposite sides of the diagram.

The second bell is inscribed with the letters A.S.

The third bell bears the following capitals, T.H.X.R.B.—R.X.H.G., with the initial letters A.S.

The fourth bell also contains the initials A.S. with *fourth sound*.

The fifth bell contains the following :—X. 63. X.—A.S. Tenar (not spelt with an *o*), and "*Hum all round*" on the centre of the bell.

The sixth, and largest bell, is inscribed as follows :—The gift of the Right Honourable John Lord Viscount Lymington, Edmund Relfe, Churchwarden, Henry Bagley, of Witney, made me 1741. And round the bell are the accompanying lines :—

> I to the Church the living call
> And to the grave I summon all
> Attend the instruction which I give
> That so you may for ever live.

In tracing the history of the bells it is evident that the H.K. and C.K., on the treble bell, refer to Henry and Ellis Knight, who were bell-founders in Reading in 1667, the date on the bell. We have seen that the St. Mary Bourne bells were sent to Reading for repair; and among the Whitchurch bells the third and fifth, the former bearing date 1612, and the latter 1611, bear the initials of Henry Knight. The A.S. on the second, third, fourth, and fifth bells imply that they must be the older, the letters most likely referring to a family named Saunders, who were bell-founders at Reading in 1547, the time probably when these bells were cast. I infer this from the fact that the initials 𝔄.𝔖., with 𝔖𝔦𝔤𝔫𝔢, appear on the treble bell, in company with those of the Knights; and there seems no doubt that this bell was first cast by Saunders, and that about 100 years later, on the bell becoming damaged, it was recast by the Knights. The big bell was evidently a fresh introduction, it being the work of a bell-founder living at Witney, in Oxfordshire.

A fine yew-tree stands in the churchyard on the south side. Its age from its stature can scarcely be less than seven or eight hundred years. It was most likely planted at the building of the Norman Church.

BENEFACTIONS.

On a board placed near the church door appears the following :—

Two hundred and forty-seven pounds, two shillings, consols, now standing in the name of the Earl of Portsmouth, in trust for the poor of the Parishes of Cliddesden, Farleigh Wallop, and Hurstbourne Priors, in the County of Hants, arising from a sum of money left by Mr. Dodington and others.

The interest of two-thirds of which is for the benefit of the poor of the Parishes of Cliddesden and Farleigh Wallop, and that of the other third for the benefit of the Poor of Hurstbourne Priors.

This account is made out by the Earl of Portsmouth in the year 1869, after careful investigation of his family deeds and papers.

Extracts from the Old Parish Books.

THE necessity of preserving extracts of this kind needs no advocacy, for it is to be regretted that parochial records too frequently find a depository in damp places in vestry rooms, in badly constructed ecclesiastical chests, and even in the church tower, and become the prey of mildew and spider.

Although many of the entries from the parish books of St. Mary Bourne will be found merely trivial and amusing, collectively they throw some light on past parochial history. From them we are enabled to learn what two hundred years have done in matters of education, as well as in the prices of some of the commodities of life. We find references to diseases then rife, and how they were treated; with extracts bearing on the operations of past laws, such as the old Poor-laws. We also learn a little respecting some old families; and there are notices concerning church usages and repairs, together with references to curious old books which were formerly employed in the church for public reading. Also what was done at vestries, and who conducted them. The earliest entry refers to the year 1633; but my first extract will be from the year 1635—exactly 250 years since. Now this period forms a large slice in the history of our country. It is the period of most of England's improvements, and should have to tell a good deal in the parochial history of any district. It takes us back to the disturbed times of Charles I. Contrast that time with the present one. It was a period of civil strife. Newspapers in the country were quite unknown. The first copy of the *Reading Mercury*, which was one of the earliest issues, lies before me in *facsimile*. It bears date 1723, and consists of four leaves measuring 10 inches by $7\frac{1}{2}$ inches, in double columns. The *English Mercurie* was nearly the only London paper in the time of Elizabeth; and the London *Weekly Newes* bears date 1622. The population of 1635 was about a fourth of what it is at the present day. The country gentry were comparatively uneducated, and the poor could neither read nor write. The means of travelling were so deficient that few ventured beyond the neighbouring market towns. Hunting in the day, and drinking and smoking at night, formed the summary of much of the country life, to which old prints and songs bear testimony. Books were but seldom published, and these only in London and a few of the principal towns. News came by post-letters, restricted chiefly to the wealthy, which were passed about from family to family till they were almost thumbed in pieces. People travelled in road-waggons chiefly, which were excessively crowded. A few coaches were introduced at the end of the seventeenth century, between places of importance, for even the roads between such towns as Newbury and Reading were almost impassable. What, then, must have been the condition of those of St. Mary Bourne?

At that time there could have been no school in the village beyond the horn-book class, where boys were taught rude discipline rather than book knowledge. We have no record of a school till nearly a century after the date of our first entry. And yet writing must have been familiar to some of the yeomanry, or the record could not have been kept; unless it was done by the parson, or by some competent person who was paid for the duty. Then the main road was merely a swampy drove, almost impassable to vehicles in winter. The river ran at will down the road and across it, and in times of flood was dangerous to travellers. The houses must have been wretched abodes, as it was thirty years later when those small homesteads were erected generally about the parish, which may now be recognised by their walls being laced together with stout oak timber. Further, a large proportion of the land now under cultivation must then have been down or forest; for at the time of James II, not more than half of the land in England and Wales had been brought into cultivation. The present owners of the manor, the Wallops, had just purchased the property of the Oxenbridges, the transfer having taken place in 1634.

The Extracts will be divided into three portions:—first, those which relate to Disease and Death; second, Entries concerning Church Expenses; third, Extracts relating to Parochial Matters.

Under the first division appear the following entries:—

1635.—For diggig a grave, 7*d*.
1659.—Pd Wm. Merry for going for y*e* bone setter, 1*s*.
1661, 17 Nov.—Pd Wm. Miles for diggig a grave for a poor alien that died, 6*d*.
1686.—Given to two empoverished by sea. (About this time a good deal of money appears to have been paid yearly to maimed soldiers and sailors.)

1687.—Payd Farmer Serle for curing Mary Hollen's lame leg and James Horns' boy 10s. 6d. (There is a surgeon of the name of Rolfe mentioned at this time. He lived at Whitchurch.)

1719.—Pd Mr. Willis for to have Sarae Freemantle cured, £5.

1720.—Rate Book—pd Lambden for laying out Bendel and for quiden (providing?) yͤ woath and woob 3s. 9d.; paid yͤ clark for yͤ grave and nell, 2s. 4d.

Providing the "woath and woob" refers to the "winding-sheet" to encase the dead and making it, which was done by means of the spinning-wheel. Spinning was an important method of administering relief to the poor, who according to the Act 43rd of Elizabeth were to be "set to work" when able-bodied. Linen-wheels were sometimes provided by the overseers for the use of the females, the cost being about 3s. each in the time of Queen Elizabeth; but they were to be seen as ordinary articles of furniture in the kitchens of the yeomanry, and their agreeable hum was a familiar sound when the wheel was in full operation. Some of the clean albeit coarse sheets made at that period are still preserved by old families. The last implement of the kind in St. Mary Bourne was used by Priscilla Goodyear of Stoke, in spinning mops. But "Granny" Bright and others spun silk, most likely in connection with the silk-mills at Whitchurch.

The grave-cloth of the period of the entry must have been of wool, the employment of wool being at that time compulsory. During the Middle Ages it was customary to wrap the dead in the sheet or shroud usually without a coffin; and the practice sometimes led to the placing the body in the grave with the face downwards. Under the Act 30th of Charles II, cap. 3 and 32 *ejusdem*, entitled "an Act for the lessening the importation of linen from beyond the seas, and the encouragement of the woollen and paper manufacture of the kingdom", the use of wool was insisted on to encourage the consumption and increase the trade of the clothiers and wool-growers. The Act was repealed 54th George III, c. 108; so that the time it was in operation was from about A.D. 1678 to 1814. Wool was always dear in ancient times. Thus, Whitaker, in his *History of Craven*, states that anno 1300, it sold for more than 6l. a sack, while the price of a cow was only 7s. 4d. The legal sack consisted of 26 stone, of 14 lbs. each; nearly 5s. a stone. The curate of every parish was required to keep a register of all burials in woollen. There was a fine for evading the Act, which was willingly paid by some, who were desirous to decorate the dead with lace, and even kid gloves, as in the case of Mrs. Oldfield, who died in 1731. Even the ligatures of the feet and the coffin-dressings were required to be of wool. The practice then in vogue has its survival in the present woollen shroud.

1721.—Pd old Charter curing Faune (Fanny?) children being bit with mad dogg, 6s.

1729.—Gave to a man at Wintoun that was burnd by litneng.

1731, Apl. 21.—Pd Farmer Serle for curing the widow Goodall's legg, 10s.

1739.—Mr. Bailey, bill for curing John Saunders, 15s.

1741, July 12.—For the small pox to Isaac Munday £5 7s. 6d. To y⁰ man for carrying to Ambrosia Saunders small pox, 17s. 6d. (This entry is expressive of the fear entertained of the disease. It became almost a standing disease in the parish for many years after this, the yearly bills being very heavy. Of £61 18s. 11½d. paid in 1741, the greater part was for small-pox. It was present in 1746, and as there were poor-houses in the various tythings the poor labouring under the disease appear to have been removed to them.)

1764-5-6.—Small pox rife.

1765.—Dr. Portsmouth's bill, £3 9s. (A Dr. Lawrence is mentioned, also a Dr. Holdway.)

1768.—Small pox very bad—many deaths. (A melancholy memento of its virulence is shown in the entry of "£1 4s. 6d. to four men for carrying the small pox people.")

1774.—Pd women for curing people's bad legs, etc.

1781.—Small pox, same year, Aug. 26th, 5s. 9d. for beer for the widow Plowman "for to make poultices". Sept. 23, 6s. 4d. for more beer. Afterwards, *item*, 4s. 6d. "for looking after widow Plowman." Again, an allowance of money for beer; and 5s. for "exteras".

1785.—Dr. Bendle for examining the body of Thomas Freemantle, £1 1s.

1791.—John Laws, broken yarm.

A Memorandum made by John Bull on " December y⁰ 23rd, 1797", contains the following :—"Small Pox ocationed by Neglect of a Child about 2 years and a half old Belonging to Wᵐ Baker of St. Mary Bourne Parish, Black Smith, to which nearly 50 was took bad in a fortnight besides as many obliged to be Inocalated."

1803, Ap. 13.—James Alright's Bill for curing Charity King's legg, 7s. 6d.

Small-pox was a terrible scourge in the village from time to time, in some cases probably more severe than it might have been under more judicious treatment. So fearful was the visitation that George Gibbons, the aged Clerk and Sexton, informed me that thirteen persons, who had died of this disease, were buried about the same time in a plot of ground close to the south wall of the graveyard, and the earth at that spot had not since been disturbed. There is no doubt that the following extract from the Church Register refers to this :—

1823.—Pd for bringing dead bodies 10s. candles 5s. 4d. (burried at night when the small pox was so bad here).

Inoculation was performed for small-pox, and those labouring under the modified form of the disease were sent to some secluded spot. The old cottage used for that purpose was, in 1855, still standing in ruins on the edge of the down near Doiley wood; and I have heard aged people talk of the fun they had there during their term of retirement.

Some of those mentioned as treating " bad legs", etc., were probably farriers, at all events they were not regular practitioners. Before the passing of the Apothecaries' Act of 1815 anyone might have practised medicine. But Portsmouth and Bendle appear to have been respectable surgeons, the former having for some years practised at Whitchurch. The name of Samuel Medhurst has been omitted; it appears in 1768 as receiving £7 5s. 10d. for attending small-pox. He was one of the earlier members of a family of surgeons who for a long period lived at Hurstbourne Tarrant. The "leech", "bone-setter", etc., were commonly herbalists of some local repute, who practised healing by simples. The last member of this fraternity wandered about the North Hampshire villages as late as 1865, dispensing gathered herbs in a dried state to the poor. He was an odd retiring kind of man, whose confidence it was difficult to obtain; but he once informed me that some of his simples were of but little service in healing unless they were "gathered at some particular phase of the moon". He sold a kind of soap, stated to contain Solomon's Seal,[1] for removing discolorations and freckles from the skin. Other helpers in times of sickness were aged matrons, who did their best with homely remedies prescribed in such books as Culpepper's *Herbal*, and Coles's *Art of Simpling*. Such ponderous works as Turner's *Herbal* of 1551, Gerarde's of 1597 (a copy in my possession bears date 1633), and Parkinson's of 1629, were unknown in St. Mary Bourne. Those ladies, whose efforts were directed in the relief of their fellow-villagers, were the latest representatives of the nuns of the Middle Ages, and of those benevolent "gentlewomen" for whom Gerarde wrote his treatise. They were the last of a class, for the herb-doctors whose custom it was to employ women as collectors, and who obtained their knowledge from tradition and not from books, had almost become obsolete. The entry of "*going for ye bonesetter*" brings before us a reminiscence of men who were general in times gone by, and of whom some examples were living and practising a century ago. Old Dr. Batter, of Market Lavington in Wiltshire, was a happy specimen of such, and really possessed considerable practical skill. He was a poor man, and lived in a cottage by the road-side, where his ancestors for a

---

[1] The use of Solomon's Seal for healing purposes was recognised in very early times. Gerarde's *Herball or Generall Historie of Plants* states that *Dioscorides* lauded the plant as "excellent good for to heale or close up greene wounds"; and, as Gerarde writes, the root of the same "stamped while it is fresh and greene, and applied, taketh away, in one night or two at the most, any bruise, blacke or blue spots gotten by falls, or Womens wilfullnesse, in stumbling upon their hasty husbands fists, or such like." Dr. A. C. Prior, in his *Popular Names of British Plants*, p. 209, says: "*Solomon's Seal*, from the flat round scars on the rootstock resembling the impressions of a seal, and called *Solomon's* from his seal being of frequent occurrence in Oriental tales, and a familiar expression."

generation or two had lived before him, and practised as a bone-setter. It was his custom to take his chair and table out alongside of a hedge, and having seated his patients he proceeded to prescribe for them with herbs gathered near; and his extensive acquaintance with wild plants and their localities enabled him to direct his visitors where to find what they wanted in the neighbourhood of their own homes.

The dentist of the village at the beginning of the present century was a blacksmith named Baker, some members of whose family had for a lengthened period relieved their neighbours of toothache by extracting their teeth. From the character of the instrument employed, it appears likely that the remedy must in many cases have proved more disastrous than the complaint. The apparatus consists of a home-manufactured iron key as a fulcrum, with a huge claw attached to it as a lever to grasp the offending tooth (Pl. XIII, fig. 2, of instrument now in the Reading Museum). But as the claw is irreversible, and made to do duty alike to teeth of various kinds, and on the opposite sides of the mouth, the injuries inflicted by the use of the instrument would have been discouraging, one would think, to an operator of greater nervous susceptibility.

On the same plate with the tooth extractor there is an interesting relic in the shape of a lengthened forceps, called Ember tongs (fig. 1). The instrument was found on a beam in an old house named "Munday's Cottage"; and it was employed to grasp small embers for the purpose of lighting the pipe. Its length is eighteen inches, and on its centre is a tobacco-stopper.

Extracts relating to Church Expenses, etc.

The first entry of interest is of the year 1676:—

1676, March 9.—For a stone wall bound, £3 3s. 7d. (As the wall in front of the church is of stone, capped with heavy blocks of sandstone, there is little doubt that the entry refers to it.)

1681-2.—The bells cast at Redding at £45 15s. with other expenses, such as dinner at King's clere, 4s., more expenses at Redding, 16s.—Ye last night, 16s.

1683.—Again a bell founder's bill of £18; "carrying them to Redding and bringing them back again, £2 5s."

1699.—They must again have proved unsound or have been damaged, for we find an entry,—"Michael Hedges and Robert Longman was churchwardens when the bells was cast by Mr. Robert Carr at Aldborne." ("Ye last night, 16s.," is suggestive. After a time the parishioners appear to have tired of these expenses, for later we fined an entry of contract to keep the bells in repair.)

In reference to the church bells being taken to Reading, it appears that, at the date 1681-2, the Knights were the bell-founders, there being notices of that family from 1618 to 1704.[1] After that

---

[1] Rev. C. Kerry, *History of St. Lawrence's Church, Reading*, pp. 83-91.

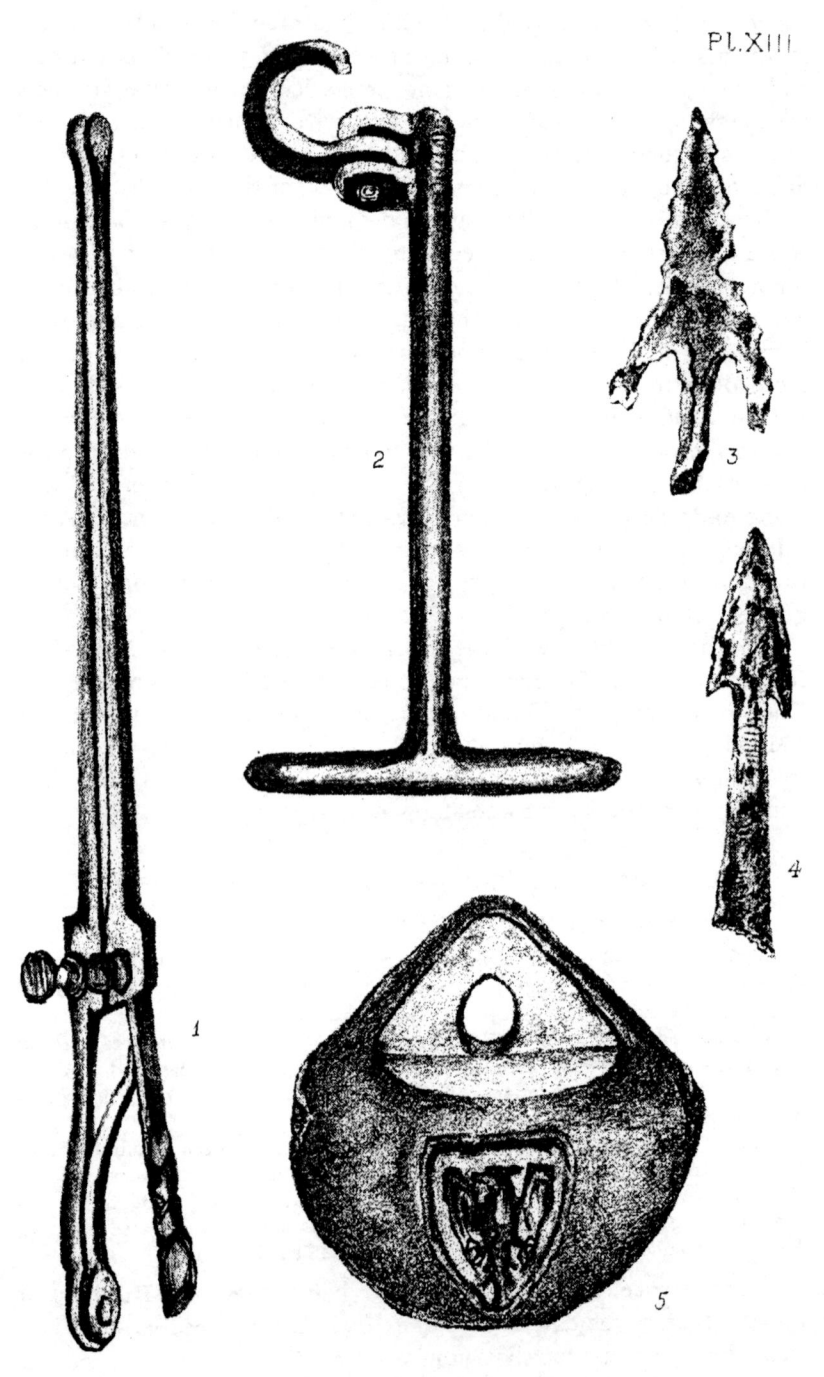

1. EMBER TONGS (⅓). 2. TOOTH EXTRACTOR. 3-4 IRON ARROW-HEADS. 5. COPPER WEIGHT (FULL SIZE).

date Robert Catlin (1748) was the founder. Previous to that time, viz., in 1593, Joseph Carter's name is mentioned. At a still earlier period Knight again is on the record, one William Knight having recast the bell "Harry" of St. Lawrence's Church in 1567. This same "Harry" was in all probability originally cast by William Hasylwood, who was a bell-founder in Reading from 1494 to 1509. That Knight's name or initials are not to be found on the St. Mary Bourne bells, evidently arises from the bells having been later cast by Carr (written *Cor* on the bells) of Aldbourne, Wilts.

Returning more minutely to the bells and their inscriptions: they consist of five, of which the first bell bears the initials H. C. * F. F.—C. W. * R. CO. 1724, meaning Henry Carter and Francis Flower, Churchwardens, and Robert Corr, who was the bell-founder.

The second bell is stamped Robert Longman—Michael Hedges C. W. * R. C. 98 (the C. W. meaning Churchwardens, and R. C. 98, Robert Corr, 1698, which is the same date as that on the fifth bell. They were evidently recast at the same time, and the dates correspond with the entry in the parish book).

The third bell is inscribed with the names Robert Rolfe—John Harbett * C. W.—John Corr * B. F. 1737 (B. F. Bell-founder).

The fourth bell is stamped with the names Robert Thorngatt—Richard Holdaway * C. W. 1683. This is one of the last bells which were sent to Reading, as the date corresponds with that in the record; it was not recast by Corr.

The fifth bell was recast at the same time as the second bell, 1698, and it contains the same names, Michael Hedges—Robert Longman * C. W. (Churchwardens). The bell bears also Rob. Cor. 1698; with the following:—

> On Earth Bells do ring
> In Heaven Angels sing—
>   Halaluiah.

Continuing with the Extracts—

1682.—Payd for an hour glasse, 2s. 7d.

The church sand-glass was in the possession of the late vicar. Some of the early glasses were supported on stands of iron, which were fixed to the side of the pulpit.[1] The cost of a glass in 1564 was

[1] *On Hour-glasses*, by H. S. Cuming, F.S.A., *Journ. Brit. Archæolog. Assoc.*, vol. for 1873, p. 130. Wood, in his *Curiosities of Clocks and Watches*, p. 244, says that the Fellows of colleges and other learned men, in the time of Elizabeth, carried sand-glasses in their hands to mark the time. In Dr. Cullen's time it was the custom of physicians to use a sand-glass to count the patient's pulse. These pulse-glasses are now exceedingly rare. They were about twice the size of the common kitchen sand-glasses.

one shilling. They were made to run from half-an-hour to twelve hours. It was not uncommon to see hour-glasses in the cottages of the poor fifty years ago; and they were used at an earlier date to measure the time in cooking, etc., when clocks and watches were expensive and difficult to obtain. An hour-glass in my possession was used about a century ago by the Wedge family, who lived in the hamlet of Dunley. It consists of an upper and lower bulb joined at their necks by a fillet or collar, and enclosed in a frame of wood formed by two disks fixed by five circular side pillars of wood.

1683.—Pd Acct. of Robert Thorngate and Robert Holdway: paid for a horse to fetch the book of martyrs from Redding, 3s.
1683.—Pd Wm. Poare for binding yᵉ book, 16s. 6d.
1683.—Pd John Lewis for looking to the church door, 4s.
1683.—Pd for 2 foxxes heads, 2s.
1686.—For the book of Homilies, 12s. 6d.
1686.—For killing of ffoxes, 9s.
1686.—Malt & expenses at church reckoning, 16s. 8d.
1687.—Payd to Farmer Monday for killing rooks, 6s.
1705.—Pd for one ould foxx, 2s. 6d. (This I suppose was old offender.)
1706.—Pd for a chaine for yᵉ book, £00 01s. 00d. (One would suppose that this chain must have been for the Book of Homilies, as further on an entry occurs of chains for the Book of Martyrs.)
1714.—Pd Goodman for a fox, 2s. 6d. Pd for 4 foxes, 6s. John Houldaway for 8 foxes.

After this foxes were killed in increasing numbers, from twenty to thirty yearly. The Bourne authorities appear to have bought them from any other neighbourhood, mention being made of Andover, Litchfield, Vernham, "*Done hosburn*", "*Up hosburn*", etc. It is evident that the destruction of poultry and game by foxes, stoats, polecats, etc., and even lambs by foxes, determined the Churchwardens to exterminate them in every way possible. Two shillings each seems to have been about the regular price. The destruction of the animal began to wane at about the end of the eighteenth century. In 1735, twenty-four foxes are mentioned; and in 1765, £1 12s. was paid for "Fockses". If similar purchases were made in other parishes the slaughter must have been enormous. The heavy, slow, old-fashioned harrier then occupied the place of the modern dashing foxhound, hare-hunting forming the principal sport of the country squire. There was more woodland as shelter for foxes; and a good deal of the land now under cultivation was down, as shown by the names of Warwick-down, Eggbury-down, Week-down, the greater part of which, if not the whole, being now arable.

1705.—A common prayer book, 11s.
1705.—Binding of yᵉ too books, 14s.
1705.—Sparrows bought in large quantities, as many as 70 dozen yearly.
1720.—Forty-to duzen sparos, 7s., John Lamden.

In past times the churches and churchyards were badly kept. Bones and even portions of corpses appeared above ground. Dogs frequented the church and churchyard, being attracted thither by the offal, which was often put there. It was the custom for the churchwardens to pay in the church for heads of foxes, badgers, stoats, moles, hedgehogs, magpies, sparrows, etc.: some of these rendering unsightly the church door, to which they were nailed. An official was paid a small sum to drive dogs out of the church; he often had the additional duty of keeping people awake during the sermon—the stick being more stirring probably than the doctrine. The church was commonly used for public business, marketing, and for the election of churchwardens, overseers, and other parish functionaries. Announcements of sales and meetings were made from the pulpit. Men drank and smoked there; and feasts, assizes, and plays have been held in churches; but the plays were in representation of Scripture subjects. During the progress of the Reformation most of the early church usages became discontinued. "King-ales", "Church-ales", and such-like were absolutely forbidden, as may be gleaned from the *Eighty-eighth Canon*, 1603, where it is stated:—"The churchwardens or questmen, and their assistants, shall suffer no plays, feasts, banquets, suppers, church-ales, drinkings, temporal courts, or leets, lay-juries, or any other profane usage to be kept in the church, chapel, or churchyard, etc."

1720.—A facetious entry,—"John Munday is my name." (A farthing trade-token was found at Hurstbourne Tarrant in 1865, which bore the name of Munday; but as no individual of that name could be found in the register of that parish, or in that of Hurstbourne Priors parish, the coin most likely referred to one of the St. Mary Bourne Mundays.)

1726.—Pd. for yͤ Church Bible, £3 12s.

1727.—Another facetious entry,—"To farmer no body pd. nothing, James Holdway" (evidently made at the wind-up of a vestry meeting).

1730.—Pd. singing master, £1 6s.

1752.—Apl. 1st, pd. for 2 chains for martyr's book, 3s.

1752.—Apl. 1st, for binding yͤ Martyr's book, 15s.

There is a later entry in the church records of a payment of "7s. 6d. for binding the Great Bible, Apl. 14th, 1773." In the year 1538, every parish priest had orders to procure an English Bible of the largest print, at the joint expense of the parish and himself. In the eighteenth century, the Bible and Fox's *Martyrs* were chained to an oak table in the church. This table came into the possession of the late vicar at the time the church was restored; and was sold after the vicar's death, and is now in the Reading Museum. It is rudely constructed, and evidently the work of the village carpenter. Two coarse chains are attached to it, secured to the supporting pillar underneath the desk, with clips at the ends for attachment to the books, a scrap of leather binding still remaining in one of the clips. The table is 4 ft. 9 ins. in height, standing on a strong pedestal with a cruciate foot; and the reading-desk is square (see figure), and made to revolve so as to bring a book on either of its sides to face the reader. The desk can be taken off by unscrewing an ornament at the top. These relics, wherever they are met with, are pretty much of one date; that of the Reformation, or soon after it, when Bible-reading was permitted among the people. They, therefore, mark an important period in ecclesiastical history. The dates of the extracts testify to the use of the St. Mary Bourne table for about one hundred years, but it must have been used much later than this. The late Mr. John Moore stated that one of his ancestors was in the habit of reading the chained Bible. This was probably the John Moore who in 1692 was one of the churchwardens. The several books mentioned were doubtless used on the table, but they might not all have been chained to it. The employment of chains expresses perhaps the great value of the books, rather than the necessity of securing them from being taken away or stolen, although security might have been an object. Books at that time were very rare and costly; and these were the only books to which the poor had access. The vicar, and the squire, or other wealthy residents might have had Bibles; but save these not a single copy probably was to be found among the whole of the parishioners. It is not, therefore, to be wondered at that the Bible should have obtained such a hold on the minds of the people, and have been held in such reverence by them.

Bell-ringing has always been a leading feature in village life. In the parochial books a general item is sometimes met with, as "ringing money". This occurs in 1754; but I imagine that this general drain on the purse at times brought about a more economical arrangement, inasmuch as later the ringers were paid annually. Thus, in 1777, the sum paid was 17s.; and in 1815, 15s. The courage of the villagers appears, however, to have roused up on special occasions, for how could even a villager sit quiet when news of the victories of Rodney, Nelson, or Wellington rang among the hamlets? The following is an enumeration of some special occasions of ringing, etc.:—

1705.—Pd. for ringing for 3 several days 15s. (After Marlborough's victories.)
1745.—pd. for ringing bells £1 10s.
1743.—Pd. for Bell ringing for the battle the King was in 5s. (After Dettingen, in which George II was engaged.)
1759.—(For the fall of Quebec.)
1802.—(For the celebration of the Peace of Amiens.)
1815, March 29th.—Ringing on account of the Peace £1. (For Peace with France.)
1835.—Ringing bell for King William, 5s.

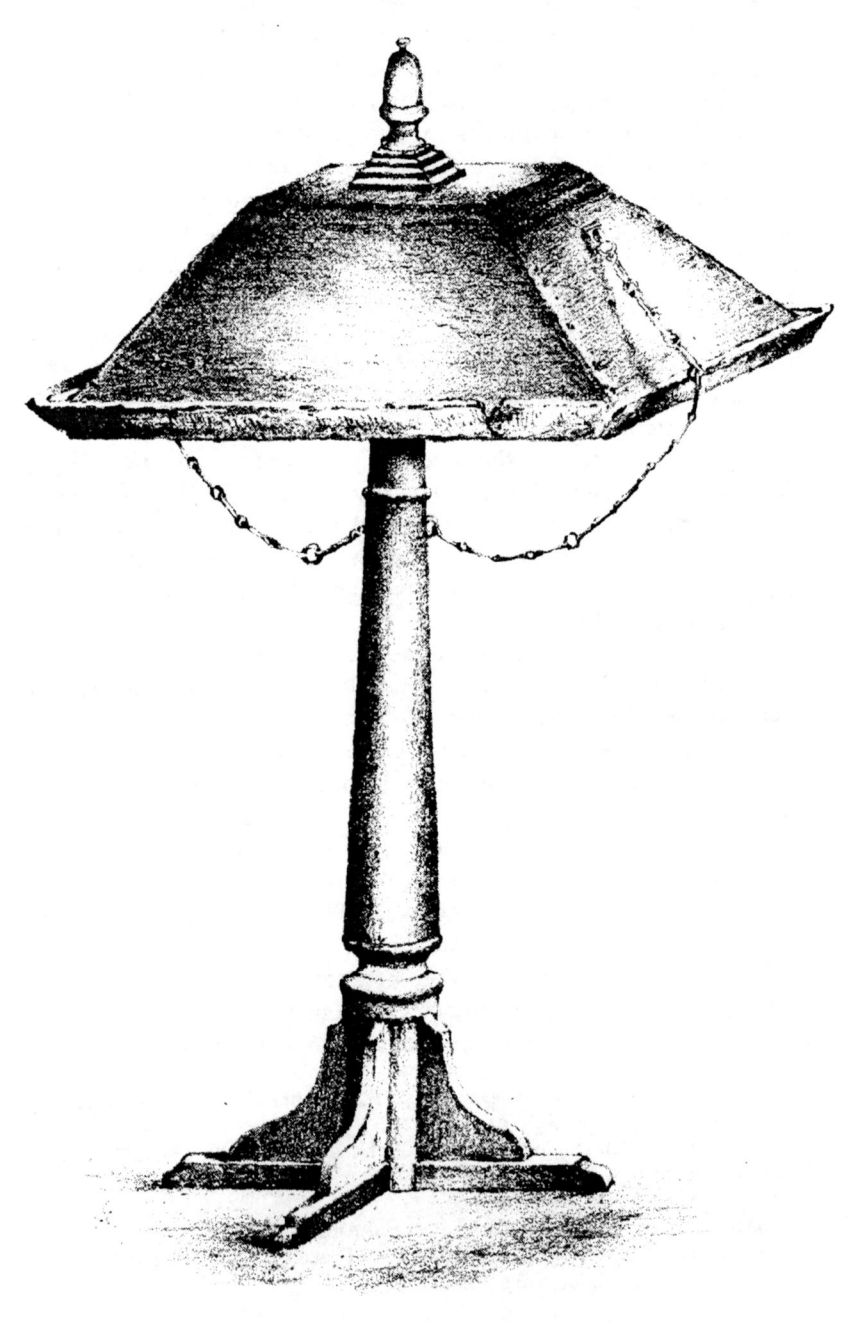

CHAINED-BIBLE TABLE,

It need not create surprise that so much money should have been spent in this way when we consider that almost every small matter out of the ordinary routine gave occasion for ringing. All the "tide times" were kept, and the annual revel at Bourne usually lasted a week. At Christmas—old Christmas—the bells had no quiet. They pealed away all day long and till midnight. Logs were dragged through the street and into the belfry, and burnt, the smoke making its way up among the bells and out at the turret-windows. Blazing firebrands were waved on the tower, and thrown into the street; the people entering the church to take part in the demonstrations. A fire occurred to the timber many years ago, and the oak to repair the mischief was brought from Tadley at 7s. 6d. a load.[1]

1759, April 11.—For setting ye yew tree, 6s. 6d.

This is the smaller tree, which was planted on the grave of Paul Holdway, so report says, to prevent the remains from being disturbed. A bushel of oats was placed in the grave, for what purpose it is difficult to conjecture. It was planted in 1759. The larger yew-tree was probably introduced at the consecration of the church, and if so its age must be about 800 years. Its girth is 21 feet, and it is hollow, the space in its interior furnishing a convenient receptacle for the implements used in preparing man's last resting-place. Some of the earlier tombstones stand underneath its spreading branches; one bearing date 1708 is the oldest recognisable date in the churchyard. The stone tells quaintly that—

The terrestrial part of Robert
Longman lys here sleeping.

In a statute of the 35th of Edward I, the felling of trees in churchyards is expressly forbidden,—" *Ne Rector arbores in cemeterio prosternat.*"

The great age of these trees, says Mr. Lower, in some churchyards, forbids the idea of their having been planted subsequently to the erection of the buildings, or any others consecrated to the same forms of faith that may have occupied their sites. According to the eminent botanist, Decandolle, the yews at Fountains Abbey and Crowhurst are each 1,200 years old; that of Fortingall, in Scotland, 1,400; while a fine specimen of *Taxus baccata* at Braborne, in Kent, must, according to the same authority, have been contemporary with Solomon's temple, having reached what Fuller would have called the "stupendous antiquitie" of thirty centuries. We know that it was the temporising policy of Augustine and the Roman missionaries to con-

---

[1] My authority for this statement was the late Mr. John Moore.

nive at many of the pagan superstitions which they found on their advent into Britain. Predilections for sacred sites and objects were indulged. Thus a druidical fountain lost none of its virtues in the popular mind if dedicated as a holy well to some saint, and many of the earliest churches arose upon spots previously dedicated to pagan worship, as within a druidical circle. I think it is highly probable, therefore, that from this feeling some churches may have been built in immediate proximity to sacred yews, and that afterwards—a symbolical meaning having been attached to the tree—it became customary to plant them in churchyards generally.

There are evidences that a cemetery of earlier date occupied the present graveyard, and extended into the field adjoining it on the east. Scraps of Romano-British pottery are sometimes found in the mould thrown out of graves, and fragments of bone, pottery, and flint flakes are brought to the surface of the field during the operations of farming.

During the repairs of the sixteenth and seventeenth centuries, the pillars and capitals of the church were plastered in a manner to hide the hollow mouldings and carvings; but these materials were scraped off during the restoration in 1855, when the edifice was re-seated. At that time some heavy links were removed from some of the pillars, which were unwarrantably attributed to Cromwell's soldiers. They had probably been placed there by some private individuals for the purpose of chaining books. Many of the dark oak pews which were then exchanged for the present series were quite as early as the time of Elizabeth.

Extracts relating to Parochial Expenses, etc.

The basis of our present system of relieving the poor in England originated in the famous Act of Elizabeth (43rd, c. 2, 1601), the professed objects of which were "to set the poor to work, to relieve the lame, impotent, old, and blind, and to put out their children as apprentices."

It was required in carrying out these objects that a fund should be raised, in every parish in England, for the maintenance of its own poor. The application of this fund was placed in the hands of the parish officers, justices of the peace having control over it. Another object of the Act was the subjecting of able-bodied men to a *test*, in order to prove that indolence was not the cause of the alleged want. Such persons were to receive relief only on condition that they should work for it.

About eight years after this, an Act was passed in the reign of James I (7 Jac. I, c. 4), ordering houses of correction to be built, provided with mills, and other appurtenances, for the purpose of setting the vagrant able-bodied poor to work. Although these houses of correction might be looked on virtually as penal establishments, they may be considered as having originated the workhouse system of England.

It seems evident from the statutes of that period, that the chief difficulty the legislature had to contend against was the indolent and vagabond disposition of a considerable section of the poor. These people preferred a life of wandering and idleness to regular employment, and thus they kept flitting about to wherever they thought they would be best supported.

Under the Act of Elizabeth, several deeds of apprenticeship lie among the parochial records of St. Mary Bourne; and bearing on the conduct of the justices in the management of the parochial system at that time, the following copy of a certificate, preserved in the Record Office, London, signed by several of the justices of the peace for the northern division of the county of Hants, will be found explanatory.

The certificate of Sir Robert Oxenbridge, Kt., William Lucy, Dr. of Divinity, Thos. Willys and Henry Reade, Esqrs., Justices of the Peace in this county of Southampton, 3rd March 1630.

We, the before named Justices of Peace, and all of us dwelling and residing within the division of Kingsclere, in this county, do purpose, God permitting us, to take care of the due performance and execution of their Lordships' orders and directions within the said division of Kingsclere, already sent or hereafter to be sent to us, as any cause or occurrence shall offer itself to us.

We have given orders at our Monthly Meetings that the Churchwardens and Overseers of the Poor in all places and parishes within the said division take present care that the old and truly impotent poor be competently relieved in their parishes, and that the poor, able and willing to work, be either set on work or relieved at the parish charge. And that all the poor be kept within the parishes and not *suffred to wander abroade a beggynge*.

We have, within this division, within this last month, *bound out fifty poor children apprentices*, and have thereby eased the poor parents and parishes of great charge, and intend to proceed against them that shall refuse to take and keep them according to the laws of the land, and their Lordships' directions therein. We have set watches and wards in this division, and relieved it of many *wandringe rogues and vagabondes*, and have sent some of them to the House of Correction, and others of them either to their dwelling places or places of birth, as their cases required, after punishment given them.

We have laboured with the *Clothiers* within this division to continue their *clothings*, which would set many or the most of the poor on work. They answer us they cannot so do, because the cloth lye upon them, and is not bought of them by the *Marchants* of London, and humbly beseech their Lordships to take it into their grand consideration. The prices of *corne* and *grayne*, in the markets of these parts, do hold and continue at the former rates, and Wheat is sold in these parts at 6s. 8d. and 7s. the bushel; Barley and Malt at 4s. and 4s. 4d. the bushel; oats at 2s. 4d. the bushel; Peas and Beans at 5s. the bushel.

ROBT. OXENBRIGGE,
THOS. WILLYS,
WILL. LUCY,
HNRY READE.

To the Right Worshipful Thomas Cotecle, Esq., High Sheriff of the County of Southampton.

The clothiers referred to here were doubtless those of Andover, Newbury, and perhaps Reading, at which places the manufacture of woollens was a staple industry. In 1666 the woollen trade of Andover was conducted by Staniford, who has left a trade-token of that date. He was a burgess, and signed the returns in 1672, 1677, and 1678. The late Mr. Samuel Shaw stated to me that he remembered a procession of Bishop Blaze and his clerks dressed in woollen, in 1818. Bishop Blaze is regarded as the patron saint of wool-combers, and the inn of that name in New Street was the place of meeting of that fraternity.

Continuing with the Parochial Extracts—

1634.—*Danley Mead* appears as an entry.

1635.—Pd for a pair of shoes for Maidde Smith 2s. 2d.

1669, June 5th.—Given to a Marchant's wife for relief to redeme her husband out of slavery 1s. Also, 1739.—Gave to a man out of Turkey 1s. (This entry refers most likely to slavery in Turkey, as similar entries occur in Church Records, notably an entry quoted by Lieut.-Col. C. King, in his *History of Berks*, of "2s. to two merchants' wives whose husbands were taken slaves in Turkey": taken from the Windsor *Register*.)

1686.—At the Petty Sessions at Up Husborne 6d. (proving that there must have been a petty court held at Hurstbourne Tarrant).

1723.—Pd for a Rideing Hood 5s.

1725.—Pd yᵉ charges for goen to yᵉ gestes 4s.

1720.—Paid yᵉ charge of yᵉ hiwayman, £2 1s. 5d.

1724.—Going to yᵉ Jestes with Mary Batchelor 6s. 6d.

1731.—To carrying yᵉ book to petty sessions and having of him signd 5s.

Danley Mead is mentioned here as being thought to refer to D'Andely, or Dandely, the name of one of the French Knights who came over with William the Conqueror, and obtained land in Hampshire (see *Richerius*).

The "Rideing Hood" was used as a cover to paupers and others, to be worn on their removal from the parish. They were generally conveyed on the backs of horses, seated on a pillion. The roads being unfavourable for vehicles, the farmers used the pillion for their wives, who sat behind them carrying their market produce in their laps. The poor often suffered terribly in being driven about to find their parishes; and were sometimes whipped through the streets, and even died during removal. Burn's *History of Parish Registers* furnishes a curious example of this. The entry states: "1578, there was comytted to the earth the body of one Johan Longley, who died in the highway as she was carried on holyback to have been conveyed from officer to officer, tyll she should have come to the p'ishe of Rayershe." Does "holyback" mean horseback, or that she was conveyed on the backs of the officers?

1750.—Bought at Weyhill, stockings, shoes, and shirt, 15s. 6d.

1751.—Agreed at vestry to pay £3 towards paying Thos. Piper's debts (debts being £10). (The Piper here referred to lived at Butler's Farm, which belonged to him at one time. He did not get on very well, and ultimately sold the property.)

1764.—Name of Hooper appears.

1765.—Alexander Neave appears as one of the overseers of the parish. He was also schoolmaster (see National Schools).

1766.—The name of Rudder appears. (He was a singular man, according to report, and one of the fraternity of Quakers. He lived at the house lately occupied by the last of the name of Munday in St. Mary Bourne parish, and it is stated that his bones repose in a meadow at Eggbury, known as "the Roman burial-ground", where his wife also lies, and a dog that had been his faithful companion.)

The notice of the purchase of goods at Weyhill deserves a word, as the fair held at Michaelmas was attended by the villagers for the purchase of their winter supplies of clothing and provisions, hops, cheese, brushes, cord, hose, horse-gear, blankets, brooms, and most other household commodities. It was a custom since the fair was established in 1599, when Queen Elizabeth granted the bailiff and Corporation of Andover a Charter to hold a fair, which Charter was confirmed by Charles II. The gathering commences on the 10th October; but before the granting of the Charter, the fair was nothing more than an ordinary revel, held on the Sunday preceding the feast of the saint—St. Michael—to whom the church of Weyhill parish is dedicated. One remarkable usage connected with it is that of the Court of *pie poudre*, provincially called "pipowder", over which the Mayor of Andover holds the jurisdiction. The court is held for the settlement of local grievances and disputes, and is a very early form of administering justice, the word meaning that the culprit shall be tried while *the dust is on the foot*, or at the moment of the offence.

In addition to the winter's stock obtained from Weyhill, the chief articles of consumption, at the time of which we are writing, consisted of bacon and salted pork, with the produce of the farmyard, among the farmers themselves, to which may be added, salt butter, cheese from skimmed-milk, and ropes of onions. A good deal of the sweetening was done with honey, as sugar was expensive; tea was a luxury, and tobacco almost worth its weight in silver.[1] Wines, when such were introduced at the family table, were universally the produce of the garden, extracted from gooseberries, currants, and home-grown grapes; but as sugar was expensive these articles were not very palatable. The kitchen-floors of stone or brick were sanded; but at an earlier period, and before the era of floors of stone, a carpet of rushes was the only relief to the native soil. The heating apparatus of the general assembly-room, the kitchen, was a huge, gabbern[2] fireplace on the hearth, flanked with spacious chimney-corners. A semi-lunar range of iron, with its lever for pot or kettle, was fixed on the right of the hearth at the base of the chimney, its stop-knobs of iron burnished as of silver. Dogs of massive iron, the handiwork of the village blacksmith, supported a rod, on and behind which was a seething fire of peat or big *maurs*,[3] coal being altogether out of reach. While overhead amidst smoke and soot were sundry sides of bacon, bronzed and snug in a capacious recess known as the bacon-loft. These were the domestic conditions of the farming community of the half-timber houses, the "better-to-do" people; but the condition of the poor bore a different and, indeed, almost a squalid feature. At the end of the eighteenth century and the beginning of the nineteenth, the state of the farm labourer was pitiable. His rations consisted of skim-cheese, a little bacon only on Sundays, sometimes a "red-herring", hardly a sufficiency of bread, and that composed of barley and wheat, with that piquant addition to his bread and cheese, a raw onion. To these might be added a little lard, and now and then "kettle-broth", which was pot-liquor from the farmer's kitchen in which bacon had been boiled. In this he sopped his bread. These were the commodities on which he lived, and on which he swung the heavy flail from morn till night.

At a time as far back as the thirteenth century, the higher class yeomen had timber-houses, housebote being, as we have seen elsewhere, a customary right of the tenants. They were built or rather framed together, the spaces between the timbers being lathed and plastered, or filled in with "mud-wall", a material composed of chalk or clay mingled with chopped straw; the floor was the bare earth, or it was sometimes pitched with flints. The bedrooms under

---

[1] In Queen Elizabeth's time tobacco was sold five pounds the ounce; and it was the custom in later times for those who indulged in the luxury to throw five-shilling pieces in the opposite scale. (*Transactions of Newbury Dist. Field Club*, 1872-75, p. 130.)

[2] Comfortless, large: see *Glossary of Provincial Words*. Halliwell, *Dictionary of Archaic and Provincial Words*.

[3] A root: see *Glossary of Provincial Words*. Used also by Wise: see *New Forest*.

the thatched roof were reached by means of a rude staircase or ladder. A few houses of this kind might have been seen in St. Mary Bourne fifty years ago; but they were occupied by the very squalid poor. These hovels were, however, somewhat in advance of the farm-houses of the Middle Ages, as they contained chimneys, and windows of a few panes of glass, which were in use only in manor-houses and castles at the more distant date. The home of the farmer of the fifteenth century had neither chimney nor window, the smoke escaping where the light came in, as in the case even now in some of the poorer cabins of the peasantry in the Western Islands of Scotland. The wood fire burnt on a hearth of clay; and apart from the light furnished by the glowing embers, but little artificial illumination could be permitted in the shape of candles, the fats being far too costly for such a purpose, being four times the price of meat. What artificial light they had consisted of dried rushes bearing a mere film of tallow, which were held in a sort of tongs called a rush-holder while being consumed. The house of the labourer was ruder still, for it had no second story; while the walls were of posts wattled and plastered with mud or clay. The floors of these homesteads, which were often below the level of the ground, were sufficiently filthy; but the surroundings were disgustingly dirty from the accumulations which were permitted to fester around the doorway. These drained where they best could in rainy weather, and polluted the dipholes and the village brook, for these houses were always near the stream, if one ran through the settlement.

Continuation of the Parochial Extracts—

1768.—Repairing parish house at Stoke 10s. 1d.
1741.—A poor-house mentioned at Swampton Green.
1781.—To Thomas Curcher £1 3s. 6d. for thatching the same. (From this and other entries it would appear that poor-houses were situated in each of the several tithings.)
1784.—For thatching parish house at Week; and for repairing the same.—Broad £42. (It stood on the site of George Gibbon's house at Week.)
1770.—Entry appears, "Thomas Beckley, now Earl Vincent."

One of this family, King Beckley, and William Brown, farmed the tithes of the parish. They were known as tithing men; and every tenth shock of wheat, and tenth pook of barley or oats were secured by them; they taking the tenths and paying the tithes to the lord of the manor. It was Brown's custom to enter a field, and direct a boy to cut boughs from the hedge, one of which he stuck into every tenth pook; the pooks so marked being left behind by the farmer in carrying the corn.

In 1724, "George Wigg of Basing, a member of a long-settled

family near Basingstoke, was prosecuted in the Exchequer for tithes, at the suit of Thomas May, tithe-farmer."[1] For a demand of about £3 5s., he was sent to Winchester gaol, May 3rd, 1712, and thence removed by habeas corpus to the Fleet, Nov. 28th, where he remained more than a year. Hampshire, up to the year 1736, reports twenty-two Quaker confessors, nineteen of whom were prosecuted in the Exchequer, two in the Church Courts, and one elsewhere. Of the twenty-two, six were thrown into prison. In this list the name of Anthony Purver, a Quaker, of Andover, and at one time of Hurstbourne Tarrant, does not appear. He was a remarkable man, and although only a shoemaker was a Hebraist of some repute, and also a schoolmaster. Perhaps he was too poor to be prosecuted. He died at Andover in 1777.

1739, April 25.—Pd for the marriage of Susan Hall and having her away £4 15s. 4d.

1782.—For a licence and ring for Charles Lewis, £2 minister and clerk's fees, also for four men for a sisting Charles Lewis. (He seems to have been a very refractory bridegroom.) Afterwards "2s. 6d. for a horse to have Charles Lewis to Kingsclere".

1786.—Expenses of taking up and marrying George Admens and Wm. Swain, £9 11s., with other expenses for rings, licences, etc., and marrying at Whitchurch.

1788.—Expenses at parish meeting, £1 0s. 6d.

The "*a sisting*" Charles Lewis might I think be more truthfully rendered by the substitution of the word *coercing*. That these marriages were compulsory there can be no doubt, for in the next entry we find "expenses of *taking up*", etc. Such transactions were wasteful of the poor-rates, and demoralising to the people; they were nevertheless of frequent occurrence under the old bastardy law, which positively gave encouragement to female unchastity. An allowance in money was made for each illegitimate child; so that the means increasing with every spurious addition, a woman with several such became as well provided for as a mother with a similar number of lawful children. The same law, further, subjected the putative father to punishment often at the woman's discretion, rendering him liable to the alternative of marriage or the prison. Of course he commonly chose the former as the least of the two present evils. All this was however small compared with the consequences of such influence on the female character. Where these measures largely prevailed chastity ceased to be valued as a virtue. In short, the woman as well as her husband and parents became in a great measure indifferent to it.

[1] Woodward and Wilkes, *Hist. of Hampshire*, p. 285, *n*.

The Loan of 1627.[1]

In 1627 there was very general discontent throughout the country, consequent on the demand made by the King (Charles I) on the people under the head of "Loan", which had been met, not merely with murmurs, but by absolute and even "contemptuous" refusal on the part of several on whom the impost was made.

"The Council impudently pretended that Parliament was not called at this crisis, only because the urgency of the case would not allow time for their assembling and deliberating; and therefore a *general loan* was enacted, and each individual was called upon to contribute according to his rating in the last subsidy. Commissioners were let loose upon the land with books and registers, and most tyrannical instructions of the King's and Council's making. The money, it was said, would all be paid back by the King to his loving subjects out of the next subsidies voted by Parliament; but people knew not when the King and Parliament would agree, and they had already ample grounds for doubting the veracity and good faith of Charles and Buckingham, who still seemed one and indivisible. Many who had refused to contribute to the loan were visited by all the vengeance of absolutism;—the rich were imprisoned—the poorer sorts sent to serve in the army or navy; *nor would Charles in any one instance step between the severity of his agents and their victims.*"

CHARLES I.—A.D. 1627.

The following is a return of such persons as were refractory, and would not appear before the Commissioners for the Loan for the Division of Kingsclere:—

OVERTON BOROUGH.

Tadly.—Bartholomew Wyatt (obstinate refuser); Henry Ludlowe, Esq. (A commissioner that never did sit or would lend.)

Hurstbourne Priors.—Maudlin White, widow; John Green; Thomas Fisher.

St. Mary Bourne.—Thomas Berkley, Robert Poore, Thomas Fisher.

Stoake.—Edward Rumboll; Thomas Knight; Anne Hayes, widow; George Bray; Henry Bray; Jeffery Ilderwell (an obstinate refuser).

Eggbury.—William Bright; John Godwin; John Broadway; William Oxenbridge, gentleman.

Weeke.—Robert Hayes; William Godwin; William Longman; Thomas Cannon (obstinate refuser, being constable); William Bunney (obstinate and

---

[1] Macfarlane's *Hist. of England*, vol. ii, p. 388; and Rushworth's *Collections*.

contemptuous). (He was doubtless an ancestor of the late Mr. Bunney, of Hurstbourne Tarrant.)

Binley.—Agnes Iserne, widow; William Poore.
Swampton.—Thomas Adnam; Thomas Morrant.
Bradley.—Edward Pierce.
Whitchurch.—Wm. Shrimpton, Valentine Hayward, Jane Barnett, Fardinando Randall, Wm. Cooper.
Freefolk.—John Silver (obstinate refuser); Elizabeth Mason.
East Woodhey.—John Kinge, John Pecock.

PASTROW HUNDRED.

Woodcot.—The Lady Ann Kingsmill (livith in London).
Hurstbourn Tarrant.—William Helliar, gentleman; Thomas Purcholl.
Tangly.—Ed. Corderoy, gentleman.
Vernham Dean.—Mrs. Frances Goddard, Thomas White, Robert Goshin, Thos. Kinge.
Okley.—Roger Wither, a Yeoman of the Guard.
Edmonstrip Benham.—Thos. Feilder.
The Parsonage.—John Cokman; John Chamberlain, livith in Barkshire.
The Lordship.—John Smith, Thomas Faukoner.

To St. John, Ths. Ellys.

The names of such persons of Kingsclere Division as are certified to be unable to lend money to his Majesty upon Loan.

OVERTON HUNDRED.

Dean.—Robt. Small, Robt. Smith, Thos. Pembroke.

OVERTON BOROUGH.

Polhampton.—John Nashe, Thos. Alrey.

CHUTELY HUNDRED.

Wortinge.—William Trews.
West Sherborne.—Ambrose Vox.
Church Okley.—John Ayloffe.

KINGSCLERE HUNDRED.

Frobery.—Walter Camber.
Okley and Hampton Lances.—Henry Soper, Ralph Jackson, gent.
Edmonstrip Benham.—Edmonstrip Lances—Richard Wither, Nicholas Bachelor.
Sandford.—Wm. French Clarke.
The Parsonage.—Hugh Hunt.
Clere Woodcut.—Nicholas Waight.
The Lordship.—Peter Bachelor, Ingram Bachelor, Jas. Holsip, John Iserne, Richard Ford, Richard Waterman.
Hurstbourne Priors.—Willm. Drake.
St. Mary Bourn.—John Damerell, George Parsons.
Stoake.—Richard Hayes.
Eggbury.—Maudlin Nervell, widow.
East Woodhay.—William Holl.
Binty.—Alice Godwin.
Itchenwell.—John White.

Whitchurch.—Wm. Poynter.
Freefolk.—Silvester Cuffy, Wm. Cuffy, Edward Flower.
Wodcot.—Wm. Sutton.
Hurstbourn Tarrant.—Robert Jeneway, Nicholas Purcholl, John Preston, gent.
Vernham Dean.—John Smith.

A note of such as being present did neither pay nor subscribe.

Robert Wallopp, Esq. (he promised to pay).
Thos. South (a councillor, he seth he hath paied in the Middle Temple £2 13s. 4d., but ought to pay by the rate of the Subsided Booke £4 13s. 4d.).
Hamden Dowse, Herbert Dodington, have not land nor in the Subsidy Books.
Sir Wm. Unedall hath paid in Westminster.
Sir Richard Young hath paid in Surrey.
Gallop of Southampton refused, and is bound over to appear before the Lords.

Poll-Tax. 12th Charles II.

The roll is in a very bad state, much of it being lost, including apparently the portion relating to Hurstbourne Priors and St. Mary Bourne.

The Hearth Tax, 1672.

Later there was the Hearth Tax of 1672, Charles II. It also gave general discontent, although it was not particularly burdensome, but from being a direct impost. Respecting it Lord Macaulay writes the following :—

"The tax on chimneys, though less productive, called forth far louder murmurs. The discontent excited by direct imposts is, indeed, almost always out of proportion to the quantity of money which they bring into the Exchequer; and the tax on chimneys was, even among direct imposts, peculiarly odious, for it could be levied only by means of domiciliary visits, and of such visits the English have always been impatient to a degree which the people of other countries can but faintly conceive. The poorer householders were frequently unable to pay their hearth-money to the day. When this happened their furniture was distrained without mercy; for the tax was farmed; and a farmer of taxes is, of all creditors, proverbially the most rapacious. The collectors were loudly accused of performing their unpopular duty with harshness and insolence. It was said that, as soon as they appeared at the threshold of a cottage, the children began to wail, and the old women ran to hide their earthenware. Nay, the single bed of a poor family had sometimes been carried away and sold. The net annual receipt from this tax was £200,000."

Lay Subsidies, Southampton, $\frac{176}{563}$. 25th Chas. II, 1672. The title of the Roll is almost entirely eaten away.

HUSBAND PRIORS.

	Hearthes.		Hearthes.
Henry Wallopp, Esq.	xxv	Rich. Camin	iiij
Joseph Leach	iij	Rob't Tompson	j
Robert Waterman	j	Marke Hunt	ij
Richard Sutton	j	Edward Smith	j
Tho. Nicholas	ij	Joane Fisher	j
Joseph Leach, now Henry Wallop, Esq.	iij	Widd' Stoners	j
		Augustin Steevens	j
John Marriner	j	James Purdey	j
Wm. Smith	ij	Tho. Nicholas	ij
Thomas Cooke	ij		
Widd' Hacke	ij	Ex.	lviij
Rob't Fisher	ij		

S'vyad by ROB'T ARNOLL, Coll', and
EDW. DRENLEY, tythingman.

These p'sons following are discharged by Certificate.

Tho. Dudman	j	John Brooker	ij
Widd' Newell	ij	Nich. Rutter	j
Wm. Peckernell	j	Rob't Holland	j
John Steele	j		
Widd' Jewell	ij		xiij
Henry Weston	j		
Tho. Dowse	j		

[Then follow Freefolke Pryors, Charlott Tything, etc. The end of the membrane is decayed, and the name of some place may have been lost.]

STOAKE TYTHING.

Mary Bray	ij	Henry Bray	ij
Mathias Rumball	ij	Geo. Phillpott	j
John Holdway	j	Rich. Bung	j
Edw. Comin	j	Wm. Lovelock	j
Nich. Hearne	j	Wm. Leach	j
Tho. Knight	ij	Wm. Rutty	j
Wm. Parker	j		
Wm. Hawkins	j	Ex.	xxj
Roger Stacey	j		
John Batchellor	ij		

S'vayd by ROB'T ARNOLL, Coll',
JOHN HOLDWAY, tythingman.

The Hearth Tax, 1672.

EGBERY TYTHING.

	Hearthes.		Hearthes.
Rob't Oxenbridge, Esq.	xiij	James Goslin	ij
Widd' Sutton	iiij	Wm. Phillice	j
Nich. Barnard	j		
Wm. Bone	j	Ex.	xxiij
John Goden	j		

S^rvayd by ROB'T ARNOLL, Coll', and
JAMES GOSLIN, tythingman.

These were most likely the people who cultivated the common fields at Swampton at the time of the Hearth Tax.

SWAMTON TYTHING.

Tho. Cannon	vij	Wm. Aldman	j
Tho. Cannon	j	Rob't Hedges	j
Joseph Hewett	j	Rob't Hedges jun.	ij
Wm. Lee	j	Wm. Burges	j
Widd' Wilkins	j	Widd' Boxell	ij
Edw. Percy	j	Rich. Figas	j
Edw. Durley	ij	Wm. Rickett	j
John Lamden	iiij	Wm. Baker	j
John Wells	j	Wm. Bond	j
Tho. Sunwest	ij		
Gregory Gisbier	ij		xxxvij
James Gosling	iij		

S^rvayd by ROB'T ARNOLL, Coll', and
WM. LEE, tythingman.

[This Impost was abolished by William and Mary, 1689.]

BINGLEY TYTHING.

Mr. Rich. Wyther	xj	John Phillpott	j
Henry Gaines	j	John Isrom	ij
Widd' Poore	j	Widd' Flood	j
Wm. Holdway	j	Widd' Fillpott	j
Wm. Pitfall	j	Tho. Isrom	ij
Wm. Andad	j		
Rob't Longman	iij	Ex.	xxviij
Rich. Holdway	ij		

Persons taken of[1] by Certificate.

Nicholas Purveyor	j	Geo. Coate	j
John Taylor	j	Geo. Dumer	j
Rob't Parker	j		
Symon Stiles	j	Ex.	vj

---
[1] *I.e.*, "off".

WEEKE TYTHING.

John Faithfull	-	-	x	John Horne -	-	j
Mr. John Markes	-	-	ij	Wm. Kedgell	-	j
Rob't Druely	-	-	j	Wm. Markes	-	j
Tho. Nicholas	-	-	j			
Tho. Powre	-	-	ij	Ex. -		xx
Rich. Caven	-	-	j			
				Wm. Beale receive Almes j		

Exchequer Depositions, Hilary, 11 and 12 William and Mary, 1698-9, 3, n. 6. *Thorngate and Izerne v. Wallop.*

Rectory of Husborne Priors and St. Mary Bourne, and the Manor of H. P. formerly belonging to Sir Robert Oxenbridge. (*Tithe* suit, apparently.)

Recovery, Easter, 1767.

Soper v. *Ellis*. Lands and ten'ts in St. Mary Bourne.—Rich'd Soper, vouchee.

Recovery, Hil., 1770.

Mountain v. *Benton*. Lands and tent's in St. Mary Bourn.—Beckley, vouchee, etc.

Boundaries, Polling District, Population, etc.

The parish of St. Mary Bourne is stated as comprehending 7,678 acres, in pasture, woodlands, and arable land. And the parochial boundaries may be broadly stated as consisting of the parish of Hurstbourne Priors on the south; that of Whitchurch on the south-east; Cold Henley, eastward; Litchfield and Woodcut on the north-east and north; Hurstbourne Tarrant, northward; Hurstbourne Tarrant and Enham, north-westward; Andover on the west; and Andover and Hurstbourne Priors on the south-west. The parish of St. Mary Bourne forms one of the three divisions of the Whitchurch Poor-law Union, and contains its own Medical Officer, who is also the Sanitary Officer of that division. Hurstbourne Priors is an outlying parish of the Whitchurch or Middle division. St. Mary Bourne is in the County Court district of Andover; and in the petty sessional division of Kingsclere.

In 1885, previous to the operation of the extended Franchise Act, St. Mary Bourne was in the polling district of Whitchurch. It is now, 1886, in the Andover division; but is itself a polling district, and exercised its function for the first time in the election on November 30th, 1885. The number of voters under the old distribution was 59; in 1886, the number was 249. Under the Redistribution scheme, the 7th of November was chosen as the day when the new register should come into operation, in order that the elections under the new Bill should take place during that month; and the new lists would be in force up to the 1st of January 1887. Hurstbourne Priors still continues in the Whitchurch district, with 74 voters; under the former distribution the number was fifteen.

The population of St. Mary Bourne parish in 1801 was 771; in 1811, 874; in 1821, 1,053; in 1831, 1,125; in 1841, 1,152; in 1851, 1,149; in 1861, 1,188; in 1871, 1246.

In Hurstbourne Priors parish the population in 1801 was 366; in 1811, 355; in 1821, 404; in 1831, 490; in 1841, 506; in 1851, 468; in 1861, 437; in 1871, 384.

The condition of the parishes as regards population, etc., in 1881, was as follows:—

	Number of separate Families.	Houses.			Males.	Females.	1881. Totals.	1871. Totals.	Increase.	Decrease.	Number of Children under five years of age.	Number of Children under thirteen years of age and over five.
		Inhabited.	Uninhabited.	Building.								
PARISH OF ST. MARY BOURNE.	276	253	6	—	569	509	1078	1246	—	168	119	147
PARISH OF HURSTBOURNE.	91	84	5	—	212	197	409	384	25	—	58	76

Elevations above sea-level of certain places in the parish of St. Mary Bourne, taken from the Ordnance Survey.

	FEET.
Hurstbourne Hill, between Doiley Copse and the milestone	520
Great Wallop Copse, Waller Hill	624
Gaston Copse	500
Upper Week Farm	476
Cross-roads, Bedlam Copse	400
Brick-kiln above Stoke	500
Binley	400
Warwick, on the road	400
Eggbury Camp, on the road at the base of the Entrenchment	432
Eggbury on the road	400
Cold Harbour	399
Stoke House, on the Road	300
St. Peter's Church	260
Viaduct, on the road	240

Village Clubs.

Several benefit societies, better know as "clubs", have had an ephemeral existence in the parish; but the earlier efforts on the part of the poorer members of the community to provide self-support during sickness, and their aims were nothing higher, were so inadequate to meet all the contingencies, that after a few years they commonly ended in failure. They were nevertheless praiseworthy endeavours to avoid parochial relief. During my residence of thirty-seven years in the parish, four of these societies carried on a struggling existence; and there was, outside of the ordinary clubs, a society by which families could obtain medical assistance by making small half-yearly payments. The later introduction of a branch of the Hampshire Friendly Society tended, in its higher aims, and in the soundness of its basis, to draw in the younger members of the population, and thus ultimately to absorb the older societies. The early clubs were all formed on a similar method, and with small modifications their rules embraced the same unsound elements. 1st. Whether young or old the members paid the same monthly contribution. 2nd. There was dissolution (*i.e.*, the club "broke up"), and distribution of the fund, or part of it, mostly septennially. 3rd. A portion of the fund was expended at monthly and general meetings. 4th. The sums paid at the death of members were large in proportion to the payments made to meet such emergencies: as all ages paid alike, the contributions were unequally levied. 5th. There were no life policies; and at the same time there was no adequate provision in the rules to suspend the payments to members in old age; members therefore often lingered on the funds from sheer inability to work. The consequence was that in times of pressing sickness the box was compelled to be "shut up" for a time. Further, there was no proper method of placing surplus funds out at interest. The box, with its three keys, one for each steward, and the other kept by the secretary, was usually placed under the bed of the innkeeper at whose house the club held its meetings. This method went on very well as long as the members were strong and healthy; indeed, they appear to have regarded "clubbing" as something rather "jolly"; and its true meaning was realised only when the dark days of sickness and infirmity dawned.

The oldest of the St. Mary Bourne clubs, known as the "Old Club", amidst its many difficulties, has shown great vitality, and may be cited as an example of the best form of the early benefit societies. It began its existence in 1820; and I am impressed with the date from the fact that thirty years after its establishment, on being informed of this at one of the anniversary meetings, the remark followed from me, "Who would have thought that when this Society was raised, a child lay in a cradle in Berkshire who would be its future Doctor?" The club-box was stolen about thirty-nine years ago (in 1848). It was taken from the bedroom where it was kept at the inn, and was discovered in a hedge-row near Derrydown Copse. The lid had been forced open and £20 taken from the box, and the books and club papers were scattered about the wood. Suspicion attached to some "navvies", who frequented the house, and who were at that time engaged on the railway then being constructed from Basingstoke to Salisbury. The club held its annual festival on Whit-Monday; and in its more prosperous days 130 members assembled, including tradesmen and small farmers. Mostly the older labourers wore the long, clean, white smock-frock, one of the last survivals of the ancient Briton, and the high hat, which never appeared except on Sundays and festivals. Each bore a tall painted stick, the emblem of his order, and a bunch of ribbons of similar colour was worn on the hat. The quiet march to church; the dinner of robust materials, and the after dinner ale and pipe of tobacco completed the annual life of the Society; and after placing two generations of men in the village churchyard, it numbered sixteen members in the year 1887, with £40 in stock.

It will not be necessary to dilate on the advantages of the Hampshire Friendly Society; its rules, drawn up and confirmed by experienced actuaries, are as suited to the fluctuating conditions of life and society as practical knowledge guided by science could make them. The St. Mary Bourne branch was initiated in September 1858. Ten years after, in 1868, the number of members reached 109. At that time the Society included members from Hurstbourne Tarrant and Hurstbourne Priors. But after this date the members from these places left the parent Society, and formed independent branches; and thus, in 1885, the numbers stood as they follow:—

St. Mary Bourne	130
Hurstbourne Tarrant	128
Hurstbourne Priors	61

The Earl of Portsmouth was the Chairman at the meeting when the branch was formed; and the following were the first officers and Committee:—

Rev. W. Temple, *Chairman.*

Honorary Members of the Committee:—
Rev. S. Lockhart.
Mr. J. W. Hooper.
Mr. J. Lywood.

Benefit Members of the Committee:—
Mr. John Freemantle.
Mr. Nathl. Goodyear.
Mr. J. S. Summerbee.
Medical Officer—Joseph Stevens, M.R.C.P.L.
Agent—Mr. Moses Butcher.
Representative Member—Mr. John Freemantle.

The annual festival was fixed, in June 1859, to take place on the first Tuesday in July, and this arrangement still remains in force.

List of Chairmen since 1858:—

Rev. W. Temple	20th Sept. 1858.
Mr. J. W. Hooper	19th June 1860.
Capt. James Harding	28th Jan. 1869.
Mr. Thos. Hooper	26th May 1869.
Dr. J. Stevens	21st Jan. 1875.
Mr. J. C. Hooper (still Chairman, 1886)	6th Jan. 1880.

The Allotment Gardens.

The first allotments granted by the Earl of Portsmouth, for the use of the poor of St. Mary Bourne, were situated on an elevation between the two copses known as Derrydown and Bedlams; but the site was found to be so inconvenient for carting manure, etc., that in 1873 the present land on the valley slope west of the village was selected. The plots extend in double series, fifty-six being in the upper series, and fifty-four in the lower one, the whole numbering 110, and covering an area of 7 acres, 2 roods, and 12 poles. Ten poles is the area of each of the lower allotments, and 12 poles of each one of the upper range, the difference in quantity being considered the equivalent of the difference in quality in the character of the soil. The same rent is therefore charged for both, viz., 2s. 6d. for each allotment, which is at the rate of £2 per acre yearly.

Although all are not equally well cultivated, that they are appreciated is shown by the full occupation of the allotments, and their generally careful cultivation, as well as by the eager competition for a vacant one. During the last few years a greater variety of vegetables has been grown, and not potatoes alone, which at one time were almost exclusively planted. This is probably due to the improvement of the ground by regular tillage, deeper digging, and proper manuring. When potatoes are grown exclusively, five sacks are regarded as a good crop, or three bushels on two poles of land, and from four to five sacks as a fair crop. These at digging are worth from 6s. 6d. to 8s. per sack, according to the market. All things considered, after deducting rent, cartage, and other small outlays, the profit on each allotment would be probably from 21s. to 25s. *per annum*, besides fresh vegetables for summer consumption.

The introduction of allotments away from the village has been of considerable advantage, in a sanitary point, to the health of the villagers. Five-and-twenty years ago there was an almost annual visitation of fever, of a typhoid character, which was due to the small gardens at the backs of the houses being crowded in the arrangement of the pig-sties, closets, and muck-heaps, which trenched too closely on the back doors. Under the operation of the Public Health Act of 1875, the Resident Medical Officer was appointed Sanitary Officer, and he having enlarged power removed the closets to healthier sites where deemed necessary. And under the surveillance of the Inspector of Nuisances greater cleanliness was exacted in the removal of all refuse materials, which found their way chiefly to the allotment gardens, and thus contamination of the water in the shallow wells or "dip-holes" was prevented, to the comparative exclusion of a long-standing menace to the health of the population.

There is overwhelming evidence of the spread of typhoid fever by water. Mr. Ernest Hart (Chairman of Council of the National Health Society) has stated that "Epidemics by the score, nay by the hundred, might be cited in which the first cause has been the pollution of the water drunk by the persons affected." In 146 epidemics of typhoid fever reported by Mr. Simon, excremental pollution of air or water—generally of both—was found in every case.[1] Prof. Frankland, in speaking of polluted water, says: "In many localities there are springs within a moderate distance of a village or group of houses; this water issuing from the spring usually joins a brook very soon after it comes from the spring, this brook is almost immediately polluted by drainage discharged into it, and the inhabitants have frequently to drink from this brook. The spring water could be easily brought in a pipe of very small diameter to the group of houses or village, and supply them with perfectly wholesome water. Another way would be the digging of a shallow well (this is done at St. Mary Bourne), where water is to be obtained by shallow wells; but the well should be at a distance of not less than 200 yards from the nearest house, or drain, or cesspool, or other source of sewage-pollution, and a pump should be erected there. The inhabitants would, of course, have to go that distance for their water, but it would then be fairly wholesome."[2]

It would appear that pollutions are readily got rid of by the soil;

---

[1] *Society of Arts Annual Conference*, 1879, pp. 119-122.
[2] *Society of Arts Congress*, 1878, *P. Inq.*, p. 82.

but not so easily when present in flowing water. Prof. Prestwich, referring to the contamination of wells, says: "Natural agencies are constantly operating to counteract the evil consequences of our neglect. The power of oxidation and absorption of the soil on underground waters, goes far to remedy the evil and restore our springs and rivers to their original purity."[1] On the other hand, with regard to running water, the Rivers Pollution Commission state in their Report:—"It has often been asserted, but without proof, that the organic matter contained in sewage and other polluting liquids is rapidly oxidised during the flow of the river into which such liquids are discharged; and that if sewage be mixed with twenty times its volume of river water, the organic matter which it contains will be oxidised and utterly destroyed whilst the river is flowing 'a dozen miles or so', we have," state the Commissioners, "made numerous observations and experiments upon the alleged destruction of sewage", and "have proved that *there is no river in Great Britain long enough to completely oxidise or destroy the soluble animal organic matter present in polluted water.*"[2]

"From numerous chemical analyses it has been established that animal matters dissolved in water, such as those contained in sewage, the contents of privies and cesspools, or farmyard manure, undergo oxidation in lakes, rivers, and streams very slowly, but in the pores of an open soil very rapidly. When this oxidation is complete, they are resolved into mineral compounds; their carbon is converted into carbonic acid, and their hydrogen into water,—products which can no longer be identified in the aërated waters of a river or spring; but their nitrogen is transformed partly into ammonia; chiefly, however, into nitrous and nitric acids, which, combining with the bases present in nearly all water that has been in contact with the earth, form nitrates and nitrites, and frequently remain dissolved in the water for a long time; there constituting a record of the sewage or other analogous contamination, to which it has been subjected since its descent to the earth as rain. . . There are several agencies at work by which this testimony, as to the amount of animal matter previously in contact with the water, may be weakened or altogether destroyed. Thus we look in vain for full evidence of previous animal pollution in the effluent water from fields irrigated with sewage; because the growing plants have removed a considerable proportion of ammonia, nitrates, and nitrites, from the liquid as it flows among their rootlets. In like manner, the aquatic vegetation of rivers, lakes, and reservoirs, slowly removes these compounds from the water, and to that extent

[1] *Society of Arts Congress*, 1878, *P. Inq.*, p. 62.
[2] *Rivers Pollution Commission*, 1868, pp. 134 and 11.

destroys the evidence of anterior animal contamination. . . . The importance of the history of water, as regards its anterior pollution with organic matters of animal origin, does not arise from the presence of the inorganic residues (nitrates, nitrites, and ammonia) of the original polluting matters, for these are in themselves innocuous, but from the risk lest some portion (not detectable by chemical or microscopical analysis) of the noxious constituents of the original animal matters should have escaped that decomposition, which has resolved the remainder into innocuous mineral compounds." "The really injurious organic suspended matters are probably not merely organic but organised matters—entozoic ova, or zymotic germs capable of reproduction in the human body with the simultaneous development of disease. Investigations of this class belong rather to microscopical than to chemical analysis."[1]

[1] *Rivers Pollution Commission*, 1868, pp. 13-17, and *ibid.*, p. 4.

The Tithings.

THERE are six tithings in the parish of St. Mary Bourne, or rather six tithings form the parish. They consist of—
1. Binley, which lies two miles on the north-east of St. Mary Bourne. In the Binley tithing the hamlet of Warwick is included, or, as it was styled in more ancient times, *Wadwick*. 2. Eggbury, which lies on the north-east, and is distant from St. Mary Bourne about two miles. 3. Week, Wick, or Wyke, from one mile to a mile and a half on the south-west. 4. Stoke, lying northward, at a mile and a half from St. Mary Bourne. 5. Swampton, which joins St. Mary Bourne at the north end. 6. St. Mary Bourne, which is the principal tithing, and contains the church.

Binley.

Binley is reached by the Wadwick Road, and along Red Lane; and from the hill at the top of the lane, the scenery of the parish offers nothing more complete in a homely way than is presented by the surroundings of this snug hamlet. The winding roads and sloping woodlands, with houses dotted here and there among the meadows and hedgerows, form a pleasing and diversified picture. Mr. William Cobbett, in his *Rural Rides* (New Edition, 1853), writes of the miserable condition of its inhabitants at the beginning of the present century. He says: "We came through a village called Woodcote, and another called Binley. I never saw any inhabited places more recluse than these; yet into these the all-searching eye of the taxing *Thing* reaches. Its exciseman can tell it what is doing even in the little odd corner of Binley, for even there I saw over the door of a place, not half so good as the place in which my fowls roost, '*Licensed to deal in*

Tea and Tobacco.' Poor half-starved wretches of Binley!" Mr. Cobbett revelled in finding fault; although much which he has penned in his *Rural Rides* respecting the scenery, and the agricultural capabilities of North Hampshire, is full of native force and careful observation.

One of the more interesting reminiscences of this period of his life is his intimacy with the late Mr. Joseph Blount, of Hurstbourne Tarrant, at whose house Mr. Cobbett was a frequent visitor, and in whose library, looking out on the fine old rookery, he penned many of his papers. The library contained many valuable books and papers, including all Mr. Cobbett's writings; and it was Mr. Blount's custom to burn logs in the peculiar grate known as "Cobbett's Register". The house has since been sold, and the rookery rooted up. Mr. Blount was the last member of a branch of the Mapledurham family. He was a remarkable man, and his life had been somewhat eventful, for having been retained as a prisoner in France at the time of the insurrection of the Jacobins, he took the opportunity of acquainting himself with the French language and literature. Although many years have since passed, Mr. Blount is still remembered for his kindness to the broken-down artisans and trade-workers, who were often passing through Hurstbourne Tarrant on their way into the West of England in search of employment. It was Mr. Blount's custom to feed these men with pickled-pork and potatoes, served on pewter vessels, which were placed on a low flat-topped wall in the front of his house. So proverbial became this hospitality that the wall received the name of the "Wayfarer's Table". It is stated that a poor tired Irishman, hearing of this arrangement, called one day and inquired if that was the " Victualling Office". For his kindness a London firm once proposed to send Mr. Blount a gold snuff-box, which he refused with the characteristic reply "that he wanted no return of that sort". Mr. Blount died at his residence at Hurstbourne Tarrant in April 1863, at the ripe age of 84 years, and lies buried under the yew-tree in Hurstbourne Churchyard.

Binley, or Bindley as it sometimes appears, is mentioned in the Tax-Roll of Edward III of 1327 as *Bynleigh*, which might be defined as coming from the Saxon, meaning a country which is tilled or inhabited—*Byn*,[1] tilled, or *Bynland*, inhabited country. But in the time of Edward I the word is written *Bylygh*, which seems to refer to its proximity to a place bearing the name of Lye or Lygh, and there is a homestead of that name at only a short distance from it. The Tax-Roll of Edward contains some remarkable names, which bear no reference to those of its present inhabitants. Thus, *Laur. dé Bynleigh*

---

[1] Bosworth, *Anglo-Saxon Dictionary.*

and *Cecilia dé Bynleigh* are evidently Norman-French, the preposition *of* (*dé*) implying that they held their land in villenage, or at the will of the lord and at customary services, and were not strictly free. They were tenants who paid rent in cash instead of in commodities. The names Joh'*e* Patrich, and Joh'*e* Willieme, which also occur, appear to be Celtic, the conjunctive *e* probably meaning that John was the son of Patrich or of Willieme. The tax paid by those people to the Crown, for that year, ranged from 1s. to 1s. 9d., which was large according to the value of money at that time. In 1545, 37th year of Henry VIII, some names appear the same as those at present living in the parish,—Purvyer (Purver) and Harrys, as the names are written in a Subsidy Roll of that period, being still parochial residents. Binley at that time is styled "*Parissche of Bynley*"; but in the 2nd and 3rd of Edward VI, it receives the title of *tithing*.

Eggbury.

From St. Mary Bourne to the tithing of Eggbury an old drove is traversed, which has been a trackway since the time of the Saxons. On the right, resting on the brow of the hill, the west rampart of the British earthwork, known as Eggbury Castle, is observable; and on the left the neatly wooded hanging called Downhams. The prefix, *Egg*, of the place-name, most likely comes from *hege*, a hedge, which is peculiarly applicable to the features of the place. This definition is supported by the fact that in the Assize Roll, 8th and 9th of Edward II, the name is spelt *Heggebire*. The suffix, *bury*, meaning fortified camp, is derived from the earthwork. In the hamlet at the right of the farm, there is a small meadow which has received the title of the "Roman burial-ground"; but there appear to be no grounds for the belief that it was used by the Romans for such a purpose, no remains being discoverable by excavations, although its surface abounds in small hollows or pits which are difficult to be accounted for. Many years ago it was chosen as the burial-place of an eccentric Quaker and his family, whose names receive record in the parish books. In *Valor Ecclesiasticus*, the manor of Eggbury with the appurtenances by the year is valued at £14 7s. 3¾d. And in the assessment for the Hearth Tax, 1672, 25th Charles II, Robert Oxenbridge of Eggbury is assessed for thirteen hearths. An ancient market-road passes through this hamlet, which was in existence long before the introduction of modern turnpikes, and was used as a market road. It conducted the traveller from Newbury to the Three-legged Cross, thence by Cruxeaston to Woodcot, and through Eggbury, passing close to the Romano-British camp on the hill, and then onwards to Whitchurch and Winchester.

The following document refers to Buckets Down, in the tithing of Eggbury. *Chancery Decree Rolls*, 3rd Division, Part 199, No. 4, 21st Geo. II. *Drake v. Etwall.*

Whereas in Easter term, 1744, Jane Drake, widow, exhibited her Bill of Complaint against Ralph Etwall, Def., setting forth that Ralph Etwall, Gent., deceased, being seized in fee of the messuage, lands, etc., hereinafter mentioned, by Indenture of mortgage, dated 3 Feb. 1740, between him and Plf., in consideration of £400 demised, granted, bargained, and sold to Plf : all that messuage in Eggbury in the parish of St. Mary Bourn in co. Southⁿ, called Buckets Down, with barns, orchards, etc. ; and also all those several closes in Eggbury belonging to the said messuage, and containing 45 acres, viz., North Croft, West Croft, Picked Close, Tell Close, Long Stringers, and Upper Stringers ; and also all that coppice or woody ground in Eggbury containing 16 acres, and also all those several inclosed grounds thereto belonging, lying at Dungley in the Tything of Eggbury, called the Lower Ground, and containing 13 acres, and [also ?] called the Upper Ground, the Two Acres, and the Meadow ; all then in the tenure of Gilbert Cole ; and all that cottage in the tenure of Robert Biggins, with commons, common of pasture, etc : all which premises had been purchased by the said Ralph Etwall, deceased, from Thomas Cannon the elder, Ann his wife, and Thomas Cannon the younger, their son : to hold to Plf. for 1000 years, subject to redemption on payment of £400 with interest. The said Ralph died 10 March 1740, leaving Def. his son and heir, without paying Plf. principal or interest. Def. gave out that no such Indenture was ever made, etc.

Def. made Answer that he never saw the said Deed, and was not privy thereto, and did not come of age till April 1744, etc.

Witnesses were examined, etc.

The cause came on for hearing on 29th May, 18th Geo. II, but Def. did not appear. It was referred to one of the Masters to ascertain how much was due to Plf., and upon Def. paying all that was due to her she should reconvey the premises to him, etc. Various other Orders were made, and the Master's Report is quoted. Def. was ordered to pay £569 10s. 10d. for principal, interest, and Plf.'s costs, but failed to do so.

Therefore, this day, 12 Nov., 21st Geo. II, 1747, it is decreed that Def. be absolutely debarred and foreclosed from all equity of redemption.

DUNLEY.

Following the course of the winding copse lane from Eggbury the hill overlooking Dunley is reached, from which an interesting view of the hamlet is obtained. The rustic homes of the poor lie in a winding hollow, with an upland capped with wood extending behind it. A little apart from the hamlet stands the old gabled farmhouse, which presents a quaint and an appropriate view from the Litchfield turnpike. Portions of its architecture are traceable to the period of Elizabeth. The manor was possessed by William Oxenbridge, who lived there at the time his elder brother, Sir Robert, lived at Hurstbourne. He was the third son of Sir Robert Oxenbridge, who died at Hurstbourne in 1591 ; and he had an elder brother, Goddard Oxenbridge, of St. Dunstan, West, who died without issue in 1634 [will proved 7th May]. William Oxenbridge of Dunley married Mary, daughter of William Kympton, of Hadley, near Barnet, son of Alderman Kympton. William had two sons, Edmund, or as Berry states, Edward, who also lived at Dunley, and died there in 1639; and Robert Oxenbridge, of Piddle Trenthyde, co. Dorset, who married for his first wife Diana, daughter of Sir John Tonstall, of Edgecumbe, co. Surrey, his second wife being Frances, daughter of James Deane, of Deaneland, Hants, and widow of William Collier. She died a widow, October 26th, 1708. There is an epitaph to this Robert Oxenbridge in Hurstbourne Priors Church. William Oxenbridge, of Dunley, had also three daughters, Catherine, Elizabeth, and Mary. According to the evidences which have been obtained, the Oxenbridges were largely represented in the district, members of the family having lived at Hurstbourne, Week, Dunley, and Eggbury.

In addition to the above elder brother, William Oxenbridge had four younger brothers, and three sisters. His brothers were Henry, Gabriel, Richard, whose will is dated 1618, and John, whose will was indited at the same time, as it also bears date 1618 (*Inquis. p. m.*). His sisters were—Elizabeth, who married Edward Woodward, Esq., Privy Chamber to King James; Susan, who was wedded, first to Edward Cason, Esq., of Pelham, Herts, Treasurer, 16th James; and second, to Sir Thomas Cecil, of Keldon, fourth son of Thomas, Earl of Salisbury, whom she survived. The third sister, Anne, lived unmarried at Windsor in 1634.

In reference apparently to the Gunpowder Plot there is a significant entry in the *Calendar of the State Papers Domestic* of November 12th, 1605, 4th James I, shortly after his accession. It refers to a letter from William Oxenbridge of Dunley, to his brother Sir Robert, of Hurstbourne Park. "Wm Oxenbridge to Sir Ro^b Oxenbridge. Speeches of Booth, Sir Arthur Hopton's servant, on Nov. 5th, about 'strange matters' to be done that day; he railed against English preachers."

Dunley is a hamlet in the tithing of Eggbury. As a definition, its name, from *dun*,[1] a hill fortress, and *ley*, a field or pasture, appears to refer to the contiguity of the village to the British encampment which encircles the crown of Beacon Hill, immediately

---

[1] *Anglo-Saxon Dictionary.*

on the north-west of the village. The Beacon must have claimed conspicuous attention in the Middle Ages, when the country was in perpetual rumour and alarm, and when fires blazed, and cresset-lights were hoisted in the centre of the camp.[1] The manor of Hurstbourne Priors was possessed by the Protector Somerset in the 2nd of Edward VI; and there is a notice of that date concerning beacons:—April, 2nd of Edward VI. Copy of a letter under the King's sign-manual and signet, countersigned by the Duke of Somerset, to the magistrates of inland shires. "For the erection of beacons, and the giving timely alarm to fighting-men *to repare sewarde for defence as occasion may serve.*"[2]

Week, or Wyke.

The Week, Wick, or Wyke tithing contains the several divisions of Upper, Middle, and Lower Week. Its name has been thought to be derived from *Vicus*, a street; but there are no remains of any street connecting the three districts, although one might have existed in former times. It comes probably from the Saxon *Wic*, a hamlet or settlement; or the name might bear reference to some occupant, at a time when Saxon families were found to cluster round some scion as a leader.

It is not improbable that the following may refer to the possession of the manor, in the early part of the thirteenth century, by Valentine de Wyke, as the entry relates to a gift of land in the manor of Hurstbourne Priors:—William de Raleigh, who held the Bishopric of Winchester from 1244 to 1250, gave to Nicholas de Rainville the two virgates of land in the manor of Husseburne Priors, which belonged to Valentine de Wyke, who had died without an heir, *de se*.

Reference to *Wix* as a name, under the head of *Wixna*, and perhaps represented in the *Weeks* of our time, occurs in an unpublished manuscript list of some of the early territorial names in England, by Mr. Walter de Gray Birch, F.S.A.[3] In this list, *inter*

---

[1] The ancient usage was revived on the night of Her Majesty's Jubilee, June 21st, 1887, when a huge beacon-fire was lighted here, and on Walbury Hill, and Cottington Hill, on the same line of the chalk elevation. It is stated by those present that seventy similar fires were visible from Beacon Hill, at least sixty from Cottington Hill, and quite seventy from Walbury. The sight must have conveyed some idea of the beacon-fires of the Middle Ages.

[2] Historical Manuscripts Commission, Appendix to Seventh Report, p. 605.

[3] *Quart. Journal Brit. Archæological Association*, March 1884.

alia, appear Week hamlet in Binstead, and Week tithing in Bourne St. Mary, co. Hants; Week tithing in Godshill, Isle of Wight; Week or Wyke parish, co. Hants; Week hamlet in Glastonbury, and several others. Four places are thus named in the county of Hants, and seven in that of Somerset. The name also appears in Essex and elsewhere. Upper Week, the more important of the three, in the parish of St. Mary Bourne, must have always held a considerable position in the parish, of which testimony is furnished in the south aisle of the church, which was formerly a chapel probably appropriated to it as "Week aisle". A field near the house, called Court-garden, bears reference to Court-place or Court-Hayes, which was its proper title at one time. *Hayes* evidently refers to *hedges*, as Week has until quite recently been completely enveloped in forest; and Court-place points to the manorial Courts, which were held there, and of which there is notice in the time of Henry VIII. The building has undergone repeated alterations; but there is a fine stack of chimneys still standing, which appears to be Jacobean.

It has been noticed that the Fawconers held Wyke manor under the title of Hurstbourne *exterius* in 1263, and after. In 1276 Martin de Roches, as we have seen, held 8 *marks of rent* in Fawconer's manor; and in 1399 Sir Bernard Brocas appears to have held the same land or part thereof. The manor of Wyke was held by Nicholas Beynton in 1422; and in 1466, time of Edward IV, the same manor was held by John Beynton. Robert Baynton held the manor in 1476; and in 1485, reign of Richard III, George Nevill had a grant of the manor. It was then called Daundelese Wyke. It would appear, further, that Sir Michael Lister had granted to him the reversion of Wyke Manor after the death of Elizabeth Baynton.[1]

That some members of the Oxenbridge family lived at Week we have the testimony of the Lay Subsidies, where the name of Mrs. "Barbarra" Oxenbridge appears in 1592, as occupying Week at the same time that her son, Sir Robert Oxenbridge, lived at Hurstbourne Priors. An extract from the will of Sir Robert Oxenbridge, 1591, the husband of the above-named lady, states that "he leaves all his brewing utensils to his son Robert, at Hurstbourn, upon condition that he allows his mother the use of them *during the time she shall dwell at Week House.*"

The son, Robert, who died in 1616, desires his wife to rest satisfied with the provision made for her, "considering how week my means to provide for my children during her life, of whom I hope she will have a godlie and motherlie care." She appears, however, to have married Mr. William Lucy a few months after his death. The

---

[1] See *Feet of Fines*, 38th Henry VIII.

Sir Robert who died in 1638, says: "I give and bequeath to John Heath all such goods and household stuff as are mine, and now remaining in the house the s'd John Heath now dwellith in called the Grange,[1] and for as much as I have delivered with mine own hand in my life time to the Churchwardens and Overseers of the poor of Hursbourne and Bourne to the use of the s'd poor, as well as the £50 given by my self, and the £50 given by Mr. Kemp, my will is that my *Exor.* shall not stand charged with the s'd several sums of £50."

During the late Mr. William Longman's occupation of Week farm a carved mantle-piece was removed from an upstairs room bearing the letters R. O.

In *Valor Ecclesiasticus* the manor of Week stands charged, with sale of wood and other appurtenances there, £16 0s. 14d.

In a document in the Probate Court, at Winchester, of which the following is a copy, it appears that Edward Lord Beauchamp occupied "Weeke" previous to 1612. It was afterwards in the occupation of Paul Alexander.[2]

"An inventory indented made the 8th December (1612) in the 10th year of the reign of King James (of England), of all such goods and chattels as sometymes were of the right honorable Edward Lord Beauchamp deceased, taken at Weeke in the parish of Husborne Priors in the county of Southt., which came into the hands and possession of Paule Alexander of Week aforesaid, gentleman; and appraized by Andrew Kingsmell, gent., Walter Waight, wollen draper, Richard Pope, inholder, and William Hinxman, inholder, as followeth."

The last entry is—"Item, the leases which were in [the hands of] the said Edward Lord Beauchamp by the demise of the said Paule Alexander on dew consideration—£100."

Sum total of Inventory, £181 2s. 2d.

Exhibited for a full and plain inventory, by Paule Alexander, gent., on the 18th December 1612.

In the house of Dr. Ridley and before him, on Monday, 28th September 1612, appeared Lancelot Thorpe, notary public and procurator of Lady Honora Beauchamp, widow, relict of the most noble Lord Edward, Lord Beauchamp, and of Francis Seymour, Esq., son of the said deceased, and renounced all right of administration; and also exhibited a letter of the Lord Edward, Lord Beauchamp, eldest son of the said deceased, renouncing the same right.

Thereupon, and on the same day, the aforesaid Mr. Thomas Ridley, LL.D., and vicar general of the lord Bishop of Winchester, granted letters of administration to Paule Alexander, one of the creditors, of Sparsholt, in the county of Berks, gentleman.

The letter of renunciation by the eldest son is dated 24th September 1612, and is signed—Edward Beauchamp. Lady Honora Beauchamp's letter of procuration

---

[1] The Grange was the old manorial residence at Hurstbourne Priors, previous to the building of the present mansion. (See account of elsewhere.)

[2] My thanks are due to Mr. F. J. Baigent for this document.

and renunciation of all right to administer, is dated 15th August 1612, and that of Francis Seymour, Esq., son of the said deceased, is dated on the same day.

The family of Longman has been associated with Week for a great number of years, and with other property in the parish of St. Mary Bourne, as proprietors, or occupiers. The first notice of the name that I can find is that of William Longman, as a holder of lands at "Weeke", in the Lay Subsidies of the 1st of Charles I. There is also an entry in the parochial books of Robert Longman being a churchwarden in 1681. But the earliest mention of the name, and probably that of an early member of the same family, occurs in the Hampshire Subsidy Roll of the 1st of Edward III, 1327, of Woodcot, written *Wodcote* (in the Hampshire *Domesday*, Odecote). For this hamlet the following assessments are returned.

Henry of Wodcote	vi*s.* vi*d.*	John Clerk	xxi½*d.*
William at the Pound	xviii*d.*	John le Blare	xviii*d.*
Philip Croc	iv*s.*	Henry Philip	xviii*d.*
William *Langman*	xiii½*d.*	Thomas de Charmyr	xviii*d.*
	Total	xix*s.* viii*d.*	

The name is here spelt with the Saxon prefix *lang*, implying that they were people of tall stature, a characteristic which distinguishes the family at the present day.[1]

In the Subsidy Rolls I find that a Lady Smyth, in 1662, time of Charles II, paid 24*s.* for Weeke farme land, standing in the valuation list at £3. Sir Richard Lucy, Knt., also possessed land at "Weeke"; but it might have been at one of the other Weeks.

Recoveries, Hilary, 30 George III, 1790, No. 223.

Recovery by John Lord Howard, of Walden, against Richard Asworth, of the manors of Husborne Priors, Swampton, Wallop, etc., site of the manor of Hursborne Fawkners, etc., etc. (long description). John Earl of Portsmouth and Urania his wife, vouchees, who call

---

[1] There was a story which I often heard respecting the way the Longman family originally obtained their property. Myths are always worth relating, as they not unfrequently refer to some tradition out of which the story grew. It is stated that an early member of the family had employed a man to grub up a "tree-stool", the name commonly used in Hampshire for the root of a tree; when he came on an iron pot, which contained something he did not wait to inspect, but went home to tell his master. The employer directed the man to sit down to his dinner, and taking advantage of the opportunity went to the tree and removed the pot, which was found to be full of coins, and that with these he founded his fortune. It is even stated that the pot lay about, and for years afterwards was to be seen at Upper Week. Now this story was current, and quite believed by the peasantry.

Charles Wallop, Esq., voucher. It has been stated that a Lord Northampton possessed Week, previous to its purchase by the present proprietors of the manor, but I can find no documents in support of this.

Stoke.

The Stoke tithing lies midway between the villages of St. Mary Bourne and Hurstbourne Tarrant. The name appears to be derived from the Saxon *Stoc*, a place. The Upper Test flows through the hamlet, and for several hundred yards the water runs along the old road down the valley, so that in times of full water it is a lengthened ford; and in autumn, when the stream has run dry, the roadway is a shingled river-bed. This was the only traffic-way in days gone by, although there is an upper road now; nevertheless, until the county bridge was built in 1869, there was no alternative but fording at the point where the stream crosses the road in the centre of the village.

The manor of "Stok", in *Valor Ecclesiasticus*, is registered with a charge on it of £19 10s. 6d.

The name of Holdway, for some time associated with property at Stoke, appears in the "Inventory of Church Goods" in the year 1600.

A charter of exchange of land at Stoke came into my possession a short time since, which, rendered from the Latin, reads as follows:—

Charter by Brother Alexander [*de Herriard*], the Prior and Convent of the Cathedral Church of St. Swythuns, Winchester [*Wynton*], to Walter atte Mere, of two acres and fifteen perches of their meadow called Runnyllemede, near the meadow of the said Walter called Wellesheard, on the south side of the King's Highway which leads towards Up Hursburne, in exchange for two parcels of meadow lying on the north side of their meadow called Stokemede, with permission to the said Walter to enclose and hold separately the said two acres and fifteen perches, and also his meadow called Wellesheard, containing by estimation half an acre and one rod.

Dated at Wynton on the Friday nearest after the feast of St. Vincent the Martyr, in the 8th year of Edward the third, 1333.

Joh'e atte More or Mere was one of the holders at Stoke in 1327, 1st of Edward III; and there is no doubt, as Walter atte Mere was permitted to enclose his meadow by the Prior, that he was a copyholder.

Chancery B. and A., James I ; H. 23, 23 ; *Hayes* v. *Hayes*. 25th May 1620.

Bill of Anne Hayes, widow of William Hayes, dec'd, alleging that about 12 years since Robert Hayes, son of the said William, understanding that the said William was to marry Plf., earnestly solicited her that if she happened to overlive the said William, she would either give him (Robert) £30 yearly out of a copyhold tenement and six yard-lands, which William then held for life in St. Mary Borne in co. Southampton, being parcel of the Manor of St. Mary Borne, or permit him to hold four of the said six yard-lands, during her widowhood. She accordingly entered into a bond to Robert. William died about 7 years since, whereupon, by the custom of the said Manor, Plf. was entitled to hold the said copyhold "for her widowhood", but she yielded to Robert the 4 yard-lands, as agreed, but he did not give up the bond, and now claims £30 a year from her, etc.

[No Answer with the Bill.]

Chancery B. and A., James I ; H. 17, 16. *Holyday* v. *Hayes and others*. 29th Nov. 1624.

I. Bill of Thomas Holyday of St. Giles' in the Fields, in co. Middx., gentleman, alleging that one Robert Hayes, late of Stoke, in co. Southampton, yeoman, in March, 9 Jas. I, by his writing obligatory stood bound to Plf. in £10, for which Plf. sued him in the Common Pleas, and obtained Judgment in Mich'as, 12 Jas. I. Understanding that Hayes was seized in fee of divers tenements and lands in St. Marie Borne, in co. South'ton, Plf. sued out a writ of *elegit* for levying the said debt and the damages adjudged, but could not obtain execution, because Hayes confederated with Thomas Boxold of St. Marie Borne, yeoman, Peter Blake of Enham, gent., and Nicholas Blake (brother of Peter), an attorney in the Common Pleas, who have contrived divers secret and fraudulent estates of the said lands, so that several successive sheriffs have been deterred from executing the said *elegit*, etc.

II. Answer of Peter Blake, denying all the allegations made in the Bill. Robert Hayes was seized in fee of a messuage and divers lands and tenements thereto belonging in Swampton and St. Maryborne, and by Indenture dated 29 Sept., 10 Jas. I, between the said Robert and Jane his wife of the one part, and Thomas Boxold of the other part, for £100. Robert and Jane bargained and sold to Boxold the reversion of the said messuage (here called a capital messuage), then or lately in the occupation of the said Robert Hayes, and of Elizabeth Cooper, widow, since deceased, for a term of years, not yet expired ; and afterwards, about two years ago, Thomas Boxold assigned, granted, bargained, and sold the same, for a sum of money paid by this Def. with the assent of Hayes, for the residue of the term, to Nicholas Blake, gent., in trust for this Deft. Subsequently Hayes and wife, for £225, conveyed the premises to this Deft.

Swampton.

The tithing of Swampton lies along the valley north of St. Mary Bourne, and is continuous with it. It has since 1723 been the site of the parochial schools, which for many years stood on what is known as Swampton Green. The tithing appears in *Domesday* as *Suantune*, in the Hundred of *Clere*.

It might be explanatory to note that, in the execution of the Survey Record called *Domesday Book*, commissioners were sent into every county and shire, and juries were summoned in each hundred, out of all orders of freemen, from barons down to the lowest farmers. These commissioners were to be informed by the inhabitants, upon oath, of the name of each manor, and that of its owner, also by whom it was held in the time of Edward the Confessor; the number of hides; the quantity of wood, of pasture, and of meadow land; how many ploughs were in the demesne, and how many in the tenanted part of it; with the value of the whole together in the time of King Edward as well as when granted by King William, and at the time of this survey; also whether it was capable of improvement, or of being advanced in its value. They were likewise directed to return the tenants of every degree, the quantity of land then and formerly held by each of them, what was the number of villeins and slaves, and also the number and kinds of their cattle and live stock.[1]

Extended Latin text of "Domesday", and translation.

Ipse Radulfus tenet, in Suantune, unam hidam. Cheping tenuit, de episcopo, et de monachis; et semper fuit de monasterio. Sed concessa est eidem. et vita sua tantum tenere; et post mortem ejus, ad ecclesiam debebat redire. Hoc monachi dicunt; sed hundredum nil scit de conventione; sed hoc scit,—quia de monasterio fuit, et geldum non dedit, nec modo facit; et nesciunt quare remansit. Terra est una carucata. Ipsa est in dominio cum 2 villanis et

Ralph (de Mortimer) holds 1 hide in Swantune (*Swampton*). Cheping held it of the Bishop and Monks (of Winchester), and it was always Abbey land. But it was granted to him for his life only; and after his death, it should revert to the Church. This the monks affirm, but the hundred know nothing of the agreement; but it is known that because it was abbey land, it neither did, nor does now, pay tax; and they know not why it remains (exempt from

---

[1] A. C. Ewald, F.S.A., *Our Public Records*, p. 50.

3 bordariis; et molinus de 15 solidis. Tempore Regis Edwardi, et post, et modo, valet 25 solidos.

tax). The land is 1 carucate, in demesne, with 2 villeins and 3 borderers; and a mill of (worth) 15s. In the time of King Edward and afterwards it was (worth), and now, is worth 25[1] shillings (*solidus*, a shilling-weight of silver; see *Ewald*).

In the reign of the Conqueror Swampton formed part of the manor of Hurstbourne, held by the Bishop of Winchester for his Cathedral.

Ralph de Mortimer held one hide of this small manor; and the demesne consisted of one carucate of land, which quantity in some cases is considered to represent the hide, or normal holding of 120 acres. It might, however, have been less; and as only two villeins and three borderers were engaged on the demesne, it is likely that the latter, in common with the villeins, took part in the cultivation. As the bovate or oxgang is considered to have employed its single beast; the virgate or two oxgangs must be looked on as the equivalent of two oxen; and the hide, consisting of four virgates, as representing eight oxen on the demesne land at Swampton. It is as likely that half that number only were engaged; and that the animals were yoked abreast. In those days the ploughs were not fashioned as they are now. The plough-beams were rude and cumbrous, necessitated to be so from the absence of iron; and being of great weight, vast animal power was requisite to drag them through the heavy soil. The ox was of advantage to the poor cultivator in various ways, the animal could be kept cheaper than the horse, be shod with less expense, and when old could be fattened for food.

The mill of the eleventh century appertained to the manor. It consisted of two horizontal stones, and the grinding was obtained by means of a heavy wheel, which was most likely turned by the hand at Swampton, where there was not a sufficiently continuous supply of water to drive a mill; or a small windmill was adopted. The servants were compelled to grind their corn there, and pay the accustomed tolls for doing so, which were a source of profit to the lord of the manor. The old *Act* of *Secta ad Molendinum* for compelling tenants to use the manorial mills has not long been abolished. The lord kept the mill in repair, provided the sails, in the case of windmills, and the more costly millstones.

The lord did not repair the holdings of his tenants whether free or otherwise. The annual accounts of bailiffs say nothing about repairs,

---

[1] In Warner's *Hants* it is stated as worth 20s.

although the rents due from cottages are duly entered, along with other rents of assize; but they were allowed the building materials for the repair or enlargement of their homesteads, and for their implements, from forest, close, or common. There is no account of the produce obtained from the holdings; but there is no doubt that it was identical in character with that produced, manipulated, and sold by the lord's bailiff.

Although there have been periods of difficulty when barley was used for food, as oats are still used in the North, nevertheless wheat has been the principal grain on which the people of England lived from the earliest times, and it was grown on every estate. The next most considerable grain was oats. Two kinds of barley; the ordinary variety with two rows for making beer; and the coarser form of four rows called *bigg* or *bere*, for feeding pigs and poultry. It, however, disappeared in the fifteenth century. Rye was more scantily cultivated; and there were three kinds of leguminous plants—beans, peas, and vetches. Among these a small amount of white peas for human consumption; beans and vetches for horse-food, and grey peas for the use of swine.[1]

In the thirteenth century there were but few handicraftsmen; and of these the carpenter and smith were the more important. Ordinary carpenter's work was commonly done by farm-hands; and the yeoman and the labourer fashioned for themselves in winter most of the tools required for their callings. The smith's place was not so easily filled; and as one demesne was hardly sufficient to find him full work he often served the wants of several manors. In most villages weaving was an industry, and tanning or tawing leather. Coarse linen and woollen clothing were doubtless manufactured in the homes of the peasantry; and occasionally flax and hemp, especially flax, were obtained in a raw state and woven at home. Woollen cloth was a much rarer commodity among the poor; although the "homespuns" were available among the wealthy.

The cost of arable farming at the same period, when the crop was wheat, may be reckoned as 6*d.* per acre for ploughing the land thrice, which was generally done first in the autumn, second in April, and the third time at midsummer. Hoeing was done by the women at 1*d.* an acre; the females also worked at piecework, as did the men. Two bushels of seed at Michaelmas, 1*s.* Hoeing a second time, ½*d.* an acre. Reaping, 5*d.* an acre. Carriage, 1*d.* per acre. The straw or forage would pay for the threshing. In this statement of cost there

---

[1] J. E. Thorold Rogers, *Six Centuries of Work and Wages*, pp. 55-60.

is no account of rent; but it is inferred that at 4s. a quarter, unless more than six bushels were reaped, there would be a loss on the operation of 1½d.

It was the custom to enter the chief articles on the farm in the annual roll. On a farm[1] where nearly 120 acres were arable land, and which was divided into at least twelve corn-fields, of which six were called furlongs, the principal articles used were:—Four iron-bound carts, and four cart frames, with four sets of rope-harness; four forks for lifting trusses, and one long fork for the rick; three ploughs, six iron dung-forks, three hoes, a reaphook, and a scythe; two mattocks, two wheelbarrows, a seed-cod, two axes, a saw, two winnowing fans, three pairs of leg-chains, divers measures and kitchen utensils, three milk-buckets, a butter-churn, three cheese-vats with cheese-cloths, and a variety of other articles. Speaking generally, the dead stock on the farm was worth in money at that time about £25. Of dead stock the most formidable item of expenditure was iron, which was bought in bars, at the great fairs, of about 4 lbs. in weight. The bailiff served it out to the smith, the weight being debited to him. Steel was employed to edge iron tools, but it was four times dearer than iron. The heavy cost of iron necessitated the frequent use of cart-wheels made from the section of a big tree and not shod with iron. Harrows made with iron tines were unknown, oak pins being used instead. The ploughshare, too, was of wood, protected with clouts or plates of iron nailed to it; and the shoes with which the hoofs of the oxen and horses were protected were very thin and light.

* * * * * *

The Cheping represented as having held one hide in the manor of Swampton was a Saxon proprietor,[1] whose name frequently figures in *Domesday*, and whose estates for the greater part appear to have fallen into the hands of the powerful baron, Ralph de Mortimer, whose possessions extended to 126 manors, in twelve different counties, of which thirteen were in the county of Southampton,[2] and six in Berkshire.

In *Domesday* it is stated, under the head of *Hantune* (Southampton), that there were sixty-five Frenchmen, and thirty-one Englishmen, who paid Customs amounting by the year to £4 0s. 6d. And

---

[1] Holywell Manor, Oxford; J. E. Thorold Rogers, *Six Centuries of Work and Wages*, pp. 86-87.
[2] Duthy, *Sketches of Hampshire*, p. 364.

the King granted to the following, among whom will be found the names of Ralph de Mortimer and Richerius de Andely, liberty of their houses without payment of the usual tax :—

The Bishop, the Abbot of Cormelies, and the Abbot of Lire, Ralph de Todeni, Hugh de Port, Humphrey (Anelf's Brother), Osborn Giffard, Richard Pugnant, Reynold Croc, each owned one house; the Earl of York, Ralph de Mortimer (who held two houses), Gilbert de Bretville, William, son of Stur, Durandus de Gloucester, Hugh de Grentmesnil, Stephen the Pilot, Turstan the Chamberlain, and another Turstan, owning two houses each; the Count of Mortaigne, and the Chamberlain Anelf, each holding five houses; the Physician Nigel (or Niel), and Richerius de Andely, owning four houses; and Anschitil, the son of Osmond, owning three houses.

With regard to the small manor of Swampton, it appears that, in 1476, it was held, in common with Wyke manor, by Robert Baynton; and in 1485 it was granted, together with Wyke, to Sir George Nevill. Subsequently it must have become amalgamated with Hurstbourne *interius*, as in 1553 it appears in the grant made to Sir John Gate. But the manor of Swampton does not appear in the list of small manors included in the purchase made by Sir Robert Oxenbridge in 1558.

Manorial Weight.

In 1860, some workmen, in removing chalk at Hurstbourne Priors, found a steelyard weight, which from the device on the three equidistant shields, on the swell of the weight, leaves but little doubt that it appertains to some member of the Mortimer family, of which family Ralph of that name, as we have seen, held in Swampton at the time of *Domesday*. The weight is globular, and weighs 2 lbs. $4\frac{1}{4}$ ozs. and 60 grains, its height being $2\frac{1}{2}$ ins., and its circumference $7\frac{1}{2}$ ins. It has a small hollow in its base, now filled with chalk, but which was probably intended for the introduction of some metal in rectification. The arms—*Or*, an eagle displayed *vert* (Plate XIII, fig. 5)—evidently refer to the Mortimers.

As heraldry did not become general till the reign of Henry III, 1216-72, the weight could hardly have belonged to any of the Mortimers living before that date. The early form of shield points to the assumption that it may be referred to the end of the thirteenth century or to the beginning of the fourteenth. There was a Ralph de Mortimer, who married, in 1296, Joan, daughter of Edward I, widow of Gilbert de Clare, Earl of Gloucester, known as the "Red Earl". By Joan, sometimes known as Joanna, he had two sons, Thomas and Edward. Sir Thomas de Monthermer had an only daughter,

Margaret, who married Sir John de Montacute, or Montague, younger son of William, first Earl of Salisbury. The monument to the memory of this Sir John is in Salisbury Cathedral, on the side of which, in quartrefoil panels, are shields of arms, two of them exhibiting the arms of Montacute impaling the spread eagle of Monthermer. He fought at Cressy, and died in 1389. Here we have the Mortimer eagle,[1] and perhaps somewhat the date of the weight; but it is impossible to assign it to any individual member of the Mortimer family. It is well known that the great landowners of the Norman period had the power of life and death, "liberty of gallows", over their retainers; they held also the control of the "Assize of bread and ale", meaning that they acted in the capacity of inspectors of weights and measures, and that this was one of the standard weights for checking those of the retailers. The weight is now in the Reading Museum.[2]

[1] Bearing on the Mortimer eagle, there is a carved device over the chantry, in the north choir aisle of Christchurch, five times repeated, representing a bird resembling a "Phœnix, collared and badged". The eagle was a cognisance of the Monthermer and Montague families. Ralph de Monthermer, Earl of Gloucester and Hereford, bore it as a crest early in the fourteenth century, and Edward III granted his own eagle crest to William de Montachute, Earl of Salisbury. (Woodward and Wilks, *Hist. of Hampshire*, vol. iii, p. 119.)

[2] Several steelyard weights are noticed in the pages of the *Archæological Institute*. Vol. viii records one found in Dorsetshire in 1860. Its weight is 3 lbs. ¼ oz., and its diameter is 2½ ins. It bears three heart-shaped shields, each charged with a crowned lion rampant. The same journal, vol. ii, gives an account of a bronze steelyard weight found near Warwick in 1840. It bears four shields, each with a lion rampant; and is thought to be of about the time of Henry III. At page 205 of the same volume two similar weights are spoken of as having been found at Norwich, and exhibited to the Society of Antiquaries in 1832. Mr. Walter Money exhibited before the same Society, in 1880, a steelyard weight which was found on property which formerly appertained to the Knights' Hospitallers of St. John of Jerusalem, at Brimpton. Its weight was 43 ozs., height 2⅝ ins., and circumference 8 ins. It carried three shields, representing the lion rampant, double-headed eagle, etc.; and, as in the case of the others, bore a cavity at its base probably to permit of adjustment being made. The first of the series mentioned here contained lead in the basal hole, which shows that rectification was the object of these depressions. In 1878, Mr. Jas. Parker exhibited a globular steelyard weight of lead, cased with brass, which was found at Blewbury. Its weight was 2 lbs. save half-an-ounce; height 2½ ins. to the top of the loop; circumference 7⅛ ins. It also bore a rampant lion on one shield; while on each of the other two was a double-headed eagle. These arms are generally referred to Richard, Earl of Cornwall. (From a note furnished by Mr. Walter Money, F.S.A.)

The Village School.

The old school-building, which stood on Swampton green, is now turned into cottages; but the date on it was 1723. And from that date, if not earlier, it was a free school in part up to 1835, when it was altered and improved, and from that date up to 1859 it became wholly a free school, and was liberally supported. It was supposed that the Oxenbridge family had left an endowment towards its support, but this it appears was a mistake. The £15 paid annually, for the free education of twelve boys and six girls, was the gratuitous and liberal provision of the various heads of the family of the Earl of Portsmouth. The filling up of the vacancies in the school, under this gift, was to be in the nomination of the tenant of Upper Wyke Farm for the time being. Many years ago, and still remembered, the higher class people of the parish did not think it beneath them to send their children to this school, at, of course, a proportionately increased payment.

The first schoolmaster on record is Alexander Neave. He died about 1778, but his grave is lost. It is about twenty years since I observed his tombstone leaning against the north wall of the graveyard, where it had been placed by the direction of the vicar. There is a notice in the parochial books that Alexander Neave was one of the overseers of the parish in 1765, as well as schoolmaster. There is no doubt that for a time he kept the records. Previous to his death he resigned the school, and was succeeded by Richard and Ann Sutton, who held it until 1828. At the death of Ann Sutton it passed into the hands of Ann Longman, who dying in 1835, Moses and Sarah Butcher succeeded to the charge. At this date the old schoolhouse was considerably enlarged by contributions from Mr. Fellowes and the inhabitants; and the annual payment of fifteen pounds, enlarged to twenty upon the first establishment of the Sunday-school, was continued, and instruction to all made free.

From this renovation the school prospered greatly under the constant supervision of Mr. Dawson, who was then vicar, and numbered variously in different years from 90 to 100 in the week-day school, and about 100 in the Sunday-school. For some few years after it ceased to be a school, the old schoolhouse was used as a parochial reading-room, and lectures on scientific and other subjects were delivered there during several successive winters. The opening commenced on January 18th, 1861; and a very small library was added.

The present National Schools bear date 1860. They were erected by subscription, aided by a Government grant. The Earl of Portsmouth was the principal donor, he having given the land. The entire cost of the building was £1,100; and the late Mr. William Gue, of Andover, was the architect and builder. A north wing was added in 1878 as a class-room for infants. It cost £139 10s., the work being completed by Mr. William Batsford, of St. Mary Bourne. For about ten years the new National Schools were fairly well supported, by means of public grants, private subscriptions, and the pence of the children; but the attendance seldom reached 100. For some few years, however, before the adoption of a Board School, the annual subscriptions became difficult to collect, on account of the losses which yearly accrued to the resident cultivators of the land, owing to unfavourable seasons; and this rendered it necessary that a Government school should be adopted. After the ordinary notices, to which no ratepayer made any special objection, a Board under the sanction of the Government was formed in November 1875. The members of the Board consisted of Joseph Stevens, Chairman; William Day, Vice-chairman; John Berry, Alfred Charles Medhurst, and John Page. The Board elected Mr. Spencer Clarke, of Whitchurch, as Clerk to the Board.

Mr. Rawlings, the first teacher at the new National Schools, began his duties in 1858, and he left on the 25th March 1864. Since that date Mr. John Orchard has been schoolmaster, his appointment bearing date the 11th April 1864.

The staff of the school has been, as a rule:—Under the National School Committee, one certificated master, a sempstress, one pupil-teacher, and occasionally a paid monitor.

Under the School Board:—One certificated master, one certificated mistress (who is also sempstress), one pupil-teacher, and two paid monitors. This account of the staff under the Board is correct only since 1880, inasmuch as during the first five years under the Board, viz., from 1876 to 1880, the staff consisted of one certificated master, a sempstress, one uncertificated female assistant over twenty years of age, and one pupil-teacher.

The average attendance at the National Schools since the year 1860 is stated below, the population of the parish of St. Mary Bourne since 1801 having already been given:—

1860	-	-	- 75	1868	-	-	- 98
1861	-	-	- 75	1869	-	-	- 104
1862	-	-	- 98	1870	-	-	- 102
1863	-	-	- 100	1871	-	-	- 98
1864	-	-	- 96	1872	-	-	- 100
1865	-	-	- 87	1873	-	-	- 96
1866	-	-	- 94	1874	-	-	- 95
1867	-	-	- 90	1875	-	-	- 90

NOTES.—The average for fourteen years under the National School Committee was 94. The emigration movement which set in about 1873, no doubt lowered the averages for 1873, 1874, 1875, and 1876.

The following figures show the average attendance during the first five years after the formation of the Board School:—

1876	-	-	-	- 92
1877	-	-	-	- 105
1878	-	-	-	- 122
1879	-	-	-	- 119
1880	-	-	-	- 104

The average for these five years is 108.

The attendance during the year 1885, under a decreased population, numbered 127.

The Government grants for the last four years under the National School Committee were as under:

					£	s.	d.
1872	-	-	-	-	40	19	3
1873	-	-	-	-	40	6	5
1874	-	-	-	-	46	19	7
1875	-	-	-	-	40	14	0

The grants to the school under the Board, for the first four years, were the following:

					£	s.	d.
1876	-	-	-	-	36	7	5
1877	-	-	-	-	67	8	5
1878	-	-	-	-	84	14	0
1879	-	-	-	-	60	13	10

As the annual capitation up to the year 1885, which was the decennial year of the Board School, averaged £72, it is evident that under the Board School there was greater efficiency in the teaching, as the increase in the number of children attending the school over and above the attendance under the former management, during a similar period, is not sufficient to account for the difference.

The Board School rate at the outset was 3½d. in the pound; but in 1885 it rose to 5d. In 1886 it was the same, the rate realising £180; at the same time the fees were £34 13s. 3d., which, with other sums, reached a total of £289 0s. 6d. The expenditure at the same period included salaries of officers, £31 15s.; legal expenses, etc., £8 3s. 2d.; salaries of teachers, £197 2s. 8d., which with the cost of books, cleaning, etc., left a balance of £25 17s. 1d.

THE TRUST DEED OF THE NATIONAL SCHOOLS.

I The Right Honorable ISAAC NEWTON EARL OF PORTSMOUTH of Hurstbourne Park in the County of Southampton under the authority of an Act passed in the fifth year of the Reign of Her Majesty Queen Victoria entitled an Act to afford further facilities for the conveyance and endowment of sites for schools and of the Act of the eighth year of the reign of her present Majesty explaining the same Do hereby freely and voluntarily and without valuable consideration Grant and Convey unto The Reverend Watkin Temple Clerk of the Parish of Hurstbourne Hants John William Hooper of Stoke in the said Parish of St. Mary Bourne in the County of Southampton Esquire and Thomas Longman of Finckley in the Parish of Andover in the said County of Southampton Esquire All that piece of land called Square Meadow containing by estimation three roods and fourteen perches situate at Swampton in the said Parish and numbered 98 on the Tithe commutation Map of the said Parish which said premises are delineated in the Map drawn in the margin hereof together with all easements appurtenances and hereditaments corporeal and incorporeal belonging thereto or connected therewith and my estate right title and interest in or to the same premises To hold the same unto and to the use of the said Reverend Watkin Temple John Willam Hooper and Thomas Longman and their heirs for the purposes of the said first recited Act and Upon trust to permit the said premises and all buildings thereon erected or to be erected to be for ever hereafter appropriated and used as and for a School for the education of children and adults or children only of the labouring manufacturing and other poorer classes in the Parish of St. Mary Bourne aforesaid and adjacent neighbourhood and for no other purpose Which said School shall be at all times open to the Inspection of the Inspector or Inspectors for the time being appointed by Her Majesty or her successors and be under the General management of a Committee to be Constituted as hereafter mentioned that is to say such Committee shall consist of myself The said Isaac Newton Earl of Portsmouth The Reverend Watkin Temple John Longman of Wadwick Esquire Walter Dowling of Middle Week Yeoman John Lywood of Week Esquire William Dowling Gentleman John Moore Farmer and William Day Farmer all of the Parish aforesaid until the month of April next and thenceforth of eight persons being subscribers to the same School to the amount of one pound at least during the current year and such Committee shall be elected annually in the said month of April by the subscribers to the said School who shall have subscribed thereto the sum of Ten Shillings at least during the current year or who have been original Dowers towards the building all subscriptions for the current year shall be considered to have become due on the first day of January thereof but may be paid at any time before or at the time of voting Provided that no default of election nor any vacancy shall prevent the managers of the past year or the continuing managers as the case may be from continuing to act in the management of the said School until the next annual election The said Committee at their first meeting shall elect a Chairman for the ensuing year who shall preside at each meeting of the said Committee and of the subscribers and in case of his absence a Chairman shall be chosen by the Meeting and in case of an equality of votes on any question the Chairman for the time being shall have a second being the casting vote and the said Committee shall annually elect one of the members thereof to act as Secretary who shall keep minutes of the proceedings at the Meetings thereof in a Book which shall be provided for the purpose and shall give due notice of all extraordinary meetings to each member of the said

Committee and such Committee shall appoint and at their discretion dismiss the Master and Mistress of the said School and shall admit and discharge all the scholars thereat and shall prescribe the times of admission and the mode and times of payment And it is hereby declared that the Instruction at the said School shall comprise at least the following branches of school learning namely Reading Writing Arithmetic Geography Scripture History and in the case of girls Needlework And it is hereby further declared that it shall be a fundamental regulation and practice of the said school that the Bible be daily read therein and that no child shall be required to learn any Catechism or religious formulary other than the Lords prayer and the ten Commandments or to attend any Sunday School or place of worship to which respectively his or her parent or guardian shall on religious grounds object but the selection of such Sunday School and place of worship shall in all cases be left to the free choice of such parent or guardian without the childs thereby incurring any loss of the benefits and privileges of the School the Trusts whereof are hereby declared And it is hereby declared that no person shall be appointed or continue to be the Master or Mistress of the School who shall not be a Member of the Church of England And it is hereby further declared that as often as any of the present or future Trustees die or go to reside beyond the seas or desire to be discharged from or decline or become incapable to act in the trusts hereby in them reposed it shall be lawful for the Committee of Management for the time being so elected as aforesaid to appoint any other person to be a Trustee in the place of the Trustee so dying or going to reside beyond the seas or desiring to be discharged or declining or becoming incapable to act as aforesaid so as to vest all hereditaments subject to the Trusts aforesaid in such new Trustees in terms of the provisions of an Act passed in the fourteenth year of the Reign of Her present Majesty entitled "An Act to render more simple and effectual the Titles by which Congregations or Societies for purposes of Religious worship or education in England and Ireland hold property for such purpose" And it is hereby expressly declared that the said School or Schools shall or may be for ever hereafter used on Sundays for the purpose of a Sunday School in connexion with the Established Church of England at which the Master or Mistress or Teacher shall assist in their several capacities as required by the Committee and the Committee may from time to time as they see fit leave the management of such Sunday School to the Vicar and Curate for the time being of the said Parish of St. Mary Bourne or to either of them In Witness whereof the said Isaac Newton Earl of Portsmouth and the said Watkin Temple John William Hooper and Thomas Longman have hereunto set their hands and seals this sixteenth day of December one thousand eight hundred and fifty-nine. [The signatures follow.]

TRUST DEED.

Enrolled in Her Majesty's High Court of Chancery the thirteenth day of January in the year of our Lord 1860 being first duly stamped according to the tenor of the Statutes made for that purpose

E. GRUBB.

By the decease of Mr. Thomas Longman of Finkley, and of Mr. John William Hooper of Stoke, two of the Trusteeships of the St. Mary Bourne National Schools became vacant. To fill one of these vacancies, Mr. Joseph Stevens, M.R.C.P.L., of St. Mary Bourne, was elected on the 5th of February 1876; consequently, in 1879, the Trustees consisted of The Right Honble. the Earl of Portsmouth, Rev. Watkin Temple, and Joseph Stevens.

Swampton Allotments of 1753.

Between 1766 and 1832, enclosures of common lands were general throughout the country, the Enclosure Acts being similar in character. There were some earlier enactments, but they were general in their operation. Thus, Act, 29th George II, 1756, was an Act for enclosing, by the mutual consent of the lords and tenants, part of any common for the purpose of planting and preserving trees fit for timber or underwood, and for preventing the unlawful destruction of trees. Recompense was agreed (in this Act) to be given to those who held common rights, either by a grant of a share of the profit from the sale of timber, or by a grant of other lands, or by some annuity or rent-charge issuing out of the said ground. Act, 31st George II, 1758, was for the purpose of rendering more effective the former Act; but in it some alterations were made in the mode of recompensing those interested in rights of common.

Act, 13th George III. *For better Cultivation, Improvement, and Regulation of Common Fields, Wastes, and Commons of Pasture.* This Act regulated the usages of common lands, such as the opening and closing of commons at particular times, which could be done by a majority of two-thirds of the commoners; the election of field-reeve or reeves [every year on the 21st May, or within three days after] to superintend the fencing, cultivating, and improving the common lands.

The lands cultivated were to be done so at the expense of the occupiers; as should be determined by three-fourths of the occupiers, with the tithe-owner or rector, twenty-one days' notice being given on places of worship, signed by one-third of such occupiers—all the expenses were to be paid *proportionately* by the occupiers.

The balks, slades, or meers which may be waste, lying among arable land (inconveniently), with the consent of the lords or ladies of manors—that is to say, any wastes in open or common fields adjoining such balks, slades, or meers, being wastes, and having also the consent of three-fourths of the value of the occupiers obtained at a meeting, such lands could be ploughed up and tilled.

From the year 1760 to 1844, 4,000 Enclosure Acts were passed,[1] showing how general was the open field system in England at so late a period. The abandonment of this system was necessitated by the increase in the population, and by the improvements made in agriculture. The Acts were drawn in the same form, reciting that the open and common fields lie intermixed, and situated inconveniently, owned by divers persons, who are entitled to rights of common on them, and being in their present state incapable of

[1] Porter's *Progress of the Nation*, p. 146.

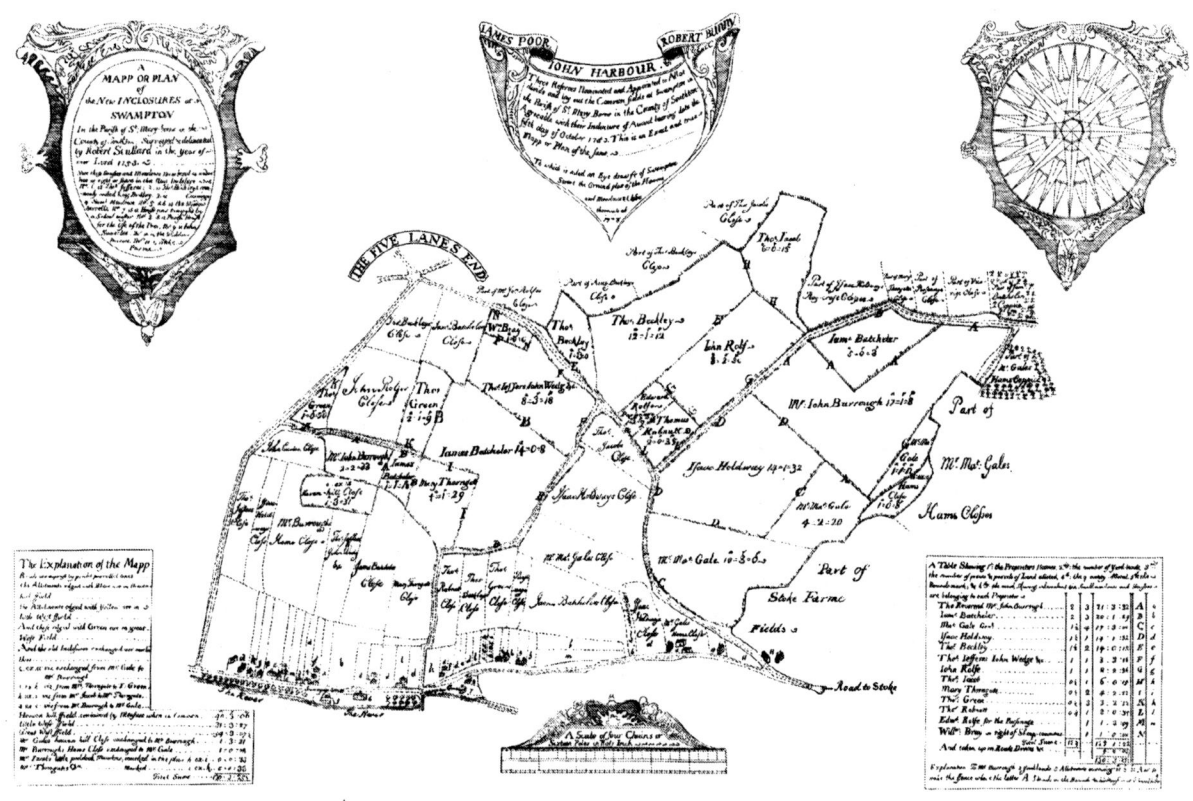

improvement, and that it is desirable that they should be divided and enclosed, each commoner having a specified share set out. On this, enclosure Commissioners were appointed, and under their award the "balks" were ploughed up, and the fields divided into parcels for the separate owners. The rearrangement and planting of hedges consequent on this quickly changed the aspect of the country.

It was previous to the Act, 29th of George II, 1756, that the common fields of Swampton were divided. From the accompanying map, which is copied from the original in the possession of Mr. Robert Colebrook, of St. Mary Bourne, the date of forming the allotments is 1753. The map is rendered half the scale of the original, or four chains or sixteen poles in half an inch, instead of one inch. A special order was obtained for setting out the common lands, when three referees were appointed, whose names are stated on the map, "to allot, divide, and lay out the common fields at Swampton agreeable with their indenture of award." From the list of names on the map it appears that there were thirteen individuals who participated in the use of the common fields before the enclosures took place, and Wm. Bray, who shared in the sheep-common only, and in lieu of which an acre of land was allotted to him. The commoners held in yardlands or virgates, the virgate representing a bundle of so many scattered strips in open fields. The number of yardlands at Swampton varied from 2 to $1\frac{1}{2}$, and $\frac{1}{2}$ virgates, down to the holding of a $\frac{1}{4}$ virgate in the case of Rabnutt, in all representing $12\frac{1}{4}$ yardlands. Taking the yardland at 30 acres, the quantity of land contained in the common fields would have been $367\frac{1}{2}$ acres; while the estimated quantity, when allotted, according to the map, is only 125 acres, 1 rood, and 22 perches, and which, with the land taken up in the roadways, etc., brings the total to rather over 130 acres, or about 11 acres to the yardland. It is evident, therefore, that the yardland named on the map differs largely in quantity from the ordinary yardland, and might refer to the half-virgate, or to some standard which had been originally fixed. At all events, some further explanation is necessary. The sheep-common was on "Heaven Hill"; and in addition to his share in the common fields, each had his close or closes for pasture or hay. In these common rights the clergyman, then the Rev. John Burrough, participated. In lieu of his 2 yardlands, he had 3 allotments, containing 21 acres, 3 roods, and 32 perches, or at the rate of about 11 acres to the yardland.[1] It will be noticed that the "droves" or early roads were

[1] As it is probable that all the land appertaining to the Priory of St. Swithin was held under a similar distribution, the manorial system adopted at Bleadon in Somersetshire might be cited. This manor appertained to the Priory; and the

necessary to the usage of the common fields. Without the plan of the common fields, as they stood when cultivated in common, it is impossible to make any statement concerning the arrangement of the strips. The map expresses that exchanges of land took place, doubtless for mutual accommodation ; and the difference in quantity obtained by some over others in lieu of their holdings in yardlands, was due most likely to the difference in the quality of the land.

A short description of a communal district furnished by Fitzherbert, in his *Treatise on Surveying*, of the early part of the sixteenth century, will serve to show the arrangement of the strips in open lands, as they then stood under cultivation in that particular case. He calls the fields "Dale Furlong",[1] in which various inhabitants have lands. In this field the parson has two strips, the lord three, a tenant one, another two, a third one, the lord four, the prior two, the parson one, a fourth tenant two, a fifth one, a sixth one, a seventh two, the prior three, the lord two and one headland, the parson having the other. Now it was almost impossible that these strips could be cultivated otherwise than collectively. The rest of the fields, of which he gives four names, are similarly divided. He then treats of a long meadow of 122 acres, which is similarly staked and bound. This appears to be used for hay, and the several tenants mow and stack their portions. In this typical manor there are also closes of various dimensions, probably as at Swampton. Each husbandman has six of these closes, three for corn and the other for pasture or hay. The rental of the common land is 6*d*. an acre, of the enclosed 8*d*., the difference in value being due to the fact that it was permitted to let oxen lie on it. The rent appears to illustrate that the average rental of arable land remained practically unchanged from the thirteenth to the sixteenth century.

The aspect of Swampton as it stood at the time of the new distribution is discernible in its present features. The houses were then all thatched, as many of them are now, and frequently lie detached, and have a small outbuilding such as a barn, stable, or granary adjoining, and behind all a strip of meadow-land. If you survey the tithing from a neighbouring elevation, it is striking how regularly the small plots of pasture are seen to extend in strips of different widths from the backs of the houses, each one divided from

tenants, of whom very few were free, held in virgates, and half-virgates ; while others were holders of quarter-virgates, and even in parcels of one-eighthvirgates. On this estate four virgates went to the hide. (Seebohm, *English Village Community*, p. 57.)

[1] J. E. Thorold Rogers, *Six Centuries of Work and Wages*, Art. "Communal Fields", p. 89.

the next by its neatly trimmed hedge, showing that at the time of the allotments every villager was a small farmer. The allotment system brought to an end a class, ranking above that of the labourer, and beneath that of the modern farmer, who tilled their few acres of land, and kept their geese, pigs, and cows. They were habited in the old British smock-frock, and worked on the land themselves, and were succeeded in their holdings by their sons, and they again by their children. It was the period—

"When every rood of ground maintained its man."

With the curtailment of common rights, this class of cultivator, which more nearly perhaps answers to the *Bordarii* of the *Domesday Survey*, became practically extinguished.

It is worthy of remark that of the allottees whose names appear on the map, the names of three only are now to be found in the parish of St. Mary Bourne, viz., Holdway, Gale, and Wedge. And showing how in the course of a century land may change owners, not one of the allotments belongs at the present time to any member of the family of its original possessor, although the names of the original allottees still cling to some of the holdings.

The allottees represent the old forty-shilling freeholders, who were the mass of the county voters previous to the passing of the Reform Bill of 1832. They were poor, and most of them mortgaged or sold their property, and became labourers. One remarkable character of this kind, living in Stoke tithing, I well remember, named Piper, who obtained a precarious livelihood by collecting wood-ashes from the cottagers, which he sold to the better-class farmers. It was his custom to traverse the parish every Monday with a string of donkeys, each bearing a bag to carry the ashes.

Of the quaint homesteads of the larger holders of land, in the parish of St. Mary Bourne, in the seventeenth century, some of the more interesting stand in Ricket's Lane leading to Stoke, and are known as Roe's, Butler's, and old Bourne farm, before it had undergone alteration. Roe's farmhouse has only recently been burnt down. The date on the chimney at Butler's, 1676, refers to the time of Charles II; but the difference in date between these dwellings is so small as to mark a common building period. They are mostly built on one plan, with long sloping roofs behind, and dormer windows in front; and the entrances in some cases are porched, and have stout oak doors, which open with heavy iron latch-loops. The walls are ribbed with oak timber interlaced and dark with age, and of sufficient stoutness to furnish material for several cottages as they are built at the present day. The lavish use of timber was due to the removal of much of the forest of the district, under disafforestation, at the time of their erection. Some of these houses are still occupied by small farmers, but others have undergone alteration, or they are tenanted by labourers, the land which formerly appertained to them having become massed in larger farms.[1]

A last remnant of the period of the common-field system, the Pound, still stands by the side of the highway leading from Swampton green to Stoke. It is used occasionally for the imprisonment of stray cattle, and the Hayward to perform the duty is still chosen in vestry; but the power now possessed by the police to report cases of animals straying on the thoroughfares has rendered impounding unnecessary.

The Chapels.

I am indebted to Mr. John Page for the following information respecting the chapels in the parish of St. Mary Bourne.

BAPTIST CHAPEL.

The chapel was formerly a barn, and was called the "Old Black Barn". The property was originally purchased at an auction by a Mr. Freeman of Whitchurch, about the year 1824; and the barn was fitted up, and used as a chapel till 1844, when a new building was erected to seat 160 people, the cost being about £180. A considerable portion of the outlay was furnished by the Baptists' Association. The chapel fell down in the spring of 1879, and the present building was erected in the autumn of the same year. A new speaking-platform, which had been put up at the south end only a short time previous to the destruction of the building, was crushed in when the walls fell. The small graveyard attached contains the body of Edward Cook, who preached here for some time, together with the body of his wife.

PRIMITIVE METHODIST CHAPELS.

The ground now occupied by the old and new chapels formerly belonged to the parish, and two cottages stood on it. It was sold by auction by the parochial officers at the Plough Inn early in the year 1838. The late Mr. John Page, and a few others, having surveyed the property by moonlight, instructed a stranger to bid for it, as the tide of opposition against Nonconformists at that time ran high in the village, when it was bought for £54. The old chapel was then erected

---

[1] These notices refer to the houses as they stood forty years ago.

at an outlay of £100, the money being furnished by the rent of one of the cottages, and by voluntary subscriptions. The building was opened on "Bourne Revel Sunday", July 18th, 1838.

The other cottage was removed in 1859, and the new chapel erected on the site, at a cost of £170, which was also liquidated by subscriptions. The building is adapted to seat 200 people.

In the little burial-ground of the old chapel, Mr. Page says, " I have a little brother buried, his name was John Page, he was the first ; and John Farr of Binley, and Elizabeth his wife, are buried just outside ; and Sophia, wife of Solomon Goodyear, and four children ; also William and Mary Parker. In the new ground are my father, mother, and sister, John Kercher and wife, William Collins and wife ; and three children in one grave, that died in one night, belonging to Charles and Emily Davis."

The Primitive Methodist Chapel at Stoke was built in the year 1864; it seats 80 people; and the charge for building it was about £100, which has all been paid.

Binley Mission Room (unsectarian) was erected in 1882, on land given by Miss Longman, daughter of the late Mr. John Longman of Warwick. It furnishes room for nearly 100 people.

WESLEYAN CHAPELS.

The old chapel was not connectional; but was built for Mr. Samuel Webb about the year 1835. It was afterwards mortgaged to Mr. William Day, who, at his death, left the sum of £40 to the Wesleyan body to purchase the building of his executors. It is now taken down, and a new building erected on land given by the Earl of Portsmouth. The memorial stone of the new building was laid on August the 23rd, 1886. It was completed and opened on October the 26th, the cost of its erection being £190 ; and it provides sittings for about 100 people. The Wesleyans also hold meetings in a cottage at Dunley.

The "Old Book Chapel", or what is now called the St. Mary Bourne Band of Hope Mission Room, seats 100 people. It was fitted up in 1866 at a cost of £25 ; and was used as a chapel by the Primitive Methodists for sixteen years. The Salvation Army now hold meetings there, and in the buildings behind it known as the "Workman's Hall".

Mr. Page writes, that the St. Mary Bourne Band of Hope was established in November 1872. "It has been", he says, "the means of reclaiming lots of drunkards and of bringing up children in the path of sobriety." Public meetings are held every fortnight in this room during the months of winter.

Pleas of the Crown.

❦ ❦ ❦

THE extracts from the Assize Rolls will be found of peculiar interest in throwing light on ancient manners and customs; and on the powers possessed by the lord of the manor of what are called the "townships of Wikes, Burne, Husseburn, and Stokes", in the hundred of Evingar. The papers show, further, the powers of juries, and furnish facts that a peculiar privilege called "Right of Sanctuary" was permitted to persons guilty of grave offences, which the following Pleas illustrate the exercise of in two cases. Sanctuary (*Sanctuarium;* see Cowel's *Interpreter*) was a place privileged by the King for the safeguard of offenders' lives. The practice of taking refuge in sacred buildings seems to have arisen from the *Cities of Refuge* mentioned in *Exodus*. There are probably some differences in the interpretation; but Cowel states that by virtue of Sanctuary persons guilty of felony and treason were permitted shelter, in order that within forty days they might acknowledge their offence and submit to banishment. If during that time any layman expelled them from the place of refuge he was excommunicated; if any clerk (*priest*) did the same he was made irregular. But after forty days no man could relieve them.

Assize of Bread and Ale was the power or privilege of assizing or adjusting the weights and measures of bread and beer. As the weight of bread prescribed by the magistrate is still called the *size* or *assize* of bread; a *Sizer* being one who has to live upon an assized allowance.

The term "*infongenthef*" expresses the privilege of lords of certain manors to seize and judge any thief taken within their fee. To this power the franchise of a gallows belonged, which power was possessed by the Prior of the manor of Hurstbourne. Three other franchises appear to have belonged to the jurisdiction of the feudal lord, viz., those of *Sac, Soc,* and *Theam*.[1] The first gave the power of hearing and determining disputes among tenants; the second, the precincts within which such power could be exercised; and the third, the right of possessing and governing bondmen and villeins and their offspring. Stocks for the punishment of offenders were an appendage of every township, an apparatus of the kind being erected, according to the 8th and 9th of Edward I, in the village (*vill*) of Stoke.

Frank-pledge (*Franci plegium*) signifies a pledge or surety for freemen for the preservation of the peace. It was the custom of English freemen to find surety for their faith towards the king and his subjects; whereupon certain neighbours became surety for each other, to see every man of their pledge forthcoming at all times, or to answer the transgression of anyone gone away. The offender in any pledge was to be produced within thirty-one days, or his fellows were called on to give satisfaction. The circuit of the pledge was called *Decenna*, because it consisted of ten households; and each particular person, who was bound for himself and his neighbours, was denominated a *Decennier*. View of Frank-pledge (*Visus Franci plegii*) was the office which the Sheriff in his County Court, or the Bailiff in his Hundred, performed in looking to the king's peace, and seeing that every man was a member of some *pledge*.

It is stated in the following Pleas that, in cases where an offender escaped or could not be found, the township or tithing to which he belonged were responsible for his appearance, and if those who had the responsibility could not, or did not, produce him, the said township or tithing were "in mercy". The explanation of this appears to be that those who were responsible were at the discretion, as regards punishment, of the king, lord, or judge; and the offenders were usually amerced in a fine.

Assize Rolls, Southampton, 20th Hen. III, 1235. M. 5 19 } 1.

(M. 1.) Pleas and Assizes before W. de Eboraco and his associates at Winchester, 20th Hen. III.

[These are not arranged under the heads of the Hundreds.]

* * * * * * *

(M. 14.) Pleas of the Crown of the County of Winchester (*sic*) before the Justices.

* * * * * * *

(M. 22*d*.) The Hundred of Evingar, of the Prior's liberty.

* * * * *

---

[1] Dr. Cowel, *The Interpreter*.

Unknown malefactors killed Roger the Reeve of Stokes. It is not known who they were, and no one is suspected thereof.

* * * * * * *

William de la Dene and Richard Woderove, Ralph Saumun [and] Sewal de Roer, having been taken for unlawful possession (*pro malo recto*), come and defend the larceny and everything. And William de la Dene and Richard Woderove put themselves upon the verdict of twelve men, and upon four townships (to wit) Wikes, Burne, Husseburn, and Stokes, for good and evil .... who come and say upon their oath that they are all thieves, and guilty of many larcenies, and therefore ..... They had no chattels.

[The judgment is not stated ; probably they were hanged.]

Tower Assize Rolls, No. 12, 33rd Hen. III. [Title lost: roll much damaged.]

[Pleas of the Crown.]

The Hundred of Evingar comes by 12 [Jurors].

Ralph, son of Reign' [Reginald ?] de Husseburne, was found dead in the mill-house in Husseburne. Peter le Parchemener of Andevere, suspected of that death, does not come: therefore let him be put in exigent and outlawed. He had no chattels, but was in the tithing of Walkelin Ercheband in Andevere: therefore [the tithing is] in mercy. And the township of Husseburne did not present this matter (*loquelam*) to the Coroner, nor make pursuit after him : therefore [the township is] in mercy.

* * * * * * *

Unknown malefactors met Thomas le Pipere and Christian at Pit (*de puteo*) in the Heath of Sandelford, in coming from the Market of Neubire, and killed them there. It is not known who they were. Henry le Pipere, the first finder comes, and is not suspected. And the townships of Echenes [*Itchingswell*], Will'i, Wydehaye, Husseburne, and Wrth, did not come to the Inquisition, nor make pursuit after them : therefore [those townships are] in mercy. A certain man, unknown, was found killed in the Wood of Badele, of the Manor of Husseburne of the Prior of Winchester. John le Engleis, the first finder, comes, and is not suspected. Judgment: misadventure. No Englishry : therefore murder.[1]

Thomas de la Wale of Thacham was found dead in the field [*i.e.*, the common field] of Hesseburn. Edmund de Wadden, the first finder, comes, and is not suspected, nor any other. Judgment: mis-

---

[1] This means that the person killed was not proved to be an Englishman ; therefore he was supposed to be a Norman ; and the hundred was liable to a fine for the murder of a Norman.

adventure. And the township of Chepmanneford and Eggebury did not come fully to the Inquisition: therefore [they are] in mercy.

* * * * * * *

Robert Calvus [*i.e.*, the Bald] of Hesseburne was found dead in the vill of Hesseburne. William Canun and John Banget, suspected of that death, come, and for good and evil put themselves upon the country. The Jurors say that the said John is not guilty of the aforesaid death: therefore [let him go] quit therefrom. But they say that the aforesaid William Canun is guilty of the aforesaid death: therefore to judgment on him. His chattels, 20*d*., for which the Sheriff shall answer.

Assize Rolls, Southampton, 40th Hen. III. $\left.\begin{array}{l}\text{M.}\\5\\19\end{array}\right\}$ 2.

(M. 1.) Pleas of Jurors and Assizes at Winchester, in co. Southampton, on the morrow of St. Hilary, before Gilbert de Preston and his associates Justices in Eyre, in the 40th year of the reign of King Henry, son of King John.

[These are not arranged under Hundreds.]

(M. 35.) Pleas of the Crown at Winchester (etc., as above).

(M. 43*d*.) *The Hundred of Evingar comes by* 12 [Jurors].

Concerning indicted persons they say that John, son of Adam the Vacher, and John, his younger brother, Nicholas, son of Philip, and William le Whyte of Wodchaye, have withdrawn themselves, and are suspected of stealing sheep and many other misdeeds. . . . Let them be put in exigent and outlawed. The chattels of John, son of Adam, senior, 3*s*., for which the Sheriff shall answer. The chattels of William le White, 12*d*., for which the same Sheriff shall answer; and he was in the tithing of John le Careter in Wodehaye; therefore [the tithing is] in mercy. The others had no chattels. And John, son of Adam, John, his brother, and Nicholas, son of Philip, were in the tithing of Silvester de Husseburne in the same [vill]: therefore [that tithing is] in mercy.

The Jurors present that Alexander, son of William Cole, was taken for burglary of the grange of the Master of Holy Cross in Husseburne, and he was delivered to the whole tithing of Husseburne to have him before the Justices, and now they have him not: therefore [they are] in mercy. And afterwards, before the coming of the Justices, the same Alexander put himself in the church of Holy Cross without Winchester, and from that church he escaped: therefore to judgment concerning that escape upon the vill of Sparkeford. And the Jurors [of the Hundred] suspect him of many larcenies. Therefore let him be put in exigent and outlawed. He had no chattels. And he was in the aforesaid tithing of Husseburne.

Assize Rolls, Southampton, 8-9 Edw. I, 1279-80. M.) 5 } 2.
21)

(M. 1.) Pleas of the Crown before Solomon de Rochester and his associates Justices in Eyre at Winchester, in the octaves of St. Martin in the eighth year of the reign of King Edward, son of King Henry, the ninth year beginning.

(M. 8.) The Hundred of Evyngar comes by 12 [Jurors]. (Rochester.)

In a long entry relating to an assault by Richard the Chapeleyn of Ekeneswell [*Itchingswell*] on Robert, parson of Nottehangre, with a knife, the flight of Richard to the church of Hycheneswell, and his death in a subsequent affray, the vill of Wyke Priors and other vills are presented for not coming to the inquest before the Coroner, and amerced.

* * * * * * *

William Godchep suddenly died between Chapmannesford and Wyke. The first finder and four neighbours come, and are not suspected, nor any other person. Judgment: misadventure. And he was buried by Richard Gower, clerk,[1] and by the vills of Wyke, Husseburne, and Heggebire; therefore [they are] in mercy. And Richard Atte Putte and William Atte Ponde falsely presented themselves to be neighbours. Therefore in mercy.

The Jurors present that a certain strange merchant (*mercator*) was killed in the royal street (*regia strata*) in the parish of Stoke, and was carried away and placed in the sheep-fold of Alexander le Grey of Stokes: whom John le Grey and William le Grey took, and carried away that body to the "said" (*sic*) Forest, and there buried the said dead man. And they say that that dead man was never found, nor seen by the Coroner. Therefore murder upon Stoke and Bendleye, because they do not take part (*participant*) with the Hundred. And the aforesaid John and William, being taken, come and defend the death and everything, and for good and evil put themselves upon the country. And the 12 Jurors of this Hundred, together with the 12 Jurors of the Hundred of Andevere, say upon their oath that they are not guilty of the aforesaid death; but they say that they removed the aforesaid dead man and carried him away to the Forest, and hid him: therefore let them be committed to gaol. Afterwards they came, and made a fine for half a mark, by

---

[1] It appears from another entry that he was clerk to the Coroner.

the pledge of Robert Durdent and Roger de Inkepenne, by [before?] W. de Braibuef and R. Fulton [two Justices?].[1]

The Jurors present that Henry Heuse obstructed a certain path, common to men passing on foot between Stoke and Frysolk, by a certain gate which he constructed there, so that they cannot pass by there, as they used. Therefore let the aforesaid way be "deobstructed" and opened, and the aforesaid gate pulled down [and] whatsoever may be a nuisance. And Henry [is] in mercy.

* * * * * * *

The Jurors present that Roger le Sepherde was taken for stealing sheep, and put in the stocks (*inceppatus*), in the custody of the vill of Stoke, and he escaped from their custody. Therefore to judgment concerning the escape upon the township of Stoke. And he fled, and withdrew himself for one year; and afterwards he returned into the country, and was taken, and delivered to the Gaol of Winchester, and there died. And afterwards it is testified by the 12 Jurors that the Prior of St. Swython's of Winchester levied from the aforesaid vill of Stoke 100 shillings for the escape, before the escape was adjudged, contrary to the Statute of the Lord the King. Therefore let the aforesaid Prior answer for the aforesaid 100 shillings for the escape; and it is commanded to the Sheriff that he distrain the aforesaid Prior that he be here to-morrow.

The Jurors present that this Hundred is the Hundred of the Prior of St. Swython of Winchester, and is worth by the year 40s.; they know not by what warrant. And the same Prior holds the manor of Hisseburne, which sometime was in the hands of the Kings of England. And the same Prior has everywhere in his lands and hundreds the returns of writs, estreats, summonses, view of frank-pledge, gallows, assize, amendment of bread and ale, infongenthef, chattels of felons, warren and free chace for taking all manner of beasts. And he holds pleas of withernam.[2] And the Bishop of

---

[1] There was a legal custom adopted at a long anterior period by the Scandinavians, that of the investigation of a crime by witnesses. A number of witnesses had to be produced by the criminal to answer for his innocence, they swearing that they believed him innocent. They could not prove an *alibi*, or anything else concerning him; but they merely asserted their opinion, and became sureties for the truth of his assertion. In the absence of proof, combat was appealed to in the presence of judges; a custom which existed on the Statute Book until about a century ago. The ordeal of hot and cold water, of hot iron and fire, and many similar modes of torture, and the trial by water in the case of witchcraft, all existed long after Christianity should have inculcated more merciful methods of dealing with suspected criminals.

[2] Withernam, according to Bracton, lib. 3, c. 37, appears to signify an unlawful distress made by him who has no right to distrain.

Winchester [has the like liberty?] in his lands and hundreds, they know not by what warrant. Therefore, as to the Bishop, let it remain until, etc. And let the aforesaid Prior be distrained that he be here. (See *Quo Warranto Rolls* of this date.)

The Jurors present that Richard Gower, the Coroner's clerk, caused Richard (*sic*) Godchep, a dead man, to be buried, and took 2s. for doing his office. Therefore it is commanded to the Sheriff that he have him here. Afterwards the said Richard comes, and cannot deny this: therefore let him be taken in charge. He made a fine, as it appears below. [Not stated on this membrane.]

M. 5 20 } 4, is a duplicate of this Roll.

Of the same date as the preceding Assize Roll, viz., 8th and 9th Edward I, Roll 36a, *Placita de quo Warranto*, shows that Robert Dandely, whose name has already appeared in connection with lands in Hampshire, and probably at Wyke, was summoned to show to the Lord the King by what warrant he claims to have return of the writs of the Lord the King, free gallows in Candover, correction of breach of the assize of bread and ale in the same vill without the will of the Lord the King, and his predecessors Kings of England, etc.

And Robert comes, and as to the return of writs he says that he hath nothing, nor doth he claim to have anything in the same. Therefore let that remain to the Lord the King. And as to the gallows and correction of the breach of assize of bread and ale, he says, that he hath the hundred of Maynesberewe, to which the aforesaid liberties are belonging, and by that warrant he claims to have them by performing the service of five shillings to the Lord the King for the hundred aforesaid.

And William of Gyselham is not able to deny this. And therefore it is considered that the aforesaid Robert go thereof without day (*sic*). Saving to the Lord the King his right and action, etc.

Subsidy Rolls.

1st Edward III, 1327.

IN the year 1327, King Edward III had granted to him by the Parliament the *twentieth* of the value of all the movable goods of every person, with the exception of the clergy. The following are the assessments for the different tithings in the parish of St. Mary Bourne:—

HUNDR'EM DE EVINGAR.
VILLATA DE BOURN.

Robt'o Chapmanford	iiis. iiid.	Joh'e Upchulli		is. iiid.
Nich'o Le Carte	iis. iiid.	Galfro Le Kyng		is. vid.
Nich'o Welward	is. iiid.	Joh'e Wacke		is.
Will'o Atte Brigge	is.	Will'o Craketail		is. iiid.
Rog'o Churcheye	is. ixd.	Henr' atte More		is. vid.
Will'o Colyere	is. vid.	Nich'o Silvestre		ixd.
Ric'o le Eir	iis.	Thom' Atte More		is.
Ric'o atte Churcheye	is. iiid.			
Will'o Stronge	iis.			
Rog'o le Mulward	ixd.	Sm'a…xxviis. vid.		
Joh'e Atte Hulle	iis. iiid.			

VILLATA DE SWAMPTONE.

Joh'e Martin	is.	Rog'o Le Irisch	is. iiid.
Joh'e Irll	ixd.	Ric'o Holfol	ixd.
Joh'e Le Yonge	is. iiid.	Sm'a…vis. vid.	
Ric'o Paryfader	is. vid.		

VILLATA DE STOKE.

Walt'o Grey	is. vid.	Nich'o Gibbe	is.
Joh'e Le Kyng	is. ixd.	Isabella Nicholl	ixd.
Joh'e Atte More	iis. ixd.	Rad'o Stricht	is.
Will'o Malgir	is. iiid.	Thom' Wytewaye	iis. viid.
Eva atte Water	is. iid.		
Will'o atte Water	vs. iiid.	Sm'a[1]…xxis. xd.	
Joh'e at Hale	iis. iiid.		

[1] There is an error at the casting; it should be xxis. iiid.

VILLATA DE BYNLYGH.

Laur' de Bynlygh	is. iiid.	Rob'to Totere	is. ixd.
Cecilia de Bynlygh	is. ivd.	Editha Toteres	is. ivd.
Ad' de Bynlygh	is.		
Joh'e Willieme	is. vid.		Sm'a...ixs. viiid.
Joh'e Patrick	is. vid.		

VILLATA DE WYKE.

Marg'ra Horn	is.	Matill' atte Nasch'	ixd.
Joh'e Hughet	is. vid.	Ric'o Rycheman	is. vid.
Joh'e Seyvere	ixd.	Will'o Le Mere	ixd.
Rog'o atte Ok	is. ixd.	Welt'o Wyrel	viid.
Thom' Stronge	is.	Nich'o Pony	is. ixd.
Rob'to Sparewe	iis. iiid.	Joh'e atte Knolle	is.
Will'o atte Ok	ixd.		
Cecilia atte Mere	ixd.		Sm'a...xviis. ivd.
Welt'o Selwyne	is. iiid.		

VILLATA DE EGGEBURY.

Rob'to Saundre	is. iiid.	Will'o Clyve	is. iiid.
Rich'o atte Barghe	iis.	Joh'a de Clyve	is. vid.
Joh'e le Cartere	is. vid.	Rob't Donlygh	iis. id.
Nich'o atte Crouche	is. iiid.	Will'o Rankyn	is. ivd.
Henr' Tacwelle	is.		
Will'o Thurstayn	is. ivd.		Sm'a...xvs. vid.
Nich'o Nyweman	is.		

1 Edward III.—Taxatio xxme Domino Reg. concessa in com. Hant. facta per Joh'em de Tycheborne et Joh'em de Roches anno regni Edwardi tertii primo.	1st of Edward III.—Taxation of the 20th, granted to our Lord the King in the county of Hants; made by John of Tycheborne and John of Roches, in the first year of the reign of Edward III.

From another source.—Taxation of Hants, 1334.

HUND' DE EVYNG'AR.

Bourne	xls. viiid.	Wyke	ls. iid.
Swampton	xiiis. iid.	Eggburi	xxxiiis.
Stoke	xlvis.	Bienlygh	xiis. xid.

No items are here given as to how these sums were made up. The totals being larger, however, show that there was a considerable increase since 1327.

Attention to some of the names comprehending the Subsidy lists, and to be met with in the *Pleas of the Crown*, will be the means of furnishing an insight into the origin of some family names still present in the district. Thus, we find the names Thomas le Pipere, Thomas de la Wall, William le Whyte, of Woodhaye, the ancestor doubtless of the Whites of that place, William de la Dene, most likely in reference to the Dean at Hurstbourne Tarrant, John le Careter, Christian at Pitt, Joh'e atte Moore, and Roger le Shepherde. Now, the *le* (*the*) becoming dropped, as in John *the* Carter, Thomas *the* Piper, and Roger *the* Shepherd, turned occupations into family names, as John Carter, Roger Shepherd, etc. In such cases as Joh'e atte Moore, Christian at Pitt, William de la Dene, etc., places of residence became surnames, the lapsing of the *att*, or the *of the*—meaning that these several persons lived at the moore, the pit, or were of the Dene—brought about such names as John Moore, Christian Pitt, and William Dean. In other well-known instances, the preposition *at* or *atte* becoming linked to the place of residence, as in *atte* Water and *atte* Well, furnished the family names Attwater and Attwell or Attewell.

The names in the early Subsidy Rolls denote that Norman-French became largely infused into this country at the Conquest. The presence of the conjunctive *de* is characteristic of the French aristocracy. The Normans adopted a corrupt Latin dialect, which continued to be the language of the Court, of the Law, and of what has been styled polite society for some centuries. During its prevalence the laws were written in Norman-French or Latin. Anglo-Saxon was used by the mass of the people; and it gained the ascendency among all ranks about the time of Henry III, and continues to be used at the present day.

Subsidy Roll, 1st Edward III, 1326 (No. 1⅓³), for Hurstbourne Priors.

HUNDR'M DE EVYNGAR (*Villata de Husseborne*).

Ric'o de Elstod .	. iij*s*. iij*d*.	Joh'e Umfray .	. xviij*d*.
Joh'e Cole .	. xxj*d*.	Joh'e le Soutere .	. ij*s*.
Will'o le Webbe .	. ij*s*. vj*d*.	Will'o Waddene .	. xv*d*.
Joh'e Keneth .	. xij*d*.	Ad. Atte Pole .	. iij*s*. iij*d*.
Joh'e Thurgond .	. xv*d*.	Rad'o le ffrye .	. xxiij*d*.
Walt'o le Hog .	. xij*d*.	Joh'e le Stur .	. xij *l*.
Will'o le Hurt .	. xviij*d*.	Joh'e Torald .	. xij*d*.
Ric'o le Waps .	. xij*d*.	Rog'o Langeford .	. ix*d*.
Nich'o Gaubed .	. ix*d*.	Joh'e Trestel .	. xxj*d*.
Joh'e Lyteman .	. xxi*d*.		
Rob'to le Yoke .	. ix*d*.	Sm'a...xxx*s*. vj*d*.	

There is a peculiarity in some of the Hurstbourne names, which leads to the opinion that they are nicknames. It was not unusual in Saxon[1] and Norman times to assign names to individuals from some

---

[1] J. M. Kemble, Esq., Secretary to the Historical Society, *On the Names, Surnames, and Nicknames of the Anglo-Saxons*.

singularity of form, feature, habit, or otherwise, as slang titles are still applied among the lower classes. History is not silent regarding lofty personages who bore peculiar epithets, such as "longshanks". Thus, *Walt'o le Hog* might be a nickname, perhaps from his employment as a feeder of swine; but *hog* might refer to him as *careful*. Again, *Joh'e le Stur*, probably John the Sturdy or Robust; *Will'o le Hurt*, William the Hurt, might have been one who had received some injury. *Ric'o le Waps*,[1] Richard the Wasp, appears to be a sobriquet applied to him on account of some individuality, perhaps he was spiteful. Of the names on the list Cole and Webb are still familiar in the district; and as the latter name is written *Will'o le Webbe*, William *the* Webbe, he might have been a weaver.

The assessments give rise to some observations on the value of property. As each person's sum was the value of the twentieth part of his goods, the first person on the list paying 3s. 3d., the value of his movable effects was £3 5s. This is high compared to the value of goods in the time of Edward III. In the Taxing Rolls of that period the household furniture of the cottagers was inventoried, the valuation being a few shillings. The whole contents of a house consisted of a few mean articles of furniture of home manufacture, a three-legged stool or two, or a settle, and a little rude earthenware crockery. The most valuable things were copper or brass pots, and common utensils of iron, all the metals being exceedingly expensive, and iron particularly so.

The Subsidy Rolls render further service as a register of the names of the earlier inhabitants of the parish; and they show when some families first became resident, or when they left the district, at all events when their names disappear from the list. From the amounts on which the taxes are levied some insight is obtained into the material prosperity of certain of the householders. It is evident from the assessments that the number of householders in several of the tithings has remained much the same for a lengthened period. In the Week and Eggbury tithings, for instance, the number of occupiers in the time of Henry VIII was much the same as at the present day. It is worthy of notice also how some of the family names still to be found in the parish have adhered to the same tithing for centuries. Horn is an example of this. We find this name, in the tithing of Week, as Marg'ra Horn (Margaret), in the reign of Edward III, as assessed at 1s. for household goods valued at £1. In the 37th of Henry VIII, the name is still at "Weke", the tax being 3s. 4d., on goods valued at £5. In the 35th of Elizabeth, Horne again appears at

---

[1] Anglo-Saxon, *waps, wesp*, a wapse or wasp.

"Weeke", in this instance bearing the old family name of M*r*gerett, a widow, she being assessed at 8s., on goods valued at £3. There is a Frizard Horne still in that tithing in the 1st of Charles I, who paid 4s., this time on lands valued at 20s., and not on goods. Thus, from 1326, 1st of Edward III, to 1625, 1st of Charles I, representing 300 years, the family of Horn is found associated with the Week tithing. It may be said that the Horns represent a family who have lived in the parish, and mostly in one tithing, under varying circumstances, during 600 years, the name being still in the list of residents.

Further, it will be observed that the assessments for purposes of taxation were made chiefly on goods and wages previous to the 1st of Charles I; after that time the taxation is largely on lands; and after the 15th of Charles II, almost wholly on lands. This is particularly observable in the tithings of Stoke and Eggbury, where all the assessments were levied on lands. In "Eggebery", in the 36th of Elizabeth, certain of the subsidies are specified as levied on copyhold lands. In the 1st of Charles I, Richard Hellier possessed lands in the "Weeke" tithing, and the place has been since known as "Hillier's Lot".

Lay Subsidies, Southampton, 174/234, 34th Hen. VIII, 1542. [No Indenture.]

HUNDRED OF EVINGAR.

STOKE.

Robert Noyse in goodes	xix*li*. ...	vj*s*. viij*d*.
Robert Fykas in goodes	xij*li*. ...	iiij*s*.
Summa	x*s*. iiij*d*.	

WEKE.

John Grove in goodes	x*li*. ...	iij*s*. iiij*d*.
Thomas Isorne in goodes	x*li*. ...	iij*s*. iiij*d*.
William Byllatt in goodes	xx*li*. ...	xiij*s*. iiij*d*.
Robert Kegyll in goodes	xx*li*. ...	xiij*s*. iiij*d*.
Summa	xxxiij*s*. iiij*d*.	

BYNLEY.

William Cynes in goodes	x*li*. ...	iij*s*. iiij*d*.
Summa	iij*s*. iiij*d*.	

KINGISHURSBORNE.

Richard Fawkener in goodes	c*li*. ...	iij*li*. vj*s*. viij*d*.
John Mylles in goodes	x*li*. ...	xxvj*s*. viij*d*.
Robert Mylles in goodes	x*li*. ...	iij*s*. iiij*d*.
William Mylles in goodes	xx*li*. ...	xiij*s*. iiij*d*.
William Sylvester in goodes	xx*li*. ...	xiij*s*. iiij*d*.
Thomas Wale in goodes	x*li*. ...	iij*s*. iiij*d*.
Summa	vi*li*. vj*s*. viij*d*.	

BORNE.

Thomas Poor in goodes	xl*li*. ...	xxvj*s*. viij*d*.
William Bray in goodes	xv*li*. ...	v*s*.
John Brekston thonger in goodes	xx*li*. ...	xiij*s*. iiij*d*.
John Becley in goodes	x*li*. ...	iij*s*. iiij*d*.
Wylliam Croke in goodes	xiij*li*. ...	iiij*s*.
Summa	lij*s*. iiij*d*.	

Lay Subsidies, Southampton, $\frac{173}{237}$, 34-35th Hen. VIII. [After "Stoke", "Weke", and "Bynley".]

EGBURY.

Xpof' Godwyn in goodes	x*li*. ...	iij*s*. iiij*d*.
Rob't Newell in goodes	x*li*. ...	iij*s*. iiij*d*.
Joh'n Goodwyn in goodes	xv*li*. ...	v*s*.
Rich. Kegill in goodes	x*li*. ...	iij*s*. iiij*d*.
Summa	xv*s*.	

[Nothing as to Dunley or Swampton.]

Lay Subsidies, Southampton, $\frac{174}{276}$, 37th Hen. VIII, 1545.

Indenture, 20th March, 1 Edw. VI, for levying a subsidy granted in the [last] Parliament of Henry VIII.

THE HUNDRED OF EVINGER.

HURSBORNE.

Richard Faukner in landes	xxx*li*. ...	iij*li*.
Wylliam Sylvester in goodes	xij*li*. ...	xij*s*.
Elyzabeth Mylles in goodes	x*li*. ...	x*s*.
William Mylles in goodes	x*li*. ...	x*s*.
John Chamberlayn in goodes	v*li*. ...	iij*s*. iiij*d*.
John Gannon (?) in goodes	vj*li*. ...	iiij*s*.
Nicholas Mylles in goodes	x*li*. ...	x*s*.
Sir Mychael Lyster in landes	clx*li*. ...	xvj*li*.
Summa	xxj*li*. ix*s*. iiij*d*.	

BORNE.

Thomas Poore in goodes	xl*li*. ...	liij*s*. iiij*d*.
John Poore in goodes	x*li*. ...	x*s*.
Austaice Braye in goodes	viij*li*. ...	v*s*. iiij*d*.
John Brekston J. in goodes	xviij*li*. ...	xviij*s*.
John Beckly in goodes	x*li*. ...	x*s*.
William Croke in goodes	x*li*. ...	x*s*.
Summa	v*li*. vj*s*. viij*d*.	

STOKE.

John Hayes in goodes	viij*li*. ...	iiij*s*. viij*d*.
Baldwyn Bright in goodes	v*li*. ...	ij*s*. iiij*d*.
Robert Noyse in goodes	x*li*. ...	x*s*.
Richard Wiggmore in goodes	vij*li*. ...	iiij*s*. viij*d*.
George Wiggmore in goodes	v*li*. ...	ij*s*. iiij*d*.
Thomas Ilderwill in goodes	vj*li*. ...	iiij*s*.
Robert Fykes in goodes	v*li*. ...	ij*s*. iiij*d*.
Summa	xxxiij*s*. iiij*d*.	

WEKE.

John Grove in goodes	x*li.* ...	x*s.*
Thomas Ilderwill in goodes	vij*li.* ...	iiij*s.* viij*d.*
Thomas Izorne in goodes	viij*li.* ...	v*s.* iiij*d.*
William Byllat in goodes	xx*li.* ...	xxvj*s.* viij*d.*
Robert Kegill in goodes	vij*li.* ...	iiij*s.* viij*d.*
William Horne in goodes	v*li.* ...	ij*s.* iiij*d.*
William Sawier in goodes	v*li.* ...	ij*s.* iiij*d.*
Summa	lviij*s.*	

BYNLEY.

Nicholas Purvyer in goodes	v*li.* ...	ij*s.* iiij*d.*
Richerd Harrys in goodes	v*li.* ...	ij*s.* iiij*d.*
Mychaell Wyggmore in goodes	v*li.* ...	ij*s.* iiij*d.*
William Gynes in goodes	v*li.* ...	ij*s.* iiij*d.*
Summa	xiij*s.* iiij*d.*	

Lay Subsidies, Southampton, 174/278, 37th Hen. VIII.
[Between Borne and Stoke]—

EGGBURY.

Will'm Goodwyn in landes	xxx*s.* ..	ij*s.*
[Xpo ?] Goodwyn in landes	xl*s.* ...	iiij*s.*
John Godwyn in goodes	x*li.* ...	x*s.*
Rich. Kegill' in goodes	viij*li.* ...	v*s.* iiij*d.*
Rob't Newell' anuyte	xl*s.* ...	iiij*s.*
Davye Stone in goodes	v*li.* ...	ij*s.* iiij*d.*
Sum'	xxix*s.* viij*d.*	

[After Weke and Bynley]—

SWAMPTON.

Thomas Gosling S. in goodes	v*li.* ...	ij*s.* iiij*d.*
Thomas Goslyng J. in goodes	v*li.* ...	ij*s.* iiij*d.*
Sum'	vj*s.* viij*d.*	

Lay Subsidies, Southampton, 173/291. "Temp. Hen. VIII." [There is nothing to show to what Subsidy this refers.]

THE HUNDRED OF EVYNGAR.

Rychard Androis and Antony Wynsore Squiers Commissioners assigned for taxing of the Subsedy in the seid Hundred.

HUSSEBORNE PRIORIS.

		Subsedy.
Thomas Myll in goodes	xl*s.* ...	xij*d.*
John Sylvester in goodes	xl*s.* ...	xij*d.*
John Prowt in goodes	xl*s.* ...	xij*d.*
Thomas Gylberd in goodes	xl*s.* ...	xij*d.*
Ric. Bokelond in goodes	xvj*li.* ...	viij*s.*
John Coper in wages	xx*s.* ...	iiij*d.*
William Newman in goodes	xx*s.* ...	iiij*d.*
John Horne in goodes	x marke ...	ij*s.* iiij*d.*
Thomas Cuttyng in goodes	xx*s.* ...	iiij*d.*
John Tapener in goodes	xx*s.* ...	iiij*d.*

William Bechyn in goodes	.	lxs. ...	xviijd.
William White in wages	.	xxs. ...	iiijd.
John Gramatt in goodes	.	lxs. ...	xviijd.
Thomas Delvys in goodes	.	xlvjs. viijd. ...	xiiijd.
Thomas Blanchard in goodes	.	xxs. ...	iiijd.
Water Savygge in wages	.	xxs. ...	iiijd.
John Cuttyng in goodes	.	lxs. ...	xviijd.
John Somersett in goodes	.	xxs. ...	iiijd.
Robert Webbe in goodes	.	iiijli. ...	ijs.
John Blanchard in goodes	.	xxs. ...	iiijd.
John Gylys in goodes	.	lxs. ...	xviijd.
Ingram Newell in goodes	.	xxs. ...	iiijd.
Crystofer Coper in goodes	.	lxli. ...	iijli.
William Ryms in wages	.	xxs. ...	iiijd.
Sum of the Subsedy .	iiijli. viijs. ijd.		

SEYNT MARY BORNE.   *Subsedy.*

John Long in goodes	.	iiijli. ...	ijs.
Thomas Power in goodes	.	iiijli. ...	ijs.
John Myller in wages	.	xls. ...	xijd.
William Jakys in goodes	.	vjli. ...	iijs.
William Hasell in goodes	.	xxs. ...	iiijd.
Richard Jakes in goodes	.	xxs. ...	iiijd.
William Bray in goodes	.	vjli. ...	iijs.
John Brytes in goodes	.	xls. ...	xijd.
Roberd Parrott in wages	.	xxs. ...	iiijd.
Richard Waterman in goodes	.	vjli. ...	iijs.
Roberd Waterman in goodes	.	xxs. ...	iiijd.
Ric. Wodcoke in goodes	.	xxs. ...	iiijd.
Jelyan Dawnsse in goodes	.	xvli. ...	vijs. vjd.
Rychard Harrold in goodes	.	xxs. ...	iiijd.
John Brekestone in goodes	.	iiijli. ...	ijs.
John Blake in goodes	.	vjli. ...	iijs.
William Blake in wages	.	xxs. ...	iiijd.
John Rose in goodes	.	xxs. ...	iiijd.
Mycaell Wygmore in goodes	.	xli. ...	vs.
John Blake in goodes	.	xls. ...	xijd.
William Parrocke in goodes	.	xls. ...	xijd.
John Bray in goodes	.	xxs. ...	iiijd.
William Becley in goodes	.	xvjli. ...	viijs.
Rogger Croke in goodes	.	vli. ...	ijs. vjd.
Sum of the Subsedy	. xlviijs.		

THE PARISSCHE OF BYNLEY.

John Downe in goodes	.	lxs. ...	xviijd.
Ryc. Phylpott in goodes	.	vli. ...	ijs. vjd.
Crystofer Phelpott in wages	.	xxs. ...	iiijd.
John Pent in wages	.	xxs. ...	iiijd.
John Dyer in goodes	.	xxs. ...	iiijd.
William Garrad in goodes	.	iiijli. ...	ijs.
Nicolas Lardener in goodes	.	vli. ...	ijs. vjd.
John Lardener in goodes	.	xls. ...	xijd.
George Issoryn in goodes	.	xli. ...	vs.
William White in wages	.	xxs. ...	iiijd.
William Skynner in goodes	.	lxs. ...	xviijd.
Sum of the Subsedy	. xvijs. iiijd.		

TETHYNG OF WYKE.

William Ildfeld in goodes	lxs. ...	xviij*d*.
Crystofer Elertton[1] in wages	xxs. ...	iiij*d*.
Ryc. Elerton[1] in wages	xxs. ...	iiij*d*.
William Lacy in wages	xxs. ...	iiij*d*.
William Horne in goodes	xls. ...	xij*d*.
Thomas Horne in wages	xxs. ...	iiij*d*.
Ryc. Brytes[2] in goodes	xviij*li*. ...	ixs.
Thomas Isschorne in goodes	viij*li*. ...	iiijs.
Jone Ilderuyld in goodes	viij*li*. ...	iiijs.
Thomas Iscchorne in goodes	viij*li*. ...	iiijs.
Thomas Thurman in wages	xxs. ...	iiij*d*.
Sum of the Subsedy	xxiijs.	

TETHYNG OF STOKE.

Roger Ilderwyld in goodes	vij*li*. ...	iijs. vj*d*.
John Wygmore in goodes	xx*li*. ...	xxs.
Thomas Broker in goodes	vij*li*. ...	iijs. vj*d*.
John Lyte in wages	xxs. ...	iiij*d*.
Thomas Bulpytt in goodes	v*li*. ...	ijs. vj*d*.
Roberd Fycas in goodes	v*li*. ...	ijs. vj*d*.
John Ilderuyld in wages	xxs. ...	iiij*d*.
Banden Wygmore in goodes	x*li*. ...	vs.
John Leche in goodes	v*li*. ...	ijs. vj*d*.
John Newell in goodes	v*li*. ...	ijs. vj*d*.
Rychard Leche in goodes	v*li*. ...	ijs. vj*d*.
John Bulpytt in goodes	xxs. ...	iiij*d*.
William Bennatt in wages	xxs. ...	iiij*d*.
Bauden Brytt in goodes	x*li*. ...	vs.
Jone Bryth in goodes	viij*li*. ..	iiijs.
Rychard Power in wages	xxs. ...	iiij*d*.
Margery Faukyner in goodes	xxs. ...	iiij*d*.
John Bulbecke in goodes	xxvij*li*. ...	xxvijs.
Thomas Goslyng in wages	xxs. ...	iiij*d*.
Thomas Ilderuyld in goodes	v*li*. ...	ijs. vj*d*.
Sum of the Subsedy	iiij*li*. vs. iiij*d*.	

The people whose names are here registered include the "free and customary tenants", who cultivated the common fields in the several tithings, and did suit and service at the Manor Court, of which some account has already been rendered, at the time the lands were held by the Crown. The rents were assessed at certain fixed sums. The tenants paid "*cert*" or head-money for the keeping of the Court; and "heriot-fines" were paid after the death of life-tenants. They also paid other fines, such as fines for the privilege of sub-letting lands, and in satisfaction for crimes or injuries committed. Officers for the services of the Court were elected at the meetings of the Court-leet; and the tenants paid their quit rents. The Court-leet of the manor of Hurstbourne Priors was held almost as a mere form, at New Barn,

---

[1] Or Eldertton? [2] Or Bryces, Brytes.

in Hurstbourne parish as late as during the lifetime of the third Earl of Portsmouth, who usually attended the meetings.

Lay Subsidies, Southampton, $\frac{174}{291}$, Hen. VIII. [After St. Mary Borne]—

THE P'ISSCHE OF EGBEREY.

		Subsedy.
Will'm Godwyn' in londes	iiij*li.* vjs. viijd.	iijs. iiijd.
John Godwyn' in goodes	xls.	xijd.
John Tyne in goodes	xxs.	iiijd.
John Haywod in goodes	iiij m'rke	xvjd.
Henr' Bechyn' in goodes	xls.	xijd.
Robert Newell' in goodes	lxs.	xviijd.
Will'm Grygge in goodes	xls.	xijd.
John Godwyn' in goodes	vj*li.*	iijs.
Will'm Brytt in goodes	xx m'rke	vjs. viijd.
Thom's Brodwey in goodes	iiij*li.*	ijs.
Will'm Penton in goodes	iiij m'rke	xvjd.
Thom's Taylour in goodes	lxs.	xviijd.
Bartelmewe Bryty in goodes	iij*li.* vjs. viijd.	xxd.
Sum of the Subsedy	xlviijs.	

[Here follows Bynley.]

THE P'ISSCHE OF SWAMTON.

Ryc' Fawken' in londes	xl m'rke	xxvjs. viijd.
Jeffery Wrynall in wages	xxs.	iiijd.
Thom's Mylsent in wages	xxs.	iiijd.
Jamys Browth[1] in wages	xxs.	iiijd.
Sybyll' Wat'ma' in goodes	xls.	xijd.
Eyde Wat'ma' in goodes	xxs.	iiijd.
Joh'n Morra't in goodes	lxs.	xviijd.
Thom's Brekestone in wages	xxs.	iiijd.
Joh'n Cuttyng' in goodes	xls.	xijd.
Rychard Nutkyng' in goodes	lxs.	xviijd.
Joh'n Nutkyng' in goodes	xls.	xijd.
John Lympis in goodes	xxs.	iiijd.
Will'm Cop' in goodes	v*li.*	ijs. vjd.
John Mylwardes in goodes	lxs.	xviijd.
Thom's Param in goodes	xls.	xijd.
John Leneley in goodes	vj*li.*	iijs.
Thom's Goslyng in goodes	lxs.	xviijd.
John Knowle in goodes	lxs.	xviijd.
Sum of the Subsedy	xlvs. viijd.	

[Nothing as to Dunley.]

Lay Subsidies, Southampton, $\frac{174}{299}$, 2-3 Edw. VI, 1547-8.

Indenture, 18th April, 3rd Edw. VI, between the Commissioners for levying a Relief granted in the last Parliament, and the petty collectors thereof: the first payment thereof to be levied on the persons named in the Schedules annexed, etc.

---

[1] Or Browt's, *i.e.*, Browtes.

THE HUNDRED OF EVINGER.

THE TYTHYNG OF BOURNE.

Thomas Powre in goodes	. . .	xl*li*. ...	xl*s*.
John Brekstone in goodes	. .	xviij*li*. ...	xviij*s*.
John Beckeley in goodes	. .	x*li*. ...	x*s*.
Will'm Croke in goodes	. .	x*li*. ...	x*s*.
Summa	.	iij*li*. xviij*s*.	

THE TYTHING OF BYNLEY.

Nicholas Purvyer in goodes	. .	x*li*. ...	x*s*.
William Gynis in goodes	. .	x*li*. ...	x*s*.
Summa	.	xx*s*.	

THE TYTHING OF STOKE.

Robert Noyis in goodes	. .	xv*li*. ...	xv*s*.
Rychard Wygmore in goodes	. .	x*li*. ...	x*s*.
Thomas Elderwell in goodes	. .	x*li*. ...	x*s*.
William Bulpytt in goodes	. .	x*li*. ...	x*s*.
Summa	.	xlv*s*.	

THE TYTHING OF WEKE.

John Grove in goodes	. .	x*li*. ...	x*s*.
Thomas Elderwell in goodes	. .	x*li*. ...	x*s*.
Will'm Byllet in goodes	. .	xx*li*. ...	xx*s*.
Summa	.	xl*s*.	

[Then follow the Tithings of Charellcott, Freffoke, and Witchurche.]

THE TYTHING OF HURSBORNE PRYORES.

Rychard Fawkener in goodes	. .	lx*li*. ...	iij*li*.
William Sylvester in goodes	. .	xij*li*. ...	xij*s*.
William Myllys in goodes	. .	xij*li*. ...	xij*s*.
John Chamberleyn in goodes	. .	x*li*. ...	x*s*.
Summa .	.	iiij*li*. xiiij*s*.	

[Then follow six other Tithings.]

Summa Totalis istius Hundredi . xlij*li*. xviij*s*.

Lay Subsidies, Southampton, $\frac{174}{337}$, 2-3rd Edw. VI.

Indenture, 7th April, 5th Edw. VI, for levying the *third* payment of the Relief (granted in 2-3rd Edw. VI).

THE HUNDRETH OF EVENGAR.

THE TEYTHYNG OF STOKE.

John Hays in goodes	. . .	xj*li*. ...	xj*s*.
Richard Wigmore in goodes	. .	x*li*. ...	x*s*.
Thomas Iderwyll in goodes	. .	x*li*. ...	x*s*.
Summa	.	xxx*s*.	

THE TEYTHYNG OF WYKE.

Thomas Ilderwill in goodes	. .	x*li*. ...	x*s*.
William Byllet in goods	. .	xx*li*. ...	xxx*s*.
Summa	.	xxx*s*.	

THE TEYTHYNGE OF BYNLEY.

William Gynes in goodes	. .	x*li.* ...	x*s.*
Nycholas Purvyer in goodes	. .	x*li.* ...	x*s.*
Summa	. . xx*s.*		

* * * * * * *

THE TEYTHYNG OF BORNE.

John Brekston in goodes	. .	xviij*li.* ...	xviij*s.*
William Croke in goodes	. .	x*li.* ...	x*s.*
Thomas Powre in goodes	. .	xl*li.* ...	xl*s.*
Summa	. iij*li.* viij*s.*		

THE TEYTHYNG OF HUSBORNE.

Sir Michaell Lister in goodes	. .	lxvj*li.* ...	iij*li.* vj*s.*
Richard Fawkener in goodes	. .	lx*li.* ...	iij*li.*
Robert Edmondes in goodes	. .	xxv*li.* ...	xxv*s.*
William Mylles in goodes	. .	xij*li.* ...	xij*s.*
William Sylvester in goodes	. .	xij*li.* ...	xij*s.*

Lay Subsidies, Southampton, $\frac{174}{337}$, 2-3rd Edw. VI. [After Bynley.]

THE TEYTHING OF EGBERY.

Richard Kedgyll' in goodes	. .	x*li.* ...	x*s.*

[Nothing as to Dunley or Swampton.]

[In $\frac{174}{299}$, of this date, there is nothing as to Eggbury, Dunley, or Swampton.]

Lay Subsidies, Southampton, $\frac{174}{416}$, "35th Elizabeth", 1592.

Indenture, 1st Oct., 36th Eliz., between the Commissioners for levying the second Subsidy granted to the Queen in 36th[1] Eliz., and the high Collector appointed by them. Schedules annexed.

HUNDRED OF EVENGARR.

HURSBORNE PRIORS.

* * * * * *

Robert Oxenbrige, Esq., in landes	.	xxvj*li.* ...	v*li.* iiij*s.*
Swythian White in goodes	.	iiij*li.* ...	x*s.* viij*d.*
John Billett in goodes	.	iiij*li.* ...	x*s.* viij*d.*
Thomas Fisher in goodes	.	iij*li.* ...	viij*s.*
John Milles in goodes	.	iij*li.* ...	viij*s.*
George Penton (?) in goodes	.	iiij*li.* ...	x*s.* viij*d.*
Randolphe Kember in goodes	.	vj*li.* ...	xvj*s.*
Richard Broker in goodes	.	iij*li.* ...	viij*s.*
Richard Dowe, alien, in coppiehold landes	.	xx*s.* ...	viij*s.*
Will'm Rogers in goodes	.	iij*li.* ...	viij*s.*
Robt. Mathew in goodes	.	iij*li.* ...	viij*s.*
Richard Blaunchard in goodes	.	iij*li.* ...	viij*s.*
Sum'	. x*li.* viij*s.* ex.		

---

[1] Defaced; looks like 36, but qu. 35.

Borne.

Jefferie Poore in goodes	vij*li*. ...	xviij*s*. viij*d*.
Benett Berkley, widd', in goodes	iij*li*. ...	viij*s*.
Will'm Jaques in goodes	iij*li*. ...	viij*s*.
Julian Breyton, widd', in goodes	iij*li*. ...	viij*s*.
Thomas Poore in goodes	iij*li*. ...	viij*s*.
M'geret Braie, widd', in landes by coppie	xx*s*. ...	iiij*s*.
John Damm'ell in goodes	iij*li*. ...	viij*s*.
Sum' . iij*li*. ij*s*. viij*d*. ex.		

Swampton.

* * * * * *

John Ayleyffe in goodes	iij*li*. ...	viij*s*.
Richard Goslinge in goodes	iij*li*. ...	viij*s*.
Will'm Coop' in landes	xx*s*. ...	iiij*s*.
Sum' . xx*s*. ex.		

Weeke.

Mrs. Barbarra Oxenbridge in landes	xij*li*. ...	xlviij*s*.
Thomas Cannon in goodes	v*li*. ...	xvj*s*.
Richard Hais in goodes	xij*li*. ...	xxxij*s*.
M'gerett Horne, widd', in goodes	iij*li*. ...	viij*s*.
Will'm Kigell in goodes	iij*li*. ...	viij*s*.
Sum' . v*li*. xij*s*. ex.		

Stooke.

John Rumbolde in goodes	iiij*li*. ...	x*s*. viij*d*.
Will'm Hais in goodes	xiij*li*. ...	xxxiiij*s*. viij*d*.
George Bachellor in landes	xx*s*. ...	iiij*s*.
Will'm Woodeeward in goodes	iij*li*. ...	viij*s*.
Anstis Ilderwill in goodes	iij*li*. ...	viij*s*.
Jefferie Ilderwill in goodes	v*li*. ...	xiij*s*. iiij*d*.
George Rumbolde in goodes	iiij*li*. ...	x*s*. viij*d*.
Will'm Philpotte in goodes	iij*li*. ...	viij*s*.
Henrie Braie in goodes	iij*li*. ...	viij*s*.
Thomas Knight in goodes	iij*li*. ...	viij*s*.
Sum' . v*li*. xiij*s*. iiij*d*. ex.		

Bynley.

John Penton in goodes	iiij*li*. ...	x*s*. viij*d*.
Xp'ofer Kigell in goodes	iiij*li*. ...	x*s*. viij*d*.
Jeames Isron in goodes	iij*li*. ...	viij*s*.
Thomas Philpott, sen., in goodes	iiij*li*. ...	x*s*. viij*d*.
Thomas Philpott, Ju., in goodes	iiij*li*. ...	x*s*. viij*d*.
Sum' . [Defaced.]		

Eggebery.

John Goddwyn	iij*li*. ..	viij*s*.
Richard Barnard in goodes	vij*li*. ...	xviij*s*. viij*d*.
Will'm Newell in goodes	iiij*li*. ...	x*s*. viij*d*.
Agnes Brodwey, widd', in coppiehold lands	xx*s*. ...	iiij*s*.
Thomas Kigell in coppiehold landes	xx*s*. ...	iiij*s*.
Will'm Bright in goodes	iiij*li*. ...	x*s*. viij*d*.
Henry (?) Godwyn in coppiehold lands	xx*s*. ...	iiij*s*.
Sum'		

Lay Subsidies, Southampton, 173/487, 7th James I.

Indenture, 1st April, 9th James I, etc. Second payment of the Subsidy granted 7th Jas. I.

KINGSCLERE DIVISION.—EVENGER HUNDRED.

* * * * * * *

HURSBORNE PRIORS.

Sir Robert Oxenbregge, Kt., lands	25*l.* …	33*s.* 4*d.*
Swithin White, goods	3*l.* …	3*s.*
Hughe Newell, goods	3*l.* …	3*s.*
Thomas Fisher, goods	3*l.* …	3*s.*
Joane Penton, by copy	20*s.* …	1*s.* 4*d.*
John Kember, by copy	20*s.* …	1*s.* 4*d.*
Robert Frowde, goods	3*l.* …	3*s.*
Summa	48*s.*	

SWAMPTON.

Robert Haies, lands	20*s.* …	1*s.* 4*d.*
John Ayleiffe, lands	20*s.* …	1*s.* 4*d.*
Summa	2*s.* 8*d.*	

BOORNE.

Widow Poore, goods	4*l.* …	4*s.*
John Damrill, goods	3*l.* …	3*s.*
Jeffery Ilderwell, goods	3*s.* …	3*s.*
Bennett Beckley, goods	3*l.* …	3*s.*
Mr. Henry Hall, lands	20*s.* …	1*s.* 4*d.*
Ralphe Romsey, goods	3*l.* …	3*s.*
Richard Purchill (?), goods	3*l.* …	3*s.*
Summa	20*s.* 4*d.*	

WEEKE.

Paule Alexander, gent. (certif.), goods	6*l.* …	6*s.*
Thomas Cannon, Senior, goods	3*l.* …	3*s.*
Richard Haise (certif.), goods	10*l.* …	10*s.*
Thomas Cannon, Junior, goods	3*l.* …	3*s.*
Thomas Kydgell, goods	3*l.* …	3*s.*
William Rumbold, lands	20*s.* …	1*s.* 4*d.*
Summa	26*s.* 4*d.*	

BYNLEY.

John Penton (?), goods	3*l.* …	3*s.*
George Godwyn, goods	3*l.* …	3*s.*
Christopher Kydgell, goods	3*l.* …	3*s.*
Janes … .[1] lands	20*s.* …	1*s.* 4*d.*
… .[1] Kydgell, lands	20*s.* …	1*s.* 4*d.*
… … .[1] goods	3*s.* …	3*s.*
Richard Browne, by copy	20*s.* …	1*s.* 4*d.*
Summa	16*s.*	

---

[1] Defaced.

EGBURY.

John Broadwaye, goods	3*l.* ...	3*s.*
Agnes Wright, by copy	20*s.* ...	1*s.* 4*d.*
Richard Barnard, goods	5*l.* ...	5*s.*
William (?) Newell, by copy	20*s.* ...	1*s.* 4*d.*
Summa		10*s.* 8*d.*

Lay Subsidies, Southampton, $\frac{175}{511}$, 1st Chas. I. Division of Kingsclere. Taxation and assessment, etc., taken at Overton, 19th Sept. 1625.

EVINGER HUNDRED.

HUSBORNE PRIORS.

Sir Robert Oxenbregge, Kt., in lands	25*l.* ...	5*l.*
Mawdlin White, widow, in goods	3*l.* ...	8*s.*
William Drake in lands	20*s.* ...	4*s.*
John Orchard in lands	20*s.* ...	4*s.*
William Penton in lands	20*s.* ...	4*s.*
John Greene in goods	4*l.* ...	10*s.* 8*d.*
Thomas Fisher in goods	4*l.* ...	10*s.* 8*d.*
		7*l.* 1*s.* 4*d.*

ST. MARYBORNE.

John Damrill in goods	3*l.* ...	8*s.*
John Nicholas in lands	20*s.* ...	4*s.*
Robert Carter in lands	20*s.* ...	4*s.*
William Beeklie in goods	3*l.* ...	8*s.*
Thomas Beckley in lands	20*s.* ...	4*s.*
Robert Power, gen., in goods	5*li.* ...	13*s.* 4*d.*
Robert Billet in goods	4*l.* ...	10*s.* 8*d.*
		2*l.* 12*s.* 0*d.*

STOAKE.

Robert Hayes, the elder, in lands	40*s.* ...	8*s.*
Edward Rombold in lands	20*s.* ...	4*s.*
Thomas Knight in goods	3*l.* ...	8*s.*
John Bachelor in lands	40*s.* ...	8*s.*
William Philpott in lands	20*s.* ...	4*s.*
William Leach in lands	20*s.* ...	4*s.*
Ann Hayes, widow, in goods	3*l.* ...	8*s.*
George Bray in lands	20*s.* ...	4*s.*
Henry Bray in goods	3*l.* ...	8*s.*
Jeffery Ilderwell in goods	3*l.* ...	8*s.*
		3*l.* 4*s.* 0*d.*

EGBURY.

Mawdlin Newell, widow, in lands	20s.	4s.
William Bright in goods	3l.	8s.
William Oxenbregge, gen., in goods	5l.	13s. 4d.
John Broadway in goods	3l.	8s.
John Godwyne in lands	20s.	4s.
		1l. 17s. 4d.

WEEKE.

William Bunney in goods	3l.	8s.
Thomas Kidgell in lands	20s.	4s.
Frizard Horne in lands	20s.	4s.
Robert Hayes, the younger, in lands	20s.	4s.
William Godwyne in lands	20s.	4s.
Thomas Cannon in goods	5l.	13s. 4d.
Richard Helliar in lands	20s.	4s.
William Longman in lands	20s.	4s.
		2l. 5s. 4d.

BINLYE.

Agnes Iserne, widow, in lands	20s.	4s.
Henry Kidgell in lands	20s.	4s.
Alice Godwine in lands	20s.	4s.
William Smythe in goods	4l.	10s. 8d.
William Poore in goods	3l.	8s.
		1l. 10s. 8d.

SWAMPTON.

Thomas Adnams in lands	20s.	4s.
Thomas Boxold in lands	20s.	4s.
Thomas Morrant in goods	3l.	8s.
		16s. 0d.

Lay Subsidies, Southampton, $\frac{176}{561}$, 15 Chas. II. Assessment to the two last of four Subsidies granted 15 Chas. II.

THE SOUTH SIDE OF EVINGAR HUNDRED.
WEEKE.

Sir Richard Lucy, Knt. (cert.), land	40s.	16s.
Mr. John Marks (cert.), land	50s.	20s.
Widdow Kidgell, per ann.	20s.	8s.
Widdow Cannon, per ann.	20s.	8s.
Clement Dorrell, per ann.	20s.	8s.
William Peirce (cert.), land	20s.	8s.
The Lady Smyth, for Weeke farme, land	3l.	24s.
Summe		4l. 12s.

* * * * * *

STOAKE.

John Batchelor, land	40s.	16s.
Thomas Knight, land	20s.	8s.
Edmond Ratue, land	20s.	8s.
Henry Bray, land	40s.	16s.
John Holdway, land	23s.	8s.
Summe		2l. 16s.

BOURNE.

Mr. Robert Poore, goods	3l.	16s.
Robert Carter, land	20s.	8s.
Richard Berkley, goods	3l.	16s.
George Parsons, goods	3l.	16s.
Mr. Peter Blake (cert.), land	40s.	16s.
Mrs. Blake, widdow (cert.), land	20s.	8s.
Mrs. Thurman, widdow (cert.), land	20s.	8s.
Summe		4l. 8s.

HUSBORNE PRYOURS.

Joane Isack, widdow, land	30s.	12s.
Joane Fisher, widdow, land	20s.	8s.
Richard Sutton, land	20s.	8s.
Walter Knight, goods	3l.	16s.
William Drake, land	20s.	8s.
Summe		2l. 12s.

SWAMPTON.

Thomas Cannon, goods	4l.	21s. 4d.
James Gosling, annuity	20s.	8s.
Edward Druly, goods	3l.	16s.
Robert Hedges, land	20s.	8s.
Summe		2l. 13s. 4d.

EGBERY.

John Deane, Esqr., Com^r., land	8l.	3l. 4s.
Robert Oxenbregg, Esqr., Com^r., land	8l.	3l. 4s.
John Goddaine, Junio^r, land	20s.	8s.
William Phillis, land	20s.	8s.
Robert Sutton, land	40s.	16s.
Nicholas Broadway, land	20s.	8s.
Summe		8l. 8s.

BINLEY.

James Issarne, goods	3l.	16s.
Henry Gynes, land	20s.	8s.
Widdow Poore, land	20s.	8s.
Robert Longman, goods	3l.	16s.
Mr. Richard Wither, goods	5l.	26s. 8d.
John Philpott of Highcleer, land	20s.	8s.
Summe		4l. 2s. 8d.

Forest of Chute and Finkley.

IN the papers relating to the forests of Finkley, and Digerley or Doiley, the names of Croc, and Columbars or Columbariis appear. The former is supposed to have originated the name of Cruxeaston. Concerning Mathew Croc, in 1155 he was warden of the forests of Andover, Wittingley, and Dingley. The forest of Andover was named "Brills";[1] and tithes of these forests were paid to the Canons of Salisbury. In 1165, the King (Henry II) gave to Salisbury Minster, by charter, among others, all the tithes of Andover. In 1213, June 7th, the King (John) sent Robert de Kerely to the Sheriff of Hants, at Andover, with two servants and their two horses, two boar hounds, three veltrariis (*dog-keepers*), twenty-eight hounds *de mota*, and sixteen greyhounds. He sent, with Robert, William Croc and Peter de Cemel, and for these men, their horses, and their dogs, the Sheriff was to supply whatever they needed. In 1217, King John re-granted the manor of Andover to William Longsword, Earl of Salisbury, who held the manor till his death. By a writ of May 20th, 1226, the Sheriff of Hants is commanded to give Matthew de Columbariis the Brills, the hunting woods of Andover, which the Sheriff had taken into the King's hands on the Earl's death.[2]

A portion of the woodlands of the forest of Chute and Finkley is situated in the parish of St. Mary Bourne, notably Wallop Hill and Frenches Copse, a part or the whole of which was grubbed not long since, the land now forming a portion of Frenches farm. And the woods of Dowles and Doiley, formerly part of the forest, lie on the north and north-west boundary, some portions extending along the separation-line of the parishes of Andover and St. Mary Bourne. Finkley

---

[1] See *Rolls of the Pipe*, 2nd of Henry II.
[2] Woodward and Wilks, *Hist. of Hampshire*, vol. iii, Art. "Andover".

was at one time known as Finkley Park, and was enclosed with a paling, portions of stout oak fence having been dug up, in 1868, on the estate of the late Mr. Thomas Longman of Finkley. Finkley was formerly the eastern walk of Chute Forest, the boundary line of which extended westward to Clanville. It appears that from Wakeswood and Finkley twenty-six loads of wood were yearly given (1589-90) to Nicholas Venables, gent., as farmer of Andover parsonage, besides forty loads claimed by Winchester College from the Finkley underwoods, then in lease. There is a notice that Charles II granted Finkley to General Monk.[1]

In early times the forest of Chute, and Hippingscombe, were held under the Crown by the family of the Columbars, whose names often occur as territorial lords in that part of North Wiltshire. And there was one part of Chute that belonged to Hyde Abbey, at Winchester. The forest ran into the counties of Wilts and Hampshire, the Hampshire portion extending to Hurstbourne Tarrant, and including the woods of Doiley and Dowles. In this portion of the forest there were one thousand acres, and twenty coppices. Chute, Wilts, fell into the hands of the Protector Somerset, who contrived to obtain possession of most of the country between Chute and Marlborough.[2]

Chute appears to be derived from the Anglo-Saxon, *Cete*, a building or cottage. In the northernmost part of the forest lies Conholt, which was formerly called Chute Park. It was made into a park by Sir Philip Medows, in the time of Charles II. He had been secretary to Oliver Cromwell, and Ambassador to Portugal; and had two male descendants, Sir Sidney Medows, who built the present house in 1762, and a Philip Medows. Philip allied himself to a Pierrepont, heiress to the Duke of Kingston, of Kingston House, at Bradford-on-Avon. Their son, Charles Medows, assumed the name of Pierrepont, and from him descended the lady who now occupies Conholt, the Lady Charles Wellesley.[3]

There was at Chute in Charles the Second's time a celebrated character, who bore nevertheless an evil reputation. His name was Sir William Scroggs, and he rose to be Lord Chief Justice of England. He was of low origin, whose birthplace was the metropolis; and being intended for the Church, was sent to Pembroke College, Oxford, in 1643. Having previously, however, been a soldier, and borne arms for Charles I as a Captain at Colchester, in 1640, he was disqualified for holy orders, and thus entered for the law, and rose to the dignified office already mentioned.[4] Along with two other judges, he was

---

[1] Woodward and Wilks, *Hist. of Hampshire*, vol. iii, p. 192.
[2] *Notes on the Border of Wilts and Hants*, by the Rev. Canon J. E. Jackson, *Wilts Magazine*, vol. xxi. [3] *Ibid.*, p. 336. [4] *Ibid.*, p. 336.

THE DIFFERENCE BETWEEN A FOREST AND A CHASE.

A forest differs from a chase in three things, viz., in particular laws, in certain officers, and in special courts, which are incident to forests, for the execution of these laws. And there are no particular laws proper to a chase alone; for all offenders in a chase are punishable by the Common Law, and not by the Forest Law, or by any other law proper only and peculiar to a chase. Neither are the officers in a chase the same as those in a forest, there being in a chase neither Verderers, Foresters, Regarders, nor Agistors, but only Keepers and Woodwards. There are no Courts of Attachments, Swainmote, or Justice-seat, in a chase; all of which are held and observed in forests; and those officers which are called Keepers in a chase are called Foresters in a forest.

The forest of Chute, Finkley, and Doiley was a forest, and not a chase, if we may judge from the officials, as mention is made, in the following papers relating to the forest, of a Chief Warden, a Justice of the Forest, and of Foresters and Verderers.[1] In 1611, the house known as Dowles Lodge was the residence of the Queen's Yeoman of the Bows, and Keeper of the forest of Dowles.

Further, parks and chases might be held by any subject, whilst a forest, truly and strictly taken, could not be in the hands of any but the King. That the forest of Chute and Finkley belonged to the King, we have a *Bill in the Exchequer*, of 1647, wherein it is stated that "*Our Sovⁿ Lord the King stands seized of the forest of Finkley*, etc." It was not, however, a forest in the same degree as was the New Forest.

A chase is in one degree the same thing as a park, only a park is enclosed, and a chase is always open.

The next in degree to a free chase is a park, and next to a park

---

[1] The *Verderer* had charge of the forest, and to his duties *Swainmote* was attached, which was a jury of freeholders, called by the Steward, in a court concerning forest matters before the Verderers. The *Court of Attachment* was a lower court, as the Swainmote had to receive the attachments against any who trespassed against the forest laws, and to enter and present the cases at the next *Justice Seat;* this last being the highest Court. The *Regarder* viewed the forest, and took cognizance of offences. The *Agistor* had care of the cattle taken in to graze, and to collect the payments for the same. The *Forester* was a keeper of the forest (Manwood. *Forest Laws*, cap. 21, Nos. 1, 2, 3, 4). The last Court of Justice Seat was held in the reign of Charles II.

is the franchise of a free warren; and therefore, because a forest is the highest and greatest franchise, being also a general and compound word, it comprehends both a chase, a park, and a warren. And for that reason the beasts of chase, and the beasts and fowls of warren, are privileged in a forest, as well as the beasts of forest; and therefore if any such beasts or fowls of chase, park, or warren, are hunted or killed in a forest, it is a trespass of the forest, and to be punished by the laws thereof, and by no other law whatsoever.[1]

SEVERE FOREST LAWS IN NORMAN TIMES.

A forest in former days did not mean merely large tracts of woodland; but a district often comprehending within its limits farms and open fields, and woods and coppices belonging to private gentlemen. It was a tract of country of so many miles in length and breadth subject to the old severe forest laws, in which the forest laws were enforced, and heavy penalties levied on any persons found killing wild animals, and especially deer, which were Royal game. In some cases the penalties were inflicted with cruel severity on the person. Thus, according to Brompton, William the Conqueror put out the eyes of a man who took either a buck or a boar. Rufus, as stated by Knighton, would hang a person for taking a doe, and for a hare he made him pay twenty shillings. Rufus further caused fifty rich men to be apprehended, and accused them of killing the bucks, which they denying, they were to clear themselves by the ordeal of fire. Henry I made no distinction between him who killed a man or a buck, and punished those who destroyed the game either by forfeiture of goods or loss of limbs. Henry II made it only imprisonment for a time. His son, Richard I, revived the old laws for punishing those who were convicted of hunting in the forest—that they should be gelt, and have their eyes taken out. He afterwards, however, appointed that such convicts should abjure the realm, or pay a fine. Edward I appointed the same punishment, but that they should be free both of life and limb.[2]

Forest Proceedings. Matthew de Columbars, in 1200, was Governor of Winchester Castle.

In 1237 he married Maud, daughter of Endo de Morwille of the Co. of Southampton. He obtained a Charter exempting himself and his heirs and all his tenants of his Manor of Chisbury (in Savernake),

---

[1] Manwood's *Forest Laws*, edit. 1717.
[2] Cowel's *Interpreter.*

also of his Manor of Luderly with its Members, Lockerly, Holebury, and Bockholt, that they should not be liable to the expeditating[1] of their dogs. He died in 1272, seized of Thunderly [query Titherly], and one Knight's fee in Enham and Crockeston [query Cruxeaston], leaving Michael, his brother, his heir, 60 years of age, of which Michael gave 200 marks for license to marry the Daughter of Elias Croc (A.D. 1207), and to have the office of forester in fee, after the death of Elias, but he died in 1234, whereupon Avice, his Widow, Daughter and heir to Elias Croc, had livery of the Baliwick of the Forest of Chute: this Avice died in 1258, as appears by the following Inquisition (43 Hen. III), made by the Oaths of Philip Kroc, Roger the Poyer, Roger Nowell, Henry of Foxcote, Thomas of Hort, John the Bel, Thomas of Anne, John of Cormail, Roger Quarel, William Wikes, William Fitz Robert, and Simon Lifith, as to how much land and what Bailiwick Avice of Columbars, who lately closed her last day, held of the Lord the King in chief, and by what service and how much land of others, and by what service, and how much that land, and that Bailiwick are worth by the year in all issues, and who is her next heir, and of what age. Who say upon their Oaths, that the said Avice of Columbars held of the Lord the King in chief, in the Co. of Southampton, one Virgate of Land at the Woodhouse near to Andover, which same Virgate of Land doth pertain to the Forestry of Fynkeley. They also say, that the said Avice held of the Lord the King, in the Co. aforesaid, the Bailiwick of Finkley and Digerley in Forestership by the service of Ten shillings, to be yielded at the Exchequer of the Lord the King, at Westminster, for the aforesaid Virgate of Land of the Woodhouse, and for the aforesaid Bailiwicks of Finkele and Digerly, together with the Bailiwick of Chet, which is in the County of Wilts: And the aforesaid Virgate of Land of the Woodhouse is worth, together with the aforesaid Bailiwick of Finkele and Digele by the year in all issues 100 shillings. They also say that the said Avice held of the Lord the King in chief, in the Co. aforesaid, one Knight's fee by the service of one Knight for 40 days when the Lord the King and other high personages shall be present in the Army, and is worth by the year in all issues 15 pounds. They also say that the said Avice held nothing else of others in the Co. aforesaid. And they say that Matthew of Columbars is the next heir of the said Avice, and that the said Matthew is of the age of 40 years and upwards. In Witness whereof to this Inquisition have set their Seals.

[1] Expeditating means the cutting out of the balls of dogs' forefeet, so that they should not be able to hunt the king's game; and anyone not specially exempt was liable to a fine of 3s. 4d. for not complying with the order.

Forest Notices in the Rolls of the Crown.

Liberate Roll, 17 Hen. III, 1232, m. 6. Of the King's Hall at Winchester.

It is commanded to the Sheriff of Southampton that, according to what Master Elias de Derham will make known to him, he shall cause to be felled in the woods of Digerle, Finkele, and Chette, timber for the work of the hall of the Castle of Winchester, and cause it to be carried to Winchester for the same work, and the cost shall be allowed him in his account. Witness, the King, at Wudestok', on the 20th day of June.

Close Roll, 19 Hen. III, 1234, p. 1, m. 20.

It is commanded to Michael de Columbar(iis) that in the grove of Digerle he shall cause the Sheriff of Southampton to have timber for making a certain new Kitchen within the Castle of Winchester, and a certain butlery and dispensary there, and for a certain drawbridge, and for the joists and boards of two turrets, and for making a certain chamber over the gate of the same Castle ; so that a tally of the timber which he shall cause him to have for this purpose, shall be made between the same Michael and the aforesaid Sheriff. Witness, the King, at Winchester, on the 8th of January.

Close Roll, 20 Hen. III, 1235.

It is commanded to Avicia de Columbariis that she shall cause the Constable of the Castle of Winchester to have, in the King's Forest of Finkele and Derhele, 16 couples [Beams, apparently] for making the King's dispensary in the aforesaid Castle, and as many couples for the King's saucery there. Witness, etc., Wudestok', 9 Nov.

NOTE.—The dispensary would be the Steward's office, and the saucery would be the place where the sauces and spices were kept.

Placita Forestæ, Southampton, 53 Hen. III, 1268.

Pleas of the Forest at Winchester on the morrow of St. Michael in 53 Hen. III, before Roger de Clifford and others, Justices.

(*Roll* 3.) Bounds of the Forest.

(*Roll* 14*d*.[1]) Alexander Prior of St. Swithin's claims to have chaces in all his demesne lands and woods, etc. This claim is rather long: no places are mentioned by name.

(*Roll* 16.) Bartholomew de Insula, son and heir of John de Insula, Forester of the Fee of the Forest of Chuyt, in cos. Wilts and Southampton, claims, etc. [claims set out]. One of his six "foot-foresters" keeps (or guards) Doules and Husseburnewode.

(*Roll* 22*d*.) Copy of the Charter of 29th year of King Edward (I), 1300, to St. Swithin's, of free warren in Husseburn and other places.

---

[1] Roll 14*d*, and Roll 22*d*, appertain to Hurstbourne Priors. In the Tower Records there are deeds relating to grants of land in the forests, forest proceedings, patents of office, perambulations, etc., in the reigns of John, Henry III, Edward I, Edward II, Edward III, Henry VIII, Edward VI, Elizabeth, James I, Charles I, and Charles II. (5*th Rep. Deputy Keeper of Records*, App. 2, pp. 46, 59.)

Perambulations of the Forest, etc.

FYNKELY.

16th Edward II, A.D. 1323.

A perambulation made in the Bailwick of the forest of *Fynkely*, in the county of Southampton, in the presence of John of Berewyk and his fellows, for this assigned by the writ of the Lord the King, as appears in the Roll of the perambulation of the forest of Wolvemere and Alsiesholt, and in the presence of John of Romesey, Lieutenant (or deputy) of the Justice of the Forest, and in the presence of John de Lisle, Forester of the Fee, of Roger of Lecford and Thomas Spircock, Verderors,—that is to say at *Dururdeshord*, and so always by the borders of the wood as far as the way that comes from *Crockerestokes*, towards *Andevere*, and from thence up to the corner of the hay that is called *Burg'hegge*, and from thence going as far as *Stotfortanggeshegges*, and so as far as the Hay of *Blomescroft*, and so by that hay as far as *Wodehouse Lane*, and so up to the corner of *Wysecroft*, and so going up by the same croft as far as *Wythonesdone*, and so going up by the hay as far as the ditch of the *Wywelond*, and so by the same ditch as far as *Blakedenesend*, and so going up by the hay of *Appelcroft* as far as the way of *Mayesgrove*, and so straight by the hay up to the corner of *Mayesgrove*, and so by the way that leads between the pasture of *Churelton* and *Knystenlese* as far as *Byles-grove*, and so by the borders of *Byles-grove* up to the ditch that is the boundary between the land of *Cherleton* and *Knyteshenham* (Knight's Enham), and so going down by the same ditch as far as the *Bruyl* of *Charleton*, and so always continuing by the same ditch between the land of *Charleton* and the aforesaid *Bruyl*,[1] as far as the way that leads from *Charleton towards Bedewynde*, and so always by the ditch near to the King's highway up to the ditch of the east corner of *Langgehangre*, and so by the ditch of the *Wodelonde* up to the *Cross in the High Street*, and so by the way that leads along into *North Wode Dell*, and so by the hay as far as *Kinggates*, and so going up by the hay and way that leads towards *Penemere* as far as the *Rydesherd*, and so from the east side by the hay that stretches up to the *Wolhouse*, and from thence by the same hay up to the east corner of the croft of *Penemere*, and so straight by the pathway that leads to the *Croft of St. Andrew*, and so by the hay of *Knoldich* up to the *Knoldich* south end, and so going up to the trench which is the boundary between the wood of the *Abbess of Tarentes*, and the wood of the *Prior of St. Swithin*, Winchester. And so always from the north side of that trench up to the *Rydesde*, and thence by the trench from the west side between the wood of the Lord the King, and the wood of the aforesaid Prior of Winchester, as far as the way that leads from *Crockerestokes towards Andevere*, and from thence as the boundaries divide between the wood of the Lord the King, and the wood of the aforesaid Prior, up to the way that comes from *Cheepemansford towards Andevere*, and so by the same way as far as *Fastendiche*, and so going down by the little ditch up to the aforesaid *Durhurdeshord*. And the Jurors say that the aforesaid metes and bounds before the time of the Coronation of the Lord the King, Henry, the great grandfather of the Lord the now King, were used to include all the aforesaid forest of *Fynkely*. And they say that the Lord the King has no demesne wood nigh to the same metes and bounds adjacent to the said Forest. And they say that all the woods, lands, and places, without the aforesaid metes and bounds which by this peram-

---

[1] "Bruyl" means wood.

bulation are deafforested, have been appropriated to the forest after the time of the Coronation of King Henry, the great grandfather of the now King, but what and how much in the time of whatsoever King separately can by no means be made evident to them.

CHUTES, HANTS.

16th Edward II, A.D. 1323.

A perambulation made in the forest of Chutes, in the presence of John Berewykes and his fellows, as above appears. And in the presence of John de Lisle, the Forester in Fee, and in the presence of Roger of Lecford, and Thomas Spircock, Verderors, and so it was proceeded, that is to say at *Grymesdichusestend*, which is the boundary between the wood of the Lord the King, and the wood of Ralph Wakes, and from thence always by the way that leads near the *Frith* up to the *Dykes-deheth* (Devils' Dyke), and from thence always by the boundaries between the wood of the Lord the King and the pasture of the *marsh*, and from thence by the borders of the wood up to the corner of *Durdauntescroft*, and from thence by the hay as far as *Burchecroft*, and so by the same croft as far as *Capyedon*, and so all along *Capyedon* up to *Okwey* (*Ox-drove*), and from thence going up by the same *Okwey*, as far as *Grymesdiches westend*, and so by the same *Grymesdich* up to *Grymesdichestend* aforesaid. And the Jurors say that the aforesaid metes and bounds before the time of the Coronation of the Lord the King Henry, the great grandfather of the Lord, the now King, were used to include the aforesaid Forest of Chutes. And the Lord the King has no demesne wood adjacent to the said Forest. And they say that all the woods, lands, and places without the aforesaid metes and bounds, of the aforesaid Forest appropriated, which by this perambulation are deafforested, were appropriated after the time of the Coronation of King Henry, the great grandfather of the Lord the now King. But what and how much in the time of whatsoever King separately can in no wise be made evident to them.

DYGHERLYE.

16th Edward II, A.D. 1323.

A perambulation made in the forest of *Dygherlye*, in the presence of John of Berewyke and his fellows as above doth appear, and in the presence of John de Lysle, the Forester in Fee, and in the presence of Roger of Leckford and Thomas Spircock, Verderors, that is to say at *Falkestaple*, and so from thence always by the King's Highway up to the corner of the wood, and so along by the borders of the wood up to the ditch of *Medmadon*, and from thence always by the same ditch up to the ditch of *Faccumbe*, and so from thence by the boundaries between the wood of the Lord the King and the wood of *Faccumbe* up to the greatway that cometh from *Bolkeputtes*, which is the boundary between the wood of the Lord the King and the wood of the Prior of St. Swithin, Winchester, up to the aforesaid *Falkestaple*.[1] And the Jurors say that the aforesaid metes and bounds before the time of the Coronation of the Lord the King

---

[1] *Falkestaple*, called *Falstable* Coppice in 1571, containing 60 acres. See Leases in the Augmentation Office.

Henry, great grandfather of the Lord the now King, were used to include all the aforesaid forest of *Dygherlye*. And that the said King hath no demesne wood adjacent without the same metes of the said forest. And they say that all the woods, lands, and places without the aforesaid metes and bounds of the aforesaid forest appropriated, which by this perambulation are deafforested, were appropriated to the forest after the time of the Coronation of King Henry, the great grandfather of the Lord, the now King. But what and how much in the time of whatsoever King separately, can in no wise be made evident to them.

Bill in the Exchequer by the Attorney General, Michael[s] term, 23rd Chas. 1st, 9th Jan. 1647.

Sheweth,—That where as our Sov[n] Lord the King's Majesty stands seized of the Forest of Finkley, which said forest hath been time out of mind, beyond the memory of man until of late years, very well wooded with timber trees of oak and other trees, and many copses of underwood, and constantly replenished with 800 of fallow deere at the least, there kept and preserved by the Ranger for the time being of the s[d] Forest, for the use, sport, pleasure, and delight of Hi Majesty, and his Royal Progenitors the Kings and Queens of this their Kingdom of England; and whereas there hath not been heretofore nor nowhere ought to be any quantity of conyes or any sheep or swine kept within the s[d] Forest, etc.; and when any visible number of coneyes have then risen there, and when there have been visible numbers, directions have been issued for their destruction, to the intent that his Majesty and his Royal Progenitors might there ride, hunt and disporte there without any danger of any coneyburies. Yet now so it is may it please your Majesty one W[m] Cook *pretending* himself to be Keeper of s[d] walk or Forest of Finkley, together with one Robert Chandler and diverse other unknown persons (whose names his Majesty's Solicitor prayeth may be here inserted and they made def[ts] when they shall be discovered) combining and confederating themselves together contrary to the laws of this kingdom and specially to the forest lawes, without any lawful warrant, etc., at several times within these seven years last past, chased, killed, and destroyed with dogges, gunnes, or bowes one hundred of his Majesty's deere within the s[d] Forest of Finkley at the least, and have from time to time divided the same deere among themselves or disposed of them to their own use "makinge merchandise and sellinge many of them to several inhabitants about the same Forest", *at greate prizes*. By which unlawful means, practises and courses of s[d] W[m] Cook and Rob[t] Chandler and other confederates the game of the s[d] Forest of Finkley is now almost utterly destroyed—there being now left at this present above fiftie head of deere in the same; and the s[d] Cook under the pretence of being keeper hath within the time aforesaid, contrary to the forest laws, used all means possible for the *nourishment and increasing of the coneyes for his own private gayne and ends*, insomuch that they have now almost utterly destroyed the underwood and copses there. And the s[d] Cook hath for the last 5 or 6 years kept and fedd fforty greate beasts, that is to say, Cowes, oxen, Horses, mules, and 100 sheepe, a greate number of swine, and bred up and fostered there nearly 10 calues at the least, and for the better mayntaining and keeping of s[d] greate beasts, etc., etc., hath enclosed many parts of s[d] Forest, and in special, that part called the Lawn where was heretofore the "call of deere", and upon the call of the keeper his servant or servants there were wont to appear a goodly shewe of Deere for His Majesty's pleasure and delight, one hundred at the least, convertinge the s[d] Forest of and from the nature of a Forest to his own private use, benefit, and behoofe; and he hath cut down without authority 100 oaken timber trees, and other trees, and much underwood, and most thereof at unseasonable times in the yeare, and yet under pretence of being Keeper of s^d Forest hath for some years presented and molested many of His Majesty's leige people by waye of indictment. Cook says in his answer that by letters patent dated 24 March 17 Chas. 1st. that he was appointed Keeper of the Forest of Finkley with the same privileges as Richard Hopgood formerly had—he says he only killed the deere when he had warrant for so doing, and denies the allegation as to the number of them stated in the bill as being in the Forest. "Albeit true it is that in these late distracted times they have been much destroyed by soldiers and others, who have against the defendant's will forcibly entered the s^d forest, as well by day as night, and have with gunns and other weapons, and with multitude of people, whom the defendant could not resist, at several times chased and slayne the said deere in the s^d forest, and when he hath offered to make resistance, and to defend the s^d deere, he hath been cruelly and barbarously beaten and wounded, and received at one tyme six woundes in his head, and had both his armes broken. And he hopes that the killing of the Deere by such misdoers and riotous persons shall not be objected against him as a cryme, considering he never assisted them therein, but opposed them so much as he could, to the hazard of his life—he denies keepinge sheep, but acknowledges keepinge 7 or 8 swine about his house, being the lodge belonging to the forest where he lives, who do in most time feed upon the mast, but do not otherwise trouble the forest. He denies most of the other charges, and those he does not he gives a different version of to the complainant.

23rd Charles I, in another Bill,

There is a bill of complaint against Andrew Mooring of Andover, Yeoman, Thos Piper of the same, Coller-Maker, Leonard Poole of the same, Victualler, Thos Young of the same, Coller-maker, Wm Blake, of Eastenton, Gent^{lm}, Jas. Hart of the same, labourer, George Hellyer, Henry Hellyer, and Robt Poore of Hurstbourne Tarrant, Gent: Robert Ash, George Merrick, and Jno. Moreing of Andover, Yeomen; and Wm Goldinge of Woodhouse, labourer, being persons of disordered, riotous, and dissolute carriage and behaviour, combining, and confederating themselves together, contrary to the laws, in the Month of June 1644, did associate unto themselves diverse other riotous, disorderly, and dissolute persons, to the number of 20 persons or more, being armed and prepared with gunnes, charged with powder and shott, crossebowes, pikes, buckstalls and other unlawful weapons, netts and engines, and also with greyhounds, mastives and fferretts did hunt, chase, and kill, and destroy or cause to be destroyed two bucks, and did divide the same among themselves, and the same persons during the last 7 years had in like manner destroyed 40 bucks, does and fawns, twenty hares, one hundred couple of coneyes, twenty pheasants, ffortie partridges, and other beests and fowles of the forest, chase, and warden. And the s^d John Moreing usually keeps one or more greyhounds for the purpose of hunting the game, and some of the defendants had destroyed the pound or pinfold of s^d forest of Finkley. They say in answer that they regret His Majesty's Solicitor should have been informed that they are persons of dissolute, riotous and disorderly carriage. They deny all the charges but killing 10 or 12 couple of rabbits, which they understood was according to the King's wish, and they are farre better than those whom the defendants conceive to be the Relators.

𝔉inkley 𝔓ark.

Part of the Protector's private property was Finkley Park, Co. Hants, as may be learned from the following Extract from the *Harleian Miscellany*, vol. viii.—" Joyce being about to buy Finkley Park in Hampshire, and having generously offered to part with all, or any part of it again to Richard Cromwell: Oliver took him in his arms and told him that himself and his son and family were more beholden to him than to all the world besides, and therefore bade him go on and prosper. Upon this Joyce went the next morning about it, and there being a full Committee (the Park belonging to the Crown) he was just upon the point of contracting for the said Park, when on a sudden in came Richard, his Father, then overtopping all in power, with three Lawyers with him, and required them to proceed no further in it, in regard it was his own inheritance, and no Park as was supposed. Whereupon Joyce informed the Committee of the whole Discourse that had passed between the General, his son and himself, the night before: upon which he fell upon him in foul words, saying, Sirrah! sirrah! hold your tongue! or I shall make you repent the time you were born; which the Committee perceiving, desired them to withdraw, and since that time he never durst meddle with the Park any further. Joyce took this usage of Cromwell's so much to heart, that it was near being the Death of him, whom no one can pity, as he had been the tool of the Protector's worst actions: and had been equally insulted before by him for his Villany."[1]

A Survey of Finkley Park, 1652.

A survey of Finkley Park *als.* Finkley Forest, with the rights, members, and appurtenances thereof, lying and being in the Parish of Andover, in the Co. of Southampton, late parcel of the possessions of Charles Stuart, late King of England, made and taken by us whose names are hereunto subscribed, by virtue of a Commission granted to us, by the Hon[ble] the Justices appointed by Act of the Commons, assembled in Parliament, for sale of the Honors, Manors, and lands, belonging to the late King, Queen and Prince, under their hands and seals.

---

[1] From Noble's *Cromwell*, family edition, 1787, vol. i, pp. 334-335.

All that parcel of inclosed Ground called or known by the name of Finkley Park, with the appurtenances lying and being in the Parish of Andover in the Co. of Southampton:

As it is bounded on the East by the "procession" way dividing the Parishes of Andover and St. Mary Bourne, and passeth between the said Park and the lands of Mr. Wallop, and with the lands of Sir Richard Lucy called Weeke Down, and with the late enclosed lands belonging to Mr. W. Bleke of Eastanton and the Common called Eastanton Down towards the South, and with the said Common called Eastanton Down and the Common called Finkley Down and the lands of Richard Pyle towards the west, and towards the north by a certain Common called Finkley Purlieus, and the Highway leading from Andover towards Nuberye, passing between the said Park and the woods and Coppices called the Ridges, hereafter abutted with the said Park, containeth by admeasurement 841 acres 1 rood and 17 perches, together with the Lodge standing thereon, all which we value to be worth per annum £210 6s. 6d.

There are Coppices in the said Park, which have been usually fenced in, containing by admeasurement 620 acres and 2 roods by 18 foot pole, the soil of all which is valued with the said Park as being comprehended within the measure of 841 a. 1 r. 17 p. as aforesaid, the vesture of them being by several (years') growth, as follows:—

Montgomery Coppice. All that Coppice called Montgomery Coppice, being of 5 years' growth, containing by admeasurement 79 a. 2 r. 0 p., whereof we estimate 19 acres to be "plekes" and voyd places, the residue being 60 a. 2 r. 0 p. of Wood, we value to be worth in the gross £15 2s. 6d.

Great Nuthill Coppice. All that Coppice called Great Nuthill Coppice, being of 19 years' growth, containing by admeasurement 55 a. 22 r. 0 p., whereof we estimate 20 acres to be plekes and bare places, the residue 35 a. 2 r. 0 p. of wood we value to be worth in gross £53 5s. 0d.

Little Nuthill Coppice. All that Coppice called Little Nuthill Coppice, being of 23 years' growth, containing 35 acres, whereof 15 acres are bare and void places, the residue, 20 acres of wood, worth in gross £50.

Little Wydell Coppice. Being of 12 years' growth, containing 19 a. 2 r., which we value in gross at £9 15s. 0d.

Great Wydell Coppice. Being of 19 years' growth, containing 59 a. 1 r. 0 p., whereof 30 acres are void and bare, and 29 a. 1 r. 0 p. we value to be worth in gross £87 15s. 0d.

Peeke Coppice. Being of 17 years' growth, containing 75 a. 1 r. 0 p., whereof 45 acres are bare and waste, residue 30 a. 1 r. 0 p., we value to be worth £30 5s. 0d.

Wayting Oak Coppice. Being of 21 years' growth, containing 58 a. 2 r. 0 p.—8½ acres bare, residue worth in gross £33 13s. 4d.

Swanhill Coppice. Being of 18 years' growth, containing 78½ acres, 31 acres to be "*pleches*", residue 44½ ac., worth £89.

Pound Coppice. Being 22 years' growth, containing 68 a. 3 r. 0 p., 40 acres void, residue 28 a. 3 r. 0 p., worth £64 13s. 9d.

Deereman Coppice. Being 30 years' growth, containing 93 a. 3 r. 0 p., 43 acres waste and void, residue 50 a. 3 r. 0 p., worth £152 5s. 0d.

Underwood. There are underwoods in the said Park, the Soil whereof is valued with the said Park as aforesaid, the worth growing in Lawns, Plots and "Ragges" in the said Park, we estimate to be 337 Loads, which we value to be worth upon the place in gross £143 4s. 6d.

Deer. There are in the said Park at present 150 deer of all sorts, which we value to be worth £100.

There are (is?) a stock of Conyes in the said Park which we value to be worth £50.

The Ridges. All that wood and wood ground called by the name of the Ridges, parcel of the said Forest of Finkley, lying and being without the enclosed ground called Finkley Park, and in the Parish of Andover aforesaid, bounded east by the "procession" way dividing Andover and St. Mary Bourne aforesaid, South by the Highway before mentioned leading from Andover to Nuberye, on the West by the Lands of Mr. Anthony Hyde, and on the North by the Common or Heath called *Dowles* heath, containing by admeasurement 192 a. 3 r. 35 p. by 18 foot pole.

Coppices in the Ridges. Three Coppices called the "Ragges" which have been usually fenced in, the vesture being of several growths, containing by estimation 74 acres, which we value *Com. Ann.* (communis annis) £9 16s.

Upper Coppice of 17 years' growth, 33 acres of wood worth £55.

Middle Coppice of 7 years' growth, 29 acres of wood worth £38 13s. 4d.

Lower Coppice of 18 years' growth, 12 acres of wood worth £12.

Trees in the Ridges. The timber trees and saplings now growing being in number 5,120, the time of converting them into money we value to be worth on the place £853 6s. 8d.

Underwoods in the said Ridges without the Coppices, consisting most part of Thorn and Bushes, we estimate at £40.

Mem. That the tithe of the Coppices, both in the Park, and also the Coppices in the Ridges, as we are informed, have been paid and so belong to the Parsonage of Andover.

We found Richard Cromwell, Esq., Chief Ranger of the Forest of Finkley, who claimeth office as an Inheritance, by means of letters patent, but inasmuch as no Patent was shewn to us, we humbly leave the said claim to be made good before the Honble The Trustees and Surveyor General.

The late King, by letters Patent 24 March 17th of his reign, granted to Wm Cook the place of Keeper of Finkley Forest, together with all Wages, Fees, Profits, etc., for his natural Life, the same as Richard Hopgood, late Underkeeper had.

The possessors of the Farm called King's Enham Farm, belonging to Magdalen College, Oxford, have had time out of mind commonage with the enclosed Park, called Finkley Park, for 20 Cows and 1 Bull, from May day to Michaelmas, for which 22s. per annum is paid as an acknowledgment to the Chief Ranger, and unto the under Keeper 9s. yearly, towards making up fences of Finkley Park, which said Commonage for 20 Cows and 1 Bull we estimate to be worth £13 6s. 8d. per annum.

We conceive the yearly Profits to Wm Cook, Keeper of Finkley Park, have been £160 arising out of the profits of the Conyes, and the herbage of said Park and other fees incident to the office.

This Survey was perfected the 5th March 1652 by us :—

Joseph Haddock, John Fiske, and Saml Coltman.

Examined by William Webb, 1652.

NOTICES IN THE "CALENDAR OF STATE PAPERS (DOMESTIC)" RELATIVE TO CHUTE AND FINKLEY.

Aug. 1st, 1606, Jas. I.—Grant to Richard Gifford of the office of Ranger of Chute Forest and others, County of Hants, for life.

Greenwich, June 5th, 1609.—Warrant to pay Andrew Kingsmill £169 18s. 4d. for his interest in certain Coppices, in Finkley Walk, in the Forest of Chute, co. Hants, purchased by the King for preservation of the deer.

Dec. 24th, 1610, Elizabeth.—Petition of Edward Thornburgh of Shoddesdon,

Hants, to the King. for a grant in fee simple, of the decayed forests of Chute, cos. Hants and Wilts, leased to him and his father, Edward Thornburgh of Hamfell, co. Lancaster, by the late Queen, at so high a rent that it has been the overthrow of an antient house.

June 1611.— Petition of Richard Withers, the Queen's Yeoman of the Bows, and keeper of the forest of Dowles (to Salisbury), to order Mr. Norden to proceed with the repair of the *Lodge of Dowles*, as he has done with that of Chute.

July 11th, 1611.—Grant to Mr. Richard Fermor, Tho' Purcell, and Adrian Kirby of certain Coppices and woodlands within the perambulation of the Forest of Chute, co. Hants.

April 4th, 1626, Charles I. — Warrant to Sir John Philpot, Ranger of the Forest of Chute, co. Southampton, to take the charge of preserving the game in the said forest, and *within seven miles* compass of the same.

Sept. 1660, Charles II.—Note of a Petition by Mr. Hughes for the purchase in fee farm of six Coppices disafforested, which are surrounded by his other lands, and have no deer in them; he is willing to surrender his lease of larger Coppices within Finkley, which are useful for the deer—at a reasonable rate.

Sept. 1660.— Petition of Edward Manning for a lease for 31 years of Finkley Coppice, co. Hants, as granted him by the late King, with clause of disafforestation—will improve its value £300 a year—lost £10,000 in the late King's cause, a Parliament Captain torturing his servant to discover his money and plate, and has spent £10,000 on the debts of his brother slain at Cheriton fight, and in support of his family—cut the new river from Colebrook to Hampton Court; walled the Great Park at Richmond, etc., etc.

Whitehall, Dec. 11th, 1660-1.—Petition of Henry Philpot to the King for an allotment of land from Finkley forest, co. Hants. His ancestors have held the chief wardenship of Finkley and Chute Forests 300 years, but the late King transferred that of Chute to Mr. Hughes, compensating him by a grant of lands, and now his Majesty has transferred that of Finkley to the Duke of Albermarle, so that he is deprived of office and estate. Notes with reference thereon to the Lord Treasurer—his reference Dec. 17th to the Solicitor and Surveyor General —report of the latter, Feb. 16th, 1661, that tho' one Cook has lately held Finkley Walk by Patent from the late King, the Petitioner might have £300 allowed for his interest therein, his father Sir John Philpot having received £600 for that of Chute forest, which is twice the size. Report of the Lord Treasurer that he should be allowed £400.

Feb. 1661.—Grants to George Duke of Albermarle, Anne his wife, and their heirs of the Manor and park of Theobald's, co. Hertford (excepting mines Royal and the passage of the new river), the Manor of Periors and other lands, cos. Hertford, Mid^x, Berks, Hants, Notts, and York; total value £4,066 18s. 4d., with the timber in Chute Manor, and leave to disforest Coppices, and have free warren in the forest of Chute, part of the said grant.

June 10th, 1662, Hampton Court, Charles II.—The Forest was now on the wane. Petition of Charles, son and heir of the late Lord Charles Paulet, to the King, for leave to disafforest Dowles wood and Dyley Coppice, sometime part of the late forest of Chute, co. Hants, all the residue of which was disafforested. This land descended to him from Willlam, late Marquis of Winchester; but burdened with great debts incurred by his father and himself for loyalty, and with provision for his Mother, and four younger brothers and sisters.

Sept. 24, 1662.—Order for warrant disfranchising that part of the Forest of Chute called *Dowles* and *Dyley*, co. Hants, belonging to Charles, Son and heir of the late Lord Charles Paulet, and granting him the deer there, in consideration of his Father's services and sufferings.

From the Journals of the House of Commons.

1648, Charles I.—Order for the granting the Custody and Command of *Finkley Chase* to Lord la Ware.

DISAFFORESTATION OF DOLES AND DYLEY WOODS, A.D. 1662.

To the King's most excellent Majesty.

The humble Petition of Charles Powlett, Esqre, son and heir of the Lord Charles Powlett deceased,

Humbly sheweth,—

That King James, by several Letters Patent, did grant to William, late Lord Marquis of Winchester, and to other persons by his appointment and his and their heirs severally, certain Woods and Wastes, now commonly called *Dowles*, and certain other woods called *Dyley* coppices, which several premises were sometimes parcels of the late Forest of Chute, in the County of Southampton, and since by settlements to the Petitioner.

That all the other parts, residue of the said late forest, have since been granted in fee to several other persons, and disafforested, so that your Majesty hath now not any land left within the said forest.

That the Petitioner's father left to the Petitioner the premises (being the greater part of his estate) charged with debts (besides the provision for the Petitioner's mother and some younger brothers and a sister, to be made out of the same), which debts were contracted by his said father's sufferings in the just cause of your Majesty's Royal Father, and your Majesty, to whom the Petitioner hath always been a loyal and dutiful subject, and hath suffered much under the late Tyrants for his so being.—That the Petitioner, by the occasions aforesaid, is become encumbered with great debts, and cannot so freely order his said estate for satisfaction of his said debts and support of the family, as is requisite, by reason that the said Dowles Wood and Waste, and Dyley Coppices (in defect of inserting sufficient clauses of disafforestation in the several letters patent and grants thereof) remain in strictness of law still subject and liable to the Forest Laws, notwithstanding all the residue of the said late Forest is wholly and absolutely disafforested and no deer remaining at all therein nor in the premises.

May it therefore please your Majesty to grant a Disafforestation of the Petitioner's said ground, now commonly called Dowles Wood and the Wastes thereunto adjoining or belonging,—

And the Petitioner shall ever pray for your Majesty.

The foregoing Petition was granted, and among the State Papers of the date 8th Jan. 1667, we find a warrant for a grant to Mary, Countess of Falmouth, of the 1,000 acres of land, wood, etc., called Doles, part of the late Forest of Chute, counties of Wilts and Hants, forfeit to the Crown by attainder of Edmund Ludlow, on whose father it devolved as a lapsed mortgage from Charles Powlett of Woodhouse, County of Hants.—And under date 4th Feb. 1667, occurs a Petition of Charles Powlett, and Nathaniel and Edmund Ludlow, to the King, stating that on the 7th July 1664, Charles Powlett borrowed £2,600 of the late Edmund Ludlow, of St. Martin's in the Fields, Middlesex, on mortgage of Hurstbourne Tarrant, and other manors in the County of Hants; the said Ludlow died, leaving Nathaniel and Edmund Ludlow his executors heirs to the debt, but the land legally devolving on the next heir, Colonel Edmund Ludlow, attainted of treason, is forfeited to the Crown, they beg a regrant of the said lands to Charles Powlett and his heirs,—upon which the Attorney General reports that the mortgagor should be admitted to a redemption, but that the executors are not entitled to the mortgaged lands in equity, though they may be by the King's goodness. After this, occurs a petition from Charles Powlett to the King, for a grant to Nathaniel Ludlow and Edward Boswell, nominees of Mary Countess of Falmouth, of the manor of Hurstbourne Tarrant, and other lands in the County of Hants, mortgaged to Edmund Ludlow by the petitioner for £2,600, but escheated to the Crown by Ludlow's death, without heir,—whereon his Majesty ordered them to be granted to the said Countess. The report of Sir Charles Harbord, Surveyor General, is that the estate will not satisfy the legatees without the money granted to the Countess of Falmouth,—that the lady can only claim the right belonging to the attainted person, and the mortgagor having the right of redemption, the property becomes personal, and then goes by will to the executors, but to save trouble they will give her a sum of money if she will resign the lands to them.

Parochial Customs.

The Wooset.

FROM time immemorial a rude demonstration was made in the parish, under the title of "Wooset",[1] or "Ooset hunting", whenever it became known that infidelity had occurred on the part of a husband or wife. The term *Ooset* appears to be derived from *Oost*, a host or army. The practice consisted of an assembling together in the evening of any desirous to take part in the proceedings. Noises were made with ox-horns, or other discordant instruments, to call the people to the place of meeting. The result was a gathering of the most heterogeneous human constituents, bearing horns, old frying-pans, marrow-bones, tongs, or, indeed, any rough article out of which noise could be elicited. It was rightly denominated "rough music". In some instances one of the leaders carried a horse's skull at the top of a piece of wood, with a cross-bar underneath the head, on which was hung a chemise with the arms extended. To the under jaw of the head a bar of wood was fixed, in order to enable the operator to open the mouth, and force the jaw back against the upper one, so as to cause a loud champing noise. A pair of horns were sometimes attached to the top of the skull. Turnip lanterns were carried in winter. The noisy processioning in front of the offender's residence continued for three nights, there was then a suspension for three nights, when the demonstration was repeated for three nights. Another interval of three nights followed, when the meeting concluded with a third visitation of three nights, making altogether nine demonstrations. The people then dispersed, believing that their programme was quite legal, and that it could not be officially prevented.

[1] Wooset might be simply a shortening of *Whore-set*, from the Saxon *Hore*.

SKIMMINGTON.

Another parochial custom was known as "Skimmington", which was practised when wife or husband-beating occurred; but it was resorted to only when family jars were unusally provocative. I have thought the word Skimmington must be derived from the employment of a skimmer or ladle in the procession. A figure was formed, generally by padding an old smock-frock with straw, and topping it with a hat or bonnet, such as in rural districts is known as a "Galley-beggar", used for scaring birds. This figure was borne past the delinquent's house, and belaboured with a skimmer or ladle. I have more than once witnessed the placing of a heap of chaff, and a small wooden flail, at night, at the door of a person guilty of wife-beating.

HARVEST HOME.

In early times "Harvest Home" was a time of great rejoicing, and the last load was taken from the field amidst a scene of merriment. The best team of horses was selected, and decorated with ribbons; and the head-boy occupied the seat of honour on the fore-horse, also profusely decorated. In most cases notice is not now taken of the event; but as late as fifty years ago the last load was never removed from the fields without the usual chorus of

> "Well ploughed, well sowed,
> Well reaped, well mowed,
> Nor a load over*drowd:*
> Hip, Hip, hurrah!
> Harvest home!"

After the clearing a harvest supper was given, and is still given, at which all the labourers and neighbours met in friendly congratulations over the successful removal of the produce of the fields. Amidst the harmony of the evening it was customary for all to join in a song of thanks to the master and mistress. The following is the form of rhyme usually heard in Hampshire:—

> "Here's a health unto our Master the founder of the feast,
> I hope to God with all my heart his soul in heaven may rest;
> That all his works may prosper that ever he takes in hand,
> For we are all his servants, and all at his command;
> Then drink, boys, drink, and mind that you do not spill,
> For if you do, you *shall* drink *two*, with a hearty free good will.
>   *Chorus*—Drink, boys, drink, etc.

> "And now we've drunk our Master's health our *Missis* shan't go free,
> For I hope and trust her soul will rest in heaven as well as he:

>   For she's a good provider, whatever she takes in hand,
>   For we are all her servants, and all at her command;
>   Then drink, boys, drink, and mind that you do not spill,
>   For if you do, you *shall* drink *two*, with a hearty free good will.
>   *Chorus*—Then drink, boys, drink, etc."

The words, "you *shall* drink *two*", in the last line, refer to the drinking a second cup as a fine, in the event any of the liquor is spilled in taking the first mug.

I was once present at what was termed a "booting", which was a sort of punishment for the overthrowing of a load of corn during the harvest. At the harvest-supper during the evening, the delinquent was laid face downwards on the table, and one of the leaders of the festival administered some blows with one of the master's boots, while holding the boot in a peculiar manner. As a physical chastisement it was of no account; but it was probably intended as a degradation in the face of the blunderer's fellow-workers.

Sheep Washing.

In the process of preparing sheep for shearing, by swimming them in a pool to cleanse the wool, it was customary in the olden times to regard it somewhat as a festival by introducing cakes and ale. For many years it was the practice of one farmer of my acquaintance to take a large cooked chine for lunch to the "wash", the chine being always one placed on the bacon-rack a year or two previously. St. Mary Bourne was famous for its sheep-wash, a pool having been used in the parish for over 300 years. As the Upper Test in dry seasons did not carry sufficient water through the villages lying at a greater elevation than St. Mary Bourne, all the surrounding flock-masters sent their fleeces to be cleansed at Bourne, where by penning back the burn or brook sufficient water was always obtainable. In wet seasons a "wash" was sometimes practicable in a meadow belonging to Mr. Thomas Miles, of Hurstbourne Tarrant. The pool at St. Mary Bourne was reached through a yard in the occupation of Mr. George Neale; and the use of the yard was granted by the late Mr. John Longman, of Warwick; but its use could not be claimed as a right.

Sheep Shearing.

The sheep-washing in May and June was followed by the shearing of the sheep in June and July, and as on all other occasions the ingatherings of produce were times of friendly greeting, so the period of shearing was regarded in early times as one for social meetings. Dinners were provided, and friends old and young were invited.

> "Wife, make us a dinner, spare flesh neither corne,
> Make wafers and Cakes, for our Sheepe must be shorne.
> At Sheepe shearing, neighbours none other things crave,
> But good cheere and welcome like neighbours to have."

Thus wrote Tusser, in his *Husbandry*, in the days of Queen Elizabeth.

The last to depart from the early custom in St. Mary Bourne was "Farmer" John Moore, whose name has more than once received notice in these pages. It was Mr. Moore's practice to introduce in the shearing barn early in the day a savoury drink called "Spice-bowl", with cakes made for the occasion. For the last quarter of a century the habit of feeding the shearers in the house has been abandoned, the men being paid by the score for taking off the fleeces. The usual charge is 4s. 6d. per score, although prices differ in places. One may look back with some regret at the friendly feeling fostered by the social intercourse of the supper-table; but the change has been for the better, in enabling the wife and family to share the shearer's wages. The following is a list of the band of shearers at St. Mary Bourne in 1845:—

Thomas Medhurst, sen., Captain.		Joseph Fifield.
William Medhurst, sen.		Isaac Goodyear.
Thomas Medhurst.		William Goodyear.
Henry Medhurst.	Sons of	William Bacon.
John Medhurst.	Thomas	Thomas Merryfield.
Nathaniel Medhurst.	Medhurst.	Isaac Parker.
William Medhurst.		George Merryfield.

The Mummers, or Christmas Boys.

When Christmas came round, its festivities were heightened by the appearance of a small band of youths, who went through a popular pantomime at most of the houses in the parish where the residents were likely to furnish some entertainment on the spot, or contribute a small sum towards the providing a supper and ale elsewhere. Mummer means a masker. The play was conducted by half-a-dozen lads dressed in blouses, decorated profusely with coloured paper ribbons, and wearing conical caps streaming with similar paper decoration. In addition, each one carried in his hand a short wooden sword. Half-a-century ago the performances of this village band began on the evening of the 24th of December, Christmas Eve; but as some of the older inhabitants were what were called "Old Christmasers", adherents of the later date for keeping Christmas Day, considerable rivalry existed regarding the time of holding the festival. It was affirmed by some of the old Christmas Day observers "that they never had eaten their Christmas dinner except on the 6th January, and that they never would do so." And thus during the lifetime of this generation of persistents in the customs of their youth the thing went on, doubtless greatly to the satisfaction of the Christmas Boys or Mummers, whose visitations continuing somewhat interruptedly during the time intervening between the two festivals, obtained thereby a lengthened term of merriment.

The plot was evidently Eastern, and founded probably on the Legend of St. George. And there can be no doubt that the usage, continued onwards from sire to son, is as old as the myth itself. There were various versions of the play, all of which were alike in the principal characters. The following is as complete an adherence to the text as I could obtain, and at which I was present at the performance of, at Dipland House, in St. Mary Bourne in 1874. The characters were the following :—

>Old Father Christmas.
>Mince Pie.
>A Turkish Knight.
>St. George.
>An Italian Doctor.
>Little John.

Divested of matter that had no relation to the play, the dialogue ran as follows :—

>*Enter* OLD FATHER CHRISTMAS.

Oh! here come I, Old Father Christmas, welcome, or welcome not,
I hope Old Father Christmas will never be forgot.
>Make room! room! I say!
>That I may lead Mince Pie this way.
>Walk in, Mince Pie, and act *thy* part,
>And show the gentles *thy* valiant heart.

>*Enter* MINCE PIE.

Room! room! good gentles all give me room to rhyme,
I'll show you some festivity this Christmas time.

>*Enter a* TURKISH KNIGHT *with a wooden sword.*

I am a valiant Turkish Knight,
And dare with any man to fight;
Bring me the man that bids me stand,
Who says he'll cut me down with his audacious hand.
I'll cut him and hack him as small as a fly,
And send him to Satan to make mince pie.

Enter ST. GEORGE *with a wooden sword.*

Oh! in come I, St. George, the man of courage bold,
With my sword and buckler I've won three crowns of gold;
I fought the fiery Dragon and brought him to the slaughter;
I won a beauteous Queen, a King of Egypt's daughter.
    If thy mind is high, my mind is bold,
    If thy blood is hot, I will make it cold.

(*They fight, and the* TURKISH KNIGHT *falls.*)

Turkish Knight. Oh! St. George, spare my life!

Father Christmas. Is there no Doctor to be found
                To cure this man who's bleeding on the ground?

Enter THE DOCTOR.

Yes! an Italian Doctor's to be found
To cure the Knight who's bleeding on the ground.
I cure the sick of every pain,
And bring the dead to life again.

Father Christmas. Doctor, what is thy fee?

The Doctor.   I'll take ten pounds of thee,
              But fifteen is my fee,
              Before I set this gallant free.

Father Christmas. Doctor! work thy will.

The Doctor.   I have a little bottle by my side,
              The fame of which spreads far and wide,
              I drop a drop on this poor man's nose.

(*The* DOCTOR *touches the* TURKISH KNIGHT'S *nose, and the* KNIGHT *rises on his feet.*)

Enter LITTLE JACK, *with sundry dolls attached to his back.*

Oh! in come I, little saucy Jack,
With all my children at my back.
Christmas comes but once a year,
And when it comes it brings good cheer:
Roast beef, plum pudding, and mince pie,
Who likes that any better than I?
Christmas ale makes us dance and sing;
Money in the purse is a very fine thing.

Ladies and Gentlemen, give us what you please.

The performance being over, a Christmas Carol is sung, and the Mummers depart.

Glossary of Provincial Words used in North Hampshire.

In framing a short glossary of the local words in use among the peasantry of St. Mary Bourne, and the district immediately surrounding it, I have adhered to such as have from time to time come under my own observation Many of the words comprising the list range over a large area outside of the county, and have probably been introduced by labourers and others, who have come out of other counties and settled in Hampshire. It is difficult to understand whence some of these provincialisms have been derived; but they have probably come from several sources, Saxon, Danish, and in some cases from Celtic roots. By passing through the mouths of illiterate people the original words have undergone such corruption as to be scarcely discoverable. In some instances the words seem intended to represent sounds, as in "blubbering", which appears to mean snivelling or crying with pouting lips; or they have been coined to express sensation, as in "quop", a word intended to apply to the peculiar throbbing feeling attending suppuration. As an illustration of the way slang is made to convey an idea, a gipsy hawker of brushes, etc., which he carried on his back, was asked how he contrived to obtain so many halfpence in a scramble at an election at Abingdon, when he replied that "he went in all mops and brooms". The glossary is arranged alphabetically, and many of the words are spelt as they are or were pronounced. I am aware that some of the words are noticed in Halliwell's *Archaic and Provincial Words;* but I refer to them as I have understood their meaning among North Hampshire people. Some of the words are slang, and others are vulgarisms of well-known words.

Ackard, awkward, "trimming ackard".
Aish, stubble "oat-ash".
Aneust, "nearst", nearly, Berks.
Bitle, a wedge-driver.
Bout, a pause in wrestling.
Brashy, applied to rough, pebbly soil.
Budge, "won't budge (move) an inch".
Burr, sweetbread, Berks.
Bungersome, clumsy, Berks.
Caddle, to hurry.

Chaff, to make fun of.
Chopper, the lower jaw of a pig.
Cheeky, impudent.
Chissel, to cheat.
Chuck, to throw underhand.
Coddle, to fuss with, "Molly-coddle".
Cotton, to beat, as "I'll cotton him".
Crib, to steal by littles.
Crick, to sprain, "I have cricked (crooked) my ankle".
Crochet, as "got a crochet in his head".

Darn, a threat, "darn", "dash", and "drat", I have heard used as a kind of threat.
Dawnt, to frighten, "dawnt or dearnt lonely".
Deedy, "peering", or looking into.
Dew-bit, early breakfast.
Dished, deceived, "he has dished or done me".
Dizend, dressed fine.
Dollop, a lump.
Dout, extinguish, as "dout the candle".
Drunge, an obstruction.
Dummul, dull, Berks.
Dunney, deaf.
Faggot, a kind of sausage, "black-pudding".
Farrow, a litter of pigs, Berks.
Featish, middling in health. "How are you, Thomas?" "Featish like"; also "fairish".
Fettle, in good or bad fettle.
Flail, for thrashing corn, consisting of handstaff and swingle, the staff made of ash, and the swingle of crab or blackthorn.
Fleck, to tear hair or fur out.
Foust, fousty, bad-smelling.
Funk, fright.
Frow, firm.
Gabbern, roomy, comfortless, Wilts.
Galley-beggar, a scarecrow.
Gied, gave.
Gna'-pooast, a niggardly fellow.
Green-meat, green food for horses.
Grouts, grits, dregs.
Haggle, to banter in trade.
Hanker after, to desire.
Haulm, stubble, from the Saxon *healm*, straw, whence *healming*, used by thatchers.
Hide, to flog on the naked skin.
Hinge, "head and pluck", sheep's head and lungs, etc.
Hoppetty-hoy, a clumsy, overgrown lad.
Hunch, a big lump of bread, also "*Nunch*" and "*Nunchin*", lunch.
Inkling, desire after.
Inwards, the entrails of a pig.
Ire, iron.
Keever, a fermenting tub.
Kettle-broth, pot-liquor in which bacon and vegetables have been boiled.

Knacker, an old horse.
Leasing, picking loose corn.
Lear, to colour.
Logy, loggy, lazy.
Lumper, to stumble.
Main, almost, as "main tired".
Maur (Celtic), a root, "stool-maur", "tree-stool".
Mazin, astonishing.
Mawkin, a long mop used in baking. Berks.
Mazard, a face.
Measter, master, Berks.
Mizzle, go!
Moke, a donkey—gipsy's term.
Mouch, to play truant, whence "blackberry-mouchers", eating them on the sly.
Moses, a frog.
Mosey, stale.
Muckle, straw half dung.
Mummer, "mummy", mother.
Nabbet, "gna'-bit", 4 o'clock meal.
Nag, nagging, persistent worrying.
Nation, very, as "nation good".
Nitch, as much as a person can carry.
Nouse, sense.
Oller, to call out.
Oust, to shoulder up.
Paddle, a spud.
Pank, pant, to breathe hard.
Panshards, crocks, broken pots.
Pelt, skin, as "thick in the pelt".
Piggin, a small pail.
Pip, a disease in fowls; "gapes".
Plim, to enlarge in boiling.
Plumm, straightforward.
Poke, a sack, "pig in a poke".
Pook, a hay-cock.
Pot-dung, farm-yard manure.
Puff, a light faggot.
Quatch, or *quitch*, not to speak, "don't quitch".
Quilt, to swallow.
Quod, slang for prison.
Quop, to throb or pulsate.
Rap, to exchange, "swop".
Randy, renty, tearing.
Rising, as applied to yeast in making dough.
Roak, reek, as "roak with sweat".
Rowty, rooty.
Rumple, to put out of temper.

Scawt, to push backwards, Berks.
Schram'd, chilled, "knit up with cold".
Scriggle, scrawl.
Scroop, to make a screwing noise.
Shard, a gap.
Shirty, angry.
Showel, a shovel.
Shore, a stake, "fold-shore".
Shuck, a shell.
Singreen, house-leek, grows on thatch, and considered a sign of good luck.
Skeeling, sloping, as a "skeeling roof".
Skruff, nape of the neck.
Slammock, a slouch.
Sliver, to cut off.
Snacks, to go halves or "snacks".
Snop, a rap on the head.
Snowl, a large lump.
Spavins, spasm.
Speil, a spark.
Spell, a charm.
Sprack, ready.
Squale, to throw with a knobbed stick.
Start, used in reference to mirth, "we had a fine start".
Stived-up, short of room.
Stub, a broken nail.
Studdle, to stir up and make muddy.
Swipes and *swankey*, small-beer.
Tab, of a shoe.
Tackle, to defeat.
Tallot, a hay-loft.

Tan, to flog, "tan his hide".
Ta'year, this year.
Thic, this.
Tickle, to set a trap "tickle", easy to go off.
Toggs, toggery, clothing.
Tommy, slang for bread.
Touchy, testy, peevish.
Trapes, a slatternly woman.
Trimming, as "trimming hot" or, "trimming strong".
Trull, or *troll*, bowl at cricket.
Tussle, struggle.
Tuggs, traces.
Twoad, a toad.
Unkid, lonely.
Vell, a calf's stomach, Berks.
Vinney, veiny, mouldy.
Wallop, to thrash with a big stick.
Want, a mole, Berks.
Waps, a wasp.
Whee! whay! or why! stop!
Wherret, to worry.
Whisket, a small twig.
Whopper, a big object.
Wicker, to neigh.
Wrick, to wrench or sprain.
Wrinkle, a hint, as "I put him up to a thing or two".
Yeath, the earth.
Yees! yes! used occasionally.
Yeo, yaw, ewe, a female sheep.

Hampshire carters often say *Toward*, when it is intended to turn horses to the left, and *Vrammard*, when they should be turned to the right. The very illiterate use *v* strongly, as *vor-hos* for fore-horse, *vorrard* for forward, and *vlee-away* for fly-away. They call vermin *varments*; and I have sometimes heard boys apply the term *Callow-wobblers* to unfledged-sparrows.

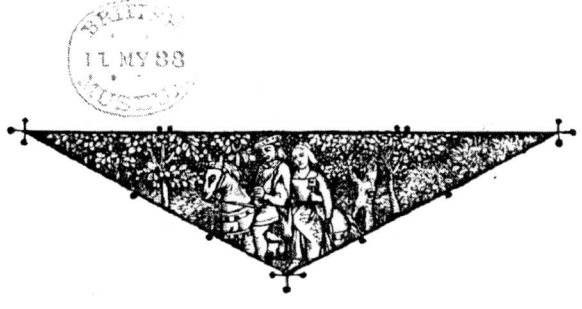

The Chalk of St. Mary Bourne.[1]

 AM indebted to Mr. E. Westlake, F.G.S., for the following notice respecting the Chalk and Tertiary beds in the district around St. Mary Bourne.

The more precise knowledge obtained of late years of the subdivisions of the Chalk made it desirable that the specimens collected by Dr. Stevens from the neighbourhood of St. Mary Bourne should be referred, as far as might be, to their particular horizons, and I therefore undertook, in the summer of 1886, an examination of the exposures of the Chalk within the limits of the parish, as well as of those seen in the cuttings of the South Western Railway which lie just without its southern boundary. In the following pages the strata and their contents are described in ascending order. Besides

[1] List of Works, Maps, etc., on the Geology of St. Mary Bourne :—

1860. BRISTOW, H. W.—Sheet 12 of the Map of the Geological Survey of England.

1862. BRISTOW, H. W., and W. WHITAKER.—The Geology of parts of Berkshire and Hampshire—Memoir Geol. Survey illustrating Sheet 12. (Clay near Stoke, pp. 28, 30 : and reprinted in *General Memoirs*, vol. iv, p. 104, 1872.)

1866. STEVENS, J. [Anon.].—Fossil Wood in Flint. *Science Gossip*, No. 13, p. 15.

1867. ,, A Descriptive List of Flint Implements found at St. Mary Bourne . . . . with a Sketch of the Geological Features of the Upper Test Valley, and a List of Fossils from the Upper and Lower Chalk of St. Mary Bourne, Hampshire. 8vo., Lond.

1872. ,, Geological Notices of North Hampshire. *Trans. Newbury Dist. Field Club*, vol. i, p. 71. Newbury.

1876. BARROIS, DR. C.—Recherches sur le Terrain Crétacé Supérieur de l'Angleterre et de l'Irlande. *Mém. Soc. Géol. Nord*, pp. 234. (Vallée de la Test à St. Mary Bourne, pp. 47, 48.

the specific interest of the remains discovered, various general inferences may be drawn from them: thus, in the pit at Stoke, it is probable that the fish and crustacea in the lower beds point to that shoaling of the Turonian sea which is still more clearly indicated by the abundance of gasteropods in the chalk rock above. It is, however, in its conjunction with similar studies in other areas that the chief use of this contribution will consist, as it is thus that we arrive at an understanding of the physical and organic changes which took place in ancient seas and oceans.

The northern part of the chalk uplands of Hampshire has an average elevation exceeding 300 ft., and consists of flinty chalk of the lower beds of the Senonian with *Marsupites* and *Micraster*. These beds, rising more steeply than the ground rises towards the axis of Kingsclere, are gradually denuded off, till the summits of the northern escarpment are formed of the chalk rock of the Turonian.

The parish of St. Mary Bourne is situated on the southern side of a small anticlinal[1] parellel to that of Kingsclere. The northerly dip, amounting to about 5°, is seen in a shallow pit on the top of a hill three-eighths of a mile N.N.W. of Ibthorpe. The southerly dip averages about 3°. This fold brings up the Middle Chalk (Turonian) at Hurstbourne Tarrant, where it is poorly seen; and at Stoke, where there is a very fine exposure of the upper beds. This latter pit was formerly worked for lime, and yielded to Dr. J. Stevens a large number of fossils.[2] The section from top to bottom is as follows :—

---

[1] This anticlinal was regarded by Dr. C. Barrois, by whom it was first noticed (*Recherches*, p. 47), as continuous with that of Peasemarsh and Froyle, which, according to J. P. Martin (*Phil. Mag.*, Ser. 4, vol. ii, p. 48; 1851), is continued westward in the high ground through Lipscomb, Ellisfield, Dummer, and to the north of Popham. I have however been unable to find any evidence of it to the north of Whitchurch, whence a continuous cutting on the Great Western Railway, extending for 1¼ mile to Larks Barrow, shows a dip increasing gradually from 0° to 1°-1½° S. (the slight northerly dip of 2° seen one mile E.S.E. in a poor exposure at Holding's Farm is probably local); about a quarter-mile further north, in a lane at Cold Henley, the dip is 1° to 2° S. (the northerly dip marked here on the Survey Map is erroneous); thence to Angle Down there is an interval of a mile without exposures, and if the anticlinal exists at all it must be here, as in the Angle Down cutting, half-mile south of Litchfield, the dip of the *cortestudinarium* chalk is 3° S. Nor is there any sign of it in the eastern branch of the Test Valley between Whitchurch and Overton, where the chalk is everywhere horizontal and shows nothing lower than the zone of *Micr. coranguinum*.

[2] The lists of fossils given by Dr. Stevens in 1867 and 1872 we have jointly revised, mostly from the original specimens, and they are therefore superseded by those now given. The species preceded by * are those collected by Dr. Stevens and now placed in the Reading Museum. A † indicates additional species, or specimens from particular beds, collected by myself in 1886. Those without a preceding mark are quoted from Dr. Stevens's former lists.

Section in Pit at the Foot of Stoke Hill.

	ft.	in.

f. SOFT CHALK with a line of flint 9 inches from the bottom . . 3 9

e. UPPER ROCK BED.—Very hard chalk, slightly ochreous, with †*Micraster*. Being near the surface this bed is much broken, but is defined at the top 2 0

d. SOFTISH WHITE CHALK, without flints 7 9

† *Ventriculites.*
† *Echinocorys gibbus*, Lamk.
† *Holaster planus*, var. *placenta*, Ag.
† *Micraster breviporus*, Ag.
† *Rhynchonella plicatilis*, Sow.
† *Rhynchonella Reedensis*, Ether.

† *Terebratula carnea* (?), Sow.
† *Terebratula semiglobosa*, Sow.
† *Inoceramus sp.*
† *Spondylus spinosus*, Sow.
† *Spondylus sp.*
† *Pleurotomaria prespectiva*, Mant.

Line of rusty flints (341 feet above Ordnance Datum), forming top of

c. SPONGE BED.—Hard nodular chalk with black specks, and many decayed irregular flints full of spicules. In places the chalk is decayed and powdery, and contains cavities . . . 1 0

† *Ventriculites cribrosus* (?), Phill.
† *Parasmilia sp.*
† *Micraster breviporus*, Ag.
* *Terebratula semiglobosa*, Sow.

† *Inoceramus* near to *cuneiformis*, d'Orb.
† *Nautilus lævigatus*, d'Orb.
* *Oxyrhina Mantelli*, Ag.

b. LOWER ROCK BED.—Two blocks of exceedingly hard chalk, the upper surfaces of which are irregular and well defined. The top 3 to 4 ins. of these blocks is nodular and pyritous, the nodules weathering greenish, and contain numerous fossils, especially in the top block, which abounds in *Turbo gemmatus*, Nautili, Corals, and small Serpulæ. Top block, 1 ft. 8 in.; bottom block, 1 ft. 2 in. 2 10

† Coral (small species).
* *Parasmilia sp.*
† *Micraster breviporus*, Ag.
† *Serpula gordialis* (?), Schlot.
† *Rhynchonella plicatilis*, Sow.
† *Rhynchonella Reedensis*, Ether.
† *Terebratula semiglobosa*, Sow.
† *Arca* (small species).
* *Inoceramus cuneiformis*, d'Orb.
† *Inoceramus Cuvieri* (?), Sow. (shell half-inch thick).

* *Modiola sp.*
* *Ostrea hippopodium* (?), Nilss.
† *Ostrea lateralis*, Nilss.
† *Spondylus spinosus*, Sow.
† *Pleurotomaria depressa*, Mant.
† *Pleurotomaria perspectiva* (?), Mant.
* *Turbo gemmatus*, Sow.
† *Turbo sp.*
†* *Ammonites Prosperianus*, d'Orb.
† *Baculites sp.*
† *Nautilus lævigatus*, d'Orb.

b. NODULAR CHALK, consisting of hard concretionary lumps, some fibrous, in a softer matrix, interspersed with wavy streaks of grey marl 2 8

† *Holaster planus*, Mant.
† *Micraster breviporus*, Ag.
† *Rhynchonella plicatilis*, Sow.

† *Terebratula semiglobosa*, Sow.
† *Inoceramus cuneiformis* (?), d'Orb.
† *Natica sp.*

		ft.	in.
5*a*. GREEN-COATED NODULES AND PYRITES		0	2

† *Terebratula semiglobosa*, Sow.

		ft.	in.
c. NODULAR CHALK, same as 5*b*.		6	6

† *Micraster breviporus*, Ag.	† *Ostrea vesicularis*, Lamk.
† *Terebratula semiglobosa*, Sow.	

		ft.	in.
b. SOFT GREY MARL .		0	4
4*a*. COMPACT GREYISH CHALK of variable hardness, weathering white with grey nodules, less concretionary than the beds above, and separating into larger blocks. Contains a few scattered flints near the top. *Spondylus spinosus* is abundant		12	0

* *Peltastes Wiltshiri*, Wright	† *Ammonites peramplus*, Mant.
* *Palæastacus Dixoni*, Bell (five specimens).	* *Belonostomus cinctus*, Ag. (five parts of jaws).
† *Terebratula semiglobosa*, Sow.	* *Beryx radians*, Ag.
* *Inoceramus Brongniarti*, Sow.	* *Beryx* (three specimens).
* *Inoceramus sp.*, concentrically ribbed.	* *Corax heterodon*, Reuss
* *Ostrea vesicularis*, Lamk.	* *Macropoma* (three coprolites).
* *Spondylus latus*, Sow.	* *Otodus obliquus* (?), Ag. (two teeth).
* *Spondylus spinosus*, Sow.	* *Ptychodus sp.* (fin ray).

The following additional species were also obtained by Dr. J. Stevens from this pit, but we are unable to refer them to particular beds.

* (*Cephalites bullatus*) (?), T. Smith	* *Inoceramus Lamarckii* (?), Brong.
* *Plocoscyphia* (*Brachiolites*) *foliacea*(?), T. Smith	* *Lima consobrina* (?), d'Orb.
* *Ventriculites infundibuliformis* (?), S. Wood.	* *Lima* (?) *spinosa*, Sow. in Dixon
	* *Lima sp.*
* *Ventriculites radiatus*, Mant.	* *Opis sp.*
Orbitolina globularis.	* *Pecten jugosus* (?), Sow. in Dixon
* *Discoidea minima*, Ag.	* *Pecten quadricostatus*, Sow.
* *Discoidea subuculus*, Klein	*Pecten sp.*
* *Palæastacus sp.* (claw and carapace).	* *Plicatula sp.*
* *Crania Parisiensis*, Defr.[1]	* *Ammonites Mantelli* (?), Sow.
* *Rhynchonella Grasiana* (?), d'Orb.	* *Drepanephorus canaliculatus*, Eg. Vertebræ of, (= Spinax major, Ag.)
* *Rhynchonella Martini*, Mant.	
* *Terebratulina striata*, Wahl.	
* *Hippurites Mortini*, Dixon (= *H. cornuvaccinum*, Bronn).	* *Ptychodus decurrens*, Ag.
	* *Ptychodus mammillaris*, Ag.

The letters appended to the beds are those used by Dr. C. Barrois in his description of this pit,[2] with the addition however of the higher rock-bed 5*e*, which corresponds with that seen in the Litchfield railway cutting four miles distant.

Zone of Terebratulina gracilis.—This zone, 4*a*, has been worked in the pit to the depth of 17 feet, of which the lower 5 feet are now

---

[1] I am uncertain as to the locality of this specimen (J. S.). [2] *Recherches*, p. 47.

concealed by *débris*. The fine series of fish and crustaceans are those which are elsewhere met with at this horizon; as at Lewes, Winchester, Warminster, etc.

Zone of Holaster planus.—I have distinguished between the upper or hard portion of 5*b*, in which I have not found *Holaster planus*, and the lower or nodular portion, in which it is fairly abundant. The similar lithological character of 4*c*, and the occurrence in it of *Micraster breviporus*, lead me to include it in the same zone. I therefore regard the marl band 4*b* as the lower limit of this zone. The occurrence of Nautili and Corals in 5*c* assimilate it also with 5*b*; so that the line of rusty flints at the top of this bed may be taken as the upper limit. The thickness of this zone is therefore 13 feet. One specimen of *Nautilus lævigatus* from the lower rock-bed measured 7 × 4½ inches. In the line of nodules, 5*a*, I found but one fossil: the "nombreux fossils" which C. Barrois quotes from this bed are evidently from the top of 5*b*, where they are abundant, and the matrix of which is similar.

Zone of Micraster breviporus.—In 5*d* I found two large specimens of *Holaster* 2¾ inches in length, with a flat base and faint marginal sulcus—a form which appears to characterise higher beds than the normal *H. planus*, and corresponds with *H. placenta*, Ag.[1] 5*d* is not well exposed at Stoke, but at Litchfield it contains numerous *M. breviporus*, and, together with 5*e*, corresponds with Mr. W. Hill's "Zone of *Micraster breviporus*".[2] This zone amounts to 16 feet at Litchfield; its thickness here is uncertain.

The Stoke pit accordingly comprises:

		ft.	in.	Zone	ft.	in.		ft.	in.
f.	Softish chalk	3	9	} Micr. breviporus	13	6	Senonian	13	6
e.	Upper rock-bed	2	0						
d.	Softish chalk	7	9						
c.	Sponge bed	1	0						
b.	Lower rock-bed	2	10						
b.	Nodular chalk	2	8	} Hol. planus	13	2			
5*a.*	Nodules		2				Turonian	25	6
c.	Nodular chalk	6	6						
b.	Marl		4	} T.-ina. gracilis	12	4			
4*a.*	Compact chalk	12	0				Total	39	0

The dip of the beds is not appreciable.

Zone of Micraster cortestudinarium.—This chalk is just seen above Butler's Farm, midway between Stoke and St. Mary Bourne, where a small scarp on the hill-side shows a dip of 3° S.

[1] Cotteau, *Echinides fossiles du Dept. de l'Yonne*, pl. 82, fig. 3.
[2] *Quart. Jour. Geol. Soc.*, vol. xlii, p. 240 (1886).

To this zone also C. Barrois has referred[1] the pit at Bedlam's Copse, near the top of the hill half a mile W. of St. Mary Bourne on the Andover road. This pit shows 15 feet of soft chalk with flints rather decayed, and two lines of tabular flint 2 or 3 inches thick and 18 to 21 inches apart.

† *Cardiaster* (?).
† *Micraster cortestudinarium* (?), Gold.
† *Serpula plexus*, Sow.
† *Inoceramus Cuvieri* (?), Sow.
† *Ostrea sp.* (small).

By a singular coincidence this pit has been opened on the axis of a small anticlinal, which after a frost is visible on both sides of the pit, so that its strike, E. 10° N., can be measured with considerable accuracy. As seen on the west side of the pit, under the copse, the dip is about 11° to the N. and S., diminishing quickly towards the S. of the pit to 7° or 8°, and according to the Survey to the same amount on the N. The evidence for the horizon of this pit is insufficient. The *Micraster* I found is intermediate between *cortestudinarium* and *coranguinum*; and I think it equally probable that the beds belong to the base of the latter zone, corresponding with those of the whiting pit at Whitchurch. If they are the top of the former, then the valley at St. Mary Bourne, which is 120 feet below the pit, should cut into Turonian.

Zone of Micraster Coranguinum.—The best section of this chalk is in the New Barn Cutting on the South Western Railway, between Hurstbourne and Whitchurch Stations, where there is a dip to the W. of ½°. The following species were obtained by Dr. J. Stevens from this cutting during its construction in 1848. *Echinoconus conicus* is the most abundant.

* *Coniferous wood* (silicified).
* *Cephalites paradoxus*, T. Smith
* *Ventriculites impressus*, T. Smith
* *Bourgueticrinus ellipticus*, Miller
* *Cidaris clavigera*, König.
* *Cidaris hirudo*, Sorig.
* *Cidaris perornata*, Forbes
* *Cidaris sceptrifera*, Mant.
* *Cyphosoma Konigi*, Mant.
* *Echinoconus conicus*, Breyn.
* *Echinocorys gibbus*, Lamk.
* *Epiaster gibbus*, Schlüt.
* *Goniaster Parkinsoni*, Forbes
* *Goniaster uncatus*, Forbes
* *Micraster coranguinum*, Forbes
* *Ophiura serrata*, Roemer
  Pentacrinus sp. (one plate on a flint).
* *Serpula plexus*, Sow.
* *Terebratula semiglobosa*, Sow.
† *Inoceramus Cuvieri* (?), Sow.
* *Lima Hoperi*, Mant.
* *Ostrea curvirostris*, Nilss. in d'Orb.
* *Pecten cretosus*, Defr.
* *Spondylus spinosus*, Sow.
* *Corax heterodon*, Reuss (=*C. falcatus*, Ag.).
* *Lamna cuspidata* (?), Ag.
* *Lamna elegans*, Ag.
* *Otodus appendiculatus*, Ag.
* *Oxyrhina crassidens*, Dixon
* *Ptychodus latissimus*, Ag.
* *Ptychodus mammillaris*, Ag.
* *Ptychodus polygyrus*, Ag.

---

[1] *Recherches*, p. 47.

The same beds are seen on the west side of the valley at Chapmansford, where C. Barrois obtained the following species.[1]

Echinoconus conicus, Breyn.
Echinocorys gibbus, Lamk.
Micraster coranguinum, Forbes
Thecidea Wetherellii, Morris

Inoceramus sp.
Ostrea hippopodium, Nilss.
Plicatula sigillina, Wood.

The railway cuttings which continue from Chapmansford for two miles to the W.S.W. to beyond the Devil's Ditch are also in the same zone, *Echinoconus conicus* being the prevailing fossil. The dip of the beds in this direction is *nil*, but they are slightly higher—the line of railway rising 20 ft. above the level at New Barn—and are described by Dr. Stevens as less fossiliferous. In the Devil's Ditch cutting there is a very good exposure of chalk, and I obtained the following species:

† *Bourgueticrinus ellipticus,* Mill.
† *Echinoconus conicus,* Breyn.
† *Micraster coranguinum,* Forbes
† *Inoceramus Cuvieri* (?), Sow.

† *Ostrea* (small sp.)
† *Belemnitella vera,* Miller
† Fish remains.

Zone of Marsupites.—To this division we may probably refer the three following pits:

(A) An old pit at the top of Stoke Hill, now grassed over, is about 15 ft. deep in chalk with large flints.

* *Cyphosoma* (three large specimens).

(B) A small pit in a field near the road, half a mile W. of Upper Wyke Farm and a quarter of a mile N.E. of Ridges Copse, shows 12 ft. of soft white chalk with two lines of large flints and two lines of tabular flint. Dip, 5° S. Spines of *Cidaris clavigera* are abundant in this chalk, and also in the flints in the adjoining field.

† *Cidaris clavigera,* König.
† *Echinocorys gibbus,* Lamk.

† *Micraster sp.*
† *Rhynchonella plicatilis,* Sow.

(C) At Frenche's Brick-kiln, about half a mile west of (B), is a soft white chalk with lines of flints about 3 ft. apart. This chalk is burnt for lime, and is mined in galleries at the bottom of a shaft 50 ft. deep; the roof being firmer at this depth. *Echinocorys* is found here, but not *Belemnitella*, and *Micraster* has not been noticed. The dip can be seen in an old pit 350 yards N. of the kiln, where a stratum of vein flint dips 3½° S.W. and 3° S. The surface-slope of the hill is 2° S.S.W.

In Frenche's Copse, about three quarters of a mile to the N., this chalk is capped by Eocene material, so that it is probably not much

[1] *Recherches,* p, 48.

below the original surface of the chalk plain of denudation. And since at Harewood and Bere Hill, only four miles to the S., the beds of this plain belong to the zone of *Belemnitella quadrata*, the beds here are probably not lower than the zone of *Marsupites*.

In addition to the species from the Upper Chalk already mentioned, the following are quoted by Dr. J. Stevens[1] from the Upper Chalk and flints[2] of St. Mary Bourne.

* *Cephalites longitudinalis*, T. Smith[3]
Chenendopora Michelini, Hinde (= *Polypothecia infundibulum*, Benett).
Clionia sp.
* *Doryderma (Spongia) ramosum*, Mant.
* *Plocoscyphia (Choanites) flexuosa* (?), Mant.
Plocoscyphia (Brachiolites) foliacea, T. Smith
Plocoscyphia (Spongus) labyrinthica, Mant.
* *Siphonia (Choanites) Königi*, Mant.
Ventriculites alcyonides, Mant.
Ventriculites decurrens (cavatus), T. Smith
* *Ventriculites radiatus*, Mant.
Orbitolina globularis
Rotalia aspera
Textularia elongata
Textularia globosa.
* *Parasmilia (Monocarya) centralis*, Mant.
* *Parasmilia (?) (Monocarya) cultrata* (?), Lons.

* *Porosphæra globularis*, Phil.
* *Porosphæra Woodwardi*, Carter
Alecto ramea, Blainv.
Diastopora ramosa, Mich.
Escharina intricata, Lons.
Flustra inelegans, Lons.
Petalopora pulchella, Roem.
Pustulopora pustulosa, Lons.
Goniaster, sp.
* *Marsupites Milleri*, Mant.[4]
* *Marsupites ornata*, Mill.[4]
* *Rhynchonella octoplicata*, Sow.
* *Terebratulina striata*, Wahl.
* *Thecidea Wetherellii*, Morris
* *Inoceramus Cuvieri*, Sow.
Inoceramus sp.
Lima (?) spinosa, Sow. in Dix.
Modiola sp.
Ostrea vesicularis, Lam. (= *O. globosa*, Sow.)
Pecten quadricostata, Sow.
Pecten quinquecostata, Sow.
Pleurotomaria sp.
* *Enchodus halocyon*, Ag. (pair of jaws).[5]

EOCENE REMANIÉ.—In Frenche's Copse (now ploughed up), at the north-east corner of Doles Wood, three quarters of a mile north of the kiln, and about half a mile north-west of Stokehill Farm, is a pit showing some 10 ft. of soft reddish-brown loam, the upper 6 ft. of which contains angular broken flints. This pit is thus described by

---

[1] *Descriptive List*, pp. 9-12.
[2] Some of the flint casts in the Reading Museum are of undetermined species of *Lima* and *Pecten*.
[3] The synonymy of these sponges I have revised in accordance with Dr. G. J. Hinde's nomenclature, but the specimens require to be redetermined.
[4] The R. M. contains a made-up specimen of single plates of these species.
[5] This specimen is probably, but not certainly, from the Upper Chalk (J. S.).

the Survey.[1] 'Within the north-eastern corner of Doles' Wood by Stokehill Farm, a ferruginous loam is dug for making bricks. At the depth of about twenty feet a bed of clay three feet thick was pierced, under which was a layer of flints resting on another bed of loam, and this last was bored into for five feet without any chalk being met with. It was stated by one of the workmen that borings had been made nearly throughout the whole extent of the wood, and that the loam did not extend more than a hundred yards from the pit in any direction,—chiefly towards the north-west." These beds, therefore, consisting apparently of Plastic Clay materials, occupy a large hollow or pipe, into which, being of a porous nature, they have been lowered bodily by the surface solution of the underlying chalk.

Assuming that the beds have not dropped many feet from their original position, we have data for ascertaining approximately the thickness of the Upper Chalk. The level of the ground at the pit is about 610 ft.; and the summit of the hill, 250 yds. to the N.N.W., is 624 ft. If therefore we take the line of rusty flint (341 ft. O. D.) at the foot of Stoke Hill as the base of the Upper Chalk (Senonian), we get 283 ft., or approximately 300 ft., as the thickness of this division.

We have here one of the stages of the overlap of the Hampshire Eocenes, which rest on successively lower beds of the Chalk as they approach the London Basin; probably the result of marine denudation in the interval between Cretaceous and Eocene times.

VALLEY DEPOSITS.—On a hill half a mile north of Stoke, and a quarter of a mile west of Slade Bottom Farm, are old disused clay-pits[2] in dark stiff red clay with angular and broken unrolled flints. This is the "Clay-with-flints" of authors. The flints are much decayed. The clay has been worked to a depth of 5 or 6 ft. It occupies the highest point of the hill, and is 450 ft. above Ordnance datum. The materials of this deposit are such as would be derived from the denudation of the Upper Chalk and the Plastic Clay. As it is 150 ft. below the Frenche's Copse deposit, and 160 ft. above the Bourne, it may be regarded as of Post-Eocene age, and related to the present valley system.

The valley of the Bourne cuts into the chalk to a depth of 300 ft., forming on its south-west side a steep scarp with precipitous coombs. On its north-east side the valley rises about 150 ft. to a kind of plain, which slopes gradually up to the north-east, and is cut into by a number of side valleys or bottoms. These bottoms are dry, and are filled to a depth of from 1 to 8 ft. with large angular flints, which pass

---

[1] Memoir to Sheet 12, p. 28; reprinted in *General Memoirs*, vol. iv, p. 104, No. 3.

[2] Stevens, *Geological Notices*, p. 75.

below into a chalky rubble, and this into rotten chalk; indicating the lines of the subsoil drainage.

The alluvial flat of the Bourne is underlain by several feet of washed subangular gravel, mixed with a good deal of fine broken gravel and sand, but no clay. Many of the larger flints are but slightly rolled. Three feet of this gravel are exposed in a pit near the Bourne in a field between Crystal Abbey and Lower Link Farm.

These later valley drifts and their contents have been noticed in an earlier part of this volume.

The Rarer Wild Flowers.

As during lengthened residence I was enabled to observe some of the rarer wild plants, or became aware of their localities through the information of others, I have thought that, as a mere record, a list of such might be of some future service. Mr. C. B. Clarke, in 1866, published an excellent list of the *Flowering Plants, Ferns, and Mosses*, observed by himself in the neighbourhood of Andover. Several plants recorded in the Andover list, as found around St. Mary Bourne, were noticed by myself many years ago; while a few to be found in the present list, of which may be named *Ophioglossum vulgatum* (Sowerby), and *Cuscuta Europæa* (Sowerby), are not in Mr. Clarke's list. Mr. Clarke selected Prof. Babington's nomenclature, and the fact that his list contains 650 plants out of 1,800 in Babington shows the pains he was at in searching out their localities. It is not my intention to do more than furnish a list of the rarer plants and their habitats. A few specimens in the following list, from the locality of Thruxton, were recorded by the late Mr. Henry Reeks.

Thalictrum flavum. Link Meadows. J. S.
Ranunculus heterophyllus. St. Mary Bourne. Clarke.
    „   *peltatus.*   Do.   Clarke.
    „   *parviflorus.* Swampton. J. S.
Papaver hybridum. Weed of cultivation, Hurstbourne Priors. Clarke.
Arabis hirsuta. Hurstbourne Hanger. Clarke. J. S.
Viola Reichenbachiana. ⎫
    „   *canina.*   ⎬ These are all given as found at Thruxton by the late Mr. H. Reeks, F.L.S.
    „   *flavicornis.* ⎭
Dianthus armeria. Derrydown Copse, west side, St. Mary Bourne. J. S.
Silene conica. Thruxton, in 1865. Reeks.
Cerastium arvense. Finkley, along Roman road. Clarke. J. S.
Hypericum quadrangulum. Link Meadows. J. S.
Hypericum calycinum. ⎫
    „   *Anglicum.*   ⎬ Reeks, Thruxton list; outcasts from gardens.
Geranium pratense. Corner of a field, east of the Roman Camp, under Fosbury Wood. J. S.
Geranium lucidum. On scattered flints, Wadwick Road. J. S.
Oxalis acetosella. Under Bedlams' Copse, St. Mary Bourne. J. S.
    „   *corniculata.* Reeks. Collingbourn Wood, 1865.
Vicia tetrasperma. Less frequent than *hirsuta.* Derrydown Copse. J. S.
Genista tinctoria, Eggbury drove. J. S.
Sarothamnus scoparius. Dowles' Wood. Clarke. J. S.
Lathyrus aphaca. Near Fox Cottage. Clarke.
Alchemilla vulgaris. Near Hillier's Lot. J. S.

Rubus idæus. Highdown Camp, Fosbury. J. S.
Potentilla argentea. Near Stoke. J. S.
Prunus avium. Dowles' Wood. Clarke. J. S.
Rosa rubiginosa. Hurstbourne Priors. Clarke. J. S.
Epilobium angustifolium. Wallop Hill. Clarke. J. S.
   „   *tetragonum.* Link Water Meadow. J. S.
   „   *palustre.*   Do.   J. S.
Circæa lutetiana. St. Mary Bourne. J. S.
Schleranthus annuus. Hillier's Lot. J. S.
Sedum telephium. Upper Wyke, also at the edge of Wakes'-wood Copse. J. S.
   „   *fabaria.* Hurstbourne Priors. Clarke.
   „   *acre.* The Ox-drove, near Fawconer's Down. Clarke. J. S.
Ribes rubrum. Escaped from gardens. Wallop Hill. J. S.
Saxifraga tridactylites. Near Fawconer's Down. Clarke.
   „   *granulata.* Finkley, 1869. J. S.
Pimpinella magna. Hurstbourne Ridge. Clarke.
Bupleurum rotundifolium. Chapmansford fields. J. S.
Caucalis daucoides. Near Hillier's Lot. J. S.
Viscum album. On Whitethorns, Hurstbourne Park. Clarke. J. S.
Galium cruciatum. St. Mary Bourne. J. S.
Dipsacus pilosus. Formerly on the side of the road below Chapmansford; apparently extinct there now (found a specimen there in 1862). J. S.
Matricaria chamomilla. Escaped specimen found by the side of Derrydown Copse. J. S.
Tanacetum vulgare. Faccombe Woods; introduced from there into gardens. Clarke. J. S.
Gnaphalium luteo-album. Hurstbourne Tarrant. Clarke.
   „   *sylvaticum.* Dowles' Wood. Clarke.
Senecio campestris. Hurstbourne Hanger. Clarke.
Centaurea cyanus. St. Mary Bourne. J. S.
Cichorium intybus. Middle Wyke. J. S.
Tragopogon porrifolius. St. Mary Bourne; escaped from Dipland garden. J. S.
Picris hieracioides. Hurstbourne Hanger. Clarke.
Lactuca muralis.   Do.   Clarke.
Phyteuma orbiculare. Barton Stacey. Clarke.
Vinca major. Escaped from gardens. St. Mary Bourne. J. S.
Cuscuta Europæa. Parasitic on nettles at Binley in 1864. J. S.
Cynoglossum officinale. Behind the Cricketer's booth, Hurstbourne Park. J. S.
Barago officinalis. Escaped from gardens, St. Mary Bourne. J. S.
Echium vulgare. Hillier's Lot. J. S.
Myosotis sylvatica. Highdown Camp, Fosbury. Clarke. J. S.
Hyoscyamus niger. Wadwick, round the pond, in 1865. J. S.
Verbascum blattaria. Under Dowles' Wood. Clarke.
Antirrhinum majus. Garden plant. St. Mary Bourne. J. S.
Linaria cymbalaria. On garden walls, Hurstbourne Tarrant and Woodhouse. J. S.
Veronica montana. Wallop Hill, 1860. Clarke. J. S.
Nepeta cataria. Lower Wyke. J. S.
Lamium purpureum. Middle Wyke. J. S.
Ajuga reptans. Found a white variety at Dunley in 1860. J. S.
Primula elatior. Gaston Copse, near Hillier's Lot. J. S.
Lysimachia vulgaris. Link Meadow. J. S.
Rumex acetosella. Doiley Down. J. S.

Daphne mezereum. Hedge-row, Dipland Hill, 1863, now almost extinct, used in gardens. J. S.
Daphne laureola. Trinley Copse and some other woods, St. Mary Bourne. J. S.
Euphorbia lathyris. Escaped from gardens. J. S.
Parietaria officinalis. (Sowerby) on Bourne Church, 1866. J. S.
Urtica urens. Binley. J. S.
Juniperus communis. Eggbury drove. J. S.
Paris quadrifolia. Hurstbourne Hanger. Clarke.
Orchis morio. Wallop Hill. J. S.
 „ *pyramidalis.* Wallop Hill and Doiley Down. J. S.
 „ *ustulata.* Kimpton. Reeks.
Gymnadenia conopsea. Doiley Down. J. S.
Habenaria viridis. Hurstbourne Hanger. Clarke.
 „ *bifolia.* Tangley, in 1862, and Moor's Wood, St. Mary Bourne. J. S.
 „ *chlorantha.* Moor's Wood, St. Mary Bourne. J. S.
Ophrys muscifera. Hurstbourne Hanger, Clarke, and Doiley Down. J. S.
Herminium monorchis. Hurstbourne Hanger. Clarke.
Ophrys apifera. Top of Doiley Down, near Binley. J. S.
Listera ovata. Derrydown Copse. J. S.
Neottia nidus avis. Becket's Down, under beeches. J. S.
Epipactis latifolia. Wallop Hill. Clarke. J. S.
Cephalanthera grandiflora. Hurstbourne Hanger. Clarke. Wallop Hill, under the beeches. J. S.
Narcissus pseudo narcissus. Warwick and Eggbury, escaped. J. S.
Asparagus officinalis. Found an escaped specimen in the drove near Chapmansford. J. S.
Allium vineale. In Breach field, St. Mary Bourne, in 1866. J. S.
Fritillaria meleagris. ⎫ (Sowerby) St. Mary Bourne. Both escaped from gardens.
Muscari racemosum. ⎭   J. S.
Ophioglossum vulgatum. Port-wine meadow, Link. J. S.
Lastræa dilatata. Found a single specimen at the west end of Derrydown Copse. J. S.
Athyrium filix fæmina. On a stone heap, Doiley bottom. J. S.
Asplenium trichomanes. ⎫ Both found on stumps in Red Lane, near Wad-
 „ *adiantum nigrum.* ⎭ wick. J. S.
 „ *ruta muraria.* Growing on south wall of Bourne Church in 1855, now extinct. J. S.
Scolopendrium vulgare. Side of the road, top of Ashmansworth Hill, in 1870. J. S.
Hordeum sylvaticum. Wallop Hill. Clarke. J. S.

GENERAL INDEX.

Abbot's Anne, 53, 58
Adstock (Stoke), 83
Ælfric, dialogue of, 80
Allen, Seymour Phillips, 180
Allotment Gardens, 264, 265, 266, 267
—— area of, 264
Almshouses, St. Mary Bourne, 211
Andely, Walter, grant by, 100
—— Godfrey, witnesses gift of chapel, 100
Andely, Richerius de, 283
Andover Corporation, Charter granted to, 251
—— West, Deanery of, 216
Anglo-Saxon, time of Henry III, 305
Anton, The, 17
Apiary, Saxon, 183
Apprenticeships under Act of Elizabeth, 249
Arch, Joseph, 10
Arthur, John, vicar, 215
Assize of Bread and Ale, 284, 296
Æthelred, laws of, 93

Babington, nomenclature of, 355
Band of Hope, 295
Baptist Chapel, 294
Barlich, manor of, 161
Batchelor, 211, 250
Barton William de, name of Wallop assumed by, 156
—— Peter de, 156
Beacons, time of Edward VI, 273
—— on Jubilee Eve, 273
—— on Beacon and Danebury hills, 38
Beauchamp, Lord Edward, 184
Beeke, Valentine, Alicia wife of, 154
Beggars, practises of, 196
Bekingham, Thomas, 122
Bell-founders of Reading, 242, 243
Bells, cast at Aldbourne, 243
—— churchwardens at casting of, 235, 243
—— of Hurstbourne Priors, 235
—— of Whitchurch, 235
—— of St. Mary Bourne, 235
—— inscriptions on, 235, 243
Bell-ringing, special occasions of, 246
—— on Old Christmas, 247
Benefactions, 236
Bennett, Dr., Dean of Windsor, 216
Bennet, Charles, Earl of Tankerville, 177

Bequests to the Churches of Farley and Old Stoke, 158
Berkley, Sir Maurice, 158
Berry, John, 286
Best, researches of, at Abbot's Anne, 58
Bible-table, 245, 246
Binley, its derivation, 269
—— Cobbett concerning, 268, 269
—— earlier occupants of, 270
—— Mission Room, 295
Bishop's Park, enclosure of, by tenants, 105
Blount, Joseph, 269
—— wayfarers fed by, 269
Board School, teachers of, 286
—— attendance at, 287
—— grants to, 287
Boc-land, 76
Bonesetters, 241, 242
Borderers (*Bordarii*), 91
Borhunte, Sir John, 120, 121
Borlase, Sir John, 176
—— William, 176
Boundaries and Polling District, 260
Bourne, Hugh, 10
Bourne, St. Mary, held by Mone, 114
—— held by Nevill, 115
—— Revel Monday, 189
—— Revel Sunday, 191
—— Revel Club, 192
—— Revel, stage erected at, 192
—— Revel, rules observed at, 192
Brank or Scolds'-Bridle, 197
Brede House, architecture of, 140
Breach-field, implements found in, 51
Brick-earths, 16
Bradshaw, John, 171
Bridges, Roman and Saxon, 199
Brills of Andover, 319
British earthworks, 55
—— *oppida*, 54
—— remains at Finkley, 65
—— tribes in Hants and Berks, 40
—— tribes, boundaries of, 40
Brocas, Sir Bernard, 120, 121, 274
—— held in Husseburn, 120
—— descendants of, 121
—— funeral of, 121
—— Sir Richard, 157
—— William, 121, 122
—— Bernard, 121, 122
—— Thomas, 121
—— John, 121, 122

Brocas, Sir Oliver, 121
—— Sir John, 121
—— Sir Pexsall, 123
—— Sir Bernard, beheaded, 121
Brocas, arms of, 124
Bucket's Down, 271
Bull, John, account of floods by, 10
Burial ground, consecration of, 230
—— presentation of, 230
Burials' Book, aged persons from, 231
—— affidavits of, 228
Burne (Bourne), Chapel of, 218
—— derivation of, 3
—— change of in *Domesday*, 4
Burrough, Rev. John, 291
Burton, Rev. Richard, 223

Calendar of State Papers relative to Chute and Finkley, 332
Calleva, Roach Smith on, 65, 67
—— Sir R. C. Hoare on, 65
—— authorities concerning, 66
Camden on Longbank, 56
—— William, Clarenceux, 119
Carnarvon, Earl of, 180
Cave-men, 22
Caverns on Cissbury Hill, 29
"Cert-money," 134
Chalk, its tenacity of water, 5
—— hills, tertiaries on, 6
—— reservoirs in, 6
—— line of saturation in, 8
—— at New Barn Cutting, 350
—— at Chapmansford Cutting, 351
—— at Upper Wyke Farm, 351
—— section of, at Stoke Hill, 347
—— fossils from, at Stoke Hill, 347
—— zones of, relative to fossils, 348, 349
Chapmansford, 149, 198
—— definition of, 198
Chancel, restoration of, by the Earl of Portsmouth, 202
Charities of St. Mary Bourne, 211
Charter settling disputes between Bishop and Prior, 105
Charter of Denewulf, 74, 80
—— serfs named in, 74
—— Hurstbourne Church referred to in, 74
Chimneys, tax on, 257
"Chinese House," 183
Christmas Boys, Pantomime of, 340, 341
Cissbury Hill, 29
Church expenses, extracts relating to, 242
—— goods, inventory of, 212
—— pillars, links removed from, 248
—— Register of Woodcut, 93
—— Register of St. Mary Bourne, 228
—— Registers, institution of, 228
—— sand-glass, 243
Church, on querns from Cirencester, 27

Church, the, 201
—— orientation of, 201
—— repair of, 201,
—— dimensions of, 203
—— Week aisle of, 204
—— architecture of, 202, 203
—— cross-legged effigy in, 205
Churchwardens of St. Mary Bourne, 224
—— duties of, 224
Churches and Churchyards, usages in, 245
Churchyard, 208, 209, 210
Churchyard, tombs of old families in, 208, 209, 210
Churchyards, festivals held in, 190
Churl's-acre, in Saxon land-boundary, 86
Churls, their services, 79, 86
—— their condition, 79, 80
—— their mode of tillage, 80
—— their common lands, 81
Chute, its derivation, 321
Chute Forest, boundary of, 321
Circular huts used by savages, 33, 34
—— huts of Wilts, Dorset, Devon, and Gloucester, 33
Clare, Gilbert de, 283
Clarke, Spencer, 286
Claybrook, Rev. John, 228
Clothiers of Andover and Newbury, 250
Cobbett at Tangley, 2
—— on North Hampshire, 14
Cobham, Lord Henry, 167
Cock, Sir Henry, 143
Colebrook, Robert, 291
Cold Harbour, derivation of, 57
Cole's Pits, Barrington on, 29
—— Godwin-Austen on, 29
Collier, researches at Redenham, 58
Columbars, 319, 323, 324
Combe Wood, British village in, 45
Common fields at Swampton, 291
—— held in yardlands, 291
—— division of, in strips, 292
Compton, Lord, 167
Compulsory marriages, 254
Conduit, John, 177
Conholt, 321
Cook and others, Bill against, in Exchequer, 328
Corbet, of Morton-Corbet, 167
Court-place, *alias* "Court-Heys", 184, 274
Courts of Attachment, 322
Cromwell, Oliver, 171
—— Richard, 171
"Crooked Billet," sign of, 12
Crown-lands, 101
Crumwell, Thomas, 126, 127
—— Gregory, 126, 127
Culture level of people of Polished Stone Age, 48, 49
Cunnington, William, 28
Dandely, Maurice, 99

Daundely, Robert, Hugh, John, Roger, and Nicholas, 99, 100
—— Keeper of Winchester Castle, 100
Dandely Robert, gallows claimed by, 302
—— Sir Richard, arms of, 205
Danebury Hill, 55
Dawson, Rev. George F., 1, 223
Day, William, 210, 286
De Blois, Henry, Charter of, 200
Deane, Sir James, 167
—— almshouses founded by, 168
De Roches, Martin, held in Husseburn, 119
—— descendants of, 120
—— Hugh, 119
Derrydown copse, 51, 56, 70, 263, 264
Desmond, Earl of, taken prisoner, 163
Devenish, Sir Richard, 140
Devil's Dyke, 41
—— a tribal boundary, 41
—— course of, 41
—— Dr. Guest concerning, 41
—— pit-habitations along, 42
—— named in Saxon boundary, 83
Difference between forest and chase, 322
—— between park and chase, 322
Dew-ponds, Mr. S. Wentworth on, 47
—— Rev. A. C. Smith on, 47
Diocesan Calendar, Winchester, 215
Disease, entries relating to, 238, 239, 240, 241
Domesday, 88, 94, 95, 97, 98, 154, 279, 282
—— tenants at time of, 91, 92
—— mills at time of, 94
—— pannage at time of, 94
Dorothy Bluet, of Bluet Hall, 176
Dowles and Doiley, Disafforestation of, 334, 335
Dowles Lodge, 322
Dowling, 209, 288
Drake v. Etwall, 271
Droves, or early roads, 291
Dunley, Oxenbridges of, 272
—— definition of, 272
Durand of Gloucester, 95

Ealdorman, presiding officer of hundred-court, 87
Earl Fortesque, 180
Easton, Lieut. William, 207
—— Rev. William, 208, 223
Easton, Manor of, 95
Echingham, Sir Thomas, 139
Education, writing as a test of, 232
Edward the Elder, gift of land by, 83
Eggbury, its derivation, 270
—— Romano-British camp at, 271
Eggbury Camp, pits found near, 37
—— used by the Celts, 37
—— Roman coins found in, 37
—— flint implements found near, 37

Eggbury Camp, probably a beacon, 38
—— thought to be Vindomis, 38
Eggbury Down, 244
Elizabeth, wife of Richard Wallop, 158
Emperor Charles V, landing at Dover, 139
Enclosure Acts, 290
Eocene Remanié, 352, 353
Eocenes, sparseness of, in North Hants, 16
Evans, Dr. J. on British coins, 35, 36
Events, entries of, 231
Expeditating of dogs, 324
Eyles, 52, 210

Fairfax, General, 171
Fairs, why held on hills, 189
—— Tanhill, Weyhill, St. Giles's, 189
Family names, origin of, 304, 305
Farley, manor of, 157
—— Church, bequest to, 158
—— seat of Sir W. Valoynes, 157
—— house, destroyed by fire, 157
—— house, rebuilt by first Earl of Portsmouth, 157
—— Church, rebuilt by first Earl of Portsmouth, 158
—— Wallop, licence to hold Court at, 169
Farmer, origin of term, 92
Farmers, houses of, in seventeenth century, 252
—— —— in fifteenth century, 253
Farming in the thirteenth century, 281
—— stock in the thirteenth century, 282
Fawconer, Richard, 184
—— Ralph le, 184
—— arms of, 118
—— Richard, pedigree of, 118
—— William, 118, 119
Fauconer, Ralph le, grant of lands to, 116
—— John le, holds in Husseburn, 117
—— Nicholas, ditto, 117
Fawconer's Manor, De Roches held in, 119
—— Brocas held in, 120
—— Brocas summoned concerning, 124
Feasts and fairs, origin of, 189
Fellows, Coulson, 178
Fellowes, Henry Arthur, 180
—— Hon. Newton, 177
—— arms of, 181
Fine of a Heriot, 134
Finkley, 41, 56, 61, 62, 65, 67, 69, 70
—— British remains at, 41
—— Forest of, 320
—— Park, 330
—— Survey of, 330, 331, 332
Firgrove, interment at, 71
Fogge, Thomas, 142
Folc-land, 76
Font, in St. Mary Bourne Church, 206

General Index.

Font, in Cathedral at Winchester, 206
—— in East Meon Church, 206
Fonts, Norman, 206
Ford Place, 137, 138, 139, 140
Forest, chief officers of, 322
—— Notices, in Crown-rolls, 325
—— of Chute and Finkley, 319
—— part of, in Hurstbourne Manor, 319
—— perambulations of, 326
Fortesque, Hon. Dudley, 180
—— Hugh, first Earl, 180
Forty-shilling freeholders, 293
Foscot, and Foxcot, 56
Fosbury, 9, 17
Foxes, purchased by churchwardens, 244
Franchise Act, 260
Frank-pledge, 297
Franks, Mr., 30
Froxfield, hospital at, 129
Fulling-mill, 94
Fynes, Sir Thomas, 139

Gallows of the Prior at Hurstbourne, 301
Gardiner, Sir Robert, 163
Gaston Copse, British dwellings in, 50
Gate, Sir John, 142, 184
—— grantee of manor, 131
—— beheaded, 131
Gilbert de Clare, 156
Gillingham, Manor of, 99
Gilmour, on the rising of the Test, 9
Gipsies, earth-cooking by, 32, 33
—— "backsword-playing" by, 32, 193
Glacial epoch, 21
Glossary of Provincial Words, 342, 343, 344
Goodyear, Mary, the centenarian, 211
Grain of the thirteenth century, 281
Grange, The, 182, 183, 184
—— burglary of, 299
Grantly, Lord William, 179
Grant of free warren in Hurstbourne, 107
—— of liberties to prior and monks, 103
Grants by Queen Elizabeth to Sir Henry Wallop, 164
Gravelly-clay, and clay-with-flints, 15
Graveyard, evidences in, of earlier interments, 248
Grey, Thomas, Earl, 167
Greenhead, Dr., 180
Griffin, James, Lord, 177
Grimes'-graves, 29
"Groaning-bridge", 139
Grymstede, John de, 157
Gue, William, 286
Guest, Dr., concerning tolls, 57
Gunpowder Plot, entry concerning, 272
Gyselham, William de, King's Attorney, 104

Halswell, Nicholas, 165
Hampshire Benefit Society, 263, 264
—— number of members of, 263

Hampshire Benefit Society, officers of, 263, 264
Hampshire, Sheriffs of, 187
—— North, scenery of, 10
Hampton, of Old Stoke, 158
Handicraftsmen of the thirteenth century, 281
Hand-mills, 27
Hanson, John, 179
Hand-stones, or mullers, 27
Hantone, 97, 99
Harewood Forest, 15
Harleston, Sir Clement, 162
Harrington, Sir James, 172
Harrow-way, derivation of, 198
Harvest Home, 337
—— "booting" connected with, 338
Hastings, Lord Edward, 138
—— imprisonment of, 138
Haydon Fort, a Roman camp, 45
—— ponds within, 46
—— Lansley, on ponds in, 46
Hanyton, Nicholas, a tenant of Hurstbourne, 108
Hearth Tax, 257
—— Egbery tithing, 259
—— Swamton tithing, 259
—— Bingley tithing, 259
—— Weeke tithing, 260
—— Husband Priors, 258
—— Stoake tithing, 258
"Heaven Hill," sheep common on, 291
Hendean (Hennadene), 86
Herbalists of past times, 241
Herberts, The, 209
Herbert, Henry, Lord, 176
—— Lady Eveline, 180
—— Lord, of Cherbury, 176
—— Hereford, Humfrey, Earl of, 156
Heseburn Church, named in papal Bull, 218
Hewett, Hund. of Compton, 40
Hide of land, value of, 90
—— carucate sometimes used for, 90
Hillier's Lot, 397
Hippenscombe, 9, 16
Hoare, Sir R. C., on British settlements, 50
Hogdiggen Copse, pottery found in, 26
—— corner, frequented by gipsies, 32
Holdway, 69, 193, 209, 211, 212, 247, 277
—— Paul, 247
Holy-wells, 191
Hooper, 61, 209, 251, 263, 264, 288, 289
Hopton, Sir Arthur, 272
Horn, a name of longstanding at Week, 306, 307
Horse-mill, 94
Howard, Lord John, of Walden, 276
Hour-glasses, 243
—— used in villages, 244
Hughes, Thomas, 193

Humphrey, Earl of Hereford, 156
Hundred of Clere, 279
—— of Evingar, 303, 304, 305, 307, 308, 309, 313, 314, 317, 318
Hund. Rolls of Beds and Bucks, 90
—— Rolls of Huntingdonshire, 90
Hungerford Lane, a packhorse road, 11
—— its former line, 11, 12
Hurstbourne Fawconers, 117, 120
Hurstbourne, James I and the Queen at, 150
—— Priors, 1, 2, 83, 90, 95, 96, 97, 98, 99, 106, 107, 108, 113, 116, 117, 126, 127, 132, 134, 145, 184, 257, 258, 260, 261, 263, 273, 274, 276, 282
—— Priors, its derivation, and name changes, 2, 3
—— Priors, the Nether Hurstbourne of Alfred, 75
—— gift of land at, by Alfred, 77
—— the Vicarage of, 215
—— manor, *interius*, 99
—— —— *exterius*, 99
—— rents of, 132
—— tithings of, 132
—— at time of *Domesday*, 87
—— Richerius held in, 89
—— Goisfrid held in, 88
—— William held in, 89
—— assessment of, at *Domesday*, 90
—— pound of, 113
—— Priors Church (St. Andrew's), 218, 233
—— Priors Church, antiquity of, 233
—— —— restoration of, 233
—— —— architecture of, 233
Hurstbourne park, 182
Hurstbourne siding, 25
—— Tarrant, 1, 2, 9, 83, 85, 101, 102, 103, 188, 193, 241, 254, 260, 263, 269, 277, 321
—— Tarrant, Saxon boundary of, 85
—— places named in boundary of, 86
—— a royal manor, 3
—— maypole at, 188
—— revel held at, 193
—— "backswording" match at, 194
Hussey, Sir Roger, 157
Hutchinson, Col. John, 172
Hyde Abbey, 321

Ikeneld Street, its various names, 55
Imp Stone (Nymph Stone?), 55
Incent, John, Master of St. Cross, 217
Ine, King of the West Saxons, 81
—— *Dooms of*, 81
"Infongenthef", 296
Inquisitions, *post mortem*, relating to Wyke, 113
Interment, Saxon, in Derrydown Copse, 71
—— Romano-Brit., at Firgrove, 71
—— at Cruxeaston, 72

Interment, Roman modes of, 73
—— Greenwell on Celtic, 72
—— near water-springs, 69
—— British, at Stoke, 70
—— Romano-Brit., at Finkley, 70
Intermittent Springs, 7, 191
Itinerary The, Iter XV of, 66
—— Horsley on, 68
—— Iter XII of, 68

Jervois, Sir J. C., 31
Judges of Charles I, survivors of, 172
Justices, management of poor by, 249
Justice-seat, 322

Kell, on pit-habitations, 26
Kemble, J. M., 90
Kemble, on Saxon slaves, 81
Kerry, Rev. Charles, 205
Kildare, Gerald, Earl of, 162
King Alfred, the will of, 74
—— buried in Old Minster, 78
—— body of, removed to New Minster, 78
King, grant by, to Dean and Chapter, 125
Kingesley, John Fitz-Williams de, 133, 184
Kingsclere Hundred, 256
Kingesmyll, Dean of Holy Trinity, 125
Kingsmill, Richard, 119, 184
—— Richard, funeral certificate of, 118
"Kingsland", 98
Kingsmill v. Oxenbridge, 149
Knights, The, Reading bell-founders, 235, 236
"Knoll-ditches", 55

Labourers, condition of, in eighteenth century, 252
—— houses of, in fifteenth century, 253
Ladle Hill, 47, 55
Lady Monson, gift to, 145
Land-boundary, in Charter of Edward, 81, 82
—— place-names mentioned in, 83
Lands, Lammas, 81
Lassels, Col. Francis, 172
Lateran, Council of, 88
Lay Subsidies, Swampton, 303, 309, 312, 315, 316, 318
—— Binley, 304, 307, 309, 310, 313, 314, 315, 316, 318, 319
—— Hurstbourne Priors, 305, 309, 313, 314, 316, 317, 319
—— Stoke, 303, 307, 308, 311, 313, 315, 317, 319
—— Week, 304, 307, 309, 311, 313, 315, 316, 318
—— Eggbury, 304, 308, 309, 312, 314, 315, 317, 318, 319
—— Bourne, 302, 308, 310, 313, 314, 315, 316, 317, 319
—— Hurstbourne Tarrant, 307

Leeke, Ralph Merrik, 180
Leland, 76
Litchfield, 83, 244, 260, 271
Livingstone, Dr., on querns used by Africans, 21
Loan, The, 255, 256, 257
Lockhart, Samuel John Ingram, 223, 263
Lockhart, C., 19
Loftus, Adam, Archbishop of Dublin, 163
Longley, Johan, death of, during removal, 251
Longman, 208, 211, 275, 276, 288, 289
—— Mrs. Hannah, 204
—— Thomas, grant of land by, 230
—— John, grant of land by, 230
—— early notice of, 276
—— myth concerning, 276
—— Thomas, of Finkley, 61, 321
Longman, Elizabeth Ann, grants of land by, 230, 295
Longsword, Earl of Salisbury, 319
Lord de la Warre, 143
—— grant to, 334
Lord Northampton, 277
Lower, M. A., 247
Lower Week, 11, 51, 59
Lucy, Sir Thomas, of Charlcot, 119
—— Sir William, 119
—— Sir Richard, 144
—— William, 274
Ludlow, Edmund, 171
Lymington, Lord Viscount, 180, 235
Lyster, Sir Mychael, 130
Lywood, J., 263, 288

Major, Richard, 171
Mammoth, The, 18, 48
Mammalia, bones of extinct, 18
Manor Court, 311
—— particulars concerning, 134, 135
—— stocks provided by, 197
Manorial weight, 283
—— weights found in England, 284
Mar, manor of, 99
Martyrs' Book, 244, 245
"Maunch gules", in heraldry, 138
May-Day, customs of, 188
"Mead-Settles", 96
Meadows, Mr., 184
Mealing-stones, 27
Medhursts, The, 210, 241
Medhurst, Alfred, 52, 286
—— Samuel, 241
Medows, Sir Philip, 321
"Meeting of the Cock and Hen", 9, 10
Mere, Walter atte, 277
Mews, for the King's hawks, 154
Mildmay, Sir Henry, 171
"Milk-stones", 31
Mill of eleventh century, 280
Molines, Lord William, 138

Moningham, family of, 138
Monk, General, held grant of Finkley, 321
Monson, Lord William, 172
—— Lady, legacy to, 145
Montachute, Sir John de, 284
Mooring and others, Bill in Exchequer, 329, 330
Moore, 12, 208, 246, 288, 339
—— William, tomb of, 209
"Mop-fairs", attendance of farm-servants at, 190
Mortimer, arms of, 283
—— Ralph de, 280, 283
Mounson v. Oxenbridge, 147
Mountain v. Benton, 260
Mummers, or Christmas Boys, 339, 340, 341
Munday, 210, 251
Munday's Cottage, 242

Nagle, Joseph Chichester, 180
National Schools, trust deed of, 288, 289
—— trustees of, 289
—— date of, 286
—— built by Gue, 286
—— attendance at, 286
—— grants to, 287
—— teachers at, 286
Neale, 210, 338
Netherton Valley, 9
Netley Fort, 3
New Barn, court-leet held at, 311
Newbury, 12, 56
Newton Manuscripts, 178
Newton, Sir Isaac, MSS. of, 177
Nicknames, origin of, 306
Norman-French, infusion of at the Conquest, 305
Nores, The, 52
Norton, Hon. Grace, 179
—— Richard, 171
Nuttle-field, Roman remains found in, 72, 73

"Old Book Chapel", 295
Old Club at St. Mary Bourne, 262, 263
Old Christmas, 247
"Old Christmasers", 340
Old Parish-books, extracts from, 237
Old stone implements, 14
Old Stoke Church, bequest to, 158
Orchard, John, 286
Ox-drove or harrow-way, 198
Oxenbridge, grant of Brede Manor to, 136
—— origin of name, 137
—— long residence of, in Sussex, 138
Oxenbridge, William, Commissioner for Oaths, 138
—— Sir Thomas, 138
—— Martyn, 138

Oxenbridge, Robert, Commissioner for Embankments, 139
—— remarkable story concerning, 139
—— Chancery rolls concerning, 147, 148, 149, 150
—— John, Canon of Windsor, 139
—— Thomas, the lawyer, 139
—— Sir Goddard, 139
—— —— tomb of, in Brede Church, 140
—— Thomas, son of Sir Goddard, 140
—— Andrew, public orator, 141
—— Sir Andrew takes Oath of Allegiance, 141
—— Elizabeth, 141
—— Sir Robert, purchaser of Hurstbourne, 141
—— Constable of the Tower, 142
—— —— funeral of, 143
—— Sir Robert, of 1638, 145
—— —— remarkable illness of, 247
—— Ursula, wife of Sir J. Monson, 145
—— William, of Dunley, 271, 272
—— Sir Robert, of 1616, 145, 272
—— —— will of, 274
—— Henry and Gabriel, 272
—— Richard and John, 272
—— William, daughters of, 272
—— —— sisters of, 272
—— Mrs. "Barbarra", 143, 274
Oxenbridge, arms of, 146
—— pedigree of, 146
—— v. Mounson, 148
—— notices of, in State Papers, 145, 151, 152
Overton borough, 255, 256
—— hundred, 256

Packhorses, 12
—— highwaymen of period of, 13
Packhorse way, 11
Page, John, 10, 286, 294, 295
Papists, levy made on, 171
Pares, Sir Francis, 167
Parham, 209
Parish, its derivation, 88
Parliament, members of, for Andover, 185
—— members of, for Whitchurch, 186
Parochial customs, 336
—— expenses, extracts relating to, 248, 249, 250, 251, 252, 253, 254
Pastrow hundred, 256
"Paunch-kettles", used by the Assineboins, 31
Pannage, payment of, 101
Pease, Sir Joseph, 181
Pen-pits, Lieut.-Gen. Pitt-Rivers on, 28
—— Sir R. C. Hoare on, 28
—— Mr. T. Kerslake on, 28

People of Polished Stone Age cognate to Basques, 53
Perambulation of Finkley, 326
—— of Chute, 327
—— of Doiley, 327, 328
Pews, free and appropriated, 231
Pexsall, Ralph, 123
—— Sir Richard, 123
Pillion, use of, by farmers, 250
Pipe Roll, 101
"Pipowder", Court of, 251
Pierrepont, heiress to Duke of Kingston, 321
Pit-dwellings, Hurstbourne Siding, 25
—— flint pitching in, 25
—— circularity of, 25
—— sloping passages of, 26
—— Albert Way on, 26
—— pottery found in, 26
—— mealing-stones found in, 26
—— bones found in, 29
—— bone implements found in, 30
—— Neolithic implements found in, 30
—— cooking conducted in, 31
—— cooking with heated stones in, 31
—— occupied by the Britons, 34
—— British coin found at, 34
—— at Highfield, 26, 27, 31
—— explored by Kell, 26
—— description of coin found at, 35
—— bearing of coin on date of, 36
Pleas of the Crown, 296, 297, 298, 299, 300, 301, 302
Ploughs of the eleventh century, 280
Poare, Richard, 204
Polished stone implements, found at Kimmer, 50
—— found at Ashmansworth, 50
—— found near Gaston copse, 50
—— makers of, occupying woods, 50
—— varieties of, 51, 52
—— places found at, on Test River, 53
—— races who wrought them, 48, 49
Poll-tax, 257
Polling district, 260
Poor, condition of, in eighteenth century, 252
Poore, 209
"Poor-houses" at St. Mary Bourne, 240, 253
Poore v. Oxenbridge, 149
Population of St. Mary Bourne, 261
—— of Hurstbourne Priors, 261
Portsmouth, the Earl of, 233, 236, 263, 264, 285, 288, 289
Portway, 54
—— its course traced, 56
—— names of places on, 56
—— pitched with flints, 57
—— Cold Harbour near, 57
Pound-fold, 86
Pound near Swampton-green, 294
Power, John, of Hurstbourne, 142

General Index.

Valor Ecclesiasticus, 270, 275, 277
Vane, Sir Harry, 170
Valoynes, Nicholas, Lord of Farley, 157
—— Sir William de, 157
Value of goods, time of Edward III, 306
Venables, Nicholas, tithe-farmer, 321
Vernham well, at George Inn, 8
Vernham Dean, in time of King John, 3
—— parish Church-book, 9
Vernon, Sir Henry, 170
Vicars, The list of, 218, 219, 220, 221, 222, 223, 224
Vicar of Hurstbourne, grant to, 214
Village clubs, 262, 263, 264
—— dentist, 242
—— herbalists, 241
—— life, 189
Village-school, kept by Neave, 285
—— kept by Sutton, 285
—— kept by Longman, 285
—— kept by Butcher, 285
Vincent, 37, 209
Vindomis, in relation to Finkley, 65, 69
—— Sir R. C. Hoare on, 65
—— Mr. C. Roach Smith on, 65, 67
—— authorities concerning, 66
—— in relation to Sorbiodunum, 67
Vine or Vyne, The, 124

Walbury Camp, a British oppidum, 42
—— flint implements found in, 44
—— correlated with Cissbury, 44
Walbury, definition of, 43
Waller, Sir William, 170
Wallop, tithes of manor of, at time of *Domesday*, 94
—— or Welhop, 153, 276
—— definition of, 154
—— Sir Henry, 153
—— —— mortgage held by, 153
—— —— specification of manor bought by, 153
—— Matthew de, lands granted to, 154
—— John de, lands in Ireland held by, 155
—— —— State papers relating to, 155
—— Sir Richard, 156
—— Sir Robert, 156
—— Sir Richard, 157
—— Sir Thomas, 157
—— John, son of Sir Thomas, 157
—— Sir Thomas, son of John Wallop, 157
—— Sir Richard, brother of Sir Robert, 158
—— Stephen, 158
—— Sir Robert, 158
—— poll-tax assessed by, 158
—— Giles, son of Stephen, 158
—— Giles, legacy to, 158
Wallop, Sir John, 159
—— serves under Sir E. Howard, 159
—— Admiral of the Fleet, 159
Wallop, Sir John, takes Morlaix, 159
—— Ambassador to France, 160
—— made Knight of the Garter, 160
—— dies at Guisnes, 160
—— Will of, 161
—— twice Commissioner, 160
—— State papers concerning, 161
—— Sir Oliver, knighted, 162
—— Sir William, 162
—— Richard, of Bugbrooke, 162
Wallop, Sir Henry, 162
—— knighted by Queen Elizabeth, 162
—— Constable of Christchurch Castle, 162
—— Treasurer of War, 163
—— purchases lands in Ireland, 164
—— Oliver, killed in Ireland, 165
—— Lady Katherine, bequests to, 165
—— Sir Henry, rebellion quelled by, 163
—— Queen Elizabeth entertained by, 164
—— State papers concerning, 165
—— tomb of, 166
—— Richard (Baron Wallop), 166
—— counsel for Lord Stafford, 166
—— Baxter defended by, 167
—— insulted by Judge Jeffreys, 167
—— Sir Henry, son of the Treasurer, 167
—— knighted by Essex, 167
—— State papers concerning, 168
Wallop, Sir Robert, 170
—— appointed a Commissioner, 171
—— State papers concerning, 171
—— Sir Robert, Member of Privy Council, 172
—— imprisoned for life, 172
—— petitions the Lords, 174
—— breviate of case of, 175
—— petitions the King, 175
—— dies in the Tower, 175
—— Sir Henry, son of Sir Robert, 176
—— John, first Viscount Lymington, 176
—— Bluet, 176
—— John, honors of, 177
—— created Earl of Portsmouth, 177
—— John, second Earl, 178
—— Barton, Master of Magdalen, 178
—— Henry, Groom of Bedchamber, 178
—— Charles, 178, 277
—— Borlase, Aide-de-Camp, 178
—— Bluet, Page of Honor, 178
—— John Charles, third Earl, 179
—— Newton, fourth Earl, 180
—— Isaac Newton, fifth Earl, 180
Wallop, Arms of, 181
Wallops, Saxon manorial lords, 154
Wallingford, flint implements found at 44
Warwick or Wadwick, 53, 268
Water, contamination of, 265, 266, 267

Way, Albert, 26
Wells, depth of, in Test Valley, 7
—— Holy, 191
Week-down, 244
Week, its derivation, 273
—— held by Beynton, 274
—— held by Nevill, 274
—— held by Lister, 274
—— held by Valentine de Wyke, 273
—— held by Fawconer, 274
—— held by Oxenbridge, 274
—— occupied by Longman, 275
—— occupied by Lord Beauchamp, 275
—— occupied by Alexander, 275
—— land held at, by Lady Smyth, 276
—— land held at, by Sir R. Lucy, 276
—— Recovery by Lord Howard, 276
—— tithing, divisions of, 273
Wellesley, Lady Charles, 321
Wellington, of Stockbridge, 157
Wesleyan Chapel, 295
Westlake, on Chalk of St. Mary Bourne, 345
Wexwood Copse, 52
Weyhill Fair, 251
—— Charter of, 251
—— purchase of goods at, by villagers, 251
Wherwell Wood, Dyke in, 41
Whipping-post, 194, 195
Whitchurch, affidavits obtained at, 228
William Rufus, Charter of, 189
William of Wykeham, Will of, 119
Winchester, Bishop of, 218, 219, 220, 221, 222, 223
—— services due to, from prior and tenants, 104

Winchester, Marquis of, 3
—— Gaol of, 154
—— Roman road from, to Cirencester, 55, 57
Wingfield, Sir Robert, 123
Winterbourne, 4
Wix or Wixna, 273
Woollen, burials in, 239
Wool, price of, in ancient times, 239
Woolwich and Reading beds, extent of, 15
Workhouses, 195
Wootton, probable derivation of, 96
Worsley, Sir Henry, 169
"Wooset", or "Ooset-hunting," 336
—— derivation of, 336
Wriothesley, Henry, Earl of Southampton, 170
—— Thomas, 126, 127
Writing as a test of education, 232
Wroxeter, Querns found at, 28
Wyatt, James, 184
Wyke, Nicholas Beynton held, 114
—— Robert Beynton held, 114
—— George Nevill held, 115
—— in reference to Dandeley, 114
—— Valentine de, 273
Wynn, Sir Richard, 170
Wynne Ellis, grant of Hurstbourne to, 124

Yeomen, houses of, in thirteenth century, 252
Yew-tree in Hurstbourne churchyard, 236
Yew-trees, in St. Mary Bourne churchyard, 247
—— Lower, on antiquity of, 247, 248

INDEX TO AUTHORITIES.

Abbrev. Rot. Orig., Hy. III, 99
—— Edw. III, 100
Act, 2 Edward III, 190
Act, 27 Henry VI, 190
Act of Convocation, Henry VIII, 190
Act for Consecration of Churchyards, 230
Act, 22 Henry VIII, 195
Act, 27 Henry VIII, 195
Act, 43 Elizabeth, 239, 248
Act, 7 James I, 249
Act, 30 Charles II, 238
Act, 29 George II, 290
Act, 31 George II, 290
Act, 13 George III, 290
Act, 54 George III, 239
Act, Secta ad Molendinum, 280
Acton, Thesaurus, Eccles. 213
Annals of King James, 167
Anstis's Register (Warner), 160
Antiquary, The, vol. xiv, 207
Archæolog. Institute, 206, 284
Assize Roll, 8 and 9, Ed. II, 270
—— 104, 298, 299, 300
Augmentation Decrees 1346, 124
—— vol. iii, 126, 127

Barrington, Pits in Berks, 29
Barrois, Rec. le Terrain Crétacé, Sup. de l'Angleterre, etc., 1876, 345, 346, 348, 350, 351
Bateman, Vestiges of Derbyshire, 29
Beale Poste, Brit. Archæol. Assoc., 1859, 67
Berry, Hampshire Genealogies, 120, 122, 156, 166, 177, 187
Bill in Exchequer 1647, 322, 328, 329
—— Sign, 20 Henry VIII, 160
—— 27 Henry VIII, 160
Bishop de Lucy's Charter, 3
Blackstone's Commentaries, 88
Bosworth's Anglo-Saxon Dictionary, 1, 2, 12, 50, 51, 52, 188, 198, 272
Brady's History, 92, 129
Brand, Pop. Antiquities, 190
Brayley and Britton, 3, 184
Brewer, Dict. of Phrase and Fable, 159
Brewster, Life of Newton, 177
Bristow and Whitaker, Memoir Geol. Survey to Sheet 12, 353
Bull of Pope Clement III, 218
Burke, Peerage, 181

Burnet, Hist. of Reformation, 141
Burn, Parish Registers, 195, 228, 251
Burrows, Brocas of Beaurepaire, 120, 121

Calendar of State Papers, 141, 142, 145, 150, 165, 168, 170, 171, 203, 216, 272, 332, 333
Calendar of State Papers, Irish, 155, 161
Calendar, House of Lords, 174
Calendarium Rotulorum, 7 John, 3
Camden's Britannia, 56, 68, 128, 154
—— Eliz. Hist. of England, 165
Cart. Roll. A. 3 John, 98
Cathedral Accounts, 173
Cæsar, De Bello Gall., 39
Chalmer's Biograph. Dictionary, 127
Chancery Decree Rolls, 149, 271
—— Miscellany, 147, 148, 153
—— Proceedings, 278
Chancellor's Roll, 102
Chandler, Antiq. of Silchester, 39
Chapter House Books, 26 Henry VIII, 126
Charta de Foresta, Henry III, 94
Charter of Denewulf, 74, 80
—— Edward the Elder, 76, 83
—— Henry de Blois, 200
—— Henry I, 3
—— Henry II, 3
—— Land Exchange, 277
—— Roll, 5 John, 154
—— —— 13 Edward I, 105
—— —— 18 Edward I, 106
—— —— 29 Edward I, 107
—— —— 1349, Edward III, 189
Chronicle of Ethelwulf, 93
Chronicles of Simeon of Durham, 97
—— of Ireland (præd.), 163
Church, Guide to Corinium Museum, 27
Church Register, St. Mary Bourne, 228
Cobbett's Rural Rides, 2, 14, 15, 268, 269
Codex Diplomaticus, No. 397, 137
—— No. 1077, 76
Clarke, Flora of Andover, 16, 355
Close Roll, 19 Henry III, 325
—— 20 Henry III, 325
—— 6 Edward I, 155
Collier, Andover and its Neighbourhood, 58

Commissioners' Report, 6 William IV, 200
Cooper, Notes on Oxenbridge, 152
Coram Rege Roll, Edward I, 79, 104
Cotteau, Echinides Fossiles, 349.
Cowel's Interpreter, 80, 94, 296, 297, 323
Cox, History of Ireland, 163
Cuming, On Hour-glasses, 243
Cunnington, H., British Pit-Dwelling, 29

Dawkins, Cave-hunting, 22
—— Early Man in Britain, 22, 34, 53
Dialogue of Ælfric, tenth century, 80
Dialogus de Scaccario, 101
Dictionary of Phrase and Fable, Brewer, 159
Disafforestation 1662, 334
Domesday Book, 1, 2, 4, 80, 89, 276, 279, 282
Duthy, Sketches of Hampshire, 98, 282
De Banco Roll, 1 Henry VII, 115
—— 16 Henry VII, 120, 124

Evans, Ancient British Coins, 34, 35, 36
—— Physiography, 5
—— The Hertfordshire Bourne, 7
—— Stone Implements of Great Britain, 51
—— on Man and his Earliest known Works, 52
Early Chancery Proceedings, 149
Edwards, Liber de Hyda, 75, 78, 90, 93
Eighty-eighth Canon, 245
Episcopal Archives, 218
Ewald, Our Public Records, 279
Ex. Regist. Buck. (Warner), 160
—— Farley (Warner), 167, 170
—— Holgrave (Warner), 158, 159
Exchequer Bill, 23 Charles I, 327
—— 23 Charles I, 328
—— Receipts, 215
—— Decrees, 217
—— Depositions, 260
Ex. Orig. Pat., 40 Elizabeth, 164
—— 14 James I, 167
Extended Franchise Act, 260
Extracts from old Parish Books, 237

Feet of Fines, 7 Richard II, 120
—— 38 Henry VIII, 131, 274
Fiske, Excursions of an Evolutionist, 49
Fitzherbert, Treatise on Surveying, 292
Forest Proceedings 1200, 323
Foss's Judges, 99, 166
Fox, Col. A. L., Hill Forts, Sussex, 29, 44
—— Cissbury Camp, Sussex, 29, 44
—— Primitive Warfare, 33
Franks, Journ. Brit. Archæol. Assoc., vol. ix, 30
Fuller's Worthies, 118
Fundi Regii, 101

Gerarde's Herball, 241
Godwin-Austen, Journ. Geolog. Soc., 20
Government "Blue Books", 185
Granger's Biog. Hist., 177
Grant to the Vicar of Hurstbourne, 214
Greenwell, Grimes' Graves, 29
—— British Barrows, 39, 53, 72
Guest, *Athenæum*, 57
Guest, Dr., Belgic Ditches, 40

Halliwell's Archaic and Prov. Words, 51, 252, 342
Hall's Chronicles, 159
Harleian MS., 100, 108, 138, 144, 211
Hatcher's Richard of Cirencester, 38
Hearth Tax, 257, 270
Hedges, History of Wallingford, 66
Henry of Huntingdon, Historia, 90
Herbert, History of England, 159
Herbert Præd. (Warner), 160
Hewett, Hund. of Compton, 40, 66
Histoire de la Croisade, 205
History of Craven, 23
Hist. Monasterii de Abingdon, 86
History of Reformation, 152
Historical Manuscripts Com. Seventh Rep., 174, 273
—— Eighth Rep., 178
Hoare, Sir R. C., Ancient Wilts, 28, 57, 65
Hills on the Itinerary, 66
Hill, Journ. Geolog. Soc. 1886, 349
Hodgetts, The Antiquary, 96
Horsley, Brit. Romana, 40
Hume, Rev. A., Remarks on Querns, 29
Hutchin's Dorset, 92
Huxley, Critiques and Addresses, 53
—— Distribution of Races of Mankind, 53
Huxley and Laing, Prehistoric Remains of Caithness, 53

Inquis. Nonarum, 213
Inquis. post mort., Beynton, 205
—— 5 Ed. I, 119
—— 7 Ed. I, 155
—— 9 Ed. III, 108
—— 49 Ed. III, 119
—— 5 Ed. IV, 114
—— 15 Ed. IV, 114
—— 19 Ed. IV, 114
—— 1 Hy. IV, 120
—— 9 Hy. V, 114
—— 12 Hy. VI, 138
—— 32 Hy. VIII, 140
—— 41 Eliz., 165
—— 5 and 6 Philip and Mary, 136
Introduction to Domesday, Ellis, 94
Itinerary of Antoninus, 66, 68
Inventory of Church Goods, 212

Jackson, Notes on Border of Wilts and Hants, 193, 321
Jervoise, Archæolog. Journ., vol. xx, 31
Jones, Intermittent Streams in Berks, 8
Journ. Brit. Archæol. Assoc., 59, 62, 273
Journ. House of Commons 1648, 334
Journ. Geol. Soc. (Quart.) 1886, 349
Joyce, Silchester, in Trans. Newbury Field Club, 66

Kell, Roman Building, 41, 60
—— Journ. Brit. Archæol. Assoc., 26
Kemble, Anglo-Saxon Charters, 78
—— Ancient Charters, 83
—— Codex Diplomaticus, 76, 85
—— Names, Surnames, etc. of Anglo-Saxons, 305
—— Saxons in England, 81, 90
King, Hist. of Berks, 19, 44, 66, 250
Kerry, Hist. of St. Lawrence's Church, 242
—— Hund. of Bray, 122
Kerslake, Caer Pensauelcoit, 28
King Alfred's Will, 2, 76
Kitchin, Chart. Edw. III, 190

Land Revenue, 212
Lansdowne MS., 129
Leland, 76
Letters of Chamberlain, Camden Soc., 165
Liberate Roll, 17 Henry III, 325
Liber Winton, 154
Lower, Sussex Families, 152
Lubbock, Prehistoric Times, 31, 34

Macaulay, History of England, 150, 167
Macfarlane, History of England, 255
Machyn's Diary, 152
Maclauchlan, Silchester, 38, 55
Memoirs, Geological Survey, 6, 15
Memoir to sheet 12, Geolog. Survey, 353
Memoranda Roll, 7 Elizabeth, 136
Manwood, Charta de Foresta, 94
—— Forest Laws, 322
Ministers' Accounts, 8, 125, 134
Moody, Sketches of Hants, 3
—— Domesday, 3, 87, 90, 95

Naturalist in Brit. Columbia, 31
Nature, 21, 22, 29
Nicholas Charles, James I, 169
Nilsson's Scandinavia, 30
Noble's Cromwell, 330
Nom. Equit. in Bibl. Cotton (Warner), 162
Notes and Queries, vol xi, 200
Notes on the Crown Lands, 101

Owen's Celtic Dictionary, 43
Ordnance Map, 6 in., 5, 25, 42, 261

Parker, Domestic Architecture, 140
Parliamentary Writs, 99, 107

Patent Roll, 15 John, 155
—— 17 John, 103
—— 16 Henry III, 103
—— 40 Henry III, 105
—— 15 Ed. II, 107
—— 3 Ed. III, 107
—— 6 Ed. III, 107, 116
—— 9 Ed. III, 108
—— 12 Ed. III, 100
—— 3 Richard III, 115
—— 33 Henry VIII, 125
—— 1 Ed. VI, 128
—— 7 Ed. VI, 131
—— Philip and Mary, 136
Pepys's Diary, 173
Perambulations, Finkley, 326
—— Chute, 199, 327
—— Digherlye, 327
Phené, Uniformity of Design, 69
Pitt-Rivers, Report on Pen-pits, 28
Plac. de quo Warranto, 8 and 9 Ed. I, 302
Placita Forestæ, 325
Pleas of the Crown, 296
Poll-Tax, 257
Pontissera's Register, 200
Porter, Progress of Nations, 290
Prestwich, Proc. Roy. Soc., 1862, 20
—— Mem. Geolog. Survey, sheet 7, 20
—— Wilts, Archæolog. and Nat. Hist. Soc., 20
—— Nature 1887, 21
Prior, Pop. Names of Plants, 188
Proc. Archæolog. Institute, 206
Probate Court Doc., 275
Prynn's Brevia Parl. (Warner), 157
Public Health Act, 265

Recovery, Hill. 1770, 260
—— Easter 1767, 260
—— 4 George III, 179
Reynolds, Prov. Constitutions, 224
Rivers Pollution Commission, 266, 267
Rogers, Six Centuries of Work, etc., 281, 282, 292
Rolls of the Pipe, 100, 101, 102, 320
Rot. Lit. Claus. 99 ; 7 John, 103 ; 154, 155 ; 6 Henry III, 155
Rushworth's Collections, 255
Russell Smith, Brief Hist. Notices, 98, 99, 111, 152
Rymer's Fœd. (Warner), 164, 167

Sandys, Consuetudines Kanciæ, 88
Seebohm, English Village Community, 80, 81, 86, 90, 91, 93, 94, 292
Selby, Jubilee Date-book, 191
Sheet 12 of Map of Geolog. Survey (Bristow), 345
Shoolcraft, vol. i, 31
Sinclair, Stat. Account of Scotland, 191
Smith, Christian Antiquities, 224
—— Rev. A. C., Guide to Brit. and Roman Antiq., 29, 33, 47, 51, 57

Smith, C. Roach, Silchester, in *Builder*, 65, 67
Society of Arts, Conference, 265
—— Congress, 265
Speede's Map of Hampshire, 3
Spence, Bate, Prehistoric Antiq. of Dartmoor, 29, 33
Stanley, Ancient Dwellings in Holyhead Island, 27, 32, 33
Statute, 35 Edward I, 247
—— 14 Edward III, 213
—— of Merton, 20 Henry III, 112
—— of Wynton, 190
Stevens, E. T., Flint Chips, 26, 31
—— Wilts County Mirror, 26
Stevens, J., Flint Implements found at St. Mary Bourne 1867, 42, 345, 352
—— Pit-dwellings, *Nature* 1872, 29
—— Notes on Worked Flints, 51
—— Relics of Early Races, 51
—— Transactions Berks and Reading Archæol. and Architect. Soc., 19
—— *Nature* 1885, 29
—— Flint Works at Cissbury, 29
—— *Science Gossip*, 345
—— Roman Remains at Finkley, 62
—— Geolog. Notices of N. Hants, 15, 16, 345, 353
—— Journ. Brit. Archæol. Assoc., 59, 71
Strype's Annals, 152, 163
Subsidies, 1 Ed. III, 269, 276, 303, 304, 305
—— 21 Ed. III, 117
—— 13 Hy. IV, 117
—— 6 Hy. VI, 117
—— 34 Hy. VIII, 307, 308, 309, 312
—— 37 Hy. VIII, 130, 270
—— 2 and 3 Edw. VI, 312, 313, 314
—— 36 Eliz., 314
—— 9 Jas. I, 316
—— 1 Charles I, 317
—— 15 Charles II, 318
—— 25 Charles II, 258
—— 1662, 276
Survey, Finkley Park 1632, 330
Swampton Allotments 1753, 290

Taylor, Words and Places, 43
Taxatio Eccles. Pope Nich., 213
Testa de Nevill, 2, 102
The Albert Nyanza, 28
The Apothecaries' Act 1815, 241

The Loan of 1627, 255
The Times 1866, 30
Thomas, Handbook to Pub. Records, 103, 105, 113, 213
Thorpe, Diplom. Angl. Ævi Saxonici, 4, 74, 78, 81
Thurnam, Crania Britan., 53
Topographer 1789, 187
Trans. Newbury Dist. Field Club, 252
Trust Deed, National Schools, 288
Turnor's Collections, 178
Tusser's Husbandry, 339
Tylor, Early Hist. of Mankind, 31

Valor Ecclesiasticus, 211, 214, 215, 270, 275, 277
Vegetius, lib. i, 43
Vernham Dean Parish Book, 9
Village Records, 5
Vincent and Charles (Warner), 160
Visitation of Hampshire 1552, 118
Visitation of Hampshire 1634, 118, 121, 138

Walford, Fairs, Past and Present, 190
Wallis's Not. Parl. (Warner), 162
Warne, Ancient Dorset, 29, 57, 66
—— Dorsetshire, its Vestiges, 33, 54
Warner's Hampshire, 1, 97, 154, 156, 177, 181, 280
Warner, Domesday, 89
Whitaker, Hist. of Craven, 239
—— On Subaërial Denudation, 16
—— Memoirs Geolog. Survey 1872, 8
—— Appendix in Memoir, do. 1881, 8
—— Proceedings Geologists' Assoc., vol. viii, 8
—— Presidential Address, 8
White, P. O. Directory, Hants, 182
Will of Henry VIII, 130
Willett, Excavations at Cissbury, 29, 44
Willis, Ex. Collect. (Warner), 176
Wilson, Prehistoric Annals, 53
Wise, New Forest, 94, 252
Wood, Curiosities of Clocks and Watches, 243
Woodward and Wilks, Hist. of Hants, 4, 39, 55, 58, 100, 118, 122, 123, 124, 152, 168, 171, 212, 216, 254, 284, 320, 321
Woolrych's Jeffreys, 166
Wright, Celt, Roman, and Saxon, 38, 66, 67, 68

ADDITIONS AND CORRECTIONS.

At page 34 it is stated, in reference to the early occupation of the pit-dwellings, that "the querns, spindle-whorl, bone articles, and pottery may be attributed to the Britons anterior to the arrival of the Romans". Now, this is hardly sufficiently definite as regards the pottery, inasmuch as the pottery found in the dwellings, as stated at page 26, was of two kinds, viz., rude, hand-made material of the British period, and the ordinary kind usually found in Romano-British dwellings. The pottery alluded to in association with the querns, etc., is the coarser British pottery.

In reference to the occupation by the Romano-Britons of the district along the line of the Roman Portway, at the top of page 27, it should be observed that at the present time a building of the Romano-British period awaits investigation on the farm of Mr. Andrew Twitchin, of New Barn. The foundations lie on the south of the Portway; and Mr. Walter Money, F.S.A., in a note to me, states that they are surrounded by a raised bank, which encloses a space of about an acre and a half. As far as it is at present known, the area of the building extends about 40 ft. south and east, and 30 ft. south and west. On hearing from Mr. Money I wrote to him stating that I was made aware of a building (if the same, which it turns out to be) on Mr. Twitchin's farm, by an angle of the foundation being laid bare about eighteen years ago; but as, on account of the cropping, it was not convenient to explore the remains at that time, its exploration was abandoned. The building lies quite near the St. Mary Bourne and Whitchurch Road, by Jamaica Farm, in an angle formed by the crossing of this road with the road from Eggbury to New Barn. It is likely its investigation will be attended with interest, as it lies near some remarkable pits or depressions in the field, and Roman coins and broken pottery of various kinds were found close by in grubbing Hogdiggen Copse. The presence of this building tends also to support the view held by those who claim that Eggbury is the site of Vindomis.

At page 40, the "Imp Stone" is stated as a block of "grey-wether" sandstone; but Lieut.-Col. Cooper-King informs me that the material of the stone is chalk-marl.

At page 99 it is stated that Hurstbourne was divided into two principal manors, *exterius* and *interius*, and that *interius* was always priory land, while *exterius* underwent change of ownership. As this may lead to the impression that *interius* alone belonged to the priory of St. Swithin, it should be observed that the Prior was also lord of the *exterior* manor, and that the so-called owners of land were persons who held *in fee* or otherwise in the manor.

Page 215. The tithe of Hurstbourne Priors *cum* St. Mary Bourne is not sufficiently rendered; but it appears that the vicarage of Hurstbourne, to which is annexed the curacy of St. Mary Bourne, is valued in *Liber Regis* (King's Book), at £12 9s. 2½d., and now (see also *Clergy List*) at £202. Warner (*Hist. of Hants*, 1795) gives an extract from Browne Willis's *Hist. of Cathedrals* (1685?):

under "Deanery of Andover", *Livings Discharged*, Hurstbourne Priors is rendered at "£32 6s. 9d. clear yearly value: yearly tenths at £1 5s. 11¼d". The large tithe of the combined parishes of St. Mary Bourne and Hurstbourne formed part of the revenue of St. Cross Hospital, Winchester, from about 1157; but it is now impropriated to the Earl of Portsmouth. The tithes of St. Mary Bourne were commuted in 1840 (White's *Hampshire Directory*)—the vicarial for £110, and the rectorial for £1,347. The tithes of Hurstbourne Priors were commuted in 1841—the small tithe for £191 8s. 10d., the large tithe for £389 18s. 10d. Combined the tithes stand thus:—

	£	s.	d.
Hurstbourne Priors, vicarial	191	8	10
St. Mary Bourne, "	110	0	0
	301	8	10
Hurstbourne Priors, rectorial	389	18	10
St. Mary Bourne, "	1,347	0	0
Total	£2,038	7	8

Mr. Charles Hooper, of Stoke, sends me word that the present (1887) apportioned vicarial tithe rent-charge for the parish of Hurstbourne Priors is £191 8s. 10d.; for St. Mary Bourne, £110; present rent of glebe at St. Mary Bourne, £45—making £346 8s. 10d.

Page 5, line 1, *for* Eisseburne, *read* Esseborne.
„ 61 „ 20 „ Finkey „ Finkley.
„ 64 „ 26 „ caliga „ caligæ.
„ 67 „ 24 „ is „ are.
„ 123 „ 20 „ Pexall „ Pexsall.
„ 141 „ 39 „ from „ after.
„ 157 „ 18 „ 33rd „ 35th.
„ 186 „ 25 „ Stopher „ Sloper.
„ 269 „ 16 „ retained „ detained.
„ 284 „ 4 „ quartrefoil „ quarter-foil.

At page 142 and page 145 reference is made to "State Papers Domestic", which should read "Calendar of State Papers Domestic", as quoted in the Index to *Authorities*, and in several parts of the book.

Powlett, Sir Hamden, 167
Pratsdown Mill, 150
Primitive Methodist Chapel, 294, 295
—— interments at, 295
Prior of St. Swithin, manorial lord, 107
—— grant to, to impark woods, 107
—— grant to, from St. Giles's fair, 108
—— lands of, after dissolution, 125
Priory, The, 183
Purver, Anthony, a Hebraist, 254
Puttingham, Sir George, 140

Quaker Confessors, 254
Quarley Hill, 55
Queen Catherine Parr, 141
Queen's Yeoman of the Bows, 322
Querns, stones used for making of, 28
—— found at Wroxeter, 28
—— found in Pen-pits, 28
Queroville, Louisa de, 177

Rainsford, Sir Henry, 170
Rainville, Nicholas de, 273
Rarer wild flowers, 355, 356, 357
Reading Free Museum, 19, 52, 64, 197, 245, 284
Reeks, Henry, 355, 356, 357
Remarkable trial by battle, 163
Renaissance tombs wrought by foreign artists, 234
Rents of Assize, 134
Reservoirs, underground, 6
Revel, prizes contended for at, 192
—— "back-sword" players of, 192, 193
Richard of Cirencester, concerning Vindomis, 38
Richerius, lands held by, 97, 98
Richerius de Andely, 98
—— probable birth-place of, 98
Ricket's Lane, half-timber houses in, 293
Rideing Hood, use of, 250
Roches, Emma de, 89
—— Sir John de, 121, 304
—— Martin de, 274
Roman burial usages, 73
Rome, Fontinalia of, 191
Romans, bye-roads of the, 55
Romano-British pottery, 27, 30, 34, 37, 59, 60, 72
Romano-Britons, solar worship by, 72
Romano-Brit. remains, at Redenham, 58
—— at Abbot's Anne, 58
—— at St. Mary Bourne, 59
—— south of Flesch stile, 59
Romano-Brit. grave at Finkley, 64
Roman coins found at Abbot's Anne, 58
—— found at Bere Hill, 59
—— found at St. Mary Bourne, 59
—— found at Finkley, 64
Roman building, Castle field, investigation of, 60, 61
—— articles found in, 61
—— probably an inn, 61

Roman building, Finkley, in relation to the Dyke, 162
—— plan of, 62
—— articles found in, 63, 64
—— at Finkley, 61
—— investigation of, 61, 62
—— surveyed by Mr. Calderwood, 61
Romans, The, conquest of Hampshire by, 45
—— line of the portway of, 55
—— vicinal ways of, 55
Rubbing-stones, 27
Rudborne, 76
Rudder, burial of in a meadow, 251

Sac, Soc, and Theam, 296
Salisbury, Canons of, 320
Sanitary officer, 265
Sanctuary, right of, 296
—— in Church of St. Cross, 299
—— in Itchingswell Church, 300
Sandstone, Old Red, 28
Saints, springs dedicated to, 191
Saxon boundaries, 86
—— theows or slaves, 80, 81
Saxons, log huts of, 96
—— land of, held by lot, 97
—— laws of, concerning tithes, 93
School Board, members of, 286
Scroggs, Sir William, 321
Sea-level, elevations above, 261
Segontiaci and Belgæ, in Hampshire, 38
Severe forest laws in Norman times, 323
Seymour, Sir John, offspring of, 128
—— Sir Edward, 128
—— Lord Treasurer, 128
—— executed, 129
—— William, 129
—— pedigree of, 129
—— Lord of Trowbridge, 129
—— Lord Robert, 180
Shaw, Mr. S., 58, 59, 64
Shearers, list of, 339
Sheep washing, 338
—— shearing, 338
Sheriff, Farmer-General of the Crown, 101
Sherard, Rev. Castel, 180
Shirley, Sir Thomas, 123
Skimmington, 337
Silchester, Caer Segeint of Nennius, 39
—— inscription found at, 39
—— the Calleva of Horsley, 39
—— British road from, 55
Slavery, redemption from, 250
Small-pox, its severity, 240
—— inoculation for, 240
Smith, Camilla Powlett, 177
Smith-Stone, tomb of, 208
Smyth, Lady, 276
Somerset, Protector, 321
—— Duke of, 148
—— Hurstbourne Manor held by, 127

Spring Hill, 10, 19
Soper v. Ellis, 260
Southampton, 12, 97, 98
South Stoneham, 97
"Spice-bowl", introduced at sheep-shearing, 339
Spinning-wheels, 239
Stair, Miss, 2
Stanley, Hon. W. O., on Ty Mawr, 27
St. Barbe, John, 171
St. Dionysius, Priory of, 97
Staniford, Andover token of, 250
St. Cross, duties of tenants of, 108
—— list of tenants of, 108, 109
—— place of the Court of, 111
—— tillage of tenants of, 111
—— officers of Court of, 112
—— revenues of, 200, 201, 212
Stevens, Joseph, 264, 286, 289
St. John, Oliver, 171
St. Mary Bourne, area of parish, 260
—— Vicar Dawson on, 1
—— dry seasons at, 5
—— 1, 2, 4, 5, 83, 90, 97, 98, 114, 115, 127, 132
St. Mary, as part of place-name, 191
Stocks, description of, 195
—— last use of, 197
—— at Stoke, 301
—— at Eggbury, 197
Stoke, 2, 15, 17, 50, 53, 69, 77, 197, 268, 277, 294, 302
—— derivation of, 277
—— exchange of land at, 277
—— Hayes v. Hayes, 278
—— Holiday v. Hayes, 278
—— gift of land at, 77
—— tithing, 277
Stoke-hill, 17
Stockmen, or Ploughmen, 80
Stone Age, Polished, 49
Stone-boiling among American Indians, 31
—— among South Sea Islanders, 31
Stourton, Lord, executed at Salisbury, 142
"Stranger's Camp", 43
Strike-light, 70
Suantune of *Domesday* translated, 279, 280
Subsidy Rolls, 303, 304, 305, 306, 307, 308, 309, 310, 311, 312, 313, 314, 315, 316, 317, 318, 319
Summerhaugh, The, 188
—— derivation of, 188
—— revel held in, 189, 192
Surnames, derived from occupations, 113, 305
Sutton, 210, 211
Swampton, 11, 87, 197, 268, 276, 280, 292, 303
—— its derivation, 11
—— tithing, 279, 294

Swampton, Green, 279
—— held by Bishop of Winchester, 280
—— held by Mortimer, 280
—— held by Beynton, 114, 283
—— held by Nevill, 115, 283
—— held by Sir John Gate, 283
—— allotments, 290
—— common fields of, 291
—— yardlands at, 291
—— its present features, 292, 293

Tarent, its derivation, 3
Temple, Rev. Watkin, 223, 264, 288, 289
Test River, in relation to "Terstan," 4
—— intermittent, 4
—— times of rising of, 5
—— its sources, 8
Thanes, tenants of, 96
—— at time of *Domesday*, 95
—— degrees of, 95
—— houses of, 95, 96
Thorngate and Izerne v. Wallopp, 217
Thruxton, Bacchus pavement at, 57
Tidbury Hill, 55
Titchbourne, Sir Benjamin, 167
Tithe-farmers, 253, 254
Tithes, 92
—— origin of, 87
—— at time of Egbert of York, 92
—— grant of, by Ethelwulf, 93
—— taken in land, 93, 94
Tithings, The, 268 to 284
Tithing of Binley, 268, 269, 270
—— of Eggbury, 270, 271
—— of Week, 273, 274, 275, 276
—— of Stoke, 277, 278
—— of Swampton, 279, 280, 281, 282, 283
Tomb of Sir Robert Oxenbridge, 234
—— inscriptions on, 234, 235
Toll, source of Church revenue, 189
Twitchen, pottery found on farm of, 26
Twyford, boundaries of, 85
Tycheborne, John de, 304
Ty Mawr, querns, found at, 27

Upper Test Basin, view of, 16
—— drainage of, 17
—— denudation of, 20
—— races who have lived in, 22
Upper Test Valley, a burial place, 69
—— drift of, 18
—— mammoth in drift of, 19
—— implements in drift of, 19
—— relation of, to Anton, 17

Vagabond money, 196
Vagrants, entries relating to, 195
—— severe treatment of, 195
—— passes given to, 195
Valley deposits, 353, 354

Lightning Source UK Ltd.
Milton Keynes UK
UKOW041919131011

180269UK00006B/35/P